Comparative
Development Perspectives

Westview Replica Editions

The concept of Westview Replica Editions is a response to the continuing crisis in academic and informational publishing. Library budgets for books have been severely curtailed. Ever larger portions of general library budgets are being diverted from the purchase of books and used for data banks, computers, micromedia, and other methods of information retrieval. Interlibrary loan structures further reduce the edition sizes required to satisfy the needs of the scholarly community. Economic pressures on the university presses and the few private scholarly publishing companies have severely limited the capacity of the industry to properly serve the academic and research communities. As a result, many manuscripts dealing with important subjects, often representing the highest level of scholarship, are no longer economically viable publishing projects--or, if accepted for publication, are typically subject to lead times ranging from one to three years.

Westview Replica Editions are our practical solution to the problem. We accept a manuscript in camera-ready form, typed according to our specifications, and move it immediately into the production process. As always, the selection criteria include the importance of the subject, the work's contribution to scholarship, and its insight, originality of thought, and excellence of exposition. The responsibility for editing and proofreading lies with the author or sponsoring institution. We prepare chapter headings and display pages, file for copyright, and obtain Library of Congress Cataloging in Publication Data. A detailed manual contains simple instructions for preparing the final typescript, and our editorial staff is always available to answer questions.

The end result is a book printed on acid-free paper and bound in sturdy library-quality soft covers. We manufacture these books ourselves using equipment that does not require a lengthy make-ready process and that allows us to publish first editions of 300 to 600 copies and to reprint even smaller quantities as needed. Thus, we can produce Replica Editions quickly and can keep even very specialized books in print as long as there is a demand for them.

About the Book and Editors

Comparative Development Perspectives
edited by Gustav Ranis, Robert L. West, Mark W. Leiserson, and Cynthia Taft Morris

A broad range of perspectives on the problems of economic development are brought together in this book, which includes contributions from eminent economists who consider needed improvements in economic institutions and policies, the workings of labor markets and their interactions with aggregate economic performance, financial aspects of development, and the general context of economic development in the 1980s. The book emphasizes a comparative historical approach, utilizing country and sectoral case studies to evaluate key policy questions. The essays reflect the influential work of Lloyd G. Reynolds in the fields of development and labor economics, and comparative economic systems.

Gustav Ranis is the Frank Altschul Professor of Economics at Yale University. Robert L. West is professor of international economics at the Fletcher School of Law and Diplomacy, Tufts University. Mark W. Leiserson is Chief, Employment and Rural Development Division, and Economic Advisor to the World Bank. Cynthia Taft Morris is professor of economics at the American University.

Published in cooperation with the
Economic Growth Center,
Yale University

Essays in Honor of Lloyd G. Reynolds

Comparative Development Perspectives

edited by Gustav Ranis, Robert L. West, Mark W. Leiserson, and Cynthia Taft Morris

Westview Press / Boulder, Colorado

A Westview Replica Edition

Copyright © 1984 by Westview Press, Inc.

Published in 1984 in the United States of America by
   Westview Press, Inc.
   5500 Central Avenue
   Boulder, Colorado 80301
   Frederick A. Praeger, President and Publisher

Library of Congress Cataloging in Publication Data
Main entry under title:
Comparative development perspectives.
   (A Westview replica edition)
   1. Economic development—Addresses, essays, lectures. 2. Comparative
economics—Addresses, essays, lectures.
I. Ranis, Gustav.
HD82.C57325   1983   338.9   83-10186
ISBN 0-86531-984-7

Printed and bound in the United States of America

10 9 8 7 6 5 4 3

Contents

Preface

I. INTRODUCTION

The product of collaboration among twenty American and Canadian economists, this volume constitutes a tribute by his colleagues and friends to the lifetime work of Lloyd G. Reynolds in comparative historical analysis, in the understanding of labor markets, and in evaluation of the development process on a domestic as well as a global basis. The contributions are organized to provide comparative perspectives on generic problems of economic development in the 1980s.

Part I emphasizes requisite improvements in economic institutions and policies associated with the development process. One of the core objectives of development management is addressed in Part I: how to accommodate the forces of technological and demographic change in ways that secure greater productivity and social welfare.

John Fei and Gustav Ranis report how technical change, at different stages of transition growth, is typified by a spatial pattern of diffusion, by sequential changes in activities at the task level, and by the emergence of new types of organization. As their central illustration of this process, they describe the substitution of modern for traditional inputs in agriculture.

Howard Pack seeks to identify the sources of productivity gains. He compares total factor productivity in the manufacturing sectors of three sharply different economies -- Israel, the Philippines, and the United States -- to account for interindustry patterns of productivity differentials. He finds that size of firm and skill requirements, but not capital-intensity differences, contribute to the explanation of factor productivity differentials.

Michael Todaro provides a framework for understanding and measuring the interactions between development policies and demographic change. He proposes criteria for relating developmental success or failure to the effects on population growth and indicates how the demographic impact of developmental projects and policies might be incorporated in the ranking of these activities in terms of improvement in social welfare.

Part II assesses the international context of development in the 1980s.

G. K. Helleiner explores three areas in which global, rather than national, analysis may be important to policymakers. He contrasts the results of adopting different scopes of analysis in measuring world economic performance, in evaluating macroeconomic management, and in appraising the efficiency of global markets.

Robert Triffin surveys the ways in which regional monetary arrangements can complement and bolster improvements needed in worldwide monetary cooperation. He finds that, in an era which he characterizes as one of near total breakdown in international monetary management, regional monetary systems may both protect member countries -- by limiting the damages flowing from the present world system -- and extend benefits to nonmembers.

ix

Two additional studies extract from the experience of the 1970s other lessons with persisting implications for the future, respecting the interplay of international and domestic factors.

Bela Balassa reports the effects of external shocks in the past decade on a dozen selected developing countries, and the varied policy responses to those shocks by groups of countries. He concludes that, in most cases, the balance of payments consequences of domestic policies aggravated the effects of adverse external shocks. Nonetheless, the domestic policies adopted were important in determining the overall impact.

Henry Bruton reviews the reasons why dramatic relief from the foreign exchange bottleneck, in some countries, has failed to produce the kind of development anticipated by both theoreticians and policymakers. He identifies the domestic barriers which have prevented oil export earnings and labor remittances from being translated into an internal dynamic force for economic growth.

Parts III, IV and V employ the comparative historical approach to evaluate key dimensions of the development process. Part III addresses the distribution of income and of poverty in the context of development.

Cynthia Taft Morris inspects the evidence that, in the period of early industrialization of high-income countries, the goal of expanding industrial capacity dominated the objective of reducing current poverty. She proposes a redirection of efforts to measure economic development in low income countries, focusing on growth of technological and institutional capacity to reduce poverty over time.

Albert Berry demonstrates the implications for income distribution trends of different ways in which subsistence income is maintained in the "traditional" sector of labor-surplus economies. He identifies the conditions in which income distribution may be expected to worsen during the labor-surplus phase, and improve subsequently.

Part IV investigates the working of labor markets and their interactions with aggregate economic performance.

Richard Freeman reviews the contribution made by Lloyd Reynolds' pioneering work to contemporary labor market analysis, with emphasis on processes of job search, implicit contracts, and disequilibrium models. He compares the results of investigative procedures similar to those generally used in developing countries today with the findings of current labor market research methods in the United States -- to show where the findings coincide and where they diverge.

Jesse Markham inspects the relation of persistent inflation, in the important case of the United States, to non-competitive elements in the structure of labor and product markets.

Peter Gregory, concentrating attention on intermediate and long-term trends in the evolution of labor markets, reports on this evolution in Mexico since 1940. Contrary to the prevailing perceptions of a secular deterioration in the conditions of employment, his data point to a much more optimistic evaluation of changes that have occurred in the Mexican labor market in the process of post-World War II economic development.

Part V places focus on the interaction of financial and economic development.

Raymond Goldsmith makes use of national and sectoral balance sheets to examine intercountry differences in economic and financial structure. He presents two illustrative, empirical applications: differences in the level and the long-term trends of relations between the tangible infrastructures and the financial superstructures of some twenty countries; and the different sectoral distributions of assets and net worth in India, Great Britain, and the United States. His review of the prospective analytical uses of national and sectoral balance sheets emphasizes their utility for international comparisons and for documenting structural changes occurring through time.

Hugh Patrick traces the historical process of development of the financial system in one country -- Japan -- to assess the interaction of real and monetary factors in distinct phases, each characterized by a different combination of government policies and market forces.

In the concluding Part VI appear country and sectoral case studies illustrating crucial policy issues and developmental processes.

Carlos Díaz Alejandro surveys, over a span of more than 100 years, the interplay of external and domestic factors in the development of Argentina, compared at each stage with performance in Australia and Brazil. His analysis indicates that it was ony with the first Peronista era, when Argentina became solidly committed to inward-looking policies, that her comparatively slower growth could be attributed mainly to domestic factors.

Frederic Pryor reviews the rapid growth of public expenditures throughout the postwar era in both East and West. To account for the increased share of national product represented by public expenditures in most countries, he compares the influence of rising demand for public services with such supply side influences as economies of scale, the rise in service sector costs, and pressures for expansion within the bureaucracy. He concludes that demand forces play the predominant role in both types of economic systems.

Walter Adams evaluates critically the performance of an industry of large absolute size under threat of foreign competition: the United States automobile industry and its appeals for import restraint. He finds little merit in the assumptions of the New Economic Darwinism and its challenge to the orthodox liberal condemnation of protection.

J. Michael Montias reports on the divergent histories of public support for the performing arts in the major market economies. His data show much higher levels of governmental support in continental Western Europe than in the United States, and he presents a systematic explanation of this difference in behavior.

Robert L. West inspects the implications for national energy management of more labor-intensive, agriculturally-oriented, development strategies in the 1980s. He shows why the intensity of energy-use is expected to rise with the adoption of more labor-intensive methods and -- from a review of sectoral energy sources and uses in developing countries -- why it is prudent to expect a future rise in the share of national energy budgets devoted to agricultural production.

II. LLOYD G. REYNOLDS: AN APPRECIATION

This volume celebrates the first fifty years of Lloyd G. Reynolds' career as an economist. His professional life has had many dimensions -- those of public service, academic administration, the study of sectoral and group behavior, and the analysis of the behavior of whole economies. But in all dimensions there is a remarkable consistency. Lloyd is a master craftsman engaged in a lifelong vocation of construction. He is always respectful of his materials, i.e. of the architecture of his predecessors; but every structure is, by his workmanship, made stronger, better organized, and more useful to his successors. In all tasks, his distinctive approach is a persistent demand for analytical rigor and a constant striving for practical relevance.

Lloyd's professional journey began in the hardest years of the Great Depression in his native Alberta, Canada. Having earned his bachelor's degree from the University of Alberta in 1931, he began his graduate studies at McGill University and completed his doctorate at Harvard. His attention, in that prewar decade, was focused on critical questions of social and economic performance in Canada. He published a half a dozen articles on the market structure and performance of Canadian industries and two books, his first on the economic and social adjustment of British immigrants (1935) and his second on the control of competition in Canada (1940).

With the outbreak of the Second World War, Lloyd accepted an appointment in the Department of Economics at the Johns Hopkins University. In 1942-43 he served as chief economist of the War Manpower Commission and in 1943-45 as a Public Member of the Appeals Committee of the National War Labor Board. He continued, in the postwar decades, to serve both governmental and private agencies as labor mediator, consultant, officer, and committee member. His organizational insights, administrative skills, and analytical powers were brought to bear at the Bureau of the Budget, the Agency for International Development, the Industrial Relations Research Association, the Ford Foundation, the National Bureau of Economic Research, and (in many roles) the American Economic Association. He has contributed generously as advisor to economic research and teaching centers at universities both in the United States and abroad.

In 1945 Lloyd came to Yale. As teacher, scholar, Fellow of Berkeley College, and as Sterling Professor of Economics, he has served the Yale community for thirty-five years. The appreciation of his colleagues was noted in the Graduate School minutes on the occasion of his recent retirement. It reads, in part: "At Yale, Lloyd Reynolds has been a master builder. He was Chairman of the Economics Department from 1951 to 1959 and it was during this period that the Department emerged from a relatively weak position to achieve a national rating as one of the very strongest. What helped was that, in the early 1950's, he was able to convert a spirited defense of the Department against right wing critics into an occasion for the substantial infusion of outside resources for graduate student fellowships. It was his great capacity to recognize talent in others which helped attract a first-rate faculty including the move of the Cowles Commission to Yale. In 1960 he convinced the Ford Foundation to help create the Economic Growth Center at Yale and served as its founding director until 1967. His vision, his organizational ability, his own shift from labor economics to development helped make the Center into an internationally recognized instrument for research on developing countries... Lloyd Reynolds' contributions to Yale extend beyond the scholarly and the teaching. He was a good citizen in every way that counts."

Lloyd introduced economics to generations of Yale students. He was a powerful force for those concerned with the welfare of society and in the profession of economics. His command of the literature, and his ability to express his thoughts with grace and clarity, made him a popular instructor -- not least in an innovative alternative to the basic introductory course in economics. He has always displayed an uncanny ability to cut through complicated ideas, lay bare the essentials, and explain them clearly and fully. Fortunately, his Yale students' contemporaries elsewhere have also benefitted from these qualities of his teaching, for the very same facility is evidenced in his writing. He has to his credit one of the best selling basic texts, Economics: A General Introduction (1963), which attained its Eighth edition in 1982. He is also the author of an extraordinarily successful labor economics text, Labor Economics and Labor Relations (1949), for which an Eighth Edition appeared in 1982, thirty-three years after its initial publication.

The wide readership and the durability of these texts are only in part attributable to Lloyd's clarity and grace of expression; more importantly, they reflect his characteristic amalgam of economic theory, insistent attention to practice and institutional frameworks, and careful empirical observation. The merger of these elements has been the hallmark of his published research.

For more than two decades Lloyd concentrated his research on labor economics and in particular on the fundamental empirical and analytical issues he identified in his review article on the "Economics of Labor" which appeared in the first volume of the American Economic Association's Survey of Contemporary Economics (1948). At the time of writing this survey he was engaged in the intensive study of the New Haven labor market for manual workers, the fruits of which appeared in his book The Structure of Labor Markets (1951). From an analysis of interviews with over 800 manufacturing workers, Lloyd and his associates developed a picture of labor market behavior by workers and employers of a much greater complexity and richness than could possibly be captured by the severe abstractions of standard labor market theory. But Lloyd's interest was not in simply demonstrating theoretical inadequacies but in laying the foundations for better analytic formulations of the interrelationships between individual job choice, worker mobility, firm wage decisions, and organizational influences on labor markets.

His next major research effort turned Lloyd from micro behavior in labor markets to the problems of relative wage rate determination. As he put it, these problems involved "that intermediate level of analysis which classical and neoclassical economists had regarded as the proper province of wage theory" but which had "simply been neglected." The Evolution of Wage Structure (with Cynthia H. Taft, 1956) perhaps represented the culmination of Lloyd's interest in the field of labor economics. It focused on movements of relative wages for different occupational groups, industrial categories, and geographical areas over substantial periods of time. The major objective was to explain the movements in relative wages and to determine how collective and organizational behavior modify the results of individual responses in the labor market. The major achievement was a significant advance toward a more integrated view of wage determination, taking account of both individual worker and employer responses in the market and the behavior of unions and other organized groups. Lloyd saw clearly at that time that the construction of a more unified theory for the determination of relative wage rates would become essential to our understanding of movements in the general wage level and to the central issues of inflation and unemployment, issues that have continued to be dominant policy concerns in the 25 years since.

These two studies, on wage structures and on the operation of labor markets, may justly be described as classics in the field with a pervasive and continuing influence on subsequent research and theoretical developments. Carried out within a carefully articulated framework of economic theory, they combined in a unique way the strong empirical traditions of institutional economics and the analytical power of neoclassical economic theory. Together, they opened up new frontiers for empirical and theoretical research and established a basis for fruitful communication between two strong traditions in U.S. economics that had all too often been marked by sterile controversy.

It is likely that future historians of economic thought will find that much of the research in labor economics over the past quarter century has concentrated on issues or drawn on empirical observations of labor market operations and wage determination processes that were originally explored in Lloyd's work. As with all such seminal works which cast new light on a whole field, many of these results were absorbed into the common perspectives of economists concerned with wage and labor markets. But the roots of a great deal in the modern analysis of job search, implicit contracts, disequilibrium models -- and more generally in the micro-foundations of macro wage and employment determination -- can be found in Lloyd's explorations.

In the early 1950's Lloyd directed a study of the manpower resources of Puerto Rico, conducted under the auspices of the University of Puerto Rico. It represented his first foray into the world of development economics. More than ten years later, working with Peter Gregory, he published Wages, Productivity, and Industrialization in Puerto Rico (1965). To the labor market of this low income society he brought the same keen theoretical interests and careful empirical observations that had characterized his work on Canada and the United States. Based on interviews with more than a thousand factory workers and field investigation of 85 manufacturing establishments, the results showed remarkably similar reactions to those found in more highly industrialized countries. With account fully taken of the special circumstances of Puerto Rico, his study decisively challenged a number of myths about the behavior of labor supply in low income countries, notably with respect to expected worker response to incentives.

At that time the relatively new and burgeoning field of development economics was experiencing the presentation of capital accumulation models and labor surplus models, often with highly simplified assumptions about the behavior of individuals offering labor. In a series of articles appearing in the latter half of the 1960s -- including "Wages and Employment in a Labor-Surplus Economy" (1965) -- Lloyd explored the relationship between his own (and other available) empirical observations of labor market behavior in less developed countries and the labor surplus models. He added substantially to the realism and practical relevance of the labor surplus models in both the Lewis and Fei-Ranis traditions. In the process, he erected an analytical framework which has been found useful for both comparative and historical development analysis in subsequent work. At the same time he was instrumental in having the Ford Foundation, under his general editorship, commission a number of comparative systems-oriented monographs in various branches of economics.

The 1970s saw Lloyd probe more fully the interstices of comparative economic systems, economic history, and development economics. His writings emphasized the limits and the extent to which the analytical "tool kit" of western economics helps our understanding of nonwestern economies. He has pointed up the importance of a long view, and of the role that a long period of slow and gradual changes has played in accounting for current economic maturity. In this process he extended the boundaries of comparative economic systems. His own major summary contribution to comparative studies, The Three Worlds of Economics (1972), was later followed by a series of insightful articles reporting on his observations of the Chinese economy. He has several times visited China and the Soviet Union in relation to these interests.

But in recent years, and currently, Lloyd's interests have increasingly focused on development. "Economic development is an activity in search of an intellectual framework" was Lloyd's observation with respect to "The Content of Development Economics" (1969). He has insisted on the distinction between the activity -- an art, something that politicians and entrepreneurs try to accomplish -- and the branch of applied economics in which scholars blend theorizing, empirical research, and policy analysis. He has never lost sight of the need for the scholar's theory to survive the test of practical relevance and for the intellectual enterprise to ground itself in empirical information.

There is a powerful interaction, in all this work, between the typologies of comparative economic systems and useful analytical models of development economics. Adopting a long-term view, Lloyd holds that development economics is concerned with disequilibrium, with how an essentially stagnant situation is disrupted, and with the course of sectoral and intersectoral development during the growth-acceleration process. Drawing on concepts from the field of comparative systems, Lloyd holds that at any moment of time -- just now, for instance -- some less developed countries are still in an essentially stagnant state; a relatively small number are experiencing a process of trend acceleration; others have entered a phase of sustained growth and have graduated from the active concern of development economics. The core of the development economics subject, then, is the analysis of growth and structural change in economies that have entered the phase of growth acceleration. This is Lloyd's empirical universe -- twenty or so sizeable developing economies -- for which he has striven to define an empirically-grounded, closed-economy framework. A classification in terms of foreign sector performance reveals a typology of open-economy models, with the impact of alternative organizational choices completing the circle. As solid empirical evidence accumulates helping us to record the growth patterns of developing economies, theoretically sound country-specific models will become available for comparative analysis -- nourishing and contributing rigor to the study of comparative systems. The pursuit of this empirical evidence and the specification of country-specific models has been among Lloyd's objectives for nearly twenty years, ever since the Yale Economic Growth Center launched its Country Analysis Program in the early 1960s under Lloyd's guidance.

Lloyd's direct contribution to this design has been to participate in clarifying the role of key sectors, to assemble and organize empirical information on sectoral performance in the universe of developing economies, and to examine the limits within which our theory contributes to our understanding of the changes seen to occur. His overview of the papers prepared for Agriculture in Development Theory (1975), for example, emphasized and endorsed the central role of rural economic activity and of the agricultural sector in the development process -- an emergent emphasis of the 1970s.

Image and Reality in Economic Development (1977) is Lloyd's major presentation of these themes. The reality of economic growth performance is seen without gimmicks -- there is no "big push," no "balanced growth," no "take-offs." Performance is assessed within the mainstream economic model -- although here, as elsewhere, he is respectful of the insights of Marx, Frank and the Sussex economists. Where the theory is incomplete, he has elaborated; where the mainstream model reveals problem areas, he has tried to explore and explain them. He has both enlarged and deepened the dual economy modernization approach of development economics. His originality is in the way ideas are brought together and in the places on which he puts emphasis. In a field of research as unwieldy and as unstructured as development economics, his has been a most useful and substantial contribution. Lloyd has helped to make the field less unwieldy by cutting through the complexity to lay bare the essentials and provide a guide for future research.

The studies assembled in this volume reflect Lloyd's impact on the world of ideas via the contributions of his friends, colleagues, and students, focused on the three related fields in which he was himself active: labor economics, comparative systems, and development economics.

III. ACKNOWLEDGEMENTS

Wordprocessing and programming to produce camera-ready copy were carried out with patience, skill, and ingenuity by Roberta M. Milano, Thomas Frenkel and Jonathan D. Putnam at Yale University's Economic Growth Center. The guidance generously provided by Zack Deal, textprocessing specialist at the Harvard Computing Center, made it feasible to design and employ the special type font required by the mathematical notations and equations. Roy E. West, with diligence and persistence in pursuit of uniform standards of style, usage, and appearance, edited the nineteen manuscripts submitted by contributors. These services, we gratefully acknowledge, made possible the publication of this volume.

The Editors

BIBLIOGRAPHY OF WORKS CITED

Reynolds, L. G. 1935. *The British immigrant*: *his economic and social adjustment in Canada*. Toronto: Oxford U. Press.

————, 1940. *The control of competition in Canada*. Cambridge: Harvard U. Press.

————, 1948. Economics of labor. In *A survey of contemporary economics*, ed. H. S. Ellis, 255-87. New York: Blakiston Co.

————, 1949. *Labor economics and labor relations*. New Jersey: Prentice-Hall, Inc.

————, 1951. *The structure of labor markets*. New York: Harper and Brothers.

————, 1963. *Economics*: *a general introduction*. Homewood, Illinois: Richard D. Irwin, Inc.

————, 1965. Wages and employment in a labor-surplus economy. *Amer. Econ. Rev.*, LV(1)(March): 19-39.

————, 1969. Economic development with surplus labor: some complications. *Oxford Econ. Papers*, (March): 89-103.

————, 1969. The content of development economics. *Amer. Econ. Rev.*, *Papers and Proceedings*, LIX(2)(May): 401-08.

————, 1972. *The three worlds of economics*. New Haven: Yale U. Press. Yale Studies in comparative Economics, Volume 12.

————, (ed.) 1975. *Agriculture in development theory*. New Haven: Yale U. Press.

————, 1977. *Image and reality in economic development*. New Haven: Yale U. Press.

Reynolds, L. G., C. H. Taft. 1956. *The evolution of wage structure*. New Haven: Yale U. Press.

Reynolds, L. G., P. Gregory. 1965. *Wages, productivity, and industrialization in Puerto Rico*. Homewood, Illinois: Richard D. Irwin, Inc.

1
Task Orientation
and Technology Change:
A Suggested Approach

John C. H. Fei and Gustav Ranis

I. INTRODUCTION

The choice of technology has long been recognized as one of the most important dimensions of LDC developmental performance but also as one which has proven most difficult and elusive. In recent years, there has been a gradual turning away from the aggregative production function, residuals-decomposition approach (e.g., Bruton 1967; Denison 1967), and towards a micro-level examination of the conditions underlying the productive system in particular industries or sectors (e.g., Pack 1975).

This paper is in the latter vein. It views "technology" not as an empty economic box, but as a phenomenon which is likely to be demystified in relation to our willingness and ability to pay more attention to engineering realities at a disaggregate or task-oriented level of concreteness. It is our view that what is required is the combination of the rational choice criteria of economics with engineering principles of scale and substitutability peculiar to particular tasks in the context of both agricultural and industrial production activities in LDCs.

II. IMPORTANCE OF AGRICULTURAL MODERNIZATION

In the process of the transition of a traditional agrarian economy into the epoch of modern growth, the most important dimension is the modernization of the agricultural sector. The idea that agricultural productivity gain is a precondition for industrialization finds ample support in both theory and empirical evidence. In the context of the so-called dualistic growth models, classical and neoclassical, the roles of the agricultural sector in supplying food surplus, manpower, and finance to fuel industrial expansion all receive prominent attention. That the "industrial revolution" was made possible by an "agricultural revolution" in both historical England and Japan has been well documented. Nevertheless, with few notable exceptions, the majority of contemporary less developed countries is still struggling with, and frustrated by, what is often referred to as the "mystery" of agricultural modernization.

The so-called modernization of agriculture is basically a technological transformation through which the various production tasks (land preparation, seeding, transplanting, fertilizing, harvesting, etc.) are increasingly performed by methods which are the product of modern science and technology--replacing traditional methods. While technological transformation in agriculture is similar to that in the industrial sector, there are certain peculiarities about agriculture which will be discussed in part III. Technological transformation of the agricultural sector involves organizational transformation. Modern technologies are usually introduced into the agricultural sector via the emergence of a new type of "organization," that is, profit-seeking firms (e.g., fertilizer factories, hybrid-seed companies, tractor manufacturers) that produce an output which substitutes for the traditional input at a particular task level. We have found this idea of "task-oriented production specialization," or TOPS, useful for our analytical purposes, as will be indicated below.

One particular type of TOPS, namely, the "cultivation firm" encountered on Taiwan, which is engaged by family farmers on a contractual basis, will be used as an example. The emergence of such cultivation firms in Taiwan in recent years is directly related to the gradual displacement of labor surplus by labor shortage brought on by successful economic development. Thus, the modernization (i.e., the mechanization) of the agricultural sector is a growth-related phenomenon induced by changes in factor prices (i.e., wage increases and/or interest-rate declines) when the surplus labor is exhausted. While such a theory can be fully stated mathematically, we will only sketch in the outline of the argument here. The general framework of economics can, however, be applied to other types of TOPS, for example, during the earlier period of biochemical-technology change in agriculture and, as we indicate below, to some parts of the industrial sector.

III. SPECIAL CHARACTERISTICS OF AGRICULTURE

Traditional LDC agriculture is endowed with three special characteristics, its spatial dimension, the production tasks involved, and the production organization chosen. The typical agricultural population is not only relatively large (e.g., typically upward of 50 percent of the total population), but also takes on a spatially dispersed pattern of location. While the nonagricultural population is spatially concentrated in the hierarchy of urban centers ($c_1, c_2, c_3, \ldots$) linked by a transportation network, the agricultural population is usually spread throughout the land space (i.e., represented by the dots in Figure 1a). Modern science and technology usually originate from the urban centers (c_1), or via imports from abroad through the port cities (e.g., c_1, c_3) which are, in turn, infused into the "rural backyard." Be it tractors, hybrid seeds, or factory-produced fertilizers, the story of agricultural modernization cannot be divorced from that of the urban-centered activities.

A local market area (represented by a circle with a center c, a local marketing town) of Figure 1a is enlarged in Figure 1b to present a more realistic view of agricultural production. Land, an

Diagram 1

Spatial Characteristic of Agricultural Modernization

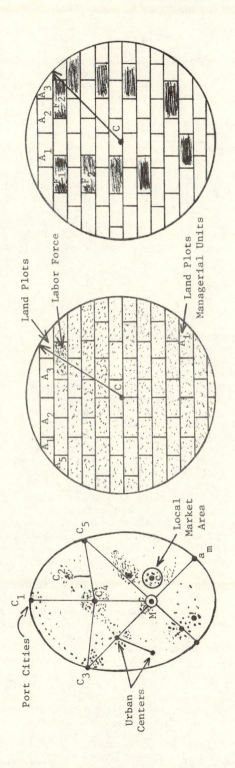

1a) Dispersed Location of Agricultural Population

1b) Land as Input and Constant Returns to Scale

1c) Spatial Spreading of Agricultural Modernization

essential agricultural input, is represented here by the rectangular plots $A_1, A_2, A_3, \ldots$, containing certain <u>areas</u>. Globally, the entire land space is covered by such "local market areas." In the process of modernization, it is useful to emphasize this localistic view as something different from a global view--as will be pointed out below. The individual plots of land $A_1, A_2, \ldots$ represent not only quantities of inputs (i.e., acreage of land area), but also, in a family farming system, managerial units of production. Because of the coexistence of a larger number of such "firms," the agricultural sector as an industry takes on a competitive nature to a degree rarely found in other industries. Modernization of the agricultural sector is thus carried out under an idealized "competitive" condition. The cotton-textiles and agricultural-machinery industries, for example, are less competitive.

When modern science and technology are infused into the agricultural sector, technological change is typified by a spatially spreading pattern. In Figure 1c, the shaded plots (i.e., managerial units) $F_1, F_2, \ldots$ are those which have already adopted modern practices, existing side by side with the "uncovered" (i.e., traditional) plots $A_1, A_2, \ldots$. In summary, the spatial perspective shows that technological transformation of the agricultural sector is a spreading process, through which modern science and technology, which originate from the urban centers, are infused into the local, rural market areas and gradually replace traditional technology.

Agricultural production is characterized by its "linearly ordered" tasks. Using the growing of rice as an illustration, for an individual firm (i.e., a farm with plot A_i and labor force L_i, measured in man-hours), these tasks are represented in Figure 2a by the activities a_1 (land preparation), a_2 (seeding), a_3 (transplanting), a_4 (applying fertilizer and insecticide), and a_5 (harvesting). While workers L_i are allocated to each activity as inputs

$$(L_i = L_1{}^i + L_2{}^i + L_3{}^i + L_4{}^i + L_5{}^i)$$

the output of each activity is sent to the next "stage," leading to the emergence of the final output q_i, that is, the rice crop. In agricultural modernization, the engineering aspect is addressed at these task levels in a time-determined sequential fashion.

When these production tasks are specified, agriculture as an industry is shown in Figure 2b. The firms $F_1, F_2, \ldots F_n$, each a replica of Figure 2a, exhibit a parallel structure. While there may exist certain cooperative arrangements between firms (e.g., joint harvesting between villagers at harvest time), each firm is, on the whole, a self-sufficient production unit perhaps typical of traditional agriculture. Thus, in agricultural modernization we do not have to stress the issue of backward and/or forward linkages between production units due to "technological complementarity" usually found between firms (e.g., subcontracting) in the urban sector.

In the typical LDC agricultural sector, there is a coincidence between the firm and the family, that is, an agricultural household formed of family working teams. While some medium- and small-scale industries in the urban sector may have the same mode of

Diagram 2

Task-Oriented Specification of Agricultural Production

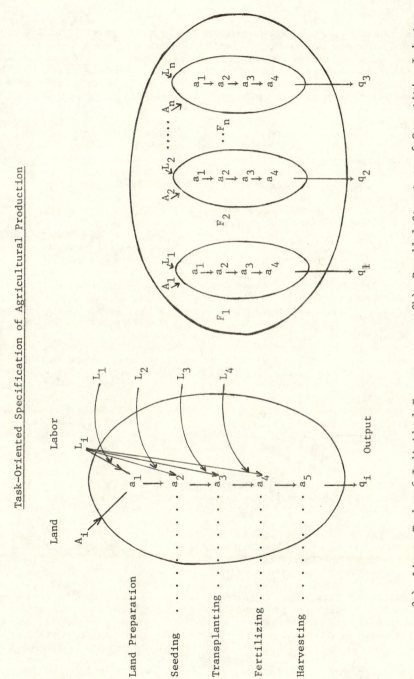

2a) Linear Tasks of Individual Farm

2b) Parallel Structure of Competitive Industry

organization, such organization is well-nigh universal for most of the food-crop production in less developed economies that preserve the family farming system. Given the initially noncommercialized orientation of the family farms, it takes the emergence of a new type of organization, namely the cultivation firm, to introduce modern mechanical technology in this particular case.

IV. TECHNOLOGICAL TRANSFORMATION OF THE AGRICULTURAL SECTOR

The modernization of the traditional agricultural sector is accomplished with the help of the emergence of an industry, serving agriculture, consisting of profit-seeking firms that engage in the production of a particular modern input, purchased by the family farm and replacing a traditional input or service.[1]

Such a process, to be modelled below, is shown in Figure 3, consisting of the family farms (a replica of Figure 2b), the industries serving agriculture (containing profit-seeking firms M_1, M_2, M_3), plus urban industries and/or research centers. The essential idea to be conveyed is that modern science and technology are infused into the agricultural sector from these urban and university centers via the emergence of a new organization, that is, industries serving the agricultural sector. Typically, it is a particular task (in Figure 3, shown as a_4, the application of fertilizer, as an illustration) which will be "performed" by the new industry M_i. The output Q (e.g., modern factories producing fertilizer) is produced by labor L_m and capital K_m carrying modern technology. These industries will require modern inputs R supplied by the urban industries, for example, certain chemical compounds used by fertilizer factories. The emergence of such an industry serving agriculture represents a form of task-oriented production specialization. From the viewpoint of the family farms, the traditional activity a_4 (traditional hand-gathered fertilizer and night soil) are now bypassed or eliminated as they are substituted for by modern inputs. This type of technological change will be referred to as TOPS or "task-oriented production specialization."

Agricultural modernization involves two types of "transformation," one basically organizational (e.g., through setting up work teams, cooperatives, farmer associations, land reform, etc.), while the other refers to certain well-known technological dimensions (e.g., the introduction of irrigation, new fertilizer-seed combinations, insecticides, tractors, etc.). A centrally planned economy, as well as a capitalist or a mixed economy, must be capable of handling both dimensions.

In the typical contemporary LDC, the organizational changes may include the emergence of new agricultural-input industries. While agricultural productivity increase can be achieved via the spreading of best traditional cultivation practices, TOPS in the post-labor surplus or mechanization phase is usually associated with productivity gains that do involve modern science and technology. That profit-seeking agricultural-input industries (e.g., hybrid-seed breeding companies, fertilizer and insecticide factories, tractors and farm-equipment manufacturers) have played a prominent role in the history of modernization of the, by now, industrially advanced countries (e.g., U.S. and Japan) is well documented by agricultural

Diagram 3

Agricultural Modernization Via Task-Oriented Production Specialization

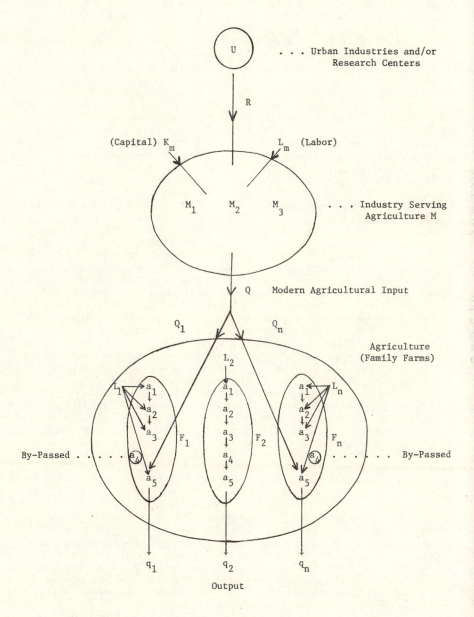

economists. Our purpose in this paper is to theorize about the usefulness of the TOPS concept as a way of improving our understanding of technological change in developing countries at different stages of their transition growth process.

A major technological principle governing the emergence of the agricultural-input industry (M in Figure 3) is the economies of scale. The fact that a single firm M_1 (or M_2) can serve many farms implies that, with the aid of modern capital equipment K_m, the firm has the conspicuous advantage of the efficiency of large-scale production. Transportation costs and the degree of scale economies tell us much about the structure of the agricultural-input industry M. When the efficiencies of large-scale production are very pronounced, outweighing the disadvantages of transportation costs, M may contain a single "fertilizer factory," located at a port city with a vast market area covering the entire economy (see Figure 4a). Conversely, when economies of scale are less conspicuous relative to transportation costs, M may contain many spatially dispersed firms M_i, each serving its own market area (see Figure 4b). This latter model deserves special emphasis in the case of contemporary LDCs aiming at agricultural modernization.

The strength of economies of scale has much to do with the nature of entrepreneurship that emerges in the agricultural-input firms M_i from the financial and/or technological standpoint. When economies of scale are conspicuous, for example, in the case of a fertilizer factory (Figure 4a), it constitutes a complex conglomeration of modern science and technology requiring heavy financial investments that far exceed the capacities of individual households. Urban-oriented entrepreneurs, financial intermediation, and/or government sponsorship become indispensable. The opposite is the case for the locally oriented industry (Figure 4b), in which the relative unimportance of economies of scale provides room for local participation from the technological and/or financial standpoint.

In the TOPS framework, a useful distinction can be made between a biochemical type of task (introduction of fertilizer, insecticides, hybrid seeds, etc.), on the one hand, and a mechanical task (introducing a new method of land preparation, harvesting, etc.), on the other. In the densely populated parts of the world (East and Southeast Asia), our main focus of attention in this paper, the biochemical type of TOPS has economic significance directly related to the development of a labor surplus economy at the early stage. On the family farms, the traditional source of power has been labor and animals, and this is likely to remain the case as long as the labor surplus condition lasts. During this period, biochemical types of tasks associated with the "Green Revolution" are likely to predominate. Once a "turning point" is reached and a shortage of unskilled labor is beginning to make itself felt, the increase in the real wage and/or the decline in the rate of interest will combine to induce the mechanical type of TOPS, so that mechanical power, burning fuel, will gradually replace the traditional human and/or animal power. Even after thirty years (1950-80) of the most successful contemporary modernization experience, including the biochemical variety of TOPS, Taiwan has now barely begun to show evidence of TOPS of the mechanical type. It is this experience which we analyze here. A similar analysis can be used, assuming availability of data, for

Diagram 4

Location Pattern of Agricultural Input Industries

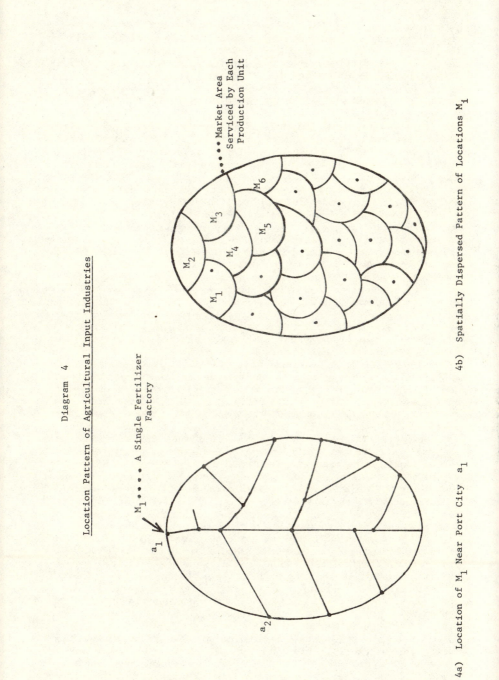

M_1 •••• A Single Fertilizer Factory

•••••Market Area Serviced by Each Production Unit

4a) Location of M_1 Near Port City a_1

4b) Spatially Dispersed Pattern of Locations M_i

the biochemical type of technology choice, likely to be more relevant to the earlier, labor surplus, period. We believe this type of analysis will provide important implications for policy for all densely populated LDCs both before and after the "turning point."

V. THE CULTIVATION FIRM AS AN EXAMPLE OF TOPS IN AGRICULTURE

In the case of Taiwan, twenty years of very successful development (1950-70) led to a turning point, with labor surplus giving way to labor shortage. The rapid increase in the real wage, and the absolute decline of the agricultural labor force after approximately 1970, created the economic backdrop for the emergence of TOPS of the mechanical type, that is, the introduction of mechanized farm equipment into the agricultural sector.

In Taiwan, this mechanical TOPS took on a particular "organizational form," that of the profit-seeking cultivation firm. In terms of our framework of analysis in Figure 3, the agricultural-input industry M consists of cultivation firms M_i which own the capital equipment K_m (mainly various types of mechanized farm equipment), hire labor L_m (mainly operators and maintainers of farm equipment), and purchase current inputs R (mainly fuel and capital-goods replacement) from the urban industries. The output Q produced by these firms constitutes cultivation services which are being sold to the family farms on a contractual basis. In this way, the traditional land-preparation tasks a_1 are being bypassed and substituted for by modern technology.

In a global, spatial perspective, the cultivation firms describe a spatially dispersed location pattern as pictured in Figure 4b. A realistic view of the operation of the cultivation firm is provided by Figure 1b, in which a cultivation firm M_i, located at a rural marketing town c, will work on the land plots A_i in a given market area.

During the ten-year period (1970-80), the TOPS introduced via the cultivation firm brought about a spatial spreading pattern of agricultural modernization on Taiwan as described in Figure 1c. According to Wang's report, by 1974 "there were 137 market areas containing 310 cultivation teams employing 4002 employees, with 1749 tractors cultivating 12.8 percent of rice land for 9 percent of the family farms."[2] It is seen that the institution of cultivation firms took root very rapidly since its beginnings in the late 1960s.

It is obvious that the cultivation firm fits our TOPS model perfectly. Furthermore, the Wang report made it clear that "while land preparation represented the initial service contracted for, the practice quickly spread to other tasks, such as the planting, transplanting, application of fertilizer and insecticides, irrigation, and harvesting." Thus, once labor shortage arrived, the mechanical type of TOPS was introduced gradually into all tasks traditionally performed by family labor on family farms.

The emergence of the institution of the cultivation firm in Taiwan can be explained in terms of the existence of economies of scale in the production of the cultivation services provided to the relatively small, family-farm plots. In contrast to the U.S., where individual farms are large enough for the individual family to own its own farm equipment, an arrangement such as "tractor stations" under socialism, or firms selling tractor services in the mixed economy, becomes the natural answer in Asia.

Unlike the case of fertilizer or insecticide manufacture, the production of cultivation services (or mechanical services in general) is characterized by only moderate scale economies. This, plus the relatively heavy transportation costs involved, are the basic reason why cultivation firms are a spatially dispersed industry, as described in Figure 4b. The short post-1970 experience of cultivation firms in Taiwan is relevant to all the densely populated agricultural economies of East and Southeast Asia which aim to develop along a mixed-economy path while maintaining the family-farm system. During the labor-surplus phase biochemical TOPS is relevant. Once labor-shortage conditions arrive, it is virtually certain that some form of locally oriented enterprise will emerge to perform the multiple mechanical types of TOPS for farming families.

In lieu of a complete statement of the underlying model, we intend to summarize briefly here the main components of our approach, focusing on the notion of technological change as a substitution and diffusion phenomenon. Given the traditional method of cultivation, let q be the labor inputs per unit of land cultivated. Similarly, let c be the units of cultivation services (as an example) needed per unit of land cultivated by the modern method. Let w be the wage rate and p be the contractual price of cultivation services. Then wq and pc are, respectively, the cost of the traditional and modern methods of cultivation (per unit of land) and hence:

$$p/w < q/c \quad \text{(or } pc < wq) \tag{1}$$

represents the substitution inequality which leads to the emergence of the cultivation firms. With a fixed q/c, the decline of p/w (the price-wage ratio) in the course of economic development induces the change in the choice of technology.

The supply of cultivation services may then be traced to the profit-maximizing behavior of the cultivation firm, that is:

$$\text{Max: } \Pi = pV - (wW + rK + p_uU) \quad \text{subject to}$$

$$V = f(W,K,U) \tag{2}$$

Thus, W (labor), K ("modern" capital goods) and U (fuel) constitute the essential inputs for the production of the cultivation services V in the production function $V = f(W,K,U)$ of the cultivation firm. We can then derive the supply function of the individual firm:

$$V = S(w,r,p_u,p) \tag{3}$$

as a function of the wage rate w, the interest rate r, the price of cultivation services p, and the price of fuel p_u. In the context of the development of a labor surplus economy, we may envision that w increases and r declines after the labor shortage condition arrives, that is:

$$dw/dt > 0 \quad \text{and}$$

$$dr/dt < 0 \tag{4}$$

Thus, in our analysis, w and r may be treated exogenously as a function of macroeconomic events related to the phasing of transition growth.

Since "cultivation" is a local industry, let A be the total land area of a local community. If all land in the local community makes use of the service, the total demand for the cultivation service is A/c and hence, equating demand and supply, we have:

$$A/c = S\ (w,r,p_u,p) \tag{5}$$

implying that p is determined by w, r, p_u, and A/c. Thus

$$p = p\ (w,r,p_u,A/c)\quad \text{and} \tag{6a}$$

$$p/w = p\ (w,\ r,\ p_u,\ A/c)/w \tag{6b}$$

From (6b) we can see that the price-wage ratio (p/w) in the substitution inequality (1) is a function of w, r, p_u, A/c. The basic analytical issue, then, is to investigate the behavior of p/w (e.g., whether it tends to fall and satisfy equation (1) when the wage declines and/or when the rate of interest rises). Properties of the production function in (2) are essential for a logical inquiry of this type.

In equations (5) and (6), the underlying assumption is that, in a given local area, there exists only one cultivation firm. In fact, there may exist a number of cultivation firms that form a local "cultivation industry." The number of firms that will eventually come into being is obviously related to the economies of scale inherent in the production function V = f (W,K,U). Imagine that the long-run average-cost curve of a cultivation firm is U-shaped, with a minimum point (and an output capacity at the minimum point) of which the magnitudes are sensitive to the economies of scale. Thus, the empirical analysis of the cultivation industry as a prototype of technological change involves the analysis of these relations using production functions with nonconstant returns to scale.

In equation (5), it was assumed that all the land in the local community is cultivated by cultivation firms. In fact, modern technology only spreads gradually across the local community (see Figure 1c). This means that, at any moment of time, not all farm families behave in the same fashion and that some families tend to demand the services of cultivation firms earlier. What is required is a framework to analyze the differentiated behavior of the farming families. That is, the problem becomes one of understanding the gradual "commercialization" of the behavior of the traditional farming families as it can be traced to a number of economic and/or sociological variables. The data inputs required by the design of our analysis are available.

In addition to the impact of growth (manifested via the changing cost-price calculation), the emergence of a new industry requires the fulfillment of certain entrepreneurial functions with respect to financial investment and technological management. The Taiwan experience shows that, in the case of the cultivation firms, the entrepreneurial functions were shared by the urban-oriented entrepreneur, the government, and the farming families themselves, either directly, or indirectly through the farmers' associations. It should be emphasized that policy issues related to the promotion of the growth of the cultivation firms center mainly on an assessment of the roles played by the government and/or the farmers' associations.

VI. APPLICATION OF THE TOPS APPROACH TO THE INDUSTRIAL SECTOR

The notion of the task-oriented production specialization type of technology change can be applied to the industrial sector as well. Indeed, the famous parable of the "needle factory" of Adam Smith makes it clear that the identification of various specific production tasks (e.g., the melting of metal, the formation of the bodies of needles, the making of holes, the packing) represents not only the foundation of the famous "division of labor", but of technological change as well. In Figure 3, we may think of F_1, F_2, F_n as traditional firms (e.g., needle factories) for which the production tasks are specialized from the engineering standpoint. The modernization of this industry very often depends upon the emergence of a "backward linkage" industry (i.e., the firms M_1, M_2, M_3 in Figure 3) that produces a modern input which substitutes for a particular task of the traditional variety.

In an engineering-oriented approach to technological change in the industrial sector, the identification of the various tasks involved in the production process is a virtual necessity. In the brick industry, for example, the four tasks of the production line consist of (1) the piling of loamy earth; (2) the formation of wet bricks; (3) sun drying; and (4) baking. In less developed countries (e.g., Taiwan or India), there are many types of brick factories designed to perform the same set of tasks. However, it is at a particular task level (e.g., the baking task) that the various types of factories are differentiated (e.g., by kiln design) into "traditional" and "modern" varieties. In previous research, we had experience with a task-oriented approach applied to the brick, textile, and shoe industries.[3] In all cases, modernization usually occurred at a particular task level based on the purchase of a modern input produced by a "backward linkage" industry. While economists recognize the importance of the interdependence of industries via an input-output approach, such interdependence is basically traced to the division of labor from a technological standpoint. As compared with the traditional input-output approach, the idea of TOPS gives a fuller and formal recognition of the engineering aspect of the production tasks linking the various industries. Unlike the "general equilibrium" nature of the input-output approach, the task-oriented approach to technology change, as formulated in the last section, is partial equilibrium in nature; it aims at the analysis of the process of technological transformation as induced by changes in the economic environment manifested in the variation of the cost-price relations.

The basic idea of TOPS is that when individual (traditional) firms are profit maximizers, new technologies will be adopted when warranted by cost-price variations brought about by economic development. The approach gives prominent recognition to the transformation aspect of technological change, that is, the aspect dealing with the abandonment of the traditional technology and the adoption of a new, modern technology via rational choice calculations (see equation (1)). But rational calculation is only a part of the story of technological change in a less developed country. In the agricultural sector, only a part of farming households make use of the modern method (Figure 1c), at least initially. Similarly, in the industrial sector, traditional and modern textile factories coexist. When the background conditions (i.e., cost-price calculations) are ripe, the technological transformation of an LDC is, at best, a slowly spreading process. Organizational differences matter, and institutional barriers must be overcome before the rational cost-price calculations can become the dominant force. The "commercialization" of the behavior of the farming household (as we indicated in the last section) is a clear-cut example of such "institutional" aspects of technological change in the agricultural sector. These "institutional" aspects may be expected to be more pronounced in rural industry, and most pronounced in the urban-centered industrial sector where non-competitive features of the environment become more relevant; hence, a model based on rational choice in a competitive environment is likely to be most relevant in the agricultural case, while one accommodating linkages and economies of scale will have relatively greater applicability in industry. The profits-function methodology can be used in both the agricultural and nonagricultural empirical applications of our approach, with adustments to the noncompetitive nature of the problem introduced where appropriate.

VII. CONCLUSIONS

In this paper we have advanced the outlines of a task-oriented approach to help us analyze the technological transformation of a traditional market-oriented economy in the course of economic development. In a rational economic system, the increase of the real wage and/or the decline of the real rate of interest induces the adoption of "modern" technology which replaces "traditional" technology based primarily on the use of labor. In the agricultural sector, this transformation may be carried out by profit-seeking firms (in our example, the cultivation firm) that produce an output which is focused at a particular engineering task level (in our example, the cultivation task) within agricultural production. The modernization of the agricultural sector also involves the commercialization of the behavior of the farming families, which leads to an increase in the demand for modern inputs (in our example, cultivation services). While we require a fuller framework to analyze this institutional aspect, it is clear that such technological transformation of an LDC's agricultural sector requires an accommodating organizational transformation. The analysis of such a task-oriented substitution process can be applied not only to the agricultural sector, but to the industrial sector as well. But, in the industrial sector, characterized by much greater diversity of both products and tasks, the engineering characteristics making for the presence or absence of scale economies have to be accommodated along with the substitution process already more fully explored.

15

FOOTNOTES

1. For example, fertilizer, new seeds, and other things which embody modern science and technology. In some other organizational contexts, some of these may be provided by non-profit-seeking firms such as government extension agencies, coops, and the like.

2. Data on Taiwan's cultivation firms are contained in a preliminary report by Professor Yi-Tao Wang (1975).

3. See Technology Choice and Employment in Developing Countries studies for USAID, including Ranis and Saxonhouse (1977); Baily (1977); Cardwell (1977); Fei (1977).

BIBLIOGRAPHY

Baily, M. A. 1977. Technology choice in the brick and men's leather shoe industries in Colombia. In *Technology Choice and Employment in Developing Countries*. Study submitted to USAID in November 1977, contract number AID/otr C-1326.

Bruton, H. 1967. Productivity growth in Latin America. *Amer. Econ. Rev.*, 57(5)(December): 1099-116.

Cardwell, L. 1977. Technology choice in the men's leather shoe and cotton spinning industries in Brazil: the relation between size, efficiency and profitability. AID/otr C-1326.

Denison, E. F. 1967. *Why growth rates differ*. Washington, D. C.: Brookings Institution.

Fei, J. 1977. Technology in a developing country: the case of Taiwan. AID/otr C-1326.

Pack, H. 1975. The choice of technique and employment in the textile industry. In *Technology and employment in industry*, ed. A. S. Bhalla. Geneva: ILO.

Ranis, G., G. Saxonhouse. 1977. Technology choice, adaptation and the quality dimension in the Japanese cotton textile industry. AID/otr C-1326.

Wang, Yi-Tao. 1975. Survey of the institution of the cultivation firm. Department of Agricultural Economics, University of Taiwan.

2
Total Factor Productivity and Its Determinants: Some International Comparisons

Howard Pack

I. INTRODUCTION

Differences in total factor productivity and factor endowment together explain the variations in per capita income across countries. Much of the analysis of developing countries has been concerned with the determinants of the levels and rates of growth of the various productive inputs as well as with increasing the static efficiency of resource use. However, there have been no systematic measurements of differences among developed and less developed countries in total factor productivity by detailed manufacturing sectors.[1] In this paper, I compare static efficiency for the Philippines, Israel, and the United States for two digit branches in manufacturing and analyze some of the sources of the measured differences.

Comparisons of total factor productivities among Israel, the Philippines, and the United States are apt for a number of reasons. Despite its rapid development, Israel's economy is still best viewed as being at the upper range of the less developed countries (LDCs), rather than being similar to that of Western Europe or North America. The industrial sector is of quite recent origin, nurtured by the typical package of import substitution policies, and, more recently, by export subsidies (see Pack 1971). Wages remain considerably lower than those in the developed countries. Moreover, many of those employed in the industrial sector have recently entered it from rural or service-sector backgrounds and bring with them few of the attitudes present in economies with a long industrial history. However, there is a substantial group of highly educated members of the labor force whose presence is likely to facilitate the industrialization process.[2]

The Philippines is, by contrast, much poorer, exhibits a lower endowment of education or other high-level skills,[3] and has a relatively short history of industrialization. Other countries could be chosen at similar levels of development; our choice of the Philippines is based upon the availability of estimates of the capital stock and effective protection rates for industrial branches, both of which are necessary for our analysis.

17

Part II presents the relevant theory, Part III a discussion of the data, and Part IV the estimates of differences in the total-factor-productivity indices. Part V attempts to explain observed productivity differentials. Part VI offers some conclusions.

The explanations, in Part V, of the intercountry differences in total factor productivity combine serveral strands of analysis that have been used in investigating the Leontief Paradox in trade patterns among advanced countries as well as in development-focused discussions. Among the variables considered are those representing skill requirements, relative capital intensity, and the size of firms. Given the cross-sectional nature of the analysis, the explanations are fairly good as measured by the coefficient of determination. Nevertheless, some of the results, particularly the low levels of relative total factor productivity in the Philippines, require additional study.[4] While additional effort at statistical analysis at the industry-wide level, including a refinement of data, will undoubtedly prove fruitful, it seems likely that a greater rate of return can be obtained from detailed studies at the firm level which will provide a better understanding of the technical and behavioral base of the more aggregative observations.

II. THEORY

Let the unit production function be:

$$q_1 = A_1 k_1{}^a z_1{}^{1-a} \tag{1}$$

where q_1 is one dollar of value added in industry i in country 1, the industry subscript being suppressed for simplicity, k_1 the capital-output ratio, and z_1 the number of man-years required to produce one unit of value added. A_1 is an efficiency index. Let this industry, in country 2, be described by a similar Cobb-Douglas function exhibiting the same output elasticities, but with a different efficiency index, A_2. As $q_1 = q_2$ the ratio of the efficiency indices is:

$$(A_1/A_2) = (k_2/k_1)^a (z_2/z_1)^{1-a} \tag{2}$$

or:

$$\log (A_1/A_2) = [a \log (k_2/k_1)] + [(1-a) \log (z_2/z_1)] \tag{3}$$

A_1/A_2 measures the ratio of total factor productivities in the two countries, assuming the same production function holds for both except for a multiplicative scalar.

Two difficulties arise in obtaining a correct measure of relative efficiencies. First, it is possible that each country produces according to a different Cobb-Douglas $a_1 \neq a_2$, in which case there is an index-number problem, A_1/A_2 depending on the particular set of output elasticities utilized. This will be discussed in the next section. Second, the specification of the underlying production function as Cobb-Douglas introduces a bias if the true (identical) function for both countries is a C.E.S. $\sigma \neq 1$, where σ is the elasticity of substitution.[5] To see the implications of this we rewrite (1) in logarithmic form:

$$\log q_1 = \log A_1 + a \log k_1 + (1-a) \log z_1 \tag{4}$$

Kmenta (1967) and Nelson (1965) have shown that the C.E.S. can be written (approximately) as (4) plus a correction factor or:

$$\log q_1 = \log A_1 + a \log k_1 + (1-a) \log z_1$$

$$+ 1/2 \ [(\sigma-1)/\sigma]a(1-a) \log (k_1-z_1)^2 \tag{5}$$

Thus, if the C.E.S. is the true production function, (3) can be rewritten as:

$$\log (A_1/A_2) = a \log (k_2/k_1) + (1-a) \log (z_2/z_1)$$

$$+ 1/2 \ a(1-a)[(\sigma-1)/\sigma] \log [(k_2-z_2)/(k_1-z_1)]^2 \tag{6}$$

If σ is significantly greater than unity, and $\log [(k_2-z_2)/(k_1-z_1)]^2$ is large, the Cobb-Douglas specification will result in an overestimate of A_1/A_2, and vice versa if σ is less than unity. However, for values of σ between .5 and 1.5, which bracket the range of estimated LDC elasticities (see Morawetz 1976), and given the actual differences in capital and labor intensities, the last term on the right-hand side of (6) is negligible.

III. DATA

In this part, I analyze two digit branches in the manufacturing sector (see the endnote for data sources). To obtain cross-country comparability, value added originating in each sector is deflated by an estimate of the ratio of domestic value added (D) to value added at world prices (W).[6] This is simply the rate of effective protection as usually calculated, (D/W) - 1, plus unity. Primary factors in each branch in all three countries are, thus, viewed as producing value added at international prices. Given the difference in the level and pattern of effective protection among the three countries, calculations based on value added at domestic prices distorted as they are by tariffs and quotas on both outputs and inputs, yield a considerably different picture of relative efficiency. In particular, when domestic prices are used, the industries in Israel and the Philippines appear much more efficient relative to the United States, and their efficiency levels show less dispersion across industries as well as different rankings.

The productivity calculations use data for the United States in 1963, the Philippines in 1961, and Israel in 1968. Both capital stock and value added have been adjusted to obtain as much comparability as possible. In particular, capital-stock estimates for the United States and Israel are both in 1958 prices, and Israel's value added has been deflated to 1963 prices.[7] No such adjustments have been made for the Philippine data given the closeness in date to that of the United States data.

Nevertheless, the capital-stock data are not entirely comparable across countries. Both the Philippines and Israel import most of the equipment used in manufacturing, and this component of the capital stock, acquired at world prices, is likely to be comparable to United States equipment prices. However, the construction component of total investment may differ in price across countries. The direction of bias is not obvious. The wages of construction workers are lower in the Philippines and Israel than in the United States, while costs of materials are likely to be higher. At the same time, techniques of production in construction, and total factor productivity in the construction sector, will differ across the countries. Insofar as we do not correct for these possible sources of bias, it is implicitly assumed that the construction component in all three countries has the same cost.

Throughout this study, capital stock, rather than the flow of services, is used, and no systematic attempt is made to determine the flow of services or the potentially different marginal productivities of the different components of the capital stock. These, and other desirable corrections suggested by Jorgenson and others, have been omitted because of the lack of data. However, in the specific country comparisons being made, these are likely to be of secondary importance compared with the large orders of magnitude of differences in total factor productivity. I have been able to determine the effect of one, potentially important source of differences in the rate of flow of capital services, namely, capacity utilization. If it is true, as often alleged, that LDCs have lower rates of utilization than do DCs, then their capital stocks will overstate the relative flow of services. Two recent studies (Hughes et al. 1976; Winston 1976) provide data that permit corrections for differences in the rate of utilization.

The utilization correction factors modify (2) by changing the (k_2/k_1) term to $[(k_2 b_2)/(k_1 b_1)]^a$, where b_2/b_1 is the ratio of capacity utilization in country 2 relative to country 1. The effect of this correction is to increase the mean value of A_1/A_2 (using U.S. factor shares as elasticities) by about 5 percent for both sets of country comparisons. Given the relatively small magnitude of the differences, I will not use the utilization-adjusted A_1/A_2 in the analysis of the sources of productivity differentials.

Labor input is measured as production workers, rather than total employment, to facilitate concentration on productive efficiency on the factory floor. Calculations using all workers as the labor input yield similar results. Data sources are indicated in the endnote.

The value of the output elasticities to be used is clearly of importance for our calculation of relative total factor productivities. Elasticities obtained from production-function estimates for the United States differ from study to study and often diverge from relative shares in the national accounts (see Solow 1964; Liu and Hildebrand 1965). The range of uncertainty in LDCs is even greater in view of the possibility of larger deviations of factor markets from the competitiveness required for measured national-accounts shares to be equal to the required elasticities. It is known that, where factor shares can be viewed as measures of output elasticities, the correct procedure is to use an arithmetic average of the two countries' factor shares in the sector in question.[8] Given the uncertainty about the closeness of observed shares in the Philippines and Israel to the "as if" imputation occurring under competitive markets, I will use three permutations of measured factor shares as elasticities in deriving A_1/A_2, namely, Israel or the Philippines, the United States, and the arithmetic average of the United States and the other country.[9]

IV. RESULTS

Single-factor unit-input coefficients are shown in Table 1, for each manufacturing branch. If both country 1 (Israel or the Philippines) and country 2 (the United States) were on the same isoquant, then the expected pattern of these coefficients would be $z_2/z_1 < 1$ and $k_2/k_1 > 1$, simply as a result of differences in relative factor prices. The typical reversal of the second inequality reveals that the capital-output ratio in most sectors, in both Israel and the Philippines, exceeds that of its United States counterpart. Nevertheless, the capital-labor ratio in the United States relative to that of the LDC (e.g., $(k_U/k_P)/(z_U/z_P)$) always exceeds unity, presumably reflecting factor price differences.

The relative single-factor labor productivities shown in Table 1 can be compared to those found in a number of other studies surveyed by Kravis (1976).[10] The unweighted mean of the Philippine-United States comparison of labor input per unit of output is .17, or .12 without petroleum refining, while for the Israel-United States comparison the mean is .27. In 1963, the unweighted mean index of relative unit-labor requirements in Japanese manufacturing was .29, close to that for Israel (Kravis 1976, 34, Table 6). To take another set of comparisons, the unweighted mean was .43 for U.S.-U.K. manufacturing in 1937, and .36 in 1950 (Kravis 1976). Thus, the relative unit-labor requirements in the United States and Israel in the 1960s fall within the range found in comparisons between such large, advanced countries as the United Kingdom and Japan. A fortiori, the average z_U/z_P figure of .12 for the Philippines does not seem surprising.

Kravis' survey also suggested some tentative hypotheses about the ranking of labor productivity among sectors. In particular, in U.S.-U.K. comparisons, U.K. unit-labor requirements are typically greater than the mean in fabricated metals, machinery, chemicals, and basic metals, and typically lower in food, beverages, tobacco, and textiles. These results are attributed to the difference in the diffusion of technological information in these sectors. Neither of our two sets of comparisons quite conforms to these patterns. For example, the food-beverage-tobacco branch in Israel and the tobacco branch in the Philippines show a higher than average, relative unit-labor requirement, while in machinery both reveal lower than average, unit inputs. Some of this reversal is likely to be due to the growing importance, particularly in the more advanced sectors, of licensing of technology as well as the presence, in the Philippines, of substantial direct foreign investment.

Table 2 presents the relative efficiency indices, A_1/A_2, for the Philippines and Israel. While the value of A_1/A_2 varies with the assumed elasticity, in both sets of columns the ranks, and usually the absolute values, are only slightly affected by the different

TABLE 1
Factor Requirements Per Unit of Value Added
(Ratios)

	Philippines		Israel	
	$\dfrac{z_U}{z_P}$	$\dfrac{k_U}{k_P}$	$\dfrac{z_U}{z_I}$	$\dfrac{k_U}{k_I}$
Food, Beverages, Tobacco			.08	.32
Food and Beverages	.13	.44		
Tobacco	.03	.17		
Textiles	.11	.14	.41	.69
Clothing	.09	.16	.24	.67
Wood and Furniture			.42	1.64
Wood	.22	.31		
Furniture	.11	.15		
Paper	.08	.23	.30	.79
Leather	–	–	.31	.40
Rubber & Plastic Products	.26	.59	.28	.74
Chemicals & Petroleum Refining			.12	.51
Chemicals	.16	.58		
Petroleum Refining	.88	1.03		
Non-metallic Minerals	.17	.40	.49	1.01
Basic Metals	.09	.36	.20	.81
Metal Products	.08	.23	.28	1.33
Machinery	.24	.80	.44	2.01
Electrical Equipment	.04	.05	.13	.61
Transport Equipment	.05	.09	.09	.24
Unweighted Average	.12	.31	.27	.83

Note: Unweighted Average for Philippines excludes petroleum refining.

elasticity assumptions.[11] As would be expected, Israel generally has considerably higher relative total factor productivity than the Philippines, with no clear pattern emerging among industries. Both countries exhibit lower total factor productivity than the United States in all industries (except in one of the calculations for petroleum refining in the Philippines), these being the mirror image of the inefficiency of import substituting industrialization induced by extensive protection.[12]

The average value of A_1/A_2 in the Israel-United States comparison (a = U.S. share) is .34, and in the Philippine-United States comparison is .16 (excluding petroleum refining). There is little correlation between the two sets of relative factor productivities, though the high relative productivity in the machinery sector in both Israel and the Philippines is of interest, given the distortions introduced that work against the sector in most LDCs.

The use of differing elasticities does not, in general, alter the ranking of A_1/A_2 across sectors within either set of comparisons. However, in some of the sectoral comparisons there is a substantial increase in relative productivity when the LDC elasticity is used. These large changes occur mainly in the "modern" sectors such as rubber, chemicals, and machinery in the Philippines, and reflect the combination of a greater capital share and relatively better capital productivity in these sectors. Whether the differences in factor shares between the Philippines and the United States represent differences in the production functions understood by manufacturers or factor market imperfections is not evident. The resulting differences in the value of A_1/A_2 are of some importance in analyzing both static comparative advantage and the cumulative impact on productivity of a sustained import-substitution regime, insofar as the newer industries exhibit higher relative productivity than might have been expected. Although A_1/A_2 varies with the elaticities used, in the effort reported below to explain observed intersectoral differences, the use of any of the three sets of A_1/A_2 yields quite similar results, reflecting the close correlation among the latter--for example, the simple correlation for the two sets of A_1/A_2, using United States and Philippine shares as elasticities, is .96.

The average value of A_1/A_2 can be viewed in a slightly different perspective using the intensive form of the Cobb-Douglas function. The average value of z_U/z_P (excluding petroleum) in Table 1 is .12; that is, Philippine average labor productivity is 12 percent of that in the United States.[13] The mean vaue of sectoral capital-labor ratios, $(k/z)_P/(k/z)_U$, is .5.[14] If the elasticity of output with respect to capital were .4 for both countries, and both operated with the same efficiency ($A_1/A_2 = 1$), then the relative average labor product in the Philippines would be .75 instead of .12. Thus, even if the Philippines had the same per capita endowment of capital as the United States, it would remain poor. A similar calculation for Israel would predict labor productivity of .64 rather than the observed .27.

TABLE 2
Total Factor Productivity Relative to United States
 (Ratios)

	Philippines			Israel		
	a equals:			a equals:		
	.5(US+ Phil.)	Phil.	U.S.	.5(US +Is.)	Israel	U.S.
Food, Beverages, Tobacco				.13	.13	.12
Food and Beverages	.24	.35	.17			
Tobacco	.10	.12	.08			
Textiles	.12	.13	.12	.47	.48	.45
Clothing	.11	.13	.10	.36	.50	.26
Wood and Furniture				.63	.76	.51
Wood	.26	.27	.24			
Furniture	.12	.12	.12			
Paper	.14	.17	.11	.40	.41	.40
Leather				.36	.37	.35
Rubber & Plastic Products	.40	.51	.31	.37	.39	.35
Chemicals & Petr.Refining				.22	.21	.23
Chemicals	.34	.44	.27			
Petroleum Refining	.99	1.02	.96			
Non-metallic Minerals	.26	.32	.22	.63	.68	.60
Basic Metals	.17	.22	.13	.30	.32	.28
Metal Products	.12	.15	.10	.43	.49	.37
Machinery	.40	.52	.30	.68	.75	.61
Electrical Equipment	.04	.05	.04	.20	.22	.18
Transport Equipment	.05	.05	.05	.12	.12	.12
Mean	.19	.24	.16	.38	.42	.34

Note: Philippines Means exclude petroleum refining.

As noted earlier there have been very few efforts to compare
total factor productivity across countries and only one, Christensen,
Cummings, and Jorgenson (1980), compares an LDC with a developed
country: they find that economy-wide total factor productivity
relative to the United States was the following for selected years:

Japan-United States

| 1955 | .45 |
| 1960 | .54 |

Korea-United States

| 1960 | .24 |
| 1970 | .32 |

These figures probably exceed those for manufacturing, as they
include the service sector in which it is likely that relative factor
productivities will be more similar across countries than is the case
in manufacturing. Thus, the Japanese-United States figure for
manufacturing in 1960 is probably below .50, exceeding the unweighted
.35 for Israel, but sufficiently close to confirm the plausibility of
the Israel-United States comparison, particularly given the
difference in size of the two poorer economies (populations of one
hundred million and three million), the emphasis on exports in Japan,
and the much longer period of Japanese industrialization.

Similarly, .24 probably overstates the relevant manufacturing
figure for Korea in 1960 which is more likely to have been below .20,
this being in roughly the same range as the figure (.19) that I have
calculated using their method (mean share) for the Philippines for
the same period. Given the substantial differences in the details of
the adjustments used by Christensen, Cummings, and Jorgenson and
those followed here, the similarities suggest that my results,
particularly the differences in total factor productivity across
countries, are not as surprising as a first glance at Table 2 would
suggest.

Nevertheless, relative total factor productivity in Philippine
textiles of 12 percent may puzzle some observers given the relatively
simple, machine-paced production processes and limited operator
skills required. A visitor to typical U.S. and Philippine weaving
sheds would not, for example, find the number of looms assigned per
weaver to be eight and a half times greater in the U.S., although
five-fold differences would be common. However, the percentage of
output of the highest quality grade is several times higher in the
American plant; part of low measured productivity stems from the poor
quality of production reflected in low product prices, rather than
from low physical productivity. Differences in the quantity and
quality of output are partly attributable to skill differentials
between operatives in the two countries, but more importantly to
managerial differences in the mastery of technology (for example, the
desirable level of humidity and the ability to correct for deviations
from it) and organization skills including the capacity to motivate
workers.[15]

V. EXPLANATION OF PRODUCTIVITY DIFFERENCES

I now attempt to explain the interindustry pattern of productivity differentials for Israel and the Philippines. At least three factors may account for the pattern of A_1/A_2, namely, relative capital intensity (the Hirschman hypothesis), skill levels, and economies of scale.

A. The Hirschman Hypothesis

Hirschman (1957) has suggested that the more mechanized a production process, the smaller the disparity between productivity in an LDC and an advanced country. Greater relative efficiency arises from the discipline imposed on both workers and management. Workers are required to conform to the inflexible tempo of machine-paced production activity. Management is forced to plan more carefully the flow of raw materials as well as to schedule preventive maintenance; if not, the entire production process may be halted by a shortage of materials, at one point, or by the breakdown of a machine which is an integral part of the production flow. Though the initial formulation emphasized the effect of machine-paced processes on labor productivity, production inefficiencies may result in higher capital-output ratios as well, though the relative "waste" of capital might be smaller than that of labor.

Relative capital-output ratios in LDCs may be raised even when there are no capital-specific inefficiencies, as a consequence of cost-minimizing substitution of capital for inefficient labor. An expanded version of the Hirschman hypothesis, analyzing total factor productivity, and its relation to capital intensity, is as appropriate as the initial formulation.[16] In this version, the LDC unit isoquant lies above that of the developed country at all capital-labor ratios, but becomes progressively closer to the latter as the relative capital-labor ratio increases. Instead of (2), the relative total factor productivities would be determined by:

$$(A_1/A_2) = (m_1/m_2) \ e^i \qquad \text{where } i = \mu(K/L)^1/(K/L)^2$$

$$= (k_2/k_1)^a \ (z_2/z_1)^{1-a} \qquad (7)$$

where (m_1/m_2) is the pure efficiency differential other than that attributable to relative capital intensity, and μ is a parameter indicating the effect of the level of relative capital intensity on relative total factor productivity.[17] Estimation of (7) using cross-industry data requires the assumption that μ is constant across industries, that is, that a 1 percent increase in capital intensity increases A_1/A_2 by the same percentage in all industries. The specification in (7) assumes that productivity in the LDC industry improves with the level of mechanization relative to that in the United States. An equally plausible specification is that relative productivity will be greater as the capital-labor ratio increases across Philippine industries regardless of the individual industry's ratio relative to its United States counterpart. Both formulations will be tested.

B. Labor Skills

There are several ways in which skilled labor may affect total factor productivity. Consider first a reformulation of (1):

$$q = m \, k^a (s \, z)^{1-a} \tag{8}$$

where the "effective" labor input now consists of two components, z, man-years of labor, and a measure of skills, s. Using this formulation to incorporate the role of skilled labor, equation (2) can be rewritten as:

$$A_1/A_2 = (m_1/m_2) \, (s_1/s_2)^{1-a}$$

$$= (k_2/k_1)^a \, (z_2/z_1)^{1-a} \tag{9}$$

Thus, the value of A_1/A_2, calculated earlier using (2), may include the effect of labor skills s_1/s_2, as well as the pure efficiency differential m_1/m_2. This view of the role of education in the production process assumes that it is simply another factor of production, increases in skill equally augmenting the marginal products of capital and labor along a given production function.[18]

Nelson and Phelps (1966) have suggested an alternative approach to the role of education or skill, namely, that higher levels of education permit workers to adjust more rapidly to changing technology, rather than increase their productivity in using a static, well-understood set of production methods. Assuming United States industries to be on the technological frontier and generating a constant stream of innovations, the differential ability to absorb this technology depends on the level of education within the LDC branches themselves; once the new methods have become familiar, the relative skill endowment will again become the determinant of relative productivity for a given vintage of equipment.

If Nelson and Phelps (1966) are correct, then education yields a payoff in terms of the greater ability to absorb newer technology successfully; the greater the absorption, the higher the value of A_1/A_2. This approach to the role of education in the determination of relative productivity will be tested by the use of two variables: (1) the calculated rate of technical change in United States manufacturing industries in the 1947-60 period, t, providing a measure of the rate of shifting of the technology frontier,[19] and hence of the potential role of skilled labor in effecting a successful transfer of technology; and (2) the absolute level of skill, E_i, within each of the LDC sectors, reflecting the absorptive ability of the domestic sector.[20]

In the Israel-United States comparisons, relative skill intensity is measured by the percentage of the labor force with thirteen or more years of education in each manufacturing sector;[21] absolute skill intensity is measured by the level of this variable in each Israeli branch, as well as by the average wage per production worker. Education by branch is not available for the Philippines. As a substitute, the annual wage per production worker is utilized.

Within the Philippines and Israel, higher wage levels may be assumed to reflect higher skill levels; however, the LDC wage relative to that of the United States will not necessarily reflect relative skill intensities.[22]

C. Economies of Scale

The productivity calculations have assumed constant returns to scale for each industry in the production process. Despite the venerability of this assumption, and the large number of empirical studies that have not disproved the hypothesis, there is a large body of engineering and cost studies that indicate the existence of scale economies at the plant level.[23] There has been relatively little effort to reconcile these two sets of results in a rigorous manner.[24]

The reconciliation of increasing returns in individual processes, and the use of a constant returns to scale production function for a firm or industry, is usually achieved by invoking a third factor such as administrative ability whose supply is limited, leading to increasing administrative costs beyond some scale. Expansion of the industry occurs by replication of plants, each of which is assumed to be operating at the point at which its average costs are a minimum. Even if this rationale is accepted for studies within a country, it does not provide a reasonable basis for the assumption that minimum average costs (or total factor productivity) will be identical across countries. Administrative and technical production management capacities will vary across countries with significantly different income levels and histories of industrialization.

Assume the "true" long-run production function exhibits increasing returns to capital and labor at the process level, but constant returns at the firm level, when the third factor, management, is included. The output level at which the firm or industry cost curve begins to exhibit constant returns to scale will depend on the relative endowments of managers, the smaller the number of managers the greater the still-to-be-exploited returns at the process level. Thus, even if the industries in the three countries under study all produce according to a constant-returns-to-scale function, such as the Cobb-Douglas assumed in our calculations, total factor productivity will vary across countries with firm size within each country.[25] The firms in the smaller country choose lower-scale higher-cost plants, and expansion of the industry will occur through replication of these. A similar process, at a larger scale, occurs in the large country. In effect, we assume that each of these average cost curves is generated by a Cobb-Douglas. The horizontal, industrywide average cost curve in the smaller country will lie above that in the larger.[26]

If the scale economies implied by this scenario do exist, then the calculated values of A_1/A_2 are maximum estimates of pure efficiency differentials; more accurate measures would be obtained if scale could be incorporated into the analysis. For example, one could allow the sum of the output elasticities to exceed unity so that the implied average cost function declines at the rate found in engineering studies. However, there is little basis in existing firm-level engineering and cost studies to permit the translation of scale economies into the respective, industrywide output elasticities of capital and labor. Thus, I have introduced a measure of scale economies as a separate variable to explain interindustry variations of A_1/A_2.

Assume that total costs C rise less than proportionally as the scale of production increases, the functional relationship being:[27]

$$C = \alpha Q^e \tag{10}$$

Average total cost (inversely proportional to total factor productivity) is:

$$c = C/Q = \alpha Q^{e-1} \tag{10a}$$

The ratio of average costs, then, in two countries will be:

$$(c_2/c_1) = (\alpha Q_2{}^{e-1})/(\alpha Q_1{}^{e-1}) = (Q_2/Q_1)^{e-1} \tag{11}$$

This last expression is proportional to A_1/A_2. As e is less than unity, the expected relation between A_1/A_2 and the relative plant size measure is negative.

As in other industrial analyses, plant size is measured by employment rather than output, as factory data by size of output are not readily available. The average plant size in an industry, Λ, is calculated as a weighted index of the relative importance of plants of different employment classes (5-10, 10-20, etc.), or:

$$\Lambda = \Sigma_i \Lambda_i \ (L_i/\Sigma_i L_i)$$

where Λ_i is the average level of employment in class i, and $L_i/\Sigma_i L_i$ is the relative share of employment in plants in this class in a given industry.[28] Use of the number of employees in the average factory will underestimate the value of Q_2/Q_1 if the average product of labor in the United States exceeds that in the LDC, which it typically does, and, thus, provides a lower-bound estimate of the difference in scale.

The value of e for each industry was obtained mainly from estimates of C. F. Pratten as follows.[29] Let c* be the percentage excess of value added per unit of output at 50 percent, compared to 100 prcent of the minimum efficient plant size in the United Kingdom; e is then defined as c*/(1+c*). The value of e, thus calculated, is assumed to hold throughout the entire range of production.

The scale variable used to explain interindustry productivity differentials substitutes L_i for each country into (11). Using S_i to denote relative scale, this yields:

$$S_i = (L_U/L_I)^{e-1} \text{ or } (L_U/L_P)^{e-1} \tag{12}$$

The equations finally estimated to explain relative total factor productivity A_1/A_2 across industries incorporating (7), (9), and (12) are:

$$(A_1/A_2)_i = b_0 + b_1 S_i + b_2 (E_I/E_U)_i + b_3 k_i \tag{13a.1}$$

$$= b_0 + b_1 S_i + b_2 (E_I/E_U)_i + b_4 (K/L)_{Ii} \tag{13a.2}$$

$$= b_0 + b_1 S_i + b_5 E_{Ii} + b_7 t_i \tag{13b.1}$$

$$= b_0 + b_1 S_i + b_6 W_{Ii} + b_7 t_i \tag{13b.2}$$

$$(A_1/A_2)_i = g_0 + g_1 S_i + g_2 W_{Pi} + g_3 k_i \tag{14a.1}$$

$$= g_0 + g_1 S_i + g_2 W_{Pi} + g_4 (K/L)_{Pi} \tag{14a.2}$$

$$= g_0 + g_1 S_i + g_2 W_{Pi} + g_6 t_i \tag{14b.1}$$

where i denotes the two digit branch; $(A_1/A_2)_i$ is relative total factor productivity in the two digit Israel-United States or Philippine-United States comparisons, calculated using United States factor shares as output elasticities; S_i is the relative size of the industry defined in the preceding paragraph; W_{Ii} and W_{Pi} are the average wage paid to production workers in sector i; t is the rate of disembodied technical change calculated for United States industries in the 1947-60 period; $(E_I/E_U)_i$ is the percentage of the labor force with thirteen or more years of formal education in Israeli sector i, relative to that in the same United States sector; and k_i is the Israeli or Philippine one-shift capital-labor ratio, relative to that in the United States; $(K/L)_{Ii}$ or $(K/L)_{Pi}$ is the Israeli or Philippine one-shift capital-labor ratio.

The measurement of the capital-labor ratio requires some elaboration. The analytic basis for the introduction of capital intensity is the presumption that mechanized processes substitute for the absence of skilled labor. Measuring mechanization indirectly through the capital-labor ratio necessitates an estimate of the capital per hour or per shift with which each worker cooperates. The use of the computed capital stock divided by average annual employment combines the two separate features of capital intensity and the utilization rate, and, thus, obscures the measure of interest, the one-shift capital-labor ratio. Using data recently presented by Hughes et al. (1976) and Winston (1976), the one-shift capital-labor ratio is calculated for the three countries by individual sector and used to obtain $(K/L)_{Ii}$, $(K/L)_{Pi}$, and k.

Equations 13a.1 and 13a.2, and 14a.1 and 14a.2, simultaneously test the scale, skill, and relative capital-intensity hypotheses for the two sets of comparisons. Given the difficulty in specifying whether the capital-labor ratio relevant to the Hirschman hypothesis is that of the LDC relative to the DC, or the absolute one across LDC industries alone, both are used, and account for the differences between the a.1 and a.2 regressions for each set of comparisons.

Equations 13b.1, 13b.2, and 14b.1 are designed to test the Nelson-Phelps hypothesis by simultaneously including measures of skill intensity across sectors and the rate of shift of technical progress in the United States, assumed to be the rate at which the technical frontier is shifting.

As noted earlier, education by sector is not available for the Philippines, and the average wage of production workers is used (as a weak proxy) in tests of both the traditional interpretation of the role of skills (14a.1 and 14a.2) as well as in the test of the Nelson-Phelps conjecture. Even though such sectoral education levels are available for Israel and the United States, the Israeli wage level is used as well in 13b.2, as it is often asserted that wages are likely to be a better measure of skill than formal education. I turn now to the empirical results.

In the Israel-United States analyses, the scale variable is significant in all of the regressions, and neither the education nor either of the capital-intensity variables are significant. The value of R^2 in 13a.1 and 13a.2 is fairly high for a cross-sectional study. Similar results in all regressions are obtained when the values of A_1/A_2, derived from alternative elasticity assumptions, are used as dependent variables. The insignificance of k_i and $(K/L)_{Ii}$ is not surprising insofar as the critical assumption of the Hirschman hypothesis is the efficiency of mechanization when a shortage of skilled labor exists. Though Israel's educational attainments are below those of the United States, they may well be beyond the threshold at which the substitution of equipment for skilled labor increases total factor productivity. The insignificance of the relative education variable in 13a.1 may be similarly explained. On the other hand, the importance of the scale variable conforms with general perceptions of the Israeli economy, which hold that an important characteristic limiting productivity is the low level of sectoral output (see Pack 1971, 106-08), which precludes both the realization of conventional economies of scale and the specialization and learning-by-doing that would accrue from longer production runs of individual products.

Given the strength and significance of the scale variable, it is worth noting that when L_I/L_U is used as the independent variable, omitting the correction for returns to scale, the regression results are uniformly insignificant. It is difficult to suggest an interpretation other than technical scale economies to account for the results of Tables 3 and 4.

The results for equations 13b.1 and 13b.2 do not confirm the Nelson-Phelps hypothesis. This failure is not surprising in an economy that had been nutured on import-substitution policies and had only recently entered a sustained phase of emphasis on exporting. Firms employing staff members with high education had many profitable opportunities for using their services in other ways than increasing productive efficiency. As these opportunities decrease, a closer association between skills and the absorption of productivity-enhancing production processes should occur, but these are not yet reflected in the data.

In equation 13b.2 the coefficient of the average production wage is positive and significant. It will be recalled that this variable was introduced as an alternative measure of skill levels given the

TABLE 3
Explanation of Relative Total Factor Productivity, A_1/A_2 : Israel-U.S.

	Constant	S_i	$(E_I/E_U)_i$	E_i	W_i	k_i	$(K/L)_I$	t_i	R^2
13a.1	1.3450 (4.03)	-.8176* (4.03)	-.0598 (0.21)			-.0450 (0.28)			.3434
13a.2	1.5746 (4.92)	-1.1027* (3.71)	-.1809 (0.72)				.00001 (1.66)		.4817
13b.1	1.4197 (4.61)	-1.0132* (3.49)		1.2503 (1.08)				1.3542 (0.42)	.4288
13b.2	1.3043 (6.23)	-1.3345* (5.79)			.0421* (3.37)			.4488 (0.19)	.7015

TABLE 4
Explanation of Relative Total Factor Productivity, A_1/A_2 : Philippines-U.S.

	Constant	S_i	W_i	k_i	$(K/L)_{Pi}$	t_i	R^2
14a.1	.1797 (0.92)	-.2731 (1.48)	.0205* (3.22)		-.00005 (0.98)		.4315
14a.2	.3049 (2.29)	-.3293** (2.36)	.0164** (2.97)	-.1059 (1.34)			.4680
14b.1	.3157 (2.20)	-.3973** (2.84)	.0173** (2.80)			.2267 (0.13)	.3825

Notes (Tables 3 and 4): For definitions of variables, see the text. t values in parentheses.
* significant at .01 level in two tail test; ** significant at .05 level in two tail test.

possible distortions associated with the use of formal education as the sole measure. Given the lack of significance of the opportunity of borrowing measure t_i, the statistical significance of W presents a quandry; in particular, is its significance specious or does it have a production theoretic basis? It is obviously a possibility that as relative factor productivity increases, an industry can afford to pay higher wages and, thus, the causality goes from A_1/A_2 to W, workers in efficient industries receiving rents above transfer earnings. This interpretation would be most plausible if lower values of A_1/A_2 were not simultaneously accompanied by greater rates of effective protection, the latter offering continued scope for wages greater than those warranted by productive efficiency. However, a negative and significant correlation between A_1/A_2 and effective protection is present in the data, (r = -.83), substantially attenuating the liklihood of a simple feedback from relative productivity to absolute wages. Moreover, when the effective rate of protection is itself introduced as a variable into regression 13b.2, the other variables, S_i and W_i, remain significant, and the ERP shows a negative and significant coefficient. The regression is:

$$A_1/A_2 = 1.1340 - .8477S_i + .0316W_i - .1163 ERP_i$$
$$(7.89) \quad (4.24) \quad (3.73) \quad (3.70)$$

$$R^2 = .8735$$

These results suggest that the higher W_i in the relatively efficient sectors at least partly reflects the use of efficiency wages to attract and retain more productive workers. The underlying production theory would suggest that skilled labor (correctly measured) should matter only insofar as the sector offers opportunities for its productive use, and the correct specification should be that in (9), employing relative skill intensity. Though it may be placing too much weight on the significance of W_i, it may be that, if a correct measure of skills were obtained, the variance across United States sectors in skills is less than that in Israel, and that, even as late as 1968, persons with relevant production skills were still in sufficiently short supply so that sectors succeeding in attracting them were able to operate relatively more effectively than other sectors.

In the Philippine-United States regressions, the role of scale and skills is confirmed, but not the capital-intensity hypothesis. Again, the Nelson-Phelps conjecture is not verified, and this fairly simple test may fail because of import substitution policies. The same question arises about the role of the wage variable, and much the same analysis may be offered; for example, the simple correlation between the effective protection rate and A_1/A_2 is -.65 and is significant, while a significant simple corelation does not hold between the latter variable and W_i. The significance of the wage variable, despite the weakness of the technical-change variable, can then be interpreted as in the case of Israel.

VI. CONCLUSIONS

Most quantitative documentation of the inefficiency of import substitution has relied on estimates of effective rates of protection in which the extent of production inefficiency is not explicit. The calculations presented in this paper may be viewed as a demonstration of the underlying productive inefficiency that necessitates high levels of protection to allow domestic industries to survive. The critical role of scale, often noted in the catalogue of difficulties presented by reliance on import substitution, is also strongly demonstrated, as well as the role of skilled labor in achieving greater productivity.

The shortcomings in achieving an effective use of extant resources cast further doubt on policy analyses that largely stress additional capital accumulation as the critical ingredient in an accelerated growth program.[30] Raising average Philippine industrial (total) productivity to half that of the United States would increase, by 100 percent, the income originating in this sector with existing primary inputs. Among the policies necessary to achieve such a goal in both the Philippines and Israel, given our empirical findings, would be the encouragement of larger scale in existing sectors in which scale economies have yet to be fully exploited. This policy would presumably require greater competitiveness within the domestic market, brought about by import liberalization, substantially to decrease the profits available at less than full utilization of capacity. In small countries such as Israel, and in larger ones characterized by low per capita income such as the Philippines, greater utilization of capacity will require a significant reliance on exports, a policy toward which Israel, but not the Philippines, has moved.

Variables such as technical knowledge and skill in labor relations are intrinsically difficult to measure. Their omission in the regressions reported in Part V undoubtedly accounts for a substantial fraction of the unexplained variance. While liberalized trade regimes may have some salutary effect on these fundamental determinants of productivity, they are almost certainly more difficult to affect through conventional policy instruments than is the level of utilization. Though there are gains to be achieved by "using the resources at hand more effectively," there also are limits to the costless realization of these benefits. Further progress in understanding the relevant issues and necessary policies requires research at the level of individual firms. The results reported in this paper demonstrate that the magnitudes involved are sufficiently large to warrant much more attention.

FOOTNOTES

Part of this research was financed by the Swarthmore College Faculty Research Fund. I have received helpful comments on earlier drafts from N. Leff, J.R. Pack, Robert West, L. Westphal and L.J. White.

1. Christensen, Cummings and Jorgenson 1980 have compared economy-wide productivity levels in eight developed countries as well as Korea. Their results will be referred to below.

2. In 1961, 5 percent of the Israeli industrial labor force had completed thirteen or more years of education compared with 14 percent for the U.S. labor force in 1960; 29 percent had nine to twelve years of education compaed with 52 percent for the U.S. See O.E.C.D. (1969).

3. In 1960, 4.5 percent of the manufacturing labor force had completed one or more years of college, and 16 percent had nine to twelve years of education. (O.E.C.D.)

4. As will be noted below, these are not that much different from the Korean levels of the same period. A comprehensive description and analysis of the Philippines is presented by the I.L.O. (1974).

5. Even more generally, the production function may be translogarithmic, as used by Christensen, Cummings, and Jorgenson (1980). The following justification for the use of the Cobb-Douglas rather than the C.E.S. extends to the translog function as well.

6. Other methods of deflation are utilized by authors of the studies surveyed by Kravis. The purchasing power parity methods employed by some are required when nontraded goods are included in the analysis. When dealing solely with traded goods, as in manufacturing, deflation by effective protection rates is appropriate.

7. The deflation procedure is the one suggested by David (1966).

8. Christensen, Cummings, and Jorgenson 1980 and references cited therein.

9. For the source of factor share data, see the endnote and Massell (1961).

10. These studies use a number of methods in deriving sector of origin output measures within each country and are not, in all cases, identical to the methods used in this study. In addition, the binary country comparisons employ several different techniques to compare output, but none uses the effective rate of protection to obtain comparability. While our single-factor productivities are, thus, not directly comparable with those summarized by Kravis, he emphasizes that very few of those are comparable among themselves.

11. Unit-labor requirements in Israel, relative to the U.S., are given by the inverse of the figures in Table 1. The high value of A_1/A_2 in petroleum refining in the Philippines is in accord with a priori expectations and provides confirmation that the

underlying data and their adjustments are reasonable.

12. For Israel, see Pack (1971, Ch. 4) and Baruh (1976). On the Philippines, see Power and Sicat (1971); and the I.L.O. (1974).

13. $z_U/z_P = (Q/L)_P/(Q/L)_U$

14. This is the average of the individual sectoral capital-labor ratios and is not the ratio of the means shown in Table 1.

15. The assertions in this paragraph are based on results of my current research on the sources of plant levels differences in productivity across countries. An interesting earlier effort along these lines can be found in Reynolds and Gregory (1965).

16. There have been few efforts to verify the Hirschman hypothesis empirically. The study most comparble to this is that of Clague (1970), who used Peru-U.S. comparisons in a number of industrial activities. His major finding is that total-productivity differentials are largest in those branches in which individual workers are offered the greatest "latitude" in the production process. Other analyses are those of Diaz-Alejandro (1965) and Gouverneur (1971). A survey of these and other studies is provided by Bhalla (1974).

17. For a discussion of the properties of this functional form, see Knox-Lovell (1968).

18. The Hirschman hypothesis suggests that a shortage of "skills" would decrease the marginal product of unskilled labor more than that of capital. For some estimates of the strength of complementarity between skilled labor and the other two factors, see Griliches (1970); and Fallon and Layard (1975).

19. t is taken from the values calculated by Massell (1961).

20. This assumes that changes in all industries are equally demanding of skilled labor to incorporate them into the production process. Other specifications of this process are clearly possible.

21. Other measures of education, such as median years, yield very similar regression results.

22. Denote the skilled wage in the U.S. by W_n, the unskilled wage by W_u and the corresponding wages in the Philippines by F_n and F_u. The average wage in the respective industries is $\Xi = m_i W_n + (1-m_i) W_u$ and $\Pi = s_i F_n + (1-s_i) F_u$ where m_i and s_i are the percentages of skilled workers in industry i in the two countries. If $m_i = s_i$ for each sector i, the relative skill intensity is the same for both countries in every branch. Yet the relative wage between the two will differ across industries with the value of m_i; differentiating $(\Xi/\Pi)_i$ with respect to m_i yields

$$[\Pi(W_n - W_u) - \Xi(F_n - F_u)]/\Pi^2$$

which will not, in general, be zero.

23. The most comprehensive surveys and analyses of these results are those of Walters (1963, 1970). Also, see Haldi and Whitcomb (1967) and Pratten (1971).

24. In some sources of growth calculations, as-if competitive imputations are used to weight factor growth rates, and then scale economies are invoked as one cause of any remaining residual. No reconciliation of the existence of scale economies and competitive-factor imputations is offered.

25. Firm size may differ across countries for other reasons as well, such as differences in the size of the domestic market combined with an unwillingness to consider exporting, often in response to a poorly designed incentive structure. Thus, firm size may capture features of the economy in addition to production-specific variables. The interpretation in the text of the source of scale differences implies that existing factor shares include a return to the third scarce factor. Thus, the observed shares contain an unknown upward bias in one or both elasticities and hence, A_1/A_2 may contain bias. In principle, the "managerial" share should be multiplied by the relevant unit-input requirement, but it is not possible to implement this procedure empirically. Thus, the size-of-firm variable used in explaining variations in productivity may partly capture these effects as well as more conventionally defined scale economies.

26. See the extensive cross-country calculations of firm size by Pryor (1973).

27. This follows the well known .6 rule. See, for example, Haldi and Whitcomb (1967).

28. This type of index is known as a Niehans index. See Pryor (1973).

29. See Pratten (1971, 269, Table 30.1). Pratten's estimates for typical activities in each of the two digit branches were augmented by those of Haldi and Whitcomb (1967) to check for consistency, and the latters' estimate was used in paper production.

30. Similar conclusions can be drawn from Kreuger's 1968 attempt to account for differences in GNP per capita across countries.

NOTES ON SOURCES OF DATA

United States

Value Added, number of production workers, distribution of firms by size. U.S. Bureau of the Census (1963).

Capital stock by industry. U.S. Office of Emergency Preparedness (1973).

Rates of effective protection. G. Basevi (1965).

Education by Industry. U.S. Bureau of the Census (1964).

Israel

Value added, number of production workers, distribution of firms by size. Israel, Central Bureau of Statistics (1971).

Capital stock by industry. Ben-Bassat, A. and A. Bergman (1974).

Rates of effective protection. J. Baruh (1976).

Education by industry. Israel, Central Bureau of Statistics (1964).

Philippines

Value added, number of production workers, distribution of firms by size, wages of production workers. Philippines, Bureau of the Census and Statistics (1961).

Capital stock by industry. J.G. Williamson, "Capital Accumulation, Labor Saving and Labor Absorption: A New Look at Some Contemporary Asian Experience."

Rates of effective protection. J. Power and G. Sicat (1971).

BIBLIOGRAPHY

Arrow, K., H. Chenery, B. Minhas, R. Solow. 1961. Capital-labor substitution and economic efficiency. *Rev. of Econ. and Statistics*, 43(August): 225-50.

Baruh, J. 1976. *Structure of protection in Israel, 1965-68.* Ph.D. Dissertation, Hebrew University, Jerusalem.

Basevi, G. 1965. *International trade restrictions and resource allocation in the United States.* Ph.D. Dissertation, University of Chicago.

Ben-Bassat, A., A. Bregman. 1974. Capital stock, capital-output ratios and capital intensity in Israeli industry. *Econ. Rev.*, 40: 29-48. Bank of Israel, Research Department.

Bhalla, A. 1974. Low cost technology, cost of labour management and industrialization. (Mimeo) Technology and Employment Programme, ILO. Geneva.

Bruno, M. 1972. Domestic resource costs and effective protection: clarification and synthesis. *J. of Pol. Econ.*, 80(January-February).

Christensen, L. R., D. Cummings, D. W. Jorgenson. 1980. Relative productivity levels, 1947-73: an international comparison. Discussion Paper No. 773, (June). Cambridge: Harvard Institute of Economic Research.

Clague, C. 1970. The determinants of efficiency in manufacturing industries in an underdeveloped country. *Econ. Dev. and Cult. Change*, 18(January).

Daniels, M. 1969. Differences in efficiency amoung industries in developing countries. *Amer. Econ. Rev.*, 59(March): 159-71.

David, P. 1966. Measuring real net output: a proposed index. *Rev. of Econ. and Statistics*, 48(November): 419-23.

Díaz Alejandro, C. 1965. Industrialization and labor productivity differentials. *Rev. of Econ. and Statistics*, 47(May).

Fallon, P. R., P. R. G. Layard. 1975. Capital-skill complementarity, income distribution, and output accounting. *J. of Pol. Econ.*, (April): 279-302.

Gouverneur, J. 1971. *Productivity and factor proportions in less developed countries.* Oxford U. Press.

Griliches, Z. 1970. Notes on the role of education in production functions and growth accounting. In *Education, income and capital*, ed. W. L. Hansen. New York: National Bureau of Economic Research.

Haldi, J., D. Whitcomb. 1967. Economies of scale in industrial plants. *J. of Pol. Econ.*, 75(August).

Hirschman, A. 1957. *The strategy of economic development.* New Haven: Yale U. Press.

Hughes, H., R. Bautista, D. Lim, D. Morawetz, F. Thoumi. 1976. Capital utilization in manufacturing in developing countries. World Bank Staff Working Paper No. 242 (September).

International Labor Office (ILO). 1974. *Sharing in development.* Geneva: ILO.

Israel, Central Bureau of Statistics. 1971. *Industry and crafts survey, 1968.* Jerusalem.

_____, 1964. Population and housing census. *Labour force, part 2.* Jerusalem.

Kmenta, J. 1967. On estimation of the CES production function. *Internat. Econ. Rev.*, 8(June): 180-89.

Kravis, I. B. 1976. A survey of international comparisons of productivity. *The Econ. J., 86(March)*.

Kreuger, A. O. 1968. Factor endowments and per capita income differences amoung countries. *The Econ. J.*, 78(September).

_____, 1972. Evaluating restrictionist trade regimes: theory and measurement. *J. of Pol. Econ.*, 80(January/February).

Liu, T. C., G. H. Hildebrand. 1965. *Manufacturing production functions in the United States, 1957.* Ithaca: Cornell U. Press.

Lovell, C., A. Knox. 1968. Capacity utilization and production function estimation in postwar American manufacturing. *Quart. J. of Econ.*, 82(May): 219-40.

Massell, B. 1961. A disaggregated view of technological change. *J. of Pol. Econ., 69(December)*.

Morawetz, D. 1975. Capital utilization in Israeli industry. (Mimeo) Falk Institute for Economic Research in Israel.

_____, 1976. Elasticities of substitution in industry: what do we learn from econometric estimates. *World Dev.* 4(April).

Nelson, R. R. 1965. The CES production function and economic growth projections. *Rev. of Econ. and Statistics, 47(August): 326-28*.

_____, 1968. A diffusion model of international productivity differences in manufacturing industry. *Amer. Econ. Rev.*, 58(December): 1219-48.

Nelson, R. R., E. Phelps. 1966. Investment in humans, technological diffusion, and economic growth. *Amer. Econ. Rev.*, 56(May): 69-75.

O.E.C.D. 1969. *Statistics of the occupational and educational structure of the labour force in 53 countries.* Paris: O.E.C.D.

Pack, H. 1971. *Structural change and economic policy in Israel.* New Haven: Yale U. Press.

Philippines, Bureau of the Census and Statistics, 1961. *Economic census of 1961.* Vol. 3.

Power, J. H., G. P. Sicat. 1971. *The Philippines: industrialization and trade policies.* New York: Oxford U. Press.

Pratten, C. F. 1971. *Economies of scale in manufacturing industry.* Cambridge: Cambridge U. Press.

Pryor, F. L. 1973. *Property and industrial organization in communist and capitalist nations.* Bloomington: Indiana U. Press.

Reynolds, L. G., P. Gregory. *Wages, productivity, and industrialization in Puerto Rico.* Homewood, Ill.: Richard D. Irwin.

Scherer, F. M. 1973. The determinants of industrial plant sizes in six nations. *Rev. of Econ. and Statistics*, 55(May).

Solow, R. M. 1964. Capital, labor and income in manufacturing. In *The behavior of income shares.* Princeton: Princeton U. Press for NBER.

U. S. Bureau of the Census. 1964. 1960 industrial characteristics. Report PC (2) 7F.

_____, 1963. *Census of manufactures.*

U. S. Office of Emergency Preparedness. 1973. *Development of capital stock series by industry sector.* Prepared by Jack Faucett Associates, Inc. Washington.

Walters, A. A. 1963. Production and cost functions: an econometric survey. *Econometrica*, 31(January-April).

_____, 1970. *An introduction to econometrics.* New York: Norton.

Winston, G. C. 1976. On measuring factor proportions in industries with different seasonal and shift patterns or did the Leontief paradox ever exist. Research Memorandum No. 71, Center for Development Economics. Williamstown, MA: Williams College.

3
Intergenerational Income-Fertility Linkages in Developing Countries: A Conceptual Framework

Michael Todaro

I. INTRODUCTION

During the 1970s, the field of population economics witnessed the emergence of a variety of complex macroeconomic-demographic models as well as an intense theoretical and quantitative examination of the microeconomic determinants of household fertility decisions. Recent research has increased our understanding of several of the major socioeconomic determinants of family size (see bibliography for selected references). Nevertheless, despite the growing sophistication of economic-demographic analysis as applied to developing countries, we do not as yet possess a practical and workable methodology to assist policymakers in systematically incorporating demographic variables into their ongoing quantitative policy and planning frameworks. Thus, the gap between conceptual generalization and practical policy advice with regard to the demographic implications of alternative development policies is still quite substantial.[1]

Although the magnitude and, in some cases, even the direction of the demographic effects of development policy are poorly understood and, thus, in need of more focused research, there does appear to be a growing consensus on "qualitative" relationships in two basic areas: (1) the demographic effects of development, and (2) the developmental effects of demographic behavior.[2]

Social and economic policies that are not specifically designed with regard to their population effects can have important influences on demographic variables. For example, policies directly designed to raise levels of living for the poorest 30 to 40 percent of a country's population (where levels of living include income, education, health delivery, housing, security, etc.) are thought to induce fertility reductions even though there may be short-run increases and short- as well as long-run improvements in the spatial distribution of the population.[3] Since lower income groups typically have the highest fertility rates and the greatest overall propensity to migrate toward increasingly congested urban slums, policies designed to attack directly the conditions of absolute poverty (e.g., through taxes and transfer payments, small-farm public investment projects, land reform accompanied by carefully designed, integrated, rural development schemes, small-town industrial development, expanded formal and informal rural education, particularly for women, labor-intensive public-works projects, credit provision to small-scale urban informal-sector activities, job creation for women, especially outside the home, etc.) are believed to create an environment that is conducive to gradual fertility reductions and to more socially desirable balances between rural and urban population distributions.[4]

On the other hand, policies focused exclusively on accelerating GNP growth through, for example, the promotion of capital-intensive, modern-sector, import-substitution schemes or the continued emphasis on promoting large-scale, private, agricultural and/or extractive activities, are likely to be partially frustrated by continued, rapid population growth, growing food shortages, and the accelerated migration of displaced rural peasants into the congested and politically explosive urban shantytowns. It follows that development policies focusing specifically on the provision of basic needs in rural areas and, particularly, those that create socially productive income-earning opportunities for the rural poor, especially for women, are also those thought most likely to have indirect positive implications for long-term fertility and mortality reduction and for modifying present excessive rates of rural-urban migration. But by how much, and over what time horizon, will group-specific, income-generating policies lead to lower aggregate population growth rates? The lacunae in existing literature and applied policy with regard to this fundamental issue remain substantial.

This paper, therefore, represents an attempt to narrow the existing gap between theory and empirical, applied policy. It will attempt to develop a framework to quantify the impact of alternative, income-generating development policies on demographic change and translate such impacts into measures of improved social welfare. Its general objectives are the following: (1) to develop a set of measurable criteria for judging the success or failure of development policies in terms of their direct and indirect effects on population gorwth; (2) to ascertain how policy-induced changes in fertility levels can be incorporated into economic indices of welfare improvement; (3) to examine how development policy affects demographic change, and detemine which policies are likely to be most effective in lowering aggregate fertility rates; and (4) to discover whether the explicit inclusion of the demographic implications of alternative development projects and policies will significantly alter the ranking of those projects and policies in terms of their contribution toward maximum welfare improvement. The present paper focuses primarily on conceptual, policy-related issues. Future work will emphasize procedures for empirical application in the context of specific developing nations.

II. THE CONCEPTUAL FRAMEWORK: INITIAL OBSERVATIONS

Traditional development theory has focused on the rate of GNP growth as a principal measure of development performance and a reflection of social-welfare growth. Such aggregate income growth in a country can conveniently be put in a formula that simultaneously reflects the size distribution of household income and the rate of income growth in various population groups. Thus, we start with the following simple measure of social-welfare growth:

$$W = \Sigma_i w_i g_i \qquad i = 1,2,\ldots,n. \tag{1}$$

where W is an index of social-welfare growth, w_i are the welfare weights, and g_i the income-growth rates for various income groups. Specifically, if each w_i equals the share of total national income accruing to each successive income class i (where $\Sigma_i w_i = 1$), and g_i equals the income-growth rate of group i in a size-distribution of income, then aggregate social-welfare increase W will be measured by the rate of national income growth (GNP). In this formulation, GNP growth is simply the weighted sum of income growth in each income group, where the relative welfare weights w_i are equal to the actual shares of national income received by each income group. Thus, equation (1) represents a convenient formula for incorporating income-distribution parameters into aggregate measures of GNP growth.

A more relevant measure of development and social-welfare progress, however, would be the overall rate of per capita income growth rather than simple GNP growth. Our social-welfare function can therefore be redefined as:

$$W' = \Sigma_i w_i' g_i' \tag{2}$$

where g_i' is now the growth rate of per capita income in each income class, and W' is the rate of per capita GNP growth. We will specify the nature of the new welfare weights w_i' later.

We assume that, for each income group, per capita income growth is equal to the average household's per capita income growth. Furthermore, household per capita income growth equals household income growth minus growth in household size:

$$g(y/p)_i = g(y)_i - g(p)_i$$

Population size can now be treated as an exogenous variable through household size. Specifically, we assume that:

$$p_i = f\,[(y/p)_i, t, X] \tag{3}$$

where p_i is the average household size in group i, $(y/p)_i$ is the average household per capita income in group i, t reflects other institutional and social changes that take place over time (trend changes) affecting population growth, and X is a vector of policies which reduce or increase population growth. Additionally:

$$g(p)_i / g(y/p)_i = z_i \tag{4}$$

where z_i measures, for group i, the percentage change in household size resulting from a percentage change in per capita household income, given no change in t or X. z_i is, for group i, the elasticity of household size with respect to per capita household income. z_i may be either positive, negative, or zero. Moreover, z_i can represent either a static elasticity at a present point in time, an intergenerational elasticity whose full effect is experienced over time between generations, or, more likely, some combination of these two time effects.[5]

A. Intergenerational Fertility Elasticities

The concept of an intergenerational income elasticity is not found in the economics literature. Such intergenerational elasticities have little relevance for the standard economic theory of consumer behavior and demand which focuses on instantaneous changes in the demand for present and future goods when incomes change. However, this concept may be highly relevant for understanding how the demand for children changes over time with changing income expectations on the part of each new generation. The "static expectations" notion of traditional demand theory in economics, therefore, needs to be modified in the context of a development process that brings about rapid economic change. Intergenerational income elasticities of demand for children are meant to represent the mechanism through which current household income changes alter the opportunity set available to the children of that household and, thus, change their attitudes, life-style expectations, and consumption preferences. They are the long-term beneficiaries of the increases in per capita family financial resources, and it is their preferences for children that are most likely to be altered as a result of their parents' improved economic situation.

In short, we hypothesize that there is a _lagged_ effect on the demand for children resulting from current income changes and that this lag operates through altered family-size preferences on the part of the children of the household whose income steadily increases. A long-term downward multiplier effect on the demand for children may thus be set in motion, one which triggers a sort of "mini" demographic transition within each income group of a country.

B. Income-Fertility Relationships: Cross-Sectional and Trend Effects

Household size decomposes into the demographic components, fertility and mortality. For the present, we deal only with changes in fertility, although the general household-size relationship can be expressed as:

$$f_i = f\ [(y/p)_i, t, X, m_i]$$

where the new variables are fertility f and mortality m. We are interested in the change in fertility with respect to the change in per capita income with all other variables given, that is, the slope (partial derivative) of the cross-sectional relationship between fertility and per capita income at any given point. The double-log form of this relationship would then be the elasticity of fertility with respect to per capita income.

In Figure 1, line t(0) represents the observed negative cross-sectional relationship between household fertility and per capita income (Kuznets 1978, 1979). From line t(0), we can trace the average household fertility (i.e., children-ever-born) of each income group as a function of its per capita income. Lines t(1), t(2) and

46

FIGURE 1

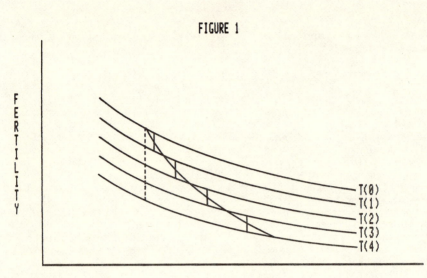

PER CAPITA INCOME

FIGURE 2

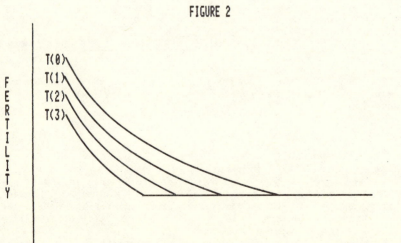

PER CAPITA INCOME

the rest represent shifts in that relationship over periods of time resulting from changes other than in a group's per capita income. For present purposes, we assume that the changes that take place over time t include mortality m and fertility-altering public-policy interventions X. Such nonincome-induced demographic changes are lumped together under the category, trend effects. The dashed line of Figure 1 is an example of the path of fertility decline for an income group which experiences no income gains, but does experience trend effects. The solid, stepwise line portrays the path of fertility decline of an income group which experiences both trend shifts and real income improvements over time. In reality, the trend effects take place as continuous change, rather than as discrete shifts. The convex, smooth line in Figure 1 represents continuous change in income and trend effects.

Movements along any time-specific, cross-sectional income-fertility relationship as, for example, along t(0) or t(1), are meant to portray how income changes of any group lead to lower fertility as a result of that group taking on the preferences and behavioral patterns of higher income groups. Trend shifts (i.e., movement of the entire income-fertility curve from, say, t(0) to t(1)) may be thought of as resulting from the more general forces of modernization in a transitional society. These shifts are assumed to be related both to general economic and social improvement and to exogenous factors such as the transfer of Western values through the internationalization of education and information. The introduction of privately or publicly supported family-planning programs may also independently contribute to secular fertility declines, but the evidence on this point is far from convincing.

Trend shifts are indirectly related to income improvements, to the extent that such improvements change the structure of the economy and society. Income growth that takes place in all income groups, as well as that which accrues to a particular income group, is likely to change both economic and societal structure. For example, income gains to higher income groups directly and indirectly change the position of lower income groups. The change takes place in occupation and residence. The landless peasant becomes the urban service worker. The change may also take place in preferences, as the poor try to emulate the new consumption patterns of the rich and middle classes. The change may also result from increased public expenditures providing public services and consumption goods to lower income groups without regard to actual income gains to these groups. How such changes take place, and which constellation of factors are most influential in inducing downward-fertility trend shifts, represents a critical but yet to be exploited area of microdemographic research.

In short, it is assumed that changes in economic and societal structure that take the form of altered industrial and occupational structures, educational opportunities, residence patterns, preference emulations, labor-force participation rates, and the availability of public goods and services, all indirectly influence fertility. These composite indirect fertility influences are represented in Figure 1 by the gradual downward trend shifts of the direct income-fertility curve from t(0) to t(4).

With regard to the fertility impacts of expanded public services X, their provision typically includes those health-promoting activities which bring about a reduction of infant and child mortality, and thereby contribute to later fertility declines. They often also include family-planning supply services which enable individual couples to close the gap between their desired and actual fertility, and family-planning educational services which change or rationalize couples' preferences. Finally, by providing a greater supply of subsidized educational opportunities, governments inevitably alter both the opportunity cost of child labor and the child's own preference set with regard to large families versus more consumption goods.

Increases in public goods and services may be independent of overall income growth. For instance, a reorientation of development strategy, away from capital-intensive industry and agriculture and toward the provision of basic needs, results in the increased supply of public goods and services to specific income groups without regard to secular income changes. Other examples of fertility-reducing factors which are not dependent on income growth include technological improvements in medicine and contraceptives, which changed the supply of health and family-planning services, and the dissemination of public information, in such areas as health and sanitation, through existing institutions. Another possibility is the alteration of relative real household incomes through progressive or regressive taxes designed to finance the provision of expanded public services.

C. The Nature of Fertility Trend Shifts

Although, in the absence of intensive micro-field studies, it may be difficult to sort out the many factors influencing fertility trend shifts, general observations about the nature of trend changes are possible.

First, trend shifts should not be expected to result in fertility levels below some minimum. Evidence from countries where the fertility transition has been completed suggests that a completed fertility of two children per couple may be a reasonable minimum from our model's operational standpoint. Figure 2 shows what trend shifts might look like with a minimum level.

Second, trend shifts are unlikely to be of the same magnitude for all income groups through all periods until a minimum fertility level is reached as depicted in Figure 2. Some groups may not even experience these shifts. Figure 3 represents such a case; the fertility of the lowest income groups, A and B, and the highest income groups, E and F, exhibits no shift between times t(0) and t(2). At any given time, depending on its absolute income level as well as its internal size distribution, a country may have a smaller range of income groups than A through F. For example, a country may only have income groups between C and D, and hence, as shown in the Figure, have the same absolute trend shifts taking place for all income groups. At a later time, the same country may have income groups ranging from C to F. Determining which range of income groups a country has could involve the problematic unraveling of the determinants of the trend effect for each income group; general

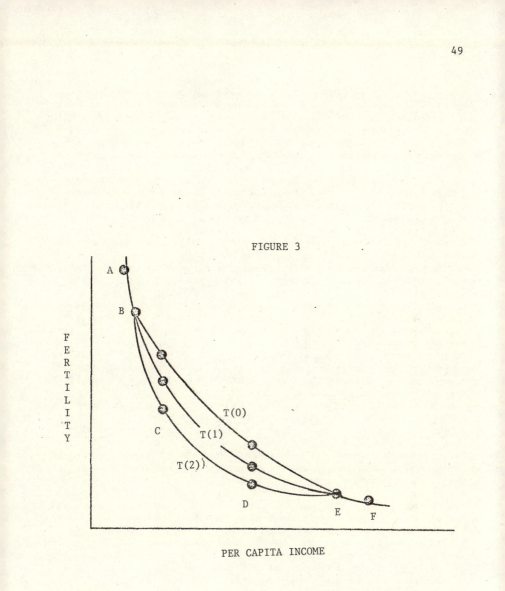

FIGURE 3

PER CAPITA INCOME

notions on the circumstances of income groups may suffice. For instance, in countries where some income groups are almost completely insulated from the dynamic elements of society, we may expect little or no trend shift, as is the case with income groups A and B in Figure 3. Among high income groups we might also expect very little trend shift as the minimum fertility level is approached.

Third, for determining the influence of alternative cross-sectional income changes on group-specific fertility behavior, only a general notion of trends may be needed. As income is not the sole determinant of fertility, we can include rates of trend changes that are chosen so that the fertility transition is completed within an expected length of time. Where we lack the information for making estimates of different trend shifts for income groups over time, using even incremental shifts is a reasonable solution. Thus, one's a priori assumption is that over time, the income-fertility relationship remains the same, while trend shifts show relatively equal movements at all income levels. For the length of the transition, recent historical demographic experience can be used. Where great uncertainty exists, several alternative lengths can be tried. This is the normal practice of demography. The United Nations projections are a prime example. Finally, to determine the reasonableness of our assumptions about trend shifts, we can test the sensitivity of different patterns of income growth between income groups to the length of the transitions and the evenness of the trend effects between groups and over time.

Fourth, income groups whose fertility is constrained by biological rather than socioeconomic determinants may not be influenced by trend shifts. Figure 4 shows a cross-sectional income-fertility relationship where income groups A and B have their fertility determined by the biological maximum in period t(0). In the next period t(1), group B experiences a fertility decline from the trend effect, while group A has no change in fertility. Figure 5 is identical to Figure 4 except that it has an upward-sloping biological constraint. The upward slope represents increased fecundity from improvements in health and nutrition associated with higher incomes. Improvements in health and nutrition independent of income increases that accrue to the low income groups would be shown by an upward trend shift of the biological constraint.

In populations where some of the low or middle income groups are constrained by the biological maximum, the best fertility-related development strategy may be to increase, first, the incomes of those groups whose fertility is not biologically constrained. Income gains to these groups will result in faster fertility declines for the aggregate population. In addition, by focusing initial economic benefits on those groups whose fertility reduction is likely to be largest (e.g., middle income groups), development planners may be able to devote fewer public resources to the provision of social and educational sevices and focus more on directly productive projects. This should lead to more rapid income growth and the eventual acceleration of fertility decline in the presently biologically constrained groups.

Where the income-fertility relationship is determined on the basis of per capita household income, and where some income groups have their fertility limited by the biological maximum, much of the

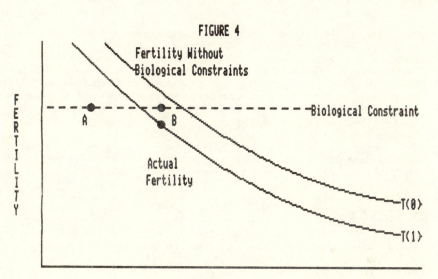

FIGURE 4

Fertility Without Biological Constraints

Biological Constraint

Actual Fertility

T(0)

T(1)

PER CAPITA INCOME

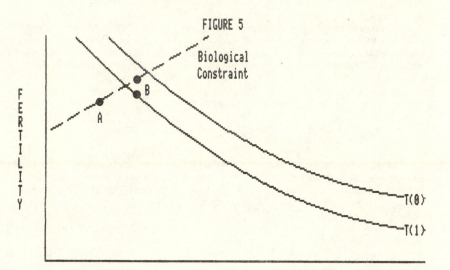

FIGURE 5

Biological Constraint

T(0)

T(1)

PER CAPITA INCOME

variation in the fertility for these groups results from variation in fecundity between women, rather than from changes in per capita income. The households of high-fecundity women have reduced per capita incomes from a large number of births. The housholds of low-fecundity women have higher per capita incomes than they would choose as a result of their lower biological constraint. Figure 6 shows the empirically observed income-fertility relationship (the solid line) and the relationship when the fecundity of all women is identical (the dashed line).

In income groups where all the variation in fertility is caused by fecundity differences, trend shifts will not take place as desired fertility is implied to be greater than actual fertility.

D. Mortality

The second major component of population or household-size growth is mortality. Where fertility and mortality both decline over time, their relative rates of decline determine the rate of population growth. If both fertility and mortality are income determined, income growth is more desirable in income groups where population growth (the difference between fertility and mortality) is most rapidly declining than where fertility is most rapidly declining.

The mortality-income effect, however, is minimized by the predominantly exogenous character of mortality decline. Mortality is decreased largely by the improved supply of public goods and sevices. Public health measures, education, sanitation, and the availability of health agents and facilities are all examples of public services which promote mortality decline. Per capita income, by contrast, does not appear to influence mortality as significantly as it does fertility.

Income improvements that reduce fertility and, thereby, improve social-welfare growth do not affect population growth or social welfare through mortality decline. Thus, the elasticity of household size with respect to per capita household income simplifies to the elasticity of fertility with respect to per capita household income:

$$z_i = g(p)/g(y/p) = g(f)/g(y/p)$$

III. THE COMPLETED FRAMEWORK

Returning to the basic framework, since per capita household-income growth equals household income growth minus growth in household size, $g(y/p) = g(y) - g(p)$ or, dividing by $g(y/p)$, we get:

$$1 = [g(y)/g(y/p)] - [g(p)/g(y/p)]$$

which can be rewritten as:

$$1 = [g(y)/g(y/p)] - z$$

It follows that we can now rewrite g_i' in equation (2) as:

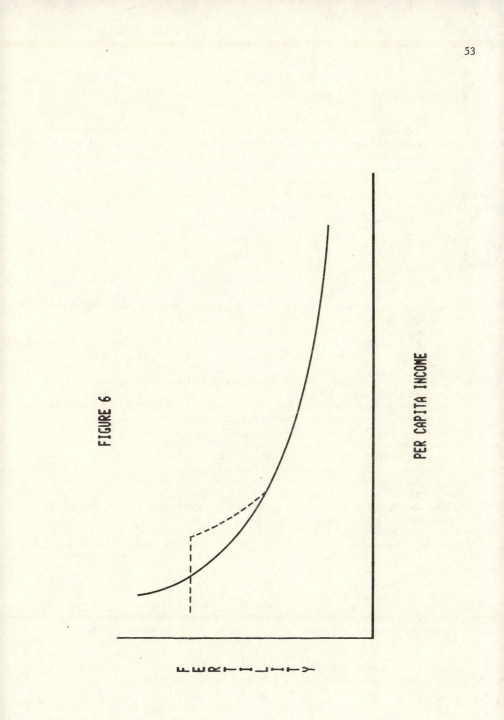

FIGURE 6

FERTILITY

PER CAPITA INCOME

$$g_i' = g_i/(1 + z_i) \tag{5}$$

since $g_i' = g(y/p)$ and $g(y) = g_i$. Thus, over time, per capita household-income growth, in any income class, will be equal to the actual household-income growth in that class, divided by one plus the elasticity of household-size growth with respect to per capita household-income growth of that specific class.

This permits us to rewrite our index of per capita welfare growth, equation (2), as:

$$W' = \Sigma_i w_i' \, [g_i/(1+z_i)] \tag{6}$$

The appropriate welfare weights w_i' in (6) should reflect the influence of two factors: (1) the relative size of group i (i.e., the proportion of the total population in group i), which we can call a_i; and (2) the objective or subjective importance of the welfare of group i (i.e., its rise in per capita income) to aggregate welfare.[6] If per capita income growth of each household group i is valued with weight v_i and the proportion of the total population in group i is a_i, then $w_i' = v_i a_i$. v_i could once again be the income share w_i, so that normalized $w_i' = (w_i a_i)/(\Sigma_i w_i a_i)$ -- where $\Sigma_i w_i = 1$ -- and W' would be a strictly empirical measure of aggregate per capita income growth.

Alternatively, v_i could be some socially determined, "normative" measure of the relative desirability of raising per capita incomes in group i, so that W' would no longer be a strict measure of per capita income growth. For example, with regard to group-specific fertility reductions, planners may decide that the marginal social benefit-cost ratio of an averted birth may not be equal across all income groups (e.g., they may be much higher for fertility reductions in low income classes) and incorporate these differential social valuations in the various welfare weights. (A suggested method is in Todaro 1977a.) Alternatively, the planners may decide income gains to lower income groups are more important than the same percentage income gains to higher income groups and, therefore, weight accordingly.

Equation (6) shows that income growth will exert a direct and indirect effect on social-welfare growth over time, depending on: (1) how national income is initially distributed or, in the normative case, how group specific birth rate changes are evaluated (the w_i'); (2) the rates of per capita income growth in different income groups (the g_i'); (3) the proportion of the total population in each group (the a_i); (4) the relative numerical value (positive, zero, or negative) of the intergenerational per capita income elasticity of population growth in each income group (z_i); and (5) the trend effects on z_i (z_i is a function of the relative trend shifts between income groups of initial relationship, $z_i = z_i(t)$). The numerical values of these five parameters will jointly determine the aggregate rates of per capita income growth (or, social-welfare growth, if the v_i are subjectively determined).

IV. POPULATION AND DEVELOPMENT POLICY

We can use the simple formulation above to examine the macro welfare implications of alternative population and development policies. The vector X in expression (3) is our starting point.

Consider first the effect of a change in policy measure x_n on the growth rate of per capita income in group i, where $g(y/p)_i = f(x_n)$. Let us assume that the benefit (or cost) of this measure to group i can be represented by an increase (or decrease) in the income growth rate of group i. Additional benefits (or costs) will accrue as a result of the anticipated direct and indirect decline (or increase) in the population growth rate of group i. Thus, assuming:[7]

$$z_i = \frac{g(p)_i}{g(y/p)_i} - \frac{\partial g(p)_i}{\partial g(y/p)_i} \qquad (4')$$

we start with the identity:

$$\frac{dg(y/p)_i}{dx_n} = \frac{dg(y)_i}{dx_n} - \frac{dg(p)_i}{dx_n}$$

Decomposing the direct and indirect effects of x_n on $g(p)_i$, and substituting z_i from (4'), we obtain:

$$\frac{dg(y/p)_i}{dx_n} = \frac{dg(y)_i}{dx_n} - \left| z_i \frac{dg(y/p)_i}{dx_n} + \frac{\partial g(p)_i}{\partial x_n} \right| \qquad (7)$$

In equation (7), the first term represents the direct income benefit (or cost) of population policy x_n for group i, the second term represents the _indirect_ effect of x_n on the population growth rate for group i as a result of the induced change in household per capita income, and the third term represents the _direct_ effect of measure x_n on the population growth rate of group i. Such population effects can only occur as direct results of changes in intermediate population variables (e.g., age of marriage, use of contraception, etc.), with the distinct liklihood that the same policy instrument may differentially affect population behavior in different groups. Note that if z_i is negative, then each of the three terms in equation (7) will be positive, so that the direct and indirect effects of population policies aimed at raising income levels will be to increase per capita income growth by _more_ than non-population-oriented general-development policies that operate only indirectly on population growth through general increases in the standard of living.

For example, providing expanded female employment opportunities outside the home might simultaneously raise household incomes (the first term), indirectly reduce the desired family size of the present and next generation through intergenerational income-elasticity effects (the second term), and directly reduce the number of desired children by delaying the age of marriage, causing greater birth spacing, and the rest (the third term). On the other hand, providing

similar employment opportunities for men at comparable wage rates may
have a smaller overall impact on per capita income growth rates by
working only through the first and, possibly, the second term of
equation (7). Family-planning programs would operate to reduce
directly the number of children by closing the gap between the actual
number of children and the desired number of children, and by
reducing the desired number of children (the third term). Family-
planning programs would indirectly reduce the desired family size of
the present and the next generation through the intergenerational
income-elasticity effects by increasing per capita income through
fertility reductions (the second term).

Table 1 provides a short-hand tabulation of the expected direct
and indirect demographic effects of a whole range of development and
population policies. Following the recent literature, policies whose
designated effect is primarily socioeconomic are labeled "demand"
policies, while those that relate to the availability and/or
provision of modern fertility control are designated "supply"
policies (Berelson and Haveman 1979).

The "pluses" and "minuses" in the Table are only illustrative
and are meant merely to indicate general directions of induced
effects. The number of "pluses" and "minuses" in each cell is
intended to give hypothetical general orders of magnitude. Thus, for
example, "development" policies that focus on women may have the
greatest long-term impact on lowering fertility and increasing per
capita incomes, even though the short-run population effects may be
less significant than, say, family-planning programs.

The formulas in equations (9) and (10) provide more specific
numerical estimates and predictions of likely impacts based on
calculated parametric values of a_i, v_i, w_i, and z_i. Theoretically,
they can be used to tell us by how much more a poverty-focused
development strategy will contribute to long-term income growth and
fertility declines than, say, a traditional GNP-maximizing strategy.
In a forthcoming paper, these parameters will be used to illustrate
the population impacts of alternative development scenarios in a
simulation exercise based on relatively high quality data on
household income and size from Colombia.

The full effect, then, of policy x_n can be written as:

$$\frac{dg(y/p)_i}{dx_n} = \frac{1}{1+z_i} \left| \frac{dg(y)_i}{dx_n} - \frac{\partial g(p)_i}{\partial x_n} \right| \tag{8}$$

Equation (8) shows, even more clearly, the importance of the
intergenerational income-elasticity measure z_i, particularly in the
expected case where $z_i < 0$ and $|z_i| < 1$. Finally, since the overall
effect of a change in policy measure x_n on social-welfare growth is
simply the weighted sum of the direct and indirect effects of the
various policy instruments, we get:

$$\frac{dW'}{dx_n} = \Sigma_i \frac{w_i}{1+z_i} \left| \frac{dg(y)_i}{dx_n} - \frac{\partial g(p)_i}{\partial x_n} \right| \tag{9}$$

or letting $w_i = a_i v_i$:

TABLE 1
An Illustrative Matrix of the Expected Demographic Impacts of Selected Population and Development Policies
(+ equals "increase"; − represents "decrease"; 0 means "no change")

Policy Variable	Direct Income Effect	Direct Population Effect	Indirect Population Effect	Total Effect On Per Capita Income
1. SUPPLY POLICIES				
a) Family Planning Programs	0	−−	−	+
b) Sterilization and Abortion	0	−−	(?)	?
c) Maternal and Child Health	0	0	−	?
d) New Technology	0	−−	−	+
2. DEMAND POLICIES				
a) Traditional Development	+	0	−	+
b) Poverty-Focused Development	+++	?	−−	++
c) Focus on Women	+++	−	−−	+++
d) Urban Development	++	?	?	?
e) Rural Development	+	+(?)	−	+
f) Incentives/Disincentives	0(+)	−(?)	−(?)	?
g) Legal sanctions	0(−)	−−	?	−(?)

$$\frac{dW'}{dx_n} = \Sigma_i \frac{a_i v_i}{1+z_i} \left| \frac{dg(y)_i}{dx_n} - \frac{\partial g(p)_i}{\partial x_n} \right| \qquad (10)$$

Equation (10) shows that the overall effects of population growth-reducing policy measures on social welfare will depend on who benefits or pays for them (say, through taxation)-- (i.e., the relative sizes of the $(dg(y)/dx_n)$)--and how the policy directly and/or indirectly influences population growth rates--the $(dg(p)_i)/(dx_n)$.

V. POLICY IMPLICATIONS

The above model is intended to be suggestive of the kind of macro theoretical framework for analyzing the direct and indirect effects on income and population growth of alternative development or population policies that our research is designed to develop. Some policies have potential direct population effects-- $(\partial g(p)_i/\partial x_n)$--for example, family-planning programs, population education, new technologies, changed marriage laws, incentive programs, and the rest; these same policies may have indirect effects on population growth through the rise in per capita household income from reduced household size working through the group-specific, intergenerational income-elasticity coefficients. Other policies can have direct effects on population growth-- expanded female employment on age of marriage; direct effects on income growth--expanded female employment opportunities raising expected household income; and indirect effects on population growth through the rise in per capita household income from increased household income working through the group-specific, intergenerational income-elasticity coefficients. Thus, for example, ceteris paribus, in providing new jobs, if a government were able to employ women instead of men at the same wage cost and the same productivity, the total effect on per capita income growth may be greater, since in addition to the direct income-growth effects and indirect population-growth-reducing effects, there would be a direct population-growth-reducing effect of expanded female job opportunities resulting, say, from delayed mariage, or more frequent use of contraception and abortion (see Table 1).

Implicit in all of the above is the assumption that sustained increases in per capita household income resulting from development and/or population programs provide expanded economic, social, and educational opportunities for the children of such households. As average levels of education increase, and concomitant income expectations rise, it is assumed that these children will reduce their fertility to below that of their parents. This is the significance of the concept of intergenerational income elasticity of household size. It prevents us from having to assume, explicitly or implicitly, a pattern of fertility behavior based on "static expectations," particularly among the lowest income groups who ordinarily exhibit the highest levels of fertility. It also allows us to introduce lagged fertility responses to household income changes that yield time paths of fertility declines that may closely parallel the path of the demographic transition in both developed and developing countries.

FOOTNOTES

Richard Monteverde provided valuable research assistance, while helpful comments and suggestions for improvement were received from Bernard Wasow and Mark Leiserson. A grant from the Compton Foundation, in partial support of this research, is gratefully acknowledged.

1. This policy-guidance gap is apparent even in one of the better studies of population policy in developing countries, Ridker (1976).

2. For a comprehensive survey of the recent literature on interrelationships between population and development, see R. H. Cassen (1976). See also attached bibliography.

3. See, for example, IBRD (1974), for one of the most well-known presentations of this viewpoint.

4. For a detailed analysis of many of these demand-oriented policy alternatives, see Ridker (1976) and Cassen (1976).

5. z_i is an elasticity in the sense that it is a percentage change with respect to a percentage change. Usually, in economics, income elasticities of demand assume preferences fixed and a movement from one set of preferences to another with a change in income. We are assuming that with a change in income, the dominant change is a change in the preferences themselves. Without a change in preferences themselves, a negative elasticity of fertility with respect to per capita income would require that children be inferior goods. If children are, in fact, inferior goods, and there are no changes in preferences, our analytic representation of income and fertility would remain intact, but with an inferior-goods interpretation.

6. a_i, the relative size of group i (i.e., the proportion of the total population in group i), is a function of per capita household income. Per capita household income determines household size. Household size determines the number of households in the next generation. The number of households in each income group, along with the average household size in that group, determines the relative size of that group.

7. The purist can drop this assumption and interpret z_i simply as $[\partial g(p)_i]/[\partial g(y/p)_i]$ in equations (7) through (10).

60

Bardhan, P. K., T. N. Srinivasan. ed. 1975. *Poverty and income distribution in India*. New Delhi: Indian Statistical Institute.

Ben-Porath, Y. 1972. Economic analysis of fertility in Israel: point and counterpoint. *J. of Pol. Econ.*, Part II, 81(2):S202-33.

Berelson, B., R. Haveman. 1979. On allocating resources for fertility reduction in developing countries. Population Council, Center for Policy Studies, Working Paper No. 40.

Bhattacharyya, A. K. 1975. Income inequality and fertility: a comparative view. *Pop. Studies*, 29(1):5-19.

Blandy, R. 1974. The welfare analysis of fertility reduction. *Econ. J.*, 84(March): 109-129.

Boulier, B. L. 1975. The effects of demographic variables on income distribution. Princeton University, Woodrow Wilson School, Research Program in Economic Development, Discussion Paper No. 61.

Carleton, R. O. 1965. Labour force participation: a stimulus to fertility in Puerto Rico? *Demography*, 2:233-39.

Cassen, R. H. 1976. Population and development: a survey. *World Dev.*, 4(10/11):785-830.

_____, 1978. *India: population, economy, society*. New York: Holmes & Meier Publishers, Inc.

Chenery, H., M. S. Ahluwalia, C. L. G. Bell, J. H. Duloy, R. Jolly. 1974. *Redistribution with growth*. London: Oxford U. Press.

Coale, A. J., ed. 1976. *Economic factors in population growth*. Proceedings of a Conference held by the International Economic Association at Valescure, France. London: Macmillan.

Daly, H. E. 1971. A Marxian-Malthusian view of poverty and development. *Pop. Studies, 25(1):25-37*.

Dinwiddy, R., D. Reed. 1977. The effects of certain social and demographic changes on income distribution. Royal Commission on the Distribution of Income and Wealth, Background Paper No. 3. London: Her Majesty's Stationery Office.

Dyson, T. P., C. L. G. Bell, R. H. Cassen. 1980. Fertility, mortality and income-changes over the long run: some simulation experiments. *The J. of Dev. Studies*, 14(4)(July).

Frejka, T. 1973. *The future of population growth*. New York: John Wiley and Sons.

Haveman, R. H. 1976. Benefit-cost analysis and family planning programs. *Pop. and Dev. Rev.*, 2(1): 37-64.

IBRD. 1974. *Population policies and economic development*: *a World Bank staff report*. Baltimore: Johns Hopkins U. Press.

Isbister, J. 1973. Birth control, income redistribution and the rate of saving: the case of Mexico." *Demography*, *10(1)*: *85-98*.

Kocher, J. E. 1973. *Rural development, income distribution and fertility decline*. Occasional Paper. New York: Population Council.

Kuznets, S. 1976. Demographic aspects of the size distribution of income: an exploratory essay. *Econ. Dev. and Cult. Change*, 25(1): 1-94.

_____, 1978. Size and age structure of family households: exploratory comparisons. *Pop. and Dev. Rev.*, 4(2): 187-224.

_____, 1979. Size of households and income disparities. Economic Growth Center, Yale University, Discussion Paper No. 318. (mimeo).

Ratcliffe, J. W. 1977. Poverty, politics and fertility: the anomaly of Kerala. *Hastings Center Rep.*, (February): 34-42.

Repetto, R. G. 1974. The Interaction of fertility and the size distribution of income. Harvard Center for Population Studies, Research Paper No. 8. (October).

_____, 1976. Inequality and the birth rate in Puerto Rico: evidence from household census data. Harvard Center for Population Studies, Research Paper No. 14. (June).

Ridker, R. G. ed. 1976. *Population and development*: *the search for selective interventions*. Baltimore: Johns Hopkins U. Press.

Robinson, W. C., ed. 1975. *Population and development planning*. New York: Population Council.

Robinson, W. C., D. Horlacher. 1971. Population growth and economic welfare. *Reports on Population/Family Planning*. New York: Population Council.

Singer, H. W. 1973. Income distribution and population growth. UN E/CONF. 60/SYM I/36, World Population Conference, Symposium on Population and Development. (June). Cairo: United Nations.

Stys, W. 1957. The influence of economic conditions on the fertility of peasant women. *Pop. Studies*, 11(2): 136-48.

Tabah, L., ed. 1976. *Population growth and economic development in the third world*. 2 Vols. Dolhain, Belgium: IUSSP, Ordina Editions.

62

_____, 1980. World population trends and projections. *Pop. and Dev. Rev.*, 6(3).

Tilly, C. ed. 1978. *Historical studies of changing fertility.* Princeton: Princeton U. Press.

Todaro, M. P. 1977a. Development policy and population growth: a framework for planners. *Pop. and Dev. Rev.*, 3(1 & 2): 23-43.

_____, 1977b. *Economic development in the third world.* Chs. 6 & 7. New York and London: Longman.

United Nations. *United Nations trends and policies*, 1979 monitoring report. (in preparation).

Wood, C., J. de Carvalho. 1980. Population growth and the distribution of household income: the case of Brazil. (February) (Manuscript).

4

The One World of Economics: Towards Global Economic Analysis

G. K. Helleiner

I. INTRODUCTION

In 1971 Lloyd Reynolds published a stimulating book on the scope and content of economics in which he called attention to some of the difficulties encountered in the transfer of traditional Western modes of economic analysis to socialist and less developed countries. In the preface to his analysis of The Three Worlds of Economics (1971) he asserted his criterion for assessing the contributions of economics, "The ultimate test of good work is explanatory and predictive power and potential relevance to important policy issues" (p. xii). In assessing what are "important policy issues" in his "three worlds" (capitalist, socialist, and less developed economies), while acknowledging some inevitable subjectivity about these matters, he assigned principal weight (1) to their quantitative importance (the numbers of people who might gain or lose from them), and (2) to the expressed views of economic policymakers and informed opinion (pp. 126-29, 146-47, 181-82). On these bases, he was able to consider fruitfully how the conventional Western tools of economic analysis could be deployed for "good work" in the "three worlds" of economics (and how they could not).

If one accepts the Reynolds' standard for "good work" and Reynolds' criteria for judging the importance of various "policy issues," one could arrive at some rather sober, indeed, even harsh, judgments of the role of economic analysis in world affairs today. I shall argue that the time has arrived for much greater conscious analytical attention on the part of economists to "the one world of economics:" the economic characteristics, behaviour, and performance of the entire global economy. I shall do this not out of visionary zeal and utopian enthusiasms such as frequently characterize those who speak of "global" issues; but out of a pragmatic assessment of the limitations of much of economics, as at present usually practiced, in the attainment of Reynolds' aspirations for the discipline. It will become apparent that there is already quite a lot of "world economics" being done, though perceptions have not quite caught up with actual practice.

The analysis of "world" economic problems is almost invariably couched in terms of a "society of nations" in which "global" problems are synonymous with "international" and usually "intergovernmental" ones. That part of economic analysis which is concerned with world problems has evolved as "international economics." (A quick glance through my list of currently available textbooks reveals only one which carries "world" rather than "international" economics in its title -- Caves and Jones' (1977) <u>World</u> <u>Trade</u> <u>and</u> <u>Payments</u> -- but its contents are not differentiated significantly, in this respect, from all of the others.) There are still sound reasons for building an analytical framework upon the fact of separate nation-states: particularly the facts of separate currencies and separate governments, and, to a lesser extent, different cultures (language, tradition, taste, etc.); the "classical" assumptions of total factor mobility within countries and total immobility between them are not so plausible today, but they have never been more than an analytical convenience -- their alteration does not in the slightest hinder orthodox analysis.

For the purposes of analyzing what is going on, rather than what governments are doing or might do, there is no logical reason for always and only adopting the conventional national (governmental) unit as the basic conceptual starting point. There are good reasons for considering the world <u>as</u> <u>a</u> <u>whole</u>.

Consider, for example, the implications of the following aspects of today's world: (1) the transnationalization of much of world business; (2) the growing need for harmonious management of the global commons -- oceans, space, the electromagnetic spectrum; (3) the vast declines in economic distance between various parts of the globe which are the result of the communications revolution; (4) the evident interdependence of activities around the world with respect to the preservation of the globe's fragile environment; (5) the increased interdependence of economic activity throughout the world in terms of purely market relationships -- trade in goods and services, financial flows, flows of people; and the increased perception on the part of the poor of the inequity of global distribution of income and wealth.

In the report of the Brandt Commission (1980) can be found the most recent, as well as the most eloquent, appeal for a global approach to analysis and policy formation. For example,

"real progress will only be made nationally if it can be assured globally" (p. 268).

"the world is a system of many different components interacting with one another -- changes in one affecting all the rest. Among the major components, apart from sovereign states, are international and regional institutions, transnational corporations, public opinion...and diverse religious, ideological, social, and political forces..." (p. 268).

The OECD Interfutures report, in its conclusion to a wide-ranging analysis of global problems and governmental policy responses, notes "not only the importance of political dialogue in the democracies of the developed countries, but also the value of informing the public very extensively about trends in the world as a whole" (OECD 1979, 423).

Holistic analyses of the global economy have been far more prominent in the Marxist, neo-Marxist, and dependencia traditions than they have in that of mainline economics. It has sometimes even been difficult to find "orthodox" holistic economic analysis with which to compare the latter writers' dramatic conclusions. Mainstream economists have not taken their writings seriously, but neither have they offered alternatives. Students of world politics can, therefore, be forgiven for appearing sometimes to have been overinfluenced by simplistic,"radical" models of global economic performance. There is no longer any logical reason for global-level economic analysis to be so neglected by mainstream economists, and there are good reasons for actively promoting it.

One may seek better understanding of the global economy primarily in order to improve the quality of national-level economic policymaking and performance. Generally speaking, that has been the apparent intention of most assessments of "world" economic events undertaken by international organizations, and much of the global-level academic analysis as well. One may also, however, seek it as a matter of inherent interest. As a matter of academic investigation there is no less reason to choose the globe as the geographic unit of analysis than there is to choose a region or a city. "International" economics is obviously still extremely important; but it may no longer be enough.

This paper will address the needs and possibilities for global-level economic analysis in three broad areas: (1) the measurement of overall economic performance; (2) macroeconomic management; and (3) the efficiency of the functioning of world markets.

II. THE MEASUREMENT OF GLOBAL ECONOMIC PERFORMANCE

Although every nation, no matter how small, is encouraged to calculate its own GNP and to develop measures of its growth over time (and debates have raged over alternative measures of national-level growth and development), there still exist only qualitative indications of the progress of the entire world economy. Even the growth of "world modelling" (e.g., Leontief 1977; Herrera 1976) has not as yet generated some of the more obvious macroeconomic performance indicators. Changes in the value and volume of international trade -- which are reported in GATT and UN sources -- are an imperfect substitute for macroeconomic performance measurements; international trade, after all, accounts for less than 20 percent of the average country's GNP. While it may be understandable that official national-statistics offices should be uninterested in the provision of "global" estimates, in the absence of effective "global" political units, it is less clear why academics and international institutions should have been so inactive in this sphere.

In the assessment of macroeconomic performance at the global level, it may be not only inherently desirable but even politically necessary to rethink our conventions concerning the weighting systems appropriate for measuring total product. Whereas the power of poor citizens within nations is typically too weak to generate much effective pressure for "poverty-weighting" or even for "proportional" weighting in the calculation of GNP, "poor power" at the international level -- at least in the agencies of the United Nations -- is considerably greater. Thus, one can take at least a step in the direction of an improved index of global economic performance by explicitly allowing, as conventional growth accounting does not, for the international, though still not the intranational, differences in per capita income levels. (The basic data on intranational income distribution, in any case, remain very weak.) As Ahluwalia and Chenery (1974) have reminded us, though most seem to continue to forget, "When we use the growth of GNP as an index of performance, we implicitly assume that a dollar of additional income creates the same additional social welfare regardless of the income level of the recipient" (p. 40). They offer as an alternative an "equal weights" index which gives the same weight to equiproportionate changes in the incomes of different (income level) classes, regardless of their income levels; this amounts to weighting by these various groups' shares of population instead of, as in conventional accounting, income. They also consider a "poverty weighted" index which explicitly grants heavier weight to the proportionate income changes of the poorest.

Table 1 illustrates the differences in measured, aggregate, global, per capita income growth estimates which result from alternative weighting systems for national growth rates. (The underlying weighting systems themselves are also shown in Table 1.) Under conventional growth-accounting practices, global per capita income can be said to have grown at an annual rate of 3.7 percent between 1960 and 1978; but this performance is significantly reduced to only 3.1 percent when population, rather than income shares, are employed as weights; and it falls even lower to 2.9 percent when a (arbitrary) poverty-weighting system, similar to that of Ahluwalia-Chenery, is employed instead. Similarly, the World Bank's projections of global economic performance can be summarized in terms which vary by substantial proportions, particularly in the case of their "low" scenario (from 2.1 percent to 2.6 percent per capita income growth), depending upon which weighting system is employed for the aggregative calculation.

The relative weights assigned to the low-income countries on the "neutral" population basis for weighting will continue to expand in response to current demographic trends, while those called for by conventional growth-accounting practices may even fail. The gap between the results of alternative global growth-accounting practices will, therefore, increase; it is important to get it "right" from the beginning.

Rather than attempting to measure an overall global average rate of unemployment which, given the variety of measurement practices even within the OECD, and the conceptual difficulties surrounding the notion of "unemployment," would be a formidable undertaking, a "global" approach would better draw on the theory of segmented labor markets (Cain 1976). Immigration restrictions are mighty sources of segmentation, but they are by no means the only ones in global labor markets, and in some instances, for example, skilled and managerial manpower within transnational corporations, international labor mobility is quite substantial. In other instances, both unskilled labor and certain types of skilled labor are already moving remarkably freely between particular national labor markets. National-level

TABLE 1
Alternative Weighting Systems for Growth Accounting: Regional and Global Real Per Capita GNP Growth Rates
(Percent)

	1978 Population Weights	1978 GNP Weights (a)	Poverty Weights (b)	Annual Growth in Real Per Capita GNP		
				1960-78 Actual	1980-85 Projections Low	1980-85 Projections High
REGIONAL WEIGHTS AND PER CAPITA GNP GROWTH						
Low Income			70.0			
Excluding China	30.5	3.1	(40.0)	1.6	1.0	1.7
China	22.4	2.6	(30.0)	3.7	3.3 (c)	3.3 (c)
Middle Income	20.6	13.0	20.0	3.7	2.1	2.7
Upper Income			10.0			
Industrialized	15.7	64.0	(6.0)	3.7	2.5	2.8
Capital surplus oil exporters	1.4	0.9	(0.5)	7.1	2.3	2.8
Centrally planned excl. China	9.4	16.5	(3.5)	4.0	3.3	3.3
	100.0	100.0	100.0			
GLOBAL PER CAPITA GNP GROWTH						
With GNP Weights				3.7	2.6	2.9
With Population Weights				3.1	2.2	2.5
With Poverty Weights				2.9	2.1	2.6

Notes: (a) Calculated from 1978 population and average per capita income data for each group.
(b) Arbitrary. Components of groups weighted by population.
(c) Average for "centrally planned economies" of which China is a component in the source document.

Source: World Bank (1981, 11, 110-111).

statistics do not always include information relating to migrant workers; nor are they covered in many national social-benefit programs. Sometimes these omissions are the product of conscious governmental policies; as often, they are the result of the incapacity of governmental authorities to monitor activities in the "grey" or illegal sectors. As the international trade union movement steps up its pressure for minimum "standards," one can expect the beginnings of rules on the provision of social benefits, the treatment of migrant labor, and the like. Is it not time to begin to consider divergent national levels of unemployment in an integrated, global framework for labor-market analysis together with demographic change, migration, information flows, and various sources of "segmentation?" Does anyone know, for example, what is happening to the total supply of various types of skills, or to average global rates of remuneration for them?

The measurement of global inflation can, in principle, be undertaken either by calculating weighted averages of national price indices or by employing indices of the world market prices for particular traded goods (e.g., raw materials, manufactures, etc.), some of which are already available. To the extent that the world moves to a new multi-currency or basket-currency (e.g., SDR, ECU) monetary system, it becomes increasingly important to have measures of the changing purchasing power of the major new "unit" of international accounting. As a beginning, a "world" price index based on the present five-currency SDR, employing its weighting system, would at least provide an indicator of SDR purchasing power, however imperfect such an index might be of the "average" rate of inflation in the total world economy.

III. GLOBAL-LEVEL MACROECONOMIC MANAGEMENT

Global economic performance is obviously not merely a matter of measurement; it is also a matter of policy concern. There are by now many signs that macroeconomic management requires more comprehensive policy approaches than those which are pursued by governments at the national level. The International Monetary Fund now publishes a World Economic Outlook for the use of decisionmakers and analysts of every description, as well as its member governments (who already previously had been receiving confidential analyses of a similar character). In its 1980 report, the IMF calls attention to "a severe worldwide problem of inflation; a general pattern of slow growth of output...; a sharp slump in the growth of volume of world trade" and asserts, "The world economic picture is rather grim" (IMF 1980, 3). IMF Annual Reports have addressed "developments in the world economy" ever since 1972. Throughout the 1970s the IMF, through its reports and the speeches of its managing directors, has advocated greater coordination of national-level macroeconomic policies. (In the Second Amendment to the Articles of Agreement, the IMF was itself authorised to exercise "firm surveillance" over the exchange-rate policies of its members.)

Since 1975, the leaders of seven major countries of the Western world, accounting for over half the value of world output, have held an annual Economic Summit Conference at which interdependence and policy coordination have been explicitly discussed. Common national solutions to global problems are difficult to achieve and impossible to negotiate in brief meetings of heads of state. "With national attitudes to economic policymaking highly individualistic and with policy stances differing widely among countries, nothing more than general statements of purpose should...be expected to emerge from summit communiqués and resolutions" (Hein 1980, 37). It is nevertheless important that, beginning in the mid-1970s, there should have been a perceived need for such meetings at all.

In the 1970s, the slowdown in the growth rates of the major industrialized countries, the universal need for "adjustment" to the sharp change in the price of oil, the preparation of contingency plans for dealing with oil-supply interruptions, and the perceived need to achieve adequate "recycling" of the surpluses of oil-exporting countries, all underlined the new "global" character of the main current macroeconomic problems. Whatever the merits of particular proposals, the arguments put forward in many places for "reflating" the industrialized world by "massive transfers" to the developing countries also employ a global approach to macroeconomic policymaking.

Again, in 1980, there was great concern over the implications for global levels of economic activity of the oil surpluses of about $115 billion expected in that and succeeding years. This "tax" was widely perceived as significantly deflationary; it amounted to about 1.7 percent of estimated, Western gross product (or about 1.4 percent of total product counting the centrally planned economies). The Keynesian multiplier which goes to work on demand changes is much larger at the global level than it is at the typical, national level because the world, being a closed economy, experiences no demand "leakage" into imports (Graham 1980). The problem of global macro-management was to ensure that adequate demand was pumped back into the world economy to compensate for this deflationary influence. Nervousness was widely expressed about the capacity of the commercial banking system and "the market" to perform this demand-maintaining function. In order to maintain demand there must be a "residual borrower" (Graham 1980) who will continue to spend -- on the basis of optimistic expectations or social considerations -- when everyone else has lost his nerve; and lenders must be willing to continue to lend to him. The difficulty that markets have in assuring such continued borrowing and lending activities in the face of uncertainties, together with the manifest imbalance in the distribution of commercial lending, have always been the problems of the "privatisation" of macro-management. The need for macroeconomic management by governmental authorities at the global level is based upon the same principles as that at the national level; and the former need has never before been so evident.

Similarly, the purported danger for the financial system in having a major, unregulated and uncontrolled segment in the money and capital markets has national-level analogues; and so does the need for some sort of backstopping system for preventing particularized crises from circulating into much more wide-ranging and costly catastrophes.

No doubt there is room for the same sort of debate as to the appropriate mode of macroeconomic analysis at the global level that there is at the national level. Indeed the global "monetarists" have already been active for some years -- relating the global quantity of paper money to the stock of real assets, and interpreting changes in exchange rates as primarily the product of differential rates of monetary expansion. Alternative approaches to short-term global macro-modelling can be found in the attempts to "link" separate, national-level econometric models, and in OECD and Western summit discussions about "locomotives" and "convoys." There is bound to be increased policy interest in global macroeconomic analysis. One can only wonder at the continuing, professional, relative lack of interest in such approaches.

IV. THE FUNCTIONING AND EFFICIENCY OF GLOBAL MARKETS

Microeconomic performance -- traditionally regarded as synonymous with allocative efficiency in the Paretian sense -- can and should be evaluated at the global level as well as the national one. While ritualistic genuflections to the optimality of free trade continue, there has been remarkably little analysis of how global markets actually function in a world of significant imperfections and instances of market concentration. There are few global-level analogues to the industrial-organization specialist, and, at least in part because of that dearth, there are few data on global market concentration, on the degree of internalization of global markets, or on the incidence of restrictive business practices at the global level.

Global-level market analysis should be distinguished from analysis of international trade. "International production", as Dunning (1973) and others call it, that part of output which is undertaken by firms owned by foreigners to the country in which it takes place, has in many sectors long exceeded the value of international trade. "World" markets for individual commodities, in any case, include purely "national" markets as well as those parts of markets which are found "between" nations in "international" exchange. Conversely, data on the degree of concentration of production in purely national markets has become of less and less analytical value as the interpenetration of national markets -- both through trade and through ownership ties -- has proceeded.

While separate national currencies provide a strong rationale for employing an "international" approach to global monetary analysis, there is no equally strong basis for an "international" approach to global production and trade. It is true that governments of nations routinely erect barriers and offer encouragements to trade and to investment, but these, unlike the consequences of separate national currencies, are typically highly variable across industries at the country level; at the industry level, global analysis can easily regard governmental trade or investment policies as analogous to differential transport costs.

In some areas global-level analyses have a fairly long tradition. In particular, there have long been attempts at forecasting demand, projecting total supplies, and modeling overall market behaviour in world primary-commodity markets. A good deal of this global-level analysis of primary-commodity markets has unfortunately been very crude and based on wholly unrealistic assumptions, typically of perfect competition between both buyers and sellers. In the discussions over stabilization of prices and/or earnings in, for instance, world cocoa, coffee, tin, rubber, and sugar markets, overly crude global-level analysis has sometimes led to the transfer of inappropriate conclusions from the global analysis to national-level circumstances; for example, while supply shocks may dominate world markets for a commodity, (net) world demand shocks may at the same time dominate all national-level experiences with respect to the same commodity, since the demand schedule facing one country is the residual when all other countries' supplies are deducted from global demand. More recently, there have been attempts to incorporate the effects of ownership ties, market concentration, government policies, and the successive stages in the processing "chain" in approaches to global-level, primary-commodity market analysis (e.g., Labys 1980).

In manufactured-goods trade, where national markets are more frequently segmented by trade barriers, and where products are typically less homogeneous, there have been far fewer attempts to assess the functioning of global markets. Global-level studies of particular manufacturing industries (steel, petrochemicals, pharmaceuticals, automobiles, etc.) have frequently been the province of "less-professional" writers such as those who write for financial newspapers and business journals. Academic specialists in international trade have rarely deigned to consider such case studies as part of their stock-in-trade; if suitable for professional investigation at all, they have been regarded as matters more for industrial-organization specialists than for international-trade ones, but the former specialists have shown relatively little interest in international trade.

Conventional approaches to the analysis of "protectionism" must be rethought. In a world of large global corporations, in which significant proportions of recorded international trade take place on an intracorporate basis, scale economies, proprietary rights over technology and marketing, and other barriers to entry are pervasive. Governmental "industrial policies" and incentives for foreign investment today merge with trade policy to influence private decision-making as to the location of productive enterprises. Private decisions are frequently made on the basis of global planning objectives rather than local or national-level ones, and they can frequently be understood only in the context of global phenomena in the relevant industries. A new "paradigm" -- based on the approaches of industrial-organization theory rather than the tenets of an obsolete, pure theory of international trade -- is overdue for application to world manufacturing industry. (For some innovative beginnings, see Newfarmer (forthcoming); and Lall 1980.)

Freight rate structures, and liner and airline "conferences" have also received short shrift in the literature on international trade. Transport costs are typically assumed away in theoretical trade models. Yet their "protective" effects -- whether reflective of real costs of transport or not -- are usually at least as important to the pattern of global investment and exchange as governmental trade barriers (Finger and Yeats 1976). The fact of market concentration and/or visible cartel activities in transportation would seem to call for more investigation but, despite the discussions over shipping in the UNCTAD during the past several years, trade economists still show little interest.

In the business world, global-level data collection and global-level analysis have been undertaken on an industry basis by global-level enterprises for some time. The growth of transnational corporations in a variety of industries and service activities has required, for effective management, an approach that looks well beyond the confines of traditional national-level analysis, and has spawned a plethora of programs, texts, and research undertakings in "international business." The difficulties encountered by national-level policymakers and policemen in monitoring, taxing, and controlling global-level enterprises quickly generated a rather weaker and less well-financed counterliterature seeking to bolster national governmental capacities.

United Nations' activities have developed as well, and there has been considerable experimentation with new governmental policies. All of this counteractivity has been designed to reduce the disadvantages of a fragmented "official" sector dealing with a global protagonist. Trade unions have also sought to globalize their activities in some sectors where transnational corporations predominate by forming international secretariats to begin to develop a counterthrust to the global firms they face. It is easy to exaggerate the degree to which these national and international reactions to transnational corporate activity have actually affected the global enterprises' capacity to "have their way," particularly in the less developed countries (see, for example, Biersteker 1980); but there certainly has been some success in reining them in, even without the global-level approaches which would presumably be necessary in order for this to be achieved with maximum effect.

The need for global-level analysis and policy in respect to corporate activity is most evident in the spheres of tax-revenue sharing and the control of restrictive business practices. The existence of different tax regimes in different countries creates -- together with other influences -- strong incentives for the manipulation of transfer prices on intracorporate transactions of all kinds. With the limited degree of transparency now required in corporate accounting, the continuing importance of "tax-haven" jurisdictions with particularly modest disclosure requirements, and the frequent weakness (or, in some cases, secrecy requirements) of the relevant investigative authorities, it is virtually impossible for independent analysts to ascertain the overall effective tax burden borne by transnational corporations or its distribution among nations. (Governmental analysts in strong countries like the U.S. may have fairly accurate data on these matters, and presumably they employ them to ensure that the U.S. Government gets a "fair share" of the total revenues, but the privacy of these data are protected by strict disclosure laws and they are not accessible to independent analysts.) As a purely analytical matter -- and not in order to "bash the multinationals" -- it should be possible to acquire far more information than is now available about the tax rate and distribution of tax payments of large firms that operate at the global level. Only with more information can one even begin to assess the feasibility or desirability of alternative, global tax regimes such as are eventually inevitable if intergovernmental squabbling is ever to be reduced.

In the field of restrictive business practices, national-level laws are themselves often quite weak or nonexistent. For the present, it is clearly too much to expect that there could be effective international control over such pratices. There already exists, nevertheless, a significant consensus as to the need to rein in possible abuses at the international level through intergovernmental cooperation and surveillance -- a consensus evident in both the OECD code on multinationals and in the much wider UNCTAD "equitable principles and rules for the control of restrictive business practices."

Intrafirm international trade is an activity about which too little is known, and about which there is still much dispute. There is ambiguity in UNCTAD's "principles and rules" on restrictive business practices in the treatment of intracorporate transactions. Following intense debate, the section on undue restraints on competition exempts intrafirm trade from its strictures, whereas the section on the abuse of dominant positions of market power does not. It seems that, following Western conceptions of "the corporate entity," some cartel-like activities will be tolerated so long as they take place within firms. This "legalistic" approach has no justification in terms of conventional economic theorizing within which all exchange is equally eligible for analysis, and social-efficiency criteria can be universally applied -- whether inside or across firms. The evident concern of national authorities with transactions within the "corporate entity" at the international level may engender increased interest at the local and national level in the implications for overall efficiency of such nonmarket modes of transaction. As in the case of measuring aggregative economic performance, there may, thus, be healthy feedback effects from global-level analysis and debates to those at the national level.

V. CONCLUSIONS

"World government" is still a long way from realisation. But economic phenomena and economic problems already are taking on dimensions which can only be adequately assessed with global-level analyses. "Important policy issues" (Reynolds 1971) in the spheres of both macroeconomics and microeconomics are involved in these global-level approaches. The policymaking institutions for their resolution are still national and international ones, rather than truly global ones.

International cooperation at the global level consists, at present, primarily of little more than the exchange of information and the joint financing of research and data collection on matters of mutual national concern. In some spheres there have been attempts to establish rules or codes governing certain governmental and international policy practices. In certain areas and in particular circumstances there may be close cooperation among subgroups of countries in the use of selected policy instruments for the attainment of mutually agreeable objectives. In only a few areas (e.g., communications, health, meteorology) can there be said to be even the beginnings of global policymaking. But summit conferences and international organizations are already groping their way towards global economic policymaking.

While these fumblings toward global approaches continue, professional economists should be accelerating their efforts to understand and predict the course of global economic events. In terms of Reynolds' criteria for assessing the "importance" of policy issues, quantitative importance and the expressed views of the informed global issues deserve more analytical attention than they have received. The time for policy-relevant, global-level economic analysis has come.

BIBLIOGRAPHY

Ahluwalia, M. S., H. Chenery. 1974. The economic framework. In *Redistribution with growth*, ed. H. Chenery, M. S. Ahluwalia, C. L. G. Bell, J. H. Duloy, R. Jolly. London: Oxford U. Press.

Biersteker, T. J. 1980. The illusion of state power: transnational corporations and the neutralization of host-country legislation. *J. of Peace Research*, 17(3).

Brandt, W., et al. 1980. *North-south: a programme for survival*. Cambridge: MIT Press.

Cain, G. G. 1976. The challenge of segmented labor market theories to orthodox theory: a survey. *J. of Econ. Lit.*, 14(4).

Dunning, J. R. 1973. The determinants of international production. *Oxford Econ. Papers*, 25(3).

Finger, J. M., A. J. Yeats. 1976. Effective protection by transportation costs and tariffs: a comparison of magnitudes. *Quart. J. of Econ.*, 90.

Graham, A. 1980. International finance: the need for a residual borrower. Paper presented to the second world scientific banking meeting on international financing of economic development. (May 26-31) Dubrovnik.

Hein, J. 1980. *From summit to summit: policymaking in an interdependent world*. The Conference Board. Report no. 774.

Herrera, A. O., et al. 1976. *Catastrophe or new society? A Latin American world model*. Ottawa: IDRC.

Labys, W. C. 1980. *Market structure, bargaining power and resource price formation*. New York: D. C. Heath.

Lall, S. 1980. The international automotive industry and the developing world. *World Development*, 8(10).

Leontief, W., et al. 1977. *The future of the world economy*. New York: Oxford U. Press.

Newfarmer, R. S., ed. Forthcoming. *Transnationals, international oligopoly and uneven development*.

Organization for Economic Co-operation and Development (OECD). 1979. *Interfutures, facing the future, mastering the probable and managing the unpredictable*. Paris.

Reynolds, L. G. 1971. *The three worlds of economics*. New Haven and London: Yale U. Press.

World Bank. 1980. *World development report, 1980*. New York: Oxford U. Press.

5

The Relationship Between the International Monetary System and Regional Monetary Systems

Robert Triffin

I. THE WORLD MONETARY DISORDER

I need not rehash once more what is known about the world monetary disorder of the last decade: an unholy alliance of recession and unemployment with the wildest inflation in world history, huge balance-of-payments disequilibria and fluctuating exchange rates, a monetary system in which reserve creation leads to the financing of the richer, more-capitalized countries by the poorer, less-capitalized ones, the abdication of any serious attempt at reform in Jamaica and in the Second Amendment to the Articles of Agreement ·of the International Monetary Fund, etc., etc. I have written abundantly on this gloomy picture over the last twenty years,[1] beginning with my book on <u>Gold</u> <u>and</u> <u>the</u> <u>Dollar</u> <u>Crisis</u> (1960). Let me merely extract today from the flood of statistics in which we are daily drowned and confused, a few figures which document the main conclusions of interest concerning the shortcomings of the present world monetary "system," which should better be labelled a chaotic "nonsystem."

A. <u>Extent and Sources of the World Inflation of the 1970s</u>

In order to place the 1970s developments to give a historical perspective to the above characterization the accompanying Tables summarize the official estimates of world monetary reserves and reserve increases over thirty years, beginning in 1949. One may note particularly the last four lines of Table 1, and the last two columns of Table 2.

The last lines of Table 1 show you that world monetary reserves, measured in dollars at current exchange rates and market gold prices, more than decupled in the last decade. Think of what "decupling" means: ten times as much in ten years as in all previous years and centuries! They were still increasing last year at an annual rate of 62 percent, that is, ten or fifteen times faster than the maximum conceivable growth of world trade and production in real, noninflationary terms, and much faster still than their actual growth in the recession that characterizes these years.

The sources of these wildly inflationary increases in world reserves are listed, in both Tables, <u>in a decreasing order of planning and acceptability</u>. The last two columns of Table 2 show that:

TABLE 1
Sources of International Monetary Reserves, 1949-1979
(Billions of U.S. Dollars)

	End of Year					10 Year Increases			One Year Increases
	1949	1959	1969	1978	1979	1950-59	1960-69	1970-79	1979
I. At $35 per ounce of Gold	45.5	57.0	78.7	279.8	302.9	11.5	21.7	224.2	23.1
1. SDR Allocations and IMF Credit	0.2	0.8	4.4	18.8	20.5	0.6	3.6	16.1	1.7
2. World Gold	34.3	40.0	41.2	39.9	39.3	5.7	1.2	-2.0	-0.6
3. Foreign Exchange	11.0	16.1	33.0	221.1	243.1	5.2	16.9	210.1	22.0
II. Impact of Fluctuations of:	-0.3	0.1	0.2	290.4	618.9	0.4	0.2	618.6	328.4
1. Dollar-SDR Exchange Rate	-	-	-	132.5	222.0	-	-	222.0	89.5
2. Gold-SDR Market Price	-0.3	0.1	0.2	157.9	396.8	0.4	0.2	396.6	239.0
III. Total Gross Reserves (I+II)	45.2	57.0	78.9	570.3	921.8	11.8	21.9	842.8	351.5
Percentage Growth Rates:									
Over Period: Measured in SDRs (I)						25	38	238	8.3
At $ Market Prices and Exchange Rates (III)						26	38	1068	62
Per Year: Measured in SDRs (I)						2.3	3.3	13	8.3
At $ Market Prices and Exchange Rates (III)						2.3	3.3	28	62

Notes and Sources: See Table 2.

TABLE 2
Sources of International Monetary Reserves, 1949-1979
(Percentage Shares of World Reserves or Reserve Increases)

	End of Year					10 Year Increases			One Year Increases
	1949	1959	1969	1978	1979	1950-59	1960-69	1970-79	1979
I. At $35 per ounce of Gold	101	100	100	49	33	97	99	27	6.6
1. SDR Allocations and IMF Credit	0.4	1.5	5.6	3.3	2.2	5.4	16	1.9	0.4
2. World Gold	76	70	52	7.0	4.3	48	5.6	-0.2	-0.2
3. Foreign Exchange	24	28	42	39	26	44	77	25	6.3
II. Impact of Fluctuations of:	-0.6	-0.1	0.3	51	67	3.1	0.7	73	93
1. Dollar-SDR Exchange Rate	-	-	-	23	24	-	-	26	25
2. Gold-SDR Market Price	-0.6	-0.1	0.3	28	43	3.1	0.7	47	68

Notes for Tables 1 and 2:
1. Sources of reserves and reserve growth are listed from the most to the least planned by the monetary authorities, ranging from SDR allocations and IMF credit, at one extreme, to gold price fluctuations, at the other.

2. This breakdown of "sources" includes, under "world gold" and "SDR allocations," reserves resulting from gold and SDR transfers to the IMF, included under "Reserve Positions in Fund" in the IFS breakdown of reserves by "composition." Note also that the European Monetary Cooperation Fund (EMCF) gold holdings are listed in IFS under "foreign exchange."

Sources: Computed from International Financial Statistics, June 1980 and Annual 1979.

1. The only source of reserve creation fully responsive to international concertation (SDR allocations and IMF credit) accounted for less than 2 percent of world reserve increases over the last decade, and less than half of 1 percent in 1979 (line I,1).

2. The contribution of world gold, measured in volume at its old price of $ or SDR 35 per ounce, was slightly negative, owing primarily to IMF and U.S. sales to the private market (line I,2).

3. National central banks' foreign-exchange purchases and retention -- welcome by some, but accepted only with increasing reluctance by others because of their inflationary impact on domestic monetary issues -- accounted for only 25 percent (one-fourth) of global reserve increases over the last decade, and fell in 1979 to little more than 6 percent, down from 77 percent in the 1960s (line I,3).

4. The major source of reserve increases, by far, was obviously the least planned of all: 73 percent (nearly three-fourths) of the global reserve increases of the 1970s, and 93 percent in 1979, originated in fluctuations of dollar exchange rates and gold prices (see line II, 1 and 2) totally deprecated by the monetary authorities theoretically in charge of the "SYSTEM"(?). Need I remind you how often governors of central banks, ministers of finance, and even heads of state or government, used to proclaim, in former days, that stability of exchange rates and gold prices -- at $35 an ounce! -- would remain forever the intangible pillars of our international monetary system, whatever the other reforms admittedly needed for its survival? Yet, the collapse of the gold-convertible dollar pillar of Bretton Woods is obviously the only major reform actually implemented so far; and the -- yet largely unrealized -- inflationary potential of the multiplication of gold prices by nearly twenty (from $35 an ounce to $666.50, on 15 September 1980), certainly does not promise us -- to use another disproved slogan -- any "light at the end of the tunnel" in which gold prices and exchange rates continue to crawl, or jump, from day to day in a most unpredicatble and deplored fashion.

5. Even if we exclude gold from these calculations of world reserves, and confine ourselves -- as International Financial Statistics' tables tend to do -- to "credit reserves" only, their increase still reached $310 billion (828 percent) at the end of the last decade, providing inflationary financing for balance-of-payments deficits that could never have been sustained otherwise on such a scale.

I might add that such financing, still under the theoretical control of the monetary authorities, has now paled into insignificance in comparison with the foreign credits extended to borrowers by the private market. The incomplete estimates published in the Annual Reports of the Bank for International Settlements show that over the four years, 1976-79, these totaled $482 billion, net of duplications ($792 million gross), that is, nearly three times as much as the foreign credits extended by the monetary authorities and more than fifty times their internationally planned credits (SDR allocations and IMF lending).

B. Regional Investment of Reserve Increases

The second major shortcoming of the system is now at the center of the North-South debate, and particularly of the Brandt Commission report. It is the ludicrous distribution of these inflationary reserve increases between the richer, more-capitalized, industrial countries, on the one hand, and, on the other, the less-capitalized and poorer countries (with the exception, now, of some of the oil-exporting countries).

The United Nations vote, year after year, pious resolutions stressing as a goal the exportation of capital by the former countries to the latter, but in the area which should be most under the control of the authorities -- that is, the international monetary system -- we do exactly the opposite.

I invite you to turn to Table 3, and particularly to Table 4 which extracts from Table 3 some significant estimates of regional shares in world reserves (under line I) and of the contribution of "borrowed" reserves to the gross reserves of the undercapitalized countries, the United States, and the other industrial countries.

1. As of the end of 1979, credit reserves other than gold totalled about $350 billion. The less-capitalized countries contributed (i.e., held as creditors) 44 percent of the total, but received, as borrowers, only 4 percent. The more-capitalized, industrial countries contributed the other 56 percent, but received as investments 96 percent. The sharpest contrast is with the United States, which contributed little more than 2 percent (less than $8 billion) of world credit reserves, but received as investments more than 52 percent ($183 billion) of the $350 billion total (See lines II and III of Table 3, and line I, 2 of Table 4).

2. Another way of looking at the same figures is to see what proportion of its gross reserves is derived by each group from "borrowed" reserves. This is shown on line II, 1 of Table 4. In brief, borrowed reserves accounted for only 6 percent of the less-capitalized countries' gross reserves (1 percent for the oil-exporting countries, and 10 percent for the others), but for 30 percent of those of industrial countries other than the United States, and 128 percent of the gross reserves of the United States, whose net reserves were, therefore, negative.

3. Finally, being minor holders of gold reserves, the less-capitalized countries benefited from less than 14 percent of the huge, gold-revaluation profits of recent years ($66 billion out of a $484 billion total) as against 26 percent for the United States, and 60 percent for the other industrial countries (See line I, 1 of Table 4, derived from line I, 2 of Table 3).

II. CHANCES AND TIMING (?) OF NEEDED WORLD REFORMS

This brief review of the present system, or nonsystem, eloquently demonstrates a far more urgent need for reform of such an absurd method of reserve creation and investments than could be suspected from official pronouncements, or even from the writings of academic economists. Most of the latters' publications in recent years -- could I hazard 90 percent as a rough "guesstimate?" -- have been devoted to the relative merits and demerits of fixed versus floating

TABLE 3
Sources and Distribution of Gross and Net International Monetary Reserves at the End of 1979
(Billions of U.S. Dollars, at Market Prices)

	World	I M F	Countries	Industrial Countries			Undercapitalized Countries		
				United States	Other	Total	Total	Oil Exporting	Other
I. World Gold, at market price	574	55	520 (d)	135	312 (e)	448	71	19	52
1. At $35 per ounce	39	3.7	36	9.3	21 (e)	31	4.8	1.3	3.6
2. Impact of fluctuations of market price	535	51	484	126	291	417	66	17	49
II. Credit Reserve Assets	364	12	352	7.8	190	198	155	72	82
1. Foreign Exchange	320	–	320	3.8	171	175	145	67	78
2. SDR Holdings	18	1.1	16	2.7	9.6	12	4.2	1.4	2.8
3. Reserve Positions in Fund	26	11 (a)	15	1.3	8.9	10	5.3	3.9	1.4
III. Credit Reserve Liabilities	364	15	348	183	152	335	14	1	13
1. Foreign Exchange	320	–	320	179 (f)	142 (f)	320	–	–	–
2. SDR Allocations	18	–	18	4.2	8.2	12	5.2	1	4.2
3. IMF Credit	26	15 (b)	11 (a)	–	2.2	2.2	8.3	–	8.3
IV. Gross Reserves (I+II)	938	66	872 (d)	143	502	645	225	91	134
V. Net Reserves (IV-III)	574	51 (c)	525 (d)	– 39	350	310	212	90	122

TABLE 4
Sources and Distribution of Gross and Net International Monetary
Reserves at the end of 1979
(Percent)

	All Countries	Undercapi- talized Countries	United States	Other Industrial Countries
I. In % of All Countries' Gross Reserve Assets	100	26	16	58
1. Gold Revaluation Profits (g)	100	14	26	60
2. Credit Reserve Assets	100	44	2.2	54
(i) Foreign Exchange	100	45	1.2	55
(ii) SDR Holdings	100	25	17	58
(iii) Reserve Positions in Fund	100	34	8.1	58
II. In % of Gross Reserves		100	100	100
1. Reserve Liabilities (−)		−6.0	−128	−30
(i) Foreign Exchange		−	−125	−28
(ii) SDR Allocations		−2.3	−2.9	−1.6
(iii) IMF Credit		−3.7	−	−0.4
2. Net Reserves		94	−28	70

Notes for Tables 3 and 4:

(a) Use of Fund Credit (Gross).
(b) Reserve Positions in Fund.
(c) Undistributed profits.
(d) Exceeds "all countries" addition by $1.2 billion = SDR 85 mil-
    lion x 512 dollars per ounce, owing to discrepancy of 2.4 mil-
    lion ounces in IFS gold total.
(e) Including EMCF gold holdings, included in IFS totals under
    "foreign exchange."
(f) Including under "other" about $17.5 billion of liabilities not
    identified by countries in IMF 1980 Annual Report, some of
    which may be U.S. liabilities. Identified Euro-dollar liabil-
    ities were estimated at $61 billion, of which $35.7 were iden-
    tified in the Federal Reserve Bulletin as liabilities of
    foreign branches of U.S. banks.
(g) Equals % of gold holdings in total reserves.

Sources: Computed from international reserve tables of International
         Financial Statistics, June 1980.

exchange rates, and to the deflationary, or inflationary, impact of the explosion of oil prices. Important as they are, these two issues are less central to the functioning of the world monetary system than the flooding proclivities imparted to it by the use of a national reserve currency, or a few such currencies -- the pound in former days, then overwhelmingly the dollar, and now also the Swiss franc, German mark, Japanese yen, etc. -- as the main instrument for international settlements and reserve accumulation, official and private.

The flooding of world reserves, politically irresistible under such a system: (1) makes absolutely impossible the satisfactory functioning of floating as well as of fixed exchange rates; and (2) bears the major responsibility for the collapse of the gold-convertible dollar and of the Bretton Woods system, in August 1971, more than two years before the explosion of oil prices in the fall of 1973. Indeed, the latter was in part impelled by a world inflation already well under way by then, and not unrelated to the doubling of world monetary reserves in the short span of the previous three years (1970-72).

I need not dwell again on my familiar prescription for world monetary reform, initially brushed off by the officials, largely endorsed by them in the swan's song of the famous Committee of Twenty after long years of debates and negotiations, but buried -- temporarily, I still hope! -- in the Second Amendment of the IMF Articles of Agreement. Let me merely point out that the objections raised against my reform proposals by central bankers have been proved devastatedly wrong by the record summarized in Part I. of this paper.

They used to denounce my reform proposals as wildly inflationary, because my proposed link between reserve creation and development financing would -- they said -- encourage the less developed countries to force excessive, inflationary issues of world reserves to increase such financing. They saw no such risk in dollar holdings, which they regarded as perfectly liquid and convertible at will into gold, at an unchangeable price of $35 an ounce. (I could quote exact comments and famous names, but this would be unkind to men who were, and still are, my friends.)

Political and financial facts proved exactly the opposite: the LDCs had far less political influence in the IMF than the richer industrial countries. Even SDR creation -- when belatedly accepted -- was distributed primarily to them (70 percent). The 100-odd less-capitalized countries were allotted less than 30 percent, that is, little more than the United States alone (24 percent).

Taken together, SDR allocations and IMF credits totalled only 3 percent of world monetary reserves at the end of last year, as against 37 percent for foreign exchange -- invested only in a few of the richer countries -- and 56 percent for the rise of the dollar price of gold. (The remaining 4 percent is the share of gold at its former price of $35 an ounce.)

One should hope that these facts are now sufficiently understood to revive the reform attempts aborted in Jamaica and in the second IMF amendment. Yet, several years are generally deemed likely -- even by the most optimistic -- to elapse before meaningful worldwide reforms can be effectively negotiated and implemented. The only hope, in the meantime, is that the countries most dissatisfied with the shortcomings denounced above will pursue their efforts at regional agreements, both to minimize -- to the extent possible -- the inevitable damages flowing from the present world system, and to demonstrate to others the feasibility and advantages of reforms which need not wait for a still-distant unanimity.

III. POTENTIALITIES OF REGIONAL MONETARY AGREEMENTS

My long career in international monetary economics has indefatigably pursued two objectives which should be regarded as inextricably complementary in fact, rather than alternative courses of action: the adjustment of both worldwide and regional monetary institutions to the realities of economic and political interdependence in a shrinking world.[2]

Regional cooperation -- and, hopefully, integration -- must, however, be outward as well as inward looking. The geographical scope of feasible, so-called optimum currency areas should entail cooperation and agreements, de jure or at least de facto, with the countries or areas of major importance in a country's foreign trade, services, and capital transactions. Close agreements -- aiming as far as full monetary union -- will be easier to negotiate, of course, among neighboring countries, linked together by a long tradition as well as by economics alone. They have, for this reason, progressed most spectacularly since the last war among the countries of the European Community and are developing also between them and other Western European countries. Intratrade encompasses about two-thirds of Western Europe's trade, that is, more than ten times its trade with the United States.

Similar agreements are less easy to negotiate among other countries wishing to build around commonly shared traditions and ideals, but whose mutual trade constitutes only a minor share of their total foreign trade. This is the case for the countries of Latin America, of the Middle East and Africa, and of Asia and the Far East. Cooperation, de facto or de jure, inevitably must for these countries encompass other countries or regional groups, including in most cases either Western Europe, the United States, or both (see Table 5).

Table 6 clearly indicates that Western Europe constitutes, in this respect, a main pole of attraction for the countries of the Middle East. Their trade with one another is only about 13 percent of their total trade, 46 percent of which is with Western Europe, and 68 percent (more than two thirds) with the broader group of countries whose trade is also primarily Europe-oriented.

Before turning, briefly, to the potentialities for Arab Monetary Arrangements, it may be of interest to summarize the experience of the European Monetary System (EMS for short), belatedly put into operation in 1979, and the high hopes placed by many of us in the development of its potentialities for other countries' benefit, as well as for its members alone.

A. The European Monetary System and the ECU

The EMS Breakthrough. The most hopeful sign of possible progress toward the international monetary reform since the breakdown of Bretton Woods is indeed, in my opinion, the breakthrough finally

TABLE 5
Regional Structure of World Trade in 1979
(Percent)

Percentage of 1979 Total Trade of:	Within Same Region or Sub- region	Within the European Commun- ity	With Western Europe	With the Europe Oriented Area	With the United States	With Japan
I. EUROPE-ORIENTED AREA	78	47	61	78	9	5
A. Western Europe	61	51	66	84	7	2
1. European Community	52	52	67	84	7	2
2. Other Countries	16	47	63	84	7	2
B. Middle East, Africa	7	39	49	60	15	12
C. Communist Countries	?	(29)	(56)	(65)	(8)	(13)
D. South Africa, Australia, New Zealand	5	29	35	49	17	17
II. WESTERN HEMISPHERE	45	19	24	38	19	9
A. United States	x	20	26	44	x	11
B. Canada	x	10	12	18	69	5
C. Latin America	19	20	27	39	31	6
III. ASIA	33	13	16	41	20	12
A. Japan	x	10	13	45	22	x
B. Other Countries	18	16	19	38	19	22
IV. WORLD	100	36	47	64	13	7

Sources: Computed by Marie Emmanuelle Vandenitte from International Monetary Fund, Direction of Trade Yearbook 1973-1979.

TABLE 6
Regional Structure of Middle East Countries' Trade, 1978 and 1979
  (Percent of Totals with the World)

Foreign Trade with:	Total		Exports		Imports	
	1978	1979	1978	1979	1978	1979
I. EUROPE-ORIENTED AREA	67	68	66	68	67	69
A. Western Europe	44	46	35	39	48	49
1. European Community	32	34	26	29	34	35
2. Other	12	12	9	10	14	13
B. Middle East	13	13	18	15	11	12
C. Other	10	10	14	13	8	8
1. Africa (excl.S.A.)	2	2	3	3	1	1
2. Communist Countries	6	6	8	7	6	5
3. South Africa, Australia, N.Z.	2	3	2	3	2	2
II. WESTERN HEMISPHERE	13	14	11	12	13	15
A. United States	11	13	10	11	12	13
B. Canada	1	1	-	-	1	1
C. Latin America	1	-	1	1	1	1
III. ASIA	10	10	15	14	8	8
A. Japan	5	5	6	6	5	4
B. Other	5	5	8	8	4	4
IV. COUNTRY UNSPECIFIED	10	8	8	6	11	8

Sources: Data from IMF, Direction of Trade Yearbook 1973-1979: 40-44

achieved in March 1979 with the initiation of the EMS and the launching -- even though very modest still -- of the ECU as a parallel world currency alongside the U.S. dollar.

Let me mention briefly three crucial features of the system most attractive to its promoters.

1. The system restores for the participating currencies a common denominator -- or numéraire -- sadly lacking in the reformed IMF Agreement. This common denominator is the ECU, defined as a weighted basket of the participating currencies. Unsatisfactory as this definition may be, it is a more realistic benchmark for exchange-rate calculations, readjustments, and progress toward stability than a widely fluctuating dollar, since trade, services, and capital transactions among the countries of the European Community and others -- in Western Europe, the Middle East, and Africa -- likely to gravitate around the ECU encompass two-thirds to three-fourths of their total external transactions, that is, close to ten times their transactions with the United States.[3]

2. One of the first consequences of this definition is to give, for the first time, an operational significance to the principle formulated in Article 107 of the Rome Treaty: "Each Member State shall treat its policy with regard to rates of exchange as a matter of common concern." Since each country's official rate is defined in terms of the ECU, and since the ECU itself is defined as a weighted average of member currencies, it is impossible for any one currency to revalue upward -- or downward -- in terms of this average without a compensatory depreciation -- or appreciation -- of all the other participating currencies. Any readjustment of mutually agreed exchange rates can thus be effected only by mutual consent.

3. Two other exchange-rate commitments are also central to the EMS agreement. The first is taken from the former "snake" agreement: the monetary authorities of each country are committed to intervene in the exchange market -- through sales or purchases of their own currency -- in order to limit bilateral exchange fluctuations between their currency and any other participating currency to a 2.25 percent margin (temporarily enlarged to 6 percent for Italy). The second, and totally novel one, is to calculate for each currency a so-called divergence indicator reflecting its market fluctuations in terms of the ECU vis-à-vis its officially agreed, central ECU rate. When these fluctuations reach a certain percentage of the maximum divergence possible under the bilateral margins system, the monetary authorities of the issuing country are automatically presumed to take appropriate action (market interventions, internal monetary policy measures and/or other economic policy measures, and/or readjustment of its central rate vis-à-vis the ECU), or, if they fail to take action, to explain and discuss with their partners the ways in which the situation should be corrected. Thus, in total contrast with Bretton Woods and all other traditional monetary "sovereignty" rules, consultations on desiderable exchange-rate readjustments may be forced upon a reluctant country, rather than left exclusively to its own initiative.

4. Beyond its "numéraire" and "divergence indicator" functions, the ECU also serves not only as a unit-of-account for an increasing number of Community transactions, but also as a real money of settlement and reserve accumulation.

Central bank stabilization interventions in the exchange market should be conducted, as far as possible, in member currencies rather than in dollars. Since, however, central banks do not in principle accumulate member currencies as reserves, such interventions require mutual credit operations between the two central banks concerned, the issuing bank of the strong currency accumulating claims against the issuing bank of the weak currency. Central banks grant each other, through the EMCF (European Monetary Cooperation Fund), unlimited, very short-term financing for their interventions and short-term monetary support, which can be supplemented further by medium-term financial assistance, granted by the council under appropriate conditions. These short- and medium-term arrangements now entail lending commitments totalling, in theory, 38.7 billion of ECU, but not all of which could in fact be simultaneously utilized.

The borrower can exercise one of several options, or combination of options, when the reimbursement falls due. In case he wishes to settle in ECUs, he cannot force upon a reluctant creditor ECU settlements exceeding 50 percent of the amount due. For any portion not settled in ECUs, the general rule -- in the absence of any other agreement between the two parties -- is to settle in reserve components in the same proportions as those in which the debtor central banks holds its reserves, gold, however, being excluded. In practice, therefore, the option is primarily between ECU and dollar repayments.

But how do central banks acquire such ECUs? They are credited in ECU accounts on the books of the EMCF against equivalent transfers[4] of gold and dollar reserves for amounts equal to 20 percent of each country's gold and dollar assets. The conversion of these gold and dollar transfers into ECUs takes place at current or (for gold) average market prices over the preceding six months. They totalled, initially, about 26 billion of ECUs, that is, about $35 billion, and ECU 45 billion, equivalent to nearly $65 billion at the end of August 1980.

The EMS baby is deemed by its parents to be reasonably healthy. Its growth to adulthood, however, will require additional and crucial agreements calling for a high degree of political vision and responsibility. I wish I could review the steps necessary to transform the EMCF into a European Monetary Fund, and, later on, into the Federal Reserve System of a full-fledged Monetary Union. This, however, deserves another paper.

Here I shall consider the external -- rather than internal -- problems confronting the EMS, in the immediate and longer-run future.

ECU and the Dollar. One of the first and most urgent problems confronting nonmember countries as well as member countries is the insertion of the EMS into the world monetary system, and particularly the uneasy relationship between the ECU and the dollar in international settlements.

An important feature of the EMS in this respect is highly welcome by our monetary authorities. This is the replacement -- in principle at least -- of the dollar by Community currencies in intra-Community interventions on the exchange market and by the ECU in the settlement of mutual credits. We have often, and justifiably, complained of the dominant use of the dollar in both of these respects, as it could exercise strong -- even though unintended -- upward or downward pressures on dollar exchange rates, irrespective of any development in the dollar competitiveness in world trade, whenever Community countries' surpluses or deficits switch from eager to reluctant dollar holders, or vice-versa.

The first months of functioning of the EMS were somewhat disappointing in this respect, dollar interventions having remained far larger than had been intended. New measures are now under discussion to make possible a further reduction in the use of the dollar in market interventions and settlements. If successful, these measures should eliminate unnecessary pressures -- upward or downward -- on the dollar rate, and restore the disciplines whose excessive relaxation has proved -- as discussed above -- the major engine of world inflation and continued balance-of-payments disequilibria for other countries as well as for the United States.

The use of the ECU outside the Community itself might, at first view, be more worrisome. As mentioned already, the ECU is likely to provide a powerful pole of attraction for other European, Middle Eastern, and African countries for which the Community accounts for a major portion of their total trade. Some of these countries are already looking, in fact, to the ECU as a potential benchmark for their exchange-rate policies and stabilization endeavors. Switches from dollars to ECUs in private and official settlements and reserve accumulation might become very tempting, if made possible by the EMS authorities, or by the imaginative Euro-currency and Euro-bond sectors of the world economy. Such switches might depress dollar rates unduly on the exhange markets, if not effected -- as suggested below -- with the EMF instead.

A close, two-way, cooperation between the EMS and the U.S. authorities will be necessary, in any case, to prevent a further weakening of an already undervalued, overcompetitive dollar. If this trend were allowed to proceed much further, it would inevitably trigger protectionist reactions abroad against so-called foreign exchange dumping by the U.S., and possibly panicky reactions in the United States itself.

The fear of such a disastrous course of events is a powerful stimulus to cooperation between the U.S. and Europe, and the EMS provides new and unprecedented instruments to make such cooperation more feasible and effective than in the past.

The first requirement in this respect will be the correction of the huge and growing U.S. deficits of recent years, and indeed the restoration of healthy surpluses in the balance of payments on current account. This, in turn, will require an even more determined and successful fight to reduce the profligate American oil consumption and imports and the rate of domestic inflation double or triple that of Germany, Japan, Belgium, the Netherlands, or Austria, to say nothing of Switzerland. The clear affirmation of these prior policy objectives by the congress as well as by the administration, and their early implementation by concrete restraints on fiscal overspending, excessive money creation, price and wage increases, oil consumption and imports, and the rest, should help restore confidence in the dollar, and reverse bearish speculation against it by Americans and by foreigners.

Yet a total and lasting correction of the U.S. deficits cannot be expected overnight. Corrective policies -- including past readjustments of the exchange rates -- produce their effects only slowly. The avoidance of an excessive depreciation of the dollar will still require considerable financing of tapering-off foreign deficits for some time to come.

The U.S. can, first of all, draw for this purpose on its own international reserves, estimated at $18 billion at the end of October 1979, but which would approximate, in fact, $200 billion if gold holdings were revalued at the current price of gold on the market. This latter estimate would, of course, be excessive since gold prices would collapse in the event of massive sales from U.S. reserves. It is relevant, however, as one of the many reassurances to prospective creditors about U.S. solvency, and as an indication of their ability to transfer gold at -- or close to -- market prices to foreign monetary authorities in settlement of their dollar claims.

Far more important, of course, is the willingness, amply demonstrated already, of foreign countries to participate in a joint defense of agreed dollar rates, including the readjustments -- upward as well as downward -- that might be deemed appropriate, or unavoidable, before any stabilization of the dollar vis-à-vis the other major currencies can be realistically envisaged, even as a presumptive goal rather than a legally binding commitment. The radical policy changes announced and put into operation since November 1978 -- and reinforced on 6 October 1979 -- are essential in this respect.

The U.S. has, first of all, accepted to intervene massively in the exchange market, rather than leave such interventions nearly exclusively to others. They have, secondly, agreed to reduce the inflationary impact of their borrowing abroad by borrowing in the financial market, rather than nearly exclusively from central banks. Thirdly, they are now ready to denominate their foreign borrowings in the creditors' currencies as well as in their own, in order to make them more attractive and acceptable to prospective lenders deterred by the risk of exchange losses on a depreciating dollar. Fourthly, they are now willing to explore actively with their IMF partners the opening of so-called substitution accounts in SDRs as a way to mop up some of the dollar overhang accumulated in the past.[5]

The EMS opens up new opportunities in all of these respects.

First of all, the adoption of the ECU as a parallel currency may soon enable the U.S. to denominate some of their foreign borrowings in ECUs. Financially, this would expose them to smaller risks of exchange losses than alternative denominations in national currencies such as the mark or the Swiss franc. Politically, it would be a concrete and spectacular demonstration of their will to support the new European Monetary System, and be far more acceptable than borrowings in any national currency other than the dollar, opening them to the accusation, for instance, of making the dollar a satellite of the mark.

Secondly, a reinforced EMCF -- and later European Monetary Fund -- should facilitate the effective concertation of joint intervention and management of European exchange rates vis-à-vis the dollar. It should also provide an additional mechanism for the "substitution accounts" envisaged above. Reluctant dollar holders could exchange them for ECUs, if they wished, as well as for SDRs.

The quid pro quo of the ECU exchange guarantee granted by the U.S. to the EMCF would be a substantial lowering of interest rates on U.S. obligations, and their consolidation into longer-term maturities. This consolidation vis-à-vis the EMCF would leave intact the "liquid" character of the ECU claims held on it by the national central banks in exchange for their dollars, insofar as intra-EMS balance-of-payments disequilibria could be settled by mere bookkeeping transfers of ECU balances from one member country to another. This liquid character would also be preserved for the financing of European deficits toward the United States -- and other dollar-area countries -- if U.S. obligations toward the EMCF were expressed in the most appropriate form, that is, in the form of "consols" without any imperative repayment date. "Consol" bonds paying interest to their holders, but repayable only at the initiative of the debtor -- mostly through open market operations -- long were a traditional and most prestigious means of borrowing for the British government, and -- under the name of "rentes perpétuelles" -- for the French government. They could be made similarly familiar and attractive today, especially if coupled with a "contingent" repayment obligation in the event that present balance-of-payments disequilibria were reversed and U.S. creditors were again to incur substantial deficits toward the United States.

It would, moreover, express operationally an obvious and inescapable truth, that is, that "real" repayment of international credits can only be effected through the recovery of a surplus position by the debtor. All that financial arrangements can do, otherwise, is to reshuffle among the creditors the claims on a deficit country, but it is equally true that these creditors can recieve "real" repayment for their claims only by running deficits. I feel that the suggestions above would help dispel the financial fog clouding these transactions -- and often misleading the transactors themselves into unfortunate and ineffective policy decisions -- and adjust international lending practices to the facts of life.

Note also that the "consols" accumulated by the EMCF -- or a reformed IMF -- should be negotiable in the market, under agreed conditions, whenever advisable to mop up excessive, inflationary, levels of liquidity.

Progress toward worldwide reforms. Some people still view regional monetary cooperation as the antithesis of worldwide monetary cooperation. I took the opposite view when I helped plan and negotiate the European Payments Union, which provided, in the 1950s, a most spectacular demonstration of the complementarity of these two approaches. The EPU did much more, indeed, than the IMF in those years to restore convertibility between the participating currencies and the dollar, as well as among themselves.

I am convinced that the success of the EMS experiment toward its basic objectives, and of the indispensable cooperation between the EMS and U.S. authorities, might at long last break the deadlock which has paralyzed, since Jamaica, the previous determination to restore a workable world monetary order. I hope I am not entirely a "loner" and a dreamer in feeling that floating rates and the Second Amendment to the IMF Articles of Agreement should not relegate to the garbage can all the previous proposals for IMF reform, ironed out over ten years of continuous, intensive negotiations. May I refer those who are open to argument in this respect to my inaugural McCloy lecture of November 1979, published in the Princeton Essays in International Finance under the title "Gold and the Dollar Crisis: Yesterday and Tomorrow" (particularly pp. 11-12). The revolutionary developments of recent years certainly require a modification of previous proposals for reform, but to enlarge them -- particularly to deal with the fantastic explosion of private international credits -- rather than to emasculate them.

First and foremost, of course, should be the actual implementation of the often-reiterated pious wish to substitute a reformed SDR for the dollar as well as for gold in international reserves and settlements. The IFS estimates show how far we are from that goal: SDR allocations and IMF credit accounted, at the end of 1979, for less than 3 percent of world reserves, as against 62 percent for gold (valued at market prices), and 35 percent for foreign-exchange holdings. The mopping up of outstanding gold and dollar holdings through "substitution accounts", however, would be useless -- and difficult to negotiate -- if it were not complemented by the radical reforms to which it should be a mere prelude, that is, those that will: (1) limit the future expansion of the world reserve system to what is needed to make it an engine of world stability rather than of world inflation; and (2) attempt to earmark this growth for the financing of high-priority economic and social objectives commonly agreed, rather than for the haphazard financing of U.S. or other reserve centers' deficits.

I would plead again, as a way to meet the first of these objectives, for a simple but only presumptive rule à la Milton Friedman: the IMF should be directed to expand its total lending and investment portfolio at a rate of 4-6 percent a year, consistent with the reserve requirements of noninflationary growth of world trade and production. Weighted voting of two-thirds, three-quarters, or even more, should be required to authorize substantial departures from this presumptive target. For it to have the desired effect, moreover, the monetary authorities should invest all of their future surpluses in SDRs -- rebaptized, of course, and made more attractive to members -- and eschew any purchase of gold and foreign exchange, except for minimum working balances in foreign currencies still needed for interventions in the market until SDRs are made available -- as they should be -- to commercial banks, and even other holders.[6] Particularly encouraging in this respect are the forward-looking "Thoughts on an International Monetary Fund based fully on the SDR" of the Economic Counsellor and director of the Research Department of the International Monetary Fund: J. J. Polak (1979).

As for the second objective, it would flow automatically from the fact that all reserve growth would become the result of agreed Fund decisions. These should include the type of operations financed in the past by the Fund -- including those covered by the "General Agreements to Borrow" -- but add to them those now made possible by the substitution of SDRs for gold and foreign exchange reserves, and not necessarily limited -- as brilliantly explained by Professor Machlup (particularly, Machlup 1965) -- to short-term lending. An expansion of IMF operations consistent with the first objective above should leave room for such operations. They might take the form of

IMF investments in long-term bonds, or even consols, issued by various agencies such as the World Bank, its affiliates, other Regional Development Banks, and even by other international agencies such as the World Health Organization, and others.

B. Potentialities of Arab Monetary Agreements

The experience of Latin America amply demonstrates that the full scope of feasible economic, financial, and monetary cooperation can be reached only by decentralized agreements, closer between some countries (in Central America or the Caribbean area, for instance, and in the Andean area) than between all the countries of Latin America. Even in Western Europe, the Community countries have negotiated with one another much more than could be negotiated, so far, between them and the EFTA countries, Benelux more than the Community as a whole, and the Belgo-Luxembourg Monetary Union still more than Benelux. I suspect that the same will be true for the Arab countries, the nations of the Gulf, for instance, proving able to conclude closer integration agreements with each other -- as the United Arab Emirates have already done -- than with some of the more distant and heterogeneous countries grouped with them in the Arab Monetary Fund. The enormous mergers -- not surrenders -- of national sovereignty indispensable to full economic and monetary union will, I hope, prove attractive and feasible, in the foreseeable future, to their statesmen and experts, and to their public opinion.

Feasible aims for the Arab world in general must probably be more modest, at least for the years immediately ahead. They should nevertheless encompass (as for all countries): (1) arrangements for balance-of-payments financing help by the richer countries to the poorer, requiring inevitably: (2) some restraints on domestic inflationary policies; and (3) determined efforts to reduce avoidable exchange-rate fluctuations.

The most topical issue to be agreed, as soon as possible, among all those willing and able to do so, is obviously -- as for the countries of the European Community -- the development of a common "exchange area" and "parallel currency" for their external transactions; far short, of course, of the full monetary union that might or might not be aimed at some day, but only after that first, and more modest step has proven successful.

Such an exchange area will have to handle, of course, its relations with other countries and exchange areas with which its trade is primarily directed, particularly the United States and Western Europe. The policies which it should try to develop in this respect would not be very different, in my opinion, from those recommended in part III., A above for the countries of the European Monetary System; and the ECU will probably prove a major center of gravity for any future Arab "parallel currency."

The richer oil-producing countries have already demonstrated their willingness to participate generously in the financing of poorer countries, outside as well as inside the Arab world. Contractual price and financing arrangements with the industrial countries also require enormous, pathbreaking innovations. The respective roles of the SDR, of the ECU, and of any Arab exchange-rate unit in these arrangements will have to be ironed out, but should provide to the creditors acceptable earnings and "maintenance of value" guarantees.

I doubt, personally, that full "purchasing power" guarantees could be realistically enforced for any length of time, in this respect. Stability in relation to the strongest, or at least stablest, exchange unit available may prove the best that should be hoped for, in practice. The ECU offers, from that point of view, undoubted advantages in the immediate future, but I continue to trust that worldwide monetary reform will make possible, someday, the generalized acceptability of a worldwide exchange unit, that is, of a vastly reformed and improved SDR.

Oil prices quoted in the agreed unit should be less volatile than in any other, national, currency, but can hardly avoid adjustments in the light of demand and supplies, affected by proper policies regarding the inevitable depletion of this scarce resource. But this problem is far beyond the scope of this paper, and of my competence.

IV. CONCLUSION

The regional monetary reforms advocated above should <u>not</u> be regarded as a mere stopgap, pending broader, worldwide agreements. They should be part and parcel of such agreements. A more decentralized -- and viable -- structure of monetary cooperation than that of the now-defunct Bretton Woods arrangements has long been overdue. It would have, to my mind, a triple advantage:

1. It would permit the fuller exploitation that can be elicited on a regional scale than a world scale, of the wider potential for realistic cooperation and enforceable commitments.

2. It would relieve the IMF of unnecessary responsibilities, and enable it to concentrate its time and attention on those areas which cannot be discharged as, or more, efficiently by regional groups.

3. It would make wholehearted participation in the IMF more attractive and feasible to disaffected countries, such as many less developed countries,[7] and particularly it would make effective participation possible and acceptable to the communist countries, for whom the rules and norms derived from the less-fully planned, so-called market-oriented economies of the capitalistic world would often be unadvisable, inapplicable, and even irrelevant in practice.

FOOTNOTES

An early version of this paper was presented to the Center for Arab Unity Studies in Abu Dhabi, on 27-29 November 1980. It draws heavily on my article, Triffin 1980.

1. See Triffin 1978, 1979, 1980.

2. I hope some of my readers may be induced to glance at some of my former writings on this subject, particularly, Triffin 1957, 256-68; 1960, 121-44; 1966, 375-543; 1975, 30-35.

3. One may argue that the somewhat larger shares of total trade contractually denominated in dollars are more relevant, but the choice of the dollar denomination in transactions with countries other than the U.S. is itself an illogical residue of past habits, no longer justified today.

4. These "transfers," however, are still, for the moment, reflected in renewable three-month's swaps, leaving the exchange risks on gold and dollars to the depositing central bank rather than sharing them through the EMCF.

5. Agreement on this technique, however, is likely to require a parallel agreement of some sort on the complementary proposal of the IMF executive directors and the Committee of Twenty on "asset settlements." See the remarks of M. Szasz and others in Szasz 1979.

6. To the extent that more substantial dollar accumulations were deemed necessary in a transition period, it should be deducted from the authorized Fund lending and investment operations.

7. Note also that it would contribute to the solution of the issue raised by the fact that the Fund system of "weighted voting," even if reformed as desired by the LDCs, will still assure them, as well as other groups, only a minority of the total voting power.

BIBLIOGRAPHY

Bank for International Settlement. 1976-1979. *Annual Report(s)*.

I. M. F. *International Financial Statistics (IFS)*. 1979. (Annual).

_____, 1980. (Annual).

_____, 1981. (July).

Machlup, F. 1965. The cloakroom rule of international reserves: reserve creation and resources transfers. *Quart. J. of Econ.*, (August).

Polak, J. J. 1979. Thoughts on an International Monetary Fund based fully on the SDR. IMF pamphlet series no. 28.

Szasz, M. et al. 1979. EMS: the emerging European Monetary System. Louvain-la-Neuve, Belgium: IRES.

Triffin, R. 1957. *Europe and the money muddle*. New Haven: Yale U. Press. Reprinted: Westport, Conn: Greenwood Press. 1976.

_____, 1966. *The world money maze*. New Haven: Yale U. Press.

_____, 1969. *Gold and the dollar crisis*. New Haven: Yale U. Press.

_____, 1975. The community and the disruption of the world monetary system. *Banca Naz. Lavoro Quart. Rev.*, (March): 30-35.

_____, 1978. Gold and the dollar crisis: yesterday and tomorrow. *Princeton essays in international finance*. (December).

_____, 1979. Some observations on the geographical structure of international deficits and their financing. *Pakistan Devel. Rev.*, (Autumn).

_____, 1980. The future of the international monetary system. English: *Banca Naz. Lavoro Quart. Rev.*, (132) (March). French: *Revue de la Banque*, (April). Revised and updated: *Kuwait business and financial review: DINAR*, (forthcoming).

6
The Policy Experience
of Twelve Less Developed
Countries, 1973–1979

Bela Balassa

I. INTRODUCTION

The non-OPEC developing countries suffered various external shocks after 1973. In the 1973-78 period, these shocks included the quadrupling of oil prices, which took full effect in 1974, and the world recession of 1974-75, which was followed by a relatively slow recovery. There were also pressures for increased protection in the developed countries.

The quadrupling of oil prices adversely affected the balance of payments of most non-OPEC developing countries. These effects were aggravated by the deterioration of the nonoil terms of trade in the case of some of the countries, and alleviated by improvements in the nonoil terms of trade in the case of others. For several non-OPEC countries, in particular those exporting cocoa and coffee, a net improvement in the terms of trade ensued, representing a favorable external shock.

The slowdown in foreign demand for their exports, whether due to lower rates of economic growth or increased protection abroad, had adverse effects on the balance of payments of OPEC and non-OPEC developing countries alike. These export-volume effects varied from country to country, depending on the composition of exports, since foreign demand for individual products and product groups changed at different rates.

Developing countries, whose terms-of-trade effects and export-volume effects combined gave rise to a deterioration in the balance of payments, adopted various policy measures to alleviate these adverse consequences. Depending on the country concerned, the policy responses included increased reliance on external financing, measures of export promotion and import substitution, as well as macroeconomic policy measures affecting imports indirectly through a decrease in the rate of economic activity. Developing countries, where the net effects of external shocks on the balance of payments were favorable, may in turn have curtailed reliance on external financing (accumulated reserves), reduced efforts aimed at export promotion and import substitution, or increased the rate of economic activity.

In this paper, estimates have been made of the balance-of-payments effects of external shocks, and of policy responses to these shocks, in twelve less developed countries that are in the range between the newly industrializing countries and the least developed countries. The paper will also examine the effects of "internal shocks," which find their origin in government policies. In the following, the analytical framework underlying the estimates will be described, and the principal characteristics of the countries in question indicated.

II. ANALYZING EXTERNAL SHOCKS AND POLICY EXPERIENCES OF LESS DEVELOPED COUNTRIES

A. External Shocks

The external shocks analyzed in the paper include changes in the terms of trade and the slowdown of foreign demand for the exports of the less developed countries. The balance-of-payments effects of these shocks have been estimated by postulating a situation that would have existed in the absence of external shocks.

Terms-of-trade effects have been derived as the difference between the current price values of exports and imports and their constant price values, calculated in the prices of the 1971-73 ("1972") base period. They have further been decomposed into a pure terms-of-trade effect, estimated on the assumption that the balance of trade, expressed in terms of "1972" prices, was in equilibrium, and an unbalanced-trade effect, indicating the impact of the rise of import prices on the deficit (surplus) in the country's balance of trade, expressed in "1972" prices. This procedure reflects the assumption that price increases since "1972" have been due to external shocks, in particular the direct and indirect effects of the quadrupling of oil prices.

The balance-of-payments effects of the slowdown of foreign demand for the exports of the less developed countries have been calculated as the difference between the trend value of exports and hypothetical exports. The trend value of exports has been derived on the assumption that the growth rate of foreign demand for traditional export commodities[1] and for major product categories, remained the same as in the 1963-73 period, and that the country concerned maintained its "1972" share in actual world exports during the period under consideration. In the case of manufactured goods, the effects of changes in foreign GNP growth rates and in "apparent" foreign income elasticities of import demand, calculated as the ratio of the rate of growth of imports to that of GNP, have further been distinguished.

B. The Policies Applied

The paper considers policy responses to external shocks which involve additional net external financing, export promotion, import substitution, and lowering the rate of economic growth. The balance-of-payments effects of these policies have again been estimated by postulating a situation that would have occurred in the absence of external shocks.

Additional net external financing has been derived as the difference between the actual trade balance, and the trade balance that would have obtained if trends in imports and exports observed in the 1963-73 period had continued and import and export prices had remained at their "1972" level. Nonfactor services and private transfers do not enter into the calculation as they are assumed to be unaffected by external shocks.

The effects of export promotion have been calculated as changes in exports associated with increases in the country's "1972" export market shares. In turn, import substitution has been defined as savings in imports resulting from a fall in the income elasticity of import demand in the country concerned. Finally, the effects on imports of changes in GNP growth rates as compared to the 1963-73 period have been calculated on the assumption of unchanged income elasticities of import demand in the importing country.

As noted above, domestic policy measures may also have been taken independently of external shocks and may themselves constitute an "internal shock." The methodology applied does not permit separating the balance-of-payments effects of policy changes taken in response to external shocks from the effects of autonomous policy changes. Correspondingly, the distinction between the two necessarily becomes a matter of interpretation.

C. Country Classification

The twelve less developed countries under study divide into four groups, depending on the character of the external shocks they have experienced and the internal shocks they may have suffered. The first group includes three North African countries, all of which showed an improvement in their "pure" terms of trade, calculated on the assumption of balanced trade in "1972" prices, as a result of the rise in the prices of their petroleum (Egypt, Tunisia) or phosphate (Morocco, Tunisia) exports. Nevertheless, these countries experienced substantial losses in their terms of trade, as defined in this paper, on account of the unfavorable effects of higher import prices on their trade deficit, expressed in "1972" prices. At the same time, increased workers' remittances and the rise in service earnings, in particular tourism, offset much -- or all -- of the adverse balance-of-payments effects of external shocks in the three countries.

There were no such offsetting factors in the second group of countries, comprising Kenya, the Philippines, and Thailand. And, in contrast to the first group, import prices rose more rapidly than export prices in these countries, thereby aggravating the adverse effects of higher import prices on their trade deficit, expressed in "1972" prices.

The third group of countries, including Jamaica, Peru, and Tanzania, experienced internal shocks that aggravated the effects of adverse external shocks. Policy changes under the Manley government in Jamaica, the military takeover in Peru, and the Uhuru movement and related policies in Tanzania may be considered as intenal shocks that adversely affected domestic production and exports.

The fourth group of countries, comprising Indonesia, the Ivory Coast, and Nigeria, experienced favorable external shocks as improvements in the terms of trade far exceeded the adverse export-volume effects. In the two OPEC member countries, Indonesia and Nigeria, increases in petroleum prices, and in the Ivory Coast, the rise in cocoa and coffee prices, explain the result.

III. THE BALANCE-OF-PAYMENTS EFFECTS OF EXTERNAL SHOCKS

In this section, empirical evidence will be provided on the balance-of-payments effects of external shocks, in the form of terms-of-trade effects and export-volume effects, for the twelve less developed countries under study. A comparative analysis of the relative importance of these sources of external shocks will also be presented.

Table 1 reports the estimated terms-of-trade and export-volume effects for the years 1974 to 1978, on the average, while Appendix Tables 2A and 2B show the result in a disaggregated framework. Table 2 relates terms-of-trade effects to the average of exports and imports (average trade), and to the gross national product, and relates export-volume effects to exports and to the gross national product, all expressed in "1972" prices. Export-volume effects are shown in a four-commodity-group breakdown in Appendix Table 1. (Data for the individual years are available from the author.)[2]

A. Terms-of-Trade Effects

The first group of North African countries showed an improvement in their "pure" terms of trade throughout the period under consideration. This was more than offset, however, by the adverse effects of higher import prices on their trade deficit, expressed in "1972" prices, which was rising over time. As a result, terms-of-trade effects increased from 1 percent of GNP in 1974 to 26 percent in 1978 in Egypt, from -4 percent to 8 percent in Morocco, and from -4 percent to 10 percent in Tunisia. (Favorable terms-of-trade effects are shown with a negative sign.)

The deterioration of the terms of trade also increasingly burdened the balance of payments of the Philippines and Thailand, where both the pure terms-of-trade effect and the impact of higher import prices on the trade deficit, measured in "1972" prices, were unfavorable. The resulting terms-of-trade loss, expressed as a percentage of GNP, increased from 2 percent in 1974 to 8 percent in 1978 in the Philippines, and from 2 percent to 6 percent in Thailand. In 1978, the pure terms-of-trade effect accounted for three-fifths of the total terms-of-trade loss in the Philippines and for one-third of the total in Thailand, reflecting a larger trade deficit in terms of "1972" prices in the latter case.

Changes in the terms of trade showed considerable similarities in Kenya and in Tanzania. Largely as a result of variations in coffee prices, both countries experienced a deterioration in their pure terms of trade in 1974 and 1975, followed by improvements in 1976 and 1977, and a further deterioration in 1978. With the effects of rising import prices on the trade deficit decreasing in 1976, and rising again afterwards, the ratio of the terms-of-trade loss to GNP fell from an average of 8 percent in 1974-75 to approximately 1 percent in 1976-77 in both countries, giving place to a loss of 16 percent in Kenya and 14 percent in Tanzania in 1978 as coffee prices declined.

Terms-of-trade effects also showed considerable fluctuations in Jamaica, with the pure terms-of-trade effect deteriorating between 1974 and 1976, and improving afterwards, largely as a result of variations in the prices of bauxite and alumina. Correspondingly,

TABLE 1
Balance of Payments Effects of External Shocks and of Policy Responses to Those Shocks: 1974-78 Av.
(US$ Million)

	EGYPT	MOROCCO	TUNISIA	KENYA	THAILAND	PHILIP.
I. EXTERNAL SHOCKS						
Terms of Trade Effects	1085	364	179	193	581	942
Export Volume Effects	166	102	95	49	63	264
Together	1251	466	274	242	644	1207
II. POLICY RESPONSES						
Additional Net External Financing	3121	980	511	108	70	1359
Increase in Export Market Share	-236	-100	42	-33	273	81
Import Substitution	-1666	-281	-230	145	275	-177
Effect of Lower GDP Growth Rate	32	-133	-49	22	25	-57
Together	1251	466	274	242	644	1207

	JAMAICA	PERU	TANZANIA	INDONES.	IV.COAST	NIGERIA
I. EXTERNAL SHOCKS						
Terms of Trade Effects	122	252	171	-3987	-340	-4053
Export Volume Effects	123	169	42	469	-145	598
Together	245	421	212	-3518	-195	-3455
II. POLICY RESPONSES						
Additional Net External Financing	-35	665	151	-3326	-258	-1029
Increase in Export Market Share	-82	-77	-98	586	165	-173
Import Substitution	146	-187	143	-696	-107	-2204
Effect of Lower GDP Growth Rate	216	20	16	-84	5	-50
Together	245	421	212	-3518	-195	-3455

Note: Numbers may not add due to rounding.
Sources: See Appendix Tables 2A and 2B. Grosss National Product from World Bank data base.

TABLE 2
Balance of Payments Effects of External Shocks and of Policy Responses to Those Shocks: 1974-78 Averages
(Percent)

	EGYPT	MOROCCO	TUNISIA	KENYA	THAILAND	PHILIP.
I. EXTERNAL SHOCKS						
Terms of Trade Effects/Average Trade	68.4	34.3	28.2	40.3	32.6	53.1
Terms of Trade Effects/GNP	14.3	4.8	5.2	6.5	4.4	6.5
Export Volume Effects/Exports	22.2	15.6	25.4	13.0	4.0	16.6
Export Volume Effects/GNP	2.2	1.3	2.8	1.6	0.5	1.8
External Shocks/GNP	16.5	6.1	8.0	8.1	4.9	8.4
II. POLICY RESPONSES						
Additional Net External Financing/Average Trade	196.8	92.3	80.7	22.5	3.9	76.6
Additional Net External Financing/GNP	41.2	12.8	14.9	3.6	0.5	9.4
Increase in Export Market Shares/Exports	-31.6	-15.2	11.3	-8.7	17.3	5.1
Import Substitution Effect/Imports	-68.8	-19.1	-25.8	24.8	13.9	-9.0
Effects of Lower GNP Growth/Imports	1.3	-9.1	-5.5	3.8	1.2	-2.9

	JAMAICA	PERU	TANZANIA	INDONES.	IV.COAST	NIGERIA
I. EXTERNAL SHOCKS						
Terms of Trade Effects/Average Trade	29.7	25.1	54.6	-133.3	-40.2	-112.9
Terms of Trade Effects/GNP	6.5	3.2	7.0	-14.9	-8.1	-14.2
Export Volume Effects/Exports	33.7	18.6	18.7	16.5	17.2	24.2
Export Volume Effects/GNP	6.5	2.2	1.7	1.8	3.5	2.1
External Shocks/GNP	13.1	5.4	8.6	-13.2	-4.7	-12.1
II. POLICY RESPONSES						
Additional Net External Financing/Average Trade	-8.6	66.3	48.1	-133.3	-30.5	-28.6
Additional Net External Financing/GNP	-1.9	8.5	6.1	-14.9	-6.2	-3.6
Increase in Export Market Shares/Exports	-22.5	-8.4	-44.0	20.6	19.6	-7.0
Import Substitution Effect/Imports	31.6	-17.1	35.5	-22.1	-12.6	-46.7
Effects of Lower GNP Growth/Imports	46.8	1.9	4.0	-2.7	0.5	-1.1

after rising from 4 percent of GNP in 1974 to an average of 11 percent in 1975-76, Jamaica's terms-of-trade loss declined again to 4 percent of GNP in 1977-78, on the average.

In conjunction with the decline in copper prices, the pure terms-of-trade effect turned increasingly unfavorable in Peru. After 1975, however, this was more than offset by reason of the improvement in the trade balance, expressed in "1972" prices. As a result, of these influences, after a slight gain in 1974, the terms-of-trade loss reached a high of 7 percent of GNP in 1975 and declined afterwards to 2 percent in 1978.

Among countries experiencing favorable external shocks, the terms-of-trade gain varied between -11 percent and -18 percent of GNP during the period under consideration in Indonesia, amounting to -17 percent in 1978. In turn, this gain declined from -22 percent in 1974 to -5 percent of GNP in 1978 in Nigeria, largely because of the effects of higher import prices on its rising trade deficit, expressed in "1972" prices. Finally, fluctuations in cocoa and coffee prices explain changes over time in the Ivory Coast, with the terms-of-trade gain amounting to -5 percent of GNP in 1974 and reaching double this level in 1978.

B. Export-Volume Effects

Except for a small gain in 1974 in Egypt, export-volume effects were unfavorable in all twelve less developed countries throughout the period under consideration. The resulting export shortfall exhibited a steady upward trend in the three North African countries and in the two countries of the Western Hemisphere, from less than 1 percent of GNP in 1974 to 2 percent in 1978 in Morocco, 3 percent in Peru, 4 percent in Egypt and Tunisia, and 14 percent in Jamaica. In the last case, unfavorable trends in world demand for bauxite and, in particular, alumina contributed to the observed result. While the world exports of alumina rose at an average annual rate of 18 percent in the 1963-73 period, the increase was 6 percent a year afterwards.

Apart from Thailand, similar developments were observed in the other countries studied, although the rebound from the world recession led to a temporary improvement in 1976. The ratio of the export shortfall to GNP reached 2 percent in Tanzania in 1978, 3 percent in Indonesia, Kenya, Nigeria, and the Philippines, and 4 percent in the Ivory Coast; it was approximately 1 percent in the countries concerned in 1974.

Thailand provides a special case, inasmuch as the peak export shortfall, amounting to 1 percent of GNP in 1975, was not again reached afterwards. The relatively small export shortfall, and its decline after 1975, is explained by the rapid growth of world demand for maize, averaging 6 percent a year during the period under consideration.

C. Terms-of-Trade Effects vs. Export-Volume Effects

The results indicate the relative importance of terms-of-trade effects in the oil-importing countries under study. In 1974, the ratio of the terms-of-trade effects to export-volume effects was especially high in Kenya (18), Tanzania (16), Thailand (13), and

Jamaica (8). With the slowdown in the rise of petroleum prices and the increase in export shortfalls, the ratio declined in subsequent years, although it increased again in 1978 in Kenya and Tanzania as coffee prices fell, and it fluctuated to a considerable extent in Thailand in response to variations in export shortfalls. The relevant results for 1978 were 9 for Thailand, 6 for Kenya and Tanzania, and practically nil in Jamaica. In the last case, the very large rise in the export shortfall was responsible for the outcome.

In 1974, the ratio of terms-of-trade effects to export-volume effects was 2 in the Philippines, which benefited from high copper and vegetable oil prices. In the same year, high copper prices led to a terms-of-trade gain in Peru, while high phosphate prices led to a similar result in Morocco and Tunisia. Finally, high petroleum prices reduced the terms-of-trade loss to practically nil in Egypt which also enjoyed a small, positive export-volume effect in 1974.

With the fall of copper prices, the ratio of terms-of-trade effects to export-volume effects rose to 4 in 1975 in Peru, but subsequently declined to 1 by 1978. A similar pattern was observed in the Philippines, where the ratio reached a peak of 7 in 1976 and decreased to 3 in 1978. In turn, due largely to the impact of increased import prices on their rising trade deficit, in terms of "1972" prices, the ratio of terms-of-trade effects to import-volume effects rose to 4 in 1978 in Morocco, 7 in Egypt, and 3 in Tunisia, notwithstanding the fact that the last two countries enjoyed an increased export surplus in petroleum.

In indicating the relative importance of terms-of-trade·effects in the oil-importing countries, the findings conflict with the conventional view that gives emphasis to the unfavorable effects of the world recession and the subsequent slow recovery in the developed countries on the balance of payments of the developing countries. Nor do the results support the view that increased protectionism in the developed countries would have adversely affected the exports of manufactured goods from the developing countries.

Thus, the data show an increase in the "apparent" income elasticity of import demand in the developed countries for manufactured goods originating in the developing countries between the pre-1973 and post-1973 periods. This increase in the income elasticity of import demand offset about one-fifth of the export shortfall due to the slowdown of economic growth in the developed countries.

In intra-LDCs trade, the favorable effects of high GNP growth rates and income elasticity of demand reinforced each other, with beneficial effects for countries, such as Egypt and the Ivory Coast, for whose manufactured exports the markets of other developing countries represent important outlets. In the case of Egypt, however, these favorable effects were far outweighed by the joint impact of lower GNP growth rates, and by the decline in the income elasticity of demand for manufactured goods in centrally planned economies which provided markets for two-thirds of Egypt's manufactured exports in the early seventies.

IV. THE POLICIES APPLIED AND THEIR BALANCE-OF-PAYMENTS EFFECTS

Section III of the paper examined the impact of external shocks, in the form of terms-of-trade and export-volume effects, on the balance of payments of twelve less developed countries, classified in four groups. Section IV will analyze the policies employed by the individual countries and indicate their balance-of-payments effects. Unless otherwise noted, the estimates pertain to the year 1978.

Table 1 shows the balance-of-payments effects of the policies applied, while Table 2 relates the results to the volume of exports, imports, average trade, and the gross national product, as the case may be, all expressed in "1972" prices; more detailed estimates are shown in Appendix Tables 1 and 2. Table 3 provides information on domestic and foreign savings ratios, incremental capital-output ratios, and rates of economic growth, while Table 4 contains summary statistics on external shocks and policy responses to these shocks as well as on debt-service ratios and on the ratio of the external debt to GNP.[3] Data on the financing of the resource gap, nominal and real interest rates, the government budget, the money supply, and nominal and real exchange rates vis-à-vis the U.S. dollar are available from the author.

A. Egypt, Morocco, Tunisia

In 1974, the combined balance-of-payments effects of external shocks equalled 1 percent of the gross national product in Egypt, -3 percent in Morocco, and -4 percent in Tunisia. The effects of these shocks turned unfavorable in 1975 in Morocco and Tunisia, and increased further in subsequent years in all three countries. By 1978, their ratio to GNP was 29 percent in Egypt, 10 percent in Morocco, and 14 percent in Tunisia.

Egypt. Increased toll revenue from the Suez Canal, tourist receipts, and workers' remittances outweighed the adverse balance-of-payments effects of external shocks in Egypt. But, additional net external financing was more than double the balance-of-payments effects of external shocks as the adverse impact of negative import substitution and losses in export market shares were offset only in small part by import savings associated with changes in GNP growth rates. The latter result represented a combination of the acceleration of economic growth and the negative income elasticity of import.

The negative income elasticity of import demand in 1963-73 had its origin in Egypt's foreign exchange shortage during the period that led to an absolute decline in the volume of imports. In turn, negative import substitution after 1973 reflected the increased availability of foreign exchange, the rapidly growing need for imported food, and the high import content of rising investment. Import liberalization had less of an influence as competing imports continued to be practically excluded in Egypt.

On the export side, large losses in market shares in Egypt's traditional export products and in its manufactured exports were not compensated by the small gains obtained in fuels and in nontraditional primary exports (mainly potatoes and onions), so that Egypt suffered a one-third loss in its average export market shares. Among traditional

TABLE 3
Savings Ratios, Incremental Capital-Output Ratios and Growth Rates

	63-73	73-76	76-79	73-79		63-73	73-76	76-79	73-79		63-73	73-76	76-79	73-79
	EGYPT					**MOROCCO**					**TUNISIA**			
Domestic Savings Ratio	9.9	12.3	17.6	15.4		13.2	14.6	11.8	12.9		17.3	23.3	22.0	22.5
Foreign Savings Ratio	4.3	16.2	13.7	14.8		1.4	10.8	15.2	13.5		4.9	4.5	8.0	6.7
Incremental Capital-Output Ratio	3.6	2.3	3.4	2.9		3.4	1.8	6.2	3.4		3.4	2.5	3.8	3.1
Rate of Growth of GNP	4.5	8.8	9.6	9.2		4.5	9.3	3.5	6.8		6.1	8.5	7.0	7.4
Growth Rate of Per Capita GNP	2.0	6.5	6.9	6.7		1.9	6.4	0.3	3.7		4.2	6.5	4.5	5.1
	KENYA					**THAILAND**					**PHILIPPINES**			
Domestic Savings Ratio	20.4	17.7	20.4	19.4		22.0	23.3	24.1	23.8		18.5	24.0	25.2	24.7
Foreign Savings Ratio	0.8	3.5	4.9	4.4		1.6	1.0	3.3	2.4		2.3	5.6	4.5	5.0
Incremental Capital-Output Ratio	2.6	3.4	3.2	3.3		3.2	2.9	2.7	2.8		3.5	3.0	3.8	3.4
Rate of Growth of GNP	6.5	5.6	6.5	6.2		7.7	6.9	8.0	7.6		5.0	5.9	5.8	5.9
Growth Rate of Per Capita GNP	3.0	2.2	3.0	2.8		4.6	4.1	5.8	5.1		2.0	3.4	3.2	3.3
	JAMAICA					**PERU**					**TANZANIA**			
Domestic Savings Ratio	26.0	12.8	14.1	13.4		17.1	13.0	16.9	14.9		16.5	11.9	10.1	10.9
Foreign Savings Ratio	5.4	10.3	0.8	5.5		-0.5	6.6	-3.3	1.8		2.8	9.2	11.0	10.3
Incremental Capital-Output Ratio	4.0	-5.7	-9.7	-6.7		3.1	3.9	-5.5	5.9		3.1	4.2	3.9	4.1
Rate of Growth of GNP	5.7	-4.8	-1.8	-3.3		4.9	3.6	-1.7	0.4		5.7	4.4	5.3	5.1
Growth Rate of Per Capita GNP	4.1	-6.4	-3.5	-5.0		2.1	0.9	-4.4	-2.4		2.9	1.5	2.2	2.1
	INDONESIA					**IVORY COAST**					**NIGERIA**			
Domestic Savings Ratio	9.0	21.9	24.2	23.3		21.9	25.9	28.9	27.9		20.4	30.8	26.8	28.4
Foreign Savings Ratio	1.4	-2.3	-3.6	-3.1		-1.6	-3.4	-0.3	-1.3		-1.1	-0.6	0.6	-1.8
Incremental Capital-Output Ratio	1.8	2.1	3.4	2.7		2.5	2.2	3.7	3.0		2.2	2.7	4.9	3.8
Rate of Growth of GNP	6.5	6.2	6.2	6.2		6.5	5.8	8.0	7.3		5.7	7.0	5.2	6.3
Growth Rate of Per Capita GNP	4.3	4.4	4.1	4.2		2.3	0.1	3.6	2.3		3.3	4.5	2.8	3.9

Source: Calculations based on data from World Bank data base.

106

TABLE 4
Summary Measures of the
Balance of Payments Effects of External Shocks and of Policy Responses to Those Shocks: Averages for 1974-78
(Percent)

	EGYPT	MOROC	TUNIS	KENYA	THAIL	PHILIP	JAMAI	PERU	TANZA	INDON	IV.CO	NIGER
External Shocks as Percentage of												
GNP	16.5	6.1	8.0	8.1	4.9	8.4	13.1	5.4	8.7	-13.2	-4.7	-12.1
Average Trade	78.9	43.9	43.2	50.5	36.1	68.0	59.3	41.9	67.9	-117.6	-23.1	-96.2
As Percentage of External Shocks:												
Terms of Trade Effects	87	78	65	80	90	78	50	60	80	-113	-174	-117
Export Volume Effects	13	22	35	20	10	22	50	40	20	13	74	17
Additional Net External Financing	250	210	187	45	11	113	-14	158	17	-101	-132	-30
Increase in Export Market Shares	-19	-21	15	-14	43	7	-34	-18	-48	17	85	-5
Import Substitution	-133	-60	-84	60	43	-15	60	-45	68	-20	-55	-64
Import Effects of Lower GNP Growth Rate	3	-29	-18	9	4	-4	88	5	8	4	2	-1
Increase in Export Market Share/Exports	-32	-15	11	-9	17	5	-23	-8	-44	21	20	-7
Import Substitution/Imports	-69	-19	-26	25	14	-9	32	-17	36	-22	-13	-47
Import Effects of Lower GNP Growth Rate/Imports	1	-9	-6	4	1	-3	47	2	4	-3	1	-1
Debt Service Ratio												
1973	24.4	13.1	30.1	33.5	20.6	23.3	10.7	46.6	14.9	3.5	9.0	1.0
1978	82.8	32.4	24.3	8.5	29.1	41.7	27.1	72.4	15.9	9.5	12.6	0.7
External Debt/GNP Ratio												
1973	47.8	18.0	32.3	19.0	7.8	16.1	18.1	35.5	21.8	22.8	17.4	2.8
1978	69.9	38.8	43.7	22.8	11.4	28.0	46.6	58.6	28.1	28.6	40.6	1.9

Source: Calculations based on data from the World Bank data base.

primary exports, Egypt's market share declined by seven-tenths in the case of rice, by one-half in the case of cotton, and by one-fourth in the case of citrus fruit.

In the same period, Egypt's market share in manufactured exports fell by one-fourth. A one-tenth loss in export shares occurred in the centrally planned economies, which traditionally took two-thirds of Egypt's manufactured exports, losses by one-half were experienced in developing country markets, reflecting largely political changes in the Middle East, and a decline by one-fifth was observed in developed country markets, reflecting the increased overvaluation of the currency. At the same time, with the unification of the exchange rate system, figures showing the Egyptian exchange rates vis-à-vis the U.S. dollar understate the appreciation of the real exchange rate after 1973.

But, Egypt improved its savings performance with the share of domestic savings in GNP reaching 18 percent towards the end of the period, as compared to 10 percent in 1963-73. Also, the share of gross domestic investment in aggregate expenditure rose from 14 percent in 1963-73 to 20 percent in 1974-76, and to 24 percent in 1977-79. As incremental capital-output ratios first declined and subsequently increased again, the rate of growth of GNP doubled in the 1973-76 period and rose slightly afterwards.

Apart from domestic savings, the high rate of investment was financed by continued foreign borrowing. As a result, the ratio of Egypt's gross external debt to GNP increased from 48 percent in 1973 to 70 percent in 1978. Given Egypt's poor export performance, the rise in its gross debt service ratio (the ratio of interest payments and amortization to export value) was even greater, from 24 percent in 1973 to 83 percent in 1978.

Morocco. In Morocco, earnings from tourism and, in particular, workers' remittances increased to a considerable extent, offsetting much of the adverse balance-of-payments effects of external shocks. However, additional net external financing was one-half larger than the balance-of-payments effects of external shocks. This result reflected the combined effects of losses in export market shares, negative import substitution, and rising imports associated with the acceleration of economic growth.

Morocco experienced losses in market shares in every major export commodity other than phosphates and fuels, as well as in nontraditional primary products and in manufactured goods. These losses rose over time as the Moroccan currency became increasingly overvalued, reaching one-fifth of total exports in 1978. The effects of the appreciation of the real exchange rate, increased food imports made necessary by the poor performance of agriculture, and the high import content of investment further gave rise to negative import substitution in Morocco.

The share of gross fixed investment in aggregate expenditure increased from 15 percent in 1963-73 to 25 percent in 1974-76 and to 27 percent in 1976-78. However, following a decline in 1974-76, the incremental capital-output ratio rose more than threefold as large investment projects of questionable efficiency were undertaken. The resulting fall in the rate of economic growth was aggravated by the deflationary policies adopted in 1978, in response to the international liquidity problems created by Morocco's increased indebtedness. Thus, after rising from 4.5 percent a year in 1963-73 to 9.3 percent in 1973-76, the average annual rate of growth of GNP fell to 3.5 percent in 1976-79.

The increase in the rate of investment was largely financed by the inflow of foreign capital as the domestic savings ratio remained at about 15 percent. Rising interest payments and amortization of the debt, in turn, raised Morocco's debt service ratio, necessitating further foreign borrowing. By 1978, the gross debt service ratio reached 32 percent and the ratio of gross external debt to GNP reached 39 percent; the corresponding ratios were 13 percent and 18 percent in 1973.

Morocco's increased indebtedness reflected the effects of expansionary policies followed in the wake of increases in phosphate prices that, however, remained temporary. These policies adversely affected the longer-term perspectives of the economy, both through the inappropriate choice of some large investments and the increased foreign indebtedness that necessitated a retrenchment which may last for several years. The situation was aggravated by the war in the Sahara.

Tunisia. While Tunisia had the same experience with phosphate prices as Morocco, given its higher trade share, the deterioration of the terms of trade represented a somewhat higher proportion of its GNP. Tunisia also suffered a larger export shortfall than Morocco, due chiefly to EEC restrictions on the importation of olive oil, its principal export. Finally, increases in tourist receipts and workers' remittances offset a smaller part of the adverse balance-of-payments effects of external shocks than in Morocco.

Nevertheless, Tunisia avoided excessive foreign indebtedness, and hence it did not have to interrupt its growth process. The ratio of gross external debt to GNP increased only from 32 percent in 1973 to 44 percent in 1978, while the debt service ratio declined from 30 percent in 1973 to 24 percent in 1978 (the results are somewhat less favorable if the ratios are calculated in net terms by adjusting for reserve changes in the first case and for interest receipts in the second).

These results are explained in part by Tunisia's successful savings effort, with domestic savings reaching one-fifth of GDP as against 15 percent in Morocco. Differences in savings ratios, in turn, may be explained by differences in real interest rates and in the government budget deficit. Apart from a slightly negative figure in 1977, Tunisia maintained positive real interest rates after 1974, whereas real interest rates were consistently negative in Morocco. Furthermore, the deficit in the government budget remained below 5 percent of the gross national product in Tunisia while it surpassed 15 percent in both 1976 and 1977 in Morocco, representing a substantial increase as compared to the 4 percent figure in 1974. In 1978, the budget deficit equalled 3 percent of GNP in Tunisia and 11 percent in Morocco.

Also, high-cost, capital-intensive investments were much less prevalent in Tunisia than in Morocco, so that its incremental capital-output ratio rose to a lesser extent. With investment shares rising from 22 percent in 1963-73 to 29 percent in 1973-79, Tunisia's GNP growth rate was 7.4 percent in the latter period as compared to 6.1 percent in the former.

In contrast to both Egypt and Morocco, Tunisia was also successful in increasing its export market shares as it provided greater incentives to exports and maintained the real exchange rate approximately constant. Increases in manufactured exports (in particular textiles) were quite spectacular, with Tunisia doubling its market share, while there was little change, on balance, in regard to primary exports. But, like the other two North African countries, Tunisia experienced negative import substitution, due largely to higher food imports and the import requirements of increased investment; its imports increased further as a result of the acceleration of the rate of economic growth.

B. Kenya, Thailand, Philippines

In 1974, the balance-of-payments effects of external shocks equalled 10 percent of the gross national product in Kenya, 2 percent in Thailand, and 3 percent in the Philippines. In Kenya, the ratio fell to 1 percent in 1976 as coffee prices increased, but it rose again to 18 percent in 1978 as coffee prices declined. In turn, the balance-of-payments effects of external shocks increased more or less continuously in the Philippines and in Thailand, reaching 11 percent and 6 percent, respectively, in 1978.

Kenya. In Kenya, additional net external financing was consistently smaller than the balance-of-payments effects of external shocks, reflecting the reliance placed on domestic measures of adjustment. In constrast with the three North African countries, which exhibited negative import substitution and increased imports in response to higher growth rates, Kenya saved foreign exchange through import substitution, as well as through a modest reduction in the rate of economic growth in the years immediately following the oil crisis.

Part of the reduction in import shares was due to the disintegration of the East African Community. For the same reason, Kenya experienced a decline in its market shares in nontraditional primary and manufactured exports. Excluding trade with Tanzania and Uganda, there was a gain in export market shares in these commodities. Kenya also increased its market shares in most traditional exports that are sold largely outside East Africa.

Increases in export market shares reflect the effects of the introduction of a 10 percent export subsidy to nontraditional exports and the alignment of agricultural prices to world market price relationships following the oil crisis and the world recession. While import protection increased also with the extension of the scope of Letters of No Objection privileges, which gave producers effective veto power over the imports of competing products, Kenya continued to maintain a relatively outward-oriented stance among developing countries.

Changes in the system of incentives, introduced in 1979, represented further steps towards outward orientation. These changes included the replacement of quantitative restrictions by tariffs, the elimination of Letters of No Objection privileges, and increases in export subsidies to nontraditional exports from 10 percent to 20 percent. The effects of these measures were mitigated, however, by increases in tariffs.

Apart from the expansionary policies followed in the years of high coffee prices, the monetary and fiscal measures applied in Kenya were generally in line with the needs of the national economy and excessive foreign borrowing was avoided. As a result, the ratio of gross external debt to GNP increased only from 19 percent in 1973 to 23 percent in 1978. And while larger increases are shown in the net external debt ratio as Kenya was drawing down reserves, both gross and net debt service ratios fell to a considerable extent.

In avoiding high-cost investment projects, Kenya was able to reduce the incremental capital-output ratio from 3.8 in 1970-73 to 3.4 in 1973-76 and 3.2 in 1976-79, although the 1963-73 ratio of 2.6 was not again reached. With domestic savings ratios rising above 20 percent of GNP, economic growth accelerated after 1976, attaining the 6.5 percent GNP growth rate observed in the 1963-73 period.

The Philippines and Thailand, two East Asian countries with similar per capita incomes and export composition, showed considerable differences in policy performance in the post-1973 period. Whereas in the Philippines additional net external borrowing exceeded the balance-of-payments effects of external shocks, in Thailand domestic policy measures carried the brunt of the adjustment and additional net external financing remained at low levels.

Thailand. Thailand experienced considerable increases in export market shares, import substitution, and, until 1977, savings in imports associated with a slight deceleration in the rate of economic growth as compared to the 1963-73 period. Increases in export shares were smaller in the Philippines, which exhibited negative import substitution and increases in imports due to a slight acceleration in the rate of economic growth.

Thailand increased market shares in its traditional exports by one-third, on the average, with gains shown in sugar, crustaceans and mollusks, tin, and rubber, and losses in rice, maize, and jute. But the largest increase occurred in tapioca which is classified among nontraditional primary exports due to the lack of comparable world market figures. The exports of tapioca rose fourfold during the period under consideration, accounting for 12 percent of Thailand's total exports by 1978. Manufactured exports also increased rapidly, with Thailand's market share rising by nearly one-half.

These changes occurred in the framework of a relatively open economy; there was little discrimination against exports, the exception being rice which was subject to tax. The openness of the economy also led to relatively efficient import substitution and to a decline in incremental capital-output ratios. With increases in the rate of investment following the granting of investment incentives, the GNP growth rates of the 1963-73 period were surpassed after 1975, and the average for the 1973-79 period (7.6 percent) was only slightly below that for 1963-73 (7.7 percent).

Thailand's balance of payments was adversely affected, however, by the decline in earnings from the Vietnam War and from private transfers, necessitating increased reliance on foreign borrowing. As a result, the ratio of gross external debt to GNP rose from 7 percent in 1973 to 11 percent in 1978, and the gross debt service ratio increased from 21 percent to 29 percent.

Philippines. The Philippines lost market shares in its traditional exports as declines in sawn logs, sugar, copra, and copper ores were not compensated by increases in edible nuts and coconut oil. However, it gained market shares in nontraditional primary exports, due to increases in the exports of bananas, canned pineapple, iron ore, and silver. Finally, it experienced a rise of export shares in manufactured goods by about one-third.

On the average, export market shares increased by one-tenth in the Philippines as compared to a one-third rise in Thailand. Smaller export increases may be explained by higher industrial protection in the Philippines that biased the system of incentives against exports. And, increases in manufactured exports were even smaller in net terms, as much of the increase was concentrated in export-processing zones where domestic value added is low.

High levels of protection notwithstanding, the Philippines experienced negative import substitution. This may be explained by the imported input needs of import-substituting industries and of export production, the high import content of rising investment, and the increase in imports associated with the appreciation of the real exchange rate to an extent much exceeding that of Thailand.

The rising cost of domestic production behind high protection also raised incremental capital-output ratios in the Philippines. While these ratios were only one-tenth higher in the Philippines than in Thailand in 1963-73, the difference in the ratios averaged one-fifth in 1973-79 and it reached two-fifths by the end of the period. Despite its higher investment share, the average annual rate of growth of GNP was nearly one-fourth lower in the Philippines than in Thailand in the 1973-79 period.

At the same time, with domestic savings accounting for about 25 percent of GNP in both countries, the higher investment share in the Philippines necessitated greater reliance on foreign borrowing. Correspondingly, its gross external debt ratio increased from 16 percent to 28 percent and the gross debt service ratio from 23 percent to 42 percent between 1973 and 1978.

C. Jamaica, Tanzania, Peru

Given the importance of coffee in the exports in Tanzania, the pattern of the balance-of-payments effects of external shocks was broadly similar to that in Kenya, declining from 7 percent of GNP in 1974 to 3 percent in 1976, and rising again to 17 percent in 1978. In Jamaica, variations in the balance-of-payments effects of external shocks increased from 4 percent of GNP in 1974 to 19 percent in 1978, with some year-to-year variations due to the business cycle, as rising export shortfalls in bauxite and alumina were only partially compensated by improvements in the terms of trade after 1974. In Peru, the balance-of-payments effects of external shocks rose from nil in 1974 to 9 percent of GNP in 1975 and declined to 6 percent by 1978, largely due to changes in copper prices.

The adverse effects of external shocks in the three countries were aggravated by internal shocks resulting from government policies that gave rise to considerable economic dislocation. In all three countries, the impact of internal shocks was most apparent in the decline of domestic savings ratios and export market shares.

In Jamaica, the share of domestic savings in GNP fell from about 25 percent, prior to the installation of the Manley government in 1972, to 10 percent in 1976-77, followed by an increase to 16 percent in 1978 which proved to be temporary. Increased government intervention in economic life, the widespread application of quantitative import restrictions, and the decline of confidence on the part of domestic and foreign investors all contributed to this result.

While favorable changes in the terms of trade aided economic activity in Peru until 1974, the chaotic management of state enterprises, the overvaluation of the currency, increased protection, and political and economic uncertainty under the military regime of General Velasco created increasing economic difficulties. These were reflected in the fall in the domestic savings ratio from 16 percent in 1970-71 to 11 percent in 1974-75. Little immediate improvement occurred following the installation of the government of General Bermudez in 1975, but savings ratios increased to 17 percent in 1978 and 24 percent in 1979 in the wake of the May 1978 policy package which included a large devaluation, the adoption of the crawling peg, as well as restraint on goverment spending.

In Tanzania, the Arusha declaration of 1967 called for increasing government intervention in economic life and for the reorganizing of agriculture. The Ujama village movement was launched shortly thereafter, but the acceleration of the villagization program began only in 1974. These developments, together with the expanded role of the government in conjunction with the 1972 reorganization of the public sector and the establishment of new parastatals, adversely affected savings in Tanzania. The domestic savings ratio declined from 17 percent in the early seventies to 9 percent in 1974-75 and 7 percent in 1978-79, with a temporary increase to 16 percent at the time of high coffee prices in 1976-77.

The three countries experiencing internal policy shocks also suffered a considerable decline in their export market shares. With increased import protection and the reduced use of price incentives, Jamaica's market share fell by 56 percent, on the average, while Tanzania experienced a decline of 44 percent, only part of which is explained by the disintegration of the East African Community. In turn, a decrease by 23 percent in 1976 gave place to a gain of 11 percent in 1978 in Peru, due to the rise of manufactured exports in response to policy changes and, to a lesser extent, increased exports of petroleum.

Jamaica. In Jamaica declines in market shares were shown for all traditional export products as well as for all major commodity groups. Shortcomings in the management of the publicly owned Banana Company, the poor performance of the newly established sugar cooperatives, and the adverse reactions of foreign companies to the 15 percent tax imposed on bauxite in 1974 led to losses in market shares amounting to 45 percent in bananas, and 27 percent in sugar, bauxite, and alumina in 1978. In the same year, Jamaica experienced losses in market shares of 75 percent in nontraditional primary exports and 60 percent in manufactured exports. In the latter commodity group, losses were even larger in developed country markets as the establishment of CARICOM led to a shift of exports to the partner countries. In response to increased political uncertainty, the growth of tourist earnings also slowed down and workers' remittances declied in absolute terms.

Losses in export market shares amounted to 10 percent of Jamaica's GNP, and equalled one-half of the balance-of-payments effects of external shocks. Furthermore, while the data appear to indicate the existence of considerable import substitution, reductions in import shares were not associated with the expansion of domestic production. Rather, output declined as losses in export earnings, together with increased difficulties encountered in borrowing abroad, gave rise to foreign exchange shortages in Jamaica.

The decline of domestic output began in 1974 and continued every year thereafter. GNP fell 4.8 percent a year, on the average, between 1973 and 1976 and 1.8 percent a year between 1976 and 1979, as against a rate of growth of 5.7 percent in the 1963-73 period and 5.9 percent between 1970 and 1973. Apart from increasing economic inefficiencies, the decline in the share of gross domestic investment in GDP from 30 percent in 1971-73 to 23 percent in 1974-76 and to 15 percent in 1977-79 contributed to this outcome.

Until the lack of creditworthiness practically eliminated foreign borrowing, the fall of the investment rate was slowed by the inflow of foreign capital, which was relied upon to alleviate the adverse balance-of-payments effects of external shocks and of losses in export market shares. As a result, Jamaica's gross debt service ratio rose from 11 percent in 1973 to 22 percent in 1976, while the ratio of gross external debt to GNP increased from 18 percent to 43 percent. With the need to finance amortization and interest payments, the gross debt service ratio rose further to 27 percent, and the gross external debt ratio to 47 percent, in 1978. Increases were even larger in the net external debt ratio, from 13 percent in 1973 to 51 percent in 1978, as Jamaica had a negative reserve position in the latter year.

Tanzania. Tanzania experienced a 13 percent average loss in market shares in its traditional exports as large declines in the exports of cotton and vegetable oil by-products were only partially compensated by increased market shares in coffee, tea, and sisal. Tanzania also had a loss of 47 percent in its market share in nontraditional primary exports and 64 percent in manufactured exports.

Losses in market shares in agricultural exports in part reflected the poor performance of agriculture. Moreover, the increased overvaluation of the exchange rate and reduced reliance on price signals adversely affected primary as well as manufactured exports, the exception being the tree crops where the production period is eight to ten years. Inefficiencies of resource allocation further led to a one-third rise in the incremental capital-output ratios as compared to the 1963-73 period.

If Tanzania did not reach a state of virtual bankruptcy as did Jamaica, the explanation lies in the increasing inflow of foreign capital that reached 14 percent of GDP in 1978. As practically all of the inflow was on concessional terms, or in the form of outright grants, Tanzania's gross debt service ratio declined from 15 percent in 1973 to 7 percent in 1975-77, although it increased again to 16 percent in 1978. In turn, the ratio of gross external debt to GNP rose from 22 percent in 1973 to 28 percent in 1978, with a rise from 15 percent to 28 percent in the net external debt ratio as Tanzania used up its foreign exchange reserves.

The inflow of funds from abroad permitted the maintenance of GNP growth rates between 4 percent to 5 percent a year in Tanzania, notwithstanding the decline in domestic savings and the rise of incremental capital-output ratios. These figures, however, reflect to a considerable extent the increased absorption of resources by the public sector, with public administration and defense growing by 9.2 percent a year between 1973 and 1979. Furthermore, the 6.1 percent reported growth rate for agriculture conflicts with data for the individual crops. At the same time, as in the case of Jamaica, Tanzania's foreign exchange difficulties largely explained the decline of import shares in GNP.

Peru. As noted above, losses in export market shares until 1976 were followed by gains in 1978 in Peru. The largest gain occurred in copper exports as the stabilization of political conditions permitted the exploitation of Peru's favorable resource endowment. Increases were further shown in manufactured exports, due in part to exports to partner countries in the Andean group and in part to the depreciation of the real exchange rate.

Increases were experienced also in petroleum and, to a lesser extent, in coffee, lead ore, and nontraditional primary exports (chiefly mining products), whereas a substantial decline occurred in the exports of iron ore, fish meal, sugar, and cotton. While natural factors were predominant in the case of fish meal, the fall in the exports of cotton and sugar reflected the poor performance of Peruvian agriculture, with production rising at a lower rate than population. Various influences contributed to this result, including the poor management of the cooperatives created after the agrarian reform, the system of quotas imposed on the use of land for producing various crops, and the nationalization of the marketing of agricultural products.

With the dislocation of production under General Velasco's reign leading to losses in export market shares and to negative import substitution, Peru incurred substantial foreign debts. The gross external debt ratio rose from 36 percent in 1973 to 48 percent in 1976, and the gross debt service ratio rose from 47 percent -- itself representing a considerable increase over earlier years -- to 60 percent. Further increases in these ratios occurred in subsequent years as the government of General Bermudez, installed in 1975, for a time continued with the expansionary policies of its predecessor. The application of the May 1978 policy package, in turn, led to a decline in GNP but, with rising amortization and interest payments, the debt situation improved only after 1978.

D. Indonesia, Nigeria, Ivory Coast

As a result of the quadrupling of petroleum prices, Indonesia and Nigeria experienced favorable external shocks in 1974, the balance-of-payments effects of which equalled -15 percent and -22 percent of GNP in the two countries, respectively. Following some fluctuations associated with changes in the real price of petroleum, these effects regained approximately their 1974 level in 1978 in Indonesia but declined to -2 percent in Nigeria which experienced a rising trade deficit in terms of "1972 " prices. Finally, in the Ivory Coast, the favorable balance-of-payments effects of external shocks equalled -3 percent of GNP in 1974 and -6 percent in 1978, with variations in the intervening years resulting from fluctuations in cocoa and coffee prices.

Indonesia. Indonesia further experienced a 45 percent increase in its average export market share, with the growth of fuel exports accounting for one-half of the total. Starting from a small base, Indonesia's market share in manufactured exports rose by three-quarters as increases in exports to its ASEAN partners more than offset loses in developed country markets.

Indonesia's market shares in its traditional exports (other than fuels) increased by one-half, on the average, during the period under consideration. Export shares more than doubled in the case of coffee and tin, rose by one-third for nonconiferous wood and by one-sixth for palm oil, remained unchanged for natural rubber, and fell by one-half in the case of crustaceans and mollusks. Indonesia also increased its market shares in nontraditional primary exports, with export growth experienced in a variety of products.

Exports rose, notwithstanding the decline in the real exchange rate that continued until the 34 percent devaluation in November 1978. Favorable developments in exports may reflect the supply-enhancing effects of investments in the pre-1973 (coffee, tea) and the post-1973 (petroleum and nontraditional primary and manufactured activities) periods. At the same time, the import needs of increased investment activity, with the share of investment in aggregate expenditure rising from 11 percent in 1963-73 to 23 percent in 1973-78, contributed to negative import substitution that was further aggravated by the appreciation of the real exchange rate.

A substantial proportion of new investment was oriented towards highly capital-intensive projects of often doubtful efficiency, undertaken or sponsored by the public sector. High-cost public investments, as well as the adverse effects of increased import, investment, and credit controls of the private sector, led to a rise in the incremental capital-output ratio from 1.8 in 1963-73 to 2.7 in 1973-78. As a result, increases in investment shares, financed largely from rising oil revenue, were not translated into higher rates of economic growth. In fact, a slight decline in GNP growth rates ocurred after 1973, giving rise to some import savings.

These savings in imports, together with increases in export market shares, exceeded the balance-of-payments impact of negative import substitution, thereby reinforcing the favorable effects of external shocks. Correspondingly, additional net external financing became increasingly negative in Indonesia. This was nearly offset, however, by the rise in nonfactor service payments that include the growing discrepancy in trade figures between trade and balance-of-payments statistics. While in "1972" the reported trade surplus was $0.3 billion larger in the trade statistics than in the balance-of-payments accounts, the difference reached $3.3 billion by 1978. To the extent that the discrepancy reflects unreported imports, negative import substitution and favorable trends in additional net external financing are overstated.

Actual net external financing was -$1.8 billion in 1974 in Indonesia, declined to -$0.2 billion in 1975 and 1976, increased again to -$1.6 billion in 1977, and fell to -$0.6 billion in 1978. The declines in 1975 and 1976 reflected substantial increases in imports for capital-intensive projects, undertaken in large part by Pertamina; these were reversed in 1977, but imports rose again in 1978.

Dividend payments to oil companies, representing a deduction from the value of petroleum exports, increased from $0.6 billion in 1973 to $1.3 billion in 1974 and to $1.9 billion in 1978. Adjusted for dividend payments, Indonesia had net external financing requirements of about $1.0 billion in 1975-76. This fell to practically zero at the time of relative austerity in 1977 but rose to $1.5 billion in 1978, motivating the November 1978 devaluation.

In 1975-76, financing took the form of drawing down reserves and borrowing abroad. After a decline in 1977, foreign borrowing increased again in 1978, in part to finance amortization and interest of debt contracted earlier, and in part to cover the balance-of-payments deficit. Nevertheless, with increasing exports and GNP, debt service and external debt ratios remained low.

Nigeria. Nigeria lost export market shares as a result of the increased overvaluation of the exchange rate and the strong pro-urban bias of the policies applied in the wake of the quadrupling of petroleum prices, which adversely affected agricultural production and exports. Agricultural output did not regain the 1970-71 level until 1979 and groundnut exports fell to zero. With Nigeria maintaining its export market share in cocoa and experiencing a decline to one-fifth in regard to tin, it had a one-third loss in its average market share in traditional primary exports. Losses were even larger in nontraditional primary exports (44 percent) while a decrease of 7 percent was shown for fuels. Finally, the overvaluation of the exchange rate and the increased absorption of domestically produced goods by home markets adversely affected manufactured exports, with a 71 percent decline in market shares.

The need for food imports, the import requirements of increased investment, and the overvaluatin of the exchange rate led to rapid increases in Nigeria's imports. In 1978, nonfuel imports were more than double the imports estimated on the assumption of unchanged income elasticities of import demand. In the early part of the period, the acceleration of economic growth also raised import levels but this effect wore off by 1978.

In fact, the rate of growth of GNP in the 1973-79 period only slightly exceeded that for 1963-73, although investment shares more than doubled. Apart from adverse developments in agriculture, this result is explained by emphasis on capital-intensive investments in the public sector and by inefficiencies in the implementation of these investments.

With the adverse balance-of-payments effects of the policies applied, additional net external financing turned positive at the end of the period under consideration as did the actual resource gap. Financial requirements were raised further by the dividends payable to the foreign oil companies. Correspondingly, Nigeria was drawing down the reserves it had earlier accumulated and, in 1978, it borrowed substantial amounts abroad. Nevertheless, gross debt service and gross external debt ratios remained negligible throughout the period.

Ivory Coast. The Ivory Coast experienced a one-fifth increase of its average market share in traditional primary exports that were dominated by two tree crops, cocoa and coffee. It experienced a four-fifths rise in its market share in cocoa beans, three-fifths in cocoa butter, and no change in cocoa paste. Increases in market shares in coffee, cotton, and palm oil approximately equalled the average increase for all traditional exports. Finally, the rise in sawn-wood exports matched the fall in the export of logs, while a small decrease was shown for bananas.

The large variety of traditional primary exports, each accounting for at least 1.5 percent of export value in "1972", indicates the success of the Ivory Coast in diversifying its primary sector during the sixties in the framework of a relatively open economy. The process of diversification continued further in the seventies, with increases in the exportation of processed fish and fruits leading to a doubling of the country's market share in nontraditional primary exports.

Notwithstanding the possibilities offered by free entry into the European Common Market and by West African integration arrangements, the Ivory Coast was less successful in developing manufactured exports. Rather, with the decline in the real exchange rate, the market share of the Ivory Coast in these commodities fell by one-fifth. Decreases were experienced in both developed country and developing country markets.

The overvaluation of the exchange rate also contributed to negative import substitution which was aggravated by the import intensity of rising investment. An increasing part of new investment was undertaken in the framework of public investment programs that often involved high-cost, capital-intensive investments. By 1976-79 the incremental capital-output ratio exceeded the 1963-73 average by one-half, fully matching the rise in investment shares.

The rise of public investment, together with increases in current public expenditures, necessitated increased borrowing from abroad. Thus, notwithstanding the favorable balance-of-payments effects of external shocks, the ratio of the gross external debt to GNP rose from 17 percent in 1973 to 41 percent in 1978 in the Ivory Coast. Increases were smaller in debt service ratios, from 9 percent in 1973 to 13 percent in 1978, as much of the borrowing occurred towards the end of the period.

E. Summary of Country Experiences

With export prices rising more rapidly than import prices, the three North African countries experienced improvements in their "pure" terms of trade, but these were more than offset by the adverse effects of higher import prices on their trade deficit, expressed in "1972" prices. And while increased tourist receipts, workers' remittances, and, in the case of Egypt, toll revenue from the Suez Canal more or less matched the adverse balance-of-payments effects of external shocks, all three countries relied on increased external financing as losses in export market shares (except for Tunisia which had a relatively open economy), negative import substitution, and the rise in GDP growth rates augmented their balance-of-payments deficit. The increased overvaluation of the exchange rate led to declines in export market shares in Egypt and Morocco, while growing food imports and the high import content of increased investment contributed to negative import substitution in all three countries.

There are differences among the three countries, however, as far as the financing and the uses of new investment are concerned. To a considerable extent, Morocco relied on foreign borrowing and undertook large investment projects of questionable efficiency which raised incremental capital-output ratios and led to a decline in the rate of economic growth. Incremental capital-output ratios rose to a lesser extent in Egypt and Tunisia, where high-cost, capital-intensive investments were much less prevalent, and these countries were also successful in improving their domestic savings effort.

In contrast to the three North African countries, Thailand utilized domestic policy measures to offset the unfavorable balance-of-payments effects of external shocks. Operating in the framework of an open economy, Thailand increased its export market shares to a considerable extent and experienced relatively efficient import substitution, leading to a decline in incremental capital-output ratios.

In the Philippines, inefficiencies associated with high protection led to increases in incremental capital-output ratios and the balance-of-payments effects of domestic policies were practically nil. Correspondingly, notwithstanding its higher investment share, the rate of economic growth was lower in the Philippines than in Thailand. Increases in the rate of investment were financed in large part by foreign borrowing in the Philippines, while Thailand relied primarily on increases in domestic savings and hence little change occurred in its foreign debt position.

Kenya also largely relied on domestic savings to finance the rise of investment activity. At the same time, Kenya maintained its relatively outward-oriented stance and eschewed large, high-cost investment projects. It was thus able to translate increased investments into higher rates of economic growth.

In Jamaica, Peru, and Tanzania, the adverse effects of external shocks were aggravated by internal shocks, entailing increased government intervention and considerable price distortions. In all three countries, the result was a substantial fall in domestic savings ratios and export shares, and an increase in incremental capital-output ratios. These adverse developments led to an absolute decline of the gross national product in Jamaica; a fall in incomes was avoided through massive foreign aid to Tanzania; and increased external indebtedness occasioned the introduction of far-reaching reforms in Peru, with subsequent increases in exports and savings.

Favorable external shocks, associated with increases in the prices of petroleum in Indonesia and Nigeria, and in cocoa and coffee prices in the Ivory Coast, gave rise to a rapid expansion of public investment in these countries. The import needs of higher investment, together with the effects of the appreciation of the real exchange rate, led to negative import substitution in all three countries. Export shares, however, rose in Indonesia and the Ivory Coast, reflecting gains in tree crops in both countries, increased petroleum exports in Indonesia, and export diversification in the relatively open economy of the Ivory Coast.

In all three countries, and especially in Nigeria, public investments were concentrated in high-cost, capital-intensive activities. Incremental capital-output ratios rose as a result, increasingly offsetting the effects of higher investment shares on GNP growth. Nevertheless, the Ivory Coast experienced an acceleration of its rate of economic growth as, on the whole, it continued to follow a policy of outward orientation.

V. CONCLUSIONS AND EVALUATION

The findings point to the importance of the policies applied in response to external shocks. Continued outward orientation in the Ivory Coast, Thailand, and Tunisia led to increases in export market shares. This conclusion also applied to Kenya if trade with Tanzania and Uganda is excluded. By contrast, the largest losses in market shares were experienced in Jamaica and Tanzania (even excluding trade with Kenya and Uganda), where government interventions in the market mechanism in general, and protectionist measures in particular, were the most far-reaching. In turn, increases in export market shares had favorable effects on the rate of economic growth whereas reliance on import substitution had the opposite effect.

These conclusions are supported by statistical analysis of the evidence for the twelve countries under study. To begin with, the Spearman rank correlation coefficient between the extent of reliance on export promotion in response to external shocks, defined as the ratio of the increment in exports associated with increases in market shares to the balance-of-payments effects of external shocks, and the rate of growth of GNP, was 0.48 during the 1973-79 period, statistically significant at the 5 percent level. The corresponding result is 0.64, statistically significant at the 1 percent level, if growth rates are calculated for the 1975-79 period, in order to take account of lags in the adjustment.

Furthermore, reliance on import substitution and the rate of economic growth are negatively correlated, with a rank correlation coefficient of -0.64 in the 1973-79 period, statistically significant at the 1 percent level. This result reflects the rising cost of import substitution in the confines of the narrow domestic markets of the developing countries, as against the lowering of costs through the exploitation of comparative advantage and the use of large-scale production methods under an outward-oriented strategy.

There was no significant statistical relationship between reliance on additional external financing in response to external shocks and the rate of growth of GNP, the rank correlation coefficient being 0.20. This finding points to the importance of domestic policy measures. Their importance is also indicated by the lack of a statistically significant correlation between the balance-of-payments effects of external shocks, expressed as a proportion of GNP, and the rate of economic growth, the Spearman rank correlation coefficient between the two variables being -0.16.

It further appears that, with the exception of Kenya and Thailand[4], the balance-of-payments effects of domestic policies, in the form of export promotion, import substitution, and lowering the rate of growth of GNP, aggravated the effects of adverse external shocks and thus necessitated additional net external financing in excess of the balance-of-payments impact of these shocks. Countries experiencing favorable external shocks, in turn, supplemented increases in their foreign exchange receipts by foreign borrowing.

The implications of investment allocation in countries that experienced a continuing (Indonesia, Ivory Coast, and Nigeria) or temporary (Morocco and Tunisia) increase in foreign exchange receipts, supplemented by foreign borrowing, are of further interest. Morocco, Indonesia, and Nigeria and, to a lesser extent, Tunisia and the Ivory Coast undertook high-cost, capital-intensive public investments that raised incremental capital-output ratios and adversely affected the rate of economic growth. Increased government intervention in economic life and reduced reliance on the price mechanism had similar effects in Jamaica, Peru, and Tanzania, where domestic savings ratios and export shares also declined to a considerable extent.

Finally, there is evidence that, unless compensated by export-promoting measures, the overvaluation of the exchange rate adversely affected exports in the countries under consideration, while negative interest rates and increased budget deficits had unfavorable effects on the rate of savings. It would appear, then, that adjustment to external shocks was conditioned to a considerable extent by the domestic policies applied.

FOOTNOTES

The author is greatly indebted to Gholam H. Azarbayejani for developing the computer program used in the calculations, to Joelle Chassard Manibog and Robert E. Therriault for the collection of information, and to Robert E. Therriault for undertaking the calculations.

The author bears full responsibility for the opinions expressed in the paper; they should not be interpreted to reflect the views of the World Bank.

1. Defined as products that accounted for at least 1.5 percent of the country's total exports in "1972".

2. All data appearing in the tables of this chapter have been derived from the World Bank data base.

3. External shocks, and ratios of policy responses to external shocks, shown in Table 4, are averages for the years 1974-78, calculated on a "1972" basis. Signs have been reversed in the case of countries with positive external shocks. The results are little affected if the increment in exports, associated with increases in market shares, is related to GNP.

4. Jamaica may also be considered an exception, although in this case the outcome was determined by the lack of availability of foreign loans.

APPENDIX TABLE 1
Trade Effects of External Shocks and Policy Responses to those Shocks, by Commodity Groups
(1974-78 Average Ratios)

	EGYPT	MOROC	TUNIS	KENYA	THAIL	PHLIP	JAMAI	PERU	TANZA	INDON	IV.CO	NIGER
EXPORTS												
TRADITIONAL PRIMARY PRODUCTS												
Hypothetical/Trend	91.9	86.7	61.7	91.6	99.1	83.1	76.1	84.3	87.8	84.3	79.4	94.8
Actual/Hypothetical	61.0	88.9	94.7	124.6	116.1	86.9	79.7	84.8	95.9	112.8	122.6	69.1
FUELS												
Hypothetical/Trend	79.6	79.6	79.6	79.6	79.6	79.6	79.6	79.6	79.6	79.6	79.6	79.6
Actual/Hypothetical	110.9	139.1	89.6	73.3	14.4	35.4	35.4	160.4	18.0	134.2	130.1	99.1
NON-TRADITIONAL PRIMARY PRODUCTS												
Hypothetical/Trend	90.2	90.2	90.2	90.2	90.2	90.2	90.2	90.2	90.2	90.2	90.2	90.2
Actual/Hypothetical	116.4	75.5	89.4	85.3	128.8	186.8	142.3	89.7	60.2	133.1	147.8	66.5
MANUFACTURED GOODS												
Hypothetical/trend	77.6	89.9	89.4	90.7	94.2	91.1	90.7	90.7	90.7	94.5	95.1	85.3
Actual/Hypothetical	80.3	92.4	171.4	69.8	130.8	114.7	55.8	183.0	49.8	133.9	102.8	48.0
TOTAL												
Hypothetical/trend	85.6	88.1	77.7	89.3	95.4	85.1	78.4	85.3	88.5	82.8	82.4	81.5
Actual/Hypothetical	76.0	86.8	112.7	92.0	120.9	103.4	81.6	92.2	69.4	126.0	124.4	93.5
IMPORTS												
FUELS												
Hypothetical/Trend	96.2	117.4	103.1	97.8	99.3	106.3	105.7	94.7	94.8	106.9	98.5	108.2
Actual/Hypothetical	125.3	85.4	119.5	95.3	92.2	83.3	65.2	103.1	40.7	217.9	116.6	473.4
NON-FUELS												
Hypothetical/Trend	95.9	112.3	108.3	97.0	98.9	102.8	104.6	98.0	97.5	103.5	99.4	102.0
Actual/Hypothetical	328.0	126.8	135.6	78.6	87.4	114.5	52.4	121.5	78.3	126.6	114.4	186.6
TOTAL												
Hypothetical/Trend	95.9	112.3	108.0	97.1	98.9	103.3	104.7	97.8	97.1	103.5	99.4	102.0
Actual/Hypothetical	320.0	123.7	134.7	80.1	87.8	109.9	53.6	120.6	73.8	128.4	114.5	187.8

APPENDIX TABLE 2A
Balance of Payments Effects of External Shocks and of Policy Responses to Those Shocks: 1974-78 Averages
($U.S. million)

	EGYPT	MOROC	TUNIS	KENYA	THAIL	PHLIP	JAMAI	PERU	TANZA	INDON	IV.CO	NIGER
I. EXTERNAL SHOCKS												
Effects of Increased Import Prices	1915	1169	721	656	2004	2167	480	900	406	2293	669	3478
of which, Fuels	116	248	137	201	658	692	164	141	83	355	129	149
Non Fuels	1798	921	584	455	1346	1475	316	759	323	1938	539	3330
Effects of Increased Export Prices	830	805	542	463	1423	1225	357	648	236	6280	1008	7531
of which, Traditional Primary	312	584	102	221	768	624	284	422	147	1061	756	281
Fuels	238	13	285	128	6	21	12	54	13	4836	53	7125
Other Non-Traditional Primary	108	109	48	53	440	402	46	92	53	324	150	119
Manufactured	172	99	106	60	208	178	16	79	22	60	50	7
Difference (Terms of Trade Effects)	1085	364	179	193	581	942	122	252	171	-3987	-340	-4053
of which, Pure Terms of Trade Effects	-271	-287	-245	-47	184	551	26	127	-19	-4216	-369	-5859
Unbalanced Trade Effects	1356	651	424	240	397	391	96	125	190	229	30	1807
Trend Value of Exports in "1972" Prices	1151	860	426	456	1368	1777	568	1153	361	2724	823	3238
Hypothetical Exports in "1972" Prices	985	757	331	407	1305	1512	446	984	319	2255	678	2640
Difference (Export Volume Effects)	166	102	95	49	63	264	123	169	42	469	145	580
of which, Traditional Primary	44	66	53	13	7	214	111	147	18	159	127	13
Fuels	16	1	25	14	4	5	3	3	6	279	3	559
Other Non-Traditional Primary	10	18	7	8	38	25	4	14	11	28	11	22
Manufactured	96	18	11	14	14	21	4	6	7	4	4	4
of which, Growth Effects	33	24	14	26	32	37	8	12	13	9	7	5
Income Elasticity Effects	63	-7	-4	-12	-18	-16	-4	-5	-6	-5	-3	-1

APPENDIX TABLE 2B
Balance of Payments Effects of External Shocks and of Policy Responses to Those Shocks: 1974-78 Averages
($U.S. Million)

	EGYPT	MOROC	TUNIS	KENYA	THAIL	PHLIP	JAMAI	PERU	TANZA	INDON	IV.CO	NIGER
II. POLICY RESPONSES												
Actual Resource Gap, in Current Prices	1031	386	202	169	747	947	72	585	310	-889	158	-699
Trend Value of Resource Gap, in "1972" Prices	-2090	-594	-308	61	677	-412	108	-80	160	2437	415	330
Difference (Additional Net External Financing)	3121	980	511	108	70	1359	-35	665	151	-3326	-258	-1029
Actual Exports, in "1972" Prices	748	658	374	375	1579	1594	364	907	222	2841	843	2468
Hypothetical Exports, in "1972" Prices	985	757	331	407	1305	1512	446	984	319	2255	678	2640
Difference (Increase in Export Market Shares)	-236	-100	42	-33	273	81	-82	-77	-98	586	165	-173
of which, Traditional Primary	-193	-48	-5	34	114	-138	-72	-120	-5	109	110	-73
Fuels	7	1	-10	-14	-12	-12	-7	6	-19	371	4	-19
Other Non Traditional Primary	16	-41	-6	-11	102	199	16	-13	-39	86	49	-70
Manufactured	-66	-12	63	-42	70	32	-19	50	-35	21	2	-11
Hypothetical Imports, in "1972" Prices	757	1186	662	728	2266	1778	608	912	547	2446	738	2511
Actual Imports in "1972" Prices	2423	1466	892	583	1990	1955	462	1100	403	3142	845	4715
Difference (Import Substitution)	-1666	-281	-230	145	276	-177	146	-188	143	-696	-107	-2204
of which, Fuels	-8	13	-7	3	18	43	8	-1	39	-58	-6	-36
Non Fuels	-1658	-294	-223	142	258	-220	138	-187	105	-637	101	-2167
Trend Value of Imports in "1972" Prices	789	1053	613	750	2290	1722	824	933	563	2363	742	2461
Hypothetical Imports in "1972" Prices	757	1186	662	728	2266	1778	608	912	547	2446	738	2511
Difference (Import Effects of Lower GNP)	32	-133	-49	22	25	-57	216	21	16	-82	5	50
of which, Fuels	1	-14	-1	2	2	-15	16	3	4	-3	1	-1
Non Fuels	31	-120	-48	21	23	-41	200	18	12	-80	4	-49

Sources: International and national statistics; World Bank data base.

7
Economic Development with Unlimited Supplies of Foreign Exchange

Henry Bruton

I. INTRODUCTION

The capacity to import has, with great frequency, been identified as the most intractable constraint to a country achieving sustained development. Labor services, on the other hand, have usually been assumed to be available in ample enough quantities to constitute no constraint at all, except possibly for specific skills here and there. During the 1970s a group of countries emerged with these conditions exactly reversed. The Middle Eastern and North African oil-producing countries have had, from the time of the 1973 oil price increase, a supply of foreign exchange which, if not exactly unlimited, has been such that no one would classify it as a constraint on the development effort. These countries are relatively sparsely populated or have very small populations. The huge foreign-exchange earnings allowed the rate of capital formation to shoot up, and a labor constraint came quickly into effect. The appearance of the labor bottleneck -- with the accompanying, high and rising wage rates and readily available employment opportunities -- resulted in another new phenomenon appearing on the development scene, international labor migrations among developing countries on a large scale.

The labor that moved into those countries newly rich in foreign exchange of course came from other countries where job opportunities and wage rates were much less attractive. So another new circumstance appeared: labor leaving its home country to travel to the oil-producing countries to work from three months to a year or two, and from there remitting large sums of foreign exchange back to their home country. These labor-supplying countries were in effect exporting labor services, often on a large scale, and receiving, in return, substantial-enough amounts of foreign exchange that their balance-of-payments position was significantly affected.[1]

Large-scale labor migrations and the accompanying remittances did not, of course, originate with the oil-price increase. Western Europe has long been relying heavily on guest workers, but the new migrations in the 1970s seem to be more relevant to the development process than the earlier ones.[2] Reference, however, will be made to the European migrations. Finally, a number of oil-producing countries (Mexico, Nigeria, Venezuela, Egypt) have ample supplies of labor, and face a situation of neither a foreign exchange constraint nor a labor bottleneck.

So during the 1970s there appeared: (1) countries with unlimited supplies of foreign exchange and heavy reliance on foreign workers; (2) countries with a significant proportion of their labor force employed outside the country and an equally significant proportion of their foreign-exchange receipts due to the remittances of these workers; and (3) countries whose foreign-exchange position improved greatly, virtually overnight, and which have an ample supply of labor at home.

These developments have brought into focus a variety of aspects of the development process that, while generally acknowledged, have been insufficiently incorporated into the theories and models of the academician and insufficiently appreciated by the policymaker. It is the purpose of this essay to explore, in a general way, some of the aspects of development thrown into relief by the various phenomena just described.

II. A TYPOLOGY

It is helpful to begin with a brief review of the major characteristics of each of the categories of countries just identified. The first, the foreign-exchange-abundant, labor-bottleneck country, is most clearly illustrated by the Middle Eastern and North African oil-producing countries, and attention will be concentrated on them. The second, the labor-exporting, remittance-receiving countries, include a much wider range of countries in virtually all parts of the world. Attention will again be concentrated on the migrations to the Middle Eastern oil-producers, with only passing reference to the flow of labor into the Western European countries and into the United States from Mexico. The third category, the foreign-exchange-abundant, labor-abundant country, includes only a few examples. Mexico, Nigeria, and Venezuela fall into this category, as does Egypt at the moment, but probably only for the moment. Mexico and Egypt are also exporters of labor services, which makes their story especially interesting.

These categories may be considered in the order just listed.

A. Foreign-Exchange Abundant, Labor-Bottleneck Countries

Kuwait, although an extreme case, may be used to give country-specific content to the general picture of the foreign-exchange-abundant, labor-short economy. Available data are open to considerable question, but do convey the correct order of magnitude. The population of Kuwait is listed at about 1.2 million, of whom somewhat less than 600,000 are nationals. Some estimates put the total population at 1.5 or 1.6 million, with the number of nationals remaining 600,000. Of an estimated 300,000-person labor force, less than one-half are Kuwaiti nationals. Less than 5,000 people are engaged in crude-oil and natural-gas production, while about 75 percent of GDP originates in this sector, and the government gets over 90 percent of its revenues from this sector. About three-quarters of the working Kuwaitis are employed in the service sector, and about two-thirds of these are in the civil service. Most observers find a great deal of underemployment among the civil services. Indeed, over 40 percent of the total labor force is employed by the government.

About one-third of the foreigners employed by the government are in the lowest salary category, while only a handful of Kuwaitis are so classified. One final point: in the middle 1970s Kuwait was saving about 75 percent of its GDP with about 17 to 20 percent utilized for physical-capital formation.

In this kind of situation, what should a country seek to accomplish? One immediately obvious answer to this question is that all Kuwaitis should simply retire, and the nation become a nation of rentiers. This is entirely possible. Net foreign assets in 1980 were probably $50 billion or more, and investment income at least $6 billion. This would yield each of the 600,000 Kuwaiti nationals about $10,000, a figure that provides a not-uncomfortable standard of living. Since Kuwait has huge oil reserves, a rentier nation with a rising per capita income is quite feasible, unless population growth greatly increases. Even Saudi Arabia with about six million nationals could become a rentier nation. As of 1980 it has about $120 billion in net foreign assets that yield some $12 billion in investment income annually, which would provide each Saudi $2,000. Such a per capita income would exceed that of about eighty-five countries of the world. It too would grow over the indefinite future. The United Arab Emirates has a resident population of possibly 1.3 million (1980), of whom about 200,000 are nationals. Its investment income is estimated at about $2.6 billion (from net foreign assets of $26 billion), which would provide each national with $13,000 annual income.[3] In 1968 over 90 percent of the residents of the UAE were nationals, and now the figure is probably below 20 percent.

To some extent Kuwait has in fact become -- or is becoming -- a nation of rentiers, in large part because it is so difficult to do otherwise. Nationals are guaranteed housing, education, health and medical care, jobs, and virtually every other social service one can name. The substantial underemployment among the civil services (and in the service sector in general) means that a large share of compensation paid to workers in the sector is simply a transfer payment. The same observation applies, to a greater or lesser degree, to most of the other oil-producing countries in the Middle East and North Africa. "Development" in such a case involves no bricks and mortar. Rather it involves only the continued purchase of safe securities in foreign markets, and providing, in one way or another, monthly checks to the nationals of the country. In the latter part of the 1970s, however, it has become increasingly evident that social utility produced by such development is considerably below that suggested by per capita GDP. Two general points seem to be at the heart of the difficulties.

Dependence on foreign workers. "Development" means, in this case, having something, rather than doing something; and that which is to be had, either domestically or abroad, is produced by others. That there is growing concern all over the area about the dependence on foreign workers is apparent in both the popular press and in government policy documents. There are explicit references to planned reductions in the demand for imported labor, and increased attention (compared to earlier years) given to "balance," the avoidance of social strains, and the importance of discipline and work. Formal projections in summaries of planning documents seem to assume that nationals will increasingly (and rapidly) replace foreigners in supervisory positions and positions requiring great skill; and foreigners will be necessary only for manual work. The manual workers are then to be gradually replaced by machines. Training programs are now operating in several countries (and of course thousands of people from some -- not all -- of the countries are sent abroad for study), aimed at securing these results. To accomplish these objectives is no small matter, however, because of the difficulty of designing the appropriate incentives in the context of (virtually) unlimited, free social services, guaranteed jobs, and so forth.

Newspaper accounts refer to statements by government officials in several countries (especially Kuwait and Saudi Arabia) to the effect that social pressure is increasing on men to do "productive work." This social pressure originates from an aim of protecting the national identity and, according to some observers, from a widespread feeling of inadequacy and even guilt, due to the heavy dependence on others for their unlimited good things. It is a slow process, however, and the task facing these communities of providing virtually everything for free, and yet creating a productive society, remains unsolved.[4]

Vulnerability. Along with these psychological and cultural consequences of unlimited supplies of foreign exchange, is the more solid one that such an economy is extremely vulnerable to the rest of the world, particularly to the rich rest of the world. The vulnerability arises not primarily from the dependence on imported labor, nor on conventional terms-of-trade arguments, but rather more from the inability of the nation to produce. They must always buy because they have not learned to produce. Thus, they depend on the rest of the world for a supply of almost everything, and as a source of assets in which to store their wealth. The vulnerability of the West and Japan to a sudden, sharp reduction in the flow of Middle Eastern oil is great indeed in the short run. In the medium and long term it would matter much less. In the medium and long term a reduced flow of oil and freezing (or confiscation) of their existing foreign assets would bring these oil-producing economies tumbling down.[5]

The awareness of this extreme vulnerability and of its origin and nature is becoming increasingly widespread. Hence the great concern of the freezing of Iranian assets by the United States after the fifty-three Americans were taken hostage in late 1979. The awareness is reflected even more clearly in their present search for policies that will enable the creation of a productive economy, not one that simply has a huge amount of money. Most rich countries are rich now because they became productive a century ago and the productivity of their resources continued to increase. The task of these countries with unlimited amounts of foreign exchange is to use that advantage to become productive, and to do this seems unusually complex.

There are very few countries that can enable their entire population to become rentiers, and most of these are located around the Persian Gulf. Libya, with investment income of around $2.5 billion, could provide each national around $800 or $1,000 per year, a figure that exceeds the per capita income enjoyed by the nationals of around sixty or seventy countries. Botswana, with its diamond mines and the high liklihood for oil, and its population of less than one million, may well fall into this category within a few years. So the issues involved in the pure Kuwait case reviewed above are common enough to be of interest in themselves, that is, in understanding the development process in the specific countries. There are other countries where there is no possibility of the population, in its entirety, becoming rentiers, but whose balance of payments is unambiguously not a constraint due to their oil exports. Iran (before recent upheavals), Indonesia, Iraq, and possibly Ecuador are all in this category. These countries have faced a number of the same problems as those identified above for the pure Kuwait case, and will occupy attention as the story proceeds.

B. Remittance-Receiving, Labor-Exporting Countries

Consider now the second kind of country, one with a large labor force relative to complementary resources, the growth of which is generally held to be constrained by the availability of foreign exchange. Such countries are, of course, the source of the workers who migrate to the Kuwait-type countries (or to Western Europe and the United States). There are now many such countries, ranging down the alphabet from Afghanistan (before the Russians moved in) to Yemen, and around the globe from the Philippines west to Portugal. Estimates on a country-by-country basis of the number of migrants are exceedingly rough.[6] There is no doubt, however, that for many countries the number is large enough to affect several important characteristics of the economy. At one extreme there is the Yemen Arab Republic with a labor force of perhaps two million, of which one-half or more are working abroad. There may be one-half of Jordan's labor force working abroad (and about 20 percent of the work force in Jordan are immigrants). At the other extreme is India. A large number of Indians are working abroad, but, as a percentage of the Indian labor force, the number is of course minute. This same observation applies to Bangladesh and Pakistan. Other large countries (Egypt, Republic of Korea, Turkey, the Philippines, Mexico) may have from 5 to 20 percent of their labor force abroad at any one time. Independently of the skill-mix of this large group, the withdrawal of that number from the labor force at a given time will have an effect on a variety of aspects of the economy.

Workers of course migrate to obtain employment at a wage higher than they can obtain at home. Whether such migration is socially beneficial to the labor-supplying country depends on a variety of circumstances.[7] The most unambiguous case would be as follows. Labor is unemployed in its home country because of the lack of complementary resources. Its marginal social product at home is zero. The growth of social welfare in the labor-supplying country is constrained by foreign exchange. Workers then may go abroad at zero social cost to their home country, and remit foreign exchange. In this event the labor-supplying country is exporting a product, labor services, which have a marginal social product of zero, and receive in return a product, foreign exchange, which has a very high social product. In this simple case it is evident that labor migration increases social welfare in the labor-supplying country.

The marginal social product (to the labor-supplying country) of a unit of labor services exported is the social welfare created within the country by the foreign exchange that the worker remits. Then the question becomes, what can be said about the productivity of the remitted foreign exchange relative to the marginal social product of labor employed domestically as more and more labor migrates? In general it seems correct to say that the marginal social product of workers going abroad (the social productivity of remittances) will fall as remittances increase.[8] Note that it is the social productivity of remittances, not of foreign exchange in general, that is assumed to fall as increasing amounts become available. Similarly, the marginal social product of domestically employed labor can be expected to rise as increasing amounts of labor are exported and increasing amounts of remittances became available. The consequences of these assumptions about the shape of the productivity curves is discussed below.

Remittances have become very large indeed for many countries, and as there are many ways to remit such funds, official estimates are usually less -- sometimes substantially less -- than actual transfers. For some countries, remittances account for virtually all of the foreign-exchange earnings. Yemen Arab Republic is perhaps the most extreme example. In 1977 exports amounted to $11 million and worker remittance to $1,000 million. Jordan's exports yield around 35 percent of the foreign exchange it receives from remittance. (Foreign workers in Jordan have remitted around $100 million annually recently.) Pakistan's exports earnings and remittances are about equal, Turkey's remittances are about 55 percent of exports, Egypt's about equal to total exports (and twice nonoil exports), and India's about 16 percent.[9] These ratios will vary from year to year, partly because the capacity of authorities to measure them varies, and partly because the remittances do, in fact, vary markedly.

Worker remittances are therefore large enough to affect, in an important way, the foreign-exchange position of the labor-exporting country. A labor-surplus, foreign-exchange-constrained economy would expect to find the arrangement one that breaks the major bottleneck to establishing the development effort on a firm basis. It is of course extremely difficult to appraise the impact of the labor-export, remittance-import experiences, but there is much evidence that leads to the view that few constraining bottlenecks have been broken, and few firm bases for sustained increases in social welfare have been established.

The increase in the price of oil imports of course affected some of the countries severely. The Philippines, for example, relaxed its efforts to prevent migrations because of the current account deficit created by the big jump in the price of oil. Inflation in general has posed additional problems, but of course a major source of the inflation has been the labor-export, remittance process.[10] A thorough, country-by-country study would doubtless reveal other, specific factors that have affected the outcome of the process. Even so, a general review of some fourteen countries leaves the impression that there have been major problems in a country taking advantage of this particular arrangement.[11] The question is, why?

C. Foreign-Exchange Abundant, Labor-Abundant Countries

Finally, a brief comment on the foreign-exchange-abundant, labor-abundant country. The experience of Nigeria is perhaps the most illuminating of this category. The rapidity with which change can take place is illustrated by the fact that in 1960 exports of agricultural products accounted for 80 percent of total exports, and now oil accounts for 95 percent. Employment in the oil sector is about 6 percent of total employment, while about 55 to 60 percent of those employed work in agriculture. Around 80 percent of federal revenue comes from the oil sector. Thus Nigeria (and Mexico, Venezuela, and Egypt to a less extent) is an oil-dominated economy with a large labor force engaged in traditional activities. Despite the ample supply of labor there are a large number of foreigners employed in the country. Estimates of any kind are apparently nonexistent, but all observers agree that there are thousands of Ghanaians, Philippinos, and Pakistanis teaching in Nigerian schools, large numbers of Europeans and North Americans serving as technicians and managers, and a large, seasonal flow of workers into the rural areas from neighboring countries at the busy season of agriculture. In a sense, Nigeria's position is the most troublesome of all: there is the enormous amount of foreign exchange readily available to be used for all kinds of modernizing projects. To implement these modernizing projects requires a wide range of skills which, despite the 80 to 100 million Nigerians, can not be supplied by the national population. The temptation to plunge ahead with the projects, using expatriate labor, is enormous. If that is done, however, not only is a large share of the population left out of the development process, but little in the way of learning and training of the labor force is taking place. The likelihood of continued dependence and vulnerability is great, even though GDP growth rates remain high.

This difficult issue is recognized in the guidelines to the Fourth Five Year Plan (1981-85).[12] Reference is repeatedly made there to increasing self-reliance and to reducing dependency on the external sector. Appeal is made to the importance of a new, national orientation conducive to greater discipline and a better outlook toward work. It is also recognized that it is necessary to "mobilize the masses directly" rather than simply to provide things. Major effort is to be concentrated on agriculture as a means to achieve this self-reliance. At the same time that these insights are made and these revealing objectives announced, the set of policies followed are quite inconsistent with their realization.

Similar questions apply to Mexico. Why is it that several million Mexicans, mainly unskilled, find it necessary to enter the United States (many illegally and at considerable risk) and to live and work in a rather inhospitable environment? The foreign-exchange bottleneck in Mexico has been broken, but something else seems at work that prevents the simple breaking of the foreign-exchange bottleneck from establishing the road to sustained development.

In the following section, an effort is made to examine the several questions raised here in further detail.

III. REASONS FOR DISAPPOINTING PERFORMANCE

It should be emphasized that most of the countries considered here have gained in a variety of ways from their greatly increased foreign-exchange receipts. Especially has infrastructure been improved in many places. Consumption has increased (or been prevented from falling) in a way that often has a favorable effect on labor productivity. Investment rates have doubtless been higher than they would have been without the new, large source of foreign exchange. At the same time, as emphasized above, the evidence is convincing that the breaking of the foreign-exchange bottleneck in this fashion did not result in the kind of development that was anticipated by theoreticians and policymakers alike. There are many, specific reasons for this failure: wars, political instability, corruption, and other things. However, there are some explanations that seem to be especially pertinent to the situations described above, and which shed some light on the development process in general. It is an examination of these issues to which attention is now given. In the following section some more specific explanations will be considered.

Foreign-exchange receipts from both oil exports and worker remittances originate independently of the "real" economy. Not only is the proportion of the labor force engaged in the oil industry very small, but linkages between oil and the rest of the economy are virtually nonexistent. This is true even where considerable refining capacity exists. Essentially, therefore, the oil revenue is equivalent to an unrequited transfer payment. It is cash made available to the country in return for nothing in the way of production by the economy in general. Obviously the same applies to worker remittances. These are cash and originate unambiguously outside the country that receives them. So oil revenue and worker remittances are very similar in this respect: they provide a cash transfer with no direct production link to any real, major productive activity within the country receiving the transfer. To help keep in mind this characteristic of the foreign exchange, it may be identified as "nonearned" foreign exchange.[13]

It is very easy to spend cash quickly and inappropriately. One of the major justifications for project loans or project aid is that a project is specified, and indeed is (presumed to be) ready to be implemented, with only the finance lacking. With oil receipts and worker remittances the development of a project on which to use the funds is not a necessary prerequisite to having foreign exchange. The notion of a "foreign-exchange bottleneck" to investment implies that all necessary conditions for investment, except foreign exchange, are met. Where funds come rolling into a country in huge amounts, the existence of enough investment projects ready for execution is unlikely. Yet the temptation to spend now is almost irresistable even to the most determined of governments. Governments that have always been without the most rudimentary of supplies suddenly have the cash to buy virtually anything. Also, regimes that are somewhat precariously situated find it convenient to allow consumption imports to rise and to provide extra services (cars, subsidized housing, etc.) to specific groups within the country. Large amounts of cash also often facilitate, or at least make less difficult, various forms of what is generally recognized as corruption. So the simple fact that the receipts accrue in the form of cash creates difficulties for governments unaccustomed to having large amounts of cash readily available.

Oil revenues, by and large, are paid directly to the government. Worker remittances are less easily captured by the government. Many governments undertake to secure a large share of these remittances, but there is no doubt that large amounts are missed. The uses to which the remittances are put are difficult to generalize about, and data that will help are just beginning to be accumulated. Much is simply sold for local currency in a routine way. Many countries allow individuals to import some items directly with foreign exchange that they acquire on their own. Hence "own-exchange imports" are effected by individuals (not necessarily the workers who earned the foreign exchange), and are often a large item. In Egypt, for example, such imports account for around 20 percent of total merchandise imports.

The argument is frequently made, especially by government officials, that remittances are used for imports of luxury consumer goods and thereby are "wasted." Empirical evidence does not generally support this position. In particular, it is rarely the case that "own-exchange imports" include a larger proportion of items classified as luxuries than do other imports. In any event, luxury importation in low-income countries is done only by the rich. Therefore, any imports of luxury goods are necessarily a consequence of income inequality, and not simply the availability of foreign exchange to individuals. It seems likely that in many countries a large share of remittances are earned by individuals in lower-income categories. Survey data show, for example, that about 60-65 percent of the Egyptians (other than teachers) working in the Gulf areas are unskilled or semiskilled. It is also known that a large proportion of migrant workers are recruited in rural areas. Similarly, the evidence is clear that many migrant workers are brought into the host country to perform menial jobs that nationals no longer are willing to perform. A safe generalization to make, therefore, is that, in most instances, low-income people benefit from the migration-remittance procedure. There is also some evidence that suggests that small-scale investment in agriculture and in small factories producing for rural markets is facilitated by the remittances. Exactly how much is involved in this kind of investment is not known, but the general evidence suggests that there is enough to matter. Rural housing also benefits.

On the other hand, the existence of remittances reveal important difficulties in "mobilizing" resources. Interest-rate policies and the availability of liquid assets that provide acceptable stores of values gain additional importance. The mechanisms for allocating investable funds begin to be seen to be especially relevant in facilitating the use of such funds for the development effort. In a number of countries, foreign exchange from remittances is placed in time deposits in banks, which in turn redeposit them in foreign banks. This occurs at the same time that some sectors of the economy are severely handicapped because of inability to obtain foreign exchange.

The malfunctioning of the market for investment funds (and other relevant markets) is due to a number of factors, the most important of which is the state of the economy, and, in particular, the set of policies in effect when the worker remittances or oil receipts shoot up. This issue, important in a variety of ways, occupies attention below.

One final generalization refers to management. Where resources, especially foreign exchange, are in such obvious short supply, management (in government, in private sector activity, in public companies, etc.) is of course important. At the same time, "bad" management is often hidden, or not easily identified, because everyone agrees that more resources are necessary before much can be done. One of the reasons that foreign exchange is so often cited as a bottleneck is simply because its nonavailability is not only obvious, but referred to with great frequency. Mismanagement is less unambiguously identifiable. On the other hand, when foreign exchange and other resources are greatly increased, the role that management plays become painfully evident, at least to some observers. Yet one of the most important characteristics of bad management is its inability to identify and appreciate good management. Also, few would-be managers back away from undertaking assignments that are beyond their capacity. The sudden availability of large amounts of foreign exchange, therefore, imposes more obvious (not greater) burdens on the functions of management, and most people and most governments are reluctant to admit that they are unable to perform these functions. Where it is accepted that a particular management skill is not available, and must be imported, the problems created by foreigners, already discussed, arise.

However, ample resources make it possible to live with bad management and bad policies. This is especially the case when the ample resources originate from outside the system, are "nonearned" in the sense used above. The argument then leads to a conundrum: foreign exchange (from "nonearned" sources) provides a strategic resource, the effective use of which requires good management and different policies from those followed in most countries. At the same time, the added foreign exchange enables a country to survive deficient management and unfortunate policies, and, since change is often painful to those in positions to thwart it, the funds are spent in a manner that leaves the real sources of underdevelopment unaffected.

These difficulties arise in large part because of the source of the foreign-exchange relief. The next section considers more specific consequences of the source.

IV. CONSEQUENCES OF THESE SOURCES OF FOREIGN EXCHANGE

There are three main issues to which attention should be paid:
(1) The state of policy at the outset of the foreign-exchange relief;
(2) the exchange rate; and (3) the migration of labor.

It is convenient to begin with the labor-migration question and work back up the list.

A. Labor Migration

As emphasized, international migrations of labor have become extremely large in recent years. In the review of the Kuwait case, it was noted that, while importing labor made possible a rate of physical-capital formation (and of conventionally measured GDP) well in excess of that which would have been possible without it, the heavy dependence on foreigners created a variety of other problems. The contribution made to the social welfare of a Kuwaiti national by a foreign worker is therefore less -- possibly much less -- than the contribution to conventionally measured GDP. However, it is this contribution to the social welfare of the Kuwaiti national that is presumably the guiding principle on the importation of labor. If such is not the criterion, then Kuwait (i.e., all labor-importing countries) is dispensing aid, and the question then becomes that of how best such countries should provide aid. It is argued below that importing labor is not the most satisfactory way for these foreign-exchange-rich countries to provide aid. The policymaker, therefore, presumably seeks to attract the number of workers such that the marginal social cost does not exceed the workers' marginal product, defined as the increment in the social welfare of the average Kuwaiti national. There is little doubt that most observers believe that, in the Persian Gulf countries, there are now too many foreigners, that is, the costs of having them there exceed their social benefit.[14] At the same time, to break away from dependence on foreigners imposes major adjustments on the communities. In particular, it requires new policies and new understanding of the content of development. It also requires recognition of the fact that the benefits to an individual firm of the large migrations may well exceed the costs that the firm itself must bear.

The impact of labor migrations on the supplying country is of greater complexity. There are several issues that may be identified.

Consider an extreme case that is approached by the Yemen Arab Republic, and to a lesser extent by Jordan. As already noted, the Yemen Arab Republic's foreign-exchange receipts from exports amounted (in 1977) to $11 million, and measured remittances were over $1,000 million. Jordan's picture was less extreme, but in the same ball park. In 1979 her imports were about $1.4 billion, exports less than $300 million, and worker remittances over $800 million. One can go a step further and imagine an economy in which all workers migrate, and leave only nonworkers at home. The domestic economy then is an economy which only consumes, it does not produce.

In this impossibly extreme case, all remittances are used exclusively to import consumer goods, and there is no investment. (People sleep under the stars.) The productivity of (physical) capital is necessarily zero, as there is no labor to serve as a complementary resource. The demand for investment is therefore nonexistent. This extreme example illustrates two points that are of considerable relevance.[15]

Profitability of investment. The migration of labor can become large enough to affect the profitability of investment. In late 1980, labor migration (in cooperation with other things) has certainly affected the productivity of investment in Egypt, Jordan, Yemen, probably Turkey, and maybe the Philippines, and possibly areas of other countries, for example, Mexico along the border with the southwestern United States. The problem is reflected most clearly in certain activities, the most obvious of which is construction. Investment in the Arab oil countries during the 1970s was heavily concentrated on construction, and many immigrants were engaged in this activity. The large-scale exodus of construction workers, therefore, penalized construction in the labor-supplying country, and in penalizing (i.e., slowing the rate of investment and the speed of completions and affecting quality) construction also penalized most other sectors of the economy. Since many of the unskilled migrants left rural areas, there emerged labor shortages in these areas that (in some countries) not only affected the profitability of investment, but the level of output as well. The level and growth of agricultural output in Jordan, Egypt, and the Sudan is doubtless lower than it would otherwise be because of the migrations, as is the rate of investment in agricultural activities.

Labor-intensive bias. Another side of the investment effect of migration can be most clearly illustrated by the migrations into Western Europe from North Africa, Turkey, and Yugoslavia. These migrations into Western Europe made possible the continuation of certain activities there that, in the absence of the immigrant, would not have been economically possible. The immigrant provide more labor and cheaper labor than is available from the national population. An activity whose continued life is possible because of the migrations is very likely to be a relatively labor-intensive activity, the very kind of activity that might provide an investment opportunity in the labor-supplying country. In this case, the migration has dampened the profitability of investment in general, and has also affected the profitability of specific activities which, in the absence of the migrations, may have provided especially attractive investment possibilities. The factor-supply situation has so changed, temporarily, that, despite the remittances, investment opportunities are adversely affected.

Another example of this phenomenon is along the Mexico-United States border. A large part of the fruit and vegetable farming and cattle ranching found on the United States side of the border would be financially unprofitable were it not for available Mexican migrants. Yet, these very activities would appear to be ideally suited for the Mexican side of the border, and if these activities could not survive in the United States because of the lack of large amounts of cheap labor, a ready export market would appear available to the Mexican producer.

These examples, and the example of Jordan and Yemen, are not far from the pure case considered above where all labor was assumed to migrate. Investment opportunities, in the labor-supplying country, so difficult to identify in the best of circumstances, are made more obscure and their risks are increased. In this event one expects that the remittances are to be used largely for consumption purposes.

One might argue, however, that the migration does result not only in "world output" being higher than it would be without the migrations, but also in the income of the migrants and their dependents being higher. There are a number of questions about this argument.

The time period is relevant, and the migration process may be sacrificing long-run development in order to gain the short-run advantage of increased consumption. The labor-supplying area or country would, therefore, find itself permanently dependent on sending its workers abroad, and using remittances for consumption purposes.

However, this arrangement leaves the labor-supplying country especially vulnerable to the labor-importing country. As already noticed, the governments of the latter countries are, to a considerable degree, increasingly convinced of the social costs of their dependency on migrant workers, especially so when they are long-term residents within the host country. Interviews with migrants and their observed behavior reveal clearly that the migrating workers (and their families) attach a great deal of disutility to working abroad. It appears that in many cases migration is acceptable only because it is assumed to be temporary.

Another aspect of this issue has to do with the kinds of jobs performed by the migrants. In many cases, in the labor-importing countries a great number of the more menial tasks are left to migrant workers. The sharp distinction between tasks performed by migrant and national, and the corresponding tendency to categorize the foreign workers in this way, contributes to the social tension to which reference has already been made. This result also contributes to the continuation of internal inequality. Migrant labor is tolerated because it performs menial tasks, and will be increasigly less acceptable if such labor begins to move -- or try to move -- into less menial jobs. Therefore, international inequality, in a very real sense, is exacerbated and perpetuated by the migration phenomenon rather than relieved by it.

The dilemma then is this: the migration-remittance process does provide foreign exchange to the labor-supplying, foreign-exchange-deficient country. However, this particular process of obtaining foreign exchange tends (except in countries with enormous populations) to dampen investment opportunities and, in a variety of cases, to remove certain, especially obvious opportunities from the investment-possibilties list. The textbook answer to this dilemma for both labor-supplying and labor-importing countries was mentioned earlier: labor should migrate to the point where marginal social benefits are no less than marginal social costs. The benefits and costs are those just reviewed. It seems that the available evidence suggests rather clearly that migration has been too large from the standpoint of most of the labor-supplying countries. The arguments above also suggest that policies in the labor-supplying countries that help to identify and exploit investment opportunities and that facilitate saving by providing appropriate assets yielding attractive rates of return, gain in importance in this kind of environment.

This way of putting the point directs attention to the question of the role that policies can play in creating a situation in which the migration-remittance process can be a more effective instrument. The exchange rate is first considered and then some more general policy issues are reviewed.

B. Exchange Rates

The exchange-rate dilemma arises from the fact that the foreign exchange originates independently of the productivity of the major sectors of the economy. This (as already emphasized) is completely true for remittances and virtually true for the foreign exchange received from oil exports. The abundance of foreign exchange obtained in this way means that an exchange rate that protects the balance of payments (given the other impediments to international trade) will misrepresent the productivity of virtually all the remaining resources within the country. Combined with a low (often negative) interest rate, the overvalued (in the sense just described) exchange rate would result in the investment that does take place going into nontradables. The most obvious nontradables are construction, trade, and finance activities.

Attention has already been directed to the difficulties in the identification of investment opportunities in the migration-remittance case because of the effect of the movement of labor on the profitability of domestic investment. Now it is recognized that the availability of substantial amounts of foreign exchange from "nonearned" sources support an exchange rate that in no sense identifies or measures the productivity of the resources remaining within the country. This then adds further to the difficulties of the identification of profitable investment opportunities.

For the Kuwaiti case a similar problem exists. To reduce the vulnerability discussed previously, nonoil activities must be created. With unlimited supplies of foreign exchange, an exchange rate that protects the balance of payments would mean that almost any nonoil activity in tradables is virtually impossible to establish. Everything can be imported more cheaply than it can be produced domestically.

Even for the plentiful-labor, plentiful-foreign-exchange countries -- Mexico, Nigeria, Venezuela (and in this instance Great Britain) -- the problem arises. In all these countries, nonoil exports have declined in recent years, and in many nonoil activities output and productivity have grown slowly or declined in the years of the big oil boom.

What, then, is the appropriate exchange-rate policy in these countries at the present time? For most of the countries included in the arguments of this paper, a strong case can be made that the domestic currency has been, over recent years, overvalued at the same time that the balance of payments has been strong. Devaluation would appear in order, but there are major questions about devaluation in the face of rising foreign-exchange reserves.

Two frequently applied arguments may be deposed of quickly. The first refers to elasticities. In the case where a single item accounts for a large proportion of total exports and the foreign demand for that item is inelastic, devaluation will reduce foreign-exchange receipts. This argument is largely inapplicable in the case of oil. Prices of oil in the international markets are quoted in dollars (or at least in foreign exchange). It is not the case that the oil importer must acquire so many Egyptian pounds, Kuwaiti dinars, or Mexican pesos in order to buy a barrel of oil. Rather, the importer simply hands over the dollars. So the demand-elasticity question is not really present insofar as exchange-rate adjustment is concerned.

The other argument has to do with the use of the exchange-rate adjustments as a means of combatting inflation. If foreign exchange is abundant, and if most of the inflation is due to the rising price of imports, then the appreciation of domestic currency is a very powerful means to control inflation. The Yemen Arab Republic, where commodity imports are many times the value of commodity exports, is an example of a country where inflation is largely imported and, hence, appreciation would serve as an effective means of offsetting the rise in the world price of imports. Jordan is very near that position. In Kuwait (also Saudi Arabia, the United Arab Emirates, Bahrain, etc.) the balance of payments would remain strong with an appreciation of several hundred percent. With a very large excess of imports relative to nonoil exports, a rising consumer-price index is largely a matter of rising import prices. As local currency rises in value, the range of tradables increases. It has been observed that it could become less expensive for a Kuwaiti lady to fly to Cairo or Beirut to "have her hair done" than to have it done in Kuwait -- if the dinar-dollar exchange rate rose sufficiently.

While limiting inflation is relevant to these countries, the discussion in Parts I and II emphasized the importance in all three categories of countries of getting investment into nonoil activities, and appreciation severely penalizes that effort. As noted in the preceding paragraph, a rising value of local currency not only makes imports cheaper (in the local currency), it also increases the range of commodities that can be imported. Even though appreciation will help control inflation and not seriously damage the balance of payments, it will contribute mightily to the defeat of the effort to strengthen the nonoil part of the oil economies and to the use of remittances in ways that add to the long-run productivity of the entire economy. To offset the rising price of imports would be inappropriate to the achievement of the more fundamental objective.

Finally, it is important to note that the relevance of this question obtains independently of how long oil or remittances are available. The problem is not, mainly, how to prepare for the time when these sources of foreign exchange are exhausted, although this is part of the question for some of the countries. The basic question is that asked above: how to develop the entire economy when the supply of foreign exchange allows an exchange rate that (to exaggerate) permits the importation of everything.

To allow the exchange rate to float will probably not do the trick, and for the kind of economies considered here, floating creates short-run difficulties that result in the emitting of misleading signals. One might also try to meet the objective by tariff policy. Tariffs, however, have difficulties of their own, and there are few guidelines that a government can follow that lead to an appropriate set of tariffs. As productivity changes, tariffs should change, and governments often have trouble changing tariffs in the appropriate way at the appropriate time. One would think, then, that the most reliable approach would include zero tariffs, or a modest rate applied equally across the board.[16]

If protecting the balance of payments is not the criterion to determine the exchange rate, then what is? The general answer is that the exchange rate should contribute to the achievement of an acceptable rate of nonoil investment and of nonoil exports. The objective (to repeat) is not only to diversify, but to provide incentives to search for new techniques and methods that lead to increasing productivity in the "real" economy. The appropriate consideration that should guide the determining of the exchange rate may well vary from country to country. Arbitrary decisions may be the most reasonable approach. For example, an exchange rate that produces a particular rate of investment and of exports outside the nonoil sectors may be settled on by trial and error. Evidently, additional instruments (e.g., subsidies) may be necessary.

For the labor-exporting, remittance-receiving country, the exchange rate may be linked in some way or another to the wage rate. The cost of earning a unit of foreign exchange by remittances is the marginal social product of the migrating labor. Unless this is zero (a doubtful situation) the domestic value of a unit of foreign exchange equal to the marginal social product of labor will measure the appropriate cost of the foreign exchange, or that part earned from remittances. In any event, tying changes in the exchange rate to changes in the marginal social product of labor provides a helpful criterion. Evidently, data do not provide easy answers, but to have the guiding principle is important.

In some (possibly most) cases, foreign assets may be accumulated, and this creates risks. Also, oil-producing countries may find it in order to reduce oil output below what oil importers think they need. These possibilities raise important questions, but (happily) are beyond the scope of the present effort. It may be worth noting in passing, however, that the provision of stores of value to these countries may well be one of the most important contributions the Western world and Japan can make towards resolving a number of the issues raised in this paper.

C. The Initial Position

The initial position of relevance here is the set of policies that obtained in 1973 when the first big increase in the price of oil took place. Of course policies were not exactly the same in all of the countries considered here, but some generalizations are possible. The structure of incentives that obtained, as well as the general planning procedure, encouraged activities that simply processed imported raw materials or assembled imported components to make final goods for the domestic market. In the other direction, manufacturing activities based on agriculture, and to a lesser degree other domestic raw materials (except crude oil in some countries), were generally discouraged. Also generally discouraged were activities producing capital and intermediate goods. The instruments include the usual array of tariffs and import controls and their discretionary application and exemptions, tax holidays, subsidized interest rates, and a direct role for the government in virtually all investment-allocation decisions. Added to this array is the exchange-rate problem already reviewed. That such a set of policies lead to distortions and bottlenecks (and employment and income-distribution problems) has been amply demonstrated in numerous empirical studies of individual countries and in equally numerous theoretical arguments.

To a considerable extent the newly available, plentiful supply of foreign exchange makes it easier for a country to live with this set of policies. Bottlenecks are overcome by imports, and distortions that result in low and nongrowing productivity are offset by the provision of a great variety of "free" social services, including the subsidization of a wide range of consumer goods. Employment problems can be resolved by expanding the government bureaucracy. Skill bottlenecks are overcome by importing foreign experts and technicians.

Inflation is blamed on the rest of the world. As previously emphasized, these ways of resolving -- of living with -- the difficulties have run into increasing disfavor.

Along with providing the range of consumer goods and services, government policy has in general included many projects that yield to the biases and incentives summarized above. Some projects -- particularly infrastructure -- serve a variety of social objectives, but the projects have often exacerbated the range of problems that government policymakers explicitly acknowledge are paramount. In Egypt, for example, government officials spend a great deal of time and effort to obtain more foreign-financed projects at the same time that they take pride in the improved balance-of-payments position and accumulated reserves. There is danger that the process will continue until the wells run dry, foreign aid is forgotten, and the country is forced to rely on its own nonoil, no-remittance economy.

V. CONCLUSIONS

What can be done varies significantly from country to country, but three generalizations do seem possible, and indeed applicable to a wider group of developing countries.

A. The Role of Policy

Even with unlimited supplies of foreign exchange, policies are strategic. The policies may be defined through a market mechanism or through a materials-balance approach to planning that is built on a thorough knowledge of factor supplies and demand conditioning the society. Foreign exchange made available from outside the system can help a country tolerate unfortunate policies or bad planning. This fact has been well learned. What seems less well appreciated -- and even less often practiced -- is that such outside foreign exchange can be used to effect policy changes, that is, to facilitate a sustained move to establish policies that are compatible with the achievement of the social and economic objectives to which everyone gives lip service. The status quo always helps some groups in the society, and if those it helps can impede change, they can be expected to do so. "Outside" funds can help in effecting policy change in a manner that inflicts few of the wounds that can lead to turmoil. In the case of the countries considered here, the problem is not only the existence of an entrenched group opposing change (though such is a problem in some of the countries), but often an entire society that has suddenly found itself in a predicament that provides very little satisfaction. To modify this situation, therefore, can constitute an effective use of the foreign exchange.

B. The Role of Investment

The rate of capital formation that a country can absorb may well be limited by things other than foreign exchange and labor. (A stronger hypothesis -- that capital accumulation is always limited by things other than foreign exchange -- is worth attention, but not explored here.) High rates of investment are generally a major policy objective, and the temptation is strong to push investment hard when foreign exchange is available to do so. As the rate of investment increases, however, the community is asked to respond and adapt in a way, and at a rate, that adds increasingly to tensions and unease. Even if none of the conventional bottlenecks (technical skills, management capacity, project-evaluation procedures, finance-allocation mechanisms, etc.) were present, a high investment rate necessarily imposes on the community a great variety of adjustments and new events and sights. Such rapid changes are impossible to ignore but difficult to accept. These problems are made more intractable in instances where the investment requires large numbers of migrant workers, and where much of the investment that takes place is aimed at an imitation of the West. This latter characteristic of investment is almost inevitable when the rapid investment occurs in an economy with the kinds of policies described above and a great deal of foreign exchange. The result, then, in this case of a high rate of investment is to create further distortions and dislocations that subtract significantly from the social welfare that the increased output might produce.

The rejoinder to the preceding kind of argument is, of course, that rapid rates of growth (and hence high rates of investment) are essential if the population problem is to be conquered, if the gap between the rich nations and poor nations is to be closed, if inhuman and inhumanizing poverty is to be relieved, and if social stability is to be achieved. If the rates of investment made possible by unlimited supplies of foreign exchange seem to create more problems than solutions, then the prospects are bleak indeed. Evidently, large amounts of resources misallocated and mismanaged can, in any event, hardly be expected to overcome these great difficulties. The experiences reviewed here, however, also suggest a third generalization.

C. The Role of an Internal Dynamic

The difficulties arise mainly from the origins of the foreign exchange, the oil revenues, and the worker remittances. The foreign-exchange receipts have not emerged from the functioning of the real economy, and accrue to a society ill prepared to use them. Large-scale, "nonearned" imports expose the community to ideas and social arrangements incompatible with, and possibly antagonistic to, their own. This exposure is so abrupt that the community cannot adapt, appraise, or screen what is available to it, so it tends to acquire things willy-nilly. It becomes a community of "unanchored souls" without a secure doctrine of its own,[17] and hence susceptible to the blandishments of the rich outsiders. Since consumption of new things can be learned more quickly than can the production of new things, the community tends to become dominated by consuming, trading, and importing, rather than producing. This helps to generate the economic vulnerability (and the social unease) previously noted.

What comes out again is that the key to development -- the key to the creation of a developing economy -- is to establish an internal, an indigenous, dynamic. Links with the rich world are useful in this effort, but unlimited imports -- even large amounts of imports -- tend to defeat, or at least to make more difficult, the search for that internal dynamic that will move the system, but move it in a way consistent with the social changes that are taking place. Therefore, it is the search for this internal dynamic (or for the replacement or avoidance of the client-culture, client-economy status) that "nonearned" foreign exchange must implement. Perhaps this is the real lesson the experience of the countries reviewed here has taught us.

FOOTNOTES

1. Large-scale labor migrations are to be distinguished from the "brain drain" question. As is discussed later in the text, a large share of migrants are unskilled or have only very limited skill. They also stay a relatively short while, but may migrate and return home often. In the brain drain problem, attention is focused on the more or less permanent migration of highly skilled professionals who perform key functions in the economy. Such people have often received much of their training at the cost of their native land, and they rarely remit foreign exchange in amounts sufficient to matter very much. The very large scale migrations discussed here create different problems to which attention is directed.

2. W. Arthur Lewis (1974) has recently examined the impact of large-scale migrations during earlier times.

3. These data on investment income are based on a study by the First National Bank of Chicago as reported in The Financial Times July 9, 1980. Data on population and make up of the labor force are from World Bank reports and summaries of planning documents reported in the press.

4. There is no evidence, that I have seen, that suggests that the objection to the large-scale use of immigrant labor rests on any sort of racialism or ethnic considerations.

5. The situation in these countries is similar to that discussed by Keynes (1932).

6. The most comprehensive set of data that I have seen is J. S. Birks and C. A. Sinclair (1980). As the title states, the authors are mainly concerned with the Middle East and have little information on the years after 1977. Equally useful, but limited to 1977 and before, is Anand G. Chandavarkar (1980). Both of these sources have a helpful bibliography. The best up-to-date sources are the country reviews published frequently in The Financial Times.

7. For a more complete discussion of this point and the following argument see Henry J. Bruton (1980).

8. See Bruton (1980).

9. Guest workers in the Federal Republic of Germany remitted about DM 6.5 billion in 1979, according to the Bundesbank.

10. Stephen R. Lewis, Jr. (1982) has examined the inflation-creating effects of quick increases in the supply of foreign exchange. Lewis also discusses other issues of relevance to the present analysis.

11. The countries considered include the following: Algeria, Egypt, Greece, India, Jordan, Korea, Mexico, Morocco, Pakistan, Philippines, the Sudan, Turkey, Yemen Arab Republic, and Yugoslavia.

12. As reported in The Financial Times, September 29, 1980.

13. Nonearned is not used unkindly. Certainly workers who go abroad earn their pay. The idea is that the foreign exchange does not result from the functioning of the "real" economy, but rather is a consequence of developments in other parts of the world.

14. No one (to my knowledge) has estimated these costs and benefits, and the statement in the text is based on the kind of general evidence provided by the press, by pronouncement of government officials, by recruitment policies and efforts, and by treatment of the immigrant worker. That the guest workers in the Western European countries are now less welcome is also clear. The real danger seems to reside in the creation of a large group of essentially and inevitably second-class citizens or residents who, as a group, are deficient in education, in experience and training, and in the traditions of European society. As this situation continues, the resentment and tensions increase as does the recognition that certain economic activities depend entirely on the presence of migrant workers.

15. For further elaboration see Bruton (1980).

16. The terms-of-trade argument for tariffs does not appear relevant here.

17. The term "unanchored souls" appears in a quite different context in Thomas Mann's (1945) The Tables of the Law.

BIBLIOGRAPHY

Birks, J. S., C. A. Sinclair. 1980. *International migration and development in the Arab region*. Geneva: International Labour Office.

Bruton, H. J. 1980. Labour migration and shadow prices. *Pakistan Dev. Rev.*, 19:65-74.

Chandavarkar, A. G. 1980. Use of migrants' remittances in labor-exporting countries. *Finance and Development*, 17 (June): 18-23.

The Financial Times. 1980. (9 July and 29 September). London.

Keynes, J. M. 1932. Economic possibilities of our grandchildren. In *Essays in persuasion*. New York: Harcourt Brace & Co.

Lewis, S. R., Jr. 1982. Development problems of the mineral-rich countries. Research memorandum no. 74. Williamstown. Center for Development Economics, Williams College.

Lewis, W. A. 1974. *Growth and fluctuations 1870-1913*. London: George Allen and Unwin.

Mann, T. 1945. *The tables of the law*. New York: Alfred A. Knopf.

8
The Measurement of Economic Development: Quo Vadis?

Cynthia Taft Morris

I. INTRODUCTION

Measurement in the social sciences starts with multidimensional theoretical concepts that can rarely be summarized by cardinal data (that is, by numbers representing physical quantities, weights, or counts of events differences between which can be meaningfully added.) These concepts usually require complex operational rules for classifying observed behavior. Particular indices of income, production, unemployment, and prices are examples of multidimensional operational definitions representing abstract economic concepts. The rules they lay down may be based on explicit theory (production or income) or may be ad hoc (concentration or industrialization). In either case, at best, they <u>rank</u> observations by the relevant theoretical concepts. This type of "measurement by definition" is the stock-in-trade of the econometrician, the practising economist, and the economic historian.[1] This paper addresses the choice of rules for ranking countries or regions by level and pace of "economic development." The focus of the paper is on the concept of economic development. It provides a critique of recent efforts at definition and proposes a possible approach.

In the fifties, "economic development" and "economic growth," then used interchangeably, were widely measured by decadal changes in per capita GNP. Many development economists became intensely dissatisfied because per capita income changes were failing to "deliver the goods" to the poor in underdeveloped countries. While no consensus emerged on what "development" was, all agreed that it was more than economic growth measured by average national income changes. To some, the "more" was greater income equity; to others, it was radical institutional changes; to still others, it was freedom from foreign domination; and to some, it was all three. "Growth with equity" became the byword of the seventies. However, plans for equitable growth made only a few dents in the conditions of the <u>world's</u> poorest 40 percent. Before the end of the decade, international lending organizations and leading development economists shifted gears once more. Meeting the "basic needs" of the poor became more frequently identified with economic development. Meantime, radical thinking followed a different path. The main emphasis of the sixties had been the freeing of underdeveloped countries from dependence on foreign investment, imports, and consumption patterns. Recently, the neo-Marxist approach has stressed the growth of total productive capacity as the best measure of economic development through capitalism.

The thesis of this paper is that a definition of economic development based on productive capacity is preferable to one based on current poverty reduction. The correlary thesis is that current poverty reduction, by no means an invariable concomitant of economic development, is best treated as a priority goal of development planning. This does not mean that an unambiguous distinction can be made between growth of productive capacity and the distribution of income. The upshot of the theoretical literature of welfare economics is that changes in aggregate productive capacity cannot be defined without judgments regarding the structure of production and associated income distribution, a theoretical result that accords with common sense. We shall, nevertheless, suggest in this paper a concept of economic development as growing capacity for eventual widespread poverty reduction, a concept requiring value judgments. Our purpose is to preserve a sufficient distinction between the growth of capacity and its detailed distributional consequences, both to obtain a partial ranking of performance on capacity growth, and to analyze the varied distributional consequences of different paths of economic development.

A key criterion for choosing among alternative definitions is how well they serve the purpose of scientific inquiry (Kaplan 1964, 198). Two lines of arguments favor definitions of economic development based on the expansion of productive capacity. First, they provide a natural link between historical and contemporary experience. We thereby avoid the anomalous position that Great Britain, Germany, France, and Belgium were "developing economically" only during those decades of their early industrialization when living standards were unambiguously rising. A definition based on current poverty reduction would require the proposition that Great Britain, for example, did not undergo economic development during the first three decades of her "industrial revolution." Only after five decades did average real incomes of all major socioeconomic groups rise significantly above their level in 1790.[2]

The second argument is that a definition based on productive capacity provides a better conceptual tool for studying the great diversity of paths, historical and contemporary, by which countries have become "economically developed." Specifically, it facilitates analysis of the varied positive and negative consequences of different paths of economic development for the structure of production and districution of income. To define economic development as an invariable "good" would appear to hamper investigation of its consequences for "welfare," by definitionally incorporating selected results, the separate analysis of which contributes to our understanding of the process of economic development.

We argue for the retention of the Kuznetsian definition of "economic growth" as sustained increases in per capita GNP over several decades, accompanied by rising population, and a major relative shift of population out of agriculture into higher productivity sectors (Kuznets 1966, 1). It provides a measure of known theoretical basis suitable for long-term comparisons among countries at reasonable, similar levels of development. We also argue that the common understanding of economic development as "more" than economic growth be retained. The question is: what type of "more" is most useful for research investigations and policy analysis? The approach we propose is to focus on the expansion of the capacity, technological and institutional, of an economic system to provide sustained reductions in the proportion of the population in poverty.

The paper is organized as follows. The next section reviews recent efforts to define economic development. The following section summarizes some historical data on what happened to the living standards of the poor during the early decades of industrialization in today's economically advanced nations. The fourth section discusses a possible approach to the definition, and this measurement, of the concept of economic development.

II. RECENT DEFINITIONS OF ECONOMIC DEVELOPMENT

A. Economic Development as Economic Growth

The interchangeability of the terms "economic growth" and "economic development" that marked the infancy of the field of development economics did not last long. The problems of using GNP to measure growth were well-known: the omission of unpriced economic outputs, negative noneconomic consequences of growth,[3] divergences between actual and efficiency prices, and intractable theoretical problems in comparisons across countries or time, among others. In underdeveloped countries, both the omission of unpriced outputs and noneconomic consequences of growth cause special problems: outputs that bypass the market system weigh more heavily than inadvanced countries; and noneconomic consequences of growth tend to be larger, especially those connected with the breakdown of traditional safeguards protecting the individual from impersonal economic forces. Institutional barriers to the transfer of resources also aggravate the deficiencies of prices used in aggregating outputs.[4]

The major theoretical problem relates to the impossibility of unambiguously defining productive capacity without reference to a particular income distribution, production structure, and consumption structure (all interrelated). There is no objective way to decide whether productive capacity with more and cheaper yachts, gold bathtubs, and golf courses is larger or smaller than productive capacity with more and cheaper cooking pots, accessible drinking water, and health care. It is typically in very underdeveloped countries that such dramatic alternatives are likely to exist. In comparing growth rates among underdeveloped countries, the choice of price weights is even more difficult than that for advanced nations, because of wider variations in tastes and distribution, and greater problems in using foreign exchange rates where more outputs are not traded or marketed.

These problems with the measurement of economic growth rates have been well known for several decades. It is not they that explain the intense dissatisfaction of the sixties with rates of growth of per capita GNP as a proxy for economic development. Rather, per capita income changes were severely criticized because quite high growth rates failed to "deliver the goods." Cross-sectional studies by

Adelman and Morris were among the earliest to suggest that along an important part of the spectrum of underdevelopment, the poorest 40 percent of the population tended, on the average, to be worse off with moves to higher national income levels.[5] Other cross-sectional studies, using samples covering a wider range of development levels, yielded more optimistic results but little evidence of marked improvements at the lower end of the income spectrum.[6] Studies of individual countries indicated that the poor often benefited little from expanding market opportunities, new technologies, and new transportation systems.[7] The handful of countries where growth benefited the poor significantly were small open economies with accumulated agricultural surpluses and quite educated populations that succeeded in developing diverse manufacturing export bases. (see Ranis 1978; and Rao 1978).

As doubts about economic growth intensified, efforts accelerated to include a much wider range of social and economic phenomena in measures of "development." Adelman and Morris and the United Nations Research Institute for Social Development (UNRISD) were among those to apply statistical methods to the measurement of development. The Adelman-Morris measure, scores on a factor representing levels of socioeconomic development, was a spin-off of an effort to study the relationship between economic and noneconomic institutional facets of development.[8] UNRISD (1970) applied correlation analysis to develop a core of social and economic indicators as the basis of a broad index of development. Other investigators formed ad hoc composites of social indicators for the study of particular aspects of development. Studies by Harbison, the World Health Organization, and the International Labour Office showed large discrepancies between per capita GNP and achievements important to social welfare in, for example, health, education, and nutrition.[9]

Major radical schools of thought expressed with renewed vigor the proposition that drastic socioeconomic and political transformations were necessary in order to improve the lot of the poor significantly. Writers such as Baran (1968), Furtado (1964), Frank (1967), and Griffin (1969) gained widespread attention for their analyses of the role of imperialism, formal and informal, as a cause of underdevelopment.

As the 1960s drew to an end, the distinction between economic growth and "economic development" became common. "Growth without development" described countries with high growth rates but little else favorable to higher standards of living. Consequently, development economists in international agencies and some national planning institutions sought ways to combine the idea of sustained growth with the goal of benefits to the poor.

B. Economic Development As "Growth With Equity"

Development economists looking for a measure of economic growth with greater equity faced problems with the measurement of equity. The well-known Gini coefficient fails to rank income distributions that are quite different, a difficulty posed by other statistics summarizing the whole distribution with a single number.[10] Ad hoc measures of the relative position of the poor, such as the percentage of income recipients in various quantiles of the income distribution, give no idea of absolute levels of poverty. Calculations of the numbers below some given poverty-line suffer from lack of sensitivity to changes within the group below the poverty-line. (An exception is a novel measure recently devised by Amartya Sen.[11]) All three of these types of measures suffer in failing to distinguish between transient and permanent income. If used to compare extents of poverty over time, they give no idea what has happened to particular income groups or classes of poor from one decade to the next.

While some very promising dynamic models for analyzing mobility between income classes or socioeconomic groups have been developed, their data requirements greatly exceed available evidence on most low-income countries.[12]

The measurement of growth with equity was also hampered by lack of precedents for combining measures of equity with those of growth. In the 1950s, James Meade in Trade and Welfare (1955) and J. de V. Graaff in Theoretical Welfare Economics (1957) had concluded that growth of productive capacity could not be measured separately from distributional changes, a conclusion now widely accepted by economic theorists. At that time, Meade proposed that income changes be weighted by policymakers according to their judgments about social welfare. Two decades later, A World Bank study, Redistribution with Growth (Chenery et al. 1974) proposed along these lines that changes in per capita income be adjusted by distributional weights; the additional income to a rich person over a given period is multiplied by a lesser weight than that of a poor person before aggregation into "national income." In this way, growth rates for countries redistributing income are higher than they would be with the conventional equality of weights. Project analysts have applied the same principle in weighting income changes generated by different projects before comparing them to determine which contributes most to national objectives (UNIDO 1972). These measures pose problems. Theoretically, it is not any clearer what is increasing when national income changes are adjusted by distributional weights than it is when they are not adjusted (Beckerman 1978). There is also the problem of whose values are to be represented, given the arbitrariness of aggregating where there are conflicts of interest (Stewart 1975).

More sophisticated efforts to develop composites of growth with equity have received less attention. Amartya Sen (1976a) reformulates the welfare theory of real national income comparisons by treating the same commodity to different persons as different goods and weighting them with distributional judgments. Atkinson (1970) starts with a social welfare function that shows, for a given degree of "society's" aversion to income inequality, how much total income society would be willing to lose to obtain a given degree of income equality. Both approaches require more data than can generally be obtained.

C. Economic Development as Meeting Basic Needs

While measures of growth with equity were being sought, some development economists proposed more dramatic changes in the concept of economic development in order that the concept directly indicate outputs critical to human welfare: adequate food, jobs, equality. Dudley Seers (1972, 22) called for a new approach:

The starting-point is that we cannot avoid what the positivists disparagingly refer to as 'value judgments'. 'Development' is inevitably a normative concept, almost a synonym for improvement. To pretend otherwise is just to hide one's value judgments.

Seers proposed that the necessary values are self-evident if we ask what are the necessary conditions for "the realization of the potential of human personality..."; food, jobs, and greater income equality are the critical dimensions (Seers 1972, 22). The "basic needs" approach is the major current effort to measure economic development along the lines suggested by Seers, that is, by outputs widely agreed to be critical inputs to human welfare.

In the mid-1970s, the International Labour Organization (ILO) and several other international groups urged that "basic needs" become the heart of development strategy.[13] The ILO underlined minimum food, shelter, clothing, and essential household equipment for each family and essential community services such as safe drinking water, sanitation, public transport, public health, and educational and cultural facilities (ILO 1977, 24). All proponents of basic needs endorsed radical structural and institutional changes, redistribution of assets and redistribution of political power. Most urged that "basic needs" include nonmaterial needs: human rights, participation, freedom, self-reliance (Ghai 1977, 14).

Most efforts to measure basic needs have focused on material needs: minimum levels of private consumption and public services. This work is the direct descendent of work on social indicators and work on "poverty-lines" that goes back to the nineteenth century.[14] One approach is to set a minimum "target" income that covers critical consumption items by surveying budgets of low income consumers.[15] The problems here are well-known: the exact cut-off income is arbitrary; the budget components vary with customs, tastes, prices, and climate; price weights depend on income distribution and supply conditions; and adequate data on family income are rarely available.

Another approach is to concentrate on a core of items such as critical foods and shelter. Minimum physical targets are set and actual and target consumption compared, item by item. Data for calculating national shortfalls are oten available but rarely permit estimates of basic needs fulfillment for socioeconomic groups or income classes.

One measurement effort, somewhat akin to the basic needs approach, is based on outputs rather than inputs. Morris David Morris (1979) has developed an index of the "physical quality of life" that combines life expectancy, infant mortality, and literacy. The index is ad hoc, but has the advantage that it is less sensitive than most measures of basic needs to differences among countries in customs, economic organization, and climate.

The strongest critics of efforts to measure basic needs underline that they are incorrectly based on current economic structures, distribution, and prices. Consumption patterns among the poor would be quite different with the kinds of radical structural changes that development requires. Foreign influences "distort" consumption patterns. Thus, neither current consumption nor current prices ought to determine basic needs targets. (Standing and Szal 1979, 3-4). As yet, little in the way of measurement has come from the "structural" critics.

D. Economic Development as Radical Transformations in Institutions

No matter how economic development is measured, everyone underlines that development will not take place without fundamental changes in economic institutions and structure. "Radical" approaches differ by placing them at the core of their definition of economic development. Why? Because to whom the national product goes depends on how production is organized and how distributed. Radical views stress that major redistributions to reduce poverty require major changes in the structure and institutions of production. To quote Haq (1973, 269):

> you have increased your GNP by producing more luxury houses and cars, it is not very easy to convert them into low cost housing or bus transport. A certain pattern of consumption and distribution inevitably follows.

Another key theme of radical approaches is that foreign domination can create or perpetuate inequality and poverty. There is a rich literature on close connections between foreign domination and inequality at low levels of development. Foreign-led dualistic growth, foreign consumption patterns, foreign technologies, and foreign domination of economic and political institutions reinforce the unfavorable impacts of economic growth.

Unfortunately, there is no agreed definition of the process of economic development as radical institutional change and liberation from foreign dependence. Sutcliffe (1972) defines development as "independent industrialization" that must be (1) directed at the home market; (2) marked by a wide range of industries; (3) independent of foreign finance (unless controlled by the country); and (4) achieved by "independent technological progress." He concludes that independent industrialization in this sense cannot be achieved through capitalism. Hence, he does not operationalize his definition in order to rank low income countries by level or pace of economic development.

E. Economic Development as the Expansion of Domestic Capitalist Productive Forces

Recently, some Marxists have diverged sharply from others by defining development as the expansion of capitalist aggregate productive forces in the Marxian sense. This approach rejects definitions based on progress in eliminating poverty. To quote Warren (1973, 4):

> Successful capitalist development is here understood as that development which provides the appropriate economic, social, and political conditions for the continuing reproduction of capital, as a social system representing the highest form of commodity production.

Warren operationalizes each component of Sutcliffe's definition of independent industrialization to help rank countries by progress toward that goal. In so doing, he shows that industrial capacity has expanded more rapidly in the underdeveloped than in the developed world; manufacturing in low-income countries has expanded mainly for the domestic market; local finance has predominated in domestic investment. Thus, in Warren's view, underdeveloped countries have made progress toward independent capitalist industrialization and the concept is, in principle, capable of measurement.[16]

What measures of economic development have these approaches provided? Only those focusing on development as outputs promoting human welfare have produced operational definitions. The rich literature on development as radical institutional change has produced little work on measurement procedures. Recent work on Marxist definitions of capitalist development shows promise, but has yet to produce an operational definition of economic development.

Thus, over the past three decades, the leading characteristic of the mainstream development literature has been to move away from a concept of economic development based on the growth of productive capacity toward a concept based on equity, currently interpreted as meeting the basic needs of the population. In part, this trend is only a shift in emphasis since those favoring the basic needs approach to measuring economic development continue to stress that to meet basic needs at very low levels of development, sustained expansions in production capacity and radical institutional changes are usually needed.

In the next section we look at some evidence on what happened to real wages during the early decades of industrialization in today's advanced nations. Our purpose is to illustrate the need for a definition of economic development that links historical and contemporary experience. Historical experience with "developing economically" was extremely varied, including cases of initial deterioration as well as cases of improvement in average standards of living. It thus suggests that it is not desirable to tie the concept of economic development to current changes in the standard of living.

III. HISTORICAL PATTERNS OF INCOME CHANGE IN THE EARLY STAGE OF INDUSTRIALIZATION

This section provides some historical evidence on changes in the incomes of lower-income groups in the early state of industrialization. We are interested in the period from the start of the "industrial revolution" until the real wages or incomes of the major socioeconomic groups started rising significantly. This period varied from close to six decades in Belgium and four to five decades in France and Switzerland, to three or four decades in Germany and much less in the United States.

Economic historians identify a marked acceleration in industrial growth in Great Britain in the 1780s and in Switzerland in the 1820s. In Germany and the United States, they see distinct regional accelerations in the 1820s and more generalized accelerations in the 1840s. In France, modern industrial growth began in the first decade of the nineteenth century and continued quite steadily thereafter without any distinct "take-off." In contrast, Belgium's industrial revolution proceeded discontinuously, from a major start about 1800, by alternating periods of upward surges in growth and relative stagnation.[17] In all six countries real per capita GNP probably rose, at least modestly, over every decade from the start of industrialization, as did output per person in both industry and agriculture, and the proportion of the labor force in agriculture steadily declined.[18]

Tables 1 through 6 (at the end of this chapter) give a picture of the diversity of changes in the incomes of poorer groups during early industrial growth. The tables indicate the probable direction of changes in real wages of factory workers and agricultural laborers, and of changes in the net income of handicraft workers, tenant farmers, and small independent landholders, insofar as data permit.

These data give only a very partial picture of the course of poverty. Several countries suffered striking increases in the numbers in extreme poverty in some periods. In Belgium, the 1830s and the 1840s were marked by dramatic surges in unemployment (Dechesne 1932). In Germany, the increase in the numbers of poor in the thirties and forties was so dramatic that it led to a flood of hundreds of pamphlets about the causes of "pauperism" and to legislation to slow population growth by limiting marriages among the poor (Matz 1980). In the United States, urban poverty increased considerably during the 1840s and 1850s (Ware 1964), a fact not reflected in the relative stability of nonfarm wages. The course of urban poverty in Great Britain has been much disputed, but, if we include Ireland in the British economic system, as Jonathan Hughes recently suggested we might, then the 1840s, when average wages were rising, saw a massive increase in regional poverty (Hughes 1983).

There is no simple relationship between the picture presented in the tables and the process of industrialization. That is, the growth of industry cannot in itself be held responsible for the patterns we observe. Subsistence crises were still a recurrent cause of poverty, particularly in Europe in the forties. Immobility, poor transportation, and other barriers to the movement of resources contributed, as they had done for centuries, to the persistence of regional poverty. Rapid population growth also played an important role. Relationships between industrial expansion and population growth were extremely complex, probably as much affected by common causes as by direct interactions. For example, it is widely argued that, in Germany, the loosening of traditional social bonds arising from preindustrial agrarian changes caused both population growth and the nexus of circumstances favoring industrial growth (Köllmann 1976). This argument is plausible since the factory sector was minute until well into the second half of the nineteenth century.

Our timing of the period when significant decadal rises in real incomes started must also be treated with caution. On the average, real incomes started rising significantly above their level at the start of industrialization, about 1840 in Great Britain, about 1850 in France and Switzerland, about 1860 in Germany and Belgium, and perhaps within a decade in the United States. A steady decadal rise in average wages and incomes did not mean necessarily that people were materially better off, since working and living conditions often worsened in the early years of industrial change. Also, the numbers unemployed or in extreme poverty sometimes rose, on occasion strikingly, while average real wages were rising. For example, a recent study of Belgium indicates that, in Brussells, real wages rose during the sixties and seventies, then stagnated to the end of the nineteenth century; while the incidence of unemployment for the average worker rose, and many workers migrated back to the countryside to find employment in the revival of domestic industries that competed with the city through extremely low piece rates (Van den Eckhout 1980). Detailed information of this type is unfortunately fragmentary for most countries. A final point is that, once these industrializing nations had achieved the capacity for a generalized rise in real incomes, cyclical crises caused recurrent failures of incomes to rise. Nevertheless, the extent of overall rise in real incomes of the major socioeconomic groups was quite marked by the end of the nineteenth century even though, by today's standard, poverty continued to persist in every country.[19]

Tables 1 through 6 thus provide some support for the thesis of this paper that, to tie a definition of economic development to current poverty reduction, goes against common understanding of the historical process of becoming "economically developed." During the periods covered by the tables, the early industrializers developed the productive and institutional capacity to provide subsequent generalized rises in average material standards of living. During that time, changes in standards of living were extremely diverse both within and across countries.

Were we to include data on countries industrializing for the first time in the last quarter of the nineteenth century, the diversity of the course of standards of living would be even greater. In Sweden and Denmark, for example, early industrialization was accompanied by rising incomes for the major socioeconomic groups. At the other end of the spectrum, in Russia and Italy, the length of the period before incomes of the major socioeconomic groups began to rise significantly was probably as long as for Belgium.[20]

IV. TOWARD A CONCEPT OF ECONOMIC DEVELOPMENT

Historical evidence on real wage changes during the early stage of industrializaton suggests that the current tendency to tie the concept of economic development in underdeveloped countries to the meeting of basic needs is unsatisfactory, because it is inconsistent with common understanding of the historical process of "developing economically." During the early period, when the now-advanced economies developed their productive and institutional capacity to provide subsequent generalized increases in material standards of living, actual changes in poverty varied greatly among countries, and included cases of little or no poverty reduction, as well as increased poverty over several decades.

Changes in per capita GNP, even sustained, have not successfully indicated the timing or extent of progress in reducing poverty. Rising per capita GNP in the early stage of industrialization often took place without much, if any, poverty reduction. Nevertheless, sustained increases in per capita GNP with Kuznets-type structural changes either preceded or accompanied all successful experiences in widespread poverty reduction. Study of history thus supports the use of per capita GNP to measure a necessary, although not sufficient, condition for eventual widespread reductions in poverty.

The main theoretical case against per capita GNP is that changes in the "size" of national product cannot be measured independently of its distribution. Even if we make judgments on distribution, a major conceptual difficulty remains which is particularly serious for underdeveloped countries. An increase in national product, that is sufficient in the aggregate to bring about desirable changes in the level and distribution of income, is irrelevant where the institutions have not the capacity to achieve an approximation of the desired distribution. This is particularly so because low-income countries rarely have sufficient governmental administrative capacity to redistribute income to the poor through entitlement programs such as social security, income maintenance, or unemployment compensation. We ignore the rare case of rentier nations such as Kuwait where productive capacity is very underdeveloped by any reasonable criterion, but is combined with widespread social-welfare entitlements.[21]

Need we then give up the effort to find a workable concept of economic development on which some degree of consensus might be reached? I think not. Let us start by concentrating on the concept we seek, ignoring, at first, problems of knowledge and measurement. We will then discuss the kinds of proxies that might serve us best. Our first proposition is that it serves no useful purpose to define economic development in terms of all the desiderata of the good life: self-fulfillment, improvements in the quality of life, greater happiness, more participation in decision-making, and so forth. These are all important goals in themselves, but analysis of progress in attaining them is not furthered by incorporating them into the definition of economic development. Furthermore, important parts of historical and contemporary literature on economic development analyze negative as well as positive consequences of different paths of development with respect to these goals. For example, discussions of the relative merits of socialist and capitalist paths to widespread poverty reduction focus on their differential achievements with respect to the quality of living, income distribution, participation in decision-making, and alienation. Yet, none would question that, broadly speaking, both the United States and the Soviet Union, for example, have become economically developed and achieved widespread poverty reduction, in spite of extremely diverse consequences with respect to other, more controversial aspects of their paths of change. While particular definitions cannot be proved right or wrong, it makes sense to formulate them in line with common understanding, and in a way that furthers comparative study and investigation of relationships among phenomena of interest.

Our second proposition is that economic development is best viewed as the growth in the capacity of the economic system. This immediately raises the question "capacity for what?" -- a question that cannot be answered without value judgments. The concept we propose is capacity to achieve reductions in poverty over time, with "poverty reduction" operationally defined as decreases in the proportion of the population living below the poverty-line. The problems in operationally defining a poverty-line are familiar and more easily soluble than most measurement problems.[22] A more complex definition of poverty reduction that takes into account the distribution of income below the poverty-line (for example, that proposed by Amartya Sen 1976a) could be substituted without much affecting the discussion that follows.

Our third proposition relates to the "output" of poverty reduction. In judging current success in raising capacity to reduce poverty, account should be taken of current contributions to future poverty reductions. Put differently, the conceptual distinction between the growth of capacity for future reductions, and current poverty reduction, should be retained in spite of the theoretical difficulties it may pose. The question is: how long may the lag be between "inputs" of increased capacity and "outputs" of poverty reduction and still have the inputs "count" toward economic development? Economic analysis suggests the application of a social discount rate to compare the present values of alternative time streams of expected poverty reductions; preferenes for earlier, rather than later, reductions can then be expressed by selection of higher discount rates. The outside limits to what can count can then be set through the selection of a discount rate that leads the present value of reductions beyond a given point in time to be negligible. Another way to set an outside limit is more pragmatic; it is based on the historical record for advanced countries. In the nineteenth and early twentieth centuries, the lag between an effective start on industrialization and the initiation of a steady expansion of benefits to the poor (both judged ex post), varied from one to six decades, but for very few cases did it exceed three decades. An outside bound of a lag of three decades is also consistent with contemporary success cases where investment in land reform and education operated slowly to diffuse poverty reductions (as, for example, in Taiwan).

Given choice of an outside bound of future poverty reductions that are to count toward economic development, the conceptual difficulty remains that different time paths of reductions must be comparatively evaluated; for example, earlier, less-widespread reductions must be evaluated against later, more-widespread reductions. The justification for applying a single discount rate for this purpose is rather weak. For very poor countries, an initially very high rate, subsequently declining, would be more consistent with common value judgment that prevention of starvation among the living takes precedence over future improvements for people not yet conceived. A possible solution is to have the rate of decline in the social discount rate depend upon both the distribution below the poverty-line and the proportion of the total population below the poverty-line.

It should be stressed that this discussion of the "output" of poverty reduction is purely for conceptual purposes, since the state of knowledge is inadequate to measure the concepts we have been discussing. Nevertheless, in seeking proxy measures, we do well to be clear on the concept we wish to measure indirectly.

Our fourth proposition relates to the input side of poverty reduction. Changes in inputs raising the capacity of a system to provide better living standards cannot be adequately represented by the usual arguments of a production function.[23] This is because of the crucial role of institutional changes in the generation and distribution of goods and services, institutional changes which may not be registered immediately in a larger total of goods and services.

Some of these institutional changes are highly correlated with conventionally measured output expansion for periods as short as a decade, for example, changes facilitating the flow of factors from lower- to higher-productivity occupations and regions, such as the growth of specialized capital or labor market institutions or major changes in business management or accounting systems. Other institutional changes do not have as immediate a counterpart in more goods and services, for example, the spread of rural credit institutions or land reforms equalizing the distribution of assets and the benefits from productivity increases; yet these changes can contribute substantially to capacity for future reductions in poverty. While these points are self-evident, the practice of measurement of economic development rarely takes account of them, for the understandable reason that our knowledge of the relationship between institutional change and poverty reduction is so uncertain. Hence, even major institutional changes greatly affecting capacity to reduce poverty, such as land reform and educational expansion, fail to count or are underestimated in conventional measures of changes in productive capacity.

In our view, indirect measures of economic development, viewed as progress toward increasing capacity to reduce poverty, should be sought in characteristics of the process of output expansion. There are two critical aspects of that process for this purpose. First, in very poor economies, the claims by the poor to a share in output increases arise primarily from entitlements gained through the production process, as wage laborers, tenants, or peasant owners, for example. Hence, the transmission of output increases across sectors, products, and regions appears to be the crucial process leading to an increase in the proportion of the population with entitlements to a share in output increases. This process of transmission appears to have been the critical common characteristic of the early phase of industrialization in the now-advanced economies. Some economies developed rapidly in this early phase, without either immediate increases in wage levels or net reductions in material poverty. In Belgium and Germany, for example, where average standards of living of the poor took several decades to rise above their preindustrial levels, the growth process was marked, nevertheless, by steadily increasing participation by those with low incomes in expanding sectors and regions. Thus, economic growth, together with the steady transmission of output expansions across the economy, serve to indicate key dimensions of historical success in expanding capacity for poverty reduction.

In choosing a concept of economic development based on the transmission of output expansion across sectors, products, and regions, we are seeking a proxy for both technological and institutional success. Direct measurement of institutional capacity is extremely difficult because of the many possible substitutions among institutions serving similar functions. Yet, an important part of successful transmission of output growth is the development of institutions for the transfer of resources, labor, capital, and technology from lower-productivity to higher-productivity sectors, occupations, and regions.

An important secondary aspect of growing capacity to reduce poverty lies in shifts in entitlements to a share of output within sectors and regions. Shifts that enhance capacity for poverty reduction establish and expand across socioeconomic groups entitlements to a share in increased output. Many institutional changes produce favorable shifts: changes in land institutions ensuring a share in output increases to the cultivator; institutions promoting wage increases as productivity rises; institutions increasing the access to inputs among poor peasants; and, at higher levels of development, the spread of unemployment insurance and social welfare entitlements. Other institutional changes produce unfavorable shifts, for example, the spread of debt and land alienation among small holders.

In our view, there are strong advantages in a concept of economic development as expanding capacity to transmit output increases and entitlements to these increases across the economy. The focus is on the functioning of the economic system: the process of output expansion, increases in the numbers participating in output expansion, and the wider spread of rights to part of the expanding product. The proposed way of looking at economic development for the purpose of measurement is consistent with a wide range of distributional consequences, particularly in the short-run, including both relative equality and relative inequality. This focus on both the common aspects and the wide variety of different paths of economic development captures the varied course of past history of now-advanced economies, both capitalist and socialist; it also appears promising as a way of distinguishing between economic growth and economic development for contemporary developing countries.

How then might we operationalize the proposed concept of economic development? We can suggest several lines along which work might proceed. Which line is preferable will depend upon the purpose at hand. A partial ranking of medium-term success over one or two decades could be sought in a measure of the dispersion of output increases across broad sectors and regions of the economy, as a proxy for the transmission of institutions and technology. Here, we would wish a ranking scheme where, ceteris paribus, the spread of productivity increases across agriculture as well as industry ranks more highly than a spread just across industry; where, within agriculture, the spread of productivity increases to more, rather than fewer, regions would rank more highly; and where, within a given region, a spread of productivity increases to more, rather than fewer, broad types of crops would rank more highly. Too fine a level of disaggregation would not be desirable because it would pose complex problems arising from the evaluation of appropriate degrees of product specialization; for example, very detailed judgments about whether output increases for one specific crop, rather than another, should rank more highly could not be made without both a production-function approach incorporating institutional inputs and the use of a social-welfare function covering the relevant range of options. Such an approach is hardly practical.

Another possibility would be to focus on linkages, ranking more highly processes of output expansion marked by more, rather than fewer, linkages. Where data permit, a multidimensional measure of changes in the density of positive cells in input-output flow tables could be devised for ranking countries partially by the spread of output expansion.[24] A similar approach could be developed using the characteristics of social-accounting matrices, their structure and shifts in structure over time. In these matrices, the allocation of factorial incomes to households, governments, and enterprises is explicitly laid out. With households distinguished by socioeconomic types, the wider spread of entitlements to shares in expanding output can be directly displayed in the pattern of shifts in the structure of factorial income distribution to households, with breakdowns by region and productive activity. While the data requirements for the social accounting approach are high, they permit the use of fragmentary and qualitative data within a consistent framework.[25]

In conclusion, this paper has briefly reviewed the current literature on the measurement of economic development and examined its relevance to the historical record. We have proposed a direction for measurement efforts by suggesting a way of looking at the concept of economic development consistent with historical understanding of the process of developing economically. We have argued against the present tendency to define economic development in low-income countries in terms of current welfare achievements. Instead, we recommend that measurement efforts be based on characteristics of the process of output expansion: especially its extent of regional and sectoral diffusion and the extent of spread across socioeconomic groups of entitlements to a share in increases in output. In our view, this approach promises more success than do approaches incorporating the size distribution of income or the meeting of basic needs, in measuring the institutional as well as the technological capacity of the economic system for steady reductions in the proportion of the population in poverty.

FOOTNOTES

1. For a basic reference on types of measurement scales, see Pfanzagl (1968, Ch. 1). For a discussion of social-science indices as a form of measurement by definition, see Torgerson (1958,Ch. 2). (See also Adelman and Morris 1972, 111-15.) It should be noted that, strictly speaking, most statistical models require cardinal data; yet economists' data are generally ordinal if interpreted to rank observations with respect to theoretical concepts of interest.

2. For data on the course of average incomes of different groups in the population in the countries mentioned here, see Part II. The classic source for wages in Great Britain during the nineteenth and early twentieth centuries is the long series of articles by A. L. Bowley and G. H. Wood, published in the Journal of the Royal Statistical Society between 1898 and 1910.

3. There is no satisfactory distinction in neoclassical economics between "economic" and "noneconomic" causes or effects. The best

that can be done is probably to say, with Graaff, that economic influences are those that interest economists, and the remainder are noneconomic (Graaff 1957, 5). The use of GNP to measure changes in productive capacity or potential social welfare does, of course, require the assumption that noneconomic influences, often interpreted as those omitted, remain unchanged.

4. For advanced nations, an unpriced effect of probably greater weight than in underdeveloped countries is the production of "leisure," the omission of which tends to bias measured growth rates downwards; the omission of negative environmental effects tends to bias measured growth rates upwards. (See Beckerman 1978.) For a good discussion of why negative economic effects of the removal of traditional safeguards tend to be strong, see Phelps Brown (1953, 22ff.).

5. (Adelman and Morris 1967.) This proposition was a hypothesis based on cross-sectional data. There is no _statistical_ justification for causal statements based on either cross-sectional or time-series analyses.

6. See the review by Ahluwalia (1976).

7. There is a large literature on unfavorable impacts of economic change on the poor. See, for example Geertz (1963); Griffin and Kahn (1977); Griffin (1978); and Dore and Weeks (1980).

8. The factor score index in the Adelman and Morris study (1967, 167ff.) was a weighted function of the following characteristics: the size of the traditional sector, the extent of dualism, the extent of urbanization, the character of basic social organization, the importance of the indigenous middle class, the extent of social mobility, the extent of mass communication, the degree of national integration, the crude fertility rate, and the degree of modernization of outlook. (Other variables with low factor loadings are ignored.) For definitions, see Adelman and Morris (1967, Ch. 2).

9. For a summary of these studies, see Ghai (1977, 5ff.).

10. The problem with the Gini coefficient is demonstrated diagrammatically in Newberry (1970). For a good review of other statistics for measuring the distribution of income, see Szal and Robinson (1977). For discussion of problems connected with the choice of income recipient, life-cycle patterns of income, the definition of income, and so forth, see Kuznets (1955).

11. Sen's measure is a composite of the gap between the mean income of the poor and the poverty-line income, the proportion of income recipients below the poverty-line, and the Gini coefficient of the distribution of income among the poor. He develops the measure axiomatically on the basis of explicit ordinally based welfare comparisons. (See Sen 1976b.)

12. See in particular Robinson and Dervis (1977). Adelman and Robinson (1977) have shown convincingly, in their study of Korea, that an analysis of the impact of government policies on the size distribution of income requires income information by occupation or socioeconomic group that can then be translated into the size distribution of income.

13. For a more detailed summary of these and other references, see Ghai (1977).

14. The work of Seebohm Rowntree (1901, 1910) on Great Britain and Belgium sets a high standard for the calculation of poverty-lines.

15. Poverty lines are currently calculated in a number of countries including the United States.

16. The line of reasoning followed in Warren's (1973) article is much more complex than is indicated by the brief reference to it here.

17. For analyses of the pattern and timing of early industrialization in these countries, see the studies by North, Deane, Hoffmann, and Marczewski, in W. W. Rostow, ed. (1963); and those by Fohlen, Borchardt, Deane, Dhondt and Bruwier, and Biucchi, in Cipolla, ed. (1973). For Belgium, see also Craeybeckx (1970); for Switzerland, see also Wittmann (1963). For the U.S.A., see also Rostow (1960); and Fogel (1964). For material on the course of wages and incomes, see the references listed in Tables 1 through 6.

18. For estimates of changes in per capita GNP, population changes, and changes in the proportion of the labor force in agriculture, see the following sources. For Great Britain, see Deane (1955-56); and Deane (1968). For France, see Perroux (1955); and Lévy-Leboyer (1968). For Germany, see Hoffmann et al. (1965); Spree (1977); and Borchardt (1973). For the U.S.A., see Gallman (1960); and the U.S. Bureau of Census (1966). For Switzerland, see Gasser (1962); and Kneschaurek (1964). (Gasser provides a chart based on unpublished estimates given him by Kneschaurek, the basis for which is unknown.) For Belgium, see Bairoch (1976). (Since Bairoch does not indicate how he arrived at his estimates and they appear to be the only ones in existence, they should be treated with caution.) Only for a short time immediately after the Napoleonic Wars did per capita GNP apparently fail to rise in Great Britain.

19. For evidence on the general rise in standards of living in France, Germany, and Great Britain, see the chapter on population and welfare in Bogart (1942).

20. The basic sources for these countries will be available in Morris and Adelman, Where Angels Fear to Tread: Quantitative Studies in History and Development (Forthcoming).

21. For an interesting treatment of these cases, see the paper in this volume by Henry Bruton.

22. See, for example, Rowntree (1901, 1910). Note that we have not taken account here of the distribution of incomes within the group below the poverty-line.

23. Graaff (1957, Ch. 5) recognizes this problem in his development of the concepts of "efficiency" and "feasibility" loci, but little attention is given to it elsewhere in the theoretical literature.

24. For interesting uses of input-output tables in the evaluation of success in economic development, see Weisskoff and Wolff (1977); and Yotopoulos and Nugent (1973). Senghaas (1982, Ch. 1) stresses the role of linkages in the concept of economic development. There is also a growing literature on the triangularization of input-output matrices that attempts to rank sectors by the strength of their links with other sectors. (See, for example, Korte and Oberhofer 1971.)

25. A good discussion of social accounting matrices may be found in Pyatt and Roe (1977).

NOTE ON APPENDIX TABLES 1 TO 6

Note that the data in Appendix Table 1 and those that follow serve only to indicate general orders of magnitude. The data on "average wages" more often reflect wage rates than earnings and are rarely ever based on proper samples. Rough estimates of the direction of change of the net income of tenants or small holders are usually based on inferences from the course of prices of outputs, major inputs, and rents.

Cost-of-living indices are sometimes based on food only and sometimes include rents.

Sometimes the sources cited are clear about the basis for the estimates and sometimes not at all clear.

Appendix Table 1

Probable Direction of Real Wage and Income Changes, Lower Income Groups

Belgium

1830s

handicraft workers, wages and income	down	Mokyr 1974, 382; Dechesne 1932, 409-10
urban population, Antwerp, consumption meat, fish, grain	down	Lis and Soly 1977, 465
income agricultural tenants (Flanders)	down	Ducpétiaux 1850, 65
textile workers, leading factory Ghent, daily wages	down	Avondts et al. 1979, viii

1840s

all categories listed under 1830s	down	Sources as above
agricultural laborers (mainly Flanders)	down	Ducpétiaux 1850, 89
textile workers (Flanders)	down	Ducpétiaux 1850, 78ff.

1850s

real wages, five major industries	fluctuating	Neyrink 1944, 182-83
agricultural wages	up	Dechesne 1932, 482
Income agricultural tenants	down	Dechesne 1932, 483

1860s

real wages, five major industries	up	Neyrink 1944, 182-83
agricultural wages	up	Dechesne 1932, 482
income agricultural tenants	down	de Laveleye 1870, 269-71

Appendix Table 2

Probable Direction of Real Wage and Income Changes, Lower Income Groups

France

1800 to 1850

Per capita food supply, Paris   down   Philippe 1970, 56

1830s and 1840s

average gross real wages (Kuczynski) (primarily nonagricultural)	up	Bogart 1942, 244
average real wages (Levasseur) -deflated by food prices only -deflated by food and nonfood prices	down up	Levasseur 1904, 704
average real wages (Lévy-Leboyer)	sharply fluctuating	Lévy-Leboyer 1968, 794
average real wages, Paris	down	Levasseur 1904, 723
net income agricultural small holders	up	Lévy-Leboyer 1968, 794
per capita consumption meat, sugar, wheat, France	up	Perroux 1955, 70
per capita consumption meat, Paris	down	Perroux 1955, 70

Appendix Table 2 (cont.)

1850s and 1860s

average real wages (Kuczynski)	up	Bogart 1942, 244
average real wages (Levasseur)	up	Levasseur 1904, 714-16
average real wages (Lévy-Leboyer) 1850s	sharply fluctuating	Lévy-Leboyer 1968, 795
1860s	up	Lévy-Leboyer 1968, 795
net income textile handicraft workers	down	Levasseur 1904, 260
average real wages, Paris	up?	Levasseur 1904, 726
agricultural wages	up	Sée 1951, 332

Appendix Table 3

Probable Direction of Real Wage and Income Changes, Lower Income Groups

Germany

1750 to 1820

average real wages   down   Saalfeld 1974, 418-19

1830s

average gross real wages
  (Kuczynski)   down   Borchardt 1976, 227

1840s

average gross real wages
  (Kuczynski)   down   Borchardt 1976, 227

average net real wages,
  1840-49 compared with
  1830-39   down   Kuczynski 1936, 96

Appendix Table 3 (cont.)

1850s

average gross real wages (Kuczynski)	sharply fluctuating	Borchardt 1976, 227
average real wages, mainly factory, based on Kuczynski	down	Spree 1977, 371
average agricultural wages	up	Hamerow 1969, 40
average net real wages, cyclical average 1852-59 compared with decadal averages 1830s and 1840s	down	Kuczynski 1936, 96
per capita consumption bread, potatoes, meat, fruit	up	Teuteberg 1976, 248, 249, 252, 264

1860s

average gross real wages (Kuczynski)	up	Borchardt 1976, 227
Average net real wages, cyclical average, 1860-67 compared with 1852-59 and 1830s and 1840s	up	Kuczynski 1936, 96
average real wages, mainly factory, based on Kuczynski	up	Spree 1977, 371

Appendix Table 4

Probable Direction of Real Wage and Income Changes, Lower Income Groups

United States

1820s and 1830s

Nonfarm workers real wages	up	Lebergott 1960, 493
Farm workers real wages	up	Lebergott 1960, 493
Industrial workers real wages	slightly up	Hansen 1925, 33
Nonfarm workers real wages	up	Kuczynski 1973, 22

1840s

Industrial workers real wages	up	Hansen 1925, 33
Nonfarm workers real wages	slightly up	Lebergott 1960, 462-93
Farm workers real wages	slightly up	Lebergott 1960, 462-93
Nonfarm workers real wages	up	Kuczynski 1973, 49

Appendix Table 4 (cont.)

1850s

Non farm workers real wages	up	Lebergott 1960, 493
Farm workers real wages	up	Lebergott 1960, 493
Industrial workers real wages	fluctuating	Hansen 1925, 32
Agricultural workers real wages	up	Bidwell and Falconer 1973, 276
Nonfarm workers real wages	fluctuating	Kuczynski 1973, 49

1860s

Industrial workers real wages	up	Bowley 1895, 381
Industrial workers real wages	up	Hansen 1925, 32
Farm workers real wages	down	Lebergott 1960, 493
Nonfarm workers real wages	fluctuating	Lebergott 1960, 462-93
Nonfarm workers real wages	fluctuating	Kuczynski 1973, 81

Appendix Table 5

Probable Direction of Real Wages and Income Changes, Lower Income Groups

Switzerland

1810 to 1830

average real wages, nonagricultural	sharply fluctuating	Hauser 1974, 606
net income agricultural small holders	sharply fluctuating	Hauser 1974, 606-07; Menzel 1979, 126

1830s

average real wages, nonagricultural	down	Hauser 1974, 606
average real wages, factory	down	Menzel 1979, 128
net income handicraft workers	down	Menzel 1979, 128; Rappard 1914, 291

1840s

average real wages, nonagricultural	down?	Hauser 1974, 606; Hauser 1961, 323
average real wages, factory	up	Menzel 1979, 128;
net income handicraft workers	down	Menzel 1979, 128; Rappard 1914, 291
net income agricultural small holders	sharply fluctuating	Hauser 1974, 606-07; Menzel 1979, 126

Appendix Table 5 (cont.)

1850s

average real wages, nonagricultural	strongly up	Hauser 1974, 606
average real wages, factory	up	Menzel 1979, 128
net income handicraft workers	down	Menzel 1979, 128
net income agricultural small holders	up?	Menzel 1979, 126

1860s

average real wages, nonagricultural	up?	Hauser 1974, 606
average real wages, factory	up	Menzel 1979, 128

Note: All data are fragmentary. Wage data in Menzel are deflated by the price of bread only and in Hauser are apparently deflated by only a few food items. Guesstimates about the net income of small holders are based on the course of a few prices only.

Appendix Table 6

Probable Direction of Real Wage and Income Changes, Lower Income Groups

Great Britain

1790 to 1830

Factory workers, real wages	slightly up	Bogart 1942, 235-36

1830s

Agricultural workers real wages	fluctuating	Kuczynski 1944, 56
Average real wages of workers (a)	up	Kuczynski 1944, 39, 56
Handicraft workers real wages	down	Lyons 1977
Factory workers real wages	up	Bogart 1942, 236
Sussex Agricultural workers; wages in terms of wheat	up	Usher 1920, 504

1840s

Agricultural workers real wages	up	Kuczynski 1944, 56
Average real wages of workers (a)	up	Kuczynski 1944, 39, 56
Handicraft workers real wages	down	Lyons 1977
Sussex agricultural workers, wages in terms of wheat	up	Usher 1920, 504

Appendix Table 6 (cont.)

1850s

Agricultural workers real wages	up	Kuczynski 1944, 89
Average real wages of workers (a)	up	Kuczynski 1944, 67, 89
Factory workers real wages	up	Bogart 1942, 236, 267
Sussex agricultural workers, wages in terms of wheat	down	Usher 1920, 504
Agricultural workers real wages	up	Jones 1964, 338

1860s

Agricultural workers real wages	up	Kuczynski 1944, 89
Average real wages of workers (a)	up	Kuczynski 1944, 67, 89
Factory workers real wages	up	Bogart 1942, 236-37
Sussex agricultural workers, wages in terms of wheat	up	Usher 1920, 504
Agricultural workers real wages	up	Jones 1964, 328, 338
Industrial workers real wages	up	Bowley 1895, 381

(a) Workers in shipbuilding, textiles, cotton, mining, printing, building, and agriculture.

BIBLIOGRAPHY

A. The Definition and Measurement of Economic Development

Adelman, I., C. Taft Morris. 1967. *Society, politics, and economic development: a quantitative approach*. Baltimore: The Johns Hopkins Press.

_____, 1972. The measurement of institutional characteristics of nations: methodological considerations. *J. of Dev. Studies*, 8 (April): 111-35.

_____, 1973. *Economic growth and social equity in developing countries*. Stanford, CA: Stanford U. Press.

Adelman, I., S. Robinson. 1977. *Income distribution policy in less developed countries: a case study of Korea*. Stanford: Stanford U. Press.

Ahluwalia, M. S. 1976. Inequality, poverty, and development. *J. of Dev. Econ.*, 3(December): 307-42.

Atkinson, A. B. 1970. On the measurement of inequality. *J. of Econ. Theory*, 2(September): 244-63.

Baran, P. A. 1968. *The political economy of growth*. New York: Modern Reader Paperbacks.

Beckerman, W. 1978. *Measures of leisure, equality, and welfare*. Paris: Organization for Economic Co-operation and Development.

Chenery, H., et al. 1974. *Redistribution with growth*. New York: Oxford U. Press.

Craeybeckx, J. 1970. The beginnings of the industrial revolution in Belgium. In *Essays in French Economic History*, ed. Rondo Cameron. Homewood, Ill.: Irwin, 187-200.

Dore, E., J. Weeks. 1980. Economic performance and basic needs in six Latin American countries. (typescript) Washington, D. C.

Frank, A. G. 1967. *Capitalism and underdevelopment in Latin America: historical studies of Chile and Brazil*. New York: Monthly Review Press.

Furtado, C. 1964. *Development and underdevelopment*. Berkeley: U. of California Press.

Geertz, C. 1963. *Agricultural involution: the processes of ecological change in Indonesia*. Berkeley: U. of California Press.

Ghai, D. P. 1977. *The basic needs approach to development*: *some issues regarding concepts and methodology*. Geneva: ILO.

Graaff, J. de V. 1957. *Theoretical welfare economics*. Cambridge, England: Cambridge U. Press.

Griffin, K. 1978. *International inequality and national poverty*. New York: Holmes and Meier Publishers.

_____, 1969. *The underdevelopment of Spanish America*. London: George Allen and Unwin.

Griffin, K., A. K. Ghose. 1979. Growth and impoverishment in rural areas of Asia. *World Dev.*, 7 (April/May): 361-81.

Griffin, K., A. R. Kahn. 1977. *Poverty and landlessness in rural Asia*. Geneva: ILO.

Haq, Mahbub ul. 1973. Employment in the 1970's: a new perspective. In *The political economy of development and underdevelopment*, ed. C. Wilber, 266-72.

Harbison, F. H., J. Maruhnic, J. R. Resnick. 1970. *Quantitative analyses of modernization and development*. Princeton: Industrial relations section, Princeton U.

Hicks, N., P. Streeten. 1979. Indicators of development: the search for a basic needs yardstick. *World Dev.*, 7(June): 567-80.

International Labour Organization (ILO). 1977. *Meeting basic needs, strategies for eradicating mass poverty and unemployment. Conclusions of the world employment conference*. Geneva.

Korte, B., W. Oberhofer. 1971. Triangularizing input-output matrices and the structure of production. *European Econ. Rev.*, (Summer): 493-521.

Kuznets, S. 1955. Economic growth and income inequality. *Amer. Econ. Rev.*, 45 (March): 1-28.

Meade, J. 1955. *Trade and welfare*. London: Oxford U. Press.

Morris, C. T., I. Adelman. (Forthcoming) *Where angels fear to tread*: *quantitative studies in history and development*. Stanford, CA: Stanford U. Press.

Morris, M. D. 1979. *Measuring the condition of the world's poor*: *the physical quality of life index*. New York: Pergamon Press.

Newberry, D. 1970. A theorem on the measurement of inequality. *J. of Econ. Theory*, 2: 264-66.

Pfanzagl, J. 1968. *Theory of measurement*. New York: Wiley.

Phelps Brown, E. H. 1953. *Economic growth and human welfare: three lectures*. Delhi: Ranjit Printers and Publishers.

Pyatt, G., A. Row. 1977. *Social accounting for development planning with special reference to Sri Lanka*. Cambridge, England: Cambridge U. Press.

Ranis, G. 1978. Equity with growth in Taiwan: how 'special' is the 'special case'? *World Dev.*, 6(March): 397-410.

Rao, D. C. 1978. Economic growth and equity in the Republic of Korea. *World Dev.*, 6(March): 383-96.

Robinson, S., K. Dervis. 1977. Income distribution and socioeconomic mobility: a framework for analysis and planning. *J. of Dev. Studies*. 13(July): 347-64.

Rowntree, B. S. 1901. *Poverty: a study of town life*. London: Macmillan.

_____, 1910. *Land and labour: lessons from Belgium*. London: Macmillan.

Seers, D. 1972. What are we trying to measure? *J. of Dev. Studies*. 8(April): 21-36.

Sen, A. 1976a. Poverty: an ordinal approach to measurement. *Econometrica*, 44(March): 219-31.

_____, 1976b. Real national income. *Rev. of Econ. Studies*, 43(1) (Feb): 19-39.

Standing, G., R. Szal. 1979. *Poverty and basic needs: evidence from Guyana and the Philippines*. Geneva: ILO.

Stewart, F. 1975. A note on social cost-benefit analysis and class conflict in LDC's. *World Dev.*, 3(January): 31-39.

Streeten, P. 1979. Development ideas in historical perspective. In *Toward a new strategy for development*, ed. K. Q. Hill, 21-52. Elmsford, NY: Pergamon Press.

Sutcliffe, B. 1972. Imperialism and industrialization in the third world. In *Studies in the theory of imperialism*, ed. R. Owen, B. Sutcliffe. London: Longman.

Szal, R., S. Robinson. 1977. Measuring income inequality. In *Income distribution and growth in the less-developed countries*, ed. C. R. Frank, Jr., R. Webb. Washington, D. C.: The Brookings Institution.

United Nations Industrial Development Organization (UNIDO). 1972. *Guidelines for project evaluation*. New York: United Nations.

United Nations Research Institute for Social Development (UNRISD). 1970. Contents and measurement of socio-economic development: an empirical enquiry. An Institute Staff Study by D. V. McGranahan et al. (Report no. 70.10)(mimeo) Geneva.

Warren, B. 1973. Imperialism and capitalist industrialization. *New Left Rev.*, (October/November).

Weisskoff, R., E. Wolff. 1977. Linkages and leakages: industrial tracking in an enclave economy. *Econ. Dev. and Cult. Change*, 25(July): 607-28.

Yotopoulos, P. A., J. B. Nugent. 1973. A balanced-growth version of the linkage hypothesis. *Quart. J. of Econ.*, 87(May): 157-71.

B. Historical

Avondts, G., J. Hanes, E. Scholliers, P. Scholliers, A. Tassin. 1979. *De Gentse Textielarbeiders in de 19e en 20e Eeuw. 4. Lonen in de Weverij van het Bedrijf A. Voortman-N.V. Texas, 1835-1925.* Brussels: Centrum vor Hedendaagse Sociale Geschiedenis.

Avondts, G., P. Scholliers. 1977. *De Gentse Textielarbeiders in de 19e en 20e Eeuw.* Vol. 5. *Gentse Prijzen, Huishuran, en Budgetonderzoeken in de 19e en 20e Eeuw.* Brussels: Centrum voor Hedendaagse Sociale Geschiedenis.

Bairoch, P. 1973. Europe's gross national products: 1800-1975. *J. of European Econ. Hist.*, 5 (2)(Fall): 273-340.

Bidwell,P. W., J. I. Falconer. 1973. *History of Agriculture in the northern United States, 1620-1860.* New York: Augustus M. Kelly. (Original published in 1925).

Bogart, E. L. 1942. *Economic History of Europe, 1760-1939.* London: Longman, Green.

Borchardt, K. 1973. Germany 1700-1914. In Cipolla (1973): 76-160.

———, 1976. Wirtschaftliches Wachstum und Weschsellagen 1800-1914. In *Handbuch der Deutschen Wirtschafts - und Sozialgeschichte.* Vol. 2. *Das 19. und 20. Jahrhundert*, ed. W. Zorn, 198-275. Stuttgart: Ernst Klett Verlag.

Bowley, A. L. 1895. Comparisons of the rates of increase of wages in the United States and Great Britain, 1860-1891. *Econ. J.*, 5: 369-83.

Bowley, A. L., G. H. Wood 1898-1906. The statistics of wages in the United Kingdon during the last hundred years: Agricultural wages. Pt. I-IV. engineering and shipbuilding. Pt. I-V. *J. of the Royal Stat. Soc.*, 61(December 1898): 702-22; 62(March, June, September 1899): 140-50, 395-404, 555-70; 68(March, June, September, December 1905): 104-37, 373-91, 563-614, 704-15; 69(March 1906): 148-92.

Cipolla, C. M., ed. 1973. *The Fontana economic history of Europe.* Vol. 4. *The emergence of industrial societies.* Two parts. London: Collins/Fontana Books.

Deane, P. 1955-56. Contemporary estimates of national income in the first half of the nineteenth century. *Econ. Hist. Rev.,* second series. 7(1, 2,& 3): 339-54.

_____, 1968. The United Kingdom 1830-1914. *Rev. of Income and Wealth,* 14(June): 95-112.

Dechesne, L. 1932. *Histoire Économique et Sociale de la Belgique Depuis les Origines Jusqu'en 1914.* Paris: Librairie du Recueil Sirey.

de Laveleye, M. É. 1870. "Land system of Belgium and Holland. In *Systems of land tenure in various countries.* The Cobden Club, ed. 233-84. 2nd ed. London: Macmillan.

Ducpétiaux, E. 1850. *Mémoire sur le Paupérisme dans les Flandres.* Brussels: M. Hayez.

Fogel, R. W. 1964. *Railroads and American economic growth: essays in econometric history.* Baltimore: The Johns Hopkins Press.

Gallman, R. S. 1960. Commodity output 1839-1899. In *Trends in the American economy in the nineteenth century,* ed. W. N. Parker, 13-71. Princeton: Princeton U. Press (Studies in Income and Wealth No. 24).

Gasser, C. 1962. Die Bodenteuerung vom Standpunkt der Industrie. *Schweizerische Zeitschrift für Volkswirtschaft und Statistik,* 98(2)(June): 121-43.

Hamerow, T. S. 1969. *The social foundations of German unification, 1858-1871.* Vol. 1. *Ideas and institutions.* Princeton: Princeton U. Press.

Hansen, A. H. 1925. Factors affecting the trend of real wages. *Amer. Econ. Rev.,* 15(March): 27-38.

Hauser, A. 1961. *Schweizerische Wirtschafts - und Sozialgeschichte: Von den Anfangen bis zur Gegenwart.* Zurich: Erlenbach.

_____, 1974. Zur Produktivität deer Schweizerischen Landwirtschaft im 19. Jahrhundert. In *Wirtschaftliche und Soziale Strukturen im Saekulären Wandel.* Vol. 3. *Wirtschaft und Gesellschaft in der Zeit der Industrialisierung.* ed. I.Bog, et al. Hannover: Verlag M., H. Schaper.

Hoffmann, W. G. et al. 1965. *Das Wachstum der Deutschen Wirtschaft seit der Mitte des 19. Jahrhunderts.* Berlin: Verlag.

Hughes, J. 1983. Correspondence with the author.

Jones, E. L. 1964. The agricultural labour market in England, 1793-1872. *Econ. Hist. Rev.* (2nd series), 17(2): 322-38.

Kaplan, A. 1964. *The conduct of inquiry: methodology for behavioral science.* San Francisco: Chandler Pub. Co.

Kneschaurek, F. 1964. Wandlungen der Schweizerischen Industriestruktur. In Schweizerische Gesellschaft für Statistik und Volkswirtschaft. *Ein Jahrundert Schweizerischer Wirtschaftsentwicklung*, 133-66. Berne: Stämpfli & Co.

Köllmann, W. 1976. Bevölkerungsgeschichte 1800-1890. *Handbuch der Deutschen Wirtschafts - und Sozialgeschichte.* Vol. 2. *Das 19, und 20. Jahrhundert*, ed. W. Zorn, 9-50. Stuttgart: Ernst Klett Verlag.

Kuczynski, J. 1936. *A short history of labour conditions under industrial capitalism.* Vol. III, Part I. *Germany 1800 to the present day.* London: Frederick Müller Ltd.

_____, 1944. *A short history of labour conditions under industrial capitalism in Great Britain and Empire.* 2nd ed. New York: Barnes and Noble.

_____, 1973. *A short history of labour conditions under industrial capitalism in the United States of America.* New York: Barnes and Noble. (Originally published in 1943).

Kuznets, S. 1966. *Modern economic growth: rate, structure, and spread.* New Haven: Yale U. Press.

Lebergott, S. 1960. Wage trends. In *Trends in the American economy in the ninetenth century*, ed. W. N. Parker. Princeton: Princeton U. Press. (Studies in Income and Wealth No. 24).

_____, 1964. *Manpower in economic growth: the American record since 1800.* New York: McGraw-Hill Book Co.

Levasseur, E. 1904. *Histoire des Classes Ouvrières et de l'Industrie en France de 1789 à 1870.* New York: AMS Press.

Lévy-Leboyer, M. 1968. La Croissance Économique en France au XIXe Siècle. Résultats Préliminaires. *Annales E.S.C.*, 23 (July/August): 788-807.

Lis, C., H. Soly. 1977. Food consumption in Antwerp between 1807 and 1859: a contribution to the standard of living debate. *Econ. Hist. Rev., 2nd series.* 30(August): 460-486.

Lyons, J. S. 1977. The Lancashire cotton industry and the introduction of the powerloom, 1815-1850. Ph.D. Dissertation. Berkeley, CA: U. of California.

Matz, K.-J. 1980. Pauperismus und Bevölkerung. *Die Gesetzlichen Ehebeschränkungen in den Süddeutschen Staaten Während des 19. Jahrhunderts.* Stuttgart: Klett-Cotta.

Menzel, U. 1979. Der Entwicklung der Schweiz (1780-1850). Ein Beitrag zum Konzept autozentrierter Entwicklung. (mimeo) Bremen: Untersuchung zurGrundlegung Einer Praxizorientierten Theorie Autozentrierter Entwicklung, Universität Bremen. (mimeo).

Mokyr, J. 1974. The industrial revolution in the Low Countries in the first half of the Nineteenth Century: a comparative case study. *J. of Econ. Hist.*, 34(June): 365-501.

Neyrinck, M. 1944. *De Lonen in Belgie Sedert 1846.* Louvain: Em. Warny.

Perroux, F. 1955. Prise de Vues sur la Croissance de l'Économie Française, 1780-1950. In *Income and wealth*, ed. S. Kuznets, series 5. London: Bowes and Bowes.

Philippe, R. 1970. Une opération pilote: L'étude du ravitaillement de Paris au temps de Lavoisier. In *Pour Une Histoire de l'Alimentation*, ed. J. J. Hémardinquer. Paris: Librairie Armand Colin. (Cahiers des Annales. 28).

Rappard, W. E. 1914. *La Révolution Industrielle et les Origines de la Protection Légale du Travail en Suisse.* Berne, Switzerland: Stämpfli & Cie.

Rostow, W. W. 1960. *The stages of economic growth: a non-Communist manifesto.* Cambridge, England: Cambridge U. Press.

———, ed. 1963. *The economics of take-off into sustained growth.* New York: St. Martin's Press.

Saalfeld, D. 1974. Lebensstandard in Deutschland 1750-1860, Einkommens Verhältnisse und Lebenshaltungs-Kosten städtischer Populationen in der Übergangsperiode zum Industriezeitalter. In *Wirtschaftliche und soziale Strukturen im säkularen Wandel. Festschrift für Wilhelm Abel zum 70. Geburtstag*, 2:417-43. Hannover. (Schriftnenreihe für Ländliche Sozialfragen Bd. 70).

Senghaas, D. 1982. *Von Europa Lernen: Entwicklungsgeschichtliche Betrachtungen.* Frankfurt am Main: Suhrkamp Verlag.

Sée, H. 1951. *Histoire Économique de la France: Les Temps Modernes (1789-1914).* Vol. 2. Paris: Armand Colin. (First published in 1942.)

Spree, R. 1977. *Die Wachstumszyklen der Deutschen Wirtschaft von 1840 bis 1880.* Berlin: Duncker & Humblot.

181

Teuteberg, H. J. 1976. Die Nähring der Sozialen Unterschichten im
Späten 19. Jahrhundert. In *Ernahrung und Ernahrungs-lehre im
19. Jahrhundert*, ed. E. Heischkel-Artelt. Gottingen, Germany:
Vandenhoeck & Ruprecht.

U.S. Bureau o the Census 1966. *Long-term economic growth, 1860-1965*.
Washington, D. C.: Government Printing Office.

Usher, A. P. 1920. *An introduction to the industrial history of
England*. Boston: Houghton Mifflin Company.

Van den Eeckhout, P. 1980. Determinentan van het 19e Eeuws Sociaal-
Economisch Levan to Brussel. Hun Betekenis voor Laagste
Bevolkingsklassen. Brussels: Vrije Universiteit Brussel,
Faculteit der Letteren en Wijsbegeerte, Doctoral Dissertation.

Ware, N. 1964. *The industrial worker, 1840-1860*. Chicago:
Quadrangle Paperbacks. (Originally published in 1924.)

Wittmann, W. 1963. Die take-off Periode der Schweizerischen
Volkswirtschaft. *Zeitschrift für die Gesamte
Staatswissenschaft*, 119 (Heft 4): 592-615.

9
Income Distribution Trends in Labor Surplus Economies

Albert Berry

I. INTRODUCTION

The last twenty or so years have seen, within the field of development, the elaboration of "labor surplus economics". For some economists this model has become a key to the interpretation of the economic structure and evolution of many less developed countries; few would disagree with the connotation of the term labor surplus -- that the less developed countries would frequently be better-off with lower populations, and correspondingly higher capital-labor and land-labor ratios. A second important trend is the increasing weight accorded to income distribution as a policy goal. This paper deals with the pessimism resulting from the confluence of these two threads of thought, pessimism with respect to the attainability in a labor surplus context of reasonable income-distribution improvements together with growth, unless the free market is rejected as the major mechanism in the economic system. When high population implies a very low equilibrium wage rate, given the country's capital stock and level of technology, maintaining an adequate income distribution under free market conditions would not seem easy. The task is complicated by the tendency of many less developed countries to adopt relatively modern and usually capital-intensive technology, and by the fact that many are undergoing more rapid population growth than before the application of modern medicine and some gains in living standards dramatically lowered their mortality rates. Another possible component of the scenario, given the low equilibrium wage rate, is the evolution of pressure groups (unions, etc.) attempting, on behalf of subgroups of the low-income population and with government backing, to attain monopoly powers over the sale of labor in certain subsectors of the economy. This would tend to increase the already severe dualism in the system, decrease labor absorption in the more capital-intensive sectors, and worsen the distribution of income within the laboring class; whether the overall income distribution would be worsened or improved is not clear and may even be a matter of definition.[1] Attempts to avoid the full weight of income inequality implicit in the relatively free working of the market[2] may have the effect of decreasing the allocative efficiency of the system and lowering its rate of growth; such a slowing down might delay the long-run improvements in income distribution which one expects to result from growth, if he accepts as "normal" and therefore more-or-less predictable the historical pattern of the now developed countries which went through periods of worsening (or at least very bad) distribution before reaching a subsequent stage of lower inequality.[3]

The objective of this paper is to probe a little further into the relationship between income-distribution trends and the labor surplus characteristic of an economy. As is fairly evident, the dynamic of such an economy could explain the worsening-improving pattern just cited.[4] But, as we see below, the effect of labor surplus on the path of income distribution may depend on the precise nature of the institutions associated with the labor surplus; a number of possible mechanisms may be at work to generate, for some people, an income level above their marginal productivity. Consideration of the relative probability of these alternative mechanisms is clearly a key component of prediction; unfortunately the empirical literature is still very limited in this area.

II. BROAD DETERMINANTS OF CHANGES IN INCOME DISTRIBUTION

Many factors affect income distribution and its trends. The effects of labor surplus must be assessed with at least the major determinants in mind. At the most general level, the before-tax and transfer distribution of income among earners can be expressed as the result of the distribution of factors of production, their prices, and the way in which the factor and product markets work. Thus, changes in distribution over time can be expressed in terms of:

1. Changes in the distribution of factors, that is, labor, human capital, and physical capital (reproducible and nonreproducible).

2. Changes in factor proportions or in the aggregate production function, which may change the relative marginal productivities of factors. Changes in the aggregate production function may be due either to technological change in the usual (microeconomic) sense of the term, or to changes in the composition of output by sector or industry. Linking distributional trends to changes in the composition of output among sectors which generate different "internal" income distributions is instructive in some cases, though an explanation for these differences in sectoral distributions is necessary for a full understanding of the process.[5]

3. Changes in market imperfections over time, which may imply that factor remunerations do not change in the same way as their marginal productivities do.[6]

The distribution of income among earners, together with family structure and intrafamily distribution, determines the distribution of income among individuals, the relevant distribution from a welfare point of view. Labor surplus economics very much involves matters of family structure, since subsidization of persons with low productivity is typically done within the family. It is, therefore, necessary to consider carefully how changes in family structure may affect the relationships among indicators of the functional distribution of income, and of personal distribution.[7]

An essential idea of labor surplus economics is that in certain countries there exist substantial reserves of labor which could be drawn into service for relatively low remuneration and whose transfer to another use, given their low current productivity and low disutility of work, would have little or no opportunity cost. Typically these would be marginal members of a family, that is, members who contribute little to family income, often less than they consume. In some cases such persons may be "surplus" for their entire life, for example, unmarried sisters of the household head. In other cases the surplus state reflects their youth or age; parents subsidize children in the expectation of being later (in old age) subsidized in turn. Again, individuals may attach themselves to a family only in bad times, and otherwise be self-supporting and live by themselves.

Family composition may be thought of as reflecting economic and social or cultural factors. The former imply that many people or groups cannot form independent households for lack of income; the latter determine that some families will be larger than economically necessary, that is, that some could break into two or more smaller families each of which would be economically self-sufficient. The tendency, where it exists, for families to be as small as economically feasible would reflect social customs, including patterns of intrafamily income distribution. The economic determinants of family size and composition change markedly over the evolution of a labor surplus economy; this complicates the monitoring and description of income-distribution trends.

The growth process has typically been characterized by: (1) an increasing capital-labor ratio, tending, per se, to lower the return to capital, raise that to labor, and decrease inequality; (2) labor-saving technological change, tending to maintain a high return to capital, lower that to labor and increase inequality; (3) an increasing share of the active population in non-agriculture, a trend whose impact is difficult to appraise, but which appears to be associated chronologically with a worsening-bettering pattern in income distribution and has been hypothesized to be causally related to it (Kuznets 1955); (4) a higher average savings rate for higher income people, probably tending to increase inequality; (5) a higher rate of return to capital for higher income people, tending to increase inequality and (6) a decrease in the prevalence of extended families (e.g., as the nuclear family becomes more and more the typical mode), with unpredictable effects on income distribution among individuals. The net effect of these forces is of course not theoretically predictable until values of the relevant parameters are specified, and other factors may be important, for example, differences in the consumption baskets of rich and poor which may lead to changes in the distribution of real income different from those of money income, and differences in family size by income level.[8]

Our main focus here is a particular market imperfection, the nonequality of income and marginal productivity in the "traditional sector" of a labor surplus economy. The easiest way to probe the effects of that imperfection is by comparing a labor surplus economy with a neoclassical system characterized by perfect markets and other simplifying assumptions.

By the most common definition, an economy is characterized by a labor surplus if marginal productivity of labor is different between a sector (sectors) where workers receive remuneration equal to their marginal product and a sector (sectors) where the marginal product of labor is below an institutionally defined subsistence level but workers receive incomes equal to or above this level.[9] The workers may receive incomes exceeding their marginal product either because they are self-employed and some of their income is from capital,[10] or because their institutional relationship with the employer (e.g., father) is such that he is willing to pay them above their marginal product. In the discussion below, a labor surplus economy is defined -- a little more broadly -- as one which has one or more sectors with marginal product of labor below a subsistence income. This would include cases in which the marginal productivity of labor is below income in all sectors (hence no misallocation of labor need be involved) with all families surviving off capital income or subsidies.

A major question in judging the relevance of the labor surplus model in a given country is the share of the labor force (and of labor income) falling in skill categories for which a surplus exists. The simplifying assumption of a homogeneous labor force is, of course, increasingly invalid as an economy becomes more complex, and as educational levels rise. Some types of labor are scarce at all stages of development, others are at some times but not at other times. Evidently the labor surplus model can be expected to provide important insights into the evolution of income distribution only if many people fall in surplus labor categories or have to subsidize people who do. The natural assumption is that unskilled workers are likely to be in surplus whereas more skilled and educated people are not. We return to this issue at the end of the paper.

III. DISTRIBUTION OVER TIME IN ALTERNATIVE LABOR SURPLUS MODELS

In this section, several different labor surplus cases are considered to assess how their income-distribution paths would differ from those of a neoclassical, perfect market model, other things being equal (e.g., the nature of technological change, etc.). The functional distribution of income between capital and labor is discussed first; this division is particularly relevant when the ownership of capital is quite concentrated -- especially likely when ownership of human capital is closely related to that of physical capital. The functional distribution then corresponds to the distribution of income between two fairly distinguishable groups of people.[11] A second division, between the (capital) income of large-scale capitalists on the one hand, and the labor and capital income of everyone else, seems more relevant for those countries characterized by a fairly wide distribution of capital in small amounts; in the early stages of development this is especially characteristic of the agricultural sector. Trends in these two distributions are of interest according to how much they tell us about the directly relevant distribution, that among persons.

In the traditional labor surplus situation (referred to here as the first labor surplus model or LSM#1), traditional sector workers receive incomes above their marginal productivity, while in the profit-maximizing modern sector marginal productivity and wages are equal. This case is portrayed in Figure 1, where the labor force is measured by the distance OO', and the marginal product of labor curves in the modern and traditional sectors are, respectively, EL(1) and FL(2). The modern sector, where marginal productivity equals the wage (assumed here to be institutionally fixed at the level OW), hires OL(0). If there is a great deal of excess labor, as here, its

186

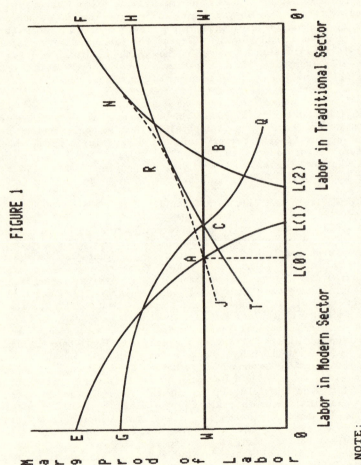

FIGURE 1

Labor in Modern Sector   Labor in Traditional Sector

Marg Prod of Labor

NOTE:
Vertical axis shows Marginal Productivity of Labor; Wages.

marginal productivity may be zero or even negative in the traditional sector. Static efficiency (relation of actual to potential output) and distribution of income depend, in part, on the production relationships in the economy and, in part, on behavioral patterns in the traditional sector. Given a modern sector wage rate of OW,[12] the static loss of production in the economy represented by Figure 1 would be the area AL(1)L(0). Loss is an increasing function of the elasticity of the modern sector, marginal product of labor curve beneath the level of the institutional wage. If there is, given equal salaries (adjusted for any differences in nonmonetary benefits or costs), a preference either to work in the modern sector or not to work there (e.g., due to poor information) the loss will be lesser or greater, respectively, than AL(1)L(0).

Two institutional situations have been most commonly hypothesized as explaining individuals' receiving an income above their marginal productivity in the traditional sector. If, as is fairly typical in the agricultural sector, the economic unit is the family consisting of several workers, then as long as average income is high enough for all to survive it is unlikely that anyone will be turned out, even though not all are needed to produce the potential output. Alternatively, it has been proposed that in more or less feudal agricultures the owner may feel a responsibility to support more workers than would maximize his profits -- a "noblesse oblige" case. In either case the support may or may not be contingent on physical presence. If it is, then individuals may be available to the modern sector only at a wage well in excess of their own marginal productivity in agriculture, the gap depending on the nature of the family's (owner's) obligation to an individual. At one extreme, the family (owner) may provide a fixed "subsistence" income, which is independent of its (his) average per capita income. We refer to this as the "minimum obligation" case. At the other extreme, the individual's income may rise, pari passu, with that of the family (or owner), what we call the "variable subsidy" case.

In the second broad model considered here (LMS#2), labor is assumed to receive its marginal product in all sectors, even though this payment is below the culturally or physically defined subsistence minimum level of real income. The model could represent a situation where the family, rather than the individual, is the income-maximizing entity;[13] maximization of the income of a family in the traditional sector would imply sending members to the modern sector at any salary above the marginal productivity in the traditional sector and subsidizing them enough to raise income to at least subsistence; if that marginal productivity is zero, members should work in the modern sector for any positive wage.[14] This theoretical extreme is implausible for a variety of practical and institutional reasons, but the possibility of a below-subsistence wage cannot be neglected, especially in societies where family relationships remain close after a person moves from a rural to urban area, or goes to work in a different "firm".[15] When some people accept wages below the institutional subsistence income, some of the static inefficiency loss characterizing LSM#1 is avoided; the extreme case where the existence of surplus labor[16] would not imply any static inefficiency is unlikely.

188

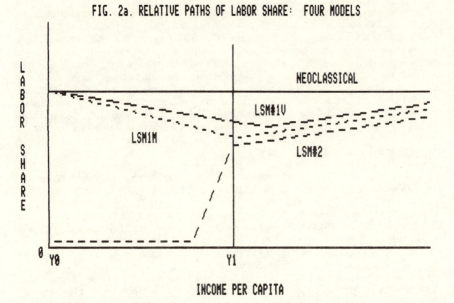

FIG. 2a. RELATIVE PATHS OF LABOR SHARE: FOUR MODELS

FIG. 2b RELATIVE PATHS OF LABOR INCOME PER CAPITA: FOUR MODELS

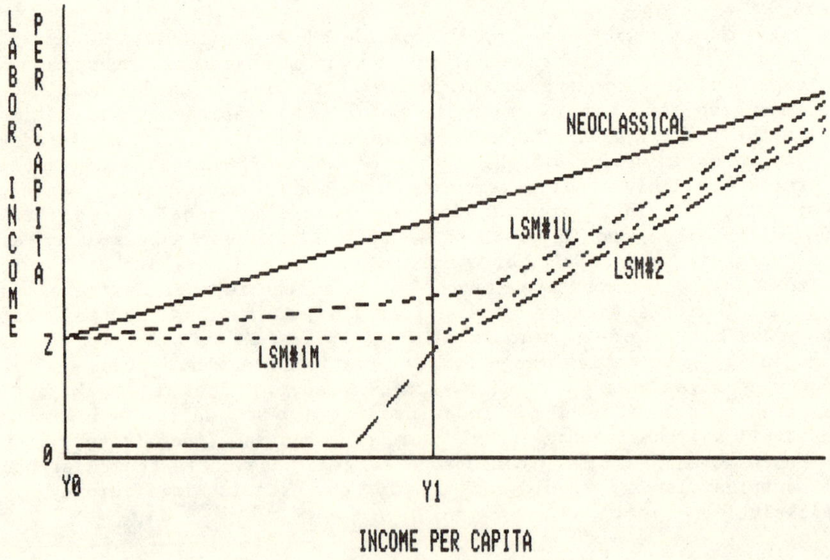

As noted above, changes in the division of income between capital and labor are of particular interest when individual families tend to have all, or almost all, of their income from only one of the two factors. Such an assumption is plausible for a modern sector where capitalists and workers are clearly defined groups, but less applicable in traditional sectors with small-scale farmers (artisans, etc.) who, although they do not operate much land (capital), do frequently own it, and thus have both labor and capital income. The capital-labor breakdown would not, thus, correspond to a distribution by (two) groups of families in either the LSM#2 or the LSM#1, family case. It would, depending on how labor income is defined, be meaningful in LSM#1 -- noblesse oblige -- since the laboring class has no capital income in the usual sense of the term.

How the labor share should be defined is not immediately clear in a labor surplus sector where income provided by the employer (usually the family head) exceeds marginal productivity. Since our concern here is with income distribution, we will define it as income received in consequence of the presence of a worker, rather than as income earned in payment for labor services.[17] Any income of persons not owning capital will thus be included as labor income. As a reference point for subsequent analysis, we consider the relative trajectories of this labor share in each of the above models, when each economy undergoes a parallel (see definition below) growth process.

Assume a given, initial per capita average income YO for each economy while defining similar production relationships (i.e., marginal product of labor curves and intersectoral distribution of output and labor) in each -- as similar as is consistent with the existence of the differences in structure and/or behavioral patterns under discussion. Figure 1 depicts the relevant assumptions used to compare initial labor shares and subsequent trends of labor income and labor share. In Figure 2b labor income is plotted as a function of average income (for average income above YO) for each case; the labor share itself is plotted in Figure 2a. In Figure 1 the two marginal productivity curves EL(1) for the modern sector and FL(2) for the traditional sector) and a subsistence income level OW define the initial state of LMS#1 (both minimum obligation and variable subsidy cases)[18]; total income is then equal to OEAL(0)+O'FL(2).[19] Labor income is OWAL(0) (from the modern sector) plus AW'O'L(0) (from the traditional sector[20]), indicated in Figure 2b as OZ. Identical, marginal productivity curves for the modern and traditional sectors and the same labor income can be assumed for the minimum obligation and variable subsidy cases. For an LSM#2 economy to have per capita income YO, one or both of the marginal productivity curves must differ from those of LSM#1, since the loss of potential production AL(1)L(0) characterizing LSM#1 does not occur in this case. Both curves are therefore assumed to be, over their full range, a little below those for LSM#1. (Small differences in the relation of the two sets of curves do not alter the results significantly.) Assuming that the marginal productivity of labor is originally zero in both sectors, labor income and share are zero when per capita income equals YO, as indicated in Figures 2a and 2b.

One or both of the marginal productivity curves representing a neoclassical economy with average income YO (and with an equilibrium wage level at least as high as W1) must have a higher output elasticity of labor; here we assume both do, the curves being GQ and HT (of Figure 1) which cut at the level W; the economy then has the same initial labor share as does LSM#1, and a higher share than LSM#2; any other neoclassical economy with the same total income would have a higher labor share.[21]

Assume now, for simplicity, a growth process which implies a constant labor share in the neoclassical economy.[22] (A sufficient set of conditions would be neutral technological change in the growing sector[23] and a Cobb-Douglas production function.) Assume further a "parallel" growth process in the other cases, where "parallel" means that, for any two rays passing through the origin, the relative percent shift (along these rays) of the growing sector's marginal product of labor curve will be the same in each of the four cases, when income per capita rises from one level (Y_i) to another level (Y_j).[24]

In the LSM#1 minimum obligation case -- the simplest to analyze -- absolute labor income would not rise at all until the marginal productivity of labor curve of the modern sector (MPL(m)) had shifted enough to cut the marginal productivity of labor curve of the traditional sector (MPL(t)) at the institutional wage level, that is, until the surplus labor was exhausted; the labor share would thus be falling during this stage as indicated in Figure 2a. After this commercialization point[25] is reached (with per capita income Y1 -- see Figure 2b) average wages would rise, in general, more quickly than in the neoclassical case -- with labor share therefore rising. The absolute income going to labor in this model could eventually (depending on the details of the production functions) rise above that in the neoclassical model, with the same being true (by definition) of the labor share.

For LSM#1-variable subsidy, labor income and share at per capita income Y0 are the same as in LSM#1-minimum obligation (assuming that the institutional income level of workers in the traditional sector is treated as labor income -- see above). Subsequently, however, labor income rises with the increase of APL in the traditional sector.[26] So, at worst, the labor share cannot fall as quickly as in the minimum obligation case; in theory it might not fall at all or could even rise, but in fact it would almost certainly fall during the early part of the growth process at least.[27] After redundancy ends, the wage in the traditional sector begins to rise relatively rapidly, and the overall labor share is then very likely to rise. The commercialization point, however, corresponds to a higher income level than in LSM#1-minimum obligation. After both economies have passed their commercialization point, they may be expected to present similar trajectories with the labor shares approaching each other; if, as is plausible, the labor shares eventually become as high as in the neoclassical case, they would have to have risen over some income range. In the real world, economies falling in the LSM#1 category would be expected to lie somewhere between these two (extreme) versions.[28]

In LSM#2, labor income is zero until MPL becomes positive; this occurs when labor redundancy ends -- at an income lower than the level (Y1) at which wages in LSM#1-minimum obligation start to rise above the subsistence level; the labor share then rises, probably rapidly, and is equal to that in LSM#1-minimum obligation at income Y1; from then on, the movements of the two curves would be the same.

IV. TRENDS IN THE DISTRIBUTION OF INCOME BETWEEN "LARGE CAPITALISTS" AND OTHERS

In three of the four cases discussed above, the labor share was either of ambiguous definition (LSM#1: both cases)[29] or not a good indicator of the income of people toward the bottom of the distribution because capital income is also important for this group (LSM#2). Thus, although it is of interest to ascertain the over-time pattern of factor shares, a better proxy for the division between rich and poor may be the shares of "modern-sector capitalists" and "others."[30] In cases where there are no noblesse oblige (presumably large-scale) capitalists in the traditional sector, then the income of "others" would include all of the capital income from the traditional sector; the division could approximate that between modern-sector capitalists and all laborers (some of whom would also have capital income from the traditional sector). It might be assumed, to make the neoclassical model as similar to the others as possible, that the capital incomes are as small in its slowly growing sector as in the traditional sectors of LSM#1-family and LSM#2.

In this context, no interesting general differences exist between the two LSM#1-family cases (minimum obligation and variable subsidy), but the noblesse oblige case does differ from the family case, so there are, once again, four models to be considered. Compare first the combined share of labor and small-scale capital in these models when per capita income in each is YO. (Note that in all cases but noblesse oblige, large-scale capital income is the same as modern or growing-sector capital income.) Assuming, as in the above discussion, a higher output elasticity of labor in each sector of the neoclassical economy than in the corresponding sector of the labor surplus models and that, at per capita income YO, the share of output in the growing sector is the same in each model, then modern or growing-sector capitalist income is less in the neoclassical model than in LSM#1-family, since more labor is employed at the same wage; hence, traditional-sector income plus modern-sector labor income (i.e., small-scale capital income and all labor income) is higher in the neoclassical model than in LSM#1-family.[31] That sum is likely to be lowest of all in the LSM#2 situation since modern-sector labor income is zero (See Figure 3b). In the noblesse oblige case where there are large capital incomes in the traditional sector also, the "labor and small capital" share at income YO is unambiguously equal to or lower than in LSM#1-family; it may be above or below that of LSM#2, being more likely to be below, the earlier the stage of development, since the traditional-sector income is then likely to be larger relative to total labor income.

During the growth process outlined earlier, the share of income going to the lower income group ("others") falls over time in the neoclassical economy (by assumption) since labor's share remains constant while the traditional-sector capital share falls; per capita income of the group rises, however. While the noblesse oblige economy is in the labor surplus condition, the real income of "others" (consisting entirely of labor income) remains constant, and the share thus falls more quickly than in the neoclassical case; when the economy leaves the labor surplus situation, the wage rate rises more quickly than in the neoclassical model, so the "others'" share also

192

FIG. 3a. RELATIVE PATHS OF INCOME SHARE OF LABOR + SSC

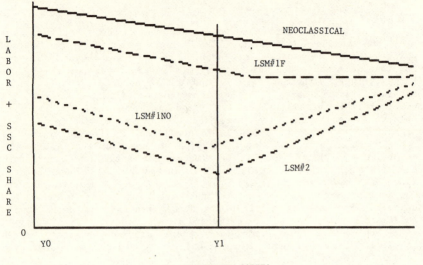

INCOME PER CAPITA

FIG. 3b RELATIVE PATHS OF LABOR + SSC INCOME PER CAPITA

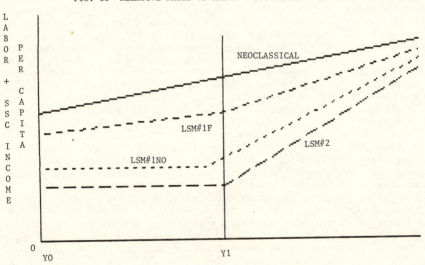

INCOME PER CAPITA

NOTE:
   In Figures 3a and 3b, 'SSC' stands for Small Scale Capitalists

rises relative to that in the neoclassical case and probably, at least over certain range, in absolute terms as well.[32]

In LSM#2 the income from labor and traditional-sector capital remains constant (at the total output of the traditional sector) until the marginal productivity of labor rises above zero (which occurs at a lower income than that at which LSM#1-noblesse oblige leaves its labor surplus state) and the labor income from the modern sector thereafter rises quickly. The share of "others", which starts lower than in LSM#1-family and either higher or lower than in noblesse oblige (see above), is unequivocally above that in the noblesse oblige case when the latter leaves the labor surplus state and wages begin to rise above their subsistence level (income level Y1), the difference at that point being roughly the income accruing to traditional-sector capital; subsequently, the paths of these two economies converge.

In LSM#1-family, the real income of "others" is initially lower than that in the neoclassical case, but higher than in both of the other labor surplus cases; it rises throughout, and may rise more or less rapidly than in the neoclassical case.[33] Under the present assumptions, "other" income is higher throughout than in the noblesse oblige case, since both labor income [34] and capital income are higher (the latter being zero in the noblesse oblige case). The income of "others" is, except for what appear to be quite unusual cases, lower at all income levels in LSM#2 than in LSM#1-family[35] (the wage rate is always lower in the former case), though the difference becomes smaller at higher income levels. The difference between the share of "others" in the noblesse oblige and family cases also becomes·smaller for higher incomes due to the decreasing income of traditional-sector capital. Thus, the three labor surplus paths converge.

V. CONCLUDING COMMENTS

One can, of course, hypothesize many mechanisms to account for a worsening followed by a bettering of income distribution during a country's development process. The discussion above -- which shows that labor surplus economies are more likely to produce such a result than neoclassical ones -- suggests the explanation that many countries are in a labor surplus condition in the early phases of development and then become more neoclassical. Since much independent evidence would support this historical sequence, at least for the densely populated LDCs, the interpretation has some plausibility.

In the labor surplus model where the labor share would be a useful indicator of the income of the poor -- the noblesse oblige case -- which we assume to be characterized by "minimum obligation", that share fell relative to its level in a "parallel" neoclassical economy (see Figure 2a) during the labor surplus phase, and subsequently rose. Of the labor surplus cases where income other than that going to modern-sector capital is a better indicator of the income of the poor, one (LSM#2) bore this same relation to the neoclassical case (see Figure 3a) and the other (LSM#1-family) might be usually expected to bear it.

The theoretical prediction that almost regardless of the institutional basis for the functioning of the labor surplus economy, it may be expected to undergo a relative worsening of income distribution during the labor surplus phase and an improvement subsequently compared to a neoclassical economy does not, as noted above, imply that an absolute worsening need occur. But it tends to suggest this, especially if one believes that much technological change is quite labor saving. And it constitutes further grounds for pessimism with respect to possibilities for improving income distribution in economies which retain the labor surplus characteristic. Such pessimism, of course, is a matter of degree, the degree depending on the importance of this factor compared to other determinants of distribution. Distribution of assets between the modern and traditional sectors may be a major determinant. In many formulations of the labor surplus model (including those presented above), the traditional sector does not grow at all. But this is, of course, not the normal experience, and many government policies impinge on the relative growth of the two sectors. Support for output growth on small farms, in small manufacturing establishments, and the rest, may exert a considerable positive impact on distribution. Expanding education, and expansion has been dramatic in most LDCs, has modified the skill composition of the labor force, decreasing labor surplus and changing the distribution of income within the modern sector. In some countries still characterized by a surplus of low-skill workers, the labor surplus model might, nevertheless, not help much in explaining income-distribution trends over time. It may be that by the time the commercialization point is reached, and no surplus labor is left, income distribution is mainly determined by asset distribution and education distribution. At early stages of development, with most workers unskilled, predictions based on the labor surplus model may be robust in the sense that the developments it highlights are the dominant ones, whereas later the trends it points to are no longer of such major importance.

FOOTNOTES

1. It is possible that these market imperfections will decrease high-capital incomes; in that case an associated increase in the dispersion of labor incomes could lower inequality by some measures and raise it by others.

2. "Free working" is, of course, not the same as "perfect"; the former may imply much monopoly and oligopoly power in product markets and monopsony power in factor markets.

3. As argued by Kuznets (1963). In almost all of the ten countries for which Kuznets presents data in this study, the relation cited was borne out. Kuznets stressed the changing relative importance of agriculture and non-agriculture in his explanation. Other authors have stressed a number of other factors.

4. This possibility has been either discussed or assumed by several authors, especially the link between the constant wage rate characteristic of some labor surplus models and a decreasing labor share. W.A. Lewis, in his original article (Lewis 1954, 139-91) observed that labor's relative income would decline in the stage

of unlimited supply of labor. Kindleberger (1967, 8), in studying the turning point in European countries, stated that the relative share of labor would decline, or remain constant, before the turning point and rise after it. Minami (1970, 8) observed that these statements were too loose, since the labor share could move the other way, depending on the elasticity of substitution in the modern sector. Considerable (though not overwhelming) empirical evidence has been adduced to support the increase-decrease pattern of inequality over time, including several cross-country studies which have presented data consistent with this conclusion. (See, for example, Ahluwalia 1976.)

5. A prominent member of this genre is Kuznets' (1955) "structural change" explanation of changes in income distribution, which stresses the increasing share of the nonagricultural sector, whose income distribution is characterized as having a higher average and a greater variance than that of the agricultural sector.

6. Schumpeter described how the process of technological change gives monopoly power to the innovator, and how this position is then eroded over the course of time. The rapidity of the erosion may be open to question, but the creation of new monopoly positions is certainly a permanent feature of growth. Market imperfections are also responsible for the fact that capital held by different groups of people earns different rates of return, a possibly important determinant of changing income and wealth distribution over time.

7. Many economic phenomena would be expected to have similar effects on the distributions among earners, among families, and among persons ranked by per capita family income; but when they involve changes in family structure this is less likely to be true.

8. This factor has been discussed by, among others, James E. Meade (1964).

9. See, for example, John C. H. Fei and Gustav Ranis (1961).

10. This case is not so frequently referred to as the second one mentioned.

11. There is, of course, a continuum of persons in terms of the share of income from labor but this complexity is set aside here.

12. Increasingly it has been recognized that by no means all surplus labor is located in agriculture. (See Lloyd G. Reynolds 1967.)

13. In the LSM#1-family case, the family as a whole does not maximize income; rather, the persons who are potential migrants to the modern sector maximize their personal incomes.

14. After allowing, of course, for transportation and other costs. An interesting phenomenon which comes close to this category has been the male migration to a number of African cities for "bachelor's

wages", that is, wages not high enough to keep a family on. Husbands would leave their families behind in the rural areas. Their earnings were often below the subsistence level for a family in the urban area, but the families were able to produce enough on the farm to bring total family income to at least subsistence. The male's marginal productivity in the rural area presumably was below what he could earn in the city, but being part of a nuclear or otherwise well-defined family, his move did not imply a branching out on his own.

15. The average earnings of many part-time workers would be below what their family might define as an appropriate, minimum living level. Young persons who spend considerable periods of time in unemployment, searching for a job, fall, in a sense, into this category.

16. Defined here in the traditional sense of labor whose marginal product is below the subsistence income level.

17. The two being equal where wages equal marginal productivity.

18. In the rest of the analysis, no distinction is made between the family and noblesse oblige versions of LSM#1, since at the level of generality used here no interestingly different results emerge. Since it seems likely that the noblesse oblige landowner will feel responsible for providing only minimum subsistence and only when the workers are on his land, this case would normally fall in the LSM#1-minimum obligation category.

19. Thus, since per capita income is YO, population is (OEAL(0) + O'FL(2))/YO. It is assumed throughout that population is constant over time.

20. As noted above, we arbitrarily define the "subsidy" that traditional-sector workers receive as labor income since it results (albeit via an unusual route) from the individual's status as a laborer.

21. It is implicitly assumed that for the economy to be neoclassical the equilibrium wage must be at least OW, that is, that it is neoclassical not because basic institutions (such as those which determine the conventional wage level) are different from the other cases but because different production functions imply a higher marginal productivity of labor for the same labor force and per capita income; thus, neither the intra- and interfamily subsidies of the LSM#1 cases nor the widespread ownership of capital of LSM#2 are necessary to keep everyone at or above the subsistence level.

22. The conditions under which distribution will become more or less concentrated over time under varying conditions within the neoclassical framework are discussed in, for example, Joseph Stiglitz (1969).

23. In fact, of course, a neoclassical economy has no "traditional" sector, using the definition applied in labor surplus economics. But to simplify the comparison with the labor surplus cases, it is convenient here to think in terms of two sectors and assume that growth occurs in only one of them; no results are altered by so doing.

24. Thus, as between any two MPL curves for the growing sector of the economy, the ratio "percent difference along ray A to percent difference along ray B" must be the same as for the two MPL curves corresponding to the same two income levels in each labor surplus case. As noted above in the context of the basic production function assumptions across the economies, there is no obviously "natural" definition of parallelism.

25. That is, the point at which the gap between income and marginal productivity disappears. See Fei and Ranis (1961).

26. This increase might be equal to or, probably, less than that of APL.

27. An increase in the labor share would be more likely, ceteris paribus, the greater the employment elasticity of output in the modern sector, the lower the ratio of traditional-sector to modern-sector employment, and the smaller the decline in the ratio of income of surplus laborers to APL in the traditional sector as APL rises. If this last ratio remained constant, and if the MPL in the traditional sector were zero, and if labor productivity were twice as high in the modern as in the traditional sector, then the overall labor share of income would remain constant, for example, for the following combinations of the share of all employment in the traditional sector ($n(t)$) and the output elasticity of employment in that sector (E).

$n(t)$:	.80	.60	.50	.40	.30
E:	1.13	1.16	.67	.50	.35

For lower E, the labor share would fall. Since the other assumptions cited are generally biased in favor of keeping the labor share up, it is clear from these figures that a decline in labor share would be virtually certain when the bulk of the labor force is in the traditional sector, and probable until the traditional sector has almost disappeared.

28. The assumption that the initial subsistence wage in the traditional sector will continue to govern the modern-sector wage until all the labor surplus is exhausted, that is, that the supply price to the modern sector is initially related to APL in the traditional sector but not thereafter, does not seem plausible. While an unchanged supply price of labor seems implausible, it seems at the same time unrealistic to assume that the modern-sector wage will permanently equal APL in the traditional sector; that assumption is plausible while income is rather evenly distributed within the family, and this appears most likely when

the family is close to subsistence and virtually all output is consumed. As average income rises, it seems more likely that the income of sons, brothers, and the rest, will fall below average family income, especially if the owner elects to save, retaining all the savings in his own name. Further, if the original equality (modern-sector wage = APL of traditional sector) was due in part to the fact that migrants from the traditional to the modern sector were not able either to retain their capital in the traditional sector (and hence the income from it) or to translate it into modern-sector capital, then the possible diminution of this problem as development proceeds, communications improve, and capital markets improve, makes it less likely that the equality be maintained. Thus, one might expect the supply price of labor in the modern sector to move further from APL(t) and closer to MPL(t) as growth proceeds.

In a number of developing countries, real wages of unskilled workers (e.g., agricultural workers, some construction workers, and other groups) have remained constant over considerable periods of time. This may suggest that the minimum obligation version of LSM#1 is indeed operative. It may also, however, simply reflect the effects of rising population, holding down APL in the traditional sector.

29. Our definition of the labor share was, as noted, necessarily arbitrary.

30. This oversimplified division permits a first step in the analysis but should not, of course, be taken to imply the nonexistence of middle groups.

31. If the appropriate comparison is between all income not going to the modern-sector capitalists in LSM#1-family and labor income in the neoclassical model, distribution may be better in the former, even for all levels of per capita income. This result may be relevant since in the neoclassical economy there is less reason to assume two different groups will receive the capital income from the two sectors; where the same group owns both capital stocks, its income will be greater than that of the modern-sector capitalists in the labor surplus cases.

32. Remember that in the neoclassical model the decision rules of firms are the same in the two sectors; the difference is that the big firms are in the growing sector and small firms in the other (by assumption).

33. That "others'" income rises throughout can be seen from the fact that, during the initial period, as total income from the traditional sector stays constant, labor income from the modern sector rises (possibly through higher wages and definitely through more people employed); then as traditional-sector output falls, labor income rises to more than offset this.

The determinants of whether this group's income grows more quickly than in the neoclassical case can be seen in terms of Figure 1. In the latter model, wages rise as the two marginal

productivity of labor curves cut at higher and higher levels. For
LSM#1-family, if we assume that the supply price of labor to the
modern sector equals average productivity in the traditional
sector, the curve JRN defines APL(t) as a function of the
traditional-sector labor force; the modern-sector salary is
defined by the intersection of the MPL(m) curve and the curve JRN
as the former curve shifts to the right. During the stage of
redundant labor (when the intersection is to the left of L(2)) JRN
is a rectangular hyperbola with focus on 0'; to the right of L(2)
it is flatter than such a hyperbola. Extensive initial labor
surplus means that the rectangular hyperbola segment of JRN will
tend to be flat. The relative increases in modern-sector capital
income (and therefore of "other" income) in the two cases depend
in part on the relative slopes of the non-growing-sector MPL curve
(HT) of the neoclassical economy and the curve JRN; the relative
slopes of these two curves determine the relative modern-sector
wage increases when MPL(m) shifts to the right by a given
proportion. A neoclassical model has, at given average income,
more elastic MPL curves than a LSM#1-family economy, suggesting a
tendency for wages to rise more slowly in that case. But JRN has
lower slope than FL(2), and this factor works in the opposite
direction. The more closely reality approximates the traditional
assumption of a constant real wage as long as there is surplus
labor, the more assured it is that the income of "others" would,
at first rise more slowly in LSM#1-family than in the neoclassical
economy.

As mentioned earlier, for higher average traditional-sector
incomes, the assumption that the supply price of labor from the
traditional sector equals average income there becomes less and
less realistic. The curve depicting the relation between the
supply price of labor to the modern sector and the quantity of
labor in that sector would thus be below JRN of Figure 1; but the
results would be altered only in degree, not in kind.

34. With any given MPL(m) curve, the wage rate in the modern sector
    will be higher in LSM#1-family than in the noblesse oblige case,
    since (in line with our earlier assumptions) it is determined not
    by its intersection with ABF but with the line JRN (Figure 1);
    this line gives APL(t) as a function of the labor employed in that
    sector.

35. This can be seen as follows. Consider a given MPL(m) curve, which
    implies a given modern-sector capital income in case LSM#2. The
    same MPL(m) curve would imply both a lower, total income level in
    the LSM#1-family case and a lower, modern-sector capital income;
    the latter variable would be lower by more than the former, and
    since it is a component of total income, its relation to total
    income would have to be lower.

BIBLIOGRAPHY

Ahluwalia, M. 1976.   Inequality, poverty, and development.   *J. of Development Economics*, 3.

Fei, J. C. H., G. Ranis. 1961.   The theory of economic development. *Amer. Econ. Rev.*, 51(4).

Kindleberger, C. P. 1967.   *Europe's postwar growth: the role of labor supply*. Cambridge, MA: Harvard U. Press.

Kuznets, S. 1955.   Economic growth and income inequality. *Amer. Econ. Rev.*, *(45)(March)*.

-----, 1963.   Quantitative aspects of the economic growth of nations: distribution of income by size.   *Econ. Devel. and Cultural Change*, 2(2)(pt.2)(January).

Lewis, W. A. 1954.   Economic development with unlimited supplies of labor. *Manchester School of Economics and Social Studies*, 22(May): 139-91.

Meade, J. E. 1964.   *Efficiency, equality, and the ownership of capital*. London.

Minami, R. 1970.   Further considerations on the turning point in the Japanese economy, parts 1 and 2.   *Hitotsubashi J. of Econ.*, 10(2)(February): 27.

Reynolds, L. G. 1967.   Economic development with surplus labor: some complications. *Oxford Econ. Papers*, 21(1).

Stiglitz, J. 1969.   Distribution of income and wealth among individuals. *Econometrica*, 37(3)(July).

10
The Structure of Labor Markets:
A Book Review Three Decades Later

Richard Freeman

When an editor of this volume sent me The Structure of Labor Markets by Lloyd Reynolds to review, I leafed quickly through the book to get an overall impression of the task before me, and I couldn't believe my eyes. Instead of the Greek symbols and tables of computerized maximum likelihood estimates of multivariate systems equations, I found carefully reasoned discussion and simple tabulations and cross-tabulations. Instead of analyses of readily available Bureau of the Census or Bureau of Labor Statistics computer data I found analyses of original data gathered through interviews of several hundred workers, management at fifty or so companies, and union officers. Had the Yale computer broken down? Where were the sophisticated theory and econometric methods that are the hallmark of current research in labor economics? Where had the author been these past thirty years? Then, noticing the publication date of the book (1951), I understood the 'primitive' analytic tools employed by Reynolds and I wondered: Is it possible to learn about the labor market without the modern apparatus? How do Reynolds' findings, based on interviews and simple data analyses, stand up in the light of current research in labor economics? Has the proliferation of analytic work on the structure of labor markets in recent decades supported or overturned his 1951 findings? Viewing the ultimate test of a body of economic research to be its ability to capture reality, as Reynolds has always stressed, rather than its mathematical elegance or technological sophistication, how fares the pathbreaking work reported in the book?

I. THE STRUCTURE OF THE STRUCTURE

The Structure of Labor Markets reports the results of an in-depth study of the New Haven labor market oriented around three basic issues: the pattern and determinants of labor mobility; the determination of wages; and the interrelation between the two. Of necessity the study also deals with the impacts of collective bargaining on mobility and wage determination. The research methodology is of a sort rarely done today in the U.S. but still undertaken in studies of labor markets in developing countries: a detailed study of an area labor market (New Haven) for manual labor. The study involved: 850 interviews of workers, of whom 450 were chosen as a cross section of the manual working population, 350 chosen because they changed jobs between 1946 and 1947 and were currently employed in manufacturing, and 50 unemployed workers; interviews with 50 companies, which yielded statistical data for about half the sample; and discussion and data gathering from diverse other market participants. An appendix to the book describes in detail the methods used in the interview procedure, gives copies of the interviewer instruments, and gives suggestions for future research. The discussion of the interview procedure makes clear the time and effort that went into the data-gathering procedure and recounts in a refreshing way what was learned about the actual mechanics of interviewing.

The data-gathering phase of the study took three years, 1946-48. What did it yield?

On one level, the study yielded a set of propositions and generalizations about mobility and wage determination, each of which can be taken as separate empirical findings which can be compared to those of ensuing work. At another level, The Structure yields a picture of the labor market which, in Reynolds' view, was sufficiently divergent from standard labor market theory to suggest the need for a revision of that theory.

Since Reynolds' broad conclusion regarding the need to revise labor market theory depends on the set of specific empirical findings, I began this review by considering those findings, divided into four areas: mobility; wage determination; collective bargaining impacts; and the interrelation between mobility and wage determination. The strategy is to summarize the findings of The Structure of Labor Markets in each area and then to compare them with those of ensuing empirical work. While I make no pretence to have obtained a complete listing of relevant studies, I believe the comparisons provide a reasonably accurate picture of the results in question.

The second half of this essay turns to Reynolds' overall evaluation of the role of competitive and institutional forces in the labor market and the need to revise labor market theory.

By way of anticipation, the main conclusion I reach is that for the most part the empirical findings which Reynolds obtained have stood up to ensuing economic analysis, with, in some instances, results which he interpreted as being deviant in terms of standard theory now incorporated into that theory. On the other hand, while Reynolds' depiction of the behavior of manual workers has not been overturned, modern human capital analyses of labor supply decisions suggest greater rationality on the supply side than is indicated in The Structure. Moreover, recent research suggests that a new labor market theory requires as much, or more, analysis of the idiosyncracies of market demand behavior than of supply behavior.

II. THE SPECIFIC FINDINGS OF THE STRUCTURE OF LABOR MARKETS IN LIGHT OF ENSUING RESEARCH

Table 1 gives some of the central findings of The Structure of Labor Markets on the issue dealt with most intensively in the book: labor mobility. Column (1) gives a quotation from Reynolds regarding his findings, column (2) shows the method by which he reached his results, while column (3) gives the results of more recent studies.

TABLE 1

Comparison of Structure of Labor Markets Findings
on Mobility with Later Empirical Work

Results on Correlates of Individual Mobility	Method	Modern Work and Partial Listing of References
1. "Propensity to change employers diminishes rapidly with increasing length of service" (39)	Tabulation of percentage of voluntary changers and non-changers by years of service	Empirical studies show a strong negative relation between quit rates and job tenure. (Freeman 1980a; Leigh 1979; Jovanovic & Mincer 1974; Parsons 1979; Blau and Kahn 1981)
2. "The minority of very mobile people accounted for a disproportionate share of the total movement" (27-28)	Table of frequency of job movement by workers who changed jobs in 1941, 1943, and 1946	Substantial core of U.S. labor force employed in long-term jobs. Unemployment largely due to small minority. (Hall 1980; Clark & Summers 1979; Akerlof & Main 1980)
3. "Unskilled workers change jobs more frequently than the semiskilled, and those in turn move more frequently than skilled workers" (39)	Interview responses	Craft workers accrue more tenure than operatives, who accrue more tenure than laborers; workers with more 'specific' human capital quit less and are laid off less. (Parsons 1972; Pencavel 1972; Freeman 1980b)
4. "The effective labor supply at a particular time... does not include... employed workers who are satisfied with their job" (101-102) "Satisfactorily employed workers are almost entirely uninterested in... other companies" (85)	Interview responses	Job satisfaction is a key determinant of quit rates. (Mandelbaum 1980; Freeman 1978)

TABLE 1 (cont.)

Results on Correlates of Individual Mobility	Method	Modern Work and Partial Listing of References
5. "Even those who are dissatisfied and plan to change jobs eventually realize that depression is no time to make a change. Voluntary turn-over falls to a very low level"	Interview responses	Quit rate variations largely explained by fluctuation in season of year, industry de-mand levels, and job openings, and to a lesser degree by variations in relative wage rates. (Schultz 1971; Parsons 1973)

Results on Information in the Job Market	Method	Modern Work and Partial Listing of References
6. "Workers had only a vague and frequently inaccurate idea of wages in other plants" (45) "Workers are poorly in-formed about job oppor-tunities" (84)	Interview responses	College students have good information on wages for occupations (Freeman 1971); young people are fairly real-istic about wage ex-pectations and well-informed about the going hourly pay for the kinds of jobs open to them. (Perrella 1971)
7. "A majority (56%) of workers replied they got their information (about jobs) from friends or relatives"	Interview responses	Personal contact is the predominant method of finding out about jobs (56%); better jobs found through contacts. (Rees and Gray 1979; Granovetter 1974); persons with contacts more likely to be hired by companies. (Freeman 1981; Schmeiser 1979)

TABLE 1 (cont.)

Results on Information in the Job Market	Method	Modern Work and Partial Listing of References
8. "The only way to judge (a job) accurately is to work on it a while. After a few weeks or months of work, one can tell whether a job is worth keeping" (22)	Interview responses	Empirical analysis indicates that there is a strong impact on workers' quitting of... aspects of employment for which learning on the job is likely to be of importance. (Viscusi 1979a, 1979b). Theoretical analysis stresses role of quitting as means to obtain optimal job match. (Mortensen 1975; Jovanovic 1977)

Results on Process of Job Selection	Method	Modern Work and Partial Listing of References
9. "(The worker) evaluates jobs one at a time, on the basis of his minimum standards, instead of trying to compare each job with the full array of possible alternatives. 'good' job, he takes it without worrying over whether a 'better' job may be available somewhere else" (85)	Interview responses	Rational search strategy is to search for jobs, taking the job which meets the 'reservation wage.' (Burdett 1978; Johnson 1978; Keiffer and Neumman 1979; Lippman & McCall 1976, 1980)
10. "The usual pattern is to quit an unsatisfactory job, spend some time in unemployment, then locate a new job" (215)	Tabulation of job changers shows 58% quit without a new job lined up.[1]	Majority of all quitters experience no unemployment between jobs. (Mattila 1974)

TABLE 1 (cont.)

Results on Process of Job Selection	Method	Modern Work and Partial Listing of References
11. "Much the best results were obtained by those who had lined up a new job before leaving the old one" (215)	Cross-tabulation	Analyses show employed search more productive than unemployed search. (Mattila 1974; Black 1980; Kahn & Low 1982) --but Kahn & Low find higher return to unemployed search in more complex model.
12. Reservation wages depend on: "workers' earnings on his last job; period of unemployment... with a strong inverse relation" (p. 109) "The level of (UI) benefit payments seems clearly to influence the minimum supply price" (110)		Asking wage of workers falls modestly with length of unemployment. (Kasper 1967; Barnes 1975; Sandell 1980; Stephenson 1976); level of UI influences wage changes after unemployment (Ehrenberg & Oaxaca 1976; Grubel, Maki & Sax 1975)
13. "The main criteria which workers use in evaluating a job are money income, the physical nature of the work, the degree of independence on the job and the agreeableness of supervision, the interesting or uninteresting character of the work, and the fairness with which the worker feels he has been treated by the management" (92)	Tabulation of interview responses	Workers place high value on income and job security when judging jobs (Quinn & Staines 1978; Borjas 1979; Hamermesh 1977)
14. "The growing practice of in-plant promotion might be taken into account though the concept of an 'inside market' in which workers already in a plant compete for desirable vacancies... " (45)	Employer responses to questionnaires	Internal labor markets exist, and are important in determining wages and mobility. (Doeringer & Piore 1971; Medoff & Abraham 1981a)

TABLE 1 (cont.)

Results on Process of Job Selection	Method	Modern Work and Partial Listing of References
15. "The concept of a rising supply curve to the firm (conveys) a false impression of reality" (229)		Monopsony unimportant except in internal labor markets; only limited evidence of some monopsony power in some labor markets. (Bunting 1962; Landon & Baird 1971; Cohen 1972; Landon & Pierce 1971; Scully 1974)

Note:

1. Reynolds reports 25 percent of job-changers quit with a new job lined up; 35 percent quit without a new job lined up. I have taken 35/(25 + 35) as the estimate of quitters without a new job lined up.

In the area of correlates of individual mobility, (the first subsection of Table 1), there has been considerable modern work, in large part because of the availability of large-scale longitudinal data sets. While clothed in quite different statistical methodology from Reynolds' simple tabulations and cross-tabulations, the recent work has essentially verified each of the five points listed in the table. Seniority, whether for reasons of heterogeneity or state dependence, is generally the most powerful determinant of quit and separation rates. As a result of the reduction in turnover with seniority, it is now generally accepted that a large proportion of the U.S. labor force is relatively permanent, so that most mobility and unemployment is due to a minority. This result, it should be noted, overturns the earlier assertion (Feldstein 1973; Hall 1976) that high turnover of the work force is the key to understanding unemployment. Tenure and quit rates show the greatest mobility among the less skilled and the least among the more skilled manual workers. Not surprisingly, job satisfaction turns out to be a major determinant of quit behavior, indicating that 'the effective labor supply' does not include the satisfied, while quit rates have long been recognized as highly dependent on cyclical conditions.

With respect to job market information, while two of the three survey results given in Table 1 have found considerable support in ensuing work, Reynolds' conclusion regarding the vague and inaccurate information of workers regarding wages is open to some question. The specific issue with which he dealt, knowledge of opportunities in other plants, has not been the subject of major study, and ·is thus difficult to evaluate. On the one hand, the existence of considerable dispersion of wages by plant lends some support to the plausibility of his findings. On the other hand, comparisons of unemployed individuals' expectations of wages available in the market as a whole show striking similarity to actual wages, while my 1971 survey of college students -- motivated in large measure by Reynolds' evidence on manual workers -- found that they had quite good information about earnings among occupations. As will be developed later, of all the generalizations in The Structure, that of the poorly informed workers is (rightly or wrongly) the least accepted today, though it is important to recognize that his conclusion referred to information about specific plants whereas most recent work deals with information about the job market as a whole. Reynolds' conclusion concerning the importance of personal contacts in obtaining job market information, by contrast, has been verified in numerous surveys, with analyses of actual hiring showing that companies prefer workers with relatives or friends in the firm. Finally, both empirical analyses and diverse models of workers' acquisition of information, most notably Viscusi's Bayesian search models, have put great stress on the importance of actually trying a job in order to obtain accurate information about it.

On the basis of the worker interviews, Reynolds reached several conclusions regarding the process of job selection. He pointed out that workers choose among jobs by comparing each to a "minimum standard". While Reynolds seemed to believe that this might not be rational, ensuing models of rational search have shown that it is in fact an appropriate search strategy: workers compare offers to their reservation wage, accepting the first job with wages above the reservation level. Reynolds' conclusions regarding the importance of unemployment in the search procedure, however, have not been supported by ensuing work, possibly because of differences between the Depression-scarred generation he studied and current workers. Modern studies indicate that Reynolds' "typical sequence" of job mobility, from employment to unemployment to a new job, is in fact less prevalent than job changing from one employer to another. Recent work also finds unemployment to have a _much_ smaller impact on reservation wages than Reynolds obtained with his sample, where "for people unemployed less than three months, the median expected wage (was) over 90 percent of the last previous wage. For people unemployed three to six months, the figure dropped to 60 percent" (109).

On the other hand, several studies have found that, consistent with Reynolds, workers who have a job lined up beforehand are likely to do better than those who do not, although the possibility that this pattern reflects selectivity has been raised by Kahn and Low (1982). Finally, studies of job satisfaction have tended to yield results of a comparable nature to Reynolds' regarding the importance of money income and various nonpecuniary factors in evaluation jobs.

Turning to institutional and firm aspects of mobility, Reynolds' conclusions regarding the importance of internal labor markets and monopsony in the labor market have been accepted in succeeding work, though Viscusi (1980) has noted that the internal market itself can be modelled in terms of a rising supply curve to a firm.

Overall, Reynolds' findings on patterns of labor mobility, like those of other early scholars in the area, are generally supported by modern investigators, the primary exception relating to worker knowledge of alternatives.

With respect to the findings of The Structure of Labor Markets on wages, much of the book focused on the pattern of wages or changes in wages by plant, as opposed to industry, occupation, or individuals. Due to the absence of readily available longitudinal or other data sets on plant-level wages, the amount of work against which to compare Reynolds' findings is small. Accordingly, in Table 2, I first present conclusions pertaining to other aspects of the wage determination process, although they were not the primary focus of The Structure. Certainly the most striking conclusion, in light of ensuing research, is Reynolds' denial of the existence of what has come to be called a stable Phillips curve. Reynolds was not alone, it should be stressed, in claiming that any relation between unemployment and wage changes was frail and indirect at best. I vividly remember John Dunlop pounding the table against the Phillips curve in a graduate labor economics course: he and Reynolds and others who based their assessment on firsthand knowledge of wage setting came away with a very different picture of the role of unemployment than that given by 1960s macro-economists enamored of the Phillips curve. Ensuing developments and research have supported their assessment. On the other hand, efforts to measure the effect of "ability to pay" factors which Reynolds, among others, suggested were possible major determinants of changes in wages have not yielded strong results in terms of the impact of the variables on wage changes.

The Structure reached two tentative conclusions regarding compensating differentials which have been supported in ensuing work. At a gross level, fringes and nonwage conditions of work have been

TABLE 2

Structure of Labor Markets Findings
on Wage Determination

Results	Method	Modern Work and Partial Listing of References
1. "The level of unemployment has nothing directly to do with the time at which wage increases begin or with the need of advance; this is determined mainly by the commodity pricing mechanism" (231)	Interviews	The "Phillips curve" relating wage changes to unemployment is not stable over time. Price changes are a critical determinant of many wage changes. (Wachter 1976; Eckstein 1968; Medoff & Abraham 1981a)
2. "Among factors which influence rates of change is 'ability to pay' in terms of sales or profits"	Interviews	Wage changes are not very sensitive to changes in demand or profitability. (Medoff & Fay 1983)
3. "There is a slight positive relation between the total amount of fringe benefits provided and the wage level of plant" (202-203)	Rank correlation	The income elasticity of demand for fringes dominates tradeoff of fringes for wages in the fringe-wage relation. (Duncan 1976; Freeman 1981; Goldstein & Pauly 1976; Leigh 1979; Solnick 1978; Viscusi 1980)
4. "Nonwage terms of employment thus tend to accentuate wage differentials rather than to offset them" (222)	Plant visits	It is difficult to find evidence of strong compensatory differentials in the labor market (Brown 1980)
5. "There is, in any area, a range or band of feasible wage levels, with high-wage companies and low-wage companies in an area hierarchy"	Data on company wages (Tables 24-27)	Large plants pay higher wages; dispersion of wages is considerable in local markets. (Masters 1969; Dunlop 1957)
6. "High-wage plants tend to remain high-wage over time"	Plant data	Little study

generally found to be positively related (fringes, some conditions) or perhaps unrelated (other conditions) to wage levels. Finer efforts to obtain compensatory differentials through more detailed controls of individual worker earnings capacity have, in Brown's (1980) assessment of studies, also yielded scant support for compensating factors as a major determinant of wage dispersion.

Points 5 and 6 in Table 2 focus on plant-level wage determinations, with which The Structure is primarily concerned. More recent research shows considerable dispersion among plants, with larger plants having higher wages, but has not dealt with issues of persistence of a plant's position in a wage structure over time or with determinants and effects of its position in the local labor market wage structure.

Table 3 turns to the findings of The Structure of Labor Markets with respect to collective bargaining. As can be seen, each of the five propositions which I have garnered from The Structure of Labor Markets has been supported in ensuing research. There is, however, an interesting aspect to these results, for in two of the areas Reynolds seemed to have changed his mind in light of some ensuing work. In the 6th edition of his textbook he wrote: "...it is questionable whether collective bargaining has produced a major change in the pattern of labor turnover" (1974, 568), and that "...the specific influence of unionism (on fringes) is hard to determine" (1974, 216-17). These apparent reversals of his views regarding the impact of unions on turnover (points 2 and 3 in Table 3) and on fringes (point 4) resulted from cross-sectional industry regressions which found either statistically insignificant or widely divergent coefficients on unionism (in the case of quits, the results were those of Burton and Parker (1969), Stoikov and Raimon (1958), and Pencavel (1970); in the case of fringes, the results were those of Rice (1966). Ensuing work with data tapes on thousands of individuals and establishments have, however, supported Reynolds' Structure findings. In this case, the interviews appear to have yielded more reliable results than efforts to infer union effects from cross-industry regressions, as was common in the 1960s. The lesson is that we should be less willing to surrender conclusions based on case analyses and interviews to aggregative regression analyses than was Reynolds. Reynolds' The Structure of Labor Markets appears to be closer to reality than was Reynolds in his textbook, relying on the 1960s relatively aggregative regressions.

One of the central purposes of Reynolds' analysis was to "form a reasoned judgment on the relation between mobility and the wage structure" (1951, 4). His specific conclusions regarding this relation are some of the prime ingredients in his overall view of the labor market, and in particular of what may be taken to be the chief finding of the book, that "all things considered, the processes of wage determination and labor mobility seem to be much less intimately related than one might expect a priori" (248).

Table 4 summarizes the central empirical generalizations which lead to this conclusion, as well as one interesting side point regarding the elasticity of demand for labor. In part because of the simultaneity problems involved in distinguishing demand and supply shifts (recognized by Reynolds, 223), evaluating the relation between wage and employment movements in terms of the underlying structural

TABLE 3

Comparison of the Structure of Labor Markets Findings
on Effects of Collective Bargaining with Later Empirical Findings

Results	Method	Modern Work and Partial Listing of References
1. Unionized plants have greater reliance on seniority (54)	Interview	Seniority independent of productivity is rewarded substantially more in promotion decisions among union members than among otherwise comparable nonunion employees. (Halasz 1980; Medoff & Abraham 1981b; Yanker 1980)
2. Unionized plants rely extensively on temporary layoffs, recalling workers by seniority (55)	Interview	There is much more cyclical labor adjustment through temporary layoffs in unionized manufacturing firms than in otherwise comparable firms that are nonunion. (Blau & Kahn 1981; Medoff 1979) Terminations are more likely to be on a last-in-first-out basis among union employees, ceteris paribus. (Blau & Kahn 1981; Medoff & Abraham 1981b)
3. Unionism creates 'walls around enterprises,' with lower quits and greater tenure (55, 148). Unions reduce interplant mobility in part through grievance procedures (254)	Cross-tabulations	The quit rate is much lower for unionized workers than for similar workers who are nonunion (Blau & Kahn 1981; Block 1978; Farber, OLS results, 1980; Freeman 1976, 1980a, 1980b; Kahn 1977; Leigh 1979)

TABLE 3 (cont.)

Results	Method	Modern Work and Partial Listing of References
4. Fringes are higher the higher the wages, and are greater in union than in nonunion settings	Simple data analysis	All else the same, the union/nonunion hourly fringe differential is between 20% and 30%. The fringe share of compensation is higher at a given level of compensation. (Duncan 1976; Freeman 1981; Goldstein & Pauly 1976; Leigh 1979; Solnick 1978; Viscusi 1980)
5. Union wage settlements tend to follow bargaining patterns, with, however, exceptions depending on local plant economic conditions (172-173)	Simple data analysis	(Greenberg 1968; Levinson 1960; Seltzer 1961; Alexander 1961)

TABLE 4

Findings on the Interrelation
Between Wages and Employment

Results	Method	Modern Work and Partial Listing of References
1. "Inter-plant movement typically involves a reduction in the workers' earnings" (242)	Workers reports on changes (215)	Young workers gain from mobility; older workers roughly hold their own; gains/losses depend on the reason for the change. (Borjas & Rosen 1980; Bartel & Borjas 1978)
2. "There was virtually no correlation between the rate of wage increase and the rate of change of employment in individual companies" (223) "The view that workers can be redistributed only by changes in wages seems to be mistaken... (what matters is) availability of jobs" (239) "Adaptation of labor supplies follows and is induced by changes in demand rather than the reverse" (239)	Rank correlation	Industry wage and employment changes only slightly related. (O.E.C.D. 1966; Freeman 1980c; Ulman 1965) Labor supply curves by industry are relatively elastic; variations of changes in employment exceeds variation in changes in wages. (Implicit in Salter 1966; Kendrick 1961; Freeman 1980)
3. "Wage differentials influence the volume of migration via their effect on labor demand," not labor supply: people do not "prefer to be unemployed in a high-wage area rather than a low-wage area"	Observation	Primary factor inducing geographic mobility is wages, not unemployment. (Greenwood 1975) There is a tradeoff between area wages and unemployment. (Hall 1970; Marston 1980, 1981; Reza 1978; Browne 1978; Behman 1978)

TABLE 4 (cont.)

Results	Method	Modern Work and Partial Listing of References
4. "Movement and potential movement of labor seems inadequate to prevent large and persistent differences in aggregate job attractiveness" (246)	Factory visits	There are "good" and "bad" jobs; compensating differentials do not equate the value of jobs. (Brown 1980; Doeringer and Piore 1971; Bluestone et. al. 1973)
5. "The elasticity of demand for labor rests mainly on the shiftability of consumer purchases rather than on the shiftability of production techniques" (182)	Observation	Elasticity of substitution between labor and capital may be small. (Hamermesh 1976; Clark & Freeman 1980)

forces at work is difficult, and it is in this area where some of Reynolds' conclusions, though not his major findings, have been overturned in succeeding work. On the basis of evidence of workers reporting gross weekly earnings on new jobs compared to their previous jobs, Reynolds concluded that individual mobility is generally associated with retrogression rather than progression in earnings. This may have been an artifact of the period studied or the group; modern work dealing with wage changes and mobility show gains for young workers, roughly no change for older male workers, but with noticeable differences depending on the reason for change. In addition, at least one model (Borjas and Rosen 1980) suggests that workers who change do better than they would have by staying on their job. While some of the differences between Reynolds and more recent work may result from his concentration on manual workers as opposed to the entire economy, it is likely that his generalization about the results of mobility exaggerate the frequency of lower earnings when workers change employment. On the other hand, Reynolds' primary conclusion regarding the relation between plant wage changes and employment changes, and thus between the structure of wages and mobility, has been confirmed in diverse studies of industries (though not of plants, because of the lack of plant analyses). Where modern labor economics diverges from Reynolds is in the interpretation of the lack of a wage and employment change relation: in contrast to his view that the lack of a relation indicates a failure of competitive theory, at least some modern work would regard it as the result of a competitive labor market in which firms face the neoclassical, infinitely elastic, labor supply curve and thus of rational response rather than irrational supply behavior. The point is that a lack of correlation between changes in wages and in employment (simultaneity demand considerations aside) is consistent with standard theory of the competitive firm. The competitive interpretation, however, is inconsistent with Reynolds' major point: that whatever mobility there is on the supply side is insufficient to eliminate plant wage differentials between apparently similar workers and jobs. Such differentials are inconsistent with the standard competitive market theory, a point which Segal (1982) has emphasized and to which we return later.

The one area in which Reynolds' conclusions appear to have been totally reversed relates to the effect of wage levels and unemployment on geographic mobility. A major finding of geographic mobility studies is that migration responds to wages, not to unemployment, contrary to Reynolds; and recent work sparked by Hall (1980) has found a positive compensating relation between area wages and unemployment. It is noteworthy that Reynolds' statements here are not directly based on the New Haven study.

A large literature relating to secondary labor markets provides considerable support for Reynolds' conclusion that mobility does not prevent large and persistent differences in job attractiveness (point 4 in Table 4). While there has been considerable debate between dual labor market analysts and standard economists over the meaning of the differences between 'good' and 'bad' jobs, it is difficult to gainsay the proposition that mobility has failed to equalize the attractiveness of jobs to a given set of workers.

The final point on Table 4 relates to what is really a side comment by Reynolds regarding labor demand. Like others, he expressed the belief that the elasticity of substitution among outputs is greater than the elasticity of substitution among inputs. Due to a lack of estimates of the elasticities of demand for goods by sector this suggestion has not been examined in the literature, though many economists regard it as a reasonable statement. In any case, studies of demand elasticities which operate through capital-labor substitution tend to find relatively modest responses.

In sum, a review of the specific findings of Reynolds with respect to mobility, wage determination, collective bargaining, and the interrelation between mobility and wages shows that, with some exceptions, his empirical findings have correctly captured labor market realities. Lack of sophisticated techniques and computer facilities did not hinder The Structure of Labor Markets in this regard.

III. AN OVERALL ASSESSMENT[2]

Part II of The Structure of Labor Markets uses the specific empirical findings just reviewed to evaluate the strengths and weaknesses of standard, competitive labor market theory. It also deals with the problem of judging the impact of collective bargaining (and by implication other noncompetitive factors) on resource allocation.

Reynolds' chief conclusion is that the competitive factors linking wage determination and labor mobility are sufficiently "weaker and less effective (in labor markets) than they are in most commodity markets" (223). As a result he suggests: substantial caution in application of competitive models to the labor market; need for detailed knowledge in particular cases; and ultimately a revision of labor market theory to take account of divergencies between models and reality.

Assertions that the competitive market model is insufficient in some respects for analysis of actual labor markets have, of course, a long and honorable history in economic thought, stretching back -- as Reynolds notes -- to Marshall and Pigou, among others. Reynolds' conclusions in this respect can be summarized in three related generalizations from the study:

1. While "within limits set by his knowledge and the objective characteristics of the market, the worker pursues a self-interested course...the limits on workers' knowledge and freedom of choice are...formidable in the extreme" (213). As a result, Reynolds locates actual worker behavior closer to the pole in which they "do not make a reasonably informed and systematic choice of jobs...[than]...the pole of perfect economic calculation" (210).

2. However the supply side operates, it sets "surprisingly wide" limits to wage differentials, with the result that "the wage structure is shaped mainly by variation in companies' ability to pay and by variations in the degree to which management chooses (or is forced by union pressure) to pay as much as it can" (248) rather than by "a strong tendency to set wages barely sufficient to attract an adequate labor supply" (260).

3. Because of the divergence between actual wage structures and the wages of competitive equilibrium, "the effects of collective bargaining (and other labor market institutions) can be discovered only by patient investigation of concrete situations" (256). "Whether the results of collective bargaining are better or worse than those of unilateral wage administration by employers...is basically a problem for empirical study" (p. 260).

I differentiate between the initial two propositions because, like many other readers of the book, I have tended to confuse them, believing (erroneously) that modern work on the labor supply decision, stressing responsiveness and rationality of supply, contradicts the main thrust of Reynolds' book when in fact it says nothing about the more important second proposition.

Taking Reynolds' depiction of the supply side of the market first, the review of specific propositions in Part I shows that modern work has corroborated most of Reynolds' specific findings on individual mobility and job selection. However, as noted, modern labor economics puts quite a different interpretation on several results and has obtained results more consistent with rational optimizing models in other areas. Perhaps most importantly, modern analyses of supply which have focused on labor supply decisions regarding human capital investment, labor participation, and related behavior find greater evidence of supply behavior than Reynolds found for plant mobility. On the other hand, one of Reynolds' major points on the supply side -- the existence of workers having a "firm attachment to their present employer" and thus being out of the external labor market (210) -- finds considerable support in modern work. The concepts of specific human capital, idiosyncratic or team productivity, and exit-voice have all sought, in different ways, to bring the "permanently" attached worker and internal labor markets into the corpus of our theory.

While one may have doubts about the success of the modern effort to explain labor supply behavior in terms of rational maximizing man, it is clear that modern labor economics diverges most from the analysis of The Structure in terms of its assessment of supply behavior as a major -- perhaps the major -- cause for divergencies between the competitive model and reality.

The modern perspective on labor supply does not, however, detract from Reynolds' second proposition regarding the apparently small impact of supply on the wage structure, and the importance of employer wage policy in wage determination. It is this proposition, I want to stress, that unites many of the "institutional labor economists" from Ely to Reynolds, Meyers, Dunlop, Kerr, Schultz and their generation to current institutionally oriented specialists in the field, and it is unaffected by one's belief regarding highly rationl supply behavior. (See Segal 1982 for a detailed argument in this regard). The same facts which Reynolds and his peers cited from their data on the "surprisingly wide" wage structure in markets are found today: significant dispersion in wages among plants; seniority wage policies independent of personal productivity within plants (Medoff and Abraham 1981b); and the modest influence of unemployment on wage-setting in the economy as a whole. Efforts to explain differences in terms of human capital (Mincer 1974) or in terms of search behavior (Stigler 1961) have narrowed the band some, but have not dented Reynolds' conclusion. Efforts to explain firm wage policies in terms of implicit contracts, while ingenious, yield results of questionable value due to their sensitivity to arbitrary untested assumptions (see J. Green and C. Kahn for a convincing, implicit contract model which yields results contradictory to those of previous models by altering assumptions) and fail to address the question raised by Reynolds and other "post-institutional labor economists" regarding the difference in wage levels among firms in the same market. In short, in the interim since The Structure was published we have developed a better understanding of labor supply and of the role of supply side investment in skills in wage determination without increasing our knowledge of employer wage policies and thus of the entire wage setting process. As Segal puts it, "while a great deal has been learned from recent studies of supply, the work of the "post-institutionalists [to which Reynolds was a major contributor] points toward a potential payoff in the explanation of the demand side...and in a comprehensive analysis of the factors that shape managerial behavior and policies" (1982, 54).

Finally, it should be noted that Reynolds' conclusion regarding the independence of the wage structure from labor supply provides the key to understanding his views and those of his peers towards labor unions. In contrast to economists whose views of the labor market are based on the belief that the competitive model is the world, Reynolds stressed the need for empirical study. In this regard, he made modern "second best" arguments regarding the difficulty of judging union (or other) wage structures when they are compared to actual, rather than theoretical, optimal structures (257-260), and contrasted "administrative equalization of job attractiveness" through unionism to "equalization through the painful and uncertain process of mobility" (260). Current work on trade union impacts by a wide variety of economists summarized by Freeman and Medoff (1981) highlight modern resurgence of this perspective, with results that are in line with those given in The Structure and in the work of other scholars in Reynolds' generation.

In sum, reading The Structure of Labor Markets thirty years after publication (is this a record for a delay in a review?) suggests that more often than not the book was on target in its picture of the labor market, despite the lack of technical sophistication. Most specific findings have been corroborated in succeeding work; the picture of labor supply in the book while generally valid for the issues considered has, however, been reinterpreted and developed in the direction of rational maximizing models, without altering the findings about the essential passivity of supply in wage determination. May our own work look as good thirty years hence.

FOOTNOTES

I have benefitted from discussions with Martin Segal and the comments of Mark Leiserson, and from reading Martin Segal's paper (1982), which analyzes the work of the school of labor economics to which Lloyd Reynolds was a major contributor.

2. I have benefitted here by discussions with Martin Segal and by reading his 1982 paper.

BIBLIOGRAPHY

Akerlof, G. A., B. G. M. Main. 1980. Unemployment spells and unemployment experience. *Amer. Econ. Rev.*, 70(5)(December): 885-93.

Alexander, K. 1961. Market practices and collective bargaining in automotive parts. *J. of Pol. Econ.*, 69(1)(February): 15-29.

Barnes, W.F. 1975. Job search models, the duration of unemployment, and the asking wage: some empirical evidence. *J. of Human Resources*, (Spring).

Barron, J., S. McCafferty. 1977. Job search, labor supply and the quit decision. *Amer. Econ. Rev.*, 67 (September): 683-91.

Bartel, A. P., G. J. Borjas. 1978. Wage growth and job turnover: an empirical analysis. NBER working paper No. 259, (October).

Behman, S. 1978. Interstate differentials in wages and unemployment. *Indust. Relations*, 17(May): 168-88.

Black, M. 1980. Pecuniary implications of on-the-job search and quit activity. *The Rev. of Econ. and Statistics*, 62(May): 222-29.

Blau, F. D., L. M. Kahn. 1981. The exit voice tradeoff in the labor market: some additional evidence. (mimeo).

Block, R. 1978. The impact of seniority provisions on the manufacturing quit rate. *Indust. and Labor Relations Rev.*, 31(July): 474-88.

Bluestone, B. W. M. Murphy, M. Stevenson. 1973. Low wages and the working poor. Policy papers in human resources and industrial relations, 22. Ann Arbor, Michigan: The Institute of Labor and Industrial Relations, The U. of Michigan - Wayne State U.

Borjas, G. J. 1979. Job satisfaction, wages and unions. *J. of Human Resources*, (Winter).

_____, 1981. Job mobility and earnings over the life cycle. *Indust. and Labor Relations Rev.*, (April): 365-76.

Borjas, G. J., S. Rosen. 1980. Income prospects and job mobility of younger men. *Research in Labor Econ.*, 3: 159-181.

Borjas, G. J., A. P. Bartel. 1977. Middle-age job mobility: its determinants and consequences. In *Men in the pre-retirement years*, ed. S. Wolfbein, 39-97. Temple U. Press.

Brown, C. 1980. Equalizing differences in the labor market. *Quart. J. of Econ.*, (February): 113-34.

Brown, D. 1962. Expected ability to pay and the inter-industry wage structure in manufacturing. *Indust. and Labor Relations Rev.*, 16(October): 45-62.

Browne, L. E. 1978. Regional unemployment rates -- why are they so different? *New England Econ. Rev.*, (November/December): 35-53.

Bunting, R. 1962. *Employer concentration in local labor markets.* Chapel Hill, NC: U. of North Carolina Press.

Burdett, K. 1978. A theory of employee job search and quit rates. *Amer. Econ. Rev.* 68(March): 212-20.

Burton, J., J. Parker. 1969. Inter-industry variation in voluntary labor mobility. *Indust. and Labor Relations Rev.*, (January): 199-216.

Clark, K., R. Freeman. 1980. How elastic is the demand for labor? *Rev. of Econ. and Statistics*, *47(4)*.

_____, L. Summers. 1979. Labor market dynamics and unemployment: a reconsideration. *Brookings papers on economic activity.* (1): 13-60.

Cohen, H. 1972. Monopsony and discriminating monopsony in the nursing market. *Applied Econ.*, 4(March): 39-48.

Doeringer, L., M. Piore. 1971. *Internal labor markets and manpower analysis.* Heath-Lexington.

Duncan, G. J. 1976. Earnings functions and nonpecuniary benefits. *J. of Human Resources*, 11(Fall): 462-83

Dunlop, J. T. 1957. The task of contemporary wage theory. In *New concepts in wage determination*, ed. G. W. Taylor, F. E. Pierson, 135-136. New York: McGraw-Hill Book Company.

Eckstein, O. 1968. Money wage determination revisited. *Rev. of Econ. Stud.*, 35(April): 133-43.

Ehrenberg, R., R. Oaxaca. 1976. Unemployment insurance, the duration of unemployment, and subsequent wage growth. *Amer. Econ. Rev.*, 66(5) (December).

Farber, H. 1980. Unionism, labor turnover and wages of young men. *Research in Labor Econ.*, 3: 33-53.

Feldstein, M. 1973. The economics of the new unemployment. *Public Interest*, 33 (Fall).

Freeman, R. B. 1971. *The labor market for college trained manpower.* Cambridge, Mass.: Harvard U. Press.

_____, 1978. Job satisfaction as an economic variable. *Amer. Econ. Rev.*, 68(2)(May): 135-41.

_____, 1980a. The exit-voice tradeoff in the labor market: unionism, job tenure, quits and separations. *Quart. J. of Econ.*, 94(4)(June).

_____, 1980b. The effect of unionism on worker attachment to firms. *J. of Labor Research*, 1(1)(Spring).

_____, 1980c. An empirical analysis of the fixed coefficient 'manpower requirements' model, 1960-1970. *J. of Human Resources*, 15(2)(Spring): 176-99.

_____, 1981. Changing market for young persons: who gets hired? A case study of the market for youth. D.O.L. Final Report. Grant #21-25-78-19.

Freeman, R. B., J. Medoff. 1981. The impact of collective bargaining: illusion or reality. In *U.S. industrial relations 1950-1980: a critical assessment*, ed. J. Stieber, R. B. McKersie, D. Quinn Mills, 47-97. Bloomington, Ill.: Pantagraph Printing.

Goldstein, G., M. Pauly. 1976. Group health insurance as a local public good. In *The role of health insurance in the health services sector*. Ed. R. Rosett, 73-110. New York: National Bureau of Economic Research.

Granovetter, M. S. 1974. *Getting a job: a study of contacts and careers*. Harvard U. Press.

Green, J., C. Kahn. Forthcoming. Wage-employment contracts. *Quart. J. of Econ*. NBER working paper no. 675.

Greenberg, D. 1968. Deviations from wage-fringe standards. *Indust. and Labor Relations Rev.*, 22(2)(January): 197-209.

Greenwood. 1975. Research in internal migration in the U.S.: a survey. *J. of Econ. Lit.*, (June): 397-433.

Gronau, R. 1971. Information and frictional unemployment. *Amer. Econ. Rev.*, (June).

Grubel, H., D. Maki, S. Sax. 1975. Real and insurance induced unemployment in Canada. *Canadian J. of Econ.*, 8(May): 174-91.

Halasz, P. 1980. What lies behind the slope of the age-earnings profile. Senior honors thesis, Harvard College.

Hall, R. E. 1970. Why is the unemployment rate so high at full employment? *Brookings papers on economic activity*. (3).

_____, 1976. Turnover in the labor force. *Brookings papers on economic activity*. (3): 709-64.

_____, 1980. The importance of lifetime jobs in the U.S. economy. NBER working paper no. 560. (October).

Hamermesh, D. S. 1976. Econometric studies of labor research and their application to policy analysis. *J. of Human Resources*, (Fall): 507-28.

_____, 1977. Economics of job satisfaction and worker alienation. In *Essays in labor market and population analysis*, ed. O. Ashenfelter, W. Oates. Princeton: Princeton U. Press.

Haworth, C., D. Rasmussen. 1971. Human capital and inter-industry wages in manufacturing. *Rev. of Econ. and Statistics*, 53(November): 376-79.

Johnson, W. 1978. A theory of job shopping. *Quart. J. of Econ.*, 92(May): 261-78.

Jovanovic, B. 1977. Theory of turnover in continuous time. Columbia University discussion paper.

Jovanovic, B., J. Mincer. 1978. Labor mobility and wages. (unpublished paper) Columbia University.

Kahn, L. M. 1977. Union impact: a reduced form approach. *The Rev. of Econ. and Statistics*, 59(November): 503-7.

Kahn, L. M., S. A. Low. 1982. The relative effects of employed and unemployed job search. *Rev. of Econ. and Statistics*, 64(May): 234-41.

Kasper, H. 1967. The asking wage of labor and the duration of unemployment. *Rev. of Econ. and Statistics*, 49(May): 165-72.

Keiffer, N., G. Neumman. 1979. An empirical job search model, with a test of a constant reservation wage hypothesis. *J. of Pol. Econ.*, 87(1) (February): 89-107.

Kendrick, J. 1961. *Productivity trends in the U.S.* New York: National Bureau of Economic Research.

Landon, J., R. Baird. 1971. Monopsony in the market for public school teachers. *Amer. Econ. Rev.*, (December): 966-71.

Landon, J., W. Pierce. 1971. Discrimination, monopsony and union power in the building trades: a cross-sectional analysis. IRRA Proceedings. (December): 254-261.

Leigh, D. E. 1978. Racial discrimination and labor unions: evidence from the NLS sample of middle-aged men. *J. of Human Resources*, 13(Fall): 568-77.

_____, 1979. Unions and nonwage racial discrimination. *Indust. and Labor Relations Rev.* 32(July): 439-50.

Levinson, H. M. 1960. Pattern bargaining: a case study of the automobile workers. *Quart. J. of Econ.*, 74(2)(May): 296-317.

Lippman, S. A., J. J. McCall. 1976. The economics of job search: a survey. *Econ. Inquiry*, 14(3)(September): 155-189.

_____, 1980. *Studies in the economics of search.* Amsterdam and New York: North Holland.

Mandelbaum, D. 1980. Undergraduate thesis, Harvard University.

Marston, S. T. 1980. Anatomy of persistent local unemployment. Draft prepared for National commission for employment policy conference (October).

_____, 1981. Two views of the geographic distribution of unemployment. Working paper no. 255 for the U.S. National Commission for Employment Policy. (draft) Cornell U.

Masters, S. 1969. An inter-industry analysis of wages and plant size. *Rev. of Econ. and Statistics*, 51(August): 341-45.

Mattila, J. P. 1974. Job quitting and frictional unemployment. *Amer. Econ. Rev.*, 64(1)(March): 235-39.

Medoff, J. L. 1979. Layoffs and alternatives under trade unions in United States manufacturing. *Amer. Econ. Rev.*, 69(3)(June): 380-95.

Medoff, J. L., K. G. Abraham. 1980. Experience, performance, and earnings. *Quart. J. of Econ.*, 95(December): 703-36.

_____. 1981a. Unemployment, unsatisfied demand for labor, and compensation growth in the U.S., 1956-1980. HIER #848.

_____. 1981b. The role of seniority at U.S. work places: a report on some new evidence. (Mimeographed).

_____. 1981c. Are those paid more really more productive? The case of experience. *J. of Human Resources*, (Spring): 186-216.

Medoff, J. L., J. A. Fay. 1983. Cyclical labor adjustment in U.S. manufacturing. (Mimeographed).

Mincer, J. 1974. *Schooling, experience, and earnings.* New York: National Bureau of Economic Research.

Mortensen, D. 1975. The turnover implications of learning about attributes on the job. (discussion paper) Northwestern U.

O.E.C.D. 1966. *Wages and labor mobility.* Paris.

Parsons, D. 1979. Models of labor market turnover. *Research in Labor Econ.*, ed. R. Ehrenberg. Greenwich, CT: JAI Press.

_____, 1972. Specific human capital: an application to quit rates and layoff rates. *J. of Political Econ.*, 80(November/December): 1120-43.

_____, 1973. Quit rates over time: a search and information approach. *Amer. Econ. Rev.*, 63(3)(June): 390-401.

Pencavel, J. 1972. Wages, specific training and labor turnover in U.S. manufacturing industries. *Internat. Econ. Rev.*, 13(February): 53-64.

_____, 1970. *An analysis of the quit rate in American manufacturing industry*. Princeton: Princeton U. Press.

Perrella, U. C. 1971. Young workers and their earnings. *Monthly Labor Rev.*, (July): 3-11.

Peterson, D. 1972. Economics of information and job search: another view. *Quart. J. of Econ.*, 86(February): 127-31.

Phelps, E. 1968. Money-wage dynamics and the labor-market equilibrium. *J. of Political Econ.*, (July/August): 678-711.

Quinn, R., G. Staines. 1978. *The 1977 quality of employment survey*. U. of Michigan.

Rees, A., W. Gray. 1979. Family effects in youth employment. NBER working paper no. 396. Cambridge, MA: National Bureau of Economic Research. (October).

Reynolds, L. G. 1951. *The structure of labor markets*. New York: Harper & Bros.

_____, 1974. *Labor economics and labor relations*. New York: Prentice-Hall. (Sixth Edition).

Reza, A. M. 1978. Geographical differences in earnings and unemployment rates. *Rev. of Econ. and Statistics*, 60: 201-208.

Rice, R. 1966. Skill, earnings and the growth of wage-supplements. *Amer. Econ. Rev.*, 54(2)(May): 583-93.

Salter, W. E. G. 1966. *Productivity and technological change*. Cambridge U. Press.

Sandell, S. H. 1980. Job search by unemployed women: determinants of the asking wage. *Indust. and Labor Relations Rev.*, 33(3)(April): 368-78.

Schmeiser, J. M. 1979. A comparison of hiring and performance in a low wage labor market. Harvard senior honors thesis.

Schultz, C. L. 1971. Has the Phillips curve shifted? Some additional evidence. *Brookings papers on economic activity.* (2): 452-67.

Scully, G. W. 1974. Pay and performance in professional baseball. *Amer. Econ. Rev.* 64(December): 915-30.

Segal, M. 1982. Post-institutionalism in labor economics: the forties and fifties revisited. Hanley papers in economics. Dartmouth College. (January).

Seltzer, G. 1961. The united steelworkers and unionwide bargaining. *Monthly Labor Rev.*, 84(2)(February): 129-36.

Solnick, L. 1978. Unionism and fringe benefit expenditures. *Indust. Relations*, 17(February): 102-07.

Stephenson, S. 1976. The economics of youth job search behavior. *Rev. of Econ. and statistics*, 58(February): 104-11.

Stigler, G. J. 1961. The economics of information. *J. of Political Econ.*, (June).

Stoikov, V., R. Raimon. 1958. Determinants of the differences in quit rates among industries. *Amer. Econ. Rev.*, (December): 1238-98.

Ulman, L. 1965. Labor mobility and the industrial wage structure in the post-war United States. *Quart. J. of Econ.*, 67(February): 73-97.

Viscusi, W. K. 1980. Labor market structure and the welfare implications of the quality of work. *J. of Labor Research*, 1(1).

_____, 1979a. *Employment hazards: an investigation of market performance.* Cambridge: Harvard U. Press.

_____, 1979b. Job hazards and worker quit rates: an analysis of adaptive worker behavior. *Internat. Econ. Rev.*; 20: 29-58.

Wachter, M. 1976. The changing cyclical responsiveness of wage inflation. *British J. of Indust. Relations*, 1:115-68.

Yanker, R. H. 1980. Productivity versus seniority: what is the determining factor in regard to wages and promotion? Senior honors thesis, Harvard College.

11

Inflation and the Wage-Price Issue: A Reappraisal

Jesse Markham

I. INTRODUCTION

For the better part of the decade just past, opinion polls have identified inflation as the primary public concern. Within the economics profession, generally attuned to public concerns considered to fall in its special area of expertise, enormous intellectual resources have been allocated to analyses of its causes, its cures, and its consequences. The intensity of the efforts -- not to mention the semantic creativity of their respective authors -- is measured in the titles and the voluminous outpourings of published treatises. The 1979 Proceedings of the Academy of Political Science equated our ability to solve the inflation problem with our national survival (Walton 1979); in his highly readable book The Anxious Economy, designed for the noneconomist, Ezra Solomon (1976) ranked inflation at the head of the list of America's anxieties; and in his last written work before his untimely death in 1980, the highly respected Arthur Okun (1980) urged upon all members of society to unite against inflation and subordinate their short-term interests to the long-run interests of restoring the vitality and stability of the American economy. The list of such recent treatises on inflation could be greatly expanded (See especially A. M. Okun and G. L. Perry 1978; and Center for the Study of American Business 1979).

To be sure, the restrained monetary policy pursued by the Federal Reserve Bank since Okun issued this appeal in 1980 seems to have significantly slowed down the rate of increase in prices compared to those experienced over the period from 1973 to 1981. However, for several reasons, this can scarcely be viewed as grounds for high optimism for the future. The reduction in the inflation rate has been accompanied by dramatic increases in unemployment and unused plant capacity, following a pattern similar to that of 1975, when a slowdown in the growth of money stocks (M1-A) to 4.6 percent was accompanied by an increase in the unemployment rate to 8.5 percent. Futhermore, even a modest economic recovery will very likely reignite inflationary pressures in view of the unprecedented federal deficits projected well into the 1980s.[1] The forecasts summarized in Table 1 confirm that inflation is generally held to be an enduring economic problem, not likely to disappear in the foreseeable future.

TABLE 1
Various Inflation Rate Forecasts   1981-1984
  (Percent Change from Previous Year)

	1981	1982	1983	1984
Carter Administration	12.2	9.4	8.2	7.2
Data Resources, Inc.	11.3	9.6	8.9	8.2
Merrill Lynch Economics, Inc.	9.4	7.0	6.5	6.0
Wharton Econometric Forecasting Associates	12.0	9.8	9.1	NA
Chase Econometrics	11.2	8.9	8.4	NA

Source: The New York Times, Section 4, p. 1, February 8, 1981.

TABLE 2
Changes in Hourly Earnings, Productivity, Prices, and Profit Margins
  in the United States, 1950-1967 and 1968-1980
  (Percent)

	Annual Average Percent Change	
	1950-1967	1968-1980
Hourly Earnings (a)	4.1	7.3
Productivity per Worker	2.6	1.3
Hourly Labor Costs	1.5	6.0
Consumer Price Index	1.9	6.4
Profits Margins (Annual Averages for Period)	4.9	4.9

Note: (a) Hourly earnings adjusted for overtime and interindustry
          employment shifts.

Sources: Profits margins from U.S. Federal Trade Commission.
         Other data from U.S. Department of Labor, Bureau of
         Labor Statistics, as reproduced in The Economic Report
         of the President, January 1981, Appendix B.

While this essay does not presume to prescribe a remedy for this malaise, it does propose to explore in depth the extent to which the root cause of the post-1967, persistent inflation is of the structural variety; that is, whether the unresponsiveness of prices and wages to the pressures of demand and supply, attributable to the noncompetitive structure of product and labor markets, has accounted for a significant portion of the upsurge in inflation rates beginning in the late 1960s. If it does develop that much of the recent inflation is of a structural origin, this would provide at least a partial explanation for why conventional monetary and fiscal policies, especially the constraining monetary policies used in 1969-71, 1975, and since 1979, have failed to have any perceptible effect on the spiraling inflation they were designed to arrest, or at least ameliorate, without creating high levels of unemployment.

An analysis of the relationship between market structure and economic stability -- the microeconomics of economic stabilization -- can of course lay no special claim to originality. The primary focus of the Temporary National Economic Hearings of the 1930s and of the various TNEC monographs (see especially Thorp 1941; Wilcox 1941; in addition, see Neal 1942) was on how the structure of industrial markets affected the process by which the economy adjusted to movements in aggregate demand. In particular, the central questions these studies addressed was whether the level of concentration in product markets was systematically related to the downward inflexibility of prices, and as a consequence thereof, most of the burden of adjusting to downward movements of demand in periods of recession was on the level of employment. However, I believe that John Kenneth Galbraith (1957, 124) as late as 1957 described the generally held view that "...differences in market structure -- differing degrees of monopoly and competitiveness -- have not usually been thought of central importance in their bearing on general price movements." He concluded that on theoretical grounds -- grounds that his empirical analysis, based on 1947-56 data, seemed broadly to support -- the adjustment process in the oligopolistic sectors contrasted sharply with that of the competitive sector. In oligopolies, prices rose gradually during the initial periods of inflation and continued to rise, or at least not fall, throughout the following phases of the business cycle. Oligopolies, Galbraith contended, could simply draw on their unliquidated monopoly gains. In competitive industries the initial response to a sharp upturn in the economy was rapidly rising prices, quickly to be followed by declines as output increased in response to the price increases (Galbraith 1957, 124-25). Galbraith concluded that since market structure had a bearing on inflationary price behavior, this may very well explain why monetary policy in 1955 and 1956 directed toward the post-Korean inflation met with indifferent success (p. 125).

Others soon developed Galbraith's market structure thesis into a more comprehensive explanatory hypothesis for the entire inflation process. (See Selden 1959; Markham 1964, 144-75; Bowen 1960). Strong labor unions were perceived to possess in the principal factor market a degree of monopoly power commensurate with that held by oligopolists in the product market. To the extent that oligopolists could pass on cost increases with relative impunity through the coordination that followed from conjectural interdependence, they had less incentive to put up a strong resistance to union wage demands. Unions, aware that they could press for money wage gains without inflicting unrecoverable losses on their corporate employers, strengthened their demands. Moreover, with the government committed to a full-employment policy, unions could press their wage demands without fear of increasing unemployment among union members.

Attempts to subject this hypothesis to empirical tests have met with, at best, mixed success. Both Selden (1959, 11) and Bailey (1958, 89) conclude that the upward drift in oligopoly (administered) prices in the 1950s reflected inflation rather than caused it. My own analysis of nine industries characterized by high concentration in the product market, strong labor unions, and generally considered as comprising an "administered" price group, revealed that only two industries -- automobiles and steel -- had price movements over the course of two business cycles that could not be reconciled with the changing conditions of demand and supply (Markham 1964, 172-73). Both the steel and automobile industries have strong labor unions. Leonard Weiss (1966, 177-87), in a comprehensive, cross-sectional statistical analysis of market concentration and prices for the 1950s and 1960s, reached ambivalent conclusions; correlation between concentration indices and prices was positive for some time periods, negative for others, and not significantly related in still others (McLaren 1970, Appendix). And Weston and Lustgarten (1974, 302-32) found that over the period from 1954 to 1970 wages in the more concentrated industries rose more rapidly than those in the less concentrated industries, but that productivity also rose more rapidly in the more concentrated industries, with a net result that unit labor costs rose less rapidly. They also found that, in general, concentration was inversely related to price movements.

II. ORIGINS OF INFLATION

I propose here to approach the issue with a somewhat different methodology. It is obvious from all the pertinent indices that the inflation of recent years is significantly different in magnitude, and perhaps in kind, from that experienced in the two decades following World War II. By recent standards, inflation in the 1950s and most of the 1960s was mild and sporatic, registering no more than 1.5 percent per year in ten of the eighteen years between 1950 and 1967. In one year (1955) the CPI actually declined -- a year, incidentally, historians of the future may well identify as an economic milestone. To the extent the operative mechanics of the American economy were influenced by a "permanent inflation" hypothesis, the influence was confined to a percentage point or two. In the years since 1967, the lows of inflation have exceeded the highs of the earlier period, with the CPI registering, on average, a threefold increase over the 1950-67 period.

A. Structural Hypothesis

The basic indices used to analyze the structural hypothesis for the inflation problem pertain to the two periods, 1950-67 and 1968-80. There are several persuasive reasons for singling out these particular time periods for analysis. The first and most obvious justification, as already discussed, is that inflation in the latter period has been very high, persistent, and apparently intractable. Second, it is generally agreed that the concurrence of both endogenous and exogenous events in 1967 and the several years following precipitated the initial upsurge leading to the new inflationary spiral: heavy expenditures on the Viet Nam conflict, on which President Johnson superimposed his costly programs for the "Great Society" (the fiscal deficit of $25 billion in fiscal 1968 was the largest deficit registered between 1945 and 1975, in spite of the low unemployment rate of 3.6 percent); the Russian, African, and Republic of China's agricultural misfortunes that severely strained the world's food supplies; the Middle Eastern war that led quickly to the quintupling of oil prices; productivity began to show the first signs of serious retardation in 1967; and 1968 marked the year median, union wage increases began to outpace median wage increases for the nonunion labor force, a pattern that persisted throughout the 1970s (Perry 1978; Okun and Perry 1978, 266-67).

In a purely statistical sense, it is obvious that wage-cost movements are closely associated with movements in the price level. As the data presented in Table 2 show, throughout the two relatively long periods one could have, on average, predicted 100 percent of the annual increase in the CPI from the simple linear equation:

$$\Delta CPI = \Delta MW - \Delta PPW + 0.4$$

where: MW = Money wage rates; and
PPW = Productivity per worker.

This relationship holds for both time periods. The average annual profits margin for all corporations is shown because it more closely approximates the Lerner index, and hence is a more acceptable measure of monopoly power than the rate of return on investment. The average registered no change as between the two periods. The striking difference between the two periods is that while average output per man-hour fell by 60 percent between 1950-67 and 1968-80, increases in average hourly money wages rose from 4.1 percent to 7.3 percent, with the result that increases in average hourly labor costs rose from 1.5 percent to 6 percent. The increase in average annual labor costs amounted to 94 percent of the average annual increase in the CPI.

A more detailed breakdown of inflation into its component parts for the years 1979 and 1980 combined appears in Table 3. The format follows that of Data Resources, Inc. (Eckstein 1980, 6-10) with the averages for money wages, productivity, and capital costs in column 1 derived from the actual recorded indexes, while those in column 2 are equilibrium trend line values as computed by DRI. Again it is clear that the increases in unit labor costs for the most recent two years account for a very large part (87 percent) of the rise in the CPI, and together with the shock factors add up to 12.8 percent cost-induced inflation, while the average annual recorded inflation was 12.85 percent. With cost factors alone accounting for virtually all the inflation, only an insignificant residual fraction is left to be attributed to demand factors (Eckstein 1980, 14), a feature of the recent inflation that has significant implications for the remedial policies discussed in some detail later on.

232

TABLE 3
Anatomy of the Recent Inflation, 1979-1980
  (Percent)

	Actual Annual Average Percent Change	Core Inflation Formula
Compensation per Hour.	9.9	8.6
Productivity per Man-hour	-0.4	0.8
Labor Costs	10.3	7.8
Capital Costs	9.5	10.3
Capital-Labor (Core) Inflation	10.0	8.7
Shock Inflation Factors (a)	2.5	2.5
Total "Cost-Push" Inflation	12.5	11.2
Actual Recorded Inflation CPI: December to December	12.85	12.85
: Year-to-Year	11.85	11.85

(a) Petroleum and food prices, exchange rate movements and
    government imposed wage increases such as minimum wage
    and social security rate increases.

Sources: Economic Report of the President, January, 1981.
         Business Week, February 16, 1981.
         Otto Eckstein, Tax Policy and Core Inflation,
         A Study Prepared for the Use of the Joint Committee,
         Congress of the United States, (Washington, G.P.O., 1980).

The critical problem, however, is to determine whether the calculated cost inflation of the past twelve-year period is attributable to structural factors -- the interaction of monopoly power in labor and product markets -- or is simply a reflection of the overall inflationary process. Attempts to make this determination through lead-lag regression models, while highly illuminating, have not produced unequivocal results. Perry (1978) concluded from his comprehensive analysis of the problem that "In summary, to explain current [1970s] wage behavior, the importance of ongoing inflation is well established, but the particular importance of ongoing price (as opposed to wage) inflation remains unsettled" (p. 278). And Mitchell (1980, 218-19) found that it required both an excess demand model and a structural model to explain the high inflation of recent years, but a model accomodating them both was "not wholly satisfying."

The critical issue the structural model seeks to resolve is not so much whether labor unions and their corporate employers possess sufficient power over wages and prices to drive both above some, competitive norm, but rather whether this power increased in sufficient quantity between 1950-67 and 1968-80 to explain the enormous difference in the inflation rates of the two periods. It can be reasonably concluded at the outset from the conventional measures of market structure that in some highly concentrated industries conjectural interdependence works sufficiently well to maintain prices above marginal costs -- a conclusion that is reenforced by the voluminous studies relating concentration ratios to price-cost margins. Similarly, the essential purpose of the federal statutes fostering collective bargaining of the 1930s was to protect labor from the competitive forces of the market place. It can be reasonably concluded that most unions, especially those in industries with high unionization rates, possess sufficient power to accomplish this purpose.

However, the quantitative data on both labor and product markets add up to convincing evidence that the power of unions and management over wages and prices did not increase during the 1967-80 period. While the degree of unionization of the labor force clearly does not completely measure union power, it is obviously an important indicator of the extent to which wages generally are subject to the influence of unions. Between the 1930s and the 1950s, union membership in both absolute numbers and as a percent of the labor force, rapidly increased. However, as a share of the labor force, union membership reached a peak in 1955 (Table 4) when it stood at 24.7 percent of the total work force and at 33.2 percent of all nonfarm employment. After 1955 this percentage gradually declined, until by the late 1970s union membership accounted for about one-fifth of all employees and a little over one-fifth of total nonfarm employment. Beginning in 1970 the Bureau of Labor Statistics also made available data on membership in employee associations. When these are included, all organized labor is a higher percentage of the labor force, but the downward trend is not reversed.

Students of industrial relations generally agree that union membership as a share of all employees understates the influence of unions on wages for two reasons. In establishments where unions do not have closed-shop agreements they bargain for nonunion as well as union members. According to Bok and Dunlop (1975, 1), in the late

TABLE 4
Union Membership as Percent of Labor Force, United States, 1950–1978
  (Percent)

	Percent of Labor Force		Percent of Non-farm Employment	
1950	22.3		31.5	
1955	24.7		33.2	
1960	23.6		31.4	
1965	22.4		28.4	
1970	22.6	(24.7)	27.3	(30.0)
1975	20.5	(23.5)	25.3	(28.9)
1976	20.1	(23.2)	24.5	(28.3)
1978	19.7		21.6	

Note: Figures in parentheses represent unions and employee
         associations.

Sources: Bureau of Labor Statistics as reproduced in
         Daniel J. B. Mitchell, Unions, Wages and Inflation,
         (Washington: Brookings Institution, 1980), p. 24.
         1978 data from Handbook of Labor Statistics,
         Bulletin 2070, Bureau of Labor Statistics,
         December, 1980.

1960s the number of workers covered by collective bargaining agreements exceeded the number of union members by three-quarters of a million. Also, unions may influence wages and working conditions of the nonunion work force in a variety of ways: in some instances employers follow a policy of meeting or beating union wage bargains to discourage unionization; in some cases nonunion wages are tied to union wages through informal agreements; and even where neither of these arrangements exist, one might expect collective bargaining settlements to affect nonunion wages through the normal functioning of the forces of supply and demand in labor markets. However, it is not entirely clear on theoretical grounds just what this effect will be. On the one hand, increases in union wages should lead to a reduction in the demand for unionized members, which increases the supply of nonunion members. On the other hand, the demand for nonunion labor will rise relative to the demand for union labor.

As will become evident later on, it is difficult enough to measure, with reasonable confidence, the direct effect of unions on wages, much less the various induced effects. However, there would appear to be no basis for inferring that the power of unions to affect wage movements, either directly or indirectly, increased perceptibly in the high-inflation period 1968-80. On the contrary, judged from such impressionistic evidence as their success rate in Congress and state legislatures, and the hard evidence on the relative decline in union membership, union power would appear to have eroded slightly since the 1960s. This conclusion is somewhat reenforced by the fact that the growing international competition that has reduced the market power of United States oligopolies, discussed more fully below, appears also to have begun to constrain union power. The recent wage concessions made by the United Automobile Workers to the Chrysler Corporation may be a special case, but the joint petition (up to now, unsuccessful) by the U.A.W. and Ford Motor Company to the President to impose limits on automobile imports reveals an awareness of the constraint's existence.

Judged by the standards of measurement which students of industrial organization have used since this branch of economic inquiry was initiated, the structure of American industry has changed very little since the end of the nineteenth century. More to the issue at hand, the evidence is quite persuasive that if oligopolistic market power has changed at all, it has diminished since about 1963. Between the end of World War II and 1963, the proportion of value added which originated in industries with concentration ratios of 50 percent or higher gradually increased from 24 percent to 33 percent; by 1972, the last year for which census data are available, the proportion had declined to 29 percent (Scherer 1980, 68). Or, as the data in Table 5 show, the share of total manufacturing value added which originated in industries with concentration ratios of less than 50 percent increased slightly over this period, while the percentage of all industries falling in this concentration class registered a slight decline. However, for the 136 definitionally comparable industries, the percentage registered a slight increase. The percentage changes, whether up or down, were in all cases trivial. The safest conclusion to be drawn from these data is that between 1950-67 and 1968-80 no perceptible change occurred in the market structure of the United States manufacturing economy.

TABLE 5
Number and Percent of Four-Digit S.I.C. Industries Having
Value-of-Shipments with Four-Firm Concentration Ratios of
Less than 50 Percent, 1947-1972

	Percent of Total Value Added	All Industries		136 Definitionally Comparable Industries	
		Number	Percent	Number	Percent
1947	75.6	254	66	96	71
1954	70.1	252	66	95	70
1958	69.9	255	68	95	70
1963	66.9	248	72	93	68
1967	—	240	70	96	71
1972 (a)	71.0	254	69	94	69

(a) Most recent census data available.

Source: Adapted from Conference Board Studies of Farkas and
Weinberger, as reproduced in Markham (1980, 439).

However, the competition domestic oligopolies have encountered from foreign producers has obviously increased. The impact foreign competition has had on such specific markets as motor vehicles, consumer electronic goods, and photographic equipment scarcely needs to be documented. But these highly visible signs do not measure the full extent to which industrial markets have become internationalized. As a crude measure, between 1960 and 1979 United States GNP in current dollars increased 5.2 times, while exports increased ninefold and imports fourteenfold. Even after the elimination of oil and petroleum products from imports, the ratio of imports to GNP nearly doubled between 1967 and 1977, and accounted for significant amounts of total domestic consumption of chemicals ($4.8 billion), machinery ($15.4 billion), transport equipment ($14.4 billion), iron and steel mill products ($4.8 billion), nonferrous base metals ($2.9 billion), clothing ($3.6 billion), crude materials excluding fuels ($7.0 billion), footwear ($1.7 billion), and paper and paper manufactures ($2.1 billion).

Finally, antitrust policy has been pressed with increased vigor against both the structure and practices of oligopoly since the mid-1960s. Beginning with the initiation of the famous IBM case in 1968, the Department of Justice or the Federal Trade Commission has initiated major cases against the ready-to-eat cereal companies, the eight largest domestic oil companies, the four domestic lead antiknock compound manufacturers, and, among others, A.T. & T. and its Western Electric subsidiary. In fact, the dramatic increase in the nation's resources allocated to antitrust in recent years has led serious antitrust scholars -- even antitrust sympathizers -- to question whether the entire process could meet the test of a reasonably careful cost-benefit analysis (The New York Times 1981). But whatever one's views on the matter, the intensification of antitrust has obviously sensitized companies in concentrated industries to their vulnerability to attack, which in turn, we may infer, has led to some lessening of oligopolistic behavior.

B. A Modified Structural Hypothesis

On balance then, no convincing case can be made to support the view that the dramatic upsurge in inflation since 1967 can find an explanation in appropriate changes in the structure of labor and product markets. The hypothesis that the interaction of monopolistic labor unions and highly concentrated oligopolists brought on the post-1968 inflation does not comport with the facts on the structure of labor and product markets. On the contrary, these data strongly suggest that while the threefold increase in the average annual inflation rate was taking place, between 1950-67 and 1968-80 union power and corporate market power experienced modest erosion.

This does not lead to the conclusion, however, that the interaction of union and oligopoly power played no role in the recent high inflation rates. In fact, as developed at some length earlier on (see Tables 2 and 3), the inflation over both the long time periods examined just about equalled wage inflation adjusted for productivity. There is then an apparent conflict in the results. A comparative analysis of labor and product market structures for the 1950-67 and 1968-80 periods revealed no structural changes that could explain a threefold increase in inflation; yet, in a statistical sense, the inflation rates of both periods can be almost entirely "explained" by the inflation in unit labor costs. This apparent conflict in results lends credence to a modified version of the traditional hypothesis, namely, that while the interaction of union and oligopoly power may not have been a significant factor in setting off the post-1967 inflation, it has played a critical role in perpetuating the inflation which has its origin in other endogenous and exogenous sources.

It should be made clear that this particular hypothesis lays no claim to being highly original. Mitchell (1980, 219) has advanced it in a somewhat different form, and it is implied in Perry's (1978, 269) "backward looking" relative wage-gain calculations for major union contracts for the period 1968-75. However, in view of its powerful policy implications, it can scarcely be overemphasized if the factual data support it.

First, lest the implications of the hypothesis be misunderstood, there is no question but that unions have power to gain wages and benefits above those the competitive forces in the labor market would set, and that this power has been exerted with increased force since the origin of the recent high inflation beginning in 1968. This is borne out by the data presented in Tables 6 and 7. For the long period 1953-68, average hourly earnings in highly unionized industries just about kept pace with wage movements generally, increasing at an average annual rate of 4 percent. The corresponding increase in real wages for highly unionized labor, low unionized labor, and all labor was, in each case, about 2 percent. Since 1970, union wages have outpaced all wages almost a full percentage point increase per year, and, on the basis of data available for 1976 and 1977, have outpaced nonunion wages by 1.3 percent per year (Table 7). When these wage payments are adjusted for fringe benefits, the gap between union and nonunion increases would increase to approximately 2 percentage points a year (Mitchell 1980, 82). As a consequence, union wage earners, in contrast with all wage earners, have just about managed to maintain their historical average annual increase in real wages of 2 percent during the post-1967, high-inflation period.

However, the timing of these relative gains by unionized labor and the instruments by which they have been attained make it almost certain that union power was directed toward insulating union members from upsurges in inflation initially attributable to other causes. The three major spurts of inflation occurred in 1968-69, 1973-74, and from 1978 onward. The first of these is generally attributed to the overheated economy with large, back-to-back federal deficits in 1967 and 1968 amounting to $34 billion. During this period, union wage increases just about equalled increases in all wages. The 1973-74 inflationary spurt was set off by the Middle Eastern oil crisis following on the heels of the removal of the 1971-72 wage and price controls. In the three-year period from 1973 to 1975, union wage increases barely exceeded increases in all wages, and union real wages declined at an average annual rate of 0.7 percent. During the several years following these outbreaks of inflation, union real wages rose as inflation rates declined. The upsurge in inflation beginning in 1978 is still with us, and predictions are that it will not return to pre-1968 levels in the foreseeable future. However, in contrast with the previous two periods, the recent wage increases and price

TABLE 6
Annual Rates of Change in Average Hourly Earnings
by Degree of Unionization, 1953-1968 and 1968-1976
  (Percent)

	1953-1968	1968-1976
Industries with Above Average Unionization Rates		
Survey 1	4.0	7.6
Survey 2	3.9	7.3
Survey 3	4.0	7.5
Industries with Below Average Unionization Rates		
Survey 1	3.9	6.7
Survey 2	4.0	6.6
Survey 3	4.0	6.7
All Industries - All Wages	4.0	6.9

Source: Data by unionization calculated from Mitchell (1980, 82).
        See his text for a description of the three wage surveys
        used. "All Wages" from The Economic Report of the
        President, January, 1981.

TABLE 7
Union and Total Wage Increases, 1970-1977
  (Percent per year)

	(1) Union Wages	(2) Average Hourly Earnings-- All Employees	Difference (1) - (2)	Real Unit Wage-Rate Change
1970	8.8	6.6	2.2	2.9
1971	9.2	7.0	2.2	4.9
1972	6.6	6.6	0.0	3.3
1973	7.0	6.4	0.6	0.8
1974	9.4	8.2	1.2	-1.6
1975	8.7	8.8	- 0.1	-0.4
1976	8.1	7.2	0.9 (1.3)	2.3
1977	8.0	7.3	0.7 (1.0)	1.5

Note: Figures in parentheses represent difference between
         total union and total nonunion.

Source: U.S. Bureau of Labor Statistics. Average union wage
         rate changes are based on agreements covering 1,000
         or more workers. Real union wage-rate changes are
         union wage-rate increases deflated by increases in
         the CPI.

increases were timed very closely together. Both registered increases over the preceeding year in 1977, and again in 1978. This change in the wage-price pattern may very well be explained by the rapid growth in cost-of-living escalator clauses and deferred wage premiums in collective bargaining contracts.

The principal means by which the collective bargaining mechanism perpetuates inflation, irrespective of what sets it off, is through the automatic cost-of-living adjustment formulas and the multiple-year terms incorporated in union contracts. Between 1967 and 1980 the proportion of workers covered by cost-of-living adjustments (COLA) rose from 25 percent to 59 percent (U. S. Department of Labor 1980a, 9). Approximately an additional 4.5 million government and nonunion employees receive regular increases in line with increases in the CPI (Kuhn 1979, 110). Of 521 major contracts having COLA provisions in 1980, 56 percent required quarterly adjustments, 21 percent semiannual adjustments, and 19 percent annual adjustments. A small number required monthly adjustments or some combination of time periods. The means by which such provisions perpetuated inflation are simple and obvious. The increases in the CPI in one period automatically become corresponding cost increases in the next. The continuous cycle of price-cost-price push inflation can be aggravated by multiple-year contracts; especially in the case of those contracts negotiated in, or in anticipation of, mounting and continuing inflation, which typically extend negotiated wage increases for three years into the future.

III. CONCLUSION

The findings set forth in this essay broadly comport with those of others who have analyzed the recent inflation with somewhat different methodological approaches. If these findings are reasonably reliable, they hold some obvious implications for the control of inflation. Few would contend that the continuous and ever larger federal deficits for the past twenty years have had little to do with the inflation that took off on a higher path in 1967, even though we may agree with the outgoing Council of Economic advisors that the inflation-generating consequences of federal deficits may easily be exaggerated (Econ. Rep. of the Pres. 1981, 41-42). In any case it is highly doubtful that under the unemployment and plant-capacity utilization rates that have prevailed over the high-inflation period, a reversal of fiscal policy would eliminate most of the inflation it has created. In a regime of downward inflexible wages and prices, adjustments to a reduction in aggregate money demand will be largely in the form of reduced output and employment.[2] However, a substantial reduction of public deficits would ease money markets and help offset the perversity of monetary policy. Attempts to fight inflation by use of high interest rates increase the price level through the capital cost component of core inflation, and through increasing the inflow of funds from abroad.

Recognition of these inadequacies of conventional stabilization policies to combat the high-level inflation of the past dozen years has led to proposals such as tax-based incomes policies (TIP) and wage-increase permit plans (WIPP). To these might be added tax penalties or enforceable constraints on the use of COLA provisions in wage setting. Inflation, it is said, is the cruelist of taxes. It is unlikely that the cruelty will abate unless appropriate policies can be designed and implemented to halt the inflation perpetuated by the downward inflexibility of wages and prices, and the price-wage-price sequence. In addition, a reduction in federal deficits, regulatory reform, some improvement in the nation's sagging productivity, and a generous gesture or two from OPEC would clearly help.

FOOTNOTES

Aside from the importance of the wage-price issue in the current search for effective policies to mitigate inflation, the subject to the author has a special relevance in a volume dedicated to Lloyd Reynolds. My first published article appeared while I was a student of Professor Reynolds, and without whose help and guidance it no doubt would have remained among my not altogether legible notes taken in his labor economics course. The article was concerned with labor productivity, a matter highly pertinent to the subject dealt with in this essay. See Markham (1943).

1. Economic Report of the President 1982, 318. Since writing the initial draft of this essay the projected deficits have risen to unprecedented levels.

2. Between the time of writing this essay and its publication the forecast implied in this statement all too painfully materialized. As of November 1982 the unemployment rate had reached 10.4 percent following on the heels of nearly two years of a restrictive monetary policy.

BIBLIOGRAPHY

Bailey, M. J. 1958. Administered prices in the American economy. In *The relationship of prices to economic stability and growth*. Compendium of papers submitted by panelists before the Joint Committee, 85th Cong; 22nd Session. Washington.

Bok, D., J. Dunlop. 1975. The current profile of the labor movement. In *Labor and the national economy*, ed. W. Bowen, O. Ashenfelter. Revised edition. New York: Norton & Co.

Bowen, W. G. 1960. *The wage-price issue: a theoretical analysis*. Princeton, N.J.: Princeton U. Press.

Business Week. 16 February 1981.

Center for the Study of American Business. (C.S.A.B.) 1979. *Alternative policies to combat inflation*. C.S.A.B. working paper no. 408. (January). St. Louis: Washington U.

Eckstein, O. 1980. *Tax policy and core inflation*. A study prepared for the use of the Joint Committee, U.S. Congress. Washington: G.P.O.

Economic Report of the President. 1981. Washington: G.P.O.

_____, 1982. Washington: G.P.O.

Galbraith, J. K. 1957. Market structure and stabilization policy. *Rev. Econ. and Statis.*, 39(May): 124-33.

Kuhn, J. W. 1979. The labor force. In *Inflation and national survival*, ed. C. C. Walton. *Proceedings of the Academy of Political Science*, 33(3).

Markham, J. W. 1943. Regional labor productivity in the textile industry. *Amer. Econ. Rev.*, 33(March): 110-15.

_____, 1964. Administered prices and the recent inflation. In *Inflation, growth and employment*. Commission on Money and Credit. New York: Prentice-Hall, Inc.

_____, 1980. The role of competition in the American economy. *Zeitschrift fur die Gesamte Staatswissenschaft*, 136(3) (September): 435-43.

McLaren, R. 1970. Testimony in *The 1970 midyear review of the state of the economy*. Hearings before the Joint Economic Committee, 91st Cong. 2nd Session, Part 1. Washington: G.P.O.

Mitchell, D. J. B. 1980. *Unions, wages and inflation*. Washington, D.C.: Brookings Institution.

Neal, A. C. 1942. *Industrial concentration and price inflexibility*. Washington, D.C.: American Council of Public Affairs.

The New York Times. 15 February 1981.

Okun, A. M., G. L. Perry, ed. 1978. *Curing chronic inflation*. Washington, D.C.: Brookings Institution.

Okun, A. M. 1980. *Uniting against inflation*. Brookings Bulletin 16(3). Published posthumously. Washington, D.C.: Brookings Institution.

Perry, G. L. 1978. Slowing the wage price spiral: the macroeconomic view. In *Brookings papers on economic activity*, ed. A. M. Okun, G. L. Perry. Washington, D.C.: Brookings Institution.

Scherer, F. M. 1980. *Industrial market structure and economic performance*. 2nd ed. Chicago: Rand McNally.

Selden, R. T. 1959. Cost-push versus demand-pull inflation, 1955-1957. *J. Polit. Econ.*, 57(1)(February): 1-20.

Solomon, E. 1976. *The anxious economy*. San Francisco: San Francisco Book Co.

Thorp, W., et al. 1941. *The structure of industry*. T.N.E.C. monograph no. 27. Washington: G.P.O.

U.S. Department of Labor, Bureau of Labor Statistics. 1980a. *Monthly labor review*. (January). Washington: G.P.O.

———, 1980b. *Handbook of labor statistics*. Bulletin 2070. (December). Washington: G.P.O.

Walton, C. E., ed. 1979. *Inflation and national survival*. *Proceedings of The Academy of Political Science* 33(3).

Weiss, L. W. 1966. Business pricing policies and inflation reconsidered. *J. Polit. Econ.*, 74(2)(April): 177-87.

Weston, J. F. S. Lustgarten. 1974. Concentration and wage-price changes. In *Industrial concentration: the new learning*, ed. H. J. Goldschmidt, H. M. Mann, J. F. Weston, 302-32. Boston: Little Brown & Co.

Wilcox, C. 1941. *Competition and monopoly in American industry*. T.N.E.C. Monograph no. 21. Washington, D.C.: G.P.O.

12
The Mexican Labor Market, 1940–1980

Peter Gregory

I. INTRODUCTION

The period of accelerated growth and modernization in Mexico dates from about 1940. The groundwork for change had already been laid by the sweeping changes flowing from the preceding thirty years of revolutionary activity that produced far-reaching social and institutional changes. The onset of World War II brought with it a disruption of traditional sources of supply for industrial goods and stimulated the expansion of manufacturing production for internal consumption. The large-scale land distribution program of the Cárdenas regime during the preceding decade resulted in a substantial increase in the land under cultivation and in agricultural output. Thus, the decade saw all of the principal sectors of the economy growing in tandem fashion. As is evidenced in Table 1, the rates of growth of the three broad sectors showed only small differences.

Following the end of the war and a return to more competitive conditions in product markets, the government opted for a policy of fostering the further growth of domestic industry behind protective tariff walls and import controls. It also embarked on a large-scale investment program to provide infrastructure for an emerging modern commercial agricultural sector. Large-scale irrigation and road-building projects in the sparsely populated northern and northwestern provinces provided a stimulus for a continued expansion of agricultural output for both domestic consumption and export. With the exhaustion of "easy" import substitution, incentives were adopted for domestic production of consumer durable goods and then for intermediate and capital goods. Throughout most of the past four decades, Mexico succeeded in maintaining a high and stable rate of growth, one that faltered significantly only during the middle of the past decade.

While the achievements of the Mexican economy are surely impressive, there remain areas of concern. A rapidly growing population of labor force age poses a formidable challenge to the economy's ability to absorb it in productive employment. The pattern of development, particularly in agriculture, has been dual. While a highly productive commercial agricultural sector has emerged, the bulk of the rural population is to be found in areas with scarce land and water resources and in which increases in productivity have been

TABLE 1
Gross National Product by Broad Sectors, 1940-1970
(Millions of 1950 Pesos and Percent)

| | Sectors of Gross National Product | | | | Annual Rate of Change | | |
	1940	1950	1960	1970	1940-50	1950-60	1960-70
Primary							
Bank of Mexico	5,221	9,242	11,433	16,473	5.9	2.2	3.7
Unikel			13,917	17,607		4.2	2.4
Secondary							
Bank of Mexico	6,789	12,466	20,956	48,727	6.3	5.3	8.8
Unikel			24,603	52,203		7.0	7.8
Tertiary							
Bank of Mexico	10,931	19,352	39,404	76,278	5.9	7.4	6.8
Unikel			35,696	82,431		6.3	8.7
Total							
Bank of Mexico	22,940	41,060	71,793	141,478	6.0	5.7	7.0
Unikel			74,215	152,251		6.1	7.5

Notes: Sectors are composed of the following: Primary: agriculture, cattle, forestry, fishing. Secondary: manufacturing, construction, mining, petroleum, electricity. Tertiary: transportation, communications, commerce, government, other services.

Sources: L. Unikel (1978, Tables VI-A5 to VI-A8). The revised GNP estimates originate with the Banco de México as reported by Reynolds (1979, 27).

modest. Rural poverty remains a serious problem; some students of Mexico hold that the incomes of a sizable rural population have not shared in the general increase that characterizes the country as a whole, or have shared only to an insignificant extent. The relative distribution of incomes continues to rank among the most unequal in Latin America and appears to be emerging as an acute social and political issue. The dualistic character of agriculture is reflected in the large differences between the productivity of land and labor among the various classes of agricultural holdings. In 1970, the output per hectare on farm units employing "modern technology" was four times that in subsistence farm units (those which destined only a small part of output for markets). The ratio of output per worker was even greater, on the order of twenty to one (Hernández and Córdova 1979, 506). Moreover, the dual character of the sector has strong regional associations. In 1970, for example, the output per hectare was twenty times greater in Sonora than in Quintana Roo. In twelve other states, the productivity of land was no greater than one-fourth that of Sonora (Unikel 1976, App. Table 6(A15)). Such large differences in the productivity of different classes of farm units and regions may be expected to give rise to similar differences in agricultural incomes.

Intrasectoral differences in productivity and earnings among productive units exist in other sectors, as might be expected, though they are not as pronounced as those indicated in agriculture. In 1975, value added and total remunerations per worker were 3.8 and 3.1 times greater in manufacturing establishments employing over 750 workers than in small shops with five or fewer employees.[1] In the service sector, the differential in the rate of earnings between small (five or fewer employees) and large (over fifty employees) establishments was more modest, on the order of 2.1 to 1 in 1975 (Secretaria de Industria y Comercio 1977, 305, Table 17). In 1970, the differential in earnings between small and large establishments in commerce was slightly narrower at 1.9 to 1 (Secretaría de Industria y Comercio 1975, 403, Table 22).

More impressive than the differences in productivity and earnings within each of the nonagricultural sectors enumerated here are the differences between them and agriculture. In 1970, value added per worker in the former was 5.2 times greater than in the latter; by 1976 it is estimated to have increased to 6.6.[2] It is no wonder, then, that most of the poverty in Mexico is to be found in the rural areas. On the basis of the 1975 income and expenditures survey, it has been estimated that approximately 52 percent of the poor families were in the agricultural sector. Stated in other terms, 76 percent of all families in the sector lived in poverty.[3] The prevalence and durability of large urban-rural income differentials are likely to have been important factors underlying a large rural-urban migration as well as a tendency of rural residents to seek seasonal employment in urban labor markets. Unikel estimates that 4.5 million persons moved from rural to urban areas between 1950 and 1970.[4]

There is a widespread recognition of the fact that many Mexicans are precariously employed in jobs of uncertain duration and at low levels of productivity and wages. What is disturbing, however, is the belief prevailing among government officials, scholars, and other observers that employment conditions are not only "poor" but that they have deteriorated over time. As Evans and James conclude after surveying a number of employment studies, "there is abundant evidence that Mexico...is plagued with a serious and worsening labor surplus problem."[5] Unemployment and underemployment are seen as having increased, and as affecting from 44 to 52 percent of the labor force during the early 1970s. Should this perception of deterioration prove, in fact, to be correct, then the prospects for improving the material well-being of the bulk of the world's population in the less developed countries of the world would seem grim indeed. After all, if, under the conditions of sustained growth achieved in Mexico, general improvement in employment conditions cannot be attained, then what hope can be held out for the workers of most LDCs that have achieved much less impressive rates of growth?

While one finds a widespread acceptance of the proposition that deterioration has occurred, it is harder to find convincing empirical support for it. Most of the appraisals of the Mexican labor market focus on its profile at a moment of time and conclude from the "unsatisfactory" state of employment that deterioration has occurred. Deterioration, however, implies change over time, change which cannot be inferred from conditions at a moment in time or even from a cursory review of labor force aggregates in isolation.[6] I sense a lamentable absence of analysis of the evolution of the labor market over time in its several dimensions, and of how it has responded to and facilitated the notable growth and change observable in the level and structure of output. Almost completely neglected is the course of wages over time, something that would appear critical to any evaluation of the changing quality of employment. This essay represents an attempt to redress these shortcomings of most current appraisals of employment conditions in Mexico. It reports on some preliminary findings of a larger effort to analyze the evolution of the Mexican labor market and focuses on several aspects that may be indicative of the nature and degree of qualitative change in employment conditions over time. In the sections that follow, I will discuss the changing structure of the labor force, the course of sectoral productivities and wages, and the measures of underutilization of the labor force.

II. STRUCTURE OF THE LABOR FORCE, PRODUCTIVITY, AND WAGES

Historical analyses of the Mexican labor force rely on the decennial censuses of population as the principal data source, for, until recently, these have provided the only comprehensive measures of the labor force. Ideally, one would hope that the censuses would provide a reliable data base for tracing the evolution of the labor force in the process of economic development, charting faithfully the course of labor force participation rates and recording the shifts that occur in employment among sectors and occupational groups and in the employment status of the labor force. Unfortunately, the Mexican censuses do not provide an unambiguous basis for assessing the changes that have occurred. In part, this is the result of changing classifications of the labor force over time that obscure the true extent of shifts or of changing practices in the classification of certain population groups within the labor force. A substantial problem is posed by the coding and processing errors that resulted in the reporting of an outsized agricultural and total labor force in the census of 1960. Further difficulties are posed in the interpretation of the 1970 census by the very large number of individuals in the labor force who could not be assigned to an economic sector of employment. The widespread awareness of these shortcomings has led to several attempts to adjust the data with rather different results. (Colegio de Mexico 1970; Altimir 1974; McFarland 1973). For various reasons, I have concluded that the adjustments proposed by Oscar Altimir are more persuasive than those of others and, therefore, I rely heavily on his data.[7]

Table 2 presents the adjusted distribution of the labor force over the principal economic sectors based on the population censuses dating from 1940 to 1969.[8] The changing structure of the labor force is a reflection of the pattern of economic development since 1940. The 1940s were a decade of rapid growth in output, in the labor force as a whole, and in employment in each of the principal sectors. Over the following two decades, the industrial and construction sectors retained their roles as "leading" sectors in the growth of employment with rates well in excess of the growth of the labor force. The commercial sector shows declining rates of growth in each successive decade, while the service sector shows a decline and then a recovery in its rate of growth. According to Altimir's adjusted census figures, the growth of the agricultural labor force over the 1950-69 period amounted to less than .5 percent per year. In my opinion, this is likely to understate somewhat the increase in the agricultural labor force that occurred between 1960 and 1969 relative to 1950.[9] However, I do not believe that a more accurate measure of the agricultural labor force would significantly modify the relative importance of the sector as a source of employment.

The growth of the tertiary sector has been a source of concern to some who view it as representing an "undue" expansion of very low productivity employments (e.g., McFarland 1973; Trejo 1974; Secretaría de Trabajo y Previsión Social 1979). The conventional "explanation" of this growth is posed in terms of a burgeoning labor force incapable of finding satisfactory wage employment being "forced" into a marginal employment and productive status in the subsectors of easy entry in commerce and services, often in the status of a self-employed or unremunerated family worker. Essentially, these observers would seem to hold to the view that employment growth in certain sectors has been entirely supply determined rather than a response to shifts in demand.

Unfortunately, the criteria employed for deciding that tertiary sector growth has been "excessive" are not explicitly set forth and verified empirically. Even a cursory look at the sectoral rates of growth, however, would not seem to indicate an "explosive" growth of marginal employments. Both the commerce and service sectors, for example, expanded at rates below those of the "productive" sectors of industry and construction. Furthermore, much of the expansion of the service sector has been in technical and professional occupational categories. Government employment has expanded at approximately the same rate as total service employment and accounts for just under a fourth of the total. Finally, the growth of both services and commerce are likely to be closely related to the growth of urban population, so that the growth in the latter would be expected to shift the demand for labor in the former.[10] In the case of Mexico, the urban population -- defined in the census as those residing in

TABLE 2
Sectoral Distribution of the Labor Force, and Rates of Change, 1940-1969
(Thousands of Workers and Percent)

	Labor Force (in Thousands)				Rates of Change (Percent)			
	1940	1950	1960	1969	1940-50	1950-60	1960-69	1940-69
Agriculture, forestry and fishing	3,832.4	4,864.9	5,048.3	5,292.7	2.4	0.4	0.5	1.1
Manufacturing, electricity and extractive	709.7	1,237.5	1,760.3	2,829.1	5.7	3.6	5.4	4.9
Construction	115.9	263.8	414.2	609.8	8.6	4.6	4.4	5.9
Commerce and finance	413.7	732.6	1,083.4	1,397.0	5.9	4.0	2.9	4.3
Other services	786.7	1,246.4	1,906.7	2,826.5	4.7	4.3	4.5	4.5
Total	5,858.5	8,345.2	10,212.9	12,955.1	3.6	2.0	2.7	2.8

Note: Altimir's distribution of the labor force includes his redistribution of the unclassified workers over the several sectors.

Sources: 1940 data: L. Unikel (1978, Table VI-A9).
1950-69 data: O. Altimir (1974, Table 16).

communities with a population in excess of 2,500 -- grew at a rate of 4.8 percent a year between 1940 and 1970, a rate that exceeds the growth of tertiary employment.

However, I would maintain that one cannot judge whether the growth of the tertiary sector has been "excessive" merely by looking at its absolute size. More instructive would be the course of productivity and incomes generated in the sector over time. Examination of these variables would also provide a test of the widespread notion that employment expansion in this sector has been "supply" determind and, therefore, "excessive." Consider the implications of the "labor surplus" and "overcrowding" characterizatons of the growth of tertiary employment. If the wages of the unskilled and unorganized labor force had been at the subsistence level at the beginning of the period under observation, then we shoud observe the expansion of employment in the sector proceeding at a constant level of real wages, or, in the short run, at wages falling below subsistence. If wages began at a level above the subsistence level, then one should observe a decline in wages toward the subsistence level. If one could observe declines in real wages, this would provide support for the deterioration hypothesis, at least within the sector.[11] Since it is possible to subject the hypothesis to empirical testing, let us do so, beginning first at a macroeconomic level.

A. Sectoral Growth

In Table 3, I trace the growth of output, labor force, and output per worker over the 1940-69 period for three broad sectors of the economy. One of the striking features of the development process in Mexico has been the broadly based increases in output and productivity across sectors. All the major sectors have participated in the developmental process, though to varying degrees, in each decade since 1940. The 1940s and 1950s saw strong increases in total output and output per worker in the agricultural sector as the large investments made in rural infrastructure began to yield returns. During the 1960s, this sector demonstrated less dynamism as the limits of cultivatable land were reached and the more obvious, or easy, investment opportunities in rural infrastructure (e.g., large scale irrigation projects, trunk roads, etc.) were exhausted. Gains in both output and output per worker were only modest. One should not overlook the fact, however, that the gains may not have been evenly distributed over the sector; recall the interregional differences that exist in the productivity of agriculture, to which I referred above.

The secondary sector's expansion of output by 89 percent during the decade of the 1940s was accompanied by an almost equally large increase in employment. Given the limited access to capital goods from abroad due to the Second World War, the growth of output was apparently achieved with little or no deepening of capital. Stable or declining real minimum wages from their highly inflated levels of 1940 may also have been factors encouraging the expansion of sector employment.[12] The following decade produced an equally large increase in output as Mexico actively pursued policies of import substitution. In contrast with the decade of the 1940s, however, employment growth lagged that of output. With the restoration of normal access to

TABLE 3
Output, Employment and Output Per Worker in Mexico, 1940-1969
(1960 Pesos, Thousands of Workers and Percent)

	1940	1950	1960	1969	Annual Rates of Change		
					1940-50	1950-60	1960-69
Primary Sector							
Output (millions of Pesos)	8,543	15,442	23,970	32,912	6.1	4.5	3.6
Labor Force (thousands)	3,832	4,867	5,048	5,293	2.4	0.4	0.5
Output per worker (Pesos)	2,229	3,173	4,748	6,218	3.6	4.1	3.0
Secondary Sector							
Output	12,447	23,467	43,933	94,362	6.5	6.5	8.9
Labor Force	826	1,490	2,175	3,439	6.1	3.9	5.2
Output per worker	15,069	15,750	20,199	27,439	0.4	2.5	3.5
Tertiary Sector							
Output	27,663	48,061	84,127	153,469	5.7	5.8	6.9
Labor Force	1,200	1,988	2,990	4,223	5.2	4.2	3.9
Output per worker	23,053	24,176	28,136	36,341	0.5	1.5	2.9
Total Gross Domestic Product							
Output	48,653	86,973	150,511	277,400	6.0	5.6	7.0
Labor Force	5,858	8,345	10,213	12,955	3.6	2.0	2.7
Output per worker	8,305	10,422	14,737	21,413	2.3	3.5	4.2

Notes: For composition of sectors, see Table 1 Note. Since the totals have been adjusted for the value
of interindustry financial transactions, Total GDP may be less than the sum of sectoral products.
Sources: Output data for 1940 and 1950: L. Unikel (1976); for 1960: Banco de México (1979, 61);
for 1970: Banco de México (1978, Statistical Appendix, Table 3). Employment data refer to
the adjusted data of O. Altimir (1974).

capital goods from abroad, capital deepening must have been a contributing factor to the sharp rise in output per worker of 28 percent over the decade. The rate of growth of the sector labor force declined relative to the previous decade but still managed to increase by 46 percent. The 1960s saw an acceleration in the rates of growth of sectoral output, employment, and productivity.

The tertiary sector has been a full participant in, and contributor to, growth. Output increases in each decade closely approximated the growth of GDP. This sector persistently reported the highest absolute levels of productivity in the economy, and the rate of increase in productivity accelerated in each decade. The recorded growth in productivity might be expected to follow from an increasing weight of high-skill employments within the sector, as well as from increments in physical productivity that have occurred in some component industry groups such as transportation and communications. Obviously, any expansion in marginal activities that may have occurred within this sector was too small to offset the impact of these more favorable developments.

In short, the broad sectoral data indicate a shift in employment from the sector with the lowest productivity, agriculture, to those of higher productivities. Moreover, this shift has not depressed the rate of increase in productivity to inconsequential levels in those sectors undergoing the most rapid growth of employment. In fact, the rate of increase in output per worker is seen as accelerating over the twenty-nine year period. Such a pattern of development, on its face, would not seem to be consistent with a general deterioration of employment conditions.

On the other hand, it could be argued justifiably that large increases in productivity in the aggregate are not inconsistent with a parallel decline in the absolute productivities of some component groups within any of the sectors. It may well be that the economy is becoming increasingly dualistic in nature, with productivity and wage declines in part of each sector being more than offset by increases in other parts. Income-distribution data for 1963, 1968, and 1977, however, would not seem to be consistent with such a development. The share of income accruing to the bottom 40 percent of households in these years varies within a very narrow range of 10.5 and 10.9 percent of the total (Hernández and Córdova 1979, 507). To the extent that the share of income flowing to the bottom deciles has remained virtually constant over time, this implies that their incomes grew at approximately the same rate as the average per capita income. Nevertheless, the income-distribution data for Mexico are not free of major deficiencies and may, therefore, mask the true course of wages of the marginal labor force.[13] Furthermore, since income-distribution data are compiled on a household, rather than on an individual, basis, they cannot be expected to reflect accurately the course of wages.

B. Wage Structure

We can explore the possibility that the terms of employment have deteriorated for the "marginal" labor force by examining the course of earnings in that part of the nonagricultural labor market that is generally acknowledged to be governed by supply and demand conditions rather than by institutional interventions such as legal minimum wages or collective bargaining. While legal minimum wages are supposed to be obligatory in all employments, evasion is acknowledged to be widespread among small employers. To the extent, therefore, that the wages paid in small establishments are market determined, they should also provide a rough guide to the earnings of the self-employed, since the latter represent the opportunity cost of labor to the small-enterprise sector. In Table 4, I present data tracing the course of earnings of workers employed in enterprises of different sizes, as well as an estimate of the returns to labor of the self-employed and unremunerated family labor in establishments employing no paid workers. The data are drawn from three sectors, industry, services, and commerce, and originate in the sectoral censuses that were taken at five-year intervals between 1960 and 1975.

The data reveal substantial increases in the real average total remunerations of employees in all size strata and in all sectors. Within the service sector, wages in the small establishments gained relative to the large ones.[14] The same is true in industry; workers employed in establishments with five or fewer workers gained relative to those in all size categories up to 500 workers per establishment. A similar narrowing of differentials is observable in commerce. The censuses do not provide a measure of the returns to labor in establishments with no paid employees. Thus, the earnings of the self-employed are not reported as such. Nevertheless, I made an attempt to estimate the returns to all labor employed in establishments with no paid employees by deducting from gross income all recorded outlays for inputs and other expenses as well as an imputed return to the capital employed. The residual would represent the returns to labor which are reducible to a per-worker basis by dividing the totals by the number of persons employed in such establishments. The results are presented in the first category appearing in Table 4. While the margin of error in estimating the returns in any one year may be substantial, the upward trend in returns is so strong that the direction of change is not likely, in fact, to have been negative. Thus, on the basis of these disaggregated data, support for the presumption of deterioration is lacking. On the contrary, the real wage position of workers in the most sensitive part in the labor market would seem to indicate a considerable improvement in employment conditions.[15]

A closer look at one category of service employment, domestic service, provides an additional basis for evaluating changes in employment conditions. Domestic service represents an occupation of easy entry, frequently the source of first employment in urban areas of migrants from rural areas. As such, it is reasonable to expect that it should mirror changes in labor market conditions for unskilled female workers generally. Domestics comprised the largest single group within the service sector in 1960, accounting for about 540,000 workers. From 1950 to 1969, the number so employed increased at an annual rate of just under 3 percent. Since total employment in the service sector was expanding at a rate of 4.4 percent, domestic employment declined as a proportion of total service sector employment. Again, whether this growth was simply the product of a labor surplus pressing into any available employment can be tested by reference to the course of wages over time. While data are not available over as prolonged a period as we would like, those that are

TABLE 4
Average Real Annual Total Remuneration in Services, Industry and
Commerce by Establishment Size: 1960–75
  (Pesos of 1960 and Percent)

Sector	Size of Establishment (workers)	Average Total Remunerations (Pesos)				Percent Change 1960–75
		1960	1965	1970	1975	
Establishmments with no paid employees:						
Services		5,402	4,838	5,683	7,115	31.7
Industry		2,333	4,523	4,668	6,582	182.1
Commerce		3,829	3,874	6,983	6,838	81.2
Establishments with paid employees:						
Services	1–2 (a)	5,397	–	9,799	8,655	60.4
Industry	1–5	4,973	6,005	6,855	9,610	93.2
Commerce	1–2	6,279	7,197	7,973	10,613	69.0
Services	3–8 (b)	7,869	–	10,437	11,096	41.0
Industry	6–25	8,119	8,940	10,534	12,977	59.8
Industry	1–25	6,644	7,945	9,308	12,003	80.7
Commerce	3–8	9,465	9,941	10,957	14,505	53.2
Services 9 or more (c)		16,470	–	18,637	18,044	9.6
Industry	26–100	10,272	11,969	14,419	17,185	67.3
Industry	101–500	11,854	15,058	18,148	22,116	86.6
Industry	over 500	12,877	18,241	23,225	28,236	119.3
Commerce 9 or more		14,259	16,611	16,595	20,135	41.2

Notes   (a) 1–3 workers in 1960.
         (b) 4–10 workers in 1960.
         (c) 11 or more workers in 1960.

Sources: Censo de servicios, 1961, 1966, 1971, 1976.
           Censo industrial, 1961, 1966, 1971, 1976.
           Censo commercial, 1960, 1966, 1971, 1975.

at hand do not yield an impression of a secular decline in earnings. One study of the domestic labor market in Mexico City compiled the wages offered to domestics in the classified advertisement section of two leading newspapers, Excelsior and Universal (Secretaría del Trabajo y Previsión Social 1976, 51-109). Between 1963 and the early 1970s, the real cash wage of domestic servants in Mexico City was estimated to have risen on the order of 25 to 35 percent. While this rate of increase lagged behind the increase in the real legal minimum wage for Mexico City (about 50 percent from 1963 to 1970), it did not compare unfavorably with the rate of increase in wages in consumer-goods manufacturing industries of about 36 percent. The course of real cash wages, however, took an abrupt turn following 1972 as inflation began to accelerate. By 1975, real cash wages had fallen by about 19 to 27 percent.[16] Most of the decline occurred in 1974 and coincided with the more than quadrupling of the rate of inflation in that year as compared with the rates characteristic of the first three years of the decade. The decline in real cash wages may simply reflect the lack of experience with inflation in a society which had enjoyed at least two decades of relative price stability. Lacking sophistication or any organizational support, domestic servants may not have adjusted their reservation price sufficiently rapidly to prevent a decline. The fact that they receive a very substantial proportion of their remuneration in kind (i.e., room and board) may also have tended to blunt their awareness of the full extent of the decline in the purchasing power of their cash wage.

The course of domestic servant remunerations since 1975 is not recorded in any statistical source in Mexico. As a first approximation to the measure of the change which has occurred since 1975, I culled a sample of cash wages offered for live-in household help from Excelsior and Universal, the same two newspapers employed in the survey cited above. I obtained seventy-eight observations from issues published in July 1980. These suggested that the loss suffered in the middle of the decade had not only been recouped but that substantial further gains had been made. The average real money wage offered in July 1980 was twice as great as that of 1975 and 55 percent greater than that of 1970 (see Table 5). Lest my sample not be representative of the offered wage but biased upward, I also compared the lowest frequently quoted wage with the past recorded average offers. As the minimum, I adopted a cash wage of 2,500 pesos, which was the bottom of the 2,500-3,000-peso interval within which just 50 percent of the observations fell. (Only six recorded wage offers were for less than 2,500 pesos per month.) Even this wage, in real terms, proved to be 19 percent greater than the previous-highest average cash wage, that for 1970. Thus, the course of real wages for domestic servants does not appear to be consistent with labor market conditions characterized by "overcrowding" in marginal employments.

III. UNEMPLOYMENT AND UNDEREMPLOYMENT

A critical issue for observers of Mexican development in recent years has been the degree to which the available labor resources have been utilized. As indicated earlier, it is commonly asserted that unemployment and underemployment have been increasing over time. The empirical foundations upon which this conclusion rests include the

TABLE 5
Average Monthly Cash Wages Offered Domestic Servants, Mexico City
(Current Pesos and Indices)

Year	Method I Monthly Wage in Current Pesos	Index of Real Wages (1963=100)	Method II Monthly Wage in Current Pesos	Index of Real Wages (1963=100)
1963	277	100.0	258	100.0
1964	288	101.8	283	107.3
1965	320	109.0	308	112.6
1966	349	114.1	333	117.0
1967	360	114.5	358	122.3
1968	363	113.9	383	128.9
1969	356	107.4	408	132.2
1970	447	128.2	433	133.5
1971	427	116.1	458	133.7
1972	478	123.6	483	134.1
1973	511	118.7	508	126.8
1974	532	101.1	533	108.7
1975	615	99.8	558	97.3
1980, July	3,260	198.8		
1980, July Minimum Wage Offered	2,500	152.4		

Notes:

Method I is a simple average of the sample offers in each year.

Method II estimated an annual wage from a regression line fitted by least squares to the sample averages.

Both methods are reported as published.

Sources:

Secretaría de Trabajo y Previsión Social 1976, 55-114.

The 1980 data were culled from July, 1980 issues of Excelsior and Universal.

following elements: (1) a decline in labor force participation rates that is interpreted as reflecting a response to increasingly scarce employment opportunities; (2) the secular rise in rates of open unemployment reported by the population census; (3) the census measures of the number of months in the year, or days in the reference week, worked by labor force members; and (4) the concentration of large numbers of workers employed at low wages. We consider each of these in turn.

A. Participation Rates

As is clear from the data presented in Table 6, the overall participation rate of the population twelve years of age and older has declined over the past three censuses. A substantial decline in male participation rates was only partially offset by an increase in female rates, so the total participation rate declined from 49.5 percent in 1950 to 43.5 percent in 1970. However, almost the whole of that decline is associated with an almost equal increase in the proportion of the population over twelve years old enrolled in school from 6.5 percent in 1950 to 12 percent in 1970. This increase of 5.5 percentage points accounts for all but .5 percentage point of the decline in the participation rate. The other significant reduction in participation rates occurs among men aged sixty and over. In view of the extension of retirement benefits to a wider segment of the aging population, withdrawal from the labor force might be interpreted as a voluntary measure rather than a response to shortages of employment opportunities.

The reported decline in labor force participation rates may also reflect shortcomings in the enumeration process.[17] The difficulties of accurately assessing the labor force status of populations in developing countries are too familiar to be reviewed here, and these are not entirely absent in the case of Mexico. In addition, the interpretation of reported changes over time are complicated by differences in the concepts employed, the nature of questions asked, and the time of the year in which censuses are taken. In particular, the declines reported for 1970 seem suspect. We have already referred to the unusually low participation rates reported for men in the prime labor force age groups in states which are predominantly agricultural. An anomaly that raises doubts about the female participation rates is found in a comparison of the rate based on the whole of 1969 with that based on activity in the week prior to the census. One would normally expect that a labor force defined on the basis of activity at any time during the preceding year should be larger than one based on labor force status during a single week. Yet, the 1970 census reports a larger female labor force during the week preceding the census.

Finally, a subsequent source of information serves further to cast doubt on the extent of decline in participation rates. Beginning in 1973, a wide range of labor force data has been provided by quarterly surveys of households for the three major urban concentrations of the country, Mexico City, Guadalajara, and Monterrey. Additional regions of the country have been added over time until, at the end of the decade, the whole country was being surveyed. Unfortunately, the only comparison that can be made of 1973 survey participation rates with those of the census is that for the

TABLE 6
Labor Force and Participation Rates, 1950-69, by Sex
  (Number in Thousands and Percent)

	Number (Thousands)	Participation Rate (Percent)	Number	LFPR	Number	LFPR
1950						
TOTAL	8,345.2	49.5				
Men	7,207.6	88.2				
Women	1,137.6	13.1				
1960	(a)	(a)	(b)	(b)	(c)	(c)
TOTAL	11,253.3	51.1	10,631.2	48.3	10,212.9	46.5
Men	9,235.0	85.1	8,732.0	80.5	8,496.2	78.7
Women	2,018.3	18.0	1,899.2	16.9	1,716.6	15.4
1969						
TOTAL	12,955.1	43.6				
Men	10,488.8	71.7				
Women	2,466.3	16.4				
1970 (Jan.)						
TOTAL	12,909.5	43.5				
Men	10,255.2	70.1				
Women	2,654.3	17.6				

Sources:

1950   VII Censo de poblacion.

1960(a)   VIII Censo de poblacion as reported by Altimir.

 (b) Colegio de México (1970) as reported by Altimir.

 (c) O. Altimir (1974, 50-83).

1970   IX Censo de poblacion.

Federal District; census data are not available for the other two
metropolitan areas in isolation from the states in which they are
located. For the Federal District, however, the survey data report
participation rates for both sexes well above the census rates for the
whole year of 1969 (see Table 7). Whereas the census participation
rate for men was 71.5 percent, the average of four quarterly surveys
yielded a rate of 75.1 percent; only among men over fifty-five are the
survey rates lower than those of the census. The absolute and
relative differences in the two rates are even greater for women, 29.7
to 35.0 percent (Secretaría de Progamación y Presupuesto 1973). While
it is not unusual for labor force surveys to report a larger labor
force than population censuses, these differences would seem to be
unusually large, particularly if participation rates are believed to
be in secular decline

Comparisons of census and survey participation rates in other
regions can be made for a later point in the decade. Table 8 presents
a comparison of participation rates reported for the week prior to the
census (January 1970) with those reported by the survey for the first
quarter of 1978. Data are presented only for men and are
disaggregated into three of the prime labor force age groups. The
margin by which the survey data exceed the census participation rates
is notable in all of the regions reporting in 1978. In short, because
of the large increase in school attendance among the population of
labor force age, and because of the possibility that the 1970 census
seriously underreported the size of the labor force, the reported
decline in participation rates cannot be accepted as having been
established as fact. It follows that the alarming conclusions drawn
from the reported trend, with respect to the degree of utilization of
available manpower resources, is likewise open to serious question.

B. Unemployment

The second basis for the view that unemployment has been
increasing secularly rests on the rates of open unemployment reported
by censuses since 1940. Clearly, these have been increasing as can be
seen from Table 9. However, while the rate appears to have quadrupled
between 1940 and 1970, the 3.8 percentage rate for the latter year can
hardly be considered to have reached a troublesome level. In view of
the doubling of the proportion of the urban population in the total
from 30 percent to 59 percent, it is reasonable to expect an increase
in frictional unemployment. Indeed, the 1970 level, if it could be
accepted as an accurate measure of unemployment, could be considered
to be close to the frictional level.

However, whether the trend can be accepted as an accurate
reflection of the past is open to question. Changes in the concepts
employed and in the questions asked have varied from one census to
another, rendering comparisons over time difficult to interpret.[18]
Certainly, the census measures for 1970 have proved to be conservative
when compared to the findings of the labor force surveys of the 1970s.
For example, the census reported the rate of open unemployment in the
Federal District to be on the order of 5 percent in the week preceding
the census. In contrast, the first of the household surveys of the
labor force, that for the first quarter of 1973, reported that 7.2
percent of the labor force was unemployed. However, important

TABLE 7
Labor Force Participation Rates in the Federal District by Age Group and Sex, 1969 and 1973
(Percent)

	Total	Age Groups						
		12-19	20-24	25-34	35-44	45-54	55-64	65 and Over
Males								
1969	71.7	28.0	80.0	94.9	96.4	94.5	85.9	57.9
1973	75.1	37.9	85.9	98.1	98.2	95.8	80.8	51.0
Females								
1969	29.7	23.8	44.2	33.0	31.2	29.2	23.6	13.8
1973	35.0	29.6	50.7	39.5	39.0	34.0	24.7	12.0

Sources:

Secretaría de Industria y Comercio, Dirección General de Estadística (1972b).

Secretaría de Programación y Presupuesto, Encuesta continua de mano de obra, 1973 (1977).

TABLE 8
Labor Force Participation Rates of Men in Prime Age Groups,
January 1970 and First Quarter 1978, by Region
(Percent)

Region	Age Groups		
	25-34	35-44	45-54
FEDERAL DISTRICT			
1970	92.9	92.1	92.3
1978	95.8	98.0	95.3
NORTH			
1970	87.0	89.3	88.1
1978	89.9	91.8	92.7
NORTHEAST			
1970	90.3	91.7	89.9
1978	95.0	97.5	94.7
NORTHWEST			
1970	90.5	89.2	88.2
1978	97.0	98.5	93.9
CENTRAL-NORTH			
1970	86.9	89.1	88.5
1978	93.4	94.8	93.7
PENINSULAR			
1970	90.1	91.8	91.7
1978	99.0	98.6	98.6
CENTRAL-PACIFIC			
1970	84.5	86.2	85.3
1978	94.1	95.8	93.8
CENTRAL			
1970	87.4	88.7	87.6
1978	94.9	95.8	92.6

Sources: Censo de población, 1970.

Secretaría de programación y presupuesto, Encuesta
continua sobre ocupación, Vol. 7, Trimestre 1, 1978.

TABLE 9
Unemployment in Mexico, 1940–1970
  (percent)

Year	Unemployment Rate		
	Total	Male	Female
1940	1.0	1.0	0.7
1940 (a)	3.1	–	–
1950	1.3	1.3	1.2
1960	1.8	1.9	1.3
1970	3.8	2.8	7.5

Notes:

1940   Census includes only those unemployed for at least a
        month at the time of the census.

1940 (a) The derivation of this estimate is not clear. It appear-
        ed in an unemployment series published in the Anuario
        Estadistico for 1938 and 1940, as reported by Wilkie.

1950   Of the 105,177 unemployed workers, the census reported
        32,030 unemployed for 12 weeks or less and 73,147 who
        had been seeking employment for 13 weeks or more.

1960   The measure of the labor force used here includes the
        Altimir adjustment. Of the 182,088 unemployed, only
        29,736 (16.3 percent) were reported to have been unem-
        ployed for 13 weeks or more.

1970   The measure of unemployment refers to status during the
        week preceding the census. Of the 485,187 unemployed,
        68,843 (13.4 percent) had been so for 13 weeks or more.

Sources: Censo de población, VI–IX.

        1940 (a) J. W. Wilkie (1971, Table 4).

differences in concepts employed render an interpretation of this increase difficult to make. For example, in the census, a respondent's status was defined by reference to a single week, whereas the surveys extended the reference period for the definition of unemployment to two months. This difference alone could account for a substantial part of the difference between the two measures. In any case, the data for the subsequent years of the survey do not reveal any consistent tendency for unemployment to increase in any of the regions during the 1970s. Unemployment increases did occur as the economy slid into recession in 1976, but the recovery which followed quickly reduced the rates to prerecession levels.

Of interest is the relatively short duration of reported unemployment. In all of the census years, only about 1 percent of the labor force was unemployed for as long as one month. Long-term unemployment of over thirteen weeks was particularly unusual; in 1970, only 13.3 percent of the unemployed were in this category. As in most countries, the incidence of unemployment was greatest among the young. In contrast to the national average unemployment rate of 3.8 percent reported by the 1970 census, that for teenagers was almost 6 percent, while that for labor force members aged twenty to twenty-four was 4.4 percent (Secretaría de Industria y Comercio 1972b, Table 32). The first survey reports even greater disparities in the age-specific unemployment rates in the large metropolitan areas. For example, in the Federal District, in the face of an average rate of 7.2 percent during the first quarter of 1973, the teenage rate was 18.4 percent, and that for young adults aged twenty to twenty-four was 10.1 percent. (Secretaría de Programación y Presupuesto 1973, Table 2A). In contrast, that for the prime age groups was on the order of 2 to 3 percent. The 1970 census data for the District yield a teenage rate of 11.2 percent and a young adult rate of 5.9 percent as compared to the average rate of 5 percent.

The view that a secular increase in unemployment may have occurred may be deduced from the surveys. Earlier, we suggested that such an increase, if it had indeed occurred, could be a reflection of the increasing urbanization of the country and a subsequent increase in frictional unemployment. A cross-sectional analysis of the regional unemployment rates would tend to support this view. The highest rates of unemployment are to be found in the metropolitan urban areas of the country, intermediate rates in the smaller urban centers, and the lowest in the least urbanized regions. Since the urban areas have increased their relative weight in the country as a whole, some increases in the national average rate of unemployment could be expected to occur. The significance of an increase due to such a structural change in the distribution of the labor force, however, is surely less ominous than secular increases in rates within regions. To date, the labor force surveys have not recorded such increases.

C. Underemployment

Measured open unemployment rates in Mexico would thus appear to have been below those frequently observed in other developing countries. Consequently, concern with the utilization of labor resources in Mexico has centered not so much on open unemployment as on the presumed high level of underemployment. Unfortunately, most of the discussions of underemployment of labor in Mexico reflect the same conceptual and measurement problems that prevail generally. As a result, one finds widely disparate estimates of underemployment depending on whether these are based on measures of the proportion of a year or week worked by the employed, on measures of the adequacy of incomes earned, or a combination of both. For example, a study group formed to study the employment problem in the early 1970s adopted a complex definition of underemployment that included almost all unpaid family workers, those with incomes below official regional minimum wage levels, and workers employed for considerably less than a full year. The group's estimates of underemployment, based on 1970 census data, ranged from 37.6 percent to 44.8 percent of the labor force.[19]

Empirical data of time worked per time unit are available for various points in time. The 1970 census recorded the number of months worked during 1969. The 1950 census recorded the number of days worked during a reference week. Finally, since 1973, the labor force surveys have captured information regarding the number of hours worked during the reference week. Unfortunately, the different measurements employed make it impossible to calculate a trend in the possible degree of underemployment over time. Only since 1973 can a consistent series be said to exist for a few major urban areas. Estimates of underemployment in the agricultural sector have been derived by applying labor input coefficients to regional cropping patterns to estimate the "required" quantity of labor inputs; converting these to full employment equivalents, and subtracting them from the measured labor supply, yields the "labor surplus." (Goreaux and Manne 1973). For those who define underemployment in terms of the level of earnings, sources of information include the census of 1970 and a number of household surveys of income and expenditures which have been undertaken since 1963.

Unfortunately, all of these approaches to the measurement of underemployment pose serious problems of interpretation. Those that define underemployment by reference to time worked as a proportion of some reference period considered to be "normal" cannot, in the absence of additional information, distinguish between those departures from full-time employment that are voluntary from those that are involuntary; presumably only the latter qualify as underemployment. Nor can the entire proportion of workers working less than a full year, as reported by the 1970 census, be taken to represent a measure of underemployment. Some part of these workers represent individuals who entered the labor force for the first time after the beginning of the year, or who retired permanently before the end of the year; on the basis of the age distribution of the population and labor force, I estimate that approximately 5 percent of the labor force, as measured in the 1970 census, was composed of individuals in one of these two categories.[20] Unless an adjustment is introduced in the raw data on months worked to account for this subgroup, estimates of underemployment will be exaggerated.

The estimation of the degree of underemployment which exists in the rural sector of Mexico is extremely difficult to undertake with confidence. The estimation of an agricultural "surplus" labor force derived by employing input coefficients does not necessarily mean that that "surplus" remains idle when not employed in agricultural production. Employment in other forms of home production may occupy some part of the time not spent in agricultural production of final goods. Furthermore, movement of labor from agricultural to nonagricultural employment is a common phenomenon in Mexico, so that what may appear to be a surplus to the agricultural sector may not be a surplus to the economy as a whole. Finally, some part of the agricultural labor force which is available for peak season employment may simply not be available for employment at other times.

The measurement of underemployment by reference to income levels likewise leaves a good deal to be desired. Many of those below the income level adopted to identify the underemployed may not be physically underemployed at all, in the sense that they are available for additional hours of work. Indeed, they may be working arduously long hours at socially useful tasks. Their incomes are low because their marginal productivity is low, which, in turn, is a function of the relative availabilities of labor and of physical and human capital. It is precisely this prevalence of low productivity and income that is the principal identifying characteristic of underdevelopment. The redefinition of poverty as underemployment creates a misleading impression of the degree to which available labor resources are not being utilized in productive employment. An additional difficulty with the income criterion for defining underemployment is the arbitrariness of the standard employed. For example, the legal minimum wage is frequently taken as the dividing line between underemployment and "full" employment. Yet, this wage has no unique quality that objectively distinguishes between the two classes of workers. By merely raising the legal minimum wage relative to "going" wages or the opportunity cost of labor, the number of "underemployed" workers will be increased even though no objective change has occurred in their employment or income situation. Conversely, if the legal minimum is allowed to drop relative to the opportunity cost of labor, the degree of underemployment will appear to have declined.[21]

Thus, not only is the concept of underemployment an elusive one, but mechanistic approaches to its measurement are likely to prove rather misleading. This becomes evident if one examines some of the more detailed information derived from the household labor force surveys. While these surveys have not been in progress long enough to provide a basis for observing conclusively the secular course of employment conditions, they do yield new and important insights into various observable labor market phenomena that counsel caution in the use of raw or aggregated data. The section which follows reviews some of the findings based on these surveys that have a relevance for some of the questions raised in this paper to date.

IV. RECENT LABOR MARKET OBSERVATIONS, 1973-78

Earlier we discussed the possible significance of the observed decline in labor force participation rates over time, noting that it could be interpreted as a product of the increased availability of educational opportunities rather than of an insufficiency in the availability of employments. The survey data now permit us to carry the analysis further and to bring it forward to 1978. We have indicated that the surveys, from the start, have reported higher labor force participation rates for both sexes than did the 1970 census. At the same time, however, the surveys do confirm and extend the secular declining trend in the participation rates among the youngest and oldest age groups of men, though the impact on the aggregate participation rate has become quite small. As observed in the intercensal periods, declines in participation rates among young males continue to be associated with increases in school enrollments. Among women, the participation rates have varied within a narrow range for the areas surveyed since 1973 with no evidence of a trend. One of the striking aspects of this stability is the fact that it has occurred in spite of a much greater increase in school enrollment among young females than among males. Prior to 1970, the rate of school attendance among females of post-primary school age was well below that of males, by approximately a third. During the 1970s, however, female enrollments increased more rapidly than male, so that, by 1978, the gap had narrowed substantially. What is significant, however, is an indication that there was not an equal tradeoff between increases in school enrollment and declines in labor force participation rates. Among females, for example, labor participation rates in 1978 were higher than they were reported to be by the census in spite of even larger increases in the rate of school enrollment. This was also true among males, though to a lesser extent. This can be shown by comparing the changes in labor force participation rates by sex with the change in the sum of those rates and the rate of school attendance. What the data in Table 10 suggest is that employment opportunities for the young expanded during the 1970s at a rate greater than the increase in the nonschool population.[22] Only if one interprets the increase in school enrollments as a reluctant choice by young people of a nonpreferred activity, can the labor force data be interpreted as reflecting a deterioration in job opportunities for young potential entrants to the labor force.

One of the constant preoccupations of students of Mexican economic development is the fear that employment opportunities have not increased as rapidly as the labor force, thus giving rise either to rising unemployment rates or declining labor force participation rates. This fear has been encouraged by the larger rates of unemployment uncovered by the labor force surveys than had been reported by the 1970 census. In fact, while the levels in the first quarter of 1978 were higher in five of the eight reporting regions than they were in January 1970, they were only marginally greater by and large (See Table 11). However, in the aggregate, in all but one region the absolute increases in the rates of unemployment lagged well behind the increases in the labor force participation rates. In other words, increases in labor force participation rates were associated with increased employment rates rather than simply increased

TABLE 10

Summary Comparison of Labor Force Participation Rates and School
Enrollments, January 1970 and First Quarter 1978, by Region and Sex
(Percent)

Region	Labor Force Participation Rate			Labor Force Participation Rate Plus Rate of School Enrollment		
	Total	Male	Female	Total	Male	Female
FEDERAL DISTRICT						
1970	48.4	70.6	24.7	63.9	89.2	36.5
1978	51.6	71.8	33.9	71.3	92.9	52.4
NORTH						
1970	41.7	67.9	15.5	54.5	82.0	21.0
1978	40.6	63.8	19.5	62.5	87.6	39.1
NORTHEAST						
1970	43.3	70.0	17.0	56.4	85.1	28.1
1978	44.2	70.1	18.7	62.7	90.9	35.0
NORTHWEST						
1970	43.4	68.9	17.4	56.9	83.6	29.4
1978	44.7	72.0	18.7	64.9	92.9	38.3
CENTRAL-NORTH						
1970	42.0	69.9	14.2	52.7	82.1	23.4
1978	43.7	72.4	15.3	58.6	88.2	28.3
PENINSULAR						
1970	43.9	47.4	13.3	54.2	86.4	22.2
1978	48.0	79.8	17.2	63.1	96.2	31.0
CENTRAL-PACIFIC						
1970	42.4	69.3	16.5	54.1	82.9	26.4
1978	46.0	72.5	22.2	62.0	90.5	36.8
CENTRAL (a)						
1970	42.7	70.1	15.6	53.2	82.4	24.4
1978	44.9	71.7	19.8	61.3	90.0	35.0

Note: (a) Includes those municipios which form part of the Mexico
        City Metropolitan area but which lie in the State of Mexico.
Sources: Same as Table 8.

TABLE 11
Summary of Changes Between January 1970 and January 1978 in Labor Force Participation Rates (LFPR) and
Unemployment Rates (U) Expressed as a Proportion of the Population 12 Years Old and Older
(Percent: January 1978 less January 1970)

	Total		Male		Female	
	% Point Changes		% Point Changes		% Point Changes	
	LFPR	U	LFPR	U	LFPR	U
Federal District	3.2	1.5	1.2	1.7	9.2	1.4
North	-1.1	-0.2	-4.1	0.1	4.0	-0.4
Northeast	0.9	0.5	0.1	0.8	1.7	0.2
Northwest	1.3	0.2	3.1	0.7	1.3	-0.3
Central-North	1.7	-1.1	2.5	-1.1	1.1	-1.1
Peninsular	4.1	-0.3	5.4	0.0	3.9	-0.6
Central-Pacific	3.6	0.4	3.2	0.5	5.7	0.3
Central	2.2	0.2	1.6	0.7	4.2	-0.2

Sources: Same as Table 8.

unemployment rates. However, if the data are disaggregated by sex, some differences do appear. Among men, in three regions, the Federal District, the Northeastern, and the Northern, the increases in the unemployment rate exceeded those in the participation rates, suggesting a relatively less favorable evolution of employment conditions for men there. In all the other regions, the increases in participation rates far outrun the increases in unemployment. On the other hand, the changes in the female rates suggest a universal and significant improvement in employment opportunities. In spite of significant increases in participation rates over those of the census, the rates of unemployment showed declines in five of the eight regions, while in the others they increased far less than the increases in participation rates. Indeed, there is a very striking, direct relationship between the increase in participation rates and changes in the unemployment rate. For example, the largest increase in the unemployment rate over 1970 was in the amount of 1.4 percentage points in the Federal District. But this was associated with a much greater increase in the labor force participation rate of 9.2 percentage points. What this seems to suggest is a widespread and significant improvement in employment opportunities, especially for women. The appearance of employment opportunities induces more women to enter the labor force. The rapid influx of women might be expected to lead to an increase in frictional unemployment and may account for the rather larger increases in unemployment rates in the regions of most rapid growth of female employment.

This apparent responsiveness of women to the expansion of employment opportunities may be interpreted as indicating the existence of a large pool of hidden unemployment, or of discouraged workers, workers who are desirous of employment but who do not seek employment out of a conviction that vacancies do not exist. That this is characteristic of many of labor force age is a common belief in Mexico. Support for this view would seem to exist in data from the labor force survey which asks individuals who appear to be out of the labor force whether they are available to accept employment even though they have taken no steps to seek jobs during the preceding two months. Among the surveyed populations of the three large metropolitan areas, approximately 2 percent of the male respondents and 6 to 7 percent of the female respondents answer in the affirmative.[23] In absolute terms, women represent about two-thirds of the "hidden unemployed." The incidence appears to be heaviest among teenage women. Over the first six years of the surveys, there is no discernable trend in these proportions. The rates seem to fluctuate within a narrow band of plus-or-minus 1 percentage point for men and a slightly wider band for women. These "measured" responses are widely interpreted as representing accurate indicators of labor force status; therefore, it is argued that the measured open unemployment rates seriously understate the "true" extent of unemployment.

On the other hand, it may be argued that responses to such hypothetical questions about availability are likely to be misleading, that more persons are likely to answer in the affirmative than are actually available for immediate employment. Until recently, we had no way of testing the significance of these responses. However, in a special publication by the authors of the survey, more detailed data were presented based on the survey of the second quarter of 1978.

(Secretaría de Programación y Presupuesto, No Date, Tables 59-61). In this publication the proportions of the respondents who had been identified as the "hidden unemployed" were further classified according to their availability for immediate employment. Only a small minority proved to be available in the Mexico City (4.1 percent), Guadalajara (6.7 percent), and Monterrey (7.4 percent), metropolitan areas. The vast majority were only conditionally available. While the report does not offer the conditions placed on the respondents' availability, it does record their current activity. Among men, the overwhelming majority were students, a condition that precludes an active labor force status except on a part-time basis. Among women, the bulk of the respondents were either engaged in household duties or in formal studies. It is noteworthy that between one-third and one-half of the respondents had had no previous work experience while an additional 20 to 25 percent had not held an employment for over five years. Over 40 percent were teenagers. Most of these individuals would appear to be engaged in worthwhile activities. But even if all those who professed an immediate and unconditional availability for employment were to be counted as in the labor force and as unemployed, their impact on the unemployment rate would amount to an increase on the order of only 1 percentage point.

We noted earlier that one approach to the measurement of the underutilization of the labor force classifies as underemployed all those workers whose work week in the reference period is shorter than something approximating a "normal" week of forty hours. Table 12 presents data on the proportion of the employed labor force working less than forty hours as reported by the labor force survey for the first quarter of 1978. The information is disaggregated by region and sex. As can be seen, significant proportions of the employed labor force are employed fewer than forty hours per week. Among employed men, the proportion varies over regions from 7.2 percent to 11.6 percent. Among women, the proportion varies between 16.6 percent and 41.8 percent. However, these proportions cannot be taken to represent a measure of underemployment since a considerable proportion of those working short hours do so voluntarily. The range for women is from almost two-thirds to three-fourths. The final column records the proportion of the employed labor force which is involuntarily employed for fewer than forty hours. As can be seen, the presumed level of underemployment is drastically reduced below the raw proportions. Among men and women, the ranges are from 3.7 to 8.9 percent, and from 4.4 to 13.3 percent, respectively, across regions. If these measures were to be reduced to full-time equivalents, their significance would be reduced even further. An interesting observation is the absence of a consistent relationship between the degree of urbanization of the region and the incidence of involuntary underemployment. One might have hypothesized that underemployment might prove to be more severe in regions with relatively large agricultural populations, since the rural labor force is thought to exceed by a considerable margin the technical requirements of current levels of agricultural output. On the contrary, some regions with relatively large rural sectors are among those showing the lowest rates of involuntary part-time employment, at least among men.

TABLE 12
Involuntary Underemployment among Employed Men and Women, by Region,
First Quarter, 1978
(Percent)

Region and Sex	Percent of Employed Labor Force Working Fewer Than 40 Hours	Percent of Col. 1 Voluntarily Underemployed	Percent of Employed Labor Force Involuntarily Underemployed
Metropolitan Mexico City			
Men	15.2	68.7	4.8
Women	34.5	76.7	8.0
Metropolitan Guadalajara			
Men	15.7	58.8	6.5
Women	32.8	72.1	9.2
Metropolitan Monterrey			
Men	9.9	60.6	3.9
Women	28.9	70.3	8.6
North			
Men	8.1	54.8	3.7
Women	16.6	73.7	4.4
Northeast			
Men	7.2	49.1	3.7
Women	27.2	67.5	8.8
Northwest			
Men	11.6	55.6	5.2
Women	25.1	69.6	7.6
Center—North			
Men	9.0	51.5	4.4
Women	45.7	78.1	10.0
Peninsular			
Men	16.4	45.6	8.9
Women	41.8	68.3	13.3
Central Pacific			
Men	11.8	62.2	4.5
Women	34.3	71.8	9.7
Central			
Men	10.6	49.9	5.3
Women	33.3	66.2	11.3

Source: Secretaría de Programación y Presupuesto, Encuesta continua
sobre ocupación, Trimestre 1, 1978, Table 9.

Thus, since past estimates of the amount of underemployment have not been able to take account of the voluntary component of less-than-full-time employment, those estimates are likely to overstate the volume of underutilization at any point in time. Furthermore, since there is no comparability in the measures of underutilization employed by the various censuses and surveys taken at different points in time, it is impossible to state with any degree of certainty either the direction or degree of change that has occurred over time.

V. CONCLUSION

This essay has examined a range of empirical information which is relevant to an evaluation of the changes that have occurred in the Mexican labor market in the process of post-World War II economic development. Contrary to the prevailing perceptions of a secular deterioration in the conditions of employment, the data analyzed here point to a much more optimstic conclusion. The rapid and sustained growth of the economy has been accompanied by a very substantial shift of the labor force from the agricultural sector, where productivity is relatively low, to the secondary and tertiary sectors, where productivities are much higher. Furthermore, this large shift has been achieved without depressing the productivity or wages of labor in the expanding sectors. Our analysis of the course of remunerations and productivities, in those parts of the nonagricultural sectors that are likely to reflect the uninhibited forces of supply and demand in the labor market, recorded substantial improvements in both of these measures. Finally, I have set forth reasons for believing that the degree of underutilization of labor resources may be considerably smaller than most estimates have held.

To be sure, challenging problems remain to be addressed. The labor force is growing at a rate approaching 3 percent per year. Its absorption at ever-higher average levels of productivity will require high and sustained levels of investment. The educational endownment of the labor force is quite low in comparison to other semi-industrialized countries, and much of the education provided is of questionable quality. Pockets of abject rural poverty remain only marginally affected by the changes occurring in the society at large. But these problems are less likely to appear insurmountable if proper recognition is given to the substantial improvements that have been achieved in the past and a fuller appreciation is gained of the way in which labor markets function.

FOOTNOTES

The findings reported in this essay are drawn from an extensive study of the evolution of the Mexican labor market that has been sponsored by The World Bank. The views expressed in this paper are the author's alone and are not attributable to The World Bank.

1. When the 1975 census provides data on remunerations and total employment by establishment size, it does not separate out the unremunerated component of total employment on a similar basis. The latter component was estimated on the basis of more complete data in earlier censuses by applying the past ratio of unremunerated personnel per establishment in each size class to the 1975 establishments of equivalent sizes. (Secretaría de Programación y Presupuesto 1979C, 167, Table 8.)

2. The estimated increase in the ratio may be exaggerated, for the labor force size assumed for the agricultural sector would seem to be larger than is likely. (Gómez 1978, 721.)

3. The poverty line in Mexico is drawn at a household income equal to half the estimated national mean, which, in 1975, would have been Mex. $1,621 per month, equivalent in purchasing power to approximately US $1,315 per year per family. These figures should be taken as being only roughly indicative. The 1975 survey appears to have underestimated severely the incomes of some groups, largely in the form of income in kind. The results of the 1977 survey, which are thought to be of better quality, are not yet available by sector of employment of the head of household. (Centro Nacional de Información y Estadísticas del Trabajo 1977.)

4. In 1950, the population measured 26.5 millions. By 1970 it had grown to 50.5 millions. (Unikel 1976, 213.)

5. Evans and James (1979, 4-24). For appraisals of employment conditions, see also Secretaría de Trabajo y Previsión Social (1979a); Trejo (1972, 411-16); Trejo (1974, 730-38); Programa Regional del Empleo Para América Latina y el Caribe (1976); Grupo de Estudio del Problema del Empleo (1974).

6. An example of the latter is the conclusion, drawn from reviews of the changing sectoral distribution of the labor force, that there has been an overexpansion of tertiary sector employment. The criteria employed in reaching the conclusion are not made explicit nor are the data disaggregated in a way that might indicate support for it. This question is addressed in the section that follows.

7. A full discussion of the merits and demerits of the various approaches will be included in a forthcoming research report on the Mexican labor market in the process of preparation.

8. The 1970 census distributed the labor force on the basis of the principal employment held during 1969.

9. Whereas in the 1950 census, all ejidatarios were automatically classified as part of the agricultural labor force, the 1960 census attempted, with only partial success, to verify the principal employment of ejidatarios. Since many of these held principal employments outside agriculture, the reclassification of these in 1960 would reduce the 1960 total relative to the

classification used in 1950. Furthermore, Altimir (1974) introduces additional adjustments to compensate for the imperfect classification of the ejidatarios as well as for the coding and processing errors that afflicted that census. The 1970 census appears to have underenumerated the agricultural labor force. This is suggested by the observation that unusually low labor force participation rates were reported for men in the prime labor force age groups in states which are heavily agricultural. In addition, the 1970 figure would have been biased downward with respect to 1950 by the greater success in properly classifying the ejidatarios.

10. Those who subscribe to the view that employment in the tertiary sector is supply determined naturally emphasize the impact on labor supply of the rapid growth of the urban population.

11. A decline in wages within the tertiary sector would not provide sufficient grounds for concluding that average employment conditions had deteriorated if the growth of the tertiary sector occurred at the expense of an even lower-wage agricultural sector.

12. S. Perrakis (1972); C. W. Reynolds (1970, 85-86); a much more conservative estimate of the probable extent of the decline in real wages is offered by T. King (1971). A summary of the literature on wages during the 1940s and 1950s is contained in P. Gregory (1975, 65-68).

13. All of the estimates of income distribution for Mexico are derived on the basis of assumptions that, by necessity, involve a high degree of arbitrariness. This arises from the large discrepancy, which has increased over time, between the estimates of national income based on the household income and expenditures studies and those derived from the national income accounts. Since the former serve as the basis for estimating the distribution of income, it is necessary to distribute this discrepancy over households in some manner. Different scholars have adopted their own methods of distributing the discrepancy with rather significantly different results for the shares of particular deciles.

14. It should be observed that, between 1970 and 1975, the real earnings of workers in the smallest size service establishments recorded a significant decline in contrast to all other categories and sectors. The significance of this decline is difficult to gauge. It may flow from data deficiencies which assigned to 1970 an unexpectedly high value to earnings in this stratum. The course of earnings in the sample establishments in the other sectors as well as that among domestic servants, which are reviewed below, suggest that the decline in services, if it did in fact occur, was not representative of changes in the small establishment sector generally.

15. It might be argued that the establishments likely to be included in a census are those which are "registered" and, therefore, not representative of the wage conditions prevailing in less formally

organized enterprises. However, to the extent to which the former are not bound by institutional intervention in the wage determination process, then they may be expected to be competitive in the labor market with the latter.

16. The range of increases and decreases in remunerations reflect the use by the authors of the study of two different methods to estimate the rate of change. The lower values given are derived from the data as recorded in each year of the survey. However, since the annual values showed rather sharp and irregular year-to-year variations, a trend line was fitted to the nominal wage data by least squares method and a series of estimated annual remunerations were derived. The larger values in the ranges appearing in the text are attributable to the wage series so derived. (Secretaría del Trabajo y Previsión Social 1976, 94-95.)

17. An excellent analysis of the measurement of the Mexican labor force and an interpretation of the changes is offered by D. B. Keesing (1977, 3-21).

18. Keesing (1977, 5-7) discusses at length some of the difficulties of interpreting the various census measures.

19. Grupo de Estudio del Problema del Empleo (1974, Table 2). For other estimates, see p. 4 and note 5 above.

20. It will be recalled that one of the measures of the labor force employed included all those who had worked at any time during 1969. It was to this group that a question regarding the number of months worked was addressed.

21. Employing this standard in Mexico would yield an astronomical proportion of the labor force as underemployed in 1940 when the legal minimum had been pushed up to a very high level relative to average incomes. During the succeeding decade, this proportion would have fallen as the real value of the minimum wage declined.

22. Even if the 1970 census data are biased toward an underenumeration of the labor force, the underenumeration is unlikely to have been sufficiently large so as to eliminate the large growth in the sum of the rates of labor force participation and school attendance that is recorded in Table 10 for all surveyed regions of the country.

23. These proportions are equivalent to about 2.5 and 8.5 percent of the male and female measured labor force respectively.

BIBLIOGRAPHY

Altimir, O. 1974. La medición de la población económicamente activa de México 1950-70. *Demografía y economía*, 8(1):50-83.

Banco de México. 1978. *Informe anual 1977*. Mexico, D.F.

_____, 1979. *Producto interno bruto y gasto 1970-78*. Mexico, D.F.

Centro Nacional de Información y Estadísticas del Trabajo. 1977. *Encuesta de ingresos y gastos familiares, 1975*. Mexico, D. F.

Colegio de México. 1970. *Dinámica de la población en México*. Mexico, D. F.

Evans, J. S., D. D. James. 1979. Conditions of employment and income distribution in Mexico as incentives for Mexican migration to the United States: prospects to the end of the century. *International Migration Rev.*, 13(1)(Spring): 4-24.

Excelsior. Mexico, D. F. Various issues

Gómez, O. L. 1978. Crisis agrícola, crisis de los compesinos. *Comercio exterior*, 28(6)(June): 714-27.

Goreaux, L. M., A. S. Manne. 1973. *Multi-level planning: case studies in Mexico*. Amsterdam: North-Holland Publishing Company.

Gregory, P. 1975. The impact of institutional factors on urban labor markets. Studies in Employment and Rural Development No. 27. (mimeo). Washington, D.C.: The World Bank.

Grupo de Estudio del Problema del Empleo. 1974. *El problema ocupacional en México*. Mexico, D. F.: Fondo de Cultura Económica.

Hernández L., E. Córdova C., J. 1979. Estructura de la distributión de ingreso en México. *Comercio exterior*, 29(5)(May): 505-20.

Keesing, D. B. 1977. Employment and lack of employment in Mexico, 1900-1970. In *Quantitative Latin American Studies: Methods and Findings*. ed. J. W. Wilkie, K. Ruddle, 3-21. Los Angeles: UCLA Latin American Center.

King, T. 1971. *Mexico: industrialization and trade policies since 1940*. London: Oxford U. Press. 26-27.

McFarland, E. L., Jr. 1973. Service employment: Mexico, 1950-1969. (mimeo). Washington, D.C.: The World Bank.

Perrakis, S. 1972. The labor surplus model and wage behavior in Mexico. *Industrial Relations*, 11(1)(February): 80-95.

278

Programa Regional del Empleo Para América Latina y el Caribe. 1976. *The employment problem in Latin America*: *facts, outlooks and policies*. Santiago, Chile: Oficina Internacional de Trabajo.

Reynolds, C. W. 1970. *The Mexican Economy*. New Haven: Yale U. Press.

_____, 1979. A shift-share analysis of regional and sectoral productivity growth in contemporay Mexico. (mimeo). Stanford, CA: Stanford University.

Secretaría de Industria y Comercio, Dirección General de Estadística. 1965. *IV Censo comercial 1961*. Mexico, D. F.

_____, 1968. *V Censo comercial 1966*. Mexico, D.F.

_____, 1975. *VI Censo comercial 1971*. (Datos de 1970) Mexico, D.F.

_____, 1965a. *IV Censo de servicios 1961*. Mexico, D.F.

_____, 1967a. *V Censo de servicios 1966*. Mexico, D. F.

_____, 1974. *VI Censo de servicios 1971*. Mexico, D.F.

_____, 1977. *VII Censo de servicos, 1976*. (Datos de 1975). Mexico, D.F.

_____, 1965b. *VIII Censo industrial 1961*. Mexico, D.F.

_____, 1967b. *VIII Censo industrial 1966*. Mexico, D.F.

_____, 1972a. *IX Censo industrial 1971*. Mexico, D.F.

_____, 1952. *VII Censo de población 1950*. Mexico D.F.

_____, 1962. *VIII Censo de población 1960*. Mexico, D.F.

_____, 1972b. *IX Censo de población 1970*. Mexico, D.F.

Secretaría de Programación y Presupuesto. 1979a. *VII Censo de comercio 1976*. Mexico, D.F.

_____, 1979b. *VII Censo de servicios, 1976*. Mexico, D.F.

_____, 1979c. *X Censo industrial 1976*. (Datos de 1975) Mexico, D.F.

_____, *Encuesta continua de mano de obra*. Various issues. Beginning in 1978 the survey publication was renamed *Encuesta continua sobre ocupación*.

_____, no date. *Información basica sobre estructura y caracteristicas del empleo en las areas metropolitanas de las ciudades de México Guadalajara y Monterrey*. Mexico, D.F.

Secretaría de Trabajo y Previsión Social. 1976. Análysis del mercado de los servicios domésticos en México. *Cuadernos de empleo*, 1:51-114. Mexico, D.F.

_____, 1979. *Programa nacional de empleo, 1980-82, Vol. I, presentación y diagnóstico*. (November). Mexico, D.F.

Trejo R., S. 1972. Desempleo y subocupación en México. *Comercio exterior*, 22(5)(May): 411-16.

_____, 1974. El desempleo en México: characterísticas generales. *Comercio exterior*, 24(7)(July): 730-38.

Unikel, L. 1976. *El desarrollo urbano de México*. Mexico, D.F.: El Colegio de México.

_____, 1978. *El desarrollo urbano de México*. 2nd Edition. Mexico, D.F.: El Colegio de México.

Universal. Mexico, D.F. various issues.

Wilkie, J.W. 1971. New hypotheses for statistical research in recent Mexican history. *Latin American research review*, 6(2)(Summer): 3-18.

13
National Balance Sheets as Tools of International Economic Comparisons

Raymond Goldsmith

I. INTRODUCTION

The international comparison of national and sectoral balance sheets is a delicate and laborious task, even more so than that of the other components of the system of national accounts, and its description does not make fascinating reading. Is it worth the trouble? Theoretically yes, since it should disclose differences and, possibly, similarities among nations and sectors and in changes over time, in important characteristics of the tangible infrastructure, the financial superstructure, and in the relation between them. Whether, empirically, the estimates can meet the basic test that, to vary the principle of homeopathic medicine, similia similibus comparentur, only actual work will tell. The few examples of published national and sectoral balance sheets presented in part III. of this paper are still far from doing so.

The test must be applied to the main characteristics of national and sectoral balance sheets, understood as the combination of the standardized balance sheets of all units belonging to a sector or located within a national territory, that is, the scope of tangible and financial assets covered; the definition of the various assets included; their valuation in current and constant prices; and the delimitation of the various sectors. One might think of simplifying or avoiding such a discussion by deferring to the standardized schema proposed by the Statistical Office of the United Nations (1977), but three considerations argue against such an easy way out. Firstly, to do so would be to deal essentially with the future (Zukunftsmusik), since at this time only two countries (France and Japan) have published official national balance sheets, and for a few years only (INSEE 1980). These, as well as the estimates of the two main components of national balance sheets, the stock of reproducible tangible assets and of financial assets and liabilities, which are being regularly published by a few other countries (e.g., Germany, Norway, Sweden, and the United States) do not conform entirely to the United Nations' scheme. Secondly, there is doubt whether some features of that scheme provide the most appropriate solution. Thirdly, the United Nations' publication does not deal sufficiently with the problem of actual measurement. There thus seems to be no way to avoid the admittedly dreary discussion of these problems, which are not rarely cavalierly treated by economists and econometricians who deal with data on a catch-can basis.

The following pages discuss in disparate brevity the main problems of putting together national and sectoral balance sheets. Less inadequate treatments can be found elsewhere (e.g., United Nations 1977; Goldsmith 1982b).

II. CONCEPTUAL AND MEASUREMENT PROBLEMS

A. The Scope of National Assets.

Consistency in the scope of assets and liabilities included in national and sectoral balance sheets is one of the most important requirements for using them for comparative studies of economic and financial structure, and is more important than their exact definition as is the case for the other characteristics of national and sectoral balance sheets that will be discussed below. The narrowest concept is limited to land, reproducible tangible assets for civilian use other than consumer goods, well-defined claims, and corporate stock. A broader concept includes several or all of a number of additional assets, namely, among tangible assets standing timber, subsoil assets, military durables, consumer goods (durable, semidurable, or nondurable), precious metals, collectors' items, and expenditures or research and development; and among financial assets the equity in unincorporated business enterprises, unfunded pension claims and such intangibles as patents, copyrights, and goodwill. Some students go even so far as to include human capital, considered either prospectively as discounted future earnings (e.g., Jorgenson and Pachon 1980) or retrospectively as the cost of rearing and educating the labor force (e.g., Kendrick 1976). This extension of the concept of national assets will not be considered here, as it is regarded as conceptually inappropriate and because its implementation would lead to the inclusion of almost arbitrary entries which are extremely large compared to all other items in the national balance sheet. The United Nations' standard national balance sheet adopts a position between the two extremes, but much closer to the narrow definition.

As always in the matter of definition, there is no right or wrong scope of the items included in national or sectoral balance sheets, but three criteria provide help in making a decision. The first is the importance of an item in the economy of the countries to be compared. From this point of view it would not make sense, for example, to use a balance sheet of Saudi Arabia that excluded subsoil assets. The second is the treatment of an item in the financial practice or the legal system of the countries being compared. Thus, what cannot be appropriated by private or public owner cannot be valued, and hence cannot be included among assets and liabilities. The third, and often decisive, criterion is the possibility of determining the size of the item within a reasonable margin of uncertainty. It is the difficulty of valuing forests, subsoil assets, and collectors' items which leads to their omission from most existing national balance sheets although they meet all conceptual tests for inclusion.

B. Itemization

The greater the number of assets and liabilties distinguished in national and sectoral balance sheets, the easier, in general, their arrangement in groups that can be compared among countries, but also the greater the difficulty of implementing the schedule. The choice should be guided by homogeneity with respect to cost, price movements, and interest rates as the case may be, and by the relative size of the items being shown separately. The United Nations' model balance sheet distinguishes about two dozen each of tangible and financial assets, but there is no country in the world for which all their empty boxes can be filled. In general, about half as many components will be sufficient. (Another model balance sheet, Ruggles 1980, Table C13, distinguishes twenty-two of them.) They should include among tangible assets land, distinguishing agricultural land, forests, urban land, and subsoil assets; reproducible fixed assets, separating dwellings, other civilian and military structures, and equipment; inventories; livestock; and consumer durables. Among financial assets claims against financial institutions, distinguishing monetary, insurance, and pension claims, should be shown separately, as well as short and long-term loans by financial institutions and other lenders, government and corporate securities, and trade credit.

C. Valuation

Unless similar methods of valuing the various components are consistently followed, valid comparisons are impossible. It has become generally accepted (including the United Nations' standard scheme) that market prices, or the nearest approximation to them, should be the basis of valuation in balance sheets drawn up in current prices. It is also accepted, explicitly or implicitly, that the same item should be identically valued in the balance sheets of all units. The opposite position of using the individual owner's, creditors', or debtors' valuation (Dorrance 1978) is nonoperational whatever its theoretical appeal. Adoption of the principle is, however, far from solving the problems of actual measurement, even if the often-heard objection that only a small proportion of any type of assets comes to the market at or close to the balance-sheet date is disregarded, and it is recognized that valuation is always <u>pars pro toto</u>.

In market economies the difficulties are more pronounced for tangible than for intangible assets. In particular, most if not all components of reproducible fixed assets must usually be valued by the perpetual inventory method, that is, the cumulation of past capital expenditures appropriately depreciated and adjusted for price changes between the date of investment and the balance-sheet date. On the other hand, the valuation of land encounters serious difficulties since no market exists for some types of land which must be valued by other means, for example, by capitalizing rents, and remain subject to a wide margin of uncertainty. Among financial assets claims are usually entered at par, though this is conceptually inappropriate and can be statistically misleading for long-term claims for which a market exists. This deviation from the basic principle is in line with the treatment in business accounts and is not important for short-term claims. In the case of long-term claims, however, it causes difficult statistical and conceptual problems.

For many types of economic analysis, though less so for financial comparisons, balance sheets in constant rather than in current prices are wanted, particularly if attention is directed at what may be called the "quantities" of the components of the balance sheet. Both the conceptual and the statistical problems of constructing national and sectoral balance sheets in constant prices that would measure changes and intercountry differences in "quantities" are, however, very great, and have not yet been solved satisfactorily, particularly for international comparisons. In the case of reproducible fixed assets, purchasing-power parities for total capital formation are now available for the postwar period for many countries (Summers, Kravis, and Heston 1980). For land and financial assets, however, the purchasing-power parities for national product provide only an unsatisfactory solution.

The difficulties are equally great in the derivation of time-series for national balance sheets in constant prices. In the case of reproducible fixed assets the problem of quality change is serious, since the existing indices of capital-goods prices and construction costs, which are needed in the perpetual-inventory method, probably do not take sufficient account of quality improvements and thus tend to understate the rate of growth of the capital stock in quantity terms -- a shortcoming shared by the perpetual-inventory estimates in current prices. This defect is even more serious in the case of land because reduction to constant prices by means of the national-product deflator ignores changes in the generally rising ratio of land prices, on which information is only rarely available, to the general price level. For the same reason, use of the national-product deflator to reduce the value of corporate stock to constant prices is very problematical, and reduction by an index of stock prices may be preferable.

D. Sectoring

Problems exist in most main sectors though they are generally easier to solve than in the case of scope and valuation.

Probably the most important problem is posed by unincorporated business enterprises. It is preferable to treat them as one or two (agricultural and nonagricultural) sectors, in which case their net worth becomes a financial asset of the owners, overwhelmingly households. Because of the conceptual and statistical difficulties of separating the assets and liabilities attributable to household and business activities, less acute for partnerships than for sole proprietorships, unincorporated business enterprises are generally consolidated with the household sector, with the result that their equity disappears from the national balance sheet and is excluded from national assets.

Uniformity is also needed for the treatment of residential structures and land. In some countries they are inappropriately allocated in their entirety to the business sector; in others they are treated as a separate sector. Their distribution among the owning sectors (i.e., households, unincorporated enterprises, nonfinancial corporations, and government) is the most informative solution if it can be implemented statistically.

With the growing importance of government enterprises, whether organized as corporations or as public bodies, and the great differences in the size (Pryor 1973, 14, 46), their treatment has become more important, particularly in international comparisons. If possible they should be set up as a separate sector, so that their assets and liabilities can be combined with either the government or the private corporate sector depending on the purpose of the analysis. The necessary information is unfortunately only rarely provided in the basic statistics.

A more difficult problem is presented by social security and similar organizations, and here again their growing size and the large differences among countries make it increasingly important to standardize their treatment. In the interest of providing as much relevant information as possible, it is desirable to treat them as a separate subsector, either of the government, as recommended in the United Nations' scheme, or of the financial institutions sector, which is preferable if they have substantial assets other than book claims against the government.

In most countries balance-sheet information is available for more subsectors of the financial-institutions sector than for any other, so that it is possible to construct figures for groups which are internationally comparable. The four subsectors distinguished in the United Nations' scheme (central bank; other monetary institutions; insurance companies and pension funds; other financial institutions) will generally suffice, though it would be desirable to separate public from private institutions. A problem special to this sector concerns claims and liabilities among financial institutions, which are often very large. To facilitate comparisons between countries and between the financial and nonfinancial sectors of the economy, it is desirable to show these intersectoral items separately.

E. Balance-Sheet Dates

No problem arises if the available statistics permit the construction of annual balance sheets. This, however, has hardly even been possible in the past, the only country for which a series of annual balance sheets extends from 1945 to the present being the United States (Goldsmith, Lipsey, and Mendelson 1963, Vol. 2; Goldsmith 1981a; Ruggles and Ruggles 1980; Federal Reserve System 1980) for all private sectors. In constructing national and sectoral balance sheets for the past it will, therefore, almost always be necessary to choose a limited number of balance-sheet dates. Their selection will be determined largely by the availability of data. Insofar as choice exists a decision must be made whether or not to use the same calendar date for all countries covered by the comparison. In either case the principle of selection should be the benchmark date's position in the short or long cycle to improve comparability. While the dating of such cycles varies to some extent among countries, years close to 1850, 1875, 1895, 1913, 1929, 1948, and 1973 will generally meet the condition, the last two at the start and the end of the long, upward swing of the postwar period, as well as the less important criterion of approximately equal spacing.

F. Grouping of Countries

Finally, a problem that is specific to the use of national and sectoral balance sheets in international comparisons, the arrangement of countries into groups that show significant similarities or differences in the structure of their balance sheets and of changes in them over time.

The separation of market and centrally planned economies is an obvious necessity. Within market economies, the dozen or so of developed economies must be distinguished from the more than one hundred less developed economies, which should be further divided between those in America and those in the rest of the world, the former being much closer in their economic structure, and particularly in their financial structure, to developed countries.

There are only a few countries that do not easily fit into these four groups. One is Yugoslavia which might be classified as a less developed, market economy on the basis of its financial system, but otherwise is closer to the centrally planned economies. Hong Kong and Singapore may soon have to be shifted to the group of developed, market economies. Finally the Middle Eastern, oil-producing countries with small populations and very high per head incomes may require separate treatment.

Additional problems arise in long-term comparisons when a few countries, astonishingly few, have changed their status (apart from the shift of about two dozen countries from developed, or less developed, market, to centrally planned economies), the most important being Japan, which would have to be classified as a less developed, market economy until close to the end of the nineteenth century. Questions also arise for the poorer European countries (Spain, Portugal, Greece, Rumania, Bulgaria, Albania) which, at least before World War I, would probably have to be classified as less developed, market economies or treated as a separate group, though it is very unlikely that national balance sheets for them during that period will ever be constructed.

III. THE USES OF NATIONAL AND SECTORAL BALANCE SHEETS IN INTERNATIONAL COMPARISONS

Having dealt previously in some detail with this topic (Goldsmith 1956, 1966, 1975), brevity and concentration on the use of national and sectoral balance sheets in international comparisons may be permitted here. In this field there are at least three problems that may be elucidated with the help of national and sectoral balance sheets: differences in the structure of tangible and of financial assets and changes in them over time; differences in the relation between tangible and financial assets and changes in them; and the effects of inflation on the asset and liability structure of the different sectors and on the intersectoral distributin of assets and liabilities.

With tangible assets, the most important characteristic is the ratio between natural resources (land, forests, and subsoil assets) and reproducible assets as it is one of the best indicators of economic development and is closely associated with the share of the primary sector in product and wealth. It has shown a downward trend in all countries, though starting its decline at varying dates -- in the now developed countries not later than the early nineteenth century -- and with varying speed, falling from about two-thirds to one-fourth or less, now mostly represented by nonagricultural land.

Probably the most significant breakdown within reproducible assets separates those used primarily in production, that is, nonresidential civilian structures and equipment, inventories, and livestock, from those serving primarily consumption, that is, residential structures, the tangible assets of nonprofit institutions, and consumers durables, and from military structures, equipment, and inventories. The allocation of reproducible assets of general civilian government, such as offices and schools, as well as of streets and highways is controversial, but of practical relevance only in the relatively few cases where the basic data are sufficiently detailed. The differences in the distribution of reproducible assets by type and by sector in individual countries and groups of them, as well as over time, are substantial, and their analyses constitute one of the main uses of national and sectoral balance sheets. A few relevant figures will be presented in part IV., B.

Among financial assets, five ratios are of particular interest for international comparisons, namely, the ratio of financial instruments issued by financial institutions to total financial assets; the share of corporate stock; the share of public debt; and the gross and net foreign-asset ratio. The first of these ratios, sometimes called the financial intermediation ratio, provides a means of assessing, not by itself of course, the importance of financial institutions and of their main groups in the financial superstructure of different countries, and of following their generally upward trend over the past one or two centuries. The significance of the other four ratios for international comparisons is fairly obvious.

The relations between the infrastructure of national wealth and the financial superstructure, influences running in both directions, constitute one of the most important aspects of economic developements, though one that is, as yet, far from having been satisfactorily treated in theory or studied empirically, and one that certainly cannot be adequately attacked by the use of national and sectoral balance sheets alone. One ratio derived from the national balance sheet, however, provides a first approach, the financial interrelations ratio, that is, the quotient of tangible and financial assets. It is discussed in part IV., A.

Sectoral balance sheets provide useful leads to the study of the international differences in the relation between superstructure and infrastructure in the form of debt-asset ratios either for a sector's total tangible assets and its liabilities, or, preferably, for a given type of tangible asset and the associated debt, for example, between the stock of residential structures and the mortgage debt on them.

The influence of inflation, or more generally of price changes, can be studied either from national and sectoral balance sheets alone (see Goldsmith, Lipsey, and Mendelson 1963, Vol. 1, part 2), or in combination with estimates of saving. In the first case, attention is directed in international comparison to the differences between balance-sheet structures in current and in constant prices; in the second case, it is directed to the differences between changes in the current values of assets and saving, either for the nation as a whole, or, more informatively, for sectors. Inflation is also a factor, though by no means the only one, in the level and movements of a ratio, which has recently become popular (e.g., Fellner 1980; Tobin and Brainard 1968), the quotient of the market value of all securities of corporations to the value of their net worth at current prices or to the replacement cost of their reproducible assets, derived from their sectoral balance sheet.

While not derived exclusively from balance sheets, asset-output ratios constitute another important use. The best known one, the capital-output ratio, usually defined as the quotient of the value of the stock of tangible assets and national product, must be used with great caution and should not be interpreted as a measure of productivity or efficiency, if only because it does not take account of differences in the degree of utilization of the capital stock and is just the weighted average of sectoral or instrumental ratios. More can be learned for international comparisons from the latter ratios, which may use as denominator either total national product, or, preferably, the value added by the sector, subsector, or, what is much more difficult to implement, by the type of tangible asset. Asset-output ratios can also be calculated for financial assets, in the aggregate or for specific instruments. These, of course, do not measure productivity, but can be used as a scalar in lieu of, or as a supplement to, the constant price value of these assets. They can also be regarded as utilization ratios or the inverse of income-velocity ratios, the only one in common use being the ratio of money to national product or, more appropriately, to monetized income.

IV. TWO EMPIRICAL APPLICATIONS

A. The Financial-Interrelations Ratio of Twenty Countries

One of the most important characteristics of an economy is the size of its financial superstructure, measured by the quotient of the value of all financial assets to that of tangible domestic assets, which has been called the financial-interrelations ratio. In international, as well as in intertemporal comparisons, some problems arise in the definition and measurement of the numerator and denominator of the ratio, some of which have already been discussed.

The financial-interrelations ratios shown in Table 1 include, in principle, in the numerator of financial assets (apart from the obvious components) monetary metals, foreign assets where they are substantial, and intercorporate stockholdings, but exclude unfunded pension claims and intangible financial assets (such as patents and copyrights); they consolidate the household and unincorporated business sectors, and treat financial institutions on a combined, rather than a consolidated basis. They exclude subsoil assets, consumer semidurables and nondurables, and collectors' items from the denominator of tangible assets, but include military durables. The nature of the basic data has, however, led in some cases to minor inconsistencies. The broader definition of the denominator, that is, the inclusion of subsoil assets, standing timber, and consumer semidurables and nondurables, would reduce the ratio in the twenty countries included in the study to only a minor extent, probably only in a few cases by as much as 5 percent of the values shown in Table 1.

TABLE 1A
The Financial Interrelations Ratio at Ten Benchmark Dates, 1850–1973
  (Ratio: financial assets/tangible assets)

	Standard Benchmark Year (a)								
	1850	1875	1895	1913	1929	1939	1950	1965	1978
Australia							0.78	0.70	0.63
Belgium	0.25	0.38	0.55	0.91	0.82	0.98	0.83	0.75	0.68
Canada							1.19	1.18	1.13
Denmark		1.06	1.26	1.41	1.55	1.26	1.12	1.05	1.09
France (b)	0.26	0.56		0.98	0.81		0.55	1.24	0.83
Germany (c)	0.19	0.38	0.72	0.76	0.39	0.57	0.40	0.93	0.85
Great Britain	0.68	0.93	1.96	1.96	2.45	2.70	1.77	1.50	1.11
Hungary								0.15	0.36
India (d)	0.64	0.47	0.40	0.34	0.30	0.38	0.45	0.54	0.54
Israel							0.66	0.74	1.11
Italy	0.21	0.39	0.45	0.47	0.68	0.73	0.42	0.85	1.03
Japan		0.30	0.34	0.63	1.23	1.42	0.54	0.80	1.02
Mexico					0.36	0.65	0.74	0.68	0.71
Norway		0.37	0.55	0.72	1.03	0.72	0.80	0.78	0.87
Russia/USSR				0.40	0.09	0.28	0.32	0.22	0.29
South Africa				0.52	0.70	0.93	0.94	1.14	0.76
Sweden								1.03	1.27
Switzerland (e)		1.11	1.60	1.51	1.64	1.59	1.33	1.54	1.80
United States	0.47	0.64	0.71	0.83	1.29	1.32	1.17	1.25	1.00
Yugoslavia							0.23	0.74	1.15

Notes: (a) For actual dates see Table 1B.
        (b) In addition, 1815, 0.20
        (c) In addition, 1688, 0.17; 1760, 0.40;1800, 0.57;1830, 0.76
        (d) Excluding gold and silver:
                0.21 0.17 0.16 0.18 0.21 0.26 0.32 0.44 0.45
        (e) In addition, 1774, 0.28; 1805, 0.32

TABLE 1B
Reconciliation of Actual and Standard Benchmark Years

	Standard Benchmark Year								
	1850	1875	1895	1913	1929	1939	1950	1965	1978
	Actual Benchmark Year								
Australia	–	–	–	–	–	–	1956	1965	1977
Belgium	1850	1875	1985	1913	1929	1939	1948	1965	1976
Canada	–	–	–	–	–	–	1955	1965	1978
Denmark	–	1880	1900	1913	1929	1938	1948	1965	1978
France	1850	1880	–	1913	1929	–	1950	1960	1976
Germany	1850	1875	1895	1913	1929	1938	1950	1960	1977
Great Britain	1850	1875	1895	1913	1927	1937	1948	1965	1977
Hungary	–	–	–	–	–	–	–	1959	1977
India	1860	1875	1895	1913	1929	1939	1950	1960	1975
Israel	–	–	–	–	–	–	1951	1966	1976
Italy	1861	1881	1895	1914	1929	1938	1951	1963	1977
Japan	–	1885	1900	1913	1930	1940	1955	1965	1977
Mexico	–	–	–	–	1930	1940	1948	1965	1978
Norway	–	1880	1899	1913	1930	1939	1953	1965	1978
Russia/USSR	–	–	–	1913	1928	1937	1950	1969	1977
South Africa	–	–	–	1913	1929	1938	1955	1965	1978
Sweden	–	–	–	–	–	–	–	1963	1978
Switzerland	–	1880	1900	1913	1929	1938	1948	1965	1978
United States	1850	1880	1900	1912	1929	1939	1950	1965	1978
Yugoslavia	–	–	–	–	–	–	1953	1962	1977

Moreover, this reduction would probably be offset in part or fully by the likelihood that the estimates of financial assets in many cases omit some minor types.

The 126 financial-interrelations ratios assembled in Table 1 permit the exploration of two aspects of international economic and financial comparisons, namely, differences, or similarities, in the level and in the trends of the relation, that is, the relative size of a country's financial superstructure compared to its national wealth.

In the late 1970s the financial-interrelations ratios ranged from 0.29 for the Soviet Union to 1.80 for Switzerland, with an average of 0.91, a median of 0.94, and an interquartile range of 0.68 to 1.11. The averages are 1.01 for the fifteen developed, market economies, 0.62 for the two less developed, market economies, and 0.33 for the two centrally planned economies; Yugoslavia, with 1.15, stands near the top of the developed, market economies.

A quarter of a century earlier, around 1950, the level of the ratios was slightly lower, but they were more dispersed, ranging among eighteen countries from 0.32 for the Soviet Union to 1.77 for Great Britain, with an average and a median of 0.79, and an interquartile range of 0.44 to 1.15, much wider than that of the late 1970s, while the averages are not too far apart. At the present time the ratios are higher for the developed, market economies, with 0.65, and for the Soviet Union, with 0.32.

At the eve of World War I the ratios for the thirteen countries, for which the ratio can be calculated, ranged from 0.34 for India (or 0.78 if the population's hoards of precious metals are excluded) to 1.96 for Great Britain. The average of 0.88, the median of 0.76, and the interquartile range of about 0.50 to 1.20 were not very different from their values around 1950 or, for that matter, in the late 1970s.

If we go back to the midnineteenth century the picture changes drastically. At that time the financial-interrelations ratio of the six developed, market economies, for which it can be estimated, averaged 0.34 -- lower than the present ratio for less developed countries -- with a concentration between 0.19 and 0.26 for four of them (Germany, Italy, France, and Belgium), the United States at 0.47, and Great Britain at the top with 0.68. The average for the same countries rises sharply to 0.55 for the benchmark dates around 1875, to over 0.85 two decades later, and more slowly to almost unity in 1913. Great Britain maintained its position throughout the period, its ratio staying at approximately twice the aveage of the other five countries, a clear indication of its leading role in financial development. Three smaller developed countries (Denmark, Norway, and Switzerland) showed a similar trend, while the level of their financial-interrelations ratios was considerably above that of the five large developed countries, the average difference declining from over one-half to one-fifth. Japan, whose ratio must have been minuscule even in 1870, had, by 1913, reached a level of three-fifths of the average of the nine developed countries and equal to that of theirs near 1875. The Indian ratio failed to show any trend (and if precious metals are included, declined substantially), reflecting sharp increases in land prices, a pattern almost certainly not representative of other less developed countries, particularly in Latin America.

The averages and ranges just discussed ignore specific differences in levels and movements of the financial-interrelations ratio of individual countries, a few of which it may be worthwhile to point out. One of them is the sharp decline in the ratio following open inflations. This is most clearly visible in Germany for 1929 and 1950 and in Japan and Italy for 1955, even though these benchmark dates are located about half a dozen years after the end of the inflation, at which time they were even lower. In contrast, the extraordinarily high ratio for the United States in 1945 of 1.75 (not shown in Table 1) is evidence of the repressed inflation of World War II. Another is the sharp rise in the Yugoslav ratio in the 1950s and 1960s, which reflects the shift of that country's financial superstructure from the pattern common to centrally planned economies dominated by a monobank to a more diversified, quasi-western system.

A study of the ratios of Table 1 seems to justify four conclusions. First, if a secular view is taken, the financial-interrelations ratio has shown a definite upward trend. The only exception is India, if the population's hoards of precious metals are regarded as a financial asset. Second, in the now-developed countries, the upward trend in the ratio ended with World War I or, more rarely, the 1930s, after having been particularly pronounced in the second half of the nineteenth century (in Japan, between 1885 and the 1920s) when these countries developed their modern financial system. Third, the level of the ratio throughout the past full century has been lower in less developed than in developed countries. Though the data now available do not permit a confident conclusion, it appears that the gap has been narrowing, and in the case of Latin America it may close before too long. The Mexican ratio, for example, has been not much lower since the 1930s than that of a number of developed countries, though still well below their average. Fourth, sharp open inflations reduce the ratio, but only temporarily.

What explains the differences in the levels and the movements of the financial-interrelations ratio of the twenty countries as they appear in Table 1?

A first possibility, the level of real national product per head, can be immediately rejected as far as the trend of the ratios goes. For developed countries the ratios for the late 1970s are on the average no higher than they were in 1913, although real product per head has increased severalfold, in the United States more than threefold. At any given point of time the correlation between the ratio and real national product per head is extremely weak and irregular among developed, market economies though it is still visible between them and less developed countries, while the ratio of centrally planned economies is much lower than corresponds to their level of real product per head. Thus, in the late 1970s, six developed countries with virtually the same real national product per head (Belgium, Denmark, France, Germany, Norway, and Sweden) had financial-interrelations ratios ranging from 0.68 to 1.27. Worse still, the ratio ranged from 0.63 to 1.80 for three countries (Australia, Great Britain, and Switzerland) whose real national product per head, averaging about one-eighth less than the first group, differs only by a few percent.

The differences, then, must be due to other factors. It is not possible to pursue this problem here, except to say that a satisfactory answer has not yet been found, and to point to a formula, which has been developed and statistically implemented elsewhere (e.g., Goldsmith 1969, Ch. 7; 1982b, Ch. 1). The formula, in a condensed version, is:

$$FIR = [(\delta + \phi + \xi) \; (1 + \nu) \; \alpha\beta^{-1}] \; \tau + \rho$$

where δ, ϕ, and ξ are the ratios of the net issues of domestic nonfinancial and financial claims and equities and of foreign instruments to the period's national product; ν is the ratio of valuation changes after issuance to value at issue, an item significant only in the case of equities, which is positively correlated to the share of equities in total issues and to their prices; α is the ratio of the period's national product to its level at the benchmark date, a ratio which is inversely related to the rate of growth of real national product and of the price level; β is the capital-output ratio; τ is an adjustment factor, which is the closer to unity the longer the period and the higher the rate of growth of national product; and ρ is the ratio of the value of financial assets at the beginning of the period plus valuation changes to that of tangible assets at its end, taking account of previously accumulated financial assets. (The term "benchmark date" refers to the date terminating a period.)

The value of the formula for the international -- as well as the intertemporal -- comparison of financial structures is that it measures the relative importance of the issues of the different types of financial instruments and of the rate of growth of real national product, of the price level, and of the prices of equities. It shows that the level and movement of the financial-interrelations ratio is positively correlated to the issue ratio of financial instruments and to the share of equities and their prices; but it is negatively correlated to the rate of growth of national product in current prices and, therefore, to that of real national product and the price level (hence the observed negative effect of inflation on the ratio), and to the capital-output ratio; but it is not related directly to the level of real national product per head. An explanation of the financial-interrelations ratio thus requires an analysis of specific financial parameters (the issue ratios and the price of equities) as well as of basic economic characteristics of an economy (the rate of growth of real national product, the capital-output ratio, and the price level). Obviously, there can be no question of treating these matters here.

Simply to illustrate orders of magnitude, and to make it clear that similar financial-interrelations ratios can be the result of different combinations of components of the ratios, Table 2 shows the structure of the ratio for three large market economies on the eve of World War I and in 1963. The values of the ratio derived from the formula deviate slightly from those observed due to some of the simplifying assumptions made in the formula (for example, straight-line logarithmic growth of national product) and probably also due to some inconsistencies in the statistics used.

It will be seen from Table 2 that in 1913 the excess of the German over the American ratio was due primarily to the higher issue ratios and secondarily to the higher multiplier, specifically the slower rate of growth of real national product. In 1963 the large excess of the American over the German ratio (still affected by the

TABLE 2
The Components of the Financial Interrelations Ratio
in the United States, Germany and India, 1913 and 1963

		U.S.A.		Germany		India
		1913	1963	1913	1963	1963
1.	δ	0.10	0.10	0.11	0.10	0.05
2.	ϕ	0.05	0.10	0.07	0.13	0.04
3.	ξ	0.00	0.00	0.01	0.01	$-$ 0.02
4.	$\sum(1+2+3)$	0.15	0.20	0.19	0.24	0.07
5.	ν	0.15	0.20	0.10	0.10	0.05
6.	α	24.3	19.1	26.5	10.1	23.4
7.	β	4.4	4.3	5.4	3.6	3.6
8.	τ	0.67	0.50	0.71	0.74	0.43
9.	ρ	0.07	0.70	0.15	0.15	0.15
10.	FIR	0.71	1.23	0.88	0.70	0.35

Notes: Variables are defined in the text.

Lines 1-6 and 8 refer to the periods 1881-1913 and 1949-1963,
respectively.

Sources: Goldsmith (1969, 313, 325, 332, 338) except for lines 6 and
7 [U.S.A.: U.S. Department of Commerce (1975, 224); Economic Report of the President (1980, 203-5). Germany:
Hoffmann (1965, 825 ff). India: Goldsmith (1982b, Table
3-3).]

TABLE 3
Structure of Balance Sheet of Main Sectors:
  Great Britain (1960), India (1961) and United States (1958)
  (Percent)

| | Assets | | | Liabilities | Net Worth |
	Total (1)	Tangible (2)	Financial (3)	(4)	(5)
	I. Households (a)				
Great Britain	100.0	31.7	69.3	11.3	89.7
India	100.0	73.4	26.6(b)	7.1	92.9(b)
United States	100.0	49.9	50.1	12.9	87.1
	II. Non-financial Corporations				
Great Britain	100.0	56.2	43.8	23.2	76.8
India	100.0	37.0	63.0	56.2	43.8
United States	100.0	64.0	36.0	33.6	66.4
	III. Government				
Great Britain	100.0	57.0	43.0	118.5	-18.5
India	100.0	39.0	61.0	71.0	29.0
United States	100.0	72.3	27.7	113.2	-13.2
	IV. Financial Institutions				
Great Britain	100.0	6.0	94.0	81.3	18.7
India	100.0	3.0	97.0	94.0	6.0
United States	100.0	1.4	98.6	89.8	10.2
	V. All Domestic Sectors				
Great Britain	100.0	36.7	63.3	47.8	53.2
India	100.0	59.2	40.8(b)	29.0	71.0(b)
United States	100.0	45.5	54.5	40.9	59.1

Notes: (a) Includes unincorporated business.

   (b) Includes gold and silver: 11.0 in ch.I(3) and I(5);
                                  7.3 in ch.V(3) and V(5).

Sources: Great Britain: Revell (1967, 52/53).

          India: Joshi (1966, 36) plus estimate for holdings of gold
                 and silver by population (Goldsmith 1982a).

          United States: Goldsmith, et al. (1963, Vol. II, 68-69).

TABLE 4
Distribution of National Balance Sheet Main Components Among Sectors
  Great Britain (1960), India (1961) and United States (1958)
  (Percent of Assets of Domestic Sectors)

	Non-financial business			Government		Finan- cial Insti- tution (6)	All Domes- tic (7)	Rest of the World (8)
	House- holds (1)	Non- Corp. (2)	Corp. (3)	Enter- prises (4)	Other (5)			
I. Total Assets								
Gr.Br.	41.0		21.1	4.3	14.8	18.8	100.0	8.9
India	67.0(a)		5.4	0.5	19.5	7.6	100.0	0.3(b)
U.S.	41.3	9.5	21.1	–	8.7	19.4	100.0	2.2
II. Tangible Assets								
Gr.Br.	35.3		32.1	10.3	19.3	3.1	100.0	2.5
India	83.0		3.4	0.4	12.8	0.4	100.0	–
U.S.	38.3	17.6	29.6	–	13.9	0.6	100.0	–
III. Financial Assets								
Gr.Br.	44.8		14.5	0.9	12.1	27.7	100.0	12.6
India	43.7(a)		8.6	0.6	29.4	17.7	100.0	0.8
U.S.	44.0	2.8	13.9	–	4.4	34.9	100.0	4.0
IV. Liabilities								
Gr.Br.	9.7		10.3	7.2	40.5	32.3	100.0	21.8
India	16.4		10.5	1.0	48.0	24.1	100.0	4.0
U.S.	11.8	4.2	17.3	–	24.3	42.4	100.0	2.3
V. Net Worth								
Gr.Br.	69.5		30.5	1.8	-8.5	6.7	100.0	-2.9
India	87.5(a)		3.3	0.3	8.3	0.6	100.0	-1.1
U.S.	61.9	13.2	23.6	–	-2.0	3.3	100.0	2.1

Notes: (a) Of which gold and silver 7.3 in I, 18.0 in III, 10.4 in V.

(b) Only monetary reserves.

Sources: Same as for Table 3, except for United States, Rest of the
         World data from U.S. Department of Commerce (1975, 869)

seisachtheia of the late 1940s) reflected primarily the much higher multiplier, that is, the considerably lower values of the rate of growth of real national product and of the general price level, and secondarily the lower capital-output ratio of Germany. The much lower level of the Indian ratio -- less than one-half of the German, and one-third of the American ratio -- is the result primarily of low new-issue ratios, notwithstanding a multiplier higher than those of the two developed countries, which reflects low values of the rate of growth of the price level and particularly of real national product.

The relation between the size of a country's financial superstructure and its infrastructure of national wealth, crudely measured by the levels and the movements of its financial-interrelations ratio, and international differences in levels and trends of the ratio are matters much too complicated to be encompassed in a formula, even one more elaborate than that used here for illustrative purposes, useful as such an approach may be as a first attack. A more satisfactory explanation will require a thorough analysis of each country's economic and financial history, using, among other tools, national and sectoral balance sheets and a great deal of systematic information on institutional factors, both of which are as yet missing for most countries and for most of the last 150 years which have witnessed the development of modern financial instruments and institutions.

B. Sectorized National Balance Sheets of Great Britain, India, and the United States Around 1960

Tables 3 and 4 show, respectively, the structure of the balance sheets for the half-dozen main sectors, and the distribution of the four main components of the national balance sheet (tangible and financial assets, liabilities, and net worth) among them for three large countries (Great Britain, India, and the United States) around 1960, these being the only countries for which sectorized national balance sheets have been published for approximately the same date. While the balance sheets are unduly compressed, distinguishing too few sectors and, particularly, too few components, partly because of the limitation of the sources (India) and partly because of limitations of space (Great Britain and the United States), they should suffice to indicate a little of what can be learned from a comparison of sectorized national balance sheets. Similarly, three countries are obviously insufficient to represent the wide range of structural differences among the well over 100 separate countries. Nevertheless, Great Britain may be regarded as representative of European developed countries and India as providing an indication of the structure of the balance sheet of less developed countries (save for its exceptionally large holdings of monetary metals), while the United States by itself around 1960 probably accounted for well over one-fourth of the world's assets. Before venturing a few comments on the characteristics of, and the differences among, these three sets of balance sheets, it must be repeated that the methods of estimation used by their authors and the margins of uncertainty of the estimates differ, and to a lesser extent the definition of sectors and components differ, differences for which no adjustment can be made because of the limitations of the basic data available; and it must be remembered that in some cases substantial, though not radical, changes have occurred in the two decades since the dates to which the balance sheets refer.

Starting with the structure of the balance sheets of the main sectors shown in Table 3, comments will be limited to the differences in the national balance sheets, and among the balance sheets of the same sector in the three countries, bypassing the fairly obvious differences in the structure of the balance sheets of the four sectors. For all domestic sectors together the share of tangible assets is much higher in India, with almost three-fifths (two-thirds if gold is regarded as a tangible rather than as a financial asset), than in the United States and particularly in Great Britain. This is due primarily to the much higher share of land in India, predominantly agricultural, of nearly one-half of tangible assets and close to one-third of total assets compared to shares of below one-fifth of tangible assets, accounted for mostly by urban land, in Great Britain and the United States. To reach similarly high shares of land it is necessary to go back in the United States and Great Britain to the first part of the nineteenth century (Goldsmith 1982b). The higher share of tangible assets in the United States is due in part to land -- 9 percent of total assets against 4 percent in Great Britain -- and in part to the relatively smaller size of the financial superstructure. The considerably smaller ratio of debt to assets and net worth in India primarily reflects the much more limited use of credit by the private sector.

The differences in the structure of the household· sector (including unincorporated business enterprises) are similar since it is in all three countries in the largest sector. Particularly striking is the low share of financial assets other than gold and silver hoards in India with only one-eighth of total assets compared to one-half in the United States and more than two-thirds in Great Britain. On the other hand, the share of land in total household wealth in India, with over two-fifths, is far above that in the United States, with about one-fifth, and less than one-tenth in Great Britain. The differences in households' debt ratios are much smaller in absolute terms, but still relatively large, amounting to 7 percent in India compared to close to 12 percent in Great Britain and the United States.

Differences among nonfinancial corporations are also substantial and again much smaller between Great Britain and the United States than between these two countries and India. The main difference, the much higher share of financial assets and liabilities among Indian corporations, reflects the relatively much greater importance of trade credit -- three-fourths of financial assets in India compared to about one-half in great Britain and one-fourth in the United States.

The balance sheet of the Indian public sector differs from that of the two developed countries by a much higher share of financial assets, reflecting the operation of the central government as the country's largest financial intermediary, and its lower debt ratio due to the absence of large-scale war debts, which around 1960 still dominated the central governments' liabilities in Great Britain and the United States.

The high degree of aggregation prevents the balance sheets of financial institutions from showing the differences in the structure of their assets and liabilities. The considerably lower ratio of net worth to liabilities in India is, however, of some significance.

Turning to the distribution of national assets and their main components among sectors, which can be followed in Table 4, large and significant differences appear. The share of the household sector (including unincorporated business enterprises and nonprofit institutions) declines from two-thirds in India to about one-half in the United States and not much over two-fifths in Great Britain. Nonfinancial private corporations account for fully one-fifth of national assets in Great Britain and the United States, but for only 5 percent in India. Financial institutions hold nearly one-fifth of national assets in the two developed countries, but less than one-twelfth in India. It is only in the case of the government that the share is similar for India and Great Britain and much higher than in the United States. Finally, the importance of foreign assets is much higher in Great Britain than in the United States and, of course, than in India. It would require the recital of a good part of the three countries' economic and financial history to explain these differences.

The differences in the sectoral distribution are similar to that of national assets in the case of tangibles, particularly in the ranking of the three countries. In the case of financial assets, the share of households is similar in all three countries at about 45 percent, provided that in India hoards of gold and silver are included. The extraordinarily high share of the government in India is due to the already mentioned very large loan activities of the central government.

In both Great Britain and India the share of the public sector, chiefly the central government, in debt is high, but for different reasons, in Great Britain largely (in 1960) because of heavy war debts, in India because of large-scale investment in productive tangible assets and loans to enterprises. In contrast, the borrowings of nonfinancial corporations are considerably higher compared to all liabilities in the United States than in Great Britain and India, in both of which they account for about one-tenth of the total representing, however, a much larger proportion of these corporations' assets in India than in Great Britain. The British volume of liabilities to the rest of the world to domestic debt is, relatively, about ten times as high as in the United States and five times as high as in India, evidence of the extraordinarily large international financial business of the City.

Differences in the sectoral distribution of net worth are, of course, the results of those of assets and of liabilities. Thus, households account for seven-eighths of the total in India against three-fourths in the United States and not much over two-thirds in Great Britain; the share of nonfinancial corporations, as well as of financial institutions, is minuscule in India compared to that in the two developed countries; and that of the public sector is negative in the United States and particularly in Great Britain, but is close to one-twelfth in India.

Without ignoring the reservations about differences in methods of sectorization and valuation, the limited representativeness of the three countries for the other 150-odd, particularly those operating under a system of centralized planning, and the changes that have occurred since 1960, the relations shown in Tables 3 and 4 should provide an idea of some of the differences between the balance sheets, and hence the economic and financial structure, of developed and less developed, market economies. In that connection it is well to recall that national assets, and most of their components other than land, constitute a considerably, though not radically, lower multiple of national product, around 1960, 7.6 in Great Britain and 8.1 in the United States compared to only 5.7 in India.

FOOTNOTE

This paper, written in 1981, is based on work done over the past three decades and published or forthcoming, generally in less compressed form, elsewhere. In particular, Table 1 is lifted from a forthcoming monograph, to be published by Chicago University Press, which is based on national balance sheets for twenty countries. Apart from this table, I have refrained from using material in that monograph in order not to deprive the publisher of his bread. Duplications in substance with other publications are therefore unavoidable, but to eschew autoplagiarism I have not looked at previous writings when drafting this paper.

BIBLIOGRAPHY

Dorrance, G. S. 1978. *National monetary and financial analysis*. New York: St. Martin's Press.

Economic Planning Agency. 1979. *Annual report on national accounts*. Tokyo.

Eisner, R. 1980. Capital gains and income: real changes in the value of capital in the United States, 1946-1977. In *The measurement of capital*, ed. D. Usher. Chicago: U. of Chicago Press.

Federal Reserve System, Board of Governors. 1979. *Flow of funds accounts 1949-1978*. Washington, D. C.

————. 1980. *Balance sheets for U. S. economy*. (mimeo). Washington, D. C.

Fellner, W. 1980. In *Contemporary economic problems 1980*. Washington, D. C.: American Enterprise Institute.

Goldsmith, R. W. 1956. The national balance sheet -- another tool in the economist's kit. *The Analysts J.*, 12(1)(February): 2-7.

————, 1966. The uses of national balance sheets. *Rev. of Income and Wealth*, Series 12(June): 95-133.

————, 1969. *Financial structure and development*. New Haven: Yale U. Press.

————, 1970. Prolegomènes a l'analyse comparative des structures financières, *Revue d'Economie Politique*, 80(3)(May): 395-424.

————, 1975. The quantitative international comparison of financial structure and development. *J. of Econ. Hist.*, XXXV(March): 216-37.

————, 1982a. *The national balance sheet of the United States, 1900 to 1980*. (forthcoming). Chicago: U. of Chicago Press.

————, 1982b. *National balance sheets*. (forthcoming).

Goldsmith, R. H , R. E. Lipsey, M. Mendelson. 1963. *Studies in the national balance sheet of the United States*. Princeton: Princeton U. Press.

Hoffman, W. G., 1965. *Das Wachstum des Dentulen Wictschaft Jeit des Mitte des 19th Jahrhunderts*. Berlin: Springer.

Institut National de la Statistique et des etudes Economiques (INSEE). 1980. *Les comptes de partimoine*. (Les Collection de l'INSEE, 89-90). Paris.

Jorgenson, D. W., A. Pachon. 1980. *The accumulation of human and nonhuman capital*. Harvard Institute for Economic Research, Discussion Paper no. 769. Cambridge, Mass.

Joshi, M. S. 1966. *The national balance sheet of India*. Bombay: U. of Bombay.

Kendrick, J. W. 1976. *The formation and stocks of total capital*. New York: National Bureau of Economic Research.

Pryor, F. 1973. *Property and industrial organization in communist and capitalist countries*. Bloomington: Indiana U. Press.

Revell, J. 1967. *The wealth of the nation*. Cambridge: Cambridge U. Press.

Ruggles, N., R. Ruggles. 1970. *The design of economic accounts*. New York: National Bureau of Economic Research.

Ruggles, R., N. D. Ruggles. 1980. *Integrated economic accounts for the United States 1947-1978*. Institution for Social and Policy Studies, Working Paper no. 841. New Haven.

Summers, R., I. B. Kravis, A. Heston. 1980. International comparison of real product and its composition: 1950-77. *The Rev. of Income and Wealth*, 26(1)(March): 1-18.

Tobin, J., W. Brainard. 1968. Pitfalls in financial model building. *Amer. Econ. Rev.*, LVIII(2)(May): 98-122.

United Nations. 1977. *Provisional international guidelines on the national and sectoral balance-sheet and reconciliation accounts of the system of national* accounts. New York.

U. S. Department of Commerce. 1975. *Historical statistics of the United States colonial times to 1970*. Washington, D. C.

14
Japanese Financial Development in Historical Perspective, 1868–1980

Hugh Patrick

I. INTRODUCTION

Japan presents one of the most illuminating historical cases of generally successful economic development, in terms both of overall performance and of such specific features as the development of its financial system. An isolated, autarchic, low-income traditional economy until forcibly opened by Western intervention in the 1850s, Japan became the first non-Western country to absorb the industrial revolution of the West and to achieve Kuznetsian modern economic growth. This complex process meant not only the adoption, adaptation, and innovation of Western technology, but also of many of its institutional forms. Once in Japanese culture, their evolutionary development took on lives of their own, though within well-recognizable Western forms. This was particularly true of the development and growth of the Japanese financial system, which, as elsewhere in market economies, has had at its core the banking system.

The purpose of this essay is to examine in broad terms the historical process of the development of the Japanese financial system from the beginning of the Meiji Restoration in 1868 to the present. I consider three major, interrelated themes: the growth and evolving institutional structure of the financial system; the nature and role of financial markets; and financial dualism. Since the concept of financial dualism is somewhat ambiguous in the literature, I briefly define and discuss it in the next section. The nature and changes of the financial system, markets, and dualism have been determined by an interacting combination of government policies and of market forces related to the economic development process itself. Accordingly, considerable emphasis is placed upon government policy.

Given the brevity of this essay and the long time period under consideration, detailed quantitative data are not included to substantiate the generalizations made here. While considerable evidence appears in the references cited and in the references contained within them, it must be cautioned that we do not yet have full understanding of what occurred over the long sweep of Japanese modern financial history. In particular, we do not have adequate evidence on the allocative function and efficiency of the financial system. The allocative effect of financial intermediation is so central that it deserves separate treatment; here I am limited to only broad, general statements. What follows is plausible and, I believe, correct in overview but subject to further refinement in detail.

Japanese modern financial development can be divided into four phases. Our three main concerns -- changes in the financial system, in financial markets, and in financial dualism -- are discussed for each of these phases. Each phase can be summarized as follows. The first was devoted to the initial creation of a modern financial system -- banks, other financial intermediaries, financial markets -- and its rules, and its integration across geographical regions and types of financial intermediation. It began at the start of Meiji and came to an end by the first decade of the twentieth century. The second phase evolved from the first. It was devoted to the growth, development, and increasing diversification of the financial system in a relatively free market environment. It came to an end in 1936. The third phase is characterized essentially by the replacement of market forces and institutions in finance, as elsewhere in the economy, by direct controls and new rules for the operation of the system, instituted in wartime and perpetuated with relatively modest change during the postwar Allied Occupation of Japan. This period is brief but traumatic: from approximately 1937 to 1952, when Japan once again became independent. While there are important elements of continuity between the second and third phases, the discontinuities are fundamental. The fourth phase -- the postwar era -- runs from the early 1950s to the mid to late-1970s. In most respects it embodies an evolutionary development from the patterns of regulated markets and institutions set in wartime. This evolution has now proceeded sufficiently that the Japanese financial system is probably entering a new, fifth, phase.

This phasing coincides closely with that for the real economy as described by Ohkawa and Rosovsky (1973) for the entire period, and Ohkawa and Ranis (1978) for the pre-World War II period. While different evidence is used to determine the phases in financial and real sectors, there is a clear interrelationship. World War II was such a watershed as to be an obvious delineator of phases. That the first decade of this century seems to have been a turning point in so many dimensions is analytically even more interesting but more difficult to understand and interpret fully. Two factors seem to have been of particular importance: the institutional framework for modern economic growth in both its real and financial dimensions had become well established; and industrial growth had come to supersede agriculture, bringing about an increasing demand for financial services. Phasing does not imply a single, inevitable causal path, and there seems little inevitability between second and third phases, or third and fourth; and evolution of the second from the first phase does seem somehow more natural, a hypothesis which requires further study.

II. FINANCIAL DUALISM

Financial dualism is analogous to the dualism in labor markets extensively discussed in the literature on Japan and other countries; and it frequently involves the same economic units. Conceptually, financial dualism can be defined in terms of the motivations and behavior of participants in financial markets, types of financial institutions, and the nature of financial markets. The literature often refers to financial dualism more or less synonomously in terms of traditional versus modern sectors, or unorganized (or informal) versus organized financial markets.

An important behavioral distinction is between those participants who engage in economically oriented maximization (profits, return on assets) and the nonmaximizing behavior of "traditional" economic units which make allocative decisions based on personal ties, social relationships, and the like -- in finance, lending to or borrowing from friends ·and relations, analagous to family household decisions on labor inputs and the sharing of outputs by average or other nonmarginal rules. An institutional distinction can be made between modern financial institutions which include banks, thrift institutions such as savings banks and the postal savings system, credit associations, credit cooperatives, insurance companies, and the stock and bond markets; and traditional financial arrangements, which include friends and relatives, moneylenders, and rotating credit cooperatives (tanomoshiko or mujin). The differences between banks and moneylenders well symbolize this institutional distinction, which is reflected in their respective balance sheets. The essence of modern banking is reliance upon private deposits and similar borrowed funds, that of moneylending the reliance upon own capital. Banks pool risk by diversified lending to and holding the securities of corporations; moneylenders lend to a less diversified ·set of individuals. Financial market dualism exists where there is severe segmentation among various financial markets such that there are large differentials in interest rates on borrowed funds and in access to funds by type of borrower, substantially in excess of transactions costs and default risks.

Though conceptually dichotomous, in reality financial dualism is more a continuum, a matter of degree. Moreover, in practice it is extremely difficult to obtain clear-cut evidence as to the existence or, more importantly, the degree of dualism. It is virtually impossible to know the motivations underlying, much less the terms of, loans made by persons to friends or relatives, certainly historically and even in present-day Japan. Like wage-rate differentials in labor market dualism, large interest-rate differentials are the clearest indicator of financial dualism. However, such differentials occur for a variety of reasons; only a subset can be regarded as indicating dualism.

The determinants of interest-rate differentials can be classified into three categories: those consistent with assumptions of the perfectly competitive neoclassical model; those involving deviations of market structures from perfect competition; and those involving behavior different from the standard assumptions of economically oriented, maximizing (hence marginalist, "rational") behavior. Financial instruments are heterogeneous in risk, maturity, liquidity, transactions costs; interest-rate differentials compensating for these specific features are to be expected in competitive markets. However, financial market structures may deviate from perfect competition due to government regulations (such as restrictions ·on entry or type of activity, regulation of interest rates) or to oligopoly and unequal bargaining power (market concentration, financial institutions captive of their clients, <u>zaibatsu</u> banks). These give rise to market segmentations not offset by arbitrage. The resulting interest rates can be thought of in terms of the differential-structure concept applied by Ohkawa and Rosovsky (1973) to differences within Japanese industry by firm size emerging during the second phase as defined here. Dualistic imperfections arise where financial markets are underdeveloped -- financial markets and/or information channels are inadequate or do not even exist, markets are thin, and/or traditional behavioral patterns prevail. We have too little historical evidence on interest rates, nominal, much less effective (adjusted for compensating balances, service charges, or other conditions which alter the prices actually paid), to be able to distinguish adequately among all these determinants of interest-rate differentials in the Japanese case.

Accordingly, I here use an institutional definition of financial dualism in terms of modern and traditional financial institutions, which thereby define modern and traditional financial sectors.[1] The traditional and modern financial sectors can be distinguished not just by type of financial institutions, but at the same time by their customers -- by type of participant, size of economic unit, type of activity, mode of production, availability of collateral. This concept overlaps substantially that of traditional and modern sectors in the real economy. Historically, the traditional sector in Japan consisted of very small scale units of production -- virtually all agriculture and the large numbers of miniscule industrial and commercial enterprises. These economic units were family-based, and relied heavily on unpaid family or apprentice labor. Financing came from traditional sources or internal saving. In addition, credit to most individuals for consumption came from traditional sources.

In contrast, the main participants in the modern sector have been medium to large corporate enterprises and wealthy individuals. Most have collateral for credit, and good to excellent credit ratings. By the interwar period these participants may be divided into, say, three tiers. The first tier includes large creditworthy firms, able to borrow at the equivalent of the prime rate, often listed on the stock exchange, able to issue bonds, and often having a close (ownership) relationship with a particular bank. The second tier includes independent medium-sized firms, subsidiaries of or other affiliates with first-tier enterprises, and some riskier large firms as well. The third tier includes all those smaller enterprises able to borrow from modern financial institutions. The loan market for first-tier firms is competitive -- a borrowers market. Lower tiers are lenders markets where financial institutions exercise increasing market power. This, then, is the financial differential structure -- all within the modern financial sector.

Part of the process of financial development is that the modern financial sector increasingly supersedes the traditional financial sector. Initially, at the beginning of Meiji, the traditional sector was predominant in financial intermediation. It took time for savers to develop knowledge of and confidence in the new institutions and instruments of financial intermediation; similarly, it took time for modern financial institutions to develop superior information as to lending opportunities and their risks for efficient allocation for investment purposes. Indeed, while the market power of such traditional institutions as moneylenders was a negative factor, on the positive side they undoubtedly had better information on small borrowers, and were better able to assess risk and allocate credit. Gradually, the efficiencies of modern finance overpowered the traditional financial sector, so that by the postwar era traditional sources of external finance have become insignificant,[2] and financial dualism has essentially ended (though vestiges remain as in all economies).

The interplay between the two sectors is an important part of this process. Traditional financial institutions evolve into modern ones. Moneylenders establish banks; highly personalized revolving-credit cooperatives become institutionalized-credit cooperatives, savings institutions, and (in the postwar period) mutual banks. Individuals deposit in modern-sector institutions, but borrow from traditional-sector institutions. Smaller enterprises, unable to borrow all they want from modern financial institutions, simultaneously rely on traditional sources as well. These possibilities for arbitrage increasingly link modern and traditional financial markets, and dualistic interest-rate differentials narrow. Gradually, modern financial institutions increase assets and diversify activities sufficiently that they are able to absorb essentially all borrowers and lenders into the modern financial system. This long-term process is founded upon the growth of the real economy -- the increase in savings and investment, and the increasing separation of savers and investors -- and the competitive effectiveness of modern financial institutions.

III. GOVERNMENT POLICY AND FINANCIAL DEVELOPMENT

Japanese government policy substantially affected the speed and the nature of this process of financial development. This has been important at three levels: the overall economy, macroeconomic policy, and specific measures concerning the development of the modern financial system. In Japan the government has always played an important role in shaping the economic environment in which the financial system is embedded. With the exception of the controlled economy of World War II, that environment has been based on a capitalist system of private ownership and initiative combined with reliance on relatively free market mechanisms, yet with more or less active government involvement in institutional development and in providing guidance to achieve government policy goals.

This is not the place to review the long historical sweep of Japanese macroeconomic fiscal and monetary policy. Successful financial development has been predicated upon successful economic development and growth. The most important macroeconomic variable in shaping the size, nature, and role of a financial system is the rate of inflation. With the dramatic exception of the third phase -- the Great Inflation of the 1940s -- Japan's economy has not been dominated by inflationary expectations which debilitated the financial system. Prior to World War II, Japan's experiences with inflation (at more than 10 percent annually) were associated mainly with war -- the domestic Satsuma Rebellion of 1877, Sino-Japanese, Russo-Japanese, and World War I -- and were always followed by periods of absolute price declines. For the fifty-six years between 1880 and 1937, the CPI increased more than 10 percent in only seven years, and actually decreased in twenty-two. Inflation was not expected to persist and it did not. The highly inflationary consequences of World War II wrought a major change in Japanese sensitivities to the possibilities and dangers of persistent inflation. Nonetheless, by the early 1950s price stability was regained. The sole postwar period of double-digit inflation was in 1973-75, the consequence of an expansionary domestic monetary policy, the world commodities boom, and then the oil shock. Monetary policy was subsequently able to bring inflation under control, and later to prevent its domestic spreading in the 1979-80 round of oil price increases. The monetary authorities generally have been successful in preventing inflationary expectations from becoming a major force leading to financial disintermediation except following World War II.

Government policy has been of central, direct importance in determining the structure of the financial system through a mixture of encouragement and regulation. It has set the conditions of entry, type of system (specialized versus general financial instutotions, unit versus branch banking), nature and degree of competition, and the conditions of financial markets (whether interest rates are controlled or determined by market supply and demand). It has created government (and semigovernmental) financial institutions to complement private institutions for specified objectives. Over time government financial policies in all these dimensions have changed dramatically, a significant feature of each of the four phases discussed below. It was important that Japan had already developed a diversified financial structure with a high degree of financial intermediation by the time the government moved from a market-oriented system to a regulated one. As the evidence of present-day developing-country financial markets attests, premature use of controls over interest rates and other regulations over the modern financial sector would have retarded its development and lengthened the life of the traditional financial sector.

IV. THE FOUR PHASES OF FINANCIAL DEVELOPMENT: AN OVERVIEW

Financial development is indicated by the growth and increasing diversity of type of financial institutions and by the increasing efficiency and effectiveness of financial markets. Ultimately, financial development is measured by the increased use of an ever-wider range of financial assets and liabilities, both absolutely and relative to real economic activities and to the holding of real (tangible) assets. A growing financial superstructure is indicative of increased saving and investment, increased separation of savers and investors, and more efficient allocation of real resources by means of fungible finance.

Table 1 provides summary data on Japan's modern financial development since 1885 when GNP estimates begin. Narrow and broad measures of money supply are available in time-series. In addition, Goldsmith (forthcoming), in a monumental forthcoming study, has made benchmark estimates of the ratios of financial assets to GNP and of financial assets to tangible assets (the financial interrelations ratio).[3] At first glance, the data in Table 1 suggest a

TABLE 1
Major Financial Ratios for Japan, Selected Years, 1885-1977
(Percent)

	(1)	(2)	(3)	(4)	(5)	(6)
	Currency	M1	M2	Financial Assets	Financial Assets	Real GNP per capita
	GNP	GNP	GNP	GNP	Tangible Assets	(1934-36 prices)
1885	22	27	28	190	30	102
1900	13	31	37	200	34	143
1913	13	36	55	306	62	158
1920	12	44	68	325	59	207
1930	13	46	93	568	120	221
1940	16	63	114	623	141	324
1944	31	118	189	-	-	279
1950	11	29	41	-	-	194
1955	7	25	55	231	54	282
1960	7	27	67	345	68	408
1965	7	32	79	385	80	616
1970	7	30	76	396	91	1,012
1975	8	34	84	473	93	1,221
1977	8	33	85	483	101	1,343

Sources: Columns 1-3, 1885-1950: Ohkawa and Shinohara (1979); Asakura
and Nishiyama (1973).

Columns 1-3, 1955-1977: Ohkawa and Shinohara (1979); Bank of
Japan, Economic Statistics Annual.

Columns 4-5: Raymond W. Goldsmith (Forthcoming).

Column 6: Estimated from Ohkawa and Shinohara (1979); Bank
of Japan, Economic Statistics Annual.

straightforward path of financial development: at the end of the period the currency ratio is lower, and all others are substantially higher. The startling fact, however, is that the ratio of money supply to GNP and the Goldsmith ratios are all larger in 1930 than in 1977! This despite the fact that postwar GNP per capita has been substantially higher than prewar peaks since the late 1950s. In other words, financial intermediation had progressed further relative to GNP and to GNP per capita in interwar Japan than it has in postwar Japan.

This discontinuity between prewar and postwar levels and rates of financial development is clearly illustrated in Figure 1 using a different measure of finance. The prewar data show both a higher level and greater slope (but lower intercept) of the line relating the ratio of nonfinancial-sector liabilities to GNP and GNP per capita than for the postwar period.[4] Tests reject (at the 1 percent level) the null hypothesis that the data for 1910-1936 and 1950-1977 (or 1955-1977) represent the same structural relationship.

Why has this discontinuity occurred? The fundamental answer is simple: the Great Inflation of the 1940s, suppressed during wartime (hence understating nominal GNP and raising these financial ratios) and then quite open in the Occupation period, destroyed the real value of government debt and other fixed-nominal-value claims and caused great financial retrogression. The institutional structure remained intact, but financial assets and liabilities had been stripped of most of their value. Post-World War II financial development had to start from pre-World War I levels of financial ratios.[5] The growth of the Japanese financial system over the past three decades, while rapid in amount, is somewhat less impressive relative to GNP growth in the context of Japan's historical financial development.

V. CREATION OF THE MODERN FINANCIAL SYSTEM: 1868-1905

A major feature of the Meiji government's commitment to building a modern economic system with all its institutions and appurtenances was the creation of a modern financial system centered on a modern banking system.[6] The government role was crucial. It set the basic rules. Financial markets were free, with interest rates determined in principle and in practice by supply and demand in the marketplace; this included bank deposit and loan markets as well as the nascent stock and bond markets. Entry into banking was easy, with low minimum capital requirements and little regulation.

The government did more than establish a competitive, private market framework. It actively encouraged the establishment of commercial banks (notably the national banks) by various forms of implicit subsidy (government deposits, rights of national banknote issue). I earlier (1967) termed this "supply-leading" development of the banking system, in that these institutions were created in advance of business and individual demand for their services.[7] In the early years the demand for both monetary and saving deposits was low; people held currency or real assets. Banks relied mainly upon their own capital, together with government deposits, as sources of funds. By the end of this first phase, nonetheless, deposit banking had become widespread. The early creation and widespread geographical coverage of the postal savings system contributed to the development of knowledge about savings deposits.

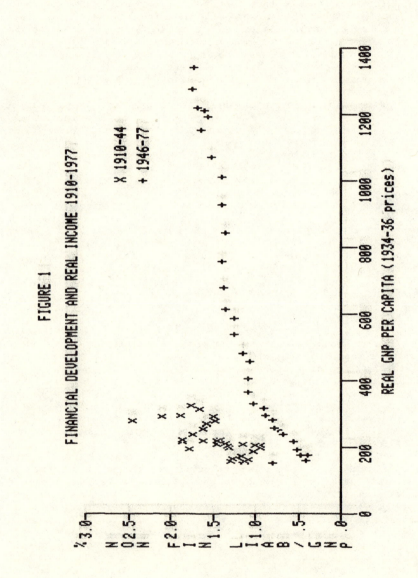

FIGURE 1

FINANCIAL DEVELOPMENT AND REAL INCOME 1910-1977

X 1910-44
+ 1946-77

REAL GNP PER CAPITA (1934-36 prices)

% N O N F I N L I A B / G N P

By the beginning of the twentieth century Japan's modern financial system was well established. There were commercial banks, savings banks, long-term credit banks, a central bank, insurance companies, and a small but active stock and bond market. The institutional structure was based upon the principle of specialization, though in practice large commercial banks were allowed to engage in a wide range of financial activities. The inherent tension between specialized and general (department-store) banking has persisted to the present. Particularly significant was the immense number and overwhelming importance of comercial banks. The number of ordinary banks peaked in 1901 at 1867; there were, in addition, 517 savings banks. It was predominantly a unit banking system, with less than one branch per bank on average. Bank size ranged enormously, from tiny "dwarf" banks to a few immense banks such as the Fifteenth, Mitsui, Dai-ichi, and Yasuda; however, it was not until later that these "big banks" (later termed "city banks") were to become of such great importance for industrial development.

Financial markets were indeed free; interest rates were not regulated. With the increase in number of banks and decrease in relative importance of government support, price competition for deposits expanded. Moreover, regional markets in finance as in commodities became increasingly integrated at the national level; regional differentials in deposit interest rates narrowed in the 1890s, though loan interest rate regional variance remained wide until the next phase (Teranishi and Patrick 1978).

This modern financial system was superimposed upon a large and relatively well developed traditional financial sector. We do not have comprehensive data on the changing absolute and relative sizes of the modern and traditional financial sectors over time. It seems clear that throughout this first phase only small proportions of both finance and real economic activity were in modern sectors. After all, even by 1909 only 46.2 percent of manufacturing production took place in factories with more than five workers; most still occurred in tiny family establishments. Modern finance went mainly to commerce and to finance working capital for factory-sized establishments. Traditional finance continued to meet the needs not just of most producers but of most production. This shows up most clearly in agriculture. In 1888 only 7.2 percent of agricultural borrowings were from modern financial institutions; by 1911 this share had increased to 35.7 percent, while traditional financial institutions (moneylenders, merchants, and pawnbrokers) provided 21.5 percent, and friends and relatives 42.9 percent.[8] Perhaps the most important point is that, while at the beginning of this period there was little connection between traditional and modern financial markets, they were somewhat integrated by about 1910. The detailed studies by Professor Ryuichi Shibuya on moneylenders (discussed in Teranishi and Patrick, 1978) indicate that movements in their interest rates were initially uncorrelated with bank loan rates, but the correlation came to be increasingly strong from about 1905 as the two sectors came into competition.

VI. FINANCIAL GROWTH AND THE DIVERSIFICATION IN FREE MARKETS,
1905-1937

Thus, the second phase began with a well-developed set of modern
financial institutions including a very large number of banks, free
and quite competitive financial markets, and considerable integration
between modern and traditional financial sectors, though the last may
have still provided most external finance to borrowers in the economy
as a whole. As a consequence of economic development, and the new
well-established institutional structure, the demand for (and supply
of) modern financial services grew very rapidly throughout this period
-- for deposits as well as loans. In contrast to the first phase,
this was a period of "demand-following," that is, market-oriented
financial development in which demand generated supply. Growth is
well reflected in comparisons of the financial ratios for 1900 and
1930 in Table 1. As one would expect, the system also became more
diversified. Modern financial institutions for agriculture and small
business, trust companies, insurance companies, and the postal savings
system all grew particularly rapidly. The relative shares of ordinary
and savings banks in modern financial-sector loans and deposits, more
than four-fifths in 1900, declined to about one-half in 1930. The
share of special banks rose somewhat over this period (from 9.8
percent in 1900 to 14.6 percent in 1930) and they played active roles
as government-sponsored institutions in foreign trade, real estate,
agriculture, and long-term industrial finance.

Despite rapid growth all was far from well, notably · in the
structure of the banking system. The banking structure was
particularly vulnerable to bank runs and panics, since it included a
large number of small banks operating in limited markets, with high
proportions of loans to a relatively few borrowers, without a system
of depositor insurance or other forms of depositor protection, and
without adequate outside inspection of the quality of bank assets.
Moreover, it was tested by a series of crises -- world and domestic
recessions and depression, the Kanto earthquake of 1923 which
generated ultimately valueless "earthquake bills" in bank portfolios,
and the resultant profound banking crisis of 1927. The government
made entry considerably more difficult (though far from impossible) by
imposing relatively high minimum paid-in capital requirements from
1927. Some 956 banks failed outright between 1905 and 1936; more
(1,333) were merged; 549 banks were established, many through mergers.
Interestingly, only a few mergers were with the "Big Five" banks. The
consolidation of the banking system was remarkable, particularly in
the interwar period. The number of commercial banks, 1,697 in 1905,
was reduced by 75 percent to 424 in 1936. However, the total number
of bank offices increased modestly; Japan moved to a branch banking
system. Consolidation was designed to strengthen the banking system
by eliminating its weakest elements while retaining a competitive
structure with small, medium, and large banks coexisting by lending in
different geographic areas and market segments.

There was some concentration of market power in the "Big Five"
banks. Their share in (ordinary and saving) bank loans and deposits,
about 17 percent in 1910, had risen to 30 percent by 1930.[9] They
behaved conservatively; they had surplus funds but sought large, safe
customers. The zaibatsu conglomerates were able to fund much of their

industrial activities from internal sources until the mid-1930s, when their first-line companies increasingly entered the new issue market for stocks and bonds. Mitsui and Mitsubishi first-line companies not only were able to finance their subsidiaries but to maintain larger deposits than loans with their affiliated banks.[10]

Financial growth and diversification increased the coverage and efficiency of financial markets. Interest rates continued to be determined by market forces, unregulated by government. The Osaka and Tokyo Bankers Associations had, from the beginning of the century, attempted to set maximum interest rates on deposits, with higher rates allowed in local areas. Apparently this price-fixing was not very effective in earlier years, but in the 1920s and 1930s these interbank agreements probably resulted in substantial price leadership. From 1927 the city banks attempted to set minimum interest rates on loans, though apparently with less impact. Restrictions on new bond and stock issues were to ensure creditworthiness, not to set prices and yields. Indeed, the government encouraged large, private-held zaibatsu firms to sell some shares to the public and be listed on the stock exchange.

Empirical evidence on prewar interest-rate differentials and financial markets is too fragmentary to assess definitively how important market segmentation among first-, second-, and third-tier firms was in the modern financial system, and how wide dualism was between modern and traditional financial sectors. First-tier companies, able to issue bonds, could obtain funds at lower cost. Otherwise there is little evidence that interest-rate differentials widened inversely with firm size. Moreover, most firms of all sizes were able to finance long-term investment internally or through equity issue.

Slightly more evidence is available on the relative reliance on modern and traditional financial sources by type of borrower. Large enterprises could rely entirely on modern financial institutions. With decrease in firm size, the proportion of external finance obtained from modern financial institutions declined and that from traditional sources increased. The myriads of tiny enterprises relied overwhelmingly on traditional sources of finance. A sample of urban manufacturers in 1932 indicates that three-fifths of total borrowings came from modern financial institutions, but for tiny firms the proportion was less than one-tenth (Teranishi and Patrick 1977). And, despite the growing role of modern financial institutions specifically designed for farmers, in 1932 agriculture obtained only 44 percent of its funds from the modern financial sector.

With the rapid growth of the modern financial system during this period, and the development of modern industry, the modern financial sector came to surpass the traditional financial sector quantitatively and qualitatively. The two sectors were ever-more-closely integrated; the degree of financial dualism declined substantially. Producers and individuals had ready access to modern financial institutions -- banks, postal savings, credit cooperatives -- for deposits, and increasing (though still limited) access for borrowing. The development of the financial system seemed to be along what might be termed a historical capitalist path of increasing, widening, deepening, and ever-more-efficient financial intermediation. And then came war.

VII. FINANCE UNDER MILITARY CONTROL, 1937-1952

Government policies during wartime wrought fundamental changes in the Japanese financial system, bringing to an end the competitive, market-oriented environment which had characterized financial development for the previous seventy years. This was no mere temporary aberration. Important features of the financial structure and policies toward financial markets developed in wartime were continued virtually unchanged during the postwar Allied Occupation. More important, many became the foundation and framework for the postwar financial system, persisting virtually to the present, even though the goals of postwar government policy shifted dramatically from military production to civilian, industry-based, rapid economic growth.

In essence the government replaced the market with planning in allocation of real resources and finance. The institutional process for financial control developed in a piecemeal fashion, and indeed was foreshadowed by mechanisms to coordinate new bond issues and prevent capital flight abroad from the early 1930s. The government obtained authority to allocate funds directly to munitions and other key war-related industries, to fund the increasingly huge government deficits through required bond purchase by financial institutions, and to absorb potential purchasing power of individuals by required deposits in financial institutions. Finance thus became the handmaiden of war. Financial planning and direct fund allocation went relatively smoothly during the war; credit was not a major problem (Cohen 1949). Most production went to the war effort; consumption dropped sharply. Rationing and price controls prevailed.

The financing of Japan's war effort flooded the economy with financial assets. Between 1937 and 1944, the ratios of currency, M1, and M2 to GNP more than doubled. Other financial claims increased even more rapidly. By war end, financial ratios to GNP and to tangible assets came to have little meaning; price controls understated the value of production, production itself was distorted and interrupted, and more than one-quarter of the nation's tangible wealth had been destroyed.

This financing of war was highly inflationary. So too was the financing of postwar reconstruction before the Dodge Plan reforms of 1949. This was the era of Japan's Great Inflation. Prices increased more than three hundredfold before inflation was finally brought under control in 1951.[11] As with all periods of great inflation, the real value of financial assets was sharply reduced, exacerbated by postwar financial reforms which wrote off a substantial proportion of wartime loans and deposits. The value of government debt evaporated, and hence, investor confidence in government and other long-term debt instruments.[12] Inflation, land reform, zaibatsu dissolution, and other measures substantially altered and reduced the inequality of the distribution of wealth. The financial infrastructure imploded from war end until early 1949 or so; the money supply-GNP ratios dropped sharply, and Goldsmith suggests the ratio of financial assets to GNP, 6.23 in 1940, was only about unity in 1948. Financial development, as measured by these summary ratios, had retrogressed to the levels of some fifty years earlier. This, however, is overly simplistic. Once inflation had been conquered, financial assets resumed their growth in real terms. More important, the financial system itself was much more developed and sophisticated in 1950 than a half century earlier.

Wartime policies fundamentally changed the structure and rules of behavior for the banking system. Under the theme "one bank for each prefecture," the government forced consolidation of the banking system through merger and a freeze on new entries, in order to make it easier to control the banking system directly. By war end, Japan had moved completely away from its Meiji system of a large number of unit banks with easy entry. The number of ordinary banks, 377 in 1937 and still 186 in 1941, had contracted to 61 in 1945; the savings-bank system was virtually eliminated. More important, however, was the concentration of financial activities to a small number of Big Banks, dominated by the Big Five, which engaged in nationwide branch banking. Of the 2,240 companies designated as munitions producers, 70.6 percent were assigned to the Big Five (Cohen 1949, 95). The Industrial Bank and other government-sponsored, long-term credit banks played an increasingly important role, as did new government financial institutions set up to fund the war effort.

This bifurcated structure of nationwide "city banks" and local banks remained virtually intact under Occupation policy. The Occupation efforts to dismantle Japan's wartime economic system and to replace it with a competitive, "democratic" system were pervasive in the real economy, but did not extend significantly to finance. There the Occupation authorities were concerned primarily with eliminating war-related institutions, dissolving the zaibatsu conglomerates, and coping both with inflation and the war-related losses of financial institutions. While specific financial institutions changed in status, the basic system remained intact based on the principle of specialized institutions for specific functions. Thus, only the ownership of the zaibatsu banks were affected; the families were dispossessed, and stock widely distributed, and control accrued to self-perpetuating management. Despite initial Occupation thinking, the Big Five banks were not broken up into smaller, independent units.[13] The "city banks" (the Big Five plus a few others engaging in widespread branch banking) retained power, prestige, and their main industrial and commercial clientele of large firms.

Even more profound than the war-forced changes in banking structure were the changes in the operations of financial markets: the structure of financial flows, and the replacing of market-determined interest rates by direct controls over the allocation of credit. Patterns were established which have persisted subsequently. For example, production was concentrated increasingly in large firms; they had to rely increasingly on external sources of funds, especially loans; they had ever-closer ties with the Big Banks. The Ministry of Finance assumed the power to decide which few companies could issue bonds, how much, and on what terms. It, and the Munitions Ministry, directly allocated bank credit to munitions firms. Bank portfolios, especially of the largest banks, shifted from commercial- and working-capital financing to increasing industrial term financing. Local banks and other small-scale financial intermediaries received savings deposits but had few customers to whom they could lend; funds were channelled to the "Big Five" banks and to government financial institutions. Their demand for loans was so huge that for the first time in history the Big Banks began to borrow substantially and continuously from the Bank of Japan.

The allocative mechanism for finance thus moved from markets based on price signals to decisions by bureaucrats and administrators based on military planning priorities. Market competition was no longer the rule. Under these circumstances, interest rates had no allocative role. Informal interbank agreements on interest rates on deposits and loans were replaced by formal regulations. Interest rates were set artificially low to ease further the financing of the war effort.

The Occupation did not fundamentally alter this war-generated system of direct controls over major components of the flows of funds and over interest rates, though somewhat more scope was given to market mechanisms.[14] The problems of reconstruction of war-ravaged Japan were so huge, the specific bottlenecks so great, that major-priority sectors -- coal, electric power, transport, chemical fertilizers, eventually steel -- had to obtain resources, especially financial, through planned, direct allocations. While the focus of priority allocation shifted from war to peace, the mechanisms remained much the same.

Even after quantitative allocations of private credit to specific industries and firms came to an end in the 1950s, the system of low interest rates and credit rationing persisted. Low interest rates were justified to encourage investment and reduce costs of production; their allocative role was not given serious attention. With the end of the war, the banks reverted to their own agreements on maximum deposit and lending rates, with government bureaucracy blessing. In 1947 the government passed the Temporary Interest Adjustment Law, which gave the Ministry of Finance and Bank of Japan control over maximum interest rates on deposits and loans, a "temporary" law still in effect. The stock market was reopened, but new bond issue was severely regulated at low interest rates. The financial system continued to be constrained to lend only for productive industrial and commercial purposes, especially to high-priority sectors.

During this third phase of financial development, Japan's financial markets became insulated and isolated from world financial markets, which also were in disarray. It is unlikely Japan could have borrowed more abroad than it succeeded in doing. Like other countries facing severe balance-of-payments problems, Japan, under the Occupation authorities, instituted tight restrictions on imports, foreign-exchange transactions, and short-term and long-term capital outflows and inflows. These too persisted in the postwar era.

We do not know exactly what took place in the interrelationships between the modern and traditional financial sectors during this period. The size and role of traditional finance became greatly reduced during wartime, and financial dualism may even have temporarily ended. The flood of government deficit expenditures extended to agriculture and other small-scale units of production. They were able to pay off debts, and were forced to deposit in credit cooperatives, credit associations, and other small-scale institutions which were now part of the modern financial system. The share of these institutions in the assets of the modern financial system rose from 5.9 percent in 1936 to 11.2 percent in 1944. The overwhelming allocation of resources directly to war production precluded much traditional-sector investment or intermediate-good expenditures, much less, need for consumption loans. The inflation-generated financial implosion during the Occupation surely increased the need for and role of traditional finance. However, modern financial institutions for agriculture and small business were now well established, and markets integrated with other financial markets. The early postwar improvement in terms of trade for agriculture and the effective elimination of debt by the inflationary process meant that traditional sources of agricultural finance became much less important.

VIII. FINANCIAL DEVELOPMENT IN THE POSTWAR ERA, 1952-1980

The rapid growth and evolution of Japan's postwar financial system and its financial intermediation of the savings-investment process in an era of high GNP growth, as well as its many specific features, have been described and analyzed elsewhere.[15] Here I stress the continuity of the postwar system with the system as it was transformed during wartime,[16] and hence, its substantial discontinuity in many, though not all, respects from pre-war. Moreover, despite all the success of financial intermediation, the postwar growth of the financial superstructure relative to prewar, as evidenced by aggregative financial ratios, is surprisingly modest.

As previously discussed, this is shown in Table 1 and Figure 1. Two facts stand out: the relative size of the financial superstructure compared to the real economy in 1977 is below that in 1930; ·and its rate of growth relative to the real economy between 1955 and 1977 was somewhat less rapid than for the prewar period (between 1900 or 1920 and 1930). These are the reality even though financial diversification and sophistication today are substantially greater than in the 1930s, the separation of saving and investment more pronounced, the amount of real financial assets much greater, and the role of traditional finance far less, even negligible. What are the probable causes?

First, the slow rate of growth of postwar financial intermediation relative to GNP and to tangible assets masks a very rapid absolute rate of growth, substantially above prewar rates. This absolute increase was concomitant with, and mainly due to, Japan's great surge of extremely rapid GNP growth and accumulation of real assets. Second, however, the lower relative levels of financial assets imply that postwar assetholders have found real assets -- land, houses, and productive fixed investment -- relatively more attractive to hold than financial assets despite much higher levels of real income and wealth. The relative price of land has increased sharply -- but land declined from 69.1 percent of national tangible wealth in 1960 to 50.3 percent in 1977. While the share of housing increased from 4.2 percent to 10.0 percent, the big increase was in productive fixed assets from 16.3 percent to 30.2 percent. Part of the preference for real assets lies in assetholder aversion to long-term, fixed-yield financial assets generated by the Great Inflation of the 1940s. But, undoubtedly, a major factor has been the perpetuation of relatively low yields on financial assets through the government's low-interest-rate policy.

The basic institutional structure of the financial system has not changed significantly in the postwar period, following the relatively minor changes made during the Occupation. The full range of institutions was already well in place, with specialization in financial activities the norm. The system has worked well, particularly given the constraints imposed by restrictions on the free operations of financial markets. Entry by banks has been severely constrained; new banks cannot be established, and the creation of new branches is severely rationed by the Ministry of Finance. The patterns of flows of funds have, nonetheless, significantly altered the relative share of different categoris of financial institutions and shaped their success. The relative position of city banks has diminished from their early postwar preeminance, due mainly to greater diversification throughout the system. Credit associations and other institutions have become more important. Segmentation among specific financial markets or different categories of financial institutions has decreased over time; aggressive institutions seek new customers and new sources of funds, even within the constraints of the system.

The persistence of war-inherited administrative controls over flows of funds, interest rates, the bond-issuance market, and related Ministry of Finance regulation of financial markets has been notable. The Government bureaucracy has long lost its direct controls over private-sector production, investment, and imports. Only in finance does its hand remain heavy. This is not simply because the Ministry of Finance has been very powerful since World War II, at least, though it certainly is reluctant to surrender its bureaucratic powers to the marketplace. The continuation into the 1970s of the wartime patterns of finance has made possible the perpetuation of administrative controls, most importantly exemplified by regulation of interest rates. While there has been considerable continuity in policy instruments, of course the purpose of the postwar low-interest-rate policy has been completely different: to stimulate rapid growth through high investment, and preferences in lending for productive purposes at the expense of housing and consumer loans.

Suzuki (1980) has characterized the postwar financial system as having four distinctive characteristics: overloan; overborrowing; imbalance of liquidity; and predominance of indirect finance. These mean, respectively: the banking system (notably the city banks) has borrowed substantially and sustainedly from the Bank of Japan; business has depended heavily on funds borrowed from the banks; local banks have surplus funds which they lend to city banks, which have the best customers but insufficient loanable funds; and both individuals as accumulators of financial assets and business as borrowers rely on banks, rather than on the stock and bond markets. All these features derive from Japan's wartime period. In addition, until the early 1970s Japanese financial markets were effectively insulated from world markets.

A system of low maximum interest rates means that markets do not clear; this has been important in postwar Japan where the demand for investment finance has been high. With demand greater than supply, the response has been credit rationing -- and in much the pattern established during World War II. The financial system strongly favored producers of goods and certain services; it was much less ready to make credit available for consumer purchases of housing or consumer durables. Within industry it favored large firms over small. Key industries received low-cost government loans, and private loans unless the industry's prospects (such as shipping) were regarded with skepticism by bankers. Moreover, small government prevailed, and its borrowing was limited until the mid-1970s. Credit allocation may not have been optimal by either static or dynamic criteria, but it was effective in financing productive investment for growth. And, importantly, within somewhat-segmented financial submarkets for first-, second-, and third-tier business loans there was substantial competition among lenders and borrowers and fairly careful evaluation of projects and creditworthiness. Rapid growth helped cover over and smooth out mistakes in allocation. So too did the widespread requirement of collateral, frequently undervalued land; the actual losses of Japanese financial institutions, despite apparent willingness to take on risk, have been very low.

Three significant qualifications should be stressed. First, credit is fungible among uses; stated purposes or actual borrowers do not provide adequate evidence of how credit is actually used at the margin. For example, interfirm trade credit, large-firm financing of subcontractors, and the role of large trading companies as de facto financial intermediaries, especially for small firms, have been of major importance. Second, there are many ways to evade or mitigate price (interest rate) controls over finance; to the extent such devices are successfully used, what may appear as credit allocation by rationing may actually be by price. In postwar Japan compensating balances have been ubiquitous; lenders, by varying deposit-balance requirements by type of borrower, have been able, somewhat, to raise and differentiate effective interest rates on short-term loans. Third, Japan's economy, including its financial system, has gone through some thirty years of very rapid growth; this dynamic has made for such change that any static characterization is misleading.

Accordingly, the financial system has gradually become increasingly market-oriented. Indeed, as of 1980 it can be argued that the short-term loan markets are now predominantly price-determined. Large firms in the first tier are able to compete effectively for relatively low-cost finance; smaller firms in the second and third tiers face oligopolistic lenders and pay higher effective rates. Only in the long-term credit market (for loans and bonds) does credit continue to be rationed, predominantly in favor of first-tier firms.

It could be argued that a financial differential structure by firm size has been more prevalent postwar than prewar; it has been enhanced by the system of specialized financial institutions and the artificially low interest-rate policy. The persistence of a low interest-rate policy is founded on the low interest rates at which new government debt issue is forced onto the financial system, and the low ceilings on savings-deposit interest rates. The Treasury-bill rate is so low that all bills are purchased by the Bank of Japan; it has almost no relationship to other short-term interest rates. However, the banks are still simply allocated a proportionate share of new government bond issue which they must purchase, even at low rates. Other bond issue rates and long-term lending rates are tied to the government bond issue rate. In the deposit market, low maximum interest rates are the rule, though they are combined with tax-exemption advantages. Additional payments have been made in practice for very large deposits, and the recently created CD (certificate of deposit) market provides a competitive outlet for very large units of short-term funds. Similar instruments, such as money market funds, are not yet available for smaller savers. In deposits, as in loans, controls over financial markets discriminate in favor of the large participant and against the small.

Over the long course of Japanese financial development, traditional finance has been absorbed by, and largely replaced by, the modern financial system. The penetration of the traditional financial sector by the modern has been through the institutional development of specialized financial intermediaries for small business and agriculture, forestry, and fishing. The immense flows of wartime credit greatly accelerated this process. While there was probably some reversion to traditional sources of funds by small borrowers in the early postwar years, by the late 1950s farmers and even very small businesses were able to obtain the overwhelming proportion of borrowed funds from the modern financial sector. For example, in 1957 even the smallest manufacturing firms (with 1 to 3 employees) obtained two-thirds from modern financial institutions (half of that from banks), 15 percent from friends and relatives, and only 0.8 percent from moneylenders (Teranishi and Patrick 1977). For the financing of production, financial dualism essentially had come to an end.

The story is less clearcut for consumption loans to wage-earners. Pawnshops and moneylenders have continued to exist. Some moneylenders have established finance companies, which can be regarded as modern institutions. However, the interest-rate differentials have been so wide -- up to 100 percent annual rates for short-term "salaryman loans" -- as to indicate some persistence of financial dualism. Consumer credit has expanded rapidly over the past decade. Accordingly, moneylenders and similar forms of traditional finance now have only a minor role, no more so than in other advanced industrial economies.

The success of financial intermediation in the postwar era cannot be credited particularly to government financial policy or to the efficacy of financial institutions. Demand for financial claims grew mainly because of rapid GNP growth, an increasing proportion of wage-earners in the labor force, an evolving economic structure in which savings and investing were done increasingly by different economic units, urbanization, high personal savings rates, and the like. The modern financial system already existed. All it had to do was supply financial claims in response to the demand for them; it was not allowed to compete effectively against real assets. If it had, the growth of financial intermediation would have been more rapid, and, probably, the allocation of resources more efficient. The main role of the financial system has been to allocate credit among alternative users through a complex combination of credit rationing and effective interest rates higher than stated nominal ceiling rates.

IX. A NEW ERA: HAS THE POSTWAR PHASE COME TO AN END?

It can be argued that Japan will move into its fifth phase of financial development when major interest-rate controls are removed and financial markets allowed to operate freely, flexibly, and competitively, because the changes in the system will be so profound. In this new era, financial markets will be, in principle, free: competitive market forces will be the main determinants of short-term and long-term interest rates and the allocation of credit. Government bond issue will be through competitive bid rather than Ministry of Finance allocation to financial institutions; accordingly, other bond issues will also be freed. The CD market will be broader and deeper, and money market funds will be allowed to develop for the benefit of a far wider range of depositors. Segmentation among financial markets will weaken. Financial institutions will take on a wider range of activities and clients. In other words, the Japanese financial system will approach the textbook perfect financial-market model. The historical problem of the absorption of the traditional financial sector by the modern will be long past. The evidence suggests that while a somewhat idealized view, this is, nonetheless, a realistic projection of underlying trends. To what extent the institutional structure of the financial system will change is problematic; major change in types of institutions is unlikely. The relative importance of the commercial banking system, particularly city banks, may well be strengthened in a more competitive environment.

This era will evolve gradually out of the postwar phase rather than through any major discontinuities in government policy, as evidenced by the various small steps taken toward financial liberalization during the decade of the 1970s. Indeed Suzuki (1980, Part 5) argues Japan has already begun its new phase. The specification of the timing of evolutionary transition from one phase to the next is not crucial. It is useful to examine both the forces bringing the postwar era of financial control to an end, and the evidence that this process is well underway.

The underlying sources of financial change lie in the real economy. Now huge, the Japanese economy is no longer dominated by superfast growth, in policy objectives and in reality. The 1974-75 recession appears to have been a major turning point. The government took strong orthodox fiscal-monetary measures to end the inflationary spiral. It was successful, but the cost was Japan's first postwar, serious recession, with an absolute decline in output, a drop in the GNP growth rate by 10 percentage points,[17] and the emergence of very large excess capacity, shown in the gap between potential and actual GNP in excess of 10 percent.

Once inflation was brought under control, private demand did not vigorously reassert itself as in past, minor recessions. Business investment demand since 1975 has become substantially less strong than earlier, while the private saving rate has remained high. With inadequate private demand, large-scale government-deficit finance through bond issue has been necessary in order to obtain a 5 to 6 percent growth rate and to reduce excess capacity gradually; in effect, the Japanese economic environment has shifted at the macro level from neoclassical (supply side) to Keynesian, while continuing to maintain considerable flexibility at the micro level. Moreover, as

Japan has become one of the largest world traders, it has been difficult and increasingly undesirable to insulate domestic financial markets from world financial markets. Institutionally, this process has been supported by the expansion of Japanese city banks abroad and foreign banks into Japan. Further, with business investment no longer the predominant focus of credit, it has spilled over into other uses -- housing, consumer credit, and especially the financing of the government debt. Inefficiencies in the allocation of financial resources have become more obvious. Moreover, the fact that the system of controlled, low interest rates on deposits, and thereby on loans to large enterprises, in effect represents a transfer of income from household savers to owners of big business is increasingly perceived as inequitable.

Over the past decade the financial system has been responding to these and to its own internal forces by evolving toward a greater market orientation (Christelow 1981). However, this evolutionary process has been gradual and slow. Those who bear the costs of financial control -- individual savers and consumers and small businessmen -- are weak and unorganized. The vested interests which benefit -- big business, specialized financial institutions, and the government bureaucracy -- are powerful. The Ministry of Finance is the key. Its officials have resisted the ending of controls over interest rates and other restrictions: free markets would reduce their power to implement monetary control, their ability to finance the government debt at low interest rates, their authority.

Nonetheless, the control mechanism is eroding under the force of domestic and international market pressures. Short-term money markets have become substantially liberalized though still discriminatorily restricted to large participants. To the earlier call-market and bill-discount markets have been added the _gensaki_ market (sale of bonds under short-term repurchase agreements), and the CD market for very large deposits. Government restrictions have been sufficiently eased that these markets are virtually free: interest rates are competitively market determined. As seven-year government bonds, issued in very large amounts since 1977, approach maturity, trading them in as short-term securities will virtually complete the process of liberalization of short-term money markets. As noted, the use of compensating balances has provided a sort of de facto market mechanism in the short-term loan market.

The main issue continues to be the long-term bond (and loan) market. Japan will not have finally moved to a new era of finance, symbolically and in reality, until long-term interest rates and credit allocations are determined in competitive markets. The key is the government bond issue market. The Ministry of Finance has been forced to adjust new issue rates closer to prevailing yields in the secondary bond market; but the system of direct allocation to city banks and other financial institutions persists. With secondary yields typically above issue yields, with the ending of Bank of Japan guarantees to purchase bonds after a one-year holding period, and with very large amounts of debt outstanding and to be issued in the next several years, the pressures to change are strong indeed. However, given the strength of the Ministry of Finance in Japan's political-economic system, one cannot predict with full confidence that the new era is upon us.

FOOTNOTES

This paper is an outgrowth of research over a number of years on Japanese finance, most recently in collaboration with Professor Juro Teranishi of Hitotsubashi University, Tokyo, as part of the Comparative Analysis Project of the International Development Center of Japan. See particularly Patrick (1967, 1971, 1972, forthcoming) and Teranishi and Patrick (1977, 1978). I express my appreciation to Teranishi, and thanks to him, Kokichi Asakura, Robert Feldman, Tsuguo Fujino, Toshihiko Kato, and Gustav Ranis for their comments on an earlier draft, while holding none responsible for this essay.

1. Inevitably, even this definition runs into some empirical problems. Many commercial banks initially relied principally upon their own capital and, hence, were little more than moneylenders in "modern" institutional guise; for some (mostly very small) banks, own capital continued to be the major source of funds well into the 1920s. Similarly, to the extent that banks rely on government funds (as was the case in the first phase), they are merely conduits of government financial intermediation rather than truly banks in the sense of obtaining private deposits.

2. The main exception continues to be, in Japan as elsewhere, the reliance by entrepreneurs starting new, small businesses on initial finance from family and friends as well as their own assets. Venture-capital institutions assist only a small proportion of new, small businesses even in the United States.

3. While specific estimates may require further refinement, the absolute numbers are less important than the trends. It should be noted that Goldsmith's data cover only modern financial institutions, so that such traditional sources as moneylenders and friends and relatives are not included since comprehensive data are not available.

4. Simple OLS regressions give the following results:

$$\underline{1910\text{-}1936}$$
$$Y = 0.2962 + 0.00508X \qquad R^2 = 0.379$$
$$\quad (1.09727) \quad (3.90772) \qquad D.W. = 0.3426$$
$$\qquad\qquad\qquad\qquad\qquad\qquad SSR = 1.13837$$
$$\qquad\qquad\qquad\qquad\qquad\qquad S.E. = 0.213389$$

$$\underline{1950\text{-}1977}$$
$$Y = 0.6179 + 0.000877X \qquad R^2 = 0.889$$
$$\quad (13.2716) \quad (14.3963) \qquad D.W. = 0.2680$$
$$\qquad\qquad\qquad\qquad\qquad\qquad SSR = 0.392780$$
$$\qquad\qquad\qquad\qquad\qquad\qquad S.E. = 0.122410$$

Where:
   Y = Non-Financial Sector Liabilities/GNP
   X = Real GNP per capita (1934-36 prices)

The basic data are derived from Sakakibara, Feldman, and Harada (1981) and Ohkawa and Shinohara (1979).

5. Goldsmith's estimates of the financial-intermediation ratio (the ratio of net new issues by nonfinancial institutions absorbed by financial institutions) shows a steady, gradual rise from about one-half in 1886-1900 to three-quarters in 1932-36, before reaching almost nine-tenths in 1937-41 as government bond issues increased dramatically. It then dropped sharply to about one-third in the mid-1950s, rising to two-fifths in the early 1970s.

6. For greater detail see Patrick (1967) and Teranishi and Patrick (1978), and references cited therein.

7. As with most conceptual dichotomizations, reality is somewhat more blurred. Teranishi has pointed out that in highly commercial industrial regions, centering particularly on silk, tea, and weaving, banks apparently were established in response to growing demand. It might be hypothesized that supply-leading lending results in lower allocative efficiency than demand-following; data on bank lending are not adequate to test this or other allocation hypotheses.

8. See Teranishi (1976-77). In 1932 the respective shares were 43.7 percent, 8.6 percent, and 44.1 percent. Modern financial institutions replaced traditional, but (traditional) personal sources continued to be of great importance.

9. The story is less clearcut than this implies. The capital of the Fifteenth National Bank at its establishment in 1877 comprised two-fifths that of the entire national banking system. It was founded by a large number of daimyo, initially lent mainly to the government, and never developed a major banking role. Accordingly, even though it was among the largest banks, it has not typically been included in the Big Five grouping. It represents an outstanding case of failure to realize potential, and was eventually merged into the Teikoku Bank in 1944.

10. The major exceptions were the trading companies which, not surprisingly, borrowed heavily for working capital -- from their own bank, from Yokohama Specie Bank for foreign-trade financing, and from other banks including major zaibatsu competitors.

11. The wholesale price index, based on a 1934-36 average of 100, was 161 in 1940, 232 in 1944, 350 in 1945, 1,627 in 1946, 20,880 in 1949, and 34,250 in 1951.

12. The ratio of government bonds to GNP was 190 percent in 1944, 10 percent in 1951 (Fuji Bank 1967, 192).

13. The one exception was the dissolution of the merger, which had been forced, between the Mitsui and Dai-ichi Banks. The Occupation did convert the semigovernmental long-term-credit banks and foreign-exchange bank into private institutions. At the same time, new governmental institutions, notably the Reconstruction Finance Bank (later transformed into the Japan Development Bank), were created.

14. The SCAP Occupation authorities did intend to end direct controls over financial markets in due course, but the problems of economic reconstruction in a highly inflationary environment took precedent. The 1949 Dodge Plan broke the back of inflation, but further reform of financial policy was left to the Japanaese government, especially once SCAP attention was diverted to the Korean War from June 1950.

15. The "conventional" view stresses the predominance of interest-rate controls and other regulation of financial markets and institutions; see Suzuki (1980) and Patrick (1972). Recently, a revisionist school has emerged which argues that financial markets have been relatively free and competitive from the early 1970s. Sakakibara, Feldman, and Harada (1981) present that case. Murakami (1982) briefly summarizes the issues and provides a good bibliography of sources in Japanese.

16. This point is well made in Sakakibara and Noguchi (1977).

17. The GNP growth rate, 8.8 percent in 1973, was -1.2 percent in 1974, and only 2.4 percent in 1975. The decline in hours worked in Japan was about the same as in the United States, but recorded unemployment only increased slightly as firms kept on redundant workers and as those losing employment were old persons and middle-aged married women who "left" the labor force in terms of employment data.

BIBLIOGRAPHY

Asakura, K., C. Nishiyama. 1973. *Nihon Keizai no Kaheiteki Bunseki 1868-1970*. (Monetary analysis of the Japanese economy 1868-1970.) Tokyo: Sobunsha.

Christelow, D. B. 1981. Financial innovation and monetary indicators in Japan. Federal Reserve Bank of New York. *Quart. Rev.*, (Spring): 42-53.

Cohen, J. B. 1949. *Japan's economy in war and reconstruction*. Minneapolis: U. of Minnesota Press.

Fuji Bank, Research Division. 1967. *Banking in modern Japan*. 2nd edition. Tokyo: Fuji Bank.

Goldsmith, R. W. Forthcoming. *The long-run financial development of India and Japan, 1860-1970*. 2 vols.: vol. 2. New Haven: Yale U. Press.

Murakami, Y. 1982. Toward a socio-institutional explanation of Japan's economic performance. In *Policies and trade issues of the Japanese economy: American and Japanese perspectives*, ed. K. Yamamura. Seattle: U. of Washington Press.

Ohkawa, K., G. Ranis. 1978. On phasing. *Papers and proceedings of the conference on Japan's historical development experience and the contemporary developing countries: issues for comparative analysis*. Tokyo: International Development Center of Japan.

Ohkawa, K., H. Rosovsky. 1973. *Japanese economic growth: trend acceleration in the twentieth century*. Palo Alto: Stanford U. Press.

Ohkawa, K., M. Shinohara. 1979. *Patterns of Japanese economic development: a quantitative appraisal*. New Haven: Yale U. Press.

Patrick, H. T. 1967. Japan. In *Banking in the early stages of industrialization*, R. Cameron et al. New York: Oxford U. Press.

———, 1971. Economic muddle of the 1920s. In *Dilemmas of growth in prewar Japan*, ed. J. M. Morley. Princeton: Princeton U. Press.

———, 1972. Finance, capital markets and economic growth in Japan. In *Financial development and economic growth*, ed. A. W. Sametz. New York: N.Y.U. Press.

———, Forthcoming. The evolution of Japan's financial system in the interwar period. In *Interwar economy of Japan in international perspective*, ed. K. Sato.

Sakakibara, E., R. Feldman, Y. Harada. 1981. Japanese financial system in comparative perspective. Paper presented to Japan Economic Seminar, 24 October 1981. (Mimeo).

Sakakibara, E., Y. Noguchi. 1977. Okurasho-Nichigin Ocho no Bunseki. *Chuo Koron*, (August).

Suzuki, Y. 1980. *Money and banking in contemporary Japan*. New Haven: Yale U. Press.

Teranishi, J. 1976-77. Noko-kan Shikin Ido Saiko. (The pattern and role of flow of funds between agriculture and non-agriculture in Japanese economic development.) *Keizai Kenkyu*, 27(4)(October 1976), and 28(1)(January 1977).

Teranishi, J., H. Patrick. 1977. Financas, dualismo e estrutura industrial diferencial do Japao. (Financial dualism and differential industrial structure of Japan.) In *Mercado de capitais e desenvolvimento economico*, A. Ferriera de Oliviera et al. Rio de Janeiro: Instituto Brasileiro de Mercado de Capitais.

_____, 1978. The establishment and early development of banking in Japan: phases and policies prior to World War I. In *Papers and proceedings of the conference on Japan's historical development experience and the contemporary developing countries: issues for comparative analysis*. Tokyo: International Development Center of Japan.

15
No Less Than One Hundred Years
of Argentine Economic History
Plus Some Comparisons

Carlos Díaz Alejandro

I. INTRODUCTION

The economic progress of the Argentine Republic since about the middle of the last century remains one of the most puzzling and misunderstood national stories in the development literature. This essay will succinctly present the salient facts of the Argentine story and will advance some interpretations regarding Argentine performance. Many big and difficult questions will remain unanswered, but it is hoped that quantification of major trends will serve at least to rule out some of the silliest nonquestions and assertions about Argentina often found in the literature.

It should be helpful to contrast Argentine evolution with those of two countries, one which has been ahead of, and another behind, the economic indicators for Argentina. Many choices are possible: early this century Argentines liked to measure their country's progress against those of the United States or Canada. Population size and geographical location suggest that Australia is a more realistic front-runner for comparative purposes.

Portuguese advances toward the River Plate led to the creation of a new Spanish viceroyalty in Buenos Aires in 1776. At least since then a certain geopolitical and economic rivalry has been perceived by many observers between the communities which today make up Argentina and Brazil. For the last fifty years or so Brazil has been catching up with Argentine per capita income, offering a suggestive contrast to the mediocre Argentine growth of that period.

II. ORIGINS

Of the three countries considered in this essay, Brazil is the oldest one, economically speaking. By the middle of the nineteenth century Brazil had already experienced a rich economic history characterized by export booms leaving behind, besides splendid architecture, little but institutional arrangements inimical to development. The seventeenth-century sugar boom of the Northeast yielded slavery and latifundia, plus a peripheral low-productivity subsistence sector. The eighteenth-century gold boom may have contributed to Brazilian national union, but its impact on sustainable per capita incomes was weak. The relatively painless way Brazil obtained independence during the 1820s could have been expected to facilitate the spread of the industrial revolution to the tropics, but by the midnineteenth century Brazil remained a patriarchal rural society, its labor market shackled by the peculiar institution. In contrast with Argentina, however, the Brazilian state by 1850 had become a going concern relying on reasonably firm institutions. At that time only Chile in Latin America could match Brazilian institutional development. The Brazilian geographical vastness and the heterogeneity of its regional economies made the political achievements of the Brazilian monarchy the more impressive, although ambiguous regarding their impact on economic development. Reflecting perhaps certain faith in its manifest destiny, that state called itself an empire.

One may conjecture that Argentine per capita income at midnineteenth century was not far above the low Brazilian levels; by then, however, slavery had dissolved in the River Plate leaving practically no imprint either ethnically or culturally. Buenos Aires had come into its own only late in the eighteenth century as a result of the Bourbon reforms; other parts of what was to become the Argentine Republic had "longer" economic histories, but mainly as peripheries to the mining centers of the Perus (including today's Bolivia). In 1861 Argentina was more of an empty land than Brazil. This emptiness was regarded both as a key barrier to economic progress and a potentially fatal geopolitical flaw; Argentine leadership was to be marked by a compulsion to "people the wilderness" with little regard for delicate benefit-cost calculations. Before the 1860s what is today the Argentine Republic was made up of fragile coalitions of regional authorities, jealous of their autonomy, and which could have gone their separate ways as in Central America. Perceived threats from the North and the West, plus the growing economic hegemony of Buenos Aires contributed to establishing national unity, a unity which may be viewed as a precondition for the rational exploitation of Pampean land.

During the nineteenth century Australia was far behind both Argentina and Brazil in the development of sovereign political institutions. The Australian colonies did not become a federation until 1901; that federation appeared to have less centralized control than those of Argentina and Brazil. Colonial status did not prevent Australia from achieving one of the highest per capita incomes and substantial industrialization in the nineteenth century, as will be seen below.

One interesting and little-known aspect of the pre-1860 period in Latin America is the early industrialization effort, which sometimes involved government support, either via tariffs or subsidies. Mythology makes Rosas with his 1832 Tariff an early industrializer in Argentina, and somewhat later the Baron of Maua undertook ambitious projects in Brazil. Portales in Chile, and Francia and the two Lopez in Paraguay are even clearer examples of conservative protectionists of the early nineteenth century, paradoxically rediscovered and glorified in recent years by some neo-Marxian authors, and by nationalist historians. These early efforts at policy-induced import substitution failed. The reasons for such failures have not been well documented, except for the tragic Paraguayan experiment, which was bloodily crushed by the Triple Alliance of Argentina, Brazil, and

Uruguay in the 1860s. The sharp decline in ocean freights plus the British technological lead made competition with imported manufactures very difficult.

III. THE BELLE EPOQUE (1860-1929)

The export-oriented growth made possible by an expanding international economy raised per capita income in a sustained and substantial way in Argentina since about the 1860s and in Brazil since the beginning of this century. The vigorous São Paulo coffee boom of the late nineteenth century was largely offset by the decline of other Brazilian export activities, such as sugar and cotton; in the River Plate the expanding export lines more clearly offset from an earlier period those in decadence, such as salted meat. The Argentine export quantum rose at a remarkable 4.8 percent per annum from 1865 to 1912, and at 4.1 percent per annum from 1912 to 1928 (Diéguez 1972). The expansion of the Australian export quantum reached 4.3 per annum during 1870-1913 (Maddison 1979, 26).

Table 1 presents estimates of per capita Gross Domestic Product (GDP) for Argentina, Australia, and Brazil. Brazilian per capita GDP growth could not have been very significant during the nineteenth century, given its 1901 level; the Table suggests significant Argentine per capita growth even before 1880. Australia, in contrast, was born rich; this point is often forgotten in comparing Argentina and Australia. Vast mineral resources and scanty population make the Australia of the second half of the nineteenth century comparable to some Persian Gulf nations of today, or to some mining states in the West of the United States also in the nineteenth century. As far back as 1861-65, Australian agriculture, livestock, dairying, and fisheries contributed only 22 percent of value added in the economy; mining and manufacturing together accounted for 19 percent, and construction 9 percent (Butlin 1962). One may conjecture that value added in agriculture and livestock in Argentina and Brazil during 1861-65 must have accounted for no less than 40 percent of GDP.

The remarkable catching up of both Argentine population and per capita product relative to Australian ones up to the late 1920s is highlighted in Tables 2 and 3. Brazil also advances in per capita product but at quite a distance from the two temperate countries of recent settlement. Australia appears to stagnate for surprisingly long periods; the aggregate figures, however, hide an impressive diversification from a rich but specialized mining and rural economy into a modern industrialized country. Australia also suffered unusually harsh weather during the 1890s.

Of the three countries, pre-1929 Argentina appears to have had the more adaptable and diversified export bill. During 1875-79 Argentine exports were still largely made up by wool, hides, and salted meat. By 1890-94 wheat had become a leading item; by 1900-04 both corn and linseed had become (each) as important as hides; and by 1910-14 frozen beef exports were about as important as wool. Wool, hides, and salted meat by 1910-14 amounted to only one-fourth of the value of merchandise exports. In contrast, the coffee share in Brazilian exports advanced secularly since the last century, so by the late 1920s Brazil had become one of the classic examples of export concentration. Much of this contrast is explained by different

TABLE 1
Estimates of Argentine, Australian and Brazilian Per Capita
Gross Domestic Product, 1880 to 1980
(U.S. Dollars of 1970 Purchasing Power)

	Argentina	Australia	Brazil
1880	470	1520	139
1901	780	1360	190
1913	1030	1690	230
1928	1200	1590	340
1939	1170	1670	430
1945	1280	1940	470
1955	1380	2340	670
1970	1960	3470	1100
1973	2049	3723	1459
1980	2184	4022	1924

Notes: Purchasing power parity dollar estimates have been
        made, backward and forward in time, centered on
        the calculations for 1970 found in Kravis, Heston
        and Summers (1978).

        Argentine and Brazilian estimates for 1880 are
        rough guesses based on export quantum data; data
        on Argentine export quantum are the revised series
        found in Dieguez (1972).

Sources: Argentine data on per capita growth since 1900
         from Diaz Alejandro (1970); Naciones Unidas
         (1978); and International Monetary Fund (1981).

         Brazilian data since 1900 from Haddad (1978) and
         International Monetary Fund (1981).

         Australian data from Butlin (1962); Butlin (1977);
         and International Monetary Fund (1981).

TABLE 2
Estimates of Argentine, Australian and Brazilian Population
(Millions)

	Argentina	Australia	Brazil
1861	1.35	1.20	8.55
1880	2.47	2.24	11.55
1901	4.92	3.83	18.39
1913	7.60	4.75	23.66
1928	11.28	6.22	32.23
1939	13.95	7.03	40.29
1945	15.39	7.58	46.22
1955	18.89	9.12	60.18
1970	23.75	12.51	92.52
1973	24.72	13.38	100.56
1980	27.06	14.62	123.03

Sources: As in Table 1, plus national statistical sources;
United Nations, Demographic Yearbook (1950 and
1955); International Monetary Fund, International Financial Statistics (July, 1980).

TABLE 3
Argentine and Brazilian GDP and Population Relative to Australia
 (Indices: Australia = 100)

	Per Capita GDP		Population	
	Argentina	Brazil	Argentina	Brazil
1861	–	–	113	713
1880	31	9	110	516
1901	57	14	128	480
1913	61	14	160	498
1928	75	21	181	518
1939	70	26	198	573
1945	66	24	203	610
1955	59	29	207	664
1970	56	32	190	740
1973	55	39	185	752
1980	54	48	185	842

Sources: Tables 1 and 2.

TABLE 4
Net Immigration into Argentina and Australia
 (Thousands of Persons during periods shown)

	Argentina	Australia
1921–25	521	183
1926–30	456	130
1931–35	51	–11
1936–40	131	43
1941–45	53	8
1946–50	505	353

Sources: Direccion Nacional de Estadistica y Censos (1956,
         28); Commonwealth Bureau of Census and Statistics
         (1950, 7).   Data exclude troop movements.

natural endowments; Brazilian efforts since 1906 to support international coffee prices plus other policies may have reinforced the trend. Wool remained the leading Australian export, representing 54 percent of all exports during the 1880s and 43 percent during the 1920s (Boehm 1979, 151); between those two decades the wheat share in Australian exports rose from 5 to 21 percent.

The ratio of exports to domestic product remained lower in Brazil than in Argentina: during 1925-29 it was about 14 percent for the former and 24 percent for the latter (data obtained from Haddad 1978; Díaz Alejandro 1970). The Argentine growth locomotive had less of a low-productivity subsistence sector to drag along than the Brazilian one. The corresponding Australian ratio was 18 percent (Butlin 1962), somewhat lower than the Argentine number in spite of a lower Australian population and lack of a significant Australian subsistence sector. A higher Australian per capita income, a more diversified productive structure, and differences in domestic relative price structures may help to explain that contrast.

The socioeconomic linkages of Australian exports, one may conjecture, were more desirable for long-term economic and political development than those of Argentina, in spite of the apparently more diversified Argentine export bill. Gold and mineral exports relied on economic agents and forms of production sharply different from those involved in rural exports; the Argentine export bill did not contain such a significant counterpoise to rural exports. Australian mining exports seem to have had powerful forward and backward industrial linkages; generated interest in scientific and technical research; and gave rise to a labor force which rapidly formed trade unions not only in mining but also among ranch hands. And those trade unions as well as entrepreneurs involved with mining coalesced into political groups opposing the creation of a permanent landowning class (Hirst 1979, 87-88, 110-12; Gallo 1979, 66-67). We now turn to an examination of the inputs of land, labor, capital, and technology feeding the export locomotives, as well as of those other goods and services generated by the pre-1929 economics. But first a few words on the institutional framework within which economic variables operated.

A political and social framework compatible with export-oriented growth had been settled in Argentina since shortly after the middle of the nineteenth century. Military campaigns expanded southward the geographical domain of the Argentine Republic during 1879-80, at the expense of indians' and Chilean claims; Chile at that time was engaged in a war against Bolivia and Peru. Brazil had some important evolutionary ch nges to make in its institutional organization as late as the 1880s and 1890s, when slavery was abolished and the empire became a republic. Australia gradually evolved toward self-rule, but retained strong ties to the British Crown. The external framework for all countries was that of the Pax Britannica until the First World War. Both internal and external frameworks being on the whole secure and satisfactory to hegemonic social forces, little public intervention was deemed necessary in the day-to-day operation of Argentine markets for outputs and inputs. The Brazilian state tended to have a more interventionist stance than the Argentine one, due partly to the requirements of an orderly abolishment of slavery. Brazilian tariffs were higher on average than Argentine ones and the Brazilian commitment to the gold standard was shakier. Both countries, however, would frequently follow financial policies which foreign bankers would find appalling. The Brazilian republic was inaugurated with an enthusiastic burst of credit expansion; the Argentine also frequently floated its currency, a practice then disparagingly labelled the inconvertible paper standard. In spite of declarations of economic liberalism, provincial and national publicly owned banks expanded in the late nineteenth century in Argentina. Influential landowners appear to have been the major beneficiaries of such departures from laissez-faire. Protectionism was the most noticeable Australian departure from pre-1929 orthodoxy regarding rules-of-the-game for international economic relations.

Both Argentina and Brazil had ample supplies of raw land to generate their land-intensive exports. The supplies were ample but not perfectly elastic: the upward tilt in the supply of economically homogeneous land was enough to generate large rents for intramarginal landowners. Both on a priori grounds and on the basis of available information, one may conclude that Pampean landowners were the major beneficiaries of the great Argentine expansion up to the 1930s. By 1880 the best Pampean land had been appropriated in a manner leading to a concentrated pattern of land ownership. Once real estate had thus been distributed, an open and competitive land market was not at all incompatible with spectacular rents falling into relatively few hands. While the Brazilian case is more complex due to its regional heterogeneity, similar conclusions seem to apply. Experiments with colonization schemes centered around family-owned farms were carried out in some regions of Argentina and Brazil. Their beneficial socioeconomic consequences, unfortunately atypical for those countries as a whole, can be seen in the Argentine province of Sante Fe and the Brazilian state of Santa Catarina. In both Argentina and Brazil landowners, particularly those producing exportable goods, became the most powerful pre-1929 political actors, and had the most to say as to how newly available land was to be distributed.

Australian land policies present a substantial contrast to those of the Argentine. For many years the British Crown did not surrender ownership of Australian land; sheep ranchers failed to get clear titles to their enormous enterprises during the crucial formative years of Australia (Gallo 1979, 100-02). Opposition to the land claims of sheep ranchers came from miners and urban groups; ranchers remained an important political force in Australia, but one which did not control the governmental machinery as landowning groups did in Argentina (Hirst 1979, 83-84). When cereals became an important Australian export, family-operated medium-size farms were relatively more important than in Argentina, where tenant farming under contracts of about five years were more widespread than in Australia. A system of rural production where tenant farmers moved frequently from one region to another apparently was not harmful for Argentine rural productivity and output growth before 1929, but had deleterious effects on income distribution as well as on social and political life. The mediocre housing, poor social services, and lamentable infrastructural facilities in most of the melancholy little towns scattered across the Pampean zone were eloquent testimony to the rootlessness of Argentine farming, and the weakness of the rural middle class. Landless tenant farmers had difficulty in obtaining credit and securing marketing arrangements which they perceived as stable and fair.

With the pattern of land ownership given by political history, and with prices of exports, imports, and capital given fundamentally by international markets, total rents depended on the conditions of labor supply. Immigration policy became the critical policy variable under the control of pre-1929 Australian, Argentine, and Brazilian governments, in the sense that public action could have an important influence on the levels of migration, and that in turn had powerful effects on the growth and distribution of GDP.

The pre-1929 world witnessed massive migrations, but the "international labor market" remained segmented by culture, policy, and prejudice. Chinese and Indians migrated, but mainly to tropical regions, northwestern Europeans moved mainly to North America, Australia, and South Africa. Argentina and Brazil (or one should say São Paulo) connected primarily with the labor markets of southern Europe. Only via the Italian labor market were there significant indirect links with the broader Atlantic labor market; Italian migrants moving back and forth between Santos and Buenos Aires also linked, but weakly, the Argentine and the Brazilian labor markets. Australia, in contrast, limited its connections with northwestern Europe, primarily the British Isles. While it is not obvious that real wages in Ireland were above those in Lombardy toward the end of the nineteenth century, it is likely that on average real wages were higher in northwestern Europe than in Italy and Spain. Emigrants from the former area also had the choice of migrating to the United States or the white dominions, a choice often made by Italians but not by Spaniards. On balance, the more restrictive Australian immigration policy placed a higher floor under Australian wages. This species of labor protectionism probably had a greater importance for the welfare of workers within Australia than the celebrated Australian tariff. But for excluded migrants the contemplation of advanced Australian social legislation must have been a small consolation.

Argentine and Brazilian landowners favored and were able to obtain more open immigration policies. The Brazilian case is particularly interesting: after the abolition of slavery in the 1880s a large pool of cheap labor existed within the country, yet São Paulo landowners pressured their state government to seek immigrants from southern Europe and even Japan. Such migration was subsidized. Internal migration into São Paulo remained surprisingly small until the 1920s. The São Paulo landowners had transitional troubles dealing with free labor not only in the case of former slaves; the Italian government early this century temporarily banned subsidized emigration to São Paulo after receiving reports of deception and mistreatment of migrants.

Migration into Argentina required fewer, if any, subsidies. The country, with a population of 2.5 million in 1880, received 3.2 million immigrants during 1880-1910, more than 80 percent coming from Italy and Spain. The architects of the Argentine liberal program had hoped for immigration from northwestern Europe, and framed post-1860 laws, including religious tolerance, to accommodate them. Some came, but Argentina was to remain predominantly Latin. Of all immigrants who came, about two-thirds stayed. While Argentine population increased by 5.1 million between 1880 and 1913, that for Australia rose only by 2.5 million. Under the influence of the interests of landowners and the urge to "people the wilderness," Argentina took many of the gains arising from export-led growth in the form of higher population; the labor-influenced Australian government "chose" to maintain a somewhat stagnant, high per capita income and a low, homogeneous population. One may note that neither Australia nor Argentina received significant numbers of nonwhite immigrants; some Japanese migrants went to Argentina, but more went to Brazil. Internal migration in Argentina, as in the Brazilian case, was surprisingly sluggish until the 1930s; it appeared easier during some of the pre-1929 Pampean harvests to bring seasonal workers from Italy than from northern Argentine provinces, which contained substantial pools of workers earning wages below those luring Italians to the Pampas. The coexistence of massive immigration with persistent pools of domestic cheap (or cheaper) labor in both Argentina and Brazil, as in the case of the United States of those days, indicates that domestic labor markets were also segmented by culture and prejudice, and perhaps also by policy.

The contrasting Australian and Argentine international migration policies may be compared to how some United States universities handle admissions to their graduate economics programs. University Y attempts to screen applicants carefully, and once one is admitted he or she can practically be sure of financial and pedagogic support for four years, almost independently of performance. University X flings its doors open but relies on competitive exams to determine who will stay and be supported after the first or second year. The atmosphere and feelings of belonging and loyalty among students at University Y are likely to present a more attractive picture than at University X. First-year students at University X, like immigrants into pre-1921 Argentina, will not rush into "citizenship" nor will they quickly join the "army." But if one could place all potential students (immigrants) behind a "veil of ignorance" regarding their prospects of admission, one would end up with different ex ante opinions regarding optimum admission policies.

While apparently not much was done in either Argentina or Brazil to select immigrants on the basis of their skills, pre-1921 Argentina engaged in important educational efforts, particularly at the level of primary education. The Argentine illiteracy rate, calculated as a percentage of the population fourteen years of age and older, dropped from 77 percent according to the 1869 census to 36 percent in the 1914 census. In 1920, comparable Brazilian illiteracy remained around 65 percent.

The pre-1929 domestic capital markets of Argentina, Australia, and Brazil became closely interwoven with those in Europe, especially London, and later with that in New York. With cyclical ups and downs, savings generated both domestically and abroad were transformed into railroads, land improvements, houses, factories, and social overhead capital. The presence of foreign capital was relatively larger in Argentina and Australia than Brazil. It has been estimated that the stock of long-term foreign investment in Argentina in 1913 was only 18 percent lower than the equivalent figure for Canada; by 1930 Argentina accounted for 12 percent of all British long-term investments overseas, while Canada accounted for 14 percent and Australia for 13 percent. Argentine creditworthiness, as measured by the market yield of her bonds, was not very different from those of Australia and Canada during the 1920s. As late as 1931 Argentina was able to roll over a loan at an interest only 90 basis points above the average rate paid by the government of the United Kingdom; in 1927 Argentine creditworthiness was ranked by British experts as seventh among foreign countries (Wortman 1981).

Associated with foreign capital, but less tightly packaged with it than in the 1950s and 1960s, came foreign technology and knowledge of various sorts. The tricks for running railroads and streetcars, meat packing and electricity plants, refrigerated ships, and coffee warehouses, were first provided by foreigners. Those tricks provided monopoly power, but of a wasting kind; too many people, including Argentines and Brazilians, could provide them sooner or later. In the meanwhile it is likely that important quasi rents were captured by foreign suppliers, feeding the debate as to whether foreigners were exploiting local residents. Note that much foreign capital was placed in activities which came close to being natural monopolies or monopsonies. Railroad and public utilities were obvious examples; less clear-cut were meatpacking, shipping, and insurance. Note also that such near monopolies (railroads) and monopsonies (meat packers) had intimate commercial and financial links with other foreign companies, decreasing competitiveness not just in the markets for their principal outputs and inputs, but also in a host of other related markets. British-owned railroads and public utility companies in Argentina are said to have bought coal, rails, and many of their other inputs exclusively from British companies with which they had common financial interests, and also engaged in what today would be called intrafirm transfer pricing (Fodor and O'Connell 1973, 16).

The fruits of technological progress generated in the leading industrial countries diffused into Argentina, Australia, and Brazil via numerous other mechanisms, besides foreign investments. Imports of capital, intermediate, and consumer goods embodied much of nineteenth and early twentieth-century advances as well as dubious fashions; migrants often carried in their hands and heads new knowledge; ideas moved freely in magazines and books eagerly sought in an age of faith in "progress." Examples of the latter with particularly beneficial impact on human welfare included advances in medicine and public health, whose diffusion also involved trips by students, researchers, and other skilled personnel.

In both Argentina and Brazil the production of exportable goods was predominantly in domestic hands, in contrast with, say, Chile and Cuba, but at least during the nineteenth century their international marketing remained controlled by foreigners to a large degree. Argentine cattlemen generated significant savings and did diversify their portfolios, but showed limited interest in investing "downstream." They had actively changed livestock technology, steadily improving cattle herds, but made only timid efforts to invest in meatpacking; Argentines were practically absent in the exporting of chilled meat (their presence was greater in frozen meat exports). This behavior contrasts with that of Tucumán landowners, who invested in sugar mills producing for domestic consumption. One may conjecture that Argentine cattlemen let foreigners handle international marketing of their products as a way of insuring foreign markets, very much as some countries rely today on transnational corporations for marketing their exports. A few large trading companies dominated Argentine grain exports; some were started by Argentine entrepreneurs and quickly became international companies. Brazilian coffee-growers significantly expanded their marketing activities since the beginning of this century.

Uneasiness about the presence of foreign capital was only one of the anxieties generated by the pre-1929 export-led growth model. Industrial activities had advanced in both Argentina and Brazil, but not enough according to some critics, including some in the armed forces, who associated industrialization with military strength and national greatness. As already noted, the Brazilian tariff seems to have been more protectionist than the Argentine one, according to average levels at least. Both countries relied heavily on manufactured imports; machinery and equipment requirements were almost totally supplied from abroad. In the case of Argentina even textiles were predominantly of foreign origin; the Argentine textile industry curiously lagged behind those of Australia, Brazil, and Mexico. Australian industrialization was encouraged not only by linkages from mineral exports but also by tariffs and other explicit government support. Australian economic historians disagree as to whether those policies advanced or retarded pre-1929 Australian development; some view protection as a wasteful luxury this early Kuwait could afford.

Commercial and exchange rate policies were debated in Argentina, Australia, and Brazil with the usual arguments and by the standard actors at least since the second half of the nineteenth century. As suggested previously, the long-run developmental and distributional consequences of the debated policy ranges were probably less than those for migration policies, which gave rise to less debate and which have received less scholarly attention. The standard scenario naturally places landowners on the side of free trade, where one also finds the Argentine Socialist party, but not the Australian Labor party. It has also been argued that in both Argentina and Brazil, producers of exportable goods favored flexible exchange rates whenever international prices of those commodities were falling, while favoring a return to the gold standard, as a check to appreciation, whenever world prices turned in their favor. Importers of goods and services also favored free trade but preferred an appreciated and stable currency. Among major importers of services one may place central governments having to service their external debt. The government also had to worry about raising revenues in local currency and found import duties an expedient mechanism for doing so. Landowners may not have been too displeased with moderate duties, as otherwise fiscal revenues may have had to come from land and other property taxes. Memories of abusive use of the inflation tax during the 1880s and 1890s in both Argentina and Brazil provided political support for the gold standard during the first three decades of this century; the Argentine Socialist party was an eloquent defender not only of free trade but also of price stability and the gold standard. One may also note that regional interests and politics in both Argentina and Brazil may explain the adoption of some protective tariffs.

Therefore, even if one considers landowners as the dominant influence on Argentine and Brazilian public policy, their enthusiasm for completely free trade and flexible currency arrangements had certain practical limits. Note also that in Argentina the middle-class Radical party controlled the government during 1916-30; radical administrations introduced (mild) social welfare measures and expanded state investments in petroleum and railroads. This has not prevented some critics from tightly associating export-oriented growth with a skewed income distribution, oligarchical political dominance, a bias against industrialization, and a masochistic dependence on foreigners, a combination sharply in contrast with the classical English case which motivated David Ricardo.

To conclude this section let us reconsider the relative Argentine position at the end of the Belle Epoque. As shown in Table 1, the late 1920s witnessed the narrowest gap between Argentine and Australian per capita incomes. But the gap remained: Argentine per capita income has never been higher than that of Australia. Besides data in Table 1 other evidence supports this conclusion. Per capita Argentine exports were below those of Australia during 1925-29; Argentine per capita apparent consumption of cement was about 60 percent that of Australia in 1928-29; Argentine infant mortality rates were twice as high as Australian ones during the 1920s, as reported by the League of Nations. The size, glitter, and cultural excellence of the city of Buenos Aires in the 1920s, unmatched by any Australian city, may have misled many a casual commentator on the Australian-Argentine comparison. It is more revealing to contrast Buenos Aires glitter to Jujuy poverty or even to the well-fed emptiness of Pampean towns, a contrast not found to the same extent in the more equalitarian Australia.

IV. ARGENTINA SLIPS: THE 1930s THROUGH THE 1950s

During the 1920s the international economic framework characterized by a free-trading, capital-exporting hegemonic power and by multilateralism in trade and payments under the gold standard, so dominant before 1914 and so convenient for the Argentine growth model, began to show serious cracks. Latecomers to the industrial revolution, such as Germany, Japan, and the United States showed limited enthusiasm for British rules-of-the-game in international economic affairs, and the old hegemony was unable to maintain clear leadership. Hints that pre-1914 normalcy would never return came in the 1920s to Brazil (and to Chile and Cuba) more forcefully than to Argentina, whose late 1920s per capita exports were the highest (so far) this century. The hints turned into blinding red signals in 1929-32. During the 1930s, the 1940s, and well into the 1950s, international economic relations witnessed nakedly mercantilistic restrictions to trade and financial flows, breached or lifted mainly by arduous political maneuvering and the establishment of special patron-client relationships. Pre-1929 Argentine economic and political history had provided a singularly poor preparation for facing this new dismal international environment. Before turning to the gloomy task of chronicling Argentine slippage, a review of the international links, attitudes, and perceptions generated by pre-1929 experience and hampering adjustment to post-1929 reality is necessary.

At least since the first Pan-American conference in 1889, Argentine foreign policy had clashed with that of the United States. Argentina came to view herself as the other major power in the Western Hemisphere, one whose strong economic and cultural links to Europe and whose desire for an independent stand in international affairs made her skeptical of U.S.-sponsored Pan-Americanism. During the early decades of this "American Century" both Right and Left in Argentina criticized United States intervention in the Caribbean and Central America, and it was an Argentine foreign minister who proclaimed the "Calvo doctrine" against the extraterritorial pretensions of direct foreign investors, whether from Europe or the United States. In spite of her close economic ties with the United Kingdom, Argentina remained strictly neutral during the First World War, and voiced opposition to the harsh terms imposed on Germany by the Treaty of Versailles. Argentina became an active and respected member of the League of Nations, adopting what today would be called a "nonaligned" stance, much more so than either Australia or Brazil.

By the 1920s Argentine trade and payments had developed a "triangular pattern" (emphasized especially by Fodor and O'Connell 1973) of minor consequence in a world of convertibility and multilateralism, but full of difficulties once the international economic system drifted away from those principles. Argentine merchandise trade showed surpluses with the United Kingdom (and Europe more generally) and deficits with the United States. Argentine grain exports competed with those of the United States; hopes that Argentina would become a major supplier of meat to the United States were dashed by the adoption in 1926 of a United States ban on fresh or frozen meat imports from areas with hoof-and-mouth disease. This measure created new friction in Argentine-United States relations. As the United Kingdom lost its industrial dynamism, Argentine importers turned to the United States for new goods; to paraphrase a 1920s slogan, Argentina was increasingly buying from those that did not buy from her.

The U.K.-U.S. rivalry in the 1920s for the Argentine market is symbolized by the competition between the old railroads and the new motor vehicles. The former were mainly British, carried linkages to British exports such as rails and coal, and generated profits and interest on old British investments (but produced meager fresh capital inflows during the 1920s). Automobiles, trucks, and tractors were predominantly a United States export, and their linkages to tires, oil-refining, and cement for road-building were also dominated by United States interests, capable of providing new capital inflows. Other traditional British exports to Argentina, such as textiles, were also under strong competitive pressure during the 1920s from both other exporters, like Japan, and incipient import-substituting entrepreneurs in Argentina.

The stock of British investments generated interest and profit remittances which, together with payments for other British services such as shipping and insurance, were roughly comparable to the Argentine export surplus with the United Kingdom. Net inflows of capital came during the 1920s mainly from the United States, offsetting the Argentine import surplus with that country. When fresh capital flows disappeared in the 1930s, United States interests would bitterly complain that Argentine authorities discriminated against imports from the United States, diverting foreign exchange to service old British capital and to purchase old-fashioned British goods (Salera 1941).

Voracious world markets and prodigious Pampean fertility made both demand and supply of Argentine exportables seem almost effortlessly and infinitely expandable at least until the First World

War. That "easy stage" of export growth had, of course, to evolve sooner or later into another where aggressive marketing had to replace passive waiting for the world to come to Argentina for foodstuffs, and where both public and private efforts had to increase land yields rather than relying on the extension of the Pampean frontier to produce more exportables. That evolution had to come even if the Great Depression and the Second World War had not occurred; the transition would have been partly induced by market signals but would have also required more active public policy in the international marketing of exportables (also involving support for domestic storage facilities) and in rural research and extension activities. Such an evolution away from a laissez-faire export policy and toward greater government attention to and support for the production of exportables has occurred at least since the 1920s in other major exporters of temperate foodstuffs, like Australia, Canada, Denmark, and the United States. Note that a more difficult selling environment and the end of empty lands in those countries did not induce them to turn away from exporting primary products.

The stormy international economic and political environment of the 1930s and 1940s was to test severely not just the Argentine economy but also its polity. Under the democratic governments of the 1920s there were flaws which opened the way to practically uninterrupted (since 1930) military presence and intervention in Argentine politics, and to governments lacking, except for brief periods, sufficiently broad and deep domestic confidence to patiently engage in the subtle and complicated international economic and political maneuvers which were necessary to maintain substantial per capita economic growth during the 1930s and 1940s.

Major chinks in the constitutional polity of the 1920s included segments of the Right which never became reconciled with post-1916, cleaner electoral processes assuring political success for the middle-class Radical party during 1916-30: immigrants who were imperfectly integrated into the national political and social life and poorly educated landless rural workers who were politically manipulated by local bosses. The nondemocratic segments of the Argentine Right were probably influenced by events and ideological ferment occurring in France, Italy, and Spain, and quietly waited (and prepared the way) for "the hour of the sword." The Radical party failed to incorporate much immigrant and working-class support, whether urban or rural, and was weakened in the late 1920s by personality clashes among major leaders.

The 1930 military coup d'etat against the charismatic but senile Radical President Hipólito Yrigoyen led to hybrid military-civilian conservative regimes during 1930-43, characterized by various degrees of electoral fraud and repression; to the nationalist-populist Peronist regimes during 1943-55; followed by attempts to restore non-Peronist civilian rule under military tutelage during 1955-66; then to outright military rule during 1966-73; to a second brief Peronist era, 1973-76; and finally to a return to military rule since 1976. The secular trend has been toward greater instability, faster turnover of economic policymakers, and a more fragmented polity.

A. The "Infamous Decade" (1930-1943)

The dismal trend was not obvious during 1930-43, when hopes for renewed economic and even political advances at times seemed justified. True enough, as shown in Table 1, per capita GDP fell slightly during the 1930s, performing worse than those of Australia and Brazil. The growth in Argentine and Australian GDPs was in fact identical between the late 1920s and the late 1930s (1.7 percent per annum); Argentine population, however, grew at nearly 2 percent per annum during those years, while that of Australia grew at only 1.1 percent per annum. It can be argued that, given external circumstances the 1930s Argentine performance, at least relative to Australia, was reasonably good. The external shock to Argentina was more severe than that received by Australia: the current dollar value of Argentine exports in 1928 was 57 percent higher than that of Australia; during 1930-34 it was only 7 percent higher; and by 1935-39 it was 10 percent higher (Kelly 1965, 51). The volume of exports per capita from Australia increased by 9 percent in the second half of the 1930s, compared with the first half, whereas in the case of Argentina it declined by 11 percent. Ruth Kelly concludes:

> Although Argentina falls behind Australia...its export performance in the thirties, compared with the rest of the world, may be considered satisfactory. Indeed, at the end of the period, it gave rise to expressions of optimism concerning the country's future prospects as one of the world's major exporters of agricultural products. (Kelly 1965, 57)

Argentine exports were hurt not only by the slump, but also by the protectionism and the discriminatory practices adopted by the United Kingdom and other industrialized countries. The grand illusions of the Belle Epoque were shattered, and Argentina, with her triangular trade and payments patterns, found herself in a difficult bargaining position vis-à-vis the British Empire. Otherwise amiable Argentines can still go for each other's throats when discussing whether or not Argentina had realistic alternatives to the humiliating Roca-Runciman Treaty, signed in 1933 to ward off further British protectionism, particularly in meat. What is generally accepted is that such a treaty was not very different from those imposed by the Nazis on Eastern European countries, and that a tougher Argentine bargaining stance would have had to be accompanied by substantial restructuring of Argentine political and economic institutions (see also Salera 1941, Ch. 3). One may speculate that a Peron in 1933 would have made more sense than in 1946; at any rate, the Roca-Runciman Treaty contributed to the spread of anti-British and pro-German nationalism throughout Argentine society, including the armed forces.

It was noted earlier that before 1929 Argentine exports were a larger fraction of GDP than those in Australia or Brazil. The greater specialization of the Argentine economy made her more vulnerable to the Great Depression; even her manufacturing sector relied heavily on the processing of exportable primary products. It is noteworthy, therefore, that the Argentine manufacturing sector grew between

1928-30 and 1937-39 at an annual rate of 3.1 percent, while that of Australia grew at only 1.3 percent per annum (Butlin 1962, 461; Naciones Unidas 1978, 78-79). Sectors of Argentine manufacturing which had lagged before 1929, such as textiles, "caught up" during the 1930s. Argentine cement production grew at an astonishing annual rate of 16.1 percent between 1928-29 and 1937-38; that of Australia grew at 1.6 percent per annum during the same nine years. Apparent cement consumption (local production plus imports) rose during that period at 4.8 percent per annum in Argentina and 1.4 percent per annum in Australia (European Cement Association 1967). Preferential treatment of British industrial exports granted under the Roca-Runciman Treaty did not block an Argentine import-substituting industrialization during the 1930s that was faster than that of Australia.

Both Argentina and Brazil, after initial confusion and hesitations, adopted during the early 1930s policies which, although primarily aimed at restoring balance-of-payments equilibrium and aiding influential producers of exportable goods, contributed to recovery in general and industrialization in particular. These measures have been discussed elsewhere (Díaz Alejandro 1980a, 1981). Here one may note that the Brazilian departure from 1920s orthodoxy was bolder than that of Argentina, although the remarkable Brazilian industrial growth during the 1930s, at least double that of the Argentine annual rate, may also be explained by the lower share of manufacturing output associated with exportable production and the more closed nature of the Brazilian economy at the start of the Great Depression.

One may conclude that the Argentine slippage behind Australia during the 1930s was minor and due more to external circumstances than to domestic policies. It may also be conjectured that the Argentine urge to "people the wilderness" had already come into conflict with faster per capita growth during the 1920s, with both Argentine birth and immigration rates remaining above those of Australia; this was to remain the case into the 1940s. While birth rates in the Argentine Federal Capital and the Province of Buenos Aires by the early 1940s were about those for the whole of Australia (less than twenty per thousand), those for the poorer provinces, such as Jujuy, Salta, and Tucumán were twice as high. Table 4 shows that net immigration into Argentina during the 1920s reached nearly one million persons, more than three times the corresponding Australian figures; even during the 1930s Argentina witnessed significant net immigration.

Income-distribution trends during the 1930s are obscure, but softer demand for labor appears to have at least maintained larger differentials in pay between skilled and nonskilled labor in Argentina relative to Australia. Evidence on this point is presented in Table 5, which also provides a rough check on Argentine-Australian per capita income comparisons. Note, however, that Table 5 uses market exchange rates (not purchasing power estimates), probably exaggerating the gap between Argentine and Australian wages. For each of the major groups shown in Table 5, such as mechanical engineering and building, the gap between Buenos Aires and Sydney wage rates appears greatest in the least-skilled category (laborers). It is also interesting that Argentine workers in printing and bookbinding had the highest relative wages; during the late 1930s Buenos Aires was the undisputed publishing center of the Spanish-speaking world, with substantial exports.

TABLE 5
Wages per Hour of Adult Male Workers, Buenos Aires, October 1936

	Wage Rates in Current U. S. Cents	Wage Rates as Percentages of Those in Sydney
Mechanical Engineering:		
Fitters and turners	0.264	60.6
Iron moulders	0.261	65.9
Patternmakers	0.322	67.4
Laborers	0.163	51.7
Building: Bricklayers and masons	0.245	46.8
Structural iron workers	0.236	65.7
Concrete workers	0.245	68.2
Carpenters and joiners	0.245	53.1
Painters	0.248	53.8
Plumbers	0.307	60.2
Electrical fitters	0.248	52.4
Laborers	0.172	47.9
Furniture Making: Cabinet makers	0.276	64.5
Upholsterers	0.276	64.5
Printing and Bookbinding:		
Hand compositors	0.353	85.3
Machine compositors	0.488	104.3
Machine minders	0.310	74.9
Bookbinders	0.267	64.5
Laborers	0.190	62.1
Food Industries: Bakers	0.263	55.1
Electric Power Distribution:		
Electrical fitters	0.282	59.6
Laborers	0.202	53.4
Transport:		
Tram and buses, drivers	0.209	55.6
Tram and buses, conductors	0.209	58.7
Cartage, motor drivers	0.301	74.9
Railroads, goods porters	0.193	57.6
Railroads, permanent way laborers	0.123	39.0
Local Authorities: Laborers	0.276	78.6
SIMPLE AVERAGE	0.257	62.5

Notes: Exchange rates used to convert wages in local currency to U.S. dollars: Argentina, 3.26 Pesos per dollar (average of import and export rates); Australia, 3.96 dollars per Pound (Aus.).

Sources: Wage rates from International Labor Organization (1937, 162)

The outbreak of the Second World War placed great pressures on the Argentine economy and polity. Within a few months major European markets disappeared, while shipping difficulties curtailed both exports and imports. New distress was visited on the Argentine rural producers of exportables, especially cereals, forcing the conservative government to decree a freezing of rural rents. Beleagured Britain could hardly supply Argentine needs of machinery, fuel, and intermediate inputs (not to mention weapons), and paid for Argentine supplies with inconvertible and low-yielding sterling. In 1941 the conservative government created the General Directorate of Military Factories, establishing the principle of military-run industries. The war exacerbated divisions within the government and armed forces between pro-Allied and pro-Axis factions; especially after 1941 the United States pressured Argentina into joining Pan-American collective actions, a course repugnant to Argentine diplomatic traditions. Few Argentines wanted departures from neutrality, and relations with the United States became tense, particularly as Brazilian-United States ties became more intimate. Ferment within the armed forces grew, and political groups maneuvered frantically against the discredited conservative civilian regime. A number of accidents and circumstances (masterfully narrated by Potash 1969) finally led to the ambiguous coup d'etat of 1943.

B. The First Peronist Era (1943-1955)

The absolute and relative decline of Argentine foreign trade which had begun in the 1930s accelerated during the Second World War and culminated during the first Peronist era, in spite of the apparently favorable terms of trade for 1946-49, according to available data, the best registered this century (Díaz Alejandro 1980b, 9). Per capita quantum indices for imports and exports are presented in Table 6 for Argentina and Australia; as during the first thirty years of this century Argentina was a major capital importer, the secular decline of imports is somewhat greater than for exports. (The Argentine terms of trade during the whole period showed considerable fluctuations, but no significant long-term trend.) Table 6 shows the sharp fall of per capita imports during the Second World War, sharper for Argentina than for Australia, and a subsequent recovery; however, during 1950-54 Argentine per capita imports were only slightly more than one-third those registered during 1925-29, and about two-thirds of the level for 1935-39. The decline in the per capita Argentine export quantum is continuous from 1925-29 through 1950-54, when it reached its lowest point for this century; even during 1945-49 it was only half the 1925-29 level, by 1950-54 it was one-third of that level and less than half of the per capita export quantum for 1935-39. Australian per capita exports during 1945-54 do not perform brilliantly relative to their favorable evolution during 1930-44, as far as quantities are concerned, but there is no dramatic collapse, as registered in the Argentine case. Indeed, the quantitative dimensions of the rise and fall of Argentine foreign trade must have few parallels in contemporary economic history; note that in 1950-54 Argentine per capita imports and exports were less than half what they had been at the beginning of this century.

TABLE 6
Per Capita Argentine and Australian Merchandise Imports and Exports
(Quantum Indices: 1930-34 = 100)

	Imports		Exports	
	Argentina	Australia	Argentina	Australia
1900-04	145	129	102	88
1905-09	198	138	118	100
1910-14	195	175	103	101
1915-19	99	133	92	81
1920-24	142	150	114	81
1925-29	186	188	121	82
1930-34	100	100	100	100
1935-39	103	160	89	109
1940-44	51	114	62	124
1945-49	89	149	60	98
1950-54	67	212	40	94
1955-59	69	197	44	109
1960-64	76	253	51	137
1965-69	66	331	55	170

Notes: Australian trade data refer to July-June years; for example,
         1900 would refer to 1900/01.

Sources: For 1930-34 and earlier years, Argentine trade data from
         Naciones Unidas (1959, Part I, 15, 110, 115). Argentine
         data for 1930-34 and later years from Naciones Unidas
         (1976, 27).

         Australian trade data from Butlin (1977).

         Population data from sources cited in Table 2.

Table 7 examines the relative decline of Argentine trade using import data at current prices, and extends the comparison to Brazil. The costs of Argentine neutrality during 1940-44 are again apparent. After a recovery during 1945-49, the Argentine relative position sinks again during 1950-54 to almost World War II levels. Argentine per capita imports, which during 1930-34 were more than five times those of Brazil, by 1950-54 were only twice Brazilian per capita imports, and less than one-third those of Australia.

Why did the decline in Argentine trade continue beyond the 1930s? The comparison with Australia, and even with Brazil, as well as other evidence regarding market shares for major Argentine exports, indicate that general world economic conditions could not be blamed for the extraordinary Argentine performance after the Great Depression. Special circumstances, such as the droughts of the early 1950s, seem overwhelmed by the quantitative dimensions and persistence of long-term trends. The answer must be sought in Argentine policies, which had the net result of giving low priority to the promotion of foreign trade.

Relevant Argentine policies go beyond those manipulating parameters affecting foreign trade. The world of the 1940s and early 1950s could not be characterized as one with open and competitive international markets. Hot and cold wars, and an uncertain recovery from depression and war circumstances and mentalities, created international markets which were politicized and segmented well into the 1950s. Buying and selling in those markets and converting currencies used in those transactions depended partly on political considerations. The Argentine vocation for an autonomous foreign policy made her highly suspect among the Allies, especially by the United States, even before the 1943 coup d'etat. As during the First World War, Argentine imports plummeted during 1940-44, more than those of Australia and Brazil, countries whose military alignment against the Axis assured them a greater flow of civilian goods, shipping services, and armaments.

Neither the Argentine declaration of war on Germany in March 1945, nor the narrow yet stunning victory of General Juan D. Perón in clean elections in February 1946, substantially improved Argentine-United States relations, which were to remain characterized by a great deal of mutual hostility until at least 1950. Unlike Ireland, Sweden, Switzerland, and even Franco's Spain, World War II neutrals which adapted to postwar political circumstances with agility, Argentina was to stick to her "Third Position," incurring the wrath of influential policymakers in the United States. The tangled web of Argentine-United States relations before and after the end of the Second World War reads at times like tragedy and at times like farce (see Escudé 1981; Macdonald 1980). What now seems clear is that such a political climate limited Argentine markets; for example, the Economic Cooperation Administration adopted from its inception a policy of preventing European procurement with Marshall Plan dollars in Argentina, and limited or increased the cost to Argentina of supplies of fuel, intermediate, and capital goods (Fodor 1975), well into the late 1940s. It may be noted that Argentina not only refused membership in the International Emergency Food Council but also refused to join the United Nations' Relief and Rehabilitation Administration and the Food and Agriculture Organization, not to

TABLE 7
Relative Value of Per Capita Argentine and Brazilian
Merchandise Imports and Brazilian Merchandise Exports,
At Current Dollar Prices
  (Percent)

	Relative to Australia		Relative to Argentina
	Argentine Merchandise Imports Per Capita (1)	Brazilian Merchandise Imports Per Capita (2)	Brazilian Merchandise Exports Per Capita (3)
1928–29	–	–	17
1930–34	63	11	21
1935–39	52	12	20
1940–44	26	9	26
1945–49	56	17	27
1950–54	28	14	48
1955–59	29	10	42
1960–64	23	8	31
1965–69	16	6	33
1970–74	17	12	47
1975–79	16	13	51

Notes: For Columns (1) and (2), per capita Australian
       imports equal 100 in each period.

       For Column (3), per capita Argentine exports equal
       100 in each period.

Sources: Merchandise imports and exports at current dollar
         prices and population for 1950–1980 obtained from
         International Monetary Fund, International Finan-
         cial Statistics (July issues of 1950, 1960, 1970,
         1980); and Naciones Unidas (1976). For earlier
         periods: United Nations, Yearbook of Internation-
         al Trade Statistics (1950, 1960, 1970, 1980); and
         United Nations, Demographic Yearbook (1950, 1960,
         1970, 1980).

mention the International Monetary Fund and the World Bank. Argentina did join the United Nations at its founding in San Francisco, with the support of the United States during a brief spell of rapprochement, but over objections of the Soviet Union that the Argentine regime had been sympathetic to the Nazis. During the early postwar years Argentina defiantly granted credits and exported foodstuffs to Portugal and Spain.

The United Kingdom, which during the 1930s used every ounce of its bargaining power to extract concessions from Argentina, during the 1940s took a tolerant stance toward Argentine nonalignment, perhaps having no realistic alternative (much of recent writings on United States hostility toward Argentina during the 1940s originates in Britain, even as much of the analysis of the British squeeze on Argentina during the 1930s originated in the United States). The halting British postwar recovery aggravated the triangularity problems in Argentine trade and payments. Britain, and Europe as a whole, were willing to buy Argentine goods using their own currencies, but Argentina already had accumulated large balances of those pieces of paper which could be used only for limited purposes in their countries of origin and not at all to buy goods in the United States. The failure of the British return to sterling convertibility, culminating in August 1947, sharply lowered the opportunity cost of Argentine sterling balances and the expected value of possible future sterling earnings.

In retrospect, difficulties in the international economy during the late 1940s appear as minor inconveniences on the road to about three decades of remarkable expansion in world trade. But at the time a case could be made that they were a prelude to a new Great Depression or to World War III. Even if those catastrophes could be avoided, it was unclear whether the protectionist barriers built by industrialized countries during the 1930s, particularly in protecting their agricultural sectors, would be significantly relaxed once recovery was completed. For Argentina, the pattern of agricultural protectionism coupled by aggressive exporting of agricultural surpluses which had emerged in industrialized countries since the 1930s was particularly worrisome.

Peronist reluctance to give high priority to the expansion of foreign trade, and to the production of exportable goods, conveniently meshed with its nationalist-populist ideology and its political inclination to reward supporters and punish opponents. Urban working-class backing was consolidated by assuring plentiful and cheap foodstuffs (another magnet attracting European immigrants during 1946-50), even if the exported share of rural output had to be reduced. A more aggressive and optimistic marketing abroad of Argentine rural produce would have clashed with the cheap food policy. Passing on favorable international postwar prices to producers of rural exportable goods, allowing them to find on their own external suppliers for their input needs, and letting those producers make their own guesses as to the outlook for primary product markets, would have strengthened groups hostile to the Peronist regime, for example, rural landowners and old import-export houses. The revenues generated by the government's trading agency in control of exports and imports helped to maintain post-1943 trends toward expansion of military payrolls, the construction of military bases and armament plants, as well as to underwrite an industrial development plan, plagued by mismanagement and corruption (Potash 1980, 4-5, 62-63). Finally, nations which had imposed unequal commercial treaties and discriminatory trading practices on Argentina during the 1930s (and which during the 1940s also engaged in state trading to maintain their bargaining power), as well as those Argentines who to Peronist eyes had collaborated with the unjust foreign powers, had weaker claims on Argentine public policies of the late 1940s than those who had swept Perón into power.

Both domestic political considerations and the bleak international political and economic outlook were probably involved in the Peronist neglect of rural research and extension services, at a time when other producers of temperate foodstuffs, notably the United States, were experiencing dramatic technological change in cereals, as a result of combined public and private sectors' efforts. Memories of unsold grain mountains, used during the Second World War as emergency fuel, and of unusable sterling mountains, weakened proposals to raise Argentine rural yields, which were around United States levels during 1920-44, but which lagged behind thereafter, especially in corn (Díaz Alejandro 1970, 163, 194).

The Argentine economy boomed during 1946-48; favorable export prices and reserves accumulated during the war, not all inconvertible, may have led to a Peronist belief that there is "nothing more elastic than the economy which everyone fears so much because no one understands it" (Hirschman 1979, 65). The 1947 census was taken during these euphoric times; conveniently a census was taken in Australia the same year. Table 8 shows the allocation of the economically active population in the two countries. One-quarter of the Argentine labor force was still in the rural sector, a share substantially higher than that for Australia. The gap in manufacturing is narrower. Although the two countries show profiles which are not too different, including the participation of women in the labor force, that for Australia indicates a higher per capita income.

The censuses also show that the percentage of the total population living during 1947 in cities of more than one hundred thousand inhabitants was higher in Australia (51.4) than in Argentina (40.6). However, the largest Argentine urban agglomeration, Greater Buenos Aires, represented a higher share of the country's total population (29.0 percent) than that in Australia, the city of Sydney (19.6 percent). A large gap separated Greater Buenos Aires from Rosario and Córdoba, the second and third largest Argentine cities, while Melbourne was close in population to Sydney. The third Australian city, Brisbane, had a share in total population (5.3 percent) similar to the combined shares of Rosario and Córdoba in total Argentine population (data for this paragraph obtained from United Nations 1952, 11, 213).

In 1949 the Argentine postwar boom came to an end. Reserves had been drawn down, international prices turned less favorable and dollar shortages became extremely severe: it was to be the first of postwar recessions induced by the need to contain balance-of-payments deficits. Per capita imports and exports levels, as shown in Table 6, reached their lowest peacetime levels this century during 1950-54. Manufacturing output, which had surged during the early postwar years,

TABLE 8
Allocation of the Economically Active Population, Argentina and Australia, 1947
(Percent)

	Percentages of Total Economically Active Population		Women as Percentage of Population in Each Category	
	Argentina	Australia	Argentina	Australia
Agriculture, forestry, hunting, fishing	25.2	15.6	5.4	4.9
Mining, quarrying	0.5	1.7	1.6	1.1
Manufacturing	22.1	25.0	28.2	22.8
Construction	5.2	7.3	1.2	0.6
Electricity, gas, water	0.5	1.0	4.6	5.8
Commerce	13.3	15.0	12.6	31.1
Transport, storage, communication	6.0	9.2	3.2	9.6
Services	21.3	17.9	43.4	47.1
Activities not adequately described	3.1	7.3	11.0	25.7
Unemployed	2.8	–	27.2	–
TOTAL	100.0	100.0	19.9	22.4

Notes: Australian data exclude full-blooded aboriginals; unemployed allocated to sectors of usual occupation

Sources: International Labor Organization, Yearbook of Labor Statistics (1950 and 1952).

after 1948 showed sharp fluctuations but a mediocre growth trend: for three-year averages, from 1943 to 1954, the annual growth rate of manufacturing was 2.5 percent (Naciones Unidas 1978). Domestic industry was unable to fully make up for the steep decline in per capita imports of manufactures. The fall in the per capita absorption of industrial commodities involved a decline in both the consumption of consumer durable goods and investment in machinery and equipment. Import substitution in intermediate and capital goods, as well as fuels, turned out to be very troublesome given the magnitude of the collapse in foreign exchange earnings, the ambivalence toward foreign capital, and difficulties in obtaining foreign machinery and equipment, especially during the late 1940s. Argentine foreign policy had a nontrivial price not only in terms of foregone exports, but also for import substitution and the maintenance and expansion of social overhead capital, especially in electricity and transport.

The low priority given to exports and other Peronist policies had a sharp negative impact on Pampean production of rual exportable goods, particularly cereals and linseed, whose per capita output in 1945-49 was 57 percent of the 1935-39 level; during 1950-54 per capita production of cereals and linseed were only 46 percent of the 1935-39 level. Livestock did better; as labor flowed out of Pampean areas that land-intensive activity actually had an incentive to expand, in spite of the overall Peronist policies toward exportable rural goods. Other rural activities selling overwhelmingly in the domestic market, as in the case of most of those outside the Pampean area, experienced substantial expansion. Taking the aggregate of all rural activities, their per capita production shows a deline of about 11 percent between 1935-44 and 1945-54. Australian rural performance during those years is far from spectacular, but per capita rural production manages to remain roughly constant (Commonwealth Bureau of Census and Statistics 1958, 114).

During the early 1950s the Peronist administration realized that the economic strategy of the late 1940s contained erroneous assumptions about the evolution of the international economy as well as inconsistencies among targets for growth, industrialization, and the balance of payments. In 1950 a loan was obtained from the U.S. Eximbank. Droughts during the early 1950s helped to make evident the decay in Pampean agriculture; in 1952 Argentina had to import wheat. Steps were taken to encourage the production of exportables. But as indicated by Tables 6 and 7 the recovery of Argentine trade was to prove arduous and halting, while the slippage of Argentine per capita GDP behind that of Australia was to continue as shown in Table 3, albeit at a slower pace than that registered between 1928 and 1955.

V. A NATION DIVIDED DOES NOT CATCH UP, BUT GROWS

Even if the steps undertaken to encourage foreign trade recovery, during the last years of the Peronist administration and by following governments, had been successful in eliminating or sharply reducing policy-induced biases against production for export, the recovery of Pampean agriculture would have probably been less than dramatic. Estancia hands were unlikely to return to the farm once they had seen Buenos Aires. The tractors, fertilizers, and improved seeds needed to replace them would take some time to be incorporated into production.

On average, export incentives were larger during 1955-73 than during the first postwar decade. But the policy tilt favoring import substitution and discriminating against exports, whether of rural or manufactured goods, which became substantial during the 1930s and extreme due to war circumstances and postwar Peronist policies, remained a feature of the Argentine economy throughout 1955-73. Argentine effective rates of protection remained among the highest in Latin America. Furthermore, incentives to Pampean production and to exports in general followed a saw-toothed pattern, diminishing their power. Why did protectionism remain so strong after the first Peronist era, and why were attempts to encourage exports so weak and transient?

By 1960 less than one-fifth of the Argentine labor force was engaged in rural activities. The Pampean production of exportable goods absorbed only part of that labor force. Furthermore, the majority of Argentines living in urban centers, whose budgets were inevitably damaged in the short run by higher prices for cereals and beef, perceived Pampean producers not as Jeffersonian farmers but as oligarchical landlords, whose large properties had emerged practically unscathed from the Peronist years. Unlike the situation in the United States and Western Europe, the Argentine farm lobby could command scanty emotional appeal, yet was strong enough to veto measures such as land taxes, which could have reconciled efficiency considerations to equity concerns.

More than two decades of sheltered industrialization had created, by the mid-1950s, vested interests opposing reductions in protection, interests which also derived support from the persistence of export pessimism, still prevalent at that time throughout Latin America. Perhaps the most powerful protectionist lobby centered around the armed forces, whose officers made up a good share of the executive ranks of state enterprises such as those producing steel and armaments. Memories of weapon shortages during the Second World War buttressed protectionist arguments.

Protectionism and hostility to Pampean rural producers, then, were hardly limited to the Peronist movement. Neither was a strong nationalist stance toward foreign capital a Peronist monopoly; indeed, it is said that one of the factors contributing to the overthrow of General Perón in 1955 was the discontent caused within the armed forces by his negotiations with foreign oil companies. As with export incentives, post-1955 governments zigzagged in their policies toward foreign capital, especially toward direct foreign investment, but on balance foreign corporations were used as key instruments in expanding industrial production in consumer durables, and intermediate and capital goods. It is a moot point whether the monsters begotten by the coupling of protectionism and direct foreign investment, such as the inchoate and spastic automobile industry, were less of an economic error than the Peronist miscalculations of the late 1940s. As in other comparisons, the Australian record on this issue (especially regarding automobiles) shows qualitative features similar to that of Argentina; it is only in the more limited quantitative dimensions of misallocation that Australia emerges in a favorable light.

Throughout 1955-73 economic policy was conducted in a turbulent political atmosphere. The exiled General Perón maintained a large following, and trade unions were dominated by Peronists. No other single group emerged to challenge Peronism as the largest coalition in Argentine political life; the old Radical party split, while conservatives and right-wing nationalists preferred to rely on favorite generals to advance their political designs. Elections were sporadically held, but Peronist candidates were banned by the armed forces. Weak civilian governments alternated with military ones; both witnessed a large turnover of economic ministers. It may be noted, however, that until the early 1970s political instability was not accompanied by much bloodletting.

In light of political instability and the limited recovery of foreign trade, the 2.2 percent per annum growth in Argentine per capita GDP between 1955 and 1973, shown in Table 1, is respectable, and should dispel the myth of Argentine economic stagnation. The Argentine per capita annual growth during 1955-73 was of course inferior to that of Australia (2.6 percent). It could be argued that Australia, not having taken protection to Argentine postwar extremes, was in a better position to benefit from the boom in international trade which occurred during 1955-73, particularly given its fresh mineral discoveries and its proximity to the fastest growing and most voracious market for primary products, that is, Japan. One may speculate that the reasonable Argentine per capita growth performance during 1955-73 may have been the result partly of an Argentine population growth rate which, for the first time since 1880, was lower than the Australian one, and partly due to a catching up with the technological change which had and was occurring abroad, particularly in the production of temperate foodstuffs. Indeed, probably the single most successful Argentine public policy since 1955 has been the support of research and extension agricultural services. One may also conjecture that the significant Argentine per capita growth during 1955-73 is often overlooked by unawareness of her low contemporary population growth (which may be lower than indicated by Table 2, for reasons to be discussed later), and has been obscured by sharp cyclical savings.

Until fairly recently, both Argentina and Brazil have been conspicuous examples of reliance on import-substituting industrialization as the engine of growth, with a corresponding neglect of exports. Yet Table 1 yields the following annual growth rates in their per capita GDPs, in percentages:

	Argentina	Brazil
1928-1955	0.5	2.5
1955-1973	2.2	4.4
1973-1980	0.9	4.1

Why this contrast in growth performance, which has carried Brazilian per capita GDP in 1980 near that of Argentina? A first, but partial, explanation was suggested in Table 7: while Brazilian foreign trade languished for more than three decades following 1928, it did not experience the postwar collapse registered in Argentina. This point is brought out more clearly in column (3) of Table 7, which presents Brazilian per capita merchandise exports, in current dollars, relative to those of Argentina. A mediocre Brazilian export performance between the late 1920s and the 1950s was sufficient to generate a sharp gain in Brazilian per capita exports relative to those of Argentina. Interestingly, about half of that gain disappears during the 1960s; it is only during the 1970s that the Brazilian export drive clearly outdistances Argentine efforts, carrying Brazilian per capita exports beyond the high relative position they reached during 1950-54. By 1980, Brazilian per capita exports were 55 percent those of Argentina; in 1928 they had been 16 percent.

As late as 1965-69, the Brazilian export quantum per capita was about what it had been during 1928-29 (Naciones Unidas 1976, 31); yet Brazilian per capita GDP in 1970 was more than three times the 1928 level. Import-substituting industrialization in Brazil was clearly more successful than in Argentina. A larger domestic market, the wartime alliance with the United States, and milder species of populism and protectionism seem doubtful or incomplete explanations for that Brazilian success. More fundamentally, it should be recalled that during the 1920s Brazil was still a Lewis-type economy with a small modern sector, including both exporting and import-competing activities, surrounded by a large subsistence sector, producing nontradeable goods and services. Average labor productivity was much higher in the modern than in the subsistence sector; similar gaps probably existed also in marginal labor productivities. In contrast, the Argentine economy by the 1920s had approached neoclassical conditions, in the sense that labor in all major sectors probably had roughly similar marginal products.

One may therefore conjecture that much of the Brazilian per capita growth of the last fifty years could be accounted for by a process not available to the same degree in Argentina, that is, a reallocation of labor from a low-productivity subsistence sector to higher-productivity occupations, whether import-competing or exporting. Such reallocation would raise the average domestic product even without an increase in per capita capitalization, or an improvement in the technology, of each sector. That process does not even require getting the balance between import-substitution and exporting exactly right, so long as an extreme foreign exchange bottleneck is avoided. The coffee and other traditional Brazilian exporting sectors have had, until recently, few worries that supply-side considerations would lead them to curtail their output, or that the growth in the domestic demand for coffee and sugar would significantly reduce their exportable surplus. There has been an awful lot of coffee in Brazil simply because there has been an awful lot of Brazilian low-productivity subsistence farmers and workers. In contrast, Argentine populism and protectionism induced a reallocation of labor, and of other inputs, away from a highly productive Pampean sector toward secondary and tertiary activities whose superior social productivity was often questionable.

The contrast between the Argentine and Brazilian growth performances is particularly striking for 1973-80: Argentina is far more self-reliant in energy than Brazil. The sharp decline in Argentine growth cannot be explained without reference to the bloodiest political turmoil the country has witnessed since the 1850s. The 1970s saw the brief return of General Juan D. Perón to the presidency; his death accelerated trends visible earlier. For the first time in Argentine history the revolutionary Left became a credible contender for power, proclaiming that "the hour of the furnaces" had come; this challenge produced a strong reaction from conservative and middle-class elements. The violent struggle between guerillas and gorillas dwarfed the old Peronists vs. anti-Peronists quarrels. Indeed, much of the violence occurred within the Peronist movement itself, which during the 1970s became even more of an ideological hodgepodge than it had been in the 1940s, as very different factions tried to inherit the mantle of the old leader. The 1970s were probably the first decade in Argentine history when the country became a net source of migrants; exact figures, however, are unavailable either for victims of the quasi civil war or for net emigration. Population data shown in Table 2 for 1973 and 1980 may represent overestimates.

Brazilian political troubles and violence look mild indeed when compared with those of Argentina, just as Brazilian inflation has never reached the wild levels registered in Argentina during the last ten years. While postwar-Argentine political life involved strong independent actors such as trade unions, landowners, and sundry military factions, leading first to "stalemate politics" and finally to the violence of the 1970s, the continuity of Brazilian policies has been based on the assurance given by a long and almost unbroken history of a state dominated by "the right people." This could be another consequence of the large Brazilian subsistence sector: its reserve army of the underemployed together with the other army have provided (so far) an unbeatable combination for assuring that political and economic leadership remains committed to unvarnished capitalist growth. Even as once it seemed perfectly natural that the Brazilian state should regulate and watch over the system of slavery, now there is a Brazilian consensus that the state is an obvious guide and ally in the process of capital accumulation, although the exact boundaries between the private and public sectors may still generate some debates. The last fifty years have shattered such feelings in the River Plate where a state once felt strong enough to tackle growth, income distribution, and national autonomy objectives, achieving little of each. Finally, one may conjecture that Brazilian geographical heterogeneity and economic diversification has left ample room for compromises and negotiations buttressing the consensus around the growth objective, while Argentina is too transparently a Stolper-Samuelson country where a zero-sum view of economic policy is plausible in the short and even the medium term.

VI. ENVOI

Did those who emigrated from Eastern Europe, Italy, and Spain to the River Plate make a mistake, now being corrected as many of their grandchildren leave Argentina? By 1970, in fact, Spain had reached a per capita GDP similar to that of Argentina, while that of Italy was about 25 percent higher (Kravis, Heston, and Summers 1978, 232-36). Argentine liberal traditions should be credited with providing migrants and their offsprings with economic and political conditions far superior to those of their countries of origin at least until quite recently; Eastern Europe, Italy, and Spain have had troubles of their own during the years of the Argentine eclipse. Paradoxically, the troubled 1970s in Argentina may have set the bases for political conditions allowing steadier and more efficient economic policies.

The murderous violence of the 1970s was unprecedented in the Argentine history of the last one hundred years, and hopefully it has discredited extremists both of the Left and the Right. A Peronist movement without a charismatic leader may become a more flexible and acceptable participant in political life. The myth that military governments will necessarily be more stable and efficient than civilian ones appears hopelessly shattered in Argentina. Perhaps swords and furnaces will be put away, and quieter hours may come. Under conditions of reasonable political stability, the unsinkable Argentine economy could recover from the catastrophes of the late 1970s and early 1980s, including a high external debt for which so little growth can be shown. Abundant foodstuffs and energy resources, plus an industry which, whatever its past costs, has shown itself capable of exporting, provide solid foundations for a growth which may or may not keep up with those of Australia and Brazil, but which could assure a good life to all Argentines.

FOOTNOTE

Earlier drafts of this essay received comments and criticisms from Pascal Arnaud, Marcelo Cavarozzi, Juan Carlos de Pablo, Ronald Findlay, Albert Fishlow, Jorge Fodor, John Fogarty, Alieto Guadagni, Nathaniel Leff, Arturo O'Connell, and Gustav Ranis. The July 1981 Oxford conference on Argentine economic history was particularly helpful for the preparation of this final version. The hard questions Lloyd Reynolds has asked me over many years regarding Argentine development have motivated much reflection. Sketches of the paper were twice presented in seminars presided over by Arthur Lewis, who kept pushing for more. Two other mentors, Albert O. Hirschman and Charles P. Kindleberger, have had an obvious influence on substance and style. Virginia Casey bravely edited and typed these pages more times than she probably cares to remember. None of the named persons should be held responsible for any errors or peculiarities of this essay.

BIBLIOGRAPHY

Boehm, E. 1979. El desarrollo económico australiano a partir de 1930. In *Argentina y Australia*, ed. J. Fogarty, E. Gallo, H. Diéguez, 115-65. Buenos Aires: Instituto Torcuato Di Tella.

Butlin, N. G. 1962. *Australian domestic product, investment and foreign borrowing, 1861-1938/39*. Cambridge: At the U. Press.

Butlin, M. W. 1977. A preliminary annual data base 1900/01 to 1973/74. Reserve Bank of Australia Research Discussion Paper 7701.

Commonwealth Bureau of Census and Statistics. 1950. *Quarterly Summary of Australian Statistics*. (December). Canberra.

———, 1958. *Primary industries, part I, rural industries*. Canberra, Bulletin no. 50.

Díaz Alejandro, C. F. 1970. *Essays on the economic history of the Argentine Republic*. New Haven: Yale U. Press.

———, 1980a. A América Latina em Depressão: 1929/39. *Pesquisa e Planejamento Econômico*, 10: 351-82.

———, 1980b. Exchange rates and terms of trade in the Argentine Republic 1913-1976. Yale Economic Growth Center Discussion Paper no. 341. (March).

———, 1981. Stories of the 1930s for the 1980s. Yale Economic Growth Center Discussion Paper no. 376. (April).

Diéguez, H. L. 1972. Crecimiento e inestablilidad del valor y el volúmen físico de las expartaciones agentinas en el período 1864-1963. *Desarrollo Económico*, 12: 333-49.

Dirección Nacional de Estadística y Censo. 1956 *Informe Demográfica de la República Argentina*. Buenos Aires.

Éscude, C. 1981. The Argentine eclipse: the international factor in Argentina's post-World-War-II decline. Ph.D. dissertation, Yale Political Science Department.

European Cement Association. 1967. *The world cement market in figures*. Paris.

Fodor, J., A. O'Connell. 1973. La Argentina y la economía atlántica en la primera mitad del siglo XX. *Desarrollo Económico*, 13(49)(April-June): 3-66.

Fodor, J. 1975. Perón's policies for agricultural exports, 1946-1948: dogmatism or commonsense? In *Argentina in the twentieth century*, ed. D. Rock, 135-62. London: Duckworth.

Gallo, E. 1979. Comentarios. In *Argentina y Australia*, ed. J. Fogarty, E. Gallo, H. Diéguez, 65-68, 99-103. Buenos Aires: Instituto Torcuato Di Tella.

Haddad, C. L. S. 1978. *Crescimento do Producto Real no Brasil 1900-1947*. Rio de Janeiro: Editora da Fundaçao Getulio Vargas.

Hirschman, A. O. 1979. The turn to authoritarianism in Latin America and the search for its economic determinants. In *The new authoritarianism in Latin America*, ed. D. Collier, 61-99. Princeton: Princeton U. Press.

Hirst, J. 1979. La sociedad rural y la política en Australia, 1959-1930. In *Argentina y Australia*, ed. J. Fogarty, E. Gallo, H. Diéguez, 77-99. Buenos Aires: Instituto Torcuato Di Tella.

International Labor Organization. 1937. *Yearbook of labor statistics*. Geneva.

————, 1950. *Yearbook of labor statistics*. Geneva.

————, 1952. *Yearbook of labor statistics*. Geneva.

International Monetary Fund. 1950. *International financial statistics*. Washington, D. C.

————, 1960. *International financial statistics*. Washington, D. C.

————, 1970. *International financial statistics*. Washington, D. C.

————, 1980. *International financial statistics*. Washington, D. C.

————, 1981. *International financial statistics*. Washington, D. C.

Kelly, R. 1965. Foreign trade of Argentina and Australia, 1930 to 1960. *Economic Bulletin for Latin America*, 10: 49-71.

Kravis, I., A. Heston, R. Summers. 1978. Real gross domestic product per capita for more than one hundred countries. *The Econ. J.*, 88(350)(June): 215-43.

Macdonald, C. \. 1980. The politics of intervention: the United States and Argentina, 1941-46. *J. of Latin American Studies*, 12(2)(November): 365-96.

Maddison, A. 1979. Long run dynamics of productivity growth. *Banca Naz. Lavoro Quart. Rev.*, no. 128(March): 1-30.

Malán, P. S., R. Bonelli, M. de Paiva Abreu, J. E. de C. Pereira. 1977. *Política Económica Externa e Industrialização no Brasil (1939/52)*. Rio de Janeiro: IPEA/INPES.

Naciones Unidas. 1959. *El Desarrollo Económico de la Argentina (Part I)*. México, Departmamento de Asuntos Económicos y Sociales.

_____, 1976. *América Latina: Relación de Precios del Intercambio*. Santiago de Chile: Naciones Unidas.

_____, 1978. *Series Históricas del Crecimento de América Latina*. Santiago de Chile: Naciones Unidas.

_____, 1979. *El Balance de Pagos de América Latina 1950-1977*. Santiago de Chile: Naciones Unidas.

Potash, R. A. 1969. *The army and politics in Argentina 1928-1945*. Stanford: Stanford U. Press.

_____, 1980. *The army and politics in Argentina 1945-1962*. Stanford: Stanford U. Press.

Salera, V. 1941. *Exchange control and the Argentine market*. New York: Columbia U. Press.

United Nations. 1950. *Demographic yearbook*. New York.

_____, 1950. *Yearbook of international trade statistics*. New York.

_____, 1952. *Demographic yearbook*. New York.

_____, 1955. *Demographic yearbook*. New York.

_____, 1960. *Demographic yearbook*. New York.

_____, 1960. *Yearbook of international trade statistics*. New York.

_____, 1970. *Demographic yearbook*. New York.

_____, 1970. *Yearbook of international trade statistics*. New York.

_____, 1980. *Demographic yearbook*. New York.

_____, 1980. *Yearbook of international trade statistics*. New York.

Wortman, C. 1981. *Argentina, Australia and Brazil: bonds in the London capital market, 1929-1939*. New Haven: Yale U. Press.

16
Interpretations of Public Expenditure Trends in East and West

Frederic Pryor

I. INTRODUCTION

For the last twenty-five years Lloyd Reynolds has displayed a keen interest in analyzing the economic behavior of the government sector from a comparative point of view. This is reflected not only in some of his articles (e.g., Reynolds 1971) but also in his aid to younger economists at Yale who were working on such problems. In particular, Lloyd Reynolds greatly encouraged and assisted basic research on differences in the public sectors in East and West which I carried out at the Yale Growth Center. This essay represents an attempt to reanalyze some of this early work, taking into account fourteen years of further developments of the nations under examination.

The concept of "public sector" refers to three major phenomena: public ownership of the means of production, public participation (directly or indirectly) in production decisions, and public financing of goods, services, and transfer payments through taxes and loans. And "public" itself can refer to various levels of government, to "social" authorities, or other groups such as nonprofit units or charitable foundations.

Although a study of the changing role of the public sector in countries with different economic systems can thus refer to a wide range of economic events, a researcher faces two major limitations. First, certain topics cannot be easily studied because of the paucity of readily available and comparable data; for instance, it would be extremely difficult to study differences in governmental participation in production decision making in many countries. Second, certain topics do not seem fruitful to study; for instance, the economies of Eastern Europe are primarily nationalized, with the exception of the agricultural and petty trade and service sectors, so that "trends" in nationalization primarily reflect changes in sectoral composition of output, rather than any dramatic change in policy.

I have chosen to focus this essay on changes in public consumption expenditures, particularly related to education, health, and social welfare, in Eastern and Western Europe. The topic is extremely important, for the single most dramatic change in the public sector in the West in the last twenty years has been rapid growth of public expenditures. For instance, the average share of total public consumption expenditures in the GNP of the OECD nations has risen from 28.5 percent in 1955-57 to 34.5 percent in 1967-69 to 41.4 percent in 1975-76, and further increases are anticipated (OECD 1978, 20-21). Leading this trend has been the rise in "welfare state expenditures," that is, expenditures for education, health, and social welfare (which includes income maintenance and pensions).

The purpose of this essay is to present some quantitative evidence on public expenditures to allow us to explore a number of hypotheses about the causes of this dramatic increase in the public sector, both traditional approaches from the demand side and more recent ideas focusing on political factors and other "supply side" considerations. By contrasting the experience of nations with different economic systems, we can also attempt to isolate the systemic factors underlying public expenditures. The major conclusions of this exercise are three: demand factors seem considerably more important than supply factors in explaining this increase in public expenditures; such expenditures appear to have grown more rapidly as a share of GNP in the market than the centrally administered economies; and in the future, such public expenditures may constitute a significantly higher share of total expenditures in the market than in the centrally administered economies.

Before turning to the analysis, it must be emphasized that comparative examination of public expenditures data raises some important statistical problems which can only be handled by circumventing them. One serious difficulty concerns the meaning of public investments, for the government can participate in the investment process in a variety of ways which may have the same end result but which utilize different institutional mechanisms. In the United States in 1975, for instance, direct investments by all levels of government amounted to roughly 24 percent of total gross investment.[1] However, governmental agencies on the federal level also lent out funds amounting to about 26 percent of total gross investment and guaranteed a group of loans that amounted to 13 percent of total gross investment. Since the degree to which these loans were used for investment purposes is quite unclear, all we can say is that government involvement in capital formation was somewhere between 24 percent and 64 percent of total gross investment. Inclusion of loans and guarantees by state and local governments would raise the upper limit and our uncertainty becomes greater. This problem is avoided by focusing only on current expenditures.

Another difficulty concerns government participation in such fields as housing, where government action having the same end effect can take place through direct investment in housing, subsidies for interest or construction costs or maintenance costs, or various types of income or rent subsidies to renters. This problem is avoided by omitting consideration of housing.

Still another difficulty concerns transfer payments, which can be either in money or in kind; the latter are extremely difficult to separate from government expenditures on goods and services (e.g., education). It might also be argued that transfer payments must also include those given by quasi-public bodies such as pension funds, an issue that leads us to considerations of "pension fund socialism" discussed by economists such as Drucker (1976) and which gives rise to enormous problems in finding comparable data. These problems are avoided by combining current expenditures and transfer payments and by focusing only upon direct agencies of government at various levels.

For these and other reasons, I have chosen to focus on public consumption expenditures (i.e., current expenditures for goods and services plus transfers) in seven specified areas which are made by various levels of government. Of course, delineation of "current expenditures" raises a number of conceptual problems which cannot be touched upon here. A number of specific statistical problems concerning the expenditures and the GNP data are discussed in the following section, a necessary but unpleasant prelude to the presentation of the data and their interpretation.

II. THE DATA

A. Sample Selection

This essay represents an extension of a previous study by the author (Pryor 1968) that analyzed public consumption expenditures in seven market, and seven centrally administered economies. The countries originally selected were matched roughly for per capita GNP in 1956. Although such levels have diverged considerably, they are sufficiently close so that the sample can still be used. Other problems arise because in one case (Hungary) a centrally administered economy has tried since 1969 to introduce a guided market economy; nevertheless, this nation has had central administration of sufficient magnitude, and a price structure sufficiently distorted by differential subsidies and taxes requiring the employment of many nonmarket allocative devices, so that it must be considered as representing some type of hybrid economic system leaning toward a centrally administered system. Furthermore, in a number of the market economies in the sample, governmental dirigisme of production has increased, so they have moved somewhat closer to central administration of production; nevertheless, their economic systems have sufficient market elements so that they may be considered as representing some type of hybrid economic system leaning toward a market economy. In short, the two groups of economies still diverge to such a degree that we need not abandon the sample and select other nations. The countries under consideration and certain basic information about them are presented in Table 1.

B. Estimation Procedures

Public consumption expenditures, on which this analysis focuses, are current governmental expenditures plus transfers that are financed either by taxes or by governmental borrowing. Expenditures for military equipment are considered as a current expenditure. Although primary attention is placed on governmental budgetary expenditures, important extrabudgetary expenditures financed through taxlike payments are also included.

Given problems of obtaining comparable data for the fourteen countries, this analysis has focused on seven functions financed through public consumption expenditures for which estimates could be made. These adjusted budgetary expenditures include: general administration, internal security (police and justice), external

TABLE 1
The Sample of Nations in 1970

Market Economies

	GNP per capita indices	Population in thousands	ABE/GNP in percent
U.S.A.	100.0	204,880	27
West Germany	78.2	60,710	28
Austria	54.2	7,430	33
Italy	49.2	53,660	28
Ireland	45.1	2,950	24
Greece	38.5	8,790	24
Yugoslavia	25.8	20,370	28

Centrally Administered Economies

	GNP per capita indices	Population in thousands	ABE/HNP in percent
East Germany	63.9	17,060	32
Czechoslovakia	62.0	14,330	26
U.S.S.R.	46.9	242,760	27
Hungary	42.7	10,340	18
Bulgaria	37.3	8,490	20
Poland	35.4	32,530	23
Romania	31.2	20,250	17

Note: ABE/GDP = adjusted budgetary expenditures / gross domestic product.

Sources: GNP per capita data from Pryor (1979) and Kravis, Heston and Summers (1978).

Population data from United Nations (1977).

Sources and calculation of the ABE/GDP data are described in the text.

security (military, diplomacy, and foreign aid), education, health, social welfare (pensions plus general social expenditures), and research and development. The exact definitions are described in the book cited above (Pryor 1968).

Adjusting the data from the various nations so that they are comparable is a wearisome task. It took me roughly two years of full-time research to make the data for the various nations compatible for the 1950-62 period that is covered in the book. I did not have the luxury of such time to extend these data to 1976; therefore, I was forced to use a number of shortcut methods that reduced the period of research but, at the same time, reduced the accuracy of the estimates. However, by focusing upon welfare state expenditures -- expenditures on education, health, and social welfare -- I have selected that subset of expenditure estimates on which I place the most confidence. The data came from a wide variety of national and international sources of data (which may be obtained from the author), and they certainly reflect the most important trends, even if certain details may be questioned. In making the estimates, some corrections were made to the data for 1962 to reflect more recent information; no corrections were made to 1956 data.[2] The result of these efforts is that for this study we have twenty-year series (from 1956 through 1976) of adjusted budgetary expenditures for fourteen nations in Eastern and Western Europe and North America.

The very difficult task of separating transfers from current expenditures could not be carried out; therefore we have no valid method of calculating fixed-price series. Since we are left with current-price series, some method must be devised to abstract from the impact of gross changes in prices. The most usual procedure found in the literature is to express these data in terms of a percentage of GDP. However, such a procedure raises a serious problem for the countries under consideration which deserves brief discussion, for some interpretive difficulties are involved.

For the market economies, it seemed appropriate to compute the ratio of public consumption expenditures to the GDP at factor costs, that is, the GDP at market costs minus net indirect business taxes (indirect business taxes minus subsidies). For the centrally administered economies, GNP data according to Western definitions are available for all countries; and GNP minus net indirect business taxes can be calculated. Since the difference between GDP and GNP for these nations is minimal, this is not a problem. However, the meaning of GNP at factor prices raises some questions, for there is no market for capital or land and the factor costs attributable to them in the GNP at factor prices do not necessarily reflect their marginal productivity as they roughly do in market economies.

Ideally, we should estimate the marginal productivity of these two factors of production, then revalue all goods and services according to their factor costs and costs of inputs at these new prices, and finally calculate the ratio of public consumption expenditures to the GNP using these adjusted prices. This task would, for the seven countries involved, take many years, and we must adopt some shortcut techniques. But it should be noted that whatever technique is involved, the results are strongly affected. In Table 2 I present ratios of adjusted budgetary expenditures and also of welfare state expenditures (i.e., education, health, and social welfare) to the GNP in prices at which the goods and services are sold or transferred (established prices), GNP minus net indirect business taxes, and GNP minus net indirect business taxes and also minus profit taxes. The results show quite clearly that the value of the ratio depends critically on which concept of GNP is chosen.

For the centrally administered economies for the rest of this study I have chosen as the denominator of the expenditures/production ratio the GNP minus net indirect business taxes (the same solution adopted in my previous study). This should not greatly affect the trend data; however, those dubious of this procedure should be careful in comparing relative levels of public consumption expenditures among nations.

C. The Results

The results of these calculations are presented in Tables 3 and 4. Between 1956 and 1976, adjusted budgetary expenditures increased dramatically in all market economies; in contrast, in the centrally administered economies, these increases were relatively small or, in the cases of the Soviet Union and Romania, decreases were registered. (In the former country, so many difficulties were encountered in estimating external security expenditures that this may be a statistical artifact.) Turning to welfare state expenditures, we see that they account for most of the dramatic increases in the market economies and, in addition, show an increase (sometimes considerable) in all centrally administered economies except Romania.

From Table 4 we see that in most countries a major share of the increase in welfare state expenditures came from increases in social welfare expenditures. It should be noted that a major share of these social welfare expenditures -- about 75 percent or more -- go for pensions and other payments to the elderly.

The tables contain some interesting information about the differential timing of these changes. For instance, in most countries, the major changes in welfare state expenditures came after 1962; and in many centrally administered economies, these payments rose especially after 1970. It is upon these data that the statistical experiments described below are performed to reveal other facets of this rising importance of the public sector.

III. INTERPRETATIONS

In early studies of the determinants of public expenditures, primary attention was paid to the demand forces underlying the level and change of these expenditures. Somewhat later, supply side considerations began to be considered. Recently we are beginning to see attempts to apply both demand and supply models. The data presented in the previous section are considered in the light of all three approaches.

A. Demand Approaches

Some statistical considerations. For at least a half a century simple demand approaches toward the determinants of public expenditures have been used. A typical equation using just such an approach is:

TABLE 2
The Impact of Various Methods of Valuation of the GNP on the Expenditures/GNP Ratio in 1970
(Percent)

Valuation Method·	Adjusted Budgetary Expenditures/GNP			Welfare State Expenditures/GNP		
	A	B	C	A	B	C
East Germany	38	32	30	23	20	18
Czechoslovakia	34	26	24	24	19	18
U.S.S.R.	32	27	23	17	14	12
Hungary	22	18	16	13	11	10
Bulgaria	24	20	18	16	14	12
Poland	27	23	19	17	15	12
Romania	19	17	15	13	12	10

Notes: Method A = GNP in established prices (prices at which goods and services are sold or trans-
        ferred) minus net indirect business taxes (indirect business taxes minus subsidies) minus
        business profits taxes.
        Method B = GNP in established prices minus net indirect business taxes.
        Method C = GNP in established prices.

Sources: These calculations were made from the public consumption expenditures data described in
         the text and from GNP data presented in Thad P. Alton, et al. (1973). The Alton esti-
         mates were supplemented with data from national sources and, for the USSR, from other
         Western recalculations of the Soviet GNP.

TABLE 3

Trends in Public Consumption Expenditures and Welfare State Expenditures, 1956-1976
(Percent of Gross Production)

	Adjusted Budget Expenditures				Welfare State Expenditures			
	1956	1962	1970	1976	1956	1962	1970	1976
Market economies								
U.S.A.	20	23	26	27	8	11	14	19
West Germany	25	29	28	38	18	19	20	29
Austria	25	28	31	35	21	23	26	30
Italy	24	25	28	33	15	17	21	16
Ireland	21	18	24	34	16	14	18	26
Greece	17	18	24	24	8	10	14	13
Yugoslavia	27	28	28	30	13	16	18	19
Centrally administered economies								
East Germany	33	30	32	36	19	20	20	22
Czechoslovakia	31	27	26	33	20	18	19	24
U.S.S.R.	30	30	27	28	14	14	14	16
Hungary	23	19	18	28	11	12	11	20
Bulgaria	28	21	20	25	14	12	14	17
Poland	21	20	23	21	12	12	15	14
Romania	20	18	17	13	10	12	12	9

Notes: The calculation of this table is described in the text. For Hungary, data are for 1955. The 1956 data are for 1955.

Sources: The 1956 data are from Pryor (1968).

TABLE 4
Education, Health, and Welfare Data
  (Percent)

| | Expenditures as a Percent of Gross Production | | | | | | Population 65 and over as Percent of Population 15 through 64 | |
| | Education | | Health | | Welfare | | | |
	1956	1976	1956	1976	1956	1976	1956	1976
Market economies								
U.S.A.	2.4	5.0	0.9	2.9	4.8	11.3	14.5	16.4
West Germany	2.2	3.8	2.6	5.1	13.1	20.6	14.8	22.9
Austria	2.5	4.6	2.8	4.6	15.5	21.1	17.1	24.4
Italy	2.7	5.0	3.0	6.1	9.8	14.8	13.2	17.6
Ireland	2.6	5.8	3.8	7.4	10.0	13.3	18.3	18.8
Greece	1.3	2.0	1.0	1.4	5.3	9.3	11.5	19.5
Yugoslavia	2.1	4.8	3.2	4.5	7.5	10.0	9.6	13.3
Centrally Administered Economies								
East Germany	3.8	4.9	4.4	5.1	10.7	11.7	19.7	26.0
Czechoslovakia	3.8	3.9	4.2	3.8	11.9	16.3	12.7	18.8
U.S.S.R.	4.4	3.7	3.0	2.6	6.4	9.3	8.9	12.4
Hungary	2.7	3.4	2.6	5.3	5.6	11.6	12.7	19.3
Bulgaria	5.1	3.9	3.4	3.1	5.5	10.3	10.9	16.2
Poland	2.6	3.2	2.6	3.3	6.5	7.1	8.7	14.7
Romania	3.4	2.5	2.7	1.9	3.8	5.0	9.6	15.1

Notes: The calculation of the expenditure ratios for 1976 is described
    in the text. For Hungary, data are for 1955 instead of 1956.
    Population data for West Germany in 1956 omit West Berlin.
    Population data for Bulgaria, Czechoslovakia, and Yugoslavia
    are for 1975 instead of 1976. Population data for the USSR
    are for 1974 instead of 1976; the age distribution for the
    USSR was, in part, estimated.

Sources: The 1956 expenditures data are from Pryor (1968). Population
    data for all market economies except Yugoslavia are from
    OECD (periodic); data for all other countries are from
    United Nations (1960 and 1977).

$$G_t = a + bX_t$$

where G is government expenditures as a percentage of GNP, X is a vector of causal variables related to the demand for public expenditures, b is a vector of coefficients, a is a constant term, and t is the time subscript. One causal variable receiving a great deal of early attention is per capita income, an hypothesis called "Wagner's Law" (Timm 1961), but discussed much earlier by other economists such as Adam Smith and J. S. Mill. A large number of other economic causal variables that are somehow related to the demand for these services have also been proposed, for example, the degree of urbanization, the density of the area, the size of the governmental unit, and various demographic variables. More recently, social scientists from other disciplines have attempted to add political variables (reviewed in Pryor 1968) or sociological variables (Wilensky 1975); the latter seem more promising than the former. Sometimes the demand for public expenditures is related to certain variables in isolation from what is happening in the rest of the economy; sometimes the demand for public expenditures is tied to the demand for private expenditures and the degree to which the private sector is able to provide services either as complements to, or a substitute for, services provided through the public sector.

In recent years this type of specificiation has been considerably modified. Some analysts have assumed that the basic causal variables influence desired, not actual, government expenditures and that there is lagged response of actual to desired expenditures (so that an additional explanatory variable representing government expenditures in the previous period is added to the above equation). Other complications in the form of various types of interactions can be introduced. For instance, we can model a mutual causation between certain response coefficients (b in the equation) and governmental expenditures or we can make some of the response coefficients functions of still other independent variables (e.g., when the growth rate of the economy influences the response to per capita income), so that some interaction terms must be added to the above equation. Unfortunately, the sample used for analysis in this study is too small to permit these various modifications of the simple demand equation to be introduced successfully.

Two very serious interpretative problems of the regression analysis based on the demand approach must also be mentioned: these relate to problems of multicollinearity and confusion between cross-sectional and time-series results.

In many of the studies using the demand approach there is considerable multicollinearity between the explanatory variables. One example occurs because per capita income and the relative price of government expenditures, both important demand elements, rise together and in a number of studies both are included as independent variables. The interpretations given to the resulting regression coefficients (and their standard errors) are open to considerable doubt since the results are so highly sensitive to those cases where one of the two variables does not predict well the other variable. In such a case, if the price variable is dropped, the calculated response coefficient of government expenditures to per capita income includes price effects as well.

In recent years perhaps the most serious interpretative problem in applying the demand approach has been a confusion of cross-sectional and time-series elasticities of government expenditures. For instance, both T. E. Borcherding (1977, ch. 3) and Sam Peltzman (1980) have argued that since the income elasticity of public expenditures is unity or less, the dramatic rise in public expenditures can not be due to demand factors. However, these demand elasticities are drawn from cross-sectional regressions of U.S. states and local governments, and then they are applied to time-series data where they do not apply. Several examples can demonstrate this point more concretely.

Among the OECD nations in recent years, the fastest growing part of public expenditures is, in most cases, transfer payments and these are primarily payments to the elderly which are included under my definition of social welfare expenditures. As one can see from the data in Table 4, for the sample nations, at any given point in time there seems to be only a weak relationship between per capita income of a country and the relative importance of retired people; but over time as per capita income has increased, the share of the elderly has increased dramatically. Further, as I discuss below, social welfare expenditures as a share of GNP are related to how long the social insurance system has been in operation, which is not strongly related to per capita income. So we have very important reasons to expect that the elasticity derived from time-series data for social welfare expenditures should be much greater than the elasticity derived from cross-sectional data.

Another example concerns education expenditures. At any single point in time, a certain level of education in the population is needed to utilize the most modern technology. Comparing two points in time for a nation with a constant per capita income, the same nation at the later time will require more educated people because the general level of world technology rises. Thus for education the time-series income elasticity should be higher than the cross-sectional income elasticity.

A final example refers to the situation where the cross-sectional elasticities are derived from governmental subunits within a nation, and the time series elasticities refer to total governmental expenditures. This is an incorrect procedure since we are comparing two different series of governmental expenditures (the time series includes federal governmental expenditures while the cross section does not). Further, on a state and local level there is a strong demonstration effect, for example, the state of Mississippi, which is relatively poor, may have governmental education expenditures per student that are almost the same as those in a much richer state such as New York, since the students from the former state must later compete against students from the latter state in the national labor market. Since state and local governments make certain decisions about their expenditures on the basis of what other states are spending, the cross-sectional income elasticities of public expenditures may be quite low vis-à-vis the time-series income elasticities where the causal role of income is more direct.

In the calculations about to be presented, I calculate cross-sectional regressions at several different points in time. I also calculate cross-sectional regressions of twenty-year changes in each country since I do not have enough time slices to calculate true time-series elasticities for the individual sample nations. One caveat must be added: the very peculiar behavior of government expenditures in Romania provides an extreme point which has some influence on the results because the sample is small; to determine this effect, I have calculated the regression results both with and without this nation. Because the major conclusions are not changed, only the former results are presented.

Some demand experiments: cross sections of levels. The most aggregative public expenditures data are the most difficult to explain; for I find no very impressive statistical relationships between total adjusted budgetary expenditures as a share of GDP and such explanatory variables as per capita income and an economic systems dummy variable in any of the four years. Similarly unsuccessful results occur when total welfare state expenditures as a share of GNP is used as the dependent variable instead.

The situation is quite different in the case of welfare expenditures, where the problem is not finding explanatory variables, but rather separating the effects of the three most promising. One variable is per capita income in a common currency;[3] and one would suspect that the higher such income, the higher the share of welfare expenditures since the greater amount of discretionary income the society would have for such purposes. A second variable is the ratio of the population aged sixty-five and over to the population fifteen through sixty-four; and one would suspect that the higher this ratio, the greater the share of welfare expenditures in the economy since pensions constitute the greatest portion of these expenditures and the need for such pensions would be greatest. A third variable is a supply variable, namely, the length of time that the social insurance system had been in operation. (The operation of this variable is discussed below.) In addition to these three intercorrelated variables, I also include an economic systems variable which plays several roles: as a measure of market versus centrally administered economy; as a measure of multiparty versus single party rulership (for the market economies, however, Yugoslavia is similar to Eastern Europe); and as an additional measure of need, since the retirement age is lower in Eastern Europe than in Western Europe. The effect of this need can be argued in several ways. Although the lower retirement age in Eastern Europe would indicate a higher ratio, the greater inequalities of income in the market economies (on which data are presented in Pryor 1973, ch. 3) would indicate a greater relative need for welfare payments to those in the lower part of the income distribution. In short, we have counteracting forces that may cancel each other out. Therefore, we are left with the economic system and the multiparty versus the single-party political systems. Evaluation of the impact of these phenomena on welfare expenditures raises a number of ideological and other issues for which no definitive answer can be given. Therefore, I include the variable as possibly important, but without prediction about its sign. Since the results for all four time slices are roughly similar, in Table 5 I present such regressions only for 1956 and 1976.

TABLE 5
Cross-Country Experiments with Welfare Expenditures

A. Variables:
AGED = ratio of population 65 and over to population 15 to 65.
YCAP = logarithm of per capita GNP in a common currency.
YEARS = years from founding of social insurance system to 1970.
SYS = 0 for market economy; 1 for centrally administered economy.
WFARE = logarithm of ratio of welfare expenditures to GDP.

B. Correlation Matrices:

	AGED 1956	YCAP 1956	YEARS	SYS	WFARE 1956
AGED 1956	1.00	.53	.52	-.33	.61
YCAP 1956		1.00	.27	-.17	.35
YEARS			1.00	.03	.72
SYS				1.00	-.32
WFARE 1956					1.00

	AGED 1976	YCAP 1976	YEARS	SYS	WFARE 1976
AGED 1976	1.00	.53	.65	-.18	.65
YCAP 1976		1.00	.34	-.18	.54
YEARS			1.00	.03	.47
SYS				1.00	-.47
WFARE 1976					1.00

C. Regressions (standard errors in parentheses):

1956

$$WFARE = 1.039 - 0.274 \ SYS + 0.0209 \ YEARS \qquad R^2 = .5172$$
$$ (0.150) (0.0053) \qquad R^2 \ adj. = .4770$$

$$WFARE = 1.192 - 0.104 \ SYS + 0.0688 \ AGED \qquad R^2 = .3752$$
$$ (0.204) (0.0301) \qquad R^2 \ adj. = .3231$$

$$WFARE = 1.284 - 0.216 \ SYS + 0.264 \ YCAP \qquad R^2 = .1255$$
$$ (0.225) (0.235) \qquad R^2 \ adj. = .0526$$

1976

$$WFARE = 1.930 - 0.364 \ SYS + 0.0127 \ YEARS \qquad R^2 = .4582$$
$$ (0.166) (0.0058) \qquad R^2 \ adj. = .3597$$

$$WFARE = 1.538 - 0.274 \ SYS + 0.0567 \ AGED \qquad R^2 = .4215$$
$$ (0.154) (0.0200) \qquad R^2 \ adj. = .3733$$

$$WFARE = 0.264 - 0.292 \ SYS + 0.571 \ YCAP \qquad R^2 = .4343$$
$$ (0.173) (0.282) \qquad R^2 \ adj. = .3414$$

Sources: See Tables 1, 3, 4 and footnote 3. Data on social insurance
systems: U.S. Dept. of Health, Educ., and Welfare (1975).

For the two years presented in the table the results are somewhat different. In 1956, the number of years of operation of the social insurance system appears unambiguously the single most important explanatory variable; in 1976, the explanatory role of the percentage of aged, and also the per capita income, appear practically the same. In both years the centrally administered economies also appear to have lower welfare expenditures; however, with one exception these coefficients designating the economic system are not statistically significant at the .05 level. In 1976, however, statistical significance at a somewhat lower level of confidence is achieved and if the trends persist, it appears from these calculations that sometime in the future the share of welfare expenditures in the GNP of the market economies may be significantly higher than in the centrally administered economies. Such conclusions can also be drawn, albeit more tentatively, if the regressions are calculated with Romania omitted.

Some demand experiments: cross sections of changes. The time-series patterns among countries have varied considerably and it is useful to attempt to separate the important causal factors underlying this phenomenon. A simple way to approach this is by comparing changes between the two ends of the twenty-year period; therefore, I have selected as a dependent variable the percentage change of the ratios of various public consumption expenditures to the GDP. That is, if the expenditures/GDP ratio rose from .10 to .15, the dependent variable is the 50 percent increase in this ratio. To explain such changes, a number of possible explanatory variables can be selected.

An obvious candidate to explain the growth of expenditures is the initial level of the variable: other things being equal, it seems likely that the growth of any expenditure would be inversely related to the initial level of this share. Another candidate for an explanatory variable is per capita income: other things being equal, the higher this income variable, the greater the share of GNP growth can be considered discretionary, and the faster the growth of expenditures might be if it were a "luxury." A third candidate for an explanatory variable is the economic system, and a variety of ideological considerations can be imagined for its justification. A fourth candidate is the growth rate of GNP, and two possible relationships could influence the results. The faster the growth of GNP, the more public expenditures might lag behind what they are desired to be, since other parts of the economy are growing so quickly; thus there might be an inverse relation between GNP growth and the growth of public expenditures. Further, the slower public expenditures grow, the more resources are available to increase growth in other parts of the economy so that an inverse relationship between GNP and public expenditures growth from this reversed causality is also possible. Unfortunately, the sample is too small for separating these effects or dealing in the most satisfactory manner with any possible simultaneous equations bias.

Some of the results with the highest degree of explanatory power are presented in Table 6. The regressions results when Romania is dropped from the sample are quite similar and are not included. It is interesting that we are able to explain time-series of the most aggregative public expenditures more easily than the more

TABLE 6
Experiments with Expenditure Share Changes

A. Variables:

PTOT = percentage change in share of total adjusted budget expenditures in GDP between 1956 and 1976.
PHEW = percentage change of share of health, education, and welfare expenditures in GDP between 1956 and 1976.
PWEL = percentage change of share of welfare expenditures in GDP between 1956 and 1976.
SYS = 0 for market economy; 1 for centrally administered economy.
GDPGR = average annual GDP growth between 1956 and 1976.
YCAP = per capita GNP in common currency.
HEW56 = share of health, education, and welfare expenditures in GDP in 1956.
WEL56 = share of welfare expenditures in GDP in 1956.

B. Regressions (standard errors in parentheses):

$$PTOT = 0.864 - 0.399 \; SYS - 0.0976 \; GDPGR \qquad R_2^2 = .8414$$
$$ (0.063) \qquad (0.0263) \qquad\qquad R^2 \; adj. = .8126$$

$$PHEW = 2.164 - 0.324 \; SYS - 0.184 \; GDPGR - 4.852 \; HEW56$$
$$ (0.129) \qquad (0.057) \qquad\quad (1.669)$$

$$R_2^2 = .6939$$
$$R^2 \; adj. = .6021$$

$$PWEL = 0.821 - 0.188 \; SYS - 0.0606 \; WEL56 + 0.0106 \; YCAP56$$
$$ (0.167) \qquad (0.0242) \qquad\quad (0.0051)$$

$$R_2^2 = .5091$$
$$R^2 \; adj. = .3698$$

Sources: Data from sources cited in Tables 1, 3, 4 and footnote 3.

disaggregated series, which is exactly the reverse of the experiments reported in Table 5. Further, for welfare state expenditures as a whole, as well as for social welfare expenditures separately, the expected negative relationship between initial level and subsequent growth appeared. This, in turn, suggests that these levels of public expenditures are converging, at least between nations with the same economic system.

An extremely puzzling result occurs in the regression experiments for the growth of welfare expenditures, namely, that neither the share of aged in the population in the initial year, nor the percentage growth of the share of the aged, nor the growth rate in the GNP, seemed to influence the results in any important manner. This is exactly contrary to the cross section results of absolute levels where the percentage of aged played an apparently important causal role. I suspect that the discrepancies between the two sets of results occurred because the role of this variable, as shown in Table 5, was somewhat different in the two time slices. Unfortunately, we have insufficient data to explore this matter more deeply and, indeed, it may be a simple statistical artifact.

B. Supply Approaches

Supply approaches toward the explanation of determinants of public expenditures depend crucially on mechanisms either directly related to the process of producing government services (e.g., economies of scale) or bureaucratic processes within the government itself. It is useful to review rapidly some of these variables which have received recent attention in order to determine their applicability to the problem at hand.

Scale and relative productivity effects. If economies of scale were important in the production of public services, one would suspect that the share of public expenditures in the GDP would decline, ceteris paribus, as the GDP increased. Of course, such a scale effect lowers the effective price and, as a result, influences demand so that one must try to take account of a complicated interaction of variables. This does not seem to provide an interpretative problem for these data since few econometric studies of government expenditures have revealed any important scale effect.

The relative productivity effect, on the other hand, does appear important. The argument is quite simple: because productivity in the production of services generally increases more slowly than in the production of goods, and because wages in the production of government services keep pace with the wages in other sectors of the economy, the relative costs of government services will rise, and we would expect a rise in the share of public expenditures in the GDP when both are defined in current prices, at least in so far as the price elasticity of demand for government services is not sufficiently great to cause a decrease in the quantity of government services demanded that totally offsets such a rise in relative costs.

A good deal of evidence is available to support this position. On a macroeconomic level, for instance, the OECD (1978) has shown that in constant prices, the ratio of production of government services to the GDP has stayed roughly constant while the current price ratio has risen considerably. The current price ratios have risen because of this price effect and also because transfers (which were not included in government services) rose. Further, a number of studies have attempted to demonstrate the extremely slow rise in productivity for particular governmental services, especially on the local level (e.g., Bradford, Malt, and Oates 1964). The role of relative productivity differences as a cause of the rising level of government expenditures to the GDP seems to be generally accepted, and to be part of the conventional wisdom in public finance.

However, the importance of the relative productivity effect has recently been challanged by Orzechowski (1974) who points out that in the United States the capital/labor ratio in the federal governmental sector (even with defense excluded) is much higher than in the manufacturing sector as a whole. Therefore, there is no reason to believe that its productivity growth (at least at this level) should be lower than the economy as a whole. Unfortunately, since government output is so difficult to measure (and, indeed, is measured in the GNP account in terms of inputs), productivity increases may not be reflected in the statistics used to compute the expenditures/GDP ratios.

Since I have measured the government services in terms of their inputs in the sample nations, the relative productivity effect certainly may play a role in the rise of the expenditures/GDP ratio. However, it is not by any means the only cause of all the rise, for, as shown in Table 4, such expenditures as welfare, which consist mostly of transfers, have risen very fast as well. Unfortunately, I have no way of measuring this relative productivity effect -- and neither does anyone else examining the problem on a macroeconomic level.

The displacement effect. In a well-known book, Alan Peacock and Jack Wiseman (1961) proposed that the pattern of government expenditures over time reveals a ratchet effect. Due to the difficulties of the political authorities in raising tax rates, government expenditures as a ratio of GNP move along some slowly changing trend line until the occurrence of a war or other national emergency. At this point, it is politically feasible to raise tax rates and, after the end of the national emergency, they may be lowered, but never to the previous level. In short, the national emergency provides a displacement of the trend. Such an argument is a particularization of a common hypothesis among historians that economic crises lead to a strengthening of government as groups attempt to utilize the government to resolve their problems.

This rather superficial theory has received considerable comment in the literature. Most attempts to test it statistically using time-series data from various nations have generally revealed the displacement to be small or negligible in most cases. More important to our purposes, this theory does not explain the dramatic increase in public expenditures as a ratio of GNP in the West during the last two decades, for most countries have not experienced war. Although to save the theory we might define this period as a "national emergency," such a step changes the theory into a tautology, which was certainly not the intention of its proponents.

A government employee voting mechanism. A number of economists (especially the authors of the essays in Borcherding 1977) have suggested that the presence of government workers in a democracy adds an impetus to the growth of governmental expenditures, for it is in their career interests to vote for candidates favoring larger budgets. Since empirical evidence has shown that governmental employees have a much higher participation in voting than the average voter, these workers may constitute a swing vote that brings about an upward spiral of government expenditures.

As economists such as Courant (1979), Greene and Munley (1979), and Pommerehne and Frey (1978) have pointed out, this approach has some theoretical difficulties which reduce its credibility. It would not be surprising that empirical tests of the hypothesis on local governmental votes have not been able to validate it. This approach also does not seem promising to explain trends in public expenditures in East and West.

A monopoly mechanism. Drawing upon the work of William Niskanen (1971), some economists (e.g., Orzechowski 1977) have pointed toward the following constellation of factors as underlying the growth of government expenditures. First, government bureaucrats try to maximize their budgets, for this allows them to increase their personal power over resources. Second, the output of government is hard to measure, as is the efficiency of the offices performing this work. Third, politicians in the legislature have neither the time nor the expertise to check thoroughly the budgets of these agencies to determine carefully what they are producing and how productive their work is. Thus, the government bureaus stand in a monopoly position vis-à-vis the politicians and, therefore, government expenditures tend to increase.

It can be argued that politicians have an incentive to be elected and since high taxes are painful to pay, they have an incentive to keep the expenditures of the government at a low level so as to maximize their votes. This would invalidate the third argument. Further, the conclusion does not follow from the assumptions. That is, although the government bureaus may stand as monopolists vis-à-vis the legislature, this means only that their budgets are somewhat higher than they ordinarily would be, and that they may be inefficient, not that the ratio of these budgetary expenditures to the GNP is constantly rising.

Another problem with this type of approach is that a static argument is being extended illegitimately to a dynamic situation. That is, the argument was originally propounded in terms of a cross-sectional comparison. Even if we assume that it is correct, it does not imply that the share of public expenditures will increase over time, something that Niskanen (1975) has pointed out.

A variant of this argument is one of the humorous laws propounded by G. Northcote Parkinson, who suggested that it is the essence of bureaucracy to increase its expenditures, even when the tasks it performs may be decreasing. There is, of course, considerable anecdotal evidence for this position. And as I have pointed out in a previous section, the ratio of such expenditures to the GNP depends in part on how long the social insurance system has been in operation: the longer the time period, the higher the ratio of public expenditures. This is because such programs increase in the share of the population served, in the extent of their programs, and in the magnitude of the payments. The crucial question, however, is whether these changes represented a demand or a supply phenomenon.

The question becomes more pointed when examining the results of a quantitative study of public expenditures by the OECD for their member nations for a period from the early 1960s to the early 1970s. The results (OECD 1978, 26) showed that for the total growth of social welfare expenditures, 16 percent was due to demographic changes (e.g., a larger number of the elderly receiving social insurance), 44 percent was due to eligibility changes, 24 percent to increased per capita payments and changes in the relative size of real benefits, and 16 percent to changes in costs. Clearly the impact of demographic factors can not be attributed to supply factors. Are the changes in eligibility, per capita payments, and real benefits a result of bureaucratic forces? Or did these changes truly reflect the demands of the voters? Unfortunately, no statistical analysis separating such factors has yet been made for this case.

Other supply effects. A number of analysts have pointed toward other supply effects. For instance, in city expenditures, the presence of a city manager versus a mayoral form of government seems to make a difference. Or the presence of grants from a central government to local governments may increase local governmental expenditures. Or the presence of competiton between local governments for enticing industry to their regions may act to lower expenditures, at least in so far as low tax rates are offered to potential investors. No believable evidence has yet been presented that such supply effects would make much difference on the national level on which we are focusing. Other types of supply effects, for example, the impact of public spending limits, appear to have more effect (Pascal 1979) but the evidence on these matters is relatively limited.

The occurrence of some special supply effects for Eastern Europe must also be noted. For the Soviet Union, Gur Ofer (1973) has shown that the analysis of the service sector (including the government sector) must take into account the presence of less-trained workers (particularly women) than in other sectors, the underpricing of defense goods (which is made up to the producers by subsidies that are not included in these calculations), the underpricing of medical services (because of the relatively low salaries of doctors), and the constant campaigns to cut down "unproductive labor." Obviously, some of these factors are offsetting so that their net effects are much smaller than their separate gross effects. Moreover, some appear to apply more to the Soviet Union than to some of the other Eastern European nations (e.g., in the DDR, the salaries of doctors are relatively high).

Two observations about such supply factors special to Eastern Europe must be made. First, in most cases, they introduce quantitative effects that are strictly of secondary importance. Second, they probably affect cross-sectional analyses more than time-series analyses since there is little reason to believe that such effects are growing or declining in importance.

C. A Combined Approach

The combined supply and demand approaches that have been proposed usually focus upon the mechanisms by which the demand for public expenditures is related to the financing of such expenditures. Perhaps the earliest exponent of such an approach was Alexis de Tocqueville (1835) who considered the relative public expenditures in three communities whose legislatures were dominated, respectively, by the richest class, by the middle class, and by the most numerous and poorest class.

De Tocqueville argued that public expenditures would be lowest when the middle class had legislative power, for this class would be loath to tax itself: "Nothing is so onerous as a large impost levied upon a small income. The government of the middle classes appears to me the most economical, I will not say the most enlightened, and certainly not the most generous, of free governments." When universal suffrage occurs, the poor are invested with the government of authority. And in this case, "[public] expenditures will always be considerable, either because the taxes cannot weigh upon those who levy them, or because they are levied in a manner as not to reach these poorer classes."

This kind of approach has been embodied in analyses of the growth of public expenditures in several different ways. Sometimes it is generalized in a manner that focuses upon the relative strength of the beneficiaries of public expenditures compared with those who pay the taxes to finance them. For instance, Meltzer (1976) argues that public expenditures rise because the beneficiaries are more organized and have more to gain by public expenditures benefiting them alone than any single individual outside the group loses. Thus, the latter have less incentive to organize around the issue than the former. Such an argument has a great deal of intuitive appeal, but it is difficult to see exactly how it could be empirically tested.

Peltzman (1980) has recast de Tocqueville's approach in an elegant model. (He reaches farther back in history and designates the poor taking from (taxing) the rich as the "Robin Hood effect.") He mathematically derives three propositions for a democracy with universal suffrage. 1. The wider the range of income between the rich and the poor, the higher the taxes on the rich and public expenditures will be. 2. The narrower the range of income among the lower-income classes, the higher the taxes on the rich and thus the public expenditures will be. 3. The more educated the lower-income classes, and the more able they are to understand and operate the political process, the higher the taxes on the rich and public expenditures will be.[4]

But what does this tell us about nations whose public expenditures are not decided through a legislature whose members are elected through universal sufferage? Certainly some nondemocratic societies (e.g., Japan before the Meiji restoration) had considerable public expenditures. However, this arose because the rich controlled the state and used the state to benefit themselves by taxing the poor. Other precapitalist societies without universal suffrage appear to have had a relatively low level of public expenditures.

What does such an approach tell us about the differences between public expenditures in East and West? Assuming away, for the moment, differences in the political structure, no firm conclusions can be drawn. Certainly the income distribution per se should play no important role, for in Eastern Europe the income differences within the lower half of the income distribution, and between the lower and the upper halves of the income distribution, seem more equal than in the West (Pryor 1973) and, according to Peltzman, these two effects work in opposite directions on public expenditures. Further, the educational levels are not very different between the two sets of countries.

Of course, in the nations of Eastern Europe the legislature plays a very minor role in the setting of the governmental budgets and, further, competition between political parties for votes does not occur. From this, Peltzman's argument suggests that welfare state expenditures would be greater in the West during the entire period. However, we only find this phenomenon appearing in the 1970s; before this, such expenditures were roughly the same. Further, Peltzman's approach does not give us any clues as to why public expenditures in the East started to rise in the 1970s.

Trying to combine the supply and demand approaches toward public expenditures gives us very few theoretical guideposts to tell us whether such expenditures will be higher in the East or West. The only relevant data presented in this essay that concerns this issue are the series on welfare, where it seems likely that there is a redistribution of income between the rich and poor. Although it appears from the regression experiments in Tables 5 and 6 that such welfare expenditures are relatively lower and are increasing less quickly in Eastern than in Western Europe, the sample is small and we can not be completely sure on this. Further, the experiment is not completely "clean" because the really important redistributional element in such welfare expenditures is from the middle aged to the old.

IV. SOME REFLECTIONS

A number of questions have been raised in this essay. To explore them empirically, it would be useful to employ a complicated multiequation model that can bring in many of the factors discussed. But the data do not permit us this luxury.

Although firm analytical conclusions can not be drawn, it appears that demand elements play the most important role in the increase in public expenditures in both East and West. With the exception of a variable indicating length of existence of the social insurance system, no supply variables appeared important in the regression analyses. Even the "relative productivity effect" does not seem very important, at least in the recent past.

The role of the systems variable is complicated. It does not appear significant in the cross-sectional regressions of expenditure levels except, perhaps, at the most disaggregated level for welfare expenditures where the centrally administered economies have a lower share of such expenditures in their GDP. However, in the cross-sectional regressions of changes in expenditures over time, it appears that for expenditures defined in the most aggregated manner, such total public consumption expenditures increased more slowly as a share of GDP in the centrally administered economies than in the market economies. However, on a disaggregated level this does not appear to be the case for certain types of expenditures such as for welfare. Together, such results suggest that in the future, for all levels of expenditures, the centrally administered economies will have a lower share of adjusted budgetary expenditures.

Certain empirical questions are even more difficult to answer. For instance, when will the share of public expenditures in the GDP stop rising, a pressing question that has been discussed both on the political level in various electoral campaigns throughout the world, as well as on a theoretical level (see, for example, the views of economists in a large number of nations in Recktenwald 1978). To help us answer this question, several conflicting factors need to be taken into account.

First, for the fastest growing components of adjusted budgetary expenditures, namely, health, education, and welfare (and for social welfare alone), the rapidity of growth is inversely proportional to the share of these expenditures in the initial period (Table 6). This suggests a slowing down of growth in the future.

Second, although many of the demand influences underlying past increases of public expenditures show no signs of abating, we can not be completely sure that these will continue to play an important causal role in the rise in the share of public expenditures. For instance, the aged continue to increase as a share of the population and, therefore, one part of social insurance expenditures might appear to continue to rise. The aged also have greater health needs and, therefore, another part of social insurance expenditures might rise. However, the change in the share of the aged did not appear to influence the change in expenditures directed to them, at least in the twenty year time period under examination.

Third, the demand forces for other types of public expenditures, for example, for education, may increase at a very slow rate or cease entirely. For education, however, offsetting factors influencing public expenditures can be cited: the lower birth rates and a falling share of children in the population make for a decline in the relative share of education; but the increasing complexity of society requires increased education expenditures. For some expenditures it is difficult to say how the major causal elements will change. For instance, for defense expenditures, it is clear that the rising international tensions in the short run will not abate; in the long run, however, the situation may be different, and nations may become more civilized to their neighbors so the need for such expenditures may decrease.

Fourth, many of the existing governmental programs in most developed countries in the West have considerable room for an expansion of the eligibility requirements (OECD 1978, 30-38). The political ability to resist these increases depends crucially on changes in the strength of these governments, and these are difficult to predict. It should be noted that effective national movements to bring about the limitation of government taxation or expenditures (as manifested through such activities as parliamentary action to limit taxes, tax evasion, and reduced work effort) seem far in the future for many countries.

The share of public consumption expenditures in the GDP has been rising in most nations in East and West and, at least in the near future, should continue along this path. Predicting the long-term future of this share is dangerous since the relative strengths of various offsetting factors can not be determined. If pressed, I would bet that a leveling off will occur in the next decade. However, I would not lay much money on such a bet.

FOOTNOTES

For assistance in obtaining data I would like to thank Thad Alton, Noel Farley, Helen Hughes, Peter Miovic, and the various national statistical agencies that sent me published and unpublished data. I would also like to thank David Muething, Gur Ofer, and Larry Seidman for their comments on a previous draft of this paper.

1. The U.S. national accounts data do not include expenditures for construction and equipment by various levels of government in the investment data. These latter expenditures (taken from U.S. Bureau of the Census 1978, 288) were added to the national accounts data to obtain total investment. Data on federal government loans and guarantees comes from Murray L. Weidenbaum (1977).

2. The major corrections for 1962 occurred not in the public expenditures data, but rather in the GNP data for several Eastern European nations. The public expenditures estimations for 1970 and 1977 were too tedious to be reported here. A desription of the methods can be obtained from the author.

3. The per capita GNPs in a common currency for 1970 are reported in Table 1. To calculate such data for other years, the following sources were used for the market economies: OECD 1979; I.B.R.D. 1975; I.B.R.D. (forthcoming). For the centrally administered economies the following sources were utilized: Alton 1977; Alton 1970; Bloch 1979; Greenslade 1976.

4. To demonstrate his theory empirically, Peltzman (1980) used four sets of data: long-time-series data for the U.S.A., the U.K., and Japan; cross-sectional OECD data; data on state and local expenditures in the various U.S. states in different years; and some cross-sectional data for various developing nations. However, such analyses can be criticized on several grounds. First, he used total government expenditures, rather than expenditures related to redistribution as his theory specified. Second, since a narrowing of income differences between the richest and the poorest, and within the poorest, groups appears highly correlated, and since these differences lead to opposite changes in public expenditures, they must be separated. However, only for the data concerning the U.S. states did this appear possible. Third, the results for the U.S. states did not validate

his theory until a cross-product term involving education was added. However, there appeared to be multicollinearity between this term and the other independent variables so that the results can be questioned. Finally, it is possible that his results were due to the causal arrows running in the opposite direction. For instance, a more progressive tax may lead to less investment in human and physical capital which will, in turn, reduce the labor supply for high-income occupations. This will later raise the wages in these groups which, in turn, will lead to a greater gap between the rich and poor. Thus a greater differentiation between rich and poor is associated with a more progressive income tax, but the tax causes the differentiation. Another instance would occur where higher social insurance payouts lead to less labor being offered by older workers which, in turn, means that their monetary income is lower (but they work less) and there is a greater gap between older and poorer workers on one hand, and richer people on the other. Thus a greater differentiation of income between rich and poor is associated with a greater social security payout, but the latter brought about the former.

BIBLIOGRAPHY

Alton, T. P. 1970. Economic structure and growth in Eastern Europe. In Joint Economic Committee, U.S. Congress, *Economic developments in countries of Eastern Europe*. Washington, D.C.: G.P.O.

_____, et al. 1973. *Estimates of military expenditures in Eastern Europe*. A report prepared for the United States Arms Control and Disarmament Agency. Processed. New York.

_____, 1977. Comparative structure and growth of economic activity in Eastern Europe. In Joint Economic Committee, U.S. Congress, *East European economies post-Helsinki*, 199-267. Washington, D.C.: G.P.O.

Bloch, H. 1979. Soviet economic performance in a global context. In Joint Economic Committee, U.S. Congress, *Soviet economy in a time of change*. Washington, D.C.: G.P.O.

Borcherding, T.E., ed. 1977. *Budgets and bureaucrats: the sources of government growth*. Durham, N.C.: Duke U. Press.

_____, W. C. Bush, R. M. Spann. 1977. The effects of public spending on the divisibility of public outputs in consumption, bureaucratic power, and the size of the tax-sharing group. In Borcherding 1977, 211-28.

_____, 1977. The sources of growth of public expenditures in the United States, 1902-1970. In Borcherding 1977, 45-70.

Bradford, D. F., R. A. Malt, W. E. Oates. 1964. The rising cost of local public services: some evidence and reflections. *National Tax J.*, 22(2)(June): 185-202.

Courant, P. N., E. M. Gramlich, D. L. Rubinfeld. 1979. Public employee market power and the level of government spending. *Amer. Econ. Rev.*, 69(3)(December): 806-818.

Drucker, P. F. 1976. *The unseen revolution: how pension fund socialism came to America*. N.Y.: Harper and Row.

Greene, K., V. G. Munley. 1979. Generating growth in public expenditures: the role of employee and constituent demand. *Public Finance Quart.*, 7(1)(January): 92-108.

Greenslade, R. 1976. The real gross national product of the U.S.S.R., 1950-1975. In Joint Economic Committee, U.S. Congress, *Soviet economy in a new perspective*, 269-301. Washington, D.C.: G.P.O.

International Bank for Reconstruction and Development (I.B.R.D.). Forthcoming. *World tables 1980*. Washington, D.C.

_____, 1975. *Yugoslavia*: *development with decentralization*. Baltimore: Johns Hopkins U. Press.

Kravis, I., A. Heston, R. Summers. 1978. Real GDP per capita for more than one hundred countries. *Econ. J.*, 88(June): 215-42.

Meltzer, A. H. 1976. Too much government. In *The economy in disarray*, ed. R. C. Blattberg. New York: N.Y.U. Press.

Niskenen, W. 1971. *Bureaucracy and representative government*. Chicago: Aldine.

_____, 1975. Bureaucrats and politicians. *J. Law and Econ.*, (December): 617-443.

OECD. Periodic. *Labour force statistics*. Paris.

_____, 1978. *Public expenditures trends*. Paris.

_____, 1979. *National accounts of OECD countries*, *1952-1977*. Vol. 1. Paris.

Ofer, G. 1973. *The service sector in Soviet economic growth*: *a comparative study*. Cambridge, Mass.: Harvard U. Press.

Orzechowski, W. P. 1974. Labor intensity, productivity, and the growth of the federal sector. *Public Choice*, 19(Fall): 123-26.

_____, 1977. Economic models of bureaucracy: survey, extensions and evidence. In Borcherding 1977, 229 ff.

Pascal, A. H., et. al. 1979. Fiscal containment of local and state government. RAND corporation paper R-2492-FF/RC. Santa Monica. (September).

Peacock, A. T., J. Wiseman. 1961. *The growth of public expenditures in the United Kingdom*. Princeton: Princeton U. Press.

Peltzman, S. 1980. The growth of government. Working paper no. 001-2, Center for the study of the economy and the state. Univ. of Chicago; Another version with the same title appeared in: *J. Law and Econ.*, 23(2)(October 1980): 204-89.

Pommerehne, W. W., B. S. Frey. 1978. Bureaucratic behavior in democracy: a case study. *Public finance/finances publiques*, 33(1-2): 98-113.

Pryor, F. L. 1968. *Public expenditures in communist and capitalist nations*. London: Allen and Unwin.

_____, 1973. *Property and industrial organization in communist and capitalist nations*. Bloomington, Ind.: Indiana U. Press.

————, 1979. Comparable GNP's per capita: an addendum. *Econ. J.*, 89(September): 666-69.

Rechtenwald, H. C., ed. 1978. *Tendances à long terme du secteur public / secular trends of the public sector.* Institut international de finances publiques. Paris; Editions Cujas.

Reynolds, L. G. 1971. Public sector savings and capital formation. In *Government and economic development*, ed. G. Ranis, 516-652. New Haven: Yale U. Press.

Timm, H. 1961. Das Gesetz der wachsenden Staatsausgaben. *Finanzarchiv*, N.F. 21(2)(September): 201-47.

De Tocqueville, A. [1835]. *Democracy in America*. Trans. by H. Reeve, F. Bowen. New York: Knopf. 1945.

United Nations. Annual. *Demographic yearbook*. New York.

U. S. Bureau of the Census. 1979. *Statistical abstract of the United States, 1978.* Washington, D.C.: G.P.O.

U. S. Department of Health, Education, and Welfare. 1975. *Social security programs throughout the world, 1975.* Washington, D.C.: G.P.O.

Weidenbaum, M. L. 1977. An economic analysis of the federal government's credit program. C.S.A.B. working paper, no. 18. (January). St. Louis: Washington U.

Wilenski, H. L. 1975. *The welfare state and equality: structural and ideological roots of public expenditure.* Berkeley: Univ. of Calif. Press.

17

"Laissez-Faire," Import Restraints, and Industry Performance: A Case Study of Automobiles

Walter Adams

I. INTRODUCTION

In recent years, it has become fashionable to deprecate the traditional antitrust philosophy and to urge its replacement by a latter-day Economic Darwinism. The leaders of this new laissez-faire movement -- primarily members of the Chicago School -- see a striking analogy between a free market system and the Darwinian theory of natural selection and physical evolution. Says Robert H. Bork: "The familiarity of that parallel, and the overbroad inferences sometimes drawn from it, should not blind us to its important truths. The environment to which the business firm must adapt is defined, ultimately, by social wants and the social costs of meeting them. The firm that adapts to the environment better than its rivals tends to expand. The less successful firm tends to contract -- perhaps, eventually, to become extinct. The Stanley Steamer and the celluloid collar have gone the way of the pterodactyl and the great ground sloth, basically for the same reasons. Since coping successfully with the economic environment also forwards consumer welfare (except in those cases that are the legitimate concern of antitrust), economic and natural selection has normative implications that physical natural selection does not have. At least there seems to me more reason for enthusiasm about the efficient firm than about the most successful physical organisms, the rat and the cockroach, though this view is, no doubt, parochial" (Bork 1978, 118).

Monopoly or market power, according to the revisionists, are of little social concern because neither is endowed with significant durability. "A market position that creates output restriction and higher prices will soon be eroded if it is not based upon superior efficiency," Bork (1978, 133) alleges. To be classified competitive, an industry needs only a single firm, say Arthur Laffer and George Gilder, because that firm "will compete against the threat of future rivals. Its monopoly can be maintained only as long as the price is kept low enough to exclude others. In this sense, monopolies are good. The more dynamic and inventive an economy, the more monopolies it will engender" (Gilder 1981, 37-38).

This vulgarized version of the Schumpeterian hypothesis rests on the dubious contention, unsubstantiated by empirical evidence, that firms are big because they are efficient; that their bigness assures superior performance and promotes consumer welfare; and that any delinquency in performance is subject to automatic correction by "natural" market forces. In this view, there is no danger per se either in relative or absolute firm size, and public policy, therefore, should primarily confine itself to the prohibition of outright, horizontal conspiracies.

Aside from the fact that it lacks a precise definition of efficiency[1] and a measurable test of performance,[2] the New Darwinism is, as I shall argue in this paper, an exercise in managerial apologetics rather than a policy for promoting the public interest. Relative firm size is significant because an industry's structure has crucial consequences for industry behavior and, ultimately, for industry performance. Absolute size is significant, because giant firms possess the political power to immunize themselves from "natural" market forces by inducing government to build storm shelters which protect them from the Schumpeterial gales of creative destruction, that is, the consequences of poor performance. In support of these propositions, I shall use the U.S. automobile industry's battle for import restraints as a (not atypical) case study.[3]

II. PERFORMANCE OF THE U. S. AUTO INDUSTRY

Most independent analysts would agree that the U.S. automobile industry -- at least since World War II -- has not been characterized by effective competition among the domestic producers. Its noncompetitive structure and noncompetitive behavior have resulted in lackluster performance.[4] Price policy has been directed at uniformity and upward inflexibility, and price competition has been virtually nonexistent.[5] Such rivalry as did exist turned on nonessential forms of product differentiation like style and model changes, accompanied by a cacophony of advertising.

On the technology front, since World War II, American automobile manufacturers, particularly the Big Three, have a record of innovative lethargy and unprogressive sluggishness. They have lagged, not led, in the battle to develop cleaner, safer, and more fuel-efficient cars. They have chosen to react to change, rather than to initiate it. They have adapted reluctantly to those exogenous pressures over which they had only limited control, namely, the government's insistence on minimum safety standards and emission control requirements, on the one hand, and rising fuel prices and foreign competition, on the other. It is noteworthy that Detroit introduced the compact car in response to the import penetration of the late fifties; that it introduced the subcompact car only after the import penetration of the late sixties; and that, in response to the influx of fuel-efficient foreign cars following the oil embargo of 1973, Detroit's "better idea" was to demand government restrictions on the import of low-priced, fuel-efficient autos.

In short, the industry's conduct and performance were precisely what one would have anticipated from a tight-knit oligopoly. The Big Three preserved their dominance in the American market -- not because of superior efficiency but by virtue of massive entry barriers confronting potential newcomers. Absent competition, there was no objective standard for measuring their efficiency, and they were left free to enjoy the fruits of their monopolistic market control. Once imports threatened to become an effective disciplining force, however, the erstwhile claims to superior efficiency and beneficent performance were no longer sustainable. Thenceforth, market dominance had to be preserved by government-sanctioned elimination of foreign competition. And this was precisely what the industry's giants, reinforced by the coalescing power of their influential trade union, proceeded to obtain. Instead of upgrading performance and competing in the marketplace, they petitioned the government (using a version of List's "infant industry" argument) for a bailout from the consequences of their self-inflicted injury. Having failed the market test, they mobilized their political power to perpetuate their market control. The net result was hardly an enhancement of consumer welfare.

III. APPEALS FOR PROTECTION: 1975

The industry's first attempt to immunize itself from foreign competition -- the only real competition which it had encountered in thirty-five years -- occurred during the last recession. On 11 July 1975, the UAW filed a complaint with the U.S. Treasury, charging that "new, on-the-highway, four-wheeled, passenger automobiles from Belgium, Canada, France, Italy, Japan, Sweden, the United Kingdom, and West Germany" were being sold in the United States at less-than-fair value in violation of Section 201(c) of the Antidumping Act of 1921, and causing injury to the domestic auto industry (U.S.I.T.C. 1975).

Specifically, the complaint charged that the increased market share of imported automobiles -- up from 15.2 percent in 1970, to 15.9 percent in 1974, to 20.3 percent in the first half of 1975 -- was "at the expense of domestic sales;" that, discounting the effects of the U.S. recession, there was still a loss of domestic sales to imports; and that the pricing of imported cars caused the resulting injury to the American automobile industry and its workers. The union demanded the imposition of dumping penalties and simultaneously asked Congress for quota protection against the imports of compacts and subcompacts from Europe and Japan.

After a careful analysis of the facts, the U.S. Council on Wage and Price Stability (1975) concluded that imports were not the primary cause of the U.S. industry's problems. Instead, the Council advised the International Trade Commission that the causes of "injury" were to be found elsewhere -- primarily in deficient industry performance.

First, a primary factor explaining the industry's travails -- one that required little elaboration -- was the national recession which drastically reduced the demand for virtually all consumer durables, including automobiles.

Second, the success of the imports was partly attributable to the delayed response by U.S. car manufacturers to a shift in consumer demand toward smaller, more fuel-efficient models. As of January 1975, according to the Council on Wage and Price Stability, no domestic cars obtained 20 MPG or more in the EPA city driving test, whereas fifteen of nineteen foreign compacts and subcompacts obtained 20 MPG or better. In the highway driving test, no U.S. compact or subcompact car had a milage rating of over 30 MPG, whereas fourteen of nineteen foreign car makes did.

    Third, while foreign producers liquidated their large inventories of 1974 models at 1974 prices well into 1975, U.S. manufacturers posted price increases of roughly 12 percent on their 1975 models which went on sale in the autumn of 1974. The counterproductive pricing policy by U.S. producers in the face of a deepening recession, combined with the realisitic market-oriented price policy of their foreign competitors, was an additional factor explaining the dramatic market penetration of the imports.

    Fourth, the fact that imported compacts and subcompacts offered consumers a far wider range of price alternatives, compared to their U.S. counterparts, may also have given imports a competitive edge over domestic models.[6]

    The Council on Wage and Price Stability concluded that the most important factors explaining the increased market share of foreign automobiles "are the pricing policies of domestic producers and the inability of domestic manufacturers to respond rapidly to changing market conditions." The Council cautioned that the imposition of special dumping penalties "would likely result in an immediate increase in the price of automobiles to the American consumer. Moreover, such penalties, or even the threat of penalties, could substantially check what has been perhaps the single most effective spur to competition in this highly concentrated industry. This, in turn, could lead to less competitive prices and a reduced level of innovation" (COWPS 1975).

    The UAW complaint was ultimately resolved by a bizarre consent settlement arranged by the U.S. Treasury Department. Under the settlement, five foreign manufacturers agreed to raise their prices in the U.S. market, and fourteen other foreign manufacturers agreed to have their prices monitored by the Treasury for the next two years. With respect to five foreign firms the Treasury took no action at all.

IV. APPEALS FOR PROTECTION: 1979-1981

    During the recession which started in 1979, the industry again demanded protection against the depredations of import competition. In parallel petitions filed with the International Trade Commission by the United Auto Workers and Ford Motor Company -- formally supported by Chrysler, and tacitly endorsed by General Motors -- industry spokesmen correctly contended that, between the first half of 1979 and the first half of 1980, there occurred a significant decline in the production, sales, capacity utilization, and employment in the domestic automobile industry as a whole. They also contended that, during the same period, there occurred a significant increase in the import penetration of the U.S. market for passenger automobiles and light trucks. Concluding that the growing volume and increased market share of imports constituted an "important" or "primary" cause of serious injury to the domestic auto manufacturers, they asked the Commission to impose mandatory controls on future imports, specifically from Japan (Ford Motor Co. 1980; UAW 1980).

    The facts, however, were not as conclusive as petitioners alleged. Thus, between January-June 1979 and January-June 1980, the drop in overall consumption of passenger automobiles and light trucks in the U.S. amounted to 2.0 million units, or a drop of 25.8 percent. During the same period, imports increased their share of U.S.

consumption by 0.9 million units, or 11.6 percent. As a Commission Staff Report noted, "for both passenger autos and light trucks, consumption decreased by more than import's share of consumption increased....Whereas the percentage decrease in passenger automobile consumption was 18.5 percent, or 1.2 million units, between January-June 1979 and January-June 1980, the increase in the ratio of imports of passenger automobiles to consumption was 9.8 percentage points, or 0.6 million units. Similarly, while the consumption of light trucks declined by 47.8 percent, or by 0.9 million units, import's share of consumption increased by 19.4 percentage points, or by 0.4 million units (U.S.I.T.C. 1980, A-64).

The explanation for this phenomenon was not an increase in imports, but a combination of three primary factors, namely: (1) the impact of the current recession on the overall demand for passenger automobiles and light trucks -- an exogenous force over which the industry had little control; (2) the failure of the U.S. manufacturers to adjust their product mix to shifts in consumer demand; and (3) the investment policies of the U.S. manufacturers which neglected the conversion, modernization, and expansion of their domestic plants, while putting substantial funds into their overseas facilities.

A. The Impact of the Recession

The automobile industry, like other durable-goods industries, is highly cyclical. This means that a recession in the national economy has a disproportionately severe impact on automobiles -- whether measured by corporate profits, consumption expenditures, industrial production, or similar indicia.

Table 1 documents this observation. It shows that during the 1973-75 recession, for example, corporate manufacturing profits increased 9.5 percent, while motor vehicles and equipment profits declined 70.7 percent; total personal consumption expenditures increased by 20.9 percent, while expenditures for motor vehicles and parts declined 3.3 percent; and total industrial production fell by 9.2 percent, while the production of motor vehicles and parts decreased by 25.3 percent. Earlier recessions since 1953 (during which, incidentally, the volume of imports was negligible in relative terms) evidence the same pattern, and there is no reason to expect that the current recession should be an exception to the rule.[7]

In the current recession, the normally severe cyclical impact on the automobile industry has been exacerbated by ancillary elements. First, while used car prices declined, as one would expect, U.S. manufacturers persisted in raising prices for new vehicles, thus widening the margin between the trade-in value of old cars and the purchase price of new cars, and making new automobiles less affordable. Moreover, the unprecedented rise in interest rates and the shortage of loanable funds further dampened the inclination of consumers to make relatively large capital outlays.[8] Finally, the exponential increase in retail prices of gasoline as well as recurrent gasoline shortages persuaded many consumers to defer car purchases or to seek alternate means of transportation. Moreover, the deregulation of oil prices, strongly advocated by domestic auto producers, had the effect of further reducing consumer demand for the kind of vehicles the industry sought to market.

TABLE 1
Comparative Impact of Recessions on the National Economy and the Motor Vehicle Industry, 1953-1975 (Percent)

Recession	Corporate Profits (a)		Consumption Expenditures (b)		Industrial Production (c)	
	Total Manufacturing	Motor Vehicles And Equipt.	Total Personal Consumption	Motor Vehicles And Parts Consumption	Total	Motor Vehicles And Parts
1953-54	-9.5	-19.2	+2.7	-6.5	-5.3	N.A.
1957-58	-19.2	-65.4	+3.2	-14.0	-6.5	-26.1
1960-61	-3.8	-16.7	+3.1	-9.6	+7.5	-12.3
1969-70	-26.4	-70.8	+6.7	-7.4	-3.0	-20.8
1973-75	+9.5	-70.7	+20.9	-3.3	-9.2	-25.3

Notes: N.A. = Not Available.

Sources: Economic Report of the President, 1980
    (a) Table B-81
    (b) Table B-13
    (c) Tables B-39 and B-41

In sum, a recession like that of 1979-81, especially when accompanied by unprecedented interest rates, escalating new car prices, rising costs of gasoline, gasoline shortages, and unappealing product offerings, was bound to have (and did have) an adverse effect on the fortunes of the domestic manufacturers, and has proven to be a primary cause of their present problems.

B. Failure to Adjust Product-Mix to Consumer Demand

Among the important causes of the problems of U.S. auto manufacturers, none was more significant than the persistent failure by the Big Three companies to recognize that the era of the gas-guzzler had come to an end, and that small, fuel-efficient cars were what the market would demand.

Despite the dramatic economic transformation precipitated by the Arab oil embargo of 1973, U.S. auto manufacturers chose not to concentrate on the development and production of small cars and to continue to rely on "intermediate" and "standard" cars as the mainstay of the domestic industry. Whatever the reasons for this decision -- whether it was to avoid competition in the small-car field where foreign producers were strong, or to capitalize on the higher profit margins on "full-sized" cars (in accordance with Henry Ford II's maxim that "mini-cars mean mini-profits"), or to profit from the more costly options (power steering and brakes, more powerful engines, automatic transmissions, etc.) required by large cars -- the decision had seriously adverse consequences for the U.S. manufacturers and, ultimately, for their employees.

The statistics tell the story. Thus, Table 2 shows that U.S. producers' shipments of subcompact and compact cars not only held their own between 1975 and 1980, but substantially increased their share of apparent U.S. consumption. By contrast, the percentage of large cars, after peaking in 1977, declined dramatically during the same period -- from 47.6 percent in 1975 to 29.2 percent in the first half of 1980. As the Commission's staff noted, "Significantly the shift from larger cars appears greater than the shift to imports. From January-June 1979 to January-June 1980, large cars' share of apparent consumption decreased by more than imports' share increased" (U.S.I.T.C. 1980, A-66; emphasis supplied). In other words, any injury suffered by domestic manufacturers was rooted primarily in their inability to sell "intermediate" and "standard and luxury" cars which they insisted on producing in lieu of the small, fuel-efficient cars increasingly demanded by the public.

The point is crucial and deserves emphasis. The observed decline in domestic automobile production, capacity utilization, and employment did not affect the industry as a whole, but was confined to the larger vehicles. Again, the Commission's staff cites the relevant evidence:

> While domestic production of subcompacts and compacts increased from 2.6 million units in 1977 to 3.7 million units in 1979, domestic production of intermediate and full-size cars decreased from 6.5 million units to 4.7 million units. These trends continued in 1980. While domestic production of compacts and subcompacts increased slightly

TABLE 2
Passenger Automobiles: Ratio of U.S. Producers' Shipments and Imports to Apparent Consumption,
By Class of Vehicle, 1975-1979, January-June 1979 and January-June 1980
(Percent of Apparent Consumption)

| | Imports | U.S. Producers' Shipments | | | | | |
| | | Small Cars | | | Large Cars | | |
		Subcompacts	Compacts	Total	Intermediate	Standard and Luxury	Total
1975	26.0	10.5	16.0	26.5	26.5	21.1	47.6
1976	25.1	7.1	17.5	24.6	29.0	21.2	50.2
1977	25.2	6.3	14.4	20.7	29.3	24.8	54.1
1978	26.2	11.6	14.5	26.1	26.3	21.4	47.7
1979	27.1	17.0	14.5	31.5	21.5	19.9	41.4
January-June							
1979	24.7	15.6	12.6	28.2	23.2	23.9	47.1
1980	34.5	18.3	18.0	36.3	17.3	11.9	29.2

Source: U.S. International Trade Commission

from January-June 1979 to January-June 1980, domestic production of intermediate and full-size cars declined by 50 percent (U.S.I.T.C. 1980, A-39).

The data for capacity utilization by size of vehicle reflect the respective differences in production trends. While the utilization of domestic capacity for producing subcompacts and compacts increased from 71.8 percent in 1977 to 79.8 percent in 1979, the utilization of domestic capacity for intermediate and full-size automobiles declined from 91.4 percent to 79.2 percent in the same period. Again, from January-June 1979 to January-June 1980, capacity utilization for smaller cars continued to increase, albeit slightly, while capacity utilization for larger cars declined from 97.3 percent to 52.6 percent (U.S.I.T.C. 1980, A-43).

In other words, the declines in aggregate production and capacity utilization figures for the industry as a whole mask the more revealing statistics broken down by size of vehicle. And these latter statistics make it quite clear that managerial decisions with respect to product mix were the principal cause of the auto industry's malaise.

The industry's battle against the government's fuel-efficiency standards lends historical perspective to these product-mix decisions. On 22 March 1977, the U.S. Department of Transportation held a hearing in Washington to invite comments on the reasonableness of the government's fuel-efficiency mandates for the 1980s which would require each U.S. manufacturer to produce a fleet with an average fuel-efficiency of 27 1/2 MPG by 1985. G.M., Ford, Chrysler, and American Motors testified in unified opposition to these requirements. Henry L. Duncombe, Jr., G.M.'s chief economist, warned that if the government moved ahead with tough gasoline economy requirements, the American consumer might just stop buying new cars. And this, he claimed, citing a study of Chase Econometrics, might cause a possible decline in sales of 2 million units in the mid-1980s, which in turn would translate into a loss of some 140,000 jobs in the auto industry and almost 400,000 jobs in other industries directly connected with the production and distribution of cars. In short, he seemed to suggest that a substantial shift to smaller, more fuel-efficient automobiles could trigger a major loss of sales by the U.S. auto producers, which, in turn, could trigger a major recession in the economy at large, and massive unemployment.[9]

As late as 26 April 1979, the U.S. auto industry was still fighting the 27 1/2 MPG fuel-efficiency requirement for the 1986 fleet. On that day, Mr. Roger B. Smith, Executive Vice-President of General Motors, told the U.S. Senate Subcommittee on Economic Stabilization:

Among all the regulations affecting the auto industry, the fuel economy standards have the greatest impact and are potentially the most disruptive to the industry and the nation. The 1985 standard of 27.5 miles per gallon requires nearly a 100 percent increase in fuel economy of the average car compared to the average 1974 model. For GM the

improvement will require a 129 percent improvement. While
we are already about half way there, having improved our
fleet average from 12 MPG in 1974 to 19 MPG in 1979, the
amount of improvement that remains to be accomplished will
be very costly (U.S. Senate 1979, 4).

Mr. Smith went on to warn the Committee that:

There is no reasonable assurance that consumers will be
willing to buy the kinds of cars and trucks we will be
forced to offer. To be marketable, these more fuel
efficient, lower polluting and, presumably, safer cars will
have to be perceived by customers to be better values. If
not, they will not buy them. In that event, older cars will
be kept in service longer which means that more fuel will be
consumed and that progress in highway safety and the control
of emissions will be impeded. Additionally, employment in
the auto and supplier industries will decrease and the used
car market will shrink, restricting the private
transportation for many who depend upon the availability of
good used cars (U.S. Senate 1979, 8).

Mr. Smith did not refer to the fact that foreign auto producers were
already meeting or exceeding these standards and doing so without
apparent difficulty.

Less than six months after this General Motors testimony, the
Environmental Protection Agency issued its semiannual ranking of cars
in terms of fuel efficiency. It found that the top ten cars on its
list were imports. The Wall Street Journal, 19 September 1979,
summarized the EPA report as follows:

The 10 best 1980 autos in terms of mileage are imports,
the Environmental Protection Agency said.
In its twice-yearly evaluation of new-car fuel economy,
the agency said only one U.S. auto maker -- financially
troubled Chrysler Corp. -- placed any models in the top 10.
But even the Chrysler cars are imports, built in Japan and
marketed here through Chrysler's dealer network.
The agency said the highest mileage car it tested was a
1980 Volkswagen Rabbit equipped with a diesel engine and
five-speed transmission. The agency said the car averaged
42 miles a gallon; the runner-up was another Rabbit diesel,
with a four-speed transmission, that averaged 40 miles a
gallon.
Two Chrysler imports, the Dodge Colt and the Plymouth
Champ, tied for third place with an average of 37 miles a
gallon. Next came a Honda Civic, imported by Honda Motor
Co., and two Volkswagen Dasher diesels, tied at 36 miles a
gallon. One of the Volkswagens, which are sold by
Volkswagen of America, Inc., was the only station wagon
among the top 10.
Completing the top-ranked models were other versions of
the Colt, Champ and Civic, all with 35 miles a gallon.

The EPA said the top-rated domestic 1980 model was a Chevrolet Chevette with a four-speed transmission. The General Motors Corp. car averaged 26 miles a gallon in its tests, the agency said.

At the other end of the scale, EPA cited two Rolls-Royce models with 10 MPG as the cars with the worst mileage. Among the domestic cars in the low-mileage category were some twenty-two Chrysler and G.M. models, which tied for the lowest mileage at 14 MPG.

C. Overseas Investment Policy and "Captive" Imports.

It is a historical fact that the major U.S. automobile manufacturers are not merely domestic producers of cars and trucks, but large multinational companies, with substantial overseas investments, which import significant quantities of automotive vehicles and parts from foreign subsidiaries, affiliates, and unrelated manufacturers. Their current worldwide investment policies, and their plans for a "world car," are further indications that their reliance on overseas supply sources in the proximate future is likely to increase -- to the detriment of automobile production and employment in the United States.

In Canada, for example, G.M. operates three assembly plants; Ford operates two; and Chrysler and American Motors operate one each. According to the Commission's staff, more than one-half of the total automobile and light truck production in these plants is exported to the United States (U.S.I.T.C. 1980, A-23).

Elsewhere, G.M. operates substantial manufacturing facilities: Vauxhall in the United Kingdom, Holden in Australia, Opel in West Germany, GM de Mexico, and plants in Brazil and Columbia. Ford is a major producer in West Germany and the United Kingdom. In addition, U.S. producers have numerous formal cooperative arrangements with foreign producers: quasimergers, joint-production and/or joint-marketing and distribution arrangements, components-purchasing agreements, and technology sharing. According to the Commission's staff, "inter-company ownership is widespread. GM, Ford, and Chrysler, for example, own substantial shares of Isuzu, Toyo Kogyo, and Mitsubishi, respectively, and jointly produce, develop, and market vehicles and components" (U.S.I.T.C. 1980, A-28).

Import statistics, in part, reflect these foreign investments and arrangements. Again according to the Commission's staff, "All five U.S. manufacturers import either automobiles, light trucks, or both, in significant quantities. Excluding VW of America, U. S. producers' imports of automobiles and light trucks accounted for nearly 28 percent and 70 percent, respectively, of all imports of these items into the U. S. in 1979" (U.S.I.T.C. 1980, A-23; emphasis is supplied). The volume of these "captive" imports is just one objective indication that the U.S. multinational companies have chosen to supply a significant part of the U.S. demand for small cars and light trucks by manufacturing or buying them abroad rather than making them here at home.

The recent investment decisions by the U.S. automobile multinationals are yet further evidence of the same proclivity. While complaining about rising import shares of the U.S. market -- and demanding mandatory import quotas (Ford and Chrysler) or "voluntary" quotas (G.M.) -- they continue to pour billions of dollars into their foreign operations, while closing down many of their domestic plants which are in dire need of modernization, conversion, or rebuilding. The General Motors (1980) Annual Report for 1979 offers dramatic documentation:

> are moving aggressively to become a more important factor in the world market. We are continuing the movement begun over a year ago to strengthen our overseas activities and to integrate them more fully into our total worldwide operation. In the past year, we have initiated major expansions or new investments in Australia, Austria, Brazil, Colombia, Mexico, Spain, and Venezuela. (p. 3)
>
> In a continuing program to improve its competitive position overseas, GM announced in June that it will build new assembly, manufacturing, and component facilities in Spain and a plant to manufacture automobile engines in Austria. Total investment in these and other European facilities will exceed $2 billion, the largest overseas expansion ever undertaken by GM. Production is scheduled to begin in Spain and Austria during late 1982. (p. 6)
>
> General Motors announced plans to build a new plant near Melbourne, Australia to manufacture four-cylinder engines. (p. 6)
>
> General Motors also announced a major expansion in Brazil including the conversion of a former diesel engine manufacturing plant to the production of automotive gasoline engines. (p. 6)
>
> GM acquired from Chrysler Corporation a car and truck assembly plant in Valencia, Venezuela, and a 77.4% equity interest in a car and truck assembly operation in Bogota, Colombia, a country where GM has not previously produced vehicles. (p. 6)
>
> Major expansion programs for the subsidiary (GM de Mexico, S.A.) announced during the year included increased assembly capacity and the addition of a new engine plant. (p. 6)
>
> An increasing proportion of GM's capital spending is for requirements outside the U.S. Key projects include GM of Canada expansions under way in Windsor and St. Catherines, Ontario, as well as those in Australia, Austria, Brazil, Mexico, and Spain, as described previously. (p. 11)

Obviously, this investment pattern is not calculated to hasten the construction of sorely needed new plants, or the conversion of existing plants, for the production of small cars and light trucks in the United States. It is not calculated to hasten the reemployment of the roughly "300,000 workers (UAW members) who were on temporary or indefinite layoff in 1980/81." Such an investment pattern is not consistent with industry emphasis on the need for capital in order to lift the U.S. auto industry out of its doldrums.

Industry hopes are focused on a "world car" which would be an amalgam of components, manufactured in different countries around the globe, rather than an automobile manufactured in the United States to combat foreign penetration of the U.S. market. The move toward the world car is already well launched, and a Ford Motor Co. executive concedes that there is "something foreign in everything" that the domestic companies turn out. Thus, the Wall Street Journal, 14 May 1980, reports:

> The parts list for some current and future U.S. autos has a global flavor: engines from West Germany and Japan, brakes from Brazil, clutches from France, and so on, from Spain to Singapore....
> Chrysler's Omni and Horizon subcompacts, for example, draw 14% of their content from abroad, including German engines, manual front-wheel-drive transmissions and starters. This fall, a large number of Chrysler's widely touted new Aries and Reliant compacts will use Japanese engines.
> Ford's long-awaited small car, the Escort, which also makes its debut this fall, will use some front-drive systems from Japan, as well as steering wheels. Other steering parts will be British, key front suspension parts will be Spanish, and fuel pumps will be Italian. GM recently went to the expense of putting up a plant in Singapore to make radio parts, and is considering buying Japanese diesel engines for some future Chevettes. Some versions of that car already use French transmissions.

The Wall Street Journal notes the irony: "at the same time it is considering foreign engines for future U.S. models, Ford is cutting back at a big Cleveland engine factory and has told some 1,200 workers they may be jobless for up to three years until a different, new engine is assigned to their plant." (Wall Street Journal 14 May 1980).

In sum, if domestic automobile manufacture has suffered injury, or is threatened with injury, a significant cause lies in the decisions of U.S. multinational manufacturers to purchase foreign automotive products and to invest abroad.

V. THE JAPANESE AGREEMENT OF 1980

Ultimately, the International Trade Commission (1980) rejected the Ford and UAW petitions, but a massive, management-labor lobbying effort, using the good offices of the federal government, persuaded the Japanese to accept "voluntary" quotas on automobile exports to the United States. Under the agreement, the Japanese promised to reduce their exports from 1.82 million vehicles (1980) to 1.68 million during the first year of the pact and, during the second year, to take no more than 16 percent of the growth (if any) in U.S. domestic automobile consumption. The effects of the agreement are not difficult to predict:

1. The quota will restrict competition in the U.S. market for passenger automobiles and light trucks. Experience shows that this normally means higher prices, poorer product quality, and less variety available to the consuming public.

2. The quota will result in an increase in small car and light truck prices and thus exacerbate the inflationary pressures which U.S. policymakers are trying to control. Prices of both imported cars and domestic small cars will rise, because of the artifically induced scarcity -- a point which Ford conceded in its petition. It admitted that the price of imported vehicles in short supply "undoubtedly would rise" (Ford Motor Co. 1980, 55), and estimated the increase to amount to 8-15 percent (Ford Motor Co. 1980, 56) -- precipitating, of course, a concomitant price increase on domestic models competing with the foreign products subject to the quota.[10]

3. The quota is not likely to induce an immediate shift from imports to domestically produced small cars because, as the commission's staff noted, "the U.S. auto industry's ability to satisfy the rapid shift in demand to smaller cars [in 1979/80 was] less than adequate. While sales of subcompacts and compacts between January 1979 and June 1980 were at least 9.3 million units, U.S. capacity to produce these was no more than 7 million units" (U.S.I.T.C. 1980, A-68). The problem of a distorted product-mix would be alleviated only when Detroit converted its production capacity from preclusive reliance on "intermediate" and "full-sized" cars to making the smaller, fuel-efficient, quality cars demanded by the market.

4. By artificially restricting the supply of small, fuel-efficient cars, the quota will not necessarily induce large numbers of consumers to buy "intermediate" or "full-sized" cars, because many of them are able to delay purchases of new automobiles by driving their old cars longer, buying a used car, or turning to alternate means of transportation.

5. The quota will adversely affect the nation's efforts to conserve energy. It will do so by artificially curtailing the availability of small, fuel-efficient cars in the U.S. market, and forcing at least some consumers to purchase or retain larger, less fuel-efficient cars which, in the absence of the quota, they would have preferred not to do.

6. The quota will not be instrumental in alleviating the national recession which is one of the major factors causing the auto industry's current malaise. Proper monetary and fiscal policies, not import restrictions, are the weapons designed for this purpose.

7. The quota -- by artificially restricting the supply of vehicles wanted by consumers -- will mean higher prices and higher profits for the U.S. producers. Thus, it will -- in theory -- increase their ability to finance the necessary conversion of domestic facilities from large-car to small-car production and hasten the adjustment of their product-mix to prevailing patterns of consumer demand. At the same time, however, it will reduce the competitive pressure on the companies to undertake such conversion or to proceed with it as rapidly as possible. The quota does not compel the companies to do what the unfettered operation of the market already indicates they must do. It does not exact a quid pro quo in return for government protection from competition. It offers no assurance that the additional funds, generated by higher prices and profits,

will indeed be invested in new production facilities <u>within</u> <u>the</u> U. S. rather than overseas or in Mexico or Canada. The quota, therefore, carries no guarantee that the U.S. auto multinationals will use the higher prices and higher profits generated by the quota to make the kind of investments which are required to enhance domestic employment in the automobile industry. Indeed, current plans for the so-called world car are not a positive omen on this score.

Perhaps, the <u>Wall</u> <u>Street</u> <u>Journal</u>, 20 March 1981, provides the most pithy summary of the consequences to be expected from the quota agreement with the Japanese:

> A quota is a quota, whether legislated or negotiated.... In both cases, a limit of Japanese imports would reduce consumers' opportunities to buy the cars they want. In both cases, it would take away the pressure on the U.S. auto industry to lower labor costs and boost production efficiencies -- in short, to regain international competitiveness. In both cases, it would raise prices and lower the quality of customer service, by reducing the intensity of competition.... Indeed, in some ways, a voluntary export restraint might even be worse. For it to work -- and according to Attorney General Smith, for it to comply with U.S. antitrust law -- the Japanese Ministry of International Trade and Industry (MITI) would have to form some kind of cartel to divvy up U.S. market shares among Japanese car-makers. So not only would GM, Ford, Chrysler and Volkswagen be spared the full force of Japanese competition. Honda, Toyota, Nissan (Datsun), Fuji (Subaru) and Toyo Kogyo (Mazda) would also stop struggling so vigorously with <u>each</u> <u>other</u> for U.S. sales.

Obviously, an increase in competitive pressure, rather than its relaxation, is required to upgrade the industry's delinquent performance. Only such pressure can compel the industry to adapt its product-mix to consumer demand; to build the modern, efficient plants to make it viable by world standards; and to undertake determined action to end its endemic price-wage-price spiral.

VI. CONCLUSION

On the basis of the foregoing evidence it is apparent that, in the U.S. automobile industry at least, corporate bigness is not necessarily endowed with superior efficiency, and it is not necessarily a felicitous instrument for promoting consumer welfare. The same is true in the U.S. steel industry (see, e.g., Adams 1982, ch. 3), and probably in other mature oligopolies which have succeeded in immunizing themselves from competition over extended periods of time. In such industries, concentration <u>does</u> make a difference in terms of firm conduct and industry performance.

So does absolute size. The giant corporation, especially when it enters into tacit, vertical collusion with a powerful trade union, becomes a political as well as an economic institution. Without necessarily exercising market power in the diverse industries in which it may operate, it possesses the political power, by virtue of its absolute (rather than relative) size, to influence the rules by which the competitive game is played. It tends to spend almost as much energy manipulating government policies for its own benefit as it does competing in the marketplace, improving productivity, or planning technological breakthroughs. It seeks governmental favors, subsidies, and privileges. It pleads for relief from "onerous" burdens like clean air, pure water, industrial safety, and energy-conservation regulations. Above all, it expects the government to compensate it for its own mistakes which, given the firm's giant size, are likely to be of gigantic proportions.

These government bailouts -- whether in the form of protection from import competition or in the form of protection from bankruptcy -- are increasingly becoming standard operating procedure. If the process is allowed to continue (under the cynical guise of a "Darwinian survival of the fittest"), the American economy may well be populated by politico-economic giants intent on pursuing the quiet life in an Ordnungswirtschaft guaranteed by the state.

FOOTNOTES

1. As Lee Preston points out, economic efficiency can be analyzed on at least three levels. Efficiency I consists of the production of the most desirable combination of goods and services from among all those that are technologically possible. This is the notion of allocative efficiency in the social sense -- broader, incidentally, than the traditional Holy Grail of Pareto optimality. Thus, Preston's Efficiency I could be regarded as equivalent to Clark's ideal of fair competition as defined in Social Control of Business, that is, the organization of production to achieve the "lowest terms of ultimate expenditure and sacrifice."

   Efficiency II has a more narrow focus, and examines the process of minimizing the level of costs incurred in producing a particular quantity of a particular product. This is the notion of managerial or engineering efficiency, which generally does not include concerns about economy-wide resource allocation.

   Finally, dynamic or innovative efficiency. Efficiency III, determines the rate at which an industry is generating useful technological or service innovations and introducing them as market alternatives. See U.S. Senate 1973, 296.

2. After touting superior efficiency and performance as the products of bigness, Bork (ironically) rejects the use of performance tests and efficiency defenses in antitrust proceedings because "they are spurious" and hence "cannot measure the factors relevant to consumer welfare" (Bork 1978, 124). He contends that neither a court nor an agency can determine "whether there exists in a particular industry a persistent divergence between price and marginal cost; the approximate size of the divergence; whether breaking up, say, eight firms into sixteen would reduce or eliminate the divergence; and whether any significant efficiencies would be destroyed by the dissolution" (Bork 1978, 125). Thus he

despairs not only about our ability to measure performance in terms of static efficiency, but also dynamic efficiency. He leaves us with the tautological faith that existing firms must be efficient; if they were not, they would have been replaced by more efficient newcomers; the fact that they have not been replaced by more efficient newcomers proves that they must be endowed by superior efficiency.

3. Another prime example, of course, is the steel industry's efforts to escape the consequences of its lamentable performance through protection from foreign competition. See Adams and Dirlam 1977; No Author 1977.

4. See White 1982; and Wright 1979. Other analysts of the industry's performance have been more charitable. Writing in 1949, Edward S. Mason concluded that, despite its high degree of concentration, the performance of the automobile industry during the decades of the twenties, thirties, and forties was "relatively good" (Mason 1949, 1265). Some twenty years later, John Kenneth Galbraith dismissed any concerns about structure-performance links in the auto industry, and applauded firm size as a beneficent planning instrument: "The size of General Motors is in the service not of monopoly or the economies of scale but of planning. And for this planning -- control of supply, control of demand, provision of capital, minimization of risk -- there is no clear upper limit to the desirable size. It could be that the bigger the better. The corporate form accomodates to this need. Quite clearly it allows the firm to be very, very large" (Galbraith 1967, 76-77).

5. Organized labor, conscious of its power to exploit the industry's oligopoly in the product market, exacerbated the Big Three's suicidal market strategy. According to Charles L. Schultze, for example:
    "In the mid-1960s hourly employment costs (wages and fringe benefits) in the major auto companies were about 20% above the average for manufacturing industries. Every three years since, the labor contract negotiated between industry and the union has widened the gap. By 1978 wages and fringes at the major auto companies had risen to almost 50% above the all-manufacturing average. Those extra costs were passed on in higher prices.
    "Finally, in 1979 -- faced with mounting interest rates, an incipient recession, sharply higher gasoline prices, growing resistance to large American cars and increased imports from Japan -- what did the industry do? It negotiated a contract that by 1980 put auto wages and fringes about 60% above the manufacturing average" (The Wall Street Journal, 20 March 1981). See also Anderson and Kreinin 1981; and Kreinin 1982.

6. A study by the U.S. Department of Commerce lent additional support to this analysis. It found that the increasing import share of the U.S. car market from late 1974 to early 1975 was not attributable to "stepped-up marketing on the part of importers," but rather appeared "to be due to the fact that the market segments in which imports generally compete -- the compact and

subcompact market -- hold up better than the market for large cars." The Commerce Department study summed up the apparent reasons for decline in production and sales of domestic automobiles as follows: "Declining real income; record interest rate levels; depressed levels of consumer confidence in the economy; and the change in consumer preference for more energy efficient vehicles, which U. S. manufacturers did not adequately perceive" (U.S. Department of Commerce 1975).

7. The cyclical character of the automobile industry is, of course, also reflected in employment statistics. As the Commission's Staff Report notes, the 29 percent drop in employment during the current downturn (amounting to some 300,000 workers) is not dissimilar from the pattern of previous recessions: "In 1969-70 the overall decline in employment was 27 percent, or about 265,000 workers, while in 1973-75 the overall decline was 25 percent, or about 244,000 workers" (U.S.I.T.C. 1980, A-51).

8. "In some States with low usury ceilings," according to the ITC Staff Report, "manufacturer's subsidiary finance companies were the only source of credit" (U.S.I.T.C. 1980, A-66). In the summer of 1981, General Motors offered 13.8 percent finance charges through GMAC in lieu of rebates in sticker prices.

9. At the same hearing, I submitted the following testimony: "If the U.S. industry persists in its recalcitrance to comply with fuel-efficiency and/or pollution control standards, this will not deter foreign manufacturers from making cars with these characteristics available to American consumers. In that event, the next fuel crisis will result once again in a massive import invasion of the American market. It will lead to renewed demands for the exclusion of foreign competition in order to avert widespread plant closings, pervasive unemployment, and untold damage to the national economy. Such demands will be a form of corporate blackmail -- an insistence on a government bailout -- to permit an industry to survive from a self-inflicted injury."

10. The pattern unfolded even before the agreement was sealed. According to The Wall Street Journal, 10 September 1980, domestic producers posted the largest price boosts for 1981 models on their smaller cars (which were selling well and were in relatively short supply) while reserving smaller price increases for their large cars (which were in relative oversupply). Nor was this pattern a novel phenomenon. Again, according to the Journal: "In October [1979], 1980-model prices rose 4.5% to 5% overall from final prices on 1979 models. Prices of many small cars rose about twice that average. During the 1979-model year, prices were raised several times in a similar pattern. As a result, some small cars are tagged more than 20% higher than a year ago. And because dealers are discounting their slow-moving stock of bigger cars, a buyer often drives home a flashy cruiser for hundreds of dollars less than a boxy compact" (The Wall Street Journal, 26 September 1979; emphasis supplied).

BIBLIOGRAPHY

Adams, W., ed. 1982. *The structure of American industry.* 6th edition. New York: Macmillan Publishing Co.

Adams, W., J. B. Dirlam. 1964. Steel imports and vertical oligopoly power. *Amer. Econ. Rev.*, (September).

Anderson, R. G., M. E. Kreinin. Labor cost and the U. S. comparative advantage in steel and motor vehicles. *The World Economy*, (July).

Bork, R. H. 1978. *The antitrust paradox.* New York: Basic Books.

Council on Wage and Price Stability (COWPS). 1975. *In the matter of the importation of passenger automobiles from Europe, Canada, and Japan.* Comments of the Staff of COWPS before the U.S.I.T.C. (September 4).

Ford Motor Company. 1980. Petition for relief from increased imports of passenger cars, light trucks, vans, and utility vehicles under Section 201 of the Trade Act of 1974. (mimeo). (August 1) Washington, D. C.

Galbraith, J. K. 1967. *The new industrial state.* Boston: Houghton Mifflin.

General Motors Corporation. 1980. *Annual report for 1979.* Detroit.

Gilder, G. 1981. *Wealth and poverty.* New York: Basic Books.

Kreinin, M. E. 1982. U. S. comparative advantage in motor vehicles and steel. In *The Michigan economy*, ed. H. Brazer. Ch. 6. Ann Arbor: U. of Michigan Press.

Mason, E. S. 1949. The current status of the monopoly problem. *Harvard Law Rev.*, (June).

No Author. 1977. Le protectionisme et l'industrie siderurgigue des Etats-Unis. *Revue d'Economie Industrielle*, (October).

United Automobile, Aerospace and Agricultural Implement Workers of America (UAW). 1980. Petition for relief under Section 201 of the Trade Act of 1974 from import competition from imported passenger cars, light trucks, vans, and utility vehicles. (mimeo). (June 12) Washington, D. C.

U. S. Department of Commerce, Office of Economic Research. 1975. The automotive industry in 1974: an international survey. (April) Washington, D. C.

U. S. International Trade Commission (U.S.I.T.C.). 1975. New, on-the-highway, four-wheeled passenger automobiles from Belgium, Canada, France, Italy, Sweden, the United Kingdom, and West

Germany. Inquiry No. AA 1921-Inq.-2. U.S.I.T.C. Publication 739. (September) Washington, D. C.

———, 1980. Certain motor vehicles and certain chassis and bodies therefor. Investigation No. TA-201-44. Prehearing report to the commission and parties. (September 10 and November) Washington, D. C.

U. S. Senate. 1973. Hearings on the Industrial Reorganization Act. Part 1. Subcommittee on Antitrust and Monopoly. Washington, D. C.

———, 1979. Statement of the General Motors Corporation on the impact of government regulation on the automobile industry. Subcommittee on Economic Stabilization of the Committee on Banking, Housing, and Urban Affairs. (April 26) (mimeo).

The Wall Street Journal. 1979a. (September 19).

———, 1979b. (December 26).

———, 1980a. (May 14).

———, 1980b. (September 10).

———, 1981. (March 20).

White, L. J. 1982. The automobile industry. In Adams 1982.

Wright, J. P. 1979. *On a clear day you can see General Motors: John Z. DeLorean's look inside the automotive giant*. Grosse Point, Mich.: Wright Enterprises.

18

Public Support for the Performing Arts in Western Europe and the United States: History and Analysis

J. Michael Montias

I. INTRODUCTION

In Western Europe, a broad variety of organizations offer plays, operas, classical music, and ballet. Some, like the Dutch orchestra foundations, are akin to American nonprofit organizations; others, especially in Germany and France, are public agencies subordinate to central, regional, or municipal organs of government. In the European capitals, and in some of the largest provincial cities, private proprietary theaters play an important role. Most European performing-arts organizations -- including many private ones -- receive subsidies, although only those that are not strictly private and proprietary are dependent for the bulk of their incomes on public support. Generally speaking, government subsidies are on a lavish scale, while the donations of individuals, businesses, and foundations, in contrast with the United States, are modest or minimal.

Ideally, I would have wanted to link each major organizational form to a pattern of behavior. Lacking information sufficiently detailed to do this, I have had to confine the analytical portions of this paper to a single organizational distinction: between "private proprietary organizations" and "all other organizations" in the performing arts. The latter group comprises nonprofit organizations of the American type and quasi-governmental organizations of the French or German type. I call all companies, enterprises, associations, foundations, or firms belonging to this group "nonprofit organizations" (NPOs), although the reader should keep in mind that some of them may differ substantially from organizations that are legally classified as nonprofits in the United States. However different they may be, most NPOs in Europe and the United States, share one characteristic: they are recognized by virtue of having been created by an organ of government or by an explicit act of a specialized government agency such as the Conseil d'Etat in France or the Internal Revenue Service in the United States, as being of public interest or utility (in German gemeinützig, in French d'utilité publique). This public-utility attribute legitimates the direct aid (subsidies) or indirect support (tax exemptions) that they receive from government agencies.

The paper is divided into several parts. In part II, I summarize the divergent histories of public support for the performing arts in continental Western Europe and the United States; in part III, I assemble statistics on the organization and the financing of theater, opera, concert, and ballet organizations in the 1970s in both parts of the world; in part IV, I analyze the theoretical behavior of nonprofit organization producing "elite" and "popular" shows in competition with a private-proprietary sector producing only "popular" shows. The chief purpose of the modeling exercise employed in part IV is to show the consequences of increased levels of subsidies on the choices made by the manager of this hypothetical NPO between the two types of shows.

II. HISTORICAL SURVEY

France. In Europe, partronage of the performing arts by ecclesiastic and secular authorities goes back to the Middle Ages. In the fifteenth century it was already common practice for the aldermen of Northern French towns to allot funds for the staging of Mystery Plays which were generally put on by members of church groups ("confraternities"). In some instances all the expenses of a play -- chiefly for costumes and staging -- were paid from the town treasury (For details see Magnin 1909, 7-12; Versillier 1973, 23-41). From the late-sixteenth century on, as European kings and princes acquired absolute power, they took over the twin roles of policing and subsidizing the stage. Monopolies and privileges were granted to royal companies that catered to elite tastes. In seventeenth century Paris, companies that did not secure royal or aristocratic patronage and sought to play for a broader public were harassed by the police; if they were not banned altogether, they had to restrict their entertainment to pantomime, puppetry, and other exhibitions that were not in direct competition with the established companies (Bourassies 1875, 4-5). In France and Sweden, theater companies and musical groups in the capital or at the seat of the court enhanced the prestige of the royal house. This was reason enough to merit support.

After the French Revolution of 1789, which proclaimed the freedom of founding new theaters, centralized controls were reimposed, first under Napoleon, then under the restoration. The modern pattern emerged in mid-nineteenth century: in the capital, a handful of subsidized theaters and opera houses coexisting with more numerous commercial establishments (forty-two private theaters in 1878); in the provinces, each municipality of any consequence financing the erection and the operation of a theater building for the free or low-cost use of theatrical and operatic companies (resident in the larger cities, itinerant in the smaller), which frequently also received an operating subsidy from the city. Controls on the repertory and even on the staff of theatrical companies were exercised by the departmental prefects and by the Ministry of the Interior until the 1870s.

Germany and Austria. From the late-seventeenth century on, German and Austrian princes set about creating theaters and opera houses, frequently providing a permanent home and financial support for companies, many of which had been regional touring groups in the past. During the Enlightenment, the notion gained currency among German-speaking intellectuals that the theater was capable of providing an essential part of a good citizen's education and that public funds deserved to be given out to advance this end, just as they were given for the purpose of educating the young (No Author 1964, p. 1776). A Kulturtheater was needed to uphold higher moral, aesthetic, and even patriotic standards. In the absence of political centralization, the emperors of Austria, the kings of Prussia, the princes, margraves, and electors of the German-speaking world created their own court theaters. Emperor Joseph II of Austria founded a national theater in 1776 "for the development of good taste and the improvement of morals" (Herterich 1937, 59-60). From 1791 on, Goethe directed the court theater of Weimar which became a showplace for German Enlightenment. Some municipalities, in emulation of the high nobility, also began to found and support their own theaters and operas about this time.

The eighteenth century debate on the value and purpose of the theater began to affect the administration of theatrical establishments in the first half of the nineteenth century. In 1808 Freiherr von Stein proposed that the Prussian theater be detached from police control and placed under the supervision of the ministry of cults and education. "The theater," he pleaded, "is an educational establishment (Bildungsanstalt)." Bildung, a word with no precise equivalent in English connoting education and cultivation, was the intellectual foundation upon which later advocates of public support for the arts were to build.

Emancipation of the theater from police authority was only accomplished in the wake of the Revolution of 1848. Shortly after that event, Edward Devrient, a leading theater man of his time who was largely responsible for drawing up a plan for reform of the Prussian theater, wrote a widely disseminated manifesto in favor of a subsidized Bildungstheater. "All that is capable of edifying and refining mankind," he argued, "should be protected by the state and be made independent of naked gain; this applies to art as well as to school and church. Competition...must be excluded once and for all. Private industry, whether in the form of rental concessions or of autonomous enterprises, under the present circumstances can bring no higher benefit to the theater; without the backstop of monetary support which will guarantee the independence of the stage from the crowds that bring money, the theater cannot be conducted on pure principles" (Herterich 1937, 60). Prussian nationalism was surely not absent from Devrient's proposals. But his ideas were also influential in cities and smaller states where the desire to base art on high principles (mixed with local pride) motivated the adoption of his policies.

Already in 1818, the general assembly of one of the German kingdoms (Wurtemberg) resolved to subsidize its national theater and opera house in Stuttgart from the regular budget. This lasted only two years, however, after which the assembly refused to meet this "wasteful expense" and the king was forced to meet the deficit of the former Court Theater from his own pocket (No Author 1964, 6). About the same time the municipality of Mannheim began to share in the burden of maintaining the National Theater created in 1774 by the Duke of Gotha. In 1839 the city placed the theater under régie (direct management) and undertook to guarantee all its losses. The city of Freiburg followed Mannheim's example in 1868. The same policy was adopted by Strasbourg in 1886, Mulhausen in 1903 (both of these presently French cities then under German suzerainty), Kiel in 1907, Essen, Hagen, and Leipzig in 1912, Breslau, Dortmund, and Eberfeld in 1913 (Herterich 1937, 9).

In the case of symphonic music, wealthy patrons and "free associations" (freie Genossenschaften) created and financed large new ensembles. Private and cooperative support provided the bridge between the patronage of princes and other potentates of the eighteenth and early-nineteenth centuries and the state-subsidized activities of the post-World War I era.[1]

The rise of publicly and cooperatively supported organizations in the second half of the nineteenth century coincided with a growing gap between bourgeois-popular and elite culture. Elite groups were able to mobilize public support for "serious" theater and music at a time when -- and perhaps because -- commercial enterprises were increasingly pandering to the "bad taste" of the dominant bourgeois public (on this point see Wahl-Ziegler 1978, 34, 35).

By the 1920s, theater, opera, and orchestral music were dominated by gemeinnützig (public-interest) organizations supported by local and state organs. In 1929 these NPOs employed 89 percent of the singers, two-thirds of the actors and actresses, and over 80 percent of the musicians engaged in professional activities (Herterich 1937, 20).

Many of the NPOs were régie enterprises, owned by and directly subordinate to municipal and state organs which covered their financial deficits. The financial guarantees against unforeseen losses, in an industry where such losses frequently occurred due to the vagaries of an uncertain demand, placed a substantial contingent burden on the budgets of the cities and states (later Länder) that had committed themselves to this Kulturpolitiek. Nevertheless, by the 1920s these included virtually all the cities and states that had any theater or opera whatsoever. Data for theater-and-opera subsidies, as initially estimated or forecast (Voränschlage) and as they were actually realized in the 1920s and early 1930s, were published shortly before World War II -- the only ones of the kind that I have come across for any country. They show wide disparities for München (2.3 million DM compared to an estimated 0.8 million), Berlin (4.4 million DM versus 2 million), Wiesbaden (1.5 versus 0.75 million), and Weimar (1.6 versus 1.1 million). On average, losses in the 1926/27 season exceeded estimates by 43.3 percent for state theaters and 35.2 percent for municipal theaters (Herterich 1937, 275, 290-92).

The same statistical source provides a valuable glimpse of the long-term structure of receipts of the German nonprofit theater and opera in 1911, 1926/27, and 1934/35. This structure is compared to data for 1973/74 in Table 1.

Imperfect as the data in Table 1 may be, the trends they reveal are too pronounced to be fortuitous. The share of subscriptions and tickets in total income fell drastically over the years covered, from over 60 percent in the pre-World War I period to 44.5 percent under Nazi rule (for municipal theaters only), down to 12 percent in 1973/74. Private support accounted for a small but significant part of total income in 1911; it has been negligible in recent years. Government support -- the obverse of the above phenomena -- has had to fill an ever-widening gap. As in the pre-World War I period, this gap has been filled by municipal and state (later Länder) subsidies, not by the central or federal government, which, for the most part, has relegated cultural policy to regional and local organs of power.

TABLE 1

Percentage Breakdown of the Earned Income and Subsidies
of the Nonprofit German Theaters   (1911, 1926/27, 1934/35, 1973/74)
  (Percent)

	1911	1926/7	1934/5	1973/4
Subscriptions and tickets (a)	63.2	60.1	44.5	12.0
Radio and TV income	–	0.1	2.3	0.2
Other earned income (b)	5.7	8.2	6.2	5.4
Private Support	3.9	1.0	–	0.1
Government subsidies	27.2	32.3	40.7	81.9
Total Income	100.0	101.7	93.7	99.6

Notes: The percentages do not add up to 100.0 in 1926/7 and 1934/5
        because they have been computed from sector-wide averages
        in each income category, some of which, for lack of detailed
        data, were based on an incomplete coverage of all theaters
        in the sector (note in the source). The data for 1911 cover
        only eight theaters, those for 1934/5 only municipal
        theaters.

   (a) Including sales to theater groups, associations, students,
       etc.

   (b) Programs, cloakroom receipts, guest appearances, tours.

Sources: F. Herterich (1937, 187, 281).
          Deutscher Buhnenverein (1974, 56).

Sweden. In Sweden, as in France, the history of patronage in early modern times coincides with the largesse of the reigning monarchs. During the period of Enlightenment, especially in the second half of the eighteenth century, the kings of Sweden emulated their fellow-autocrats in France, Austria, Prussia, and Russia by founding academies of letters, royal theaters, and opera houses (Sweden, Ministry of Education and Cultural Affairs 1970, 7). After 1809, the Riksdag, or Parliament, which now ruled over the constitutional monarchy, voted the national budget, a modest part of which was given over to support of the arts. The civil officials of the nobility wished to continue the royal patronage of the arts on an eighteenth century scale or beyond, but their pro-art policy was resisted by the economy-minded representatives of the peasantry in the riksdag. The influence of the latter was especially strong in the last forty years of the century. It was not until late in the nineteenth century that representatives of the industrial bourgeoisie and labor members of the Riksdag were able to muster the votes for a more generous arts policy (Sweden, Ministry of Education and Cultural Affairs 1970, 8). But the sluices only became wide open a decade after World War II, once the social democratic governments had met the most pressing social welfare needs of the nation: the arts were now ready for the benefactions that government officials, intent on recreating the brilliant patronage of the enlightened monarchy of the eighteenth century, could at last lavish on them.

The Netherlands. The Dutch national government launched a serious program of support for the performing arts later than the other European countries so far considered; but its commitment, once made, went very deep. The watershed here was World War II, shortly after which a dramatic increase in subsidies to all cultural and welfare activities took place.[2] Symptomatic of the government's enhanced commitment was the decision taken in 1948 to help symphony orchestras break their dependence on the box office by guaranteeing the full salaries of all accredited ochestra players (Netherlands 1977, 12). Since that time the salaries of actors employed by national theaters have also been guaranteed. Thus, when the Nieuw Rotterdamse Toneel and the Nederlandse Comedie closed "under popular pressure" during the course of the 1970/71 season, for reasons discussed below, the government saved very little money because it continued to pay the two theaters' salaries.[3]

The Dutch experience with the large-scale subsidization of music and theater in the 1960s and 1970s is so interesting and instructive that it deserves separate consideration. In the late 1960s, as part of the European youth revolt which culminated in the French university riots of 1968, Dutch students and intellectuals assailed the repertoire of subsidized orchestras and theaters. The Notenkraker (Nutcracker) group raised an outcry against the performance of esoteric music. The "Tomato Action Group" castigated and forced the closing of De Nieuw Rotterdamse Toneel and the Nederlandse Comedie for their failure to stage serious plays relevant to their social concerns. Soon thereafter, in the early 1970s, new companies (Werk Theater, Satyr, Baal, de Appel) were created that specialized in tragedies and serious social plays. The old, established state and municipal theaters adapted their repertoire to this "activist" demand. Light and middle-brow plays and operettas which had helped to stretch out subsidies and sustain socially redeeming works in the past were thrust aside.

This virtual seizure of the subsidized theaters by activist minorities was, from the viewpoint of attendance, a disaster. Attendance at all professional subsidized theaters, which had been hovering around 1.4 to 1.5 million from 1965 to 1969, fell to 1.1 million in the 1972/73 season and 907,000 in the 1974/75 season.[4] What is more, the professional private theater, which had been gradually edged out of the market by the mid-1960s, underwent a brilliant revival in the 1970s. Attendance at private theaters which had fluctuated between 150,000 and 250,000 in the period from 1965-1969 rose to 750,000 in the 1974/75 season. As the director of the Association of the Netherlandish Theater companies put the matter in an interview, the subsidized theater, by specializing in tragedies and serious plays, had left a gap in the market which was soon filled by the private theater. In part IV, a stylized version of this development is analyzed theoretically.

United States. The lack of a tradition of royal patronage combined with a strong Puritan tradition helps to explain the almost total absence of government support for the performing arts in eighteenth and early-nineteenth century America.

New England and Dutch calvinists, the Quakers, and other religious groups strongly disapproved of the theater, which, according to a widely shared view, encouraged "shiftlessness, idleness, and immorality" (cited in Nye 1960, 262). As late as 1774, the Continental Congress issued a resolution calling for the suspension of "horseracing, gambling, cockfighting, exhibition of shows, plays, and other expensive diversions and entertainments" (Nye 1960, 263). In the last one or two decades of the eighteenth century, religious prejudice against theater was still so strong that plays had to be advertised as "moral lectures" (Nye 1960, 264). In a cultural climate of this sort, when cities were still small and most taxpayers were farmers who had not the time, the money, or the inclination to attend performances, the expenditure of government revenue to subsidize the theater was unthinkable.

In the first half of the nineteenth century, British touring companies supplied most of the better theatrical fare. Native companies -- including the popular minstrel shows -- appealed to an uneducated public, which also patronized the circus, the exhibition of freaks, and other outlandish curiosities. The great P.T. Barnum offered both "high" and "low" art. In his autobiography, he explained his policy as follows: "Show business has all phases and grades of dignity, from the exhibition of a monkey to the exposition of that highest art in music or the drama, which entrances empires and secures for the gifted artist a worldwide fame" (Barnum 1871, 71). To be sure, he made more money exhibiting curious animals and freaks than presenting high art, with the exception of singer Jenny Lind's prodigiously successful tours. Barnum expressed views on the business of art that were widely held at the time. "Art," he argued, "is merchantable, and so with the whole range of amusements, from the highest to the lowest.... People cannot live on gravity alone; they need something to satisfy their gayer, lighter moods and hours, and he who ministers to this want is in a business established by the Author of our nature" (Barnum 1871, 72). If God Himself smiled on such enterprises, why should government tamper with them?

Not all Americans conceived of art as an ordinary consumption activity that private enterprise could satisfy just as any other. Already in the 1830s the painter William Dunlap had called for government support of the fine arts including especially the theater, on the model of France and Germany where the theater was flourishing under government auspices (Miller 1966, 36). He proposed that the states establish their own theaters "in order to eliminate the profit motive from theatrical enterprises and thus improve the quality of both the plays and the performances themselves" (Miller 1966, 37). But his plan found no political support and withered on the vine.

Another painter, Rubens Peale, sought to introduce high culture to Baltimore in the 1820s and 1830s by mounting an operation with the aid of civic-minded patrons that combined business and art. His was a farraginous mixture of high and low art and of natural science, typical of his time. The "Baltimore Museum" that he dedicated to the "improvement of public taste and the diffusion of science" exhibited contemporary paintings, copies of old masters, and natural-history specimens; it also staged theatrical performances "in order to meet the annual deficits of the institution" (Miller 1966, 132). When the enterprise began to fail, Peale attributed his difficulties to "the sordid calculations of shortsighted commercial avarice" -- by which he meant his patrons' unwillingness to put up the funds that were necessary to turn it into a success. The subsequent fate of the institution, according to cultural historian Lillian Miller, "is a story of gradual deterioration from a museum devoted to art and science to a theatrical 'saloon' and finally to a P. T. Barnum showcase" (Miller 1966, 234). The city of Baltimore itself, as far as I can make out, never contributed a penny to bail out the failing enterprise.

At the federal level, if there was any serious consideration of subsidizing the arts at all in pre-Civil War days, it was directed toward the plastic arts -- chiefly to the decoration of public buildings. But the government's participation was limited by the apathy of a Congress engrossed in the controversies between North and South, free and slave interests, and national power and states' rights (Miller 1966, 36).

The alternative to commercial theater and opera in the eighteenth and nineteenth centuries was not the state-subsidized quasi-governmental enterprise, but the amateur, religious, or other noncommercial group. Church music and college theatricals flourished already in the eighteenth century.[5] "Thespian" and "Aeolian" musical societies began to mushroom in colleges and cities. The New York Philharmonic Society was founded in 1842 as a cooperative venture, almost exclusively with foreign-born musicians, who paid the expenses and divided the profits. New York's Concordian and Euterpian Societies, Boston's Händel and Haydn Society, and Philadelphia's Musical Fund Society began to cater to the tastes of city elites. After the Civil War, conservatories were founded in all the larger cities. In the late 1870s and early 1880s, wealthy patrons banded together to launch new orchestras and build opera houses. The Metropolitan Opera, founded in 1883, was one such enterprise. Paul DiMaggio has recently shown how in Boston, the traditional "Brahmin" elite, after yielding its dominant position in city politics to a new class of immigrants and parvenus around the time of the Civil War, founded "a system of nonprofit organizations that permitted them to maintain some control over the community even as they lost their command of its political institutions" (DiMaggio 1982, 33-50). The Boston Symphony Orchestra, together with the Museum of Fine Arts, were the kingpins of these NPOs in the arts. These organizations drew their sustenance from a tightly knit group of rich, civic-minded patrons, not from the city treasury. The growing gulf between cultural and political elites of nineteenth century America, which had no evident counterpart in Europe, made it much more difficult to transfer the responsibility for supporting cultural activities from private to public patronage when the old Maecenates could (or would) no longer carry the burden.

The rise of a professional theater "for art rather than for profit" lagged behind the parallel development in music. It was not until shortly before World War I that the first attempts were made to found professional theaters to high-minded artistic ideals.[6] The financial deficits incurred by these avant-garde theaters were met -- if they were met -- by private backers and members' contributions. With the exception of the well-endowed New Theatre founded in New York in 1909, which folded after two seasons of heavy losses, the art theaters were small and economically run. Actors who were not yet unionized were paid very small salaries when they were paid at all. In the 1920s the "noncommercial movement" developed rapidly -- from fifty groups in 1917 to over a thousand by 1929, including college and university theaters (Poggi 1966, 107). The first municipal theaters were founded in this period, including one supported by the town of Northampton in Massachusetts. Large cities, however, did not begin to subsidize the theater until the 1930s, and very few are doing so systematically to this day.

A handful of states, spearheaded by New York, made their initial moves toward a policy of regular support of the performing arts in the late 1960s and early 1970s. The federal government, with the exception of the generously funded Federal Theatre (1935-39), did not, so to speak, get into the act until Congress passed a bill establishing the National Foundation on the Arts and Humanities in 1965 and money was appropriated for its component organization, the National Endowment for the Arts, in the following year (Netzer 1978, 59). Federal government subsidies in the 1970s in part supplemented, in part supplanted, the help given by the major foundations (Ford, Rockefeller)in the 1960s.

To sum up, government at all levels in the United States came to subsidize the arts at least a century after such support had become a regular practice in Western Europe. The lack of a tradition of princely patronage, lingering puritanical attitudes, the dominance of a mercantile spirit, a widespread ideology of self-reliance, the generosity and enterprise of wealthy patrons cooperating to found "societies" to supply the cultural activities they desired, all help to explain the distinct American pattern of development.[7]

We should also take into consideration the more democratic way of running cities and state government in this country that did not give music and theater-loving elites as much opportunity to impose their tastes on the public as in Europe.[8] The idea, fostered by European elites, that theater and music should be part of a good citizen's Bildung never took root in America. Finally, as we shall see in the next section, the more generous provisions for deducting donations to the arts in the U.S. Internal Revenue code stimulated private patronage in the U.S. and staved off the necessity of government help to keep arts institutions on an even keel.

III. A STATISTICAL OVERVIEW OF THE CONTEMPORARY ORGANIZATION AND FINANCING OF THE PERFORMING ARTS

Organizations. Official European statistics cover the heavily subsidized non-profit sector fairly well; data for the private proprietary sector, however, are scarce, and when available, frequently of mediocre quality. What is called "private" may be an amalgam of proprietary organizations and struggling theaters and ballet companies that are too small or too recently founded to be recognized as worthy objects of subsidization by the state. Table 2 illustrates the multiplicity of organizational forms in the theater and opera of the German Federal Republic. The registered associations in Table 2, like the French associations reconnues d'utilité publique, are those judged by a government agency to be of public benefit. In my analysis of public subsidies in the Tables that follow I have taken the registered associations out of the private sector and included them in the nonprofit sector.

"Régie management" refers to direct management by agents appointed by a state (Land) or municipality (Gemeinde) for the account of that agency. The expenditures of theaters and operas under régie management are comprised in the budget of the founding agency. Limited liability companies, by contrast, are responsible for covering their expenditures from their receipts and such subsidies as they may receive from one or more government agencies. Some of these companies were private, others public. The shareholders of the public ones may be states, municipalities, or a mixture of both. Private individuals, as far as I am aware, do not hold shares in these public companies.

Of the forty-five German "culture orchestras" -- essentially, orchestras playing "classical music" -- four were organized under Länder and twenty-one under municipalities, eight were associations, one was a limited-purpose association, and one a corporation under public law (Körperschaft des öffentliches Rechts) (Deutscher Bühnenverein 1974, 49-50).

The organizational status of French theaters and orchestras is as variegated as the German. The Comédie Française, although legally an association (the full-fledged sociétaires still draw part of their income in the form of shares), is in reality a national theater receiving a large part of its income from the central government budget, as do other national theaters (Chaillot, l'Odéon, L'Est Parisien, Strasbourg).[9] Major subsidized theaters in the provinces -- chiefly founded by municipalities -- are linked to the central government by "conventions" or contracts that specify the number of new plays and the total number of performances they must "produce" in a three-year period to earn a fixed amount of subsidies for that period.

In 1979, there were twenty-seven major regional theaters linked to the central government by such "conventions". Most of these theaters were originally founded by municipalities and operated as

TABLE 2
Organizational Forms of Theaters and Operas in the German Federal Republic, 1973/74
(Number of organizations)

	Grand Total	"Private"	"Public" Theaters or Operas Organized Under:			
			Total	States (Lander)	Municipal-ities	Mixed Sponsorship
Individually owned	38	38	-	-	-	-
Registered associations	24	17	7	-	-	7
Regie management	49	-	49	13	36	-
Limited liability companies (a)	40	24	16	3	6	7
Others (b)	17	4	13	-	2	11
TOTAL	168	83	85	16	44	25

Notes: (a) Gesellschaften mit beschrankten Haftung.

(B) Civil law corporations (Gesellschaften burgerliches Rechts), limited purpose associations (Zwechverbanden), companies in which liability of one partner is limited (Kommand Gesell-schaften) and private firms (Offene Handelsgesellschaften).

Sources: Deutscher Buhnenverein (1974, 12-14, 52).

concessions; they have of late been placed under the direct management (régie) of their municipal governments because of the difficulty of finding "concessionaires" willing to take on substantial risks of incurring unforeseen losses (Hue 1979, 19). These provincial theaters make up what the Ministry of Culture and Communications calls "la décentralisation dramatique." More authentically decentralized are the 300-odd "independent companies," most of which apply for central-government aid; of these only about a tenth are successful in the national competition for subsidies. The legal status of some of the small, financially weak companies is often ill-suited to their operation. For if they are organized as associations, the law of July 1901 which regulates such organizations does not allow them to engage in commercial activities and hence to obtain a theater license.[10] Some theaters, nevertheless, are organized as informal associations and even receive subsidies from the central government. A few have opted for the status of "Societé Ouvrière de Production" (workers' cooperative), created "by workers or employees desirous of exercising their profession in common" (Hue 1979, 234). A few theaters have no juridical status to speak of: they are classified as "de facto companies" (societés de fait) and are not eligible for subsidies at all (Hue 1979, 128). All these small "decentralized" companies are essentially nonprofits. But even individually owned theaters and theaters organized as limited-liability companies -- representing the so-called private sector -- may receive subsidies if they produce new plays by French authors or stage old plays in substantially new ways.

In Holland, most subsidized theaters, orchestras, and ballet companies are organized as foundations. The Nederlandse Opera of Amsterdam, for instance, is a foundation covering 75 percent of its expenditures from state subsidies and a part of the rest from hosting provincial municipalities when the opera goes on tour (d'Arschot 1974, 472-85). Such foundations are administered by boards on which representatives of subsidizing government agencies are assured a seat and a measure of influence. In Sweden, national theaters are typically administered by five-member boards, two of which are appointed by the government. The directors of municipal theaters are appointed by the town council which covers the theaters' financial deficits.

The financing of the performing arts. The statistics of receipts and expenditures of performing arts organizations in Tables 3 and 4 below cover exclusively autonomous professional organizations. They exclude orchestras that are part of a radio network and military bands (because they are not professional), and school theaters (because they are neither).[11] In accord with the basic principle of classification set forth in my introductory remarks, nonprofit organizations comprise public institutions, associations, foundations, and joint-stock companies whose shares are held by public institutions. "Private" organizations are strictly proprietary (although they may also receive public subsidies).

In Austria and France, the total receipts including subsidies -- which approximately equal the expenditures or factor costs -- of nonprofit performing-arts organizations vastly exceed those of private organizations. No precise statistics are available for the other countries, but a comparison of the size of audience in the two types of German and Dutch theaters indicates that the predominance of the nonprofit sector holds for these two countries as well.[12]

Table 4, showing the percentage distribution of the total incomes of performing-arts organizations, throws into relief the enormous difference between Western Europe and the United States in financing the arts. In the dominant nonprofit sector, earned income in the five European countries listed represented between a tenth and a third of total income (approximately equal to total expenditures). The Swedes have gone farthest down that route: ticket income accounted for only 10.5 percent of total income in the 1974/75 season (3 percent of the Royal Opera's and 7 percent of the symphony orchestras' total incomes in that season) (Sweden, Statistica Centralbryan 1976, 330-36). Comparable figures for the Paris Opera and the Comédie Francaise were 20 and 21 percent, respectively, in 1974 (France, Ministère de la Culture 1977). In Austria, earned income came to 23.2 percent of total income in the subsidized sector. In contrast, in the United States even the nonprofit sector in the Ford Foundation survey of 166 NPOs covered 55 percent of its expenditures from ticket incomes. In the aggregate, the earned income of the thirty-two U.S. operas covered 65 percent of their total income (Ford Foundation 1974). Even the private theater received generous state and local subsidies in Austria and Germany, amounting to over 50 percent in the former and to roughly a quarter of total income in the latter.

Although the financing of the performing arts in the English-speaking countries other than the United States is not systematically examined in the present study, it may nevertheless be observed that the patterns of public and private support in the United Kingdom, Australia, Canada, and New Zealand more closely resemble those prevailing in the United States than they do those in continental Europe. The share of earned income in the total receipts of NPOs in the United Kingdom, Australia, and New Zealand in the early 1970s may not have been quite so high as in the U.S. and Canada (32 to 49 percent in the first group, 55 to 60 percent in the second), but it was still appreciably higher than in Austria (23.2 percent), Germany (17.7 percent), the Netherlands (20.8 percent), and Sweden (10.5 percent). France, with 31.9 percent, representing the highest share of earned-to-total income in my sample of European countries, was on a par with New Zealand's 32 percent (Throsby and Withers 1979, 148).

In the United Kingdom, Australia, and New Zealand, there was a marked disparity between theater and opera on the one hand, and orchestral music on the other, in the extent to which NPOs covered their expenditures from their own receipts. The share of earned income exceeded 50 percent in theater and opera companies, but it was only 16 to 21 percent for orchestral groups (Throsby and Withers 1978). This difference was not nearly as marked in the United States and Canada. In fact, when orchestras are removed from our list of performing arts organizations, the overall averages are remarkably similar in all the English-speaking countries. On the continent, no clear pattern of privileged public support for music or any of the other arts emerges from the statistics: all forms of "high art" were, and are, heavily subsidized.[13]

Among the sources of support ("nonearned income"), the national government provided a major share in Austria, France, Holland, and Sweden. In the federated system of West Germany, support for the arts is the near-exclusive responsibility of the states (Länder) and the municipalities. In no country of Western Europe did private, business, and foundation support contribute more than a few percent of

TABLE 3
Financing of the Performing Arts, Western Europe and the United States
in the Early 1970s*
(Millions of National Currency Units)

	Date	Earned Income	Direct Subsidies		Private or Foundation	Other Income	Total
			National or Federal	State and Local			
AUSTRIA							
Nonprofit opera and theater	1973	282.2	680.3	253.5	2.1(a)	–	1218.1
Priv.theater (b)	1973	43.0	31.7	21.5	0.5(a)	–	96.7
FRANCE							
Public/nonprofit	1973	136.0	178.0	113.0	–	–	427.0
Private	1973	80.0	1.0	–	–	–	81.0
GERMANY							
Nonprofit (c)	1973/4	195.3	2.9	883.4	5.0	10.6(d)	1097.2
Private	1973/4	n.a.	–	14.3	–	–	n.a.
NETHERLANDS							
Nonprofit theater	1972/3	6.5	12.1	10.8	1.9(e)	–	31.3
other (f)	1972	3.6	16.5	7.6	–	–	27.7
SWEDEN							
Nonprofit	1974/75	29.4	181.7	69.7	–	–	280.8
UNITED STATES							
Nonprofit (g)	1970/1	90.4	3.4	4.9	58.2	10.5(h)	167.4
Priv.theater(i)	1970/1	105.1	–	–	–	–	105.1

Notes: * Operational budgets only, excludes capital expenditures.
(a) Proceeds from lotteries.
(b) Three large private theaters in Vienna.
(c) Theater, opera, and symphony orchestras, only.
(d) Subsidies from public radio-television stations, public
     lotteries ("lotto") and "other public sources".
(e) Financial aid from Omroep Foundation.
(f) Nederlandse Opera, Het Nationale Ballet, and Concert Gebouw
     Orchestra, only.
(g) These estimates, based on the Ford Foundation survey of 166
     performing arts organizations, may seriously underestimate
     the contribution of state and local subsidies, due to under-
     representation in the Ford sample of small companies which
     were more dependent on state support. State legislative
     appropriations to all the arts were $25.2 million, of which
     at least 40 percent, or $10.8 million, were allotted to pro-
     fessional performing arts agencies (see DiMaggio 1981,4-9).
(h) Corpus earnings used for operations plus certain transfers
     from endowments.
(i) Broadway and commercial touring, only (23.5 million audience
     in 1977); excludes small summer stock (4.9 million estimated
     audience), large musical arenas and hard tops (6.6 million),
     and summer theater (11.1 million).

TABLE 4
Financing of the Performing Arts, Western Europe and the United States
in the Early 1970s
(Percent of Total Income)

	Date	Earned Income	Direct Subsidies National or Federal	Direct Subsidies State and Local	Private or Founda- tion	Other Income	Total
AUSTRIA Nonprofit opera							
and theater	1973	23.2	55.8	20.8	0.2	–	100.0
Private theatre	1973	44.5	32.8	22.2	0.5	–	100.0
FRANCE							
Public/nonprofit	1973	31.9	41.7	26.5	–	–	100.0
Private	1973	98.8	1.2	–	–	–	100.0
GERMANY							
Nonprofit	1973/4	17.8	0.3	80.5	0.5	1.0	100.0
NETHERLANDS Nonprofit							
theater	1972/3	20.8	38.7	34.5	6.1	–	100.0
other	1972	13.0	59.6	29.4	–	–	100.0
SWEDEN							
Nonprofit	1974/5	10.5	64.7	24.8	–	–	100.0
UNITED STATES							
Nonprofit	1970/1	54.0	2.0	2.9	34.8	6.3	100.0
Private theater	1970/1	100.0	–	–	–	–	100.0

Sources for Tables 3 and 4:

Austria and Germany: Deutscher Buhnenverein (1974).

France: For Paris-based private and public nonprofit theaters
and orchestras, Ministere de la Culture et de
l'Environnement (1977); for provincial theaters,
orchestras and opera houses, data were extrapolated
from fragmentary statistics for 1970-71 in d'Arschot
(1974, Annex 1).

Netherlands: Ministerie van Cultuur, Recreatie en Maatschappelijk
Werk (1976, 5, 57); data for other nonprofit from
d'Arschot (1974, annex 3).

United States: Ford Foundation (1974).

Sweden: Statistika centralbyran (1976, 330-36).

total income. The United States again marks a sharp departure from the European pattern of finance. Here, private and foundation support made up about four-fifths of the total unearned income of the NPOs in the Ford Foundation sample and perhaps 55 to 60 percent for all NPOs.[14] Even in the English-speaking countries other than the United States, which in this as in other respects represented an intermediate position between the United States and continental Europe, the share of private, business, and foundation support was relatively modest, namely, 8 percent in Australia, 13 percent in the United Kingdom, 6 percent in New Zealand, and 15 percent in Canada (Throsby and Withers 1978, 146).

The relatively low federal subsidies listed for the United States in Tables 3 and 4 are now, of course, antiquated. Total subventions from the National Endowment for the Arts, expressed in 1972 prices, went up from $10 million in 1972 to $90 million in 1980 (Baumol and Baumol 1980, 12). Appropriations by State Art Councils rose from $28 million in 1971 to about $40 million in 1980, also in constant prices. Unfortunately, we do not have financial statistics for performing arts organizations, such as the Ford Foundation collected for the early 1970s, to assess the impact of the increase in government subsidies on the "income gaps" of these organizations. The data available for symphony orchestras alone -- major regional and metropolitan organizations -- do not point to a radical increase in the percentage of total incomes accounted for by government subsidies. Tax-supported grants (federal, state, and local) represented 14.5 percent of the total income of 160 orchestras in 1973/74 and 14.7 percent in 1978/79 (Baumol and Baumol 1980, 3). When the data are in for the entire decade of the 1970s they are likely to show some widening of the "income gap" -- government subsidies accounting for a larger share of total incomes -- but nothing like the preponderance of such subsidies in the budgets of comparable organizations in Western European countries.

So far we have looked only at current government support for the performing arts -- essentially at the operating subsidies of theaters, opera houses, symphony orchestras, and ballet companies. But the total contribution of government to the arts is a good deal larger than just operating subsidies: it includes capital expenditures, which in domains other than the performing arts typically exceed current expenditures, and specialized arts education (music schools and so forth). In France, where the accounts of central government carefully distinguish current and capital expenditures, the capital expenditures in 1973 amoun.ed to about half the level of current government expenditures on the theater and music in 1973, compared to nearly three-quarters of such expenditures in the plastic arts (chiefly for art museums).[15] The statistics of Table 5, wherever possible, comprise both current and capital expenditures as well as specialized arts education (chiefly music and art schools).

Of the data in Table 5 only those for the Netherlands have been published by the government in the desired format. They include both current and capital expenditures and cover central, provincial, and municipal support for the performing and for the plastic arts; they segregate subsidies to special schools, training young people and adults in the various arts; and they are net of any receipts received directly by government organs in each sector. France's data for support of the arts at the central government level are also

TABLE 5
Total Government Support for the Performing Arts in Western Europe and the United States

	Percentage Share of the Performing Arts in:				Government Support for Performing Arts as % of National Income	Per capita Government Support	
	Federal or National Support for the Arts	Total Government Support for the Arts	Federal or National Budget	All Government Budgets		In National Currencies	In U.S. Dollars
Austria (1973) (a)	n.a.	n.a.	0.6	0.51	0.19	166	8.30
France (1973)	27.2	n.a.	0.13	n.a.	0.04 (b)	8.5	2.10 (b)
German Fed.Rep.(1976)(a)	12.0	53.1	0.005	0.30	0.13	17.9	7.00
Great Britain (1970/1)(a)	39.0 (d)	35.4	0.05	0.04 (c)	0.023	0.18	0.44
Netherlands (1975)	38.3	54.5	0.24	0.50	0.23	32.6	13.40
Sweden (1970/1)	63.4	67.0	0.37	0.33	0.19	36.4	6.90
U.S.A. (1974)	40.0	47.0 (b)	0.014	0.02 (b)	0.008 (b)	0.44	0.44

Note: Total government support for the arts includes specialized arts education, museums and conservation of monuments. It excludes television and radio, archives, literature, cinema, and libraries. Current and capital expenditures as well as transfers are covered, except as otherwise indicated.

(a) Current expenditures, only.
(b) Based on a very rough estimation of municipal and other local expenditures.
(c) Exclusive of professional training in the arts.
(d) Includes central government subsidy to the BBC for music and ballet.

Sources: Austria and France: Same sources as Table 3.   Germany: Deutscher Buhnenverein (1979)
Great Britain: Peacock and Godfrey (1976, 91).   Sweden: C.Fabrizio (1975).
Netherlands: Central Bureau voor de Statistiek (1979, 8,24).   U.S.A.: D.Netzer (1978,46,79,90-5).

Government budgets and national income data from each country's official statistical yearbooks.

excellent, but those for local support are at best fragmentary. The British data assembled by Peacock and Godfrey (1976, 90) exclude capital expenditures and professional training in the arts as well, in the case of "total government support," as subventions to historic homes. The United States data are poor at all levels and represent only an approximation to the desired statistics.[16] Nevertheless, the disparity between the level of government support of the performing arts between Austria, Germany, the Netherlands, and Sweden (seven to thirteen dollars per capita), and Great Britain and the United States (less than half a dollar per capita) is so large it cannot possibly be bridged by more comprehensive coverage of expenditures in the Anglo-Saxon countries. Indeed, the inclusion of capital expenditures and specialized arts education in Germany and Austria would in all likelihood widen their lead over the United States and Britain in their level of government support for the performing arts. I doubt whether more complete statistics for French expenditures on the arts at the municipal level would alter France's overall record, about midway between the high-expenditure and the low-expenditure countries.

Indirect support. The data in Tables 2 through 4 refer to direct government support only. They do not reflect the indirect expenditures in the form of tax exemptions, tax deductions, and free rent of government-owned facilities. Tax exemptions are especially important in Western Europe, tax deductions in the United States. In France, the normal rate of the value added tax (VAT) was 17.6 percent in the period covered in the Table. For the arts the tax is legally reduced to 6 percent. But in fact the actual rate, paid by both nonprofit and profit theaters, is still lower. The tax base (base imposable) for the first 140 performances of "dramatic, lyrical, musical or choreographic works newly created in France or of new productions of classical works" (oeuvres classiques faisant l'objet d'une nouvelle mise en scène) is only 30 percent of the ticket price (which is itself, in the case of subsidized works, only a fraction of value added). As a result, a VAT of 2.1 percent of receipts "has almost become the rule in the theater" (Versillier 1973, 90-91). Supposing the full 17.6 percent rate had applied to an estimated 80 percent share of value added in the total expenditures of all professional performing-arts organizations,[17] the tax bill would then have come to 72 million francs in 1973 instead of 5.4 million francs that were actually paid (on the assumption that all performing-arts organizations remitted 2.1 percent of their earned income to the Treasury in the form of VAT). If these numbers are correct, the national government's contribution should be raised from 179 million francs to 246 million francs, or 42.7 percent of the total income of performing-arts organizations. For the nonprofit sector alone, the national government share would then rise from 41.7 percent to 48.5 percent of total income.

In Germany, performing-arts organizations are totally exempt from the VAT (and as far as I can make out pay no other taxes of any significance). If the normal rate of 12 percent of VAT were applied to 80 percent of the expenditures of nonprofit organizations in the sector, they would have to remit 106 million DM to the treasury. However approximate this figure may be, it clearly shows that the indirect contribution of the federal government is many times greater than its direct contribution (of the order of 9 percent of all expenditures including VAT taxes at the 12 percent rate).

Free or subsidized rent of opera houses, theaters, and concert halls make an important "hidden" contribution to nonprofit performing arts organizations all over Europe but one that is difficult to capture statistically. In the Federal Republic of Germany, rental expenses account for only 0.7 percent of the total expenses of all nonprofit theaters and opera houses (Deutscher Bühnenverein 1974, 57). According to a French author's analysis of the expenditures of a "typical" private theater in Paris, rent and rental expenses came to 4.5 percent of total yearly expenditures (Versillier 1973, 76). If we assume comparability of real expenditures in Germany and France, the implicit subsidies stemming from free or concessionary rentals may amount to 3 to 5 percent of the total expenditures of German nonprofit theaters and opera houses.

If indirect aid in the form of rental subsidies and tax exemptions is counted, total government support for the performing arts in the Federal Republic rises above the figures in the last column of Table 5 by about 15 percent, to at least $9.00 per capita.

In Holland, municipalities run their own (subsidized) theaters which sign contracts with theater groups, and opera and ballet companies for performances. They may pay outright for a performance, share in the ticket receipts, or charge rent for the hall placed at the disposal of the performers. A governmental study of seven major Dutch theaters (Schouwburgen) shows that, in the season 1972/73, precisely two-thirds of their total expenditures were covered by subsidies (5.6 million Ft) and only one-third from their rental and other receipts (2.8 million Ft).[18] The subsidy of municipalities to all fifty-four theaters in activity in the season was 16.7 million Ft (but it should be kept in mind that the theaters held opera and ballet performances as well as theatricals). In the same season, the eleven subsidized theater groups covered in the data for Table 3 received subsidies equal to 14.8 million Ft, amounting to 79.2 percent of their total expenditures (Netherlands, Ministerie van Cultuur 1976, 18). When subsidies to theater groups and to theaters are consolidated, they rise up to 39.6 million Ft of which 24.6 million Ft (82.2 percent) from the municipalities, 12.1 million Ft from the central government (30.5 percent), and 2.9 million Ft from the provincial authorities (7.3 percent). The data in Table 5, however, are not affected by these adjustments, since they already comprise both subsidies to theaters and to theater groups.

In France, most of the larger nonprofit theaters and opera houses in the provinces are owned by either a municipality or one of the twenty-one Maisons de la Culture, which themselves are jointly owned by the central government and one or more municipalities. I have not found statistics that would enable me to compute the subsidies associated with the operation of these theaters and opera houses as distinguished from the costs of the performances that took place in them.[19]

Indirect government expenditures on the arts in the United States are of a different nature altogether. The bulk of these expenditures are in the taxes foregone by the federal government whenever individuals make deductible contributions to the performing arts. Mark Schuster, in his doctoral dissertation Income Taxes and the Arts: Tax Expenditures as Cultural Policy (1972, 55), estimated that cultural institutions of all kinds received contributions amounting to $530 million in 1973, of which $310 million, or 59 percent, was in the form of tax expenditures. If this percentage is applied to the estimated $58.2 million donated to the performing arts in 1970/71, we obtain a figure for indirect support of $34 million. This rough estimate is of course intended to cover all NPOs, not just those comprised in the Ford Foundation sample which tallied only $8.3 million in the way of direct subsidies from all governmental services. If this sum of $34 million is added to the $94 million in direct support at all levels of government estimated for 1974, we obtain a figure for total per capita government support of almost $0.60. This is of course still way below the level of government support in the Western European countries in our sample.

The tax legislation of European Countries also encourages donations to the arts, but it is generally less permissive in the provisions it makes for deductions than in the United States. In Germany, individuals may deduct up to 5 percent of their taxable income, and enterprises up to 2 percent of their gross income, for donations aimed at promoting the public interest. In France, individuals may deduct only 0.5 percent of their net income for donations to "organismes d'intéret general" (an additional 0.5 percent is permitted in case the donation is made out to the Fondation de France). Enterprises may deduct up to 1 per 1,000 of their gross income for such purposes. In most instances, aggregate donations came to far less than the permissible limit obtained by applying the maximum percentage to estimated total incomes. Thus, in France, a study made in 1965 showed that donations in a sample of 300 enterprises only amounted to 0.22 per 1,000 of their gross income as against the 1 per 1,000 permitted.[20] Private philanthropic activity in Europe may well be more inhibited by a lack of tradition of giving and by high levels of government support of welfare, educational, and arts institutions. In France especially the patronage of private individuals and firms is regarded with suspicion, for fear of money-minded interference. The tendency is to "demand more state intervention because it offers better guarantees of liberty and equality" (de Varine 1977).

Conclusion. No matter how the financial statistics of the performing arts are put together -- whether or not, for instance, they include capital outlays and indirect government expenditures -- the inference is inescapable that total per capita government support is many times greater in continental Western Europe than in the English-speaking countries.

This conclusion applies to the arts in general. I have already speculated about the origins of these differences in the historical section of the paper. A subsidiary question that I have not addressed is this. What accounts for the differing shares of the performing arts in total government support for the arts in various countries? I have no conclusive answer to this question, but I am struck by the influence on these shares of the historically conditioned burden that the federal or central government must bear for conserving the monuments inherited from past generations. In France and Holland, where about a third of all central-government expenditures for the arts are normally earmarked for conservation, this onerous responsibility exerts an adverse influence on the size and share of the budget for the performing arts. In Sweden, conservation expenditures amount to a much smaller share of the total government support -- less than 10 percent. Here, the performing arts represent a larger share of total support than in the other countries. In this country, which is less encumberd (and embellished) by vestiges of the past, there should be more leeway, given the total amounts budgeted for the arts at all levels of government, to finance the performing arts. I am not confident enough of the data in Table 5, which show that less than 50 percent of total support to the arts went to the performing arts, to assert that this proportion was abnormally low by European standards. In any case, we should recall that the tradition of government aid to museums and to the adornment of public monuments is older here, and perhaps better entrenched, than that of government aid to theaters, opera societies, and orchestra groups. It may be that the proportion will gradually change in favor of the performing arts as American levels and patterns of public support for the arts come to resemble European precedents.

IV. A RETROSPECTIVE ANALYSIS

The story of the European financing of the performing arts may be summarized in the following points.

1. Government support has deep historical roots but has grown especially rapidly in the period after World War II. It now represents the bulk of receipts of professional organizations.

2. The level of private donations, which were never a preeminent source of support (if we except princely patronage which may be likened to government support), has declined over time. They are now a very minor source of receipts in all countries surveyed.

3. Nonprofit organizations (as defined in this paper to include quasi-governmental organizations) have gradually acquired a dominant place in music and theater. In the last ten years, however, the private (commercial) theater in Holland, for reasons that will be explored in the text below, has regained some of the ground it lost to the nonprofit theater in the 1960s.

In this analytical section I outline a model, fully fleshed out in a mathematical note which is available from the author. The model can be made to yield a pattern of behavior consistent with the historical evolution described under points 1., 2., and 3. above.[21] The model is, of course, a stark simplification of this complex history. It abstracts from reality, in particular, by assuming that the costs of producing shows and the preferences of consumers of the performing arts remain constant as government support increases. This approach assumes away the possbility that the widening gap between the expenditures and receipts of performing-arts oganizations was actually due to rising wage costs unmatched by increased consumer expenditures on the products of the industry. Such a rise in wage costs, according to William Baumol's well-known diagnosis of the deteriorating financial conditions of the performing arts, might be ascribed to the fact that performing-arts organizations must pay their personnel wages and salaries that are more or less competitive with those paid in rising labor-productivity sectors (such as manufacturing), despite their failure to match the productivity gains of these sectors. The model also ignores the inroads of the motion pictures, television, and phonograph records on consumer demand for the performing arts which have historically contributed to the gap between box-office receipts and expenses. As we shall see below, the model can accommodate rising production costs or declining consumer demand, but it focuses exclusively on the effects of a change in a single variable -- government support -- all others being held constant.

The model analyzes the behavior of a single nonprofit organization assumed to be representative of all the NPOs in the performing-arts sector. This NPO is engaged in competition with a private (profit-oriented) sector, but only the first-round effects of this competition are tracked in this analysis. When the NPO, for example, reduces the price of a popular type of show that is competitive with shows produced in the private sector, it necessarily encroaches on the sales of the latter. No consideration is given to the possibility that private enterprises might lower their prices to regain at least some of their customers.

Suppose the NPO were offering a single type of show for a uniform price per attendee. It faces a demand schedule for tickets showing what the audience for the show would be at every price. There will normally be a capacity limitation for the size of the audience attending any one performance. Provided customers are indifferent between attending sooner or later, the total audience at any given price may be defined as the capacity attendance multiplied by the number of days during which the show is put on. For an NPO constrained from incurring losses or earning profits, the total audience at which price equals average total cost per attendee determines the number of days during which the show will be performed. If there are two audience levels for which this equality holds -- the first where average cost per attendee is falling, the second where it is rising -- the NPO will presumably choose the higher level of total audience. The only limit that needs to be taken into consideration is the number of days in the season during which shows are normally staged. In the absence of a binding constraint on the limited run of the production, it is evident that, when total costs are reduced, the demand schedule will intersect with average total cost at a point corresponding to a lower price and a larger audience. This will also be the result if the NPO receives government subsidies or private donations which will, in effect, offset its fixed costs.

This one-product model has been subjected to econometric tests. Burkhauser and Getz have estimated the impact of subsidies on the output, measured by the number of performances, and on the employment of nonprofit symphony orchestras. They found that, because the elasticity of demand for tickets was small (from -0.128 to -0.132), subsidies caused only very moderate increases in output and that their main impact was in reducing ticket prices (Burkhauser and Getz 1982, 9-10).

Consider now an NPO producing two kinds of shows -- elite and popular -- where only popular shows compete for the audience of the private profit-oriented sector. Let v and w represent the size of the audience (number of tickets sold) attending elite and popular shows respectively. Normally the demand for the each type of show is represented as a function of its price. But we can also regard prices as inverse functions of audience size. Since the two types of shows are substitutes in consumption, we also want the price corresponding to a given audience size for each type of show to decline whenever the audience of the other type of show increases. An example of two linear price functions satisfying these conditions might be:

$$\Pi = 5 - 2v - .1w$$
$$\Psi = 10 - w - .1v$$

where Π is the price of elite shows and Ψ of popular shows.

In this example, the demand for popular shows is more elastic and greater at any price than that for elite shows. In each equation, own-demand (v in the case of Π and w in the case of Ψ) has a greater impact on price than the demand for the other type of show. (If this were not so, simultaneous equilibrium in the two markets would not be possible.)

The net revenue of the NPO may be written:

$$NR = \Pi v + \Psi w + S + D - C$$

where S denotes government subsidies, D private donations, and C total costs, which will normally be an increasing function of v and w.[22] If the organization is neither to make profit nor to suffer a loss, this expression must be set equal to zero.

In contrast to the one-product model discussed above, there will generally be an infinite number of combinations of v and w that will satisfy the net-revenue-equal-zero constraint, for given levels of subsidies and donations. In Figure 1 each ellipse-like countour is the locus of all such combinations corresponding to a certain level of S and D (both assumed here to be constants, exogenous to the problem). With the smallest S and D, only the innermost contour is attainable. Since it does not intersect either axis, we know that some of both types of shows must be produced if no losses are to be incurred. Points on a given contour located below the straight line marked d(NR)/dv = 0 and to the left of the line marked d(NR)/dw = 0 are inefficient in the sense that more of both types of shows could be produced without violating the constraint. (They are equivalent to a point equating average cost and average revenue at a low level of output in a one-product model.) A point such as q located inside the contour would generate profits. By definition, it would be shunned by the NPO. A point outside a given contour would be unattainable, given the level of S and D corresponding to this contour, because it would be conducive to losses. As the level of S and D increases, we pass on to successively higher contours. With the second contour, it becomes possible (though inefficient) to meet the no-loss constraint while producing nothing but popular shows. The third contour indicates a level of S and D so large as to make it possible to produce nothing but elite shows, even though there was less demand for them than for popular shows. In this particular case S and D are even large enough to cover all fixed costs so that both shows could be staged at no charge at all to consumers.

This rather laborious introduction is intended to drive home a key point of this paper: the imposition of a no-profit-no-loss constraint leaves the manager of an NPO with considerable scope to choose the mix of popular and elite shows that best suits his preferences or whatever goal he may be pursuing (including the satisfaction of his administrative superiors or the support of the constituency that elected him to his job). The mathematical analysis (presented fully in the note, available from the author) may be used to ascertain the choices that a manager would make, for various levels of S and D, if he were bent on maximizing his audience for elite

FIGURE 1

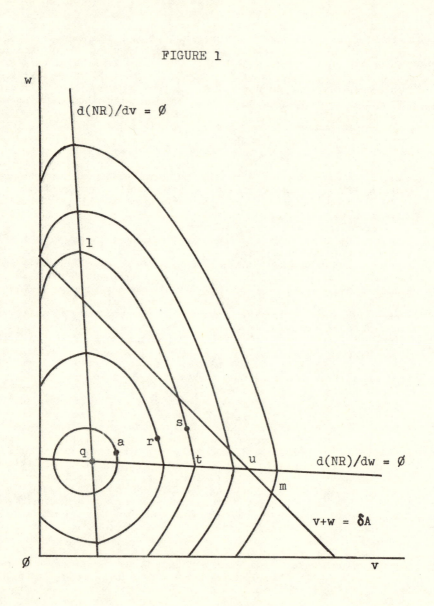

shows. It is readily shown that he would set a price for popular
shows that would maximize his net revenue from staging such shows and
expand the level of output of elite shows to a point where their price
Ⅱ would fall below marginal cost. Indeed, the manager, given
sufficiently high S and D, might wish to drive the price of elite
shows below zero: he might use the profits made on popular shows to
pay audiences to attend his elite shows. This is an example of the
well-known phenomenon of cross-subsidization familiar to students of
NPOs (James 1981). Less immediately obvious is the conclusion of the
model that an increase in subsidies will normally cause the manager to
increase v at the expense of w, the audience for popular shows. This
point is illustrated in Figure 1 by the negative slope of the line
marked d(NR)/dw = 0, the locus of all combinations of v and w selected
by a manager maximizing v, given increasing levels of S and D. (It is
easily verified that this line will be straight if the price and cost
equations are all linear in v and w.)[23] The reason why w must
diminish as subsidies and donations increase is that these outside
sources of finance obviate the need for cross-subsidizing elite shows
from the profits of the more popular shows.

A second aim of the model is to predict the impact of higher
levels of S and D on the prices of the two types of shows. Now it is
immediately obvious that as v increases in response to higher levels
of S and D, the price of v must fall (since the decline in w is only
moderate compared to the increase in v, which has a stronger impact on
Ⅱ than does w). But what happens to the price of popular shows,
competitive with the shows put on in the private sector, as the level
of S and D. rises? We have seen that the level of w will undergo a
moderate decline. This should, other things equal, cause a rise in Ψ.
But there is also the larger increase in v to take into account, which
should have a depressing effect on Ψ. It is shown in the mathematical
note that if the cross-effects of v on Ψ and of w on Ⅱ are about the
same size, the net impact of the two tendencies will be to leave Ψ
unchanged.

The capacity limitation mentioned earlier stems from the limited
length of the season. The constraint will only bind if the total
demand for both types of shows is high enough for the NPO to run a
number of performances in excess of the days available in the season.
Such situations -- possible for various combinations of v and w -- are
represented in the figure by the straight line with a unit negative
slope marked v + w = δA, where δ is the number of days in the season
and A is the daily capacity of the theater or hall available to the
NPO. Starting from a demand-constrained regime, an increase in
subsidies may eventually cause the NPO to run up against its capacity
constraint. If it is expanding along the line d(NR)/dw = 0
(consistent with the manager's maximization of v), it will hit the
constraint at point u. Any further increase of S and D would involve
a sharper trade-off between v and w than before. Moving along the
capacity constraint from u to m, for instance, would require the NPO
to reduce w at the same rate as it is increasing v, which implies in
effect that every extra day during which it stages an elite-type show
must be compensated by a one-day reduction in the run of the popular-
type shows. This will necessarily cause an increase in Ψ (since Ψ is
necessarily more sensitive to a decrease in w than to an increase in v
of the same magnitude).[24]

The model is more flexible than this stripped-down version might indicate. The analysis in the mathematical note introduces separate quality variables for elite and popular shows. As the quality variable increases (e.g., as the number of different productions of a given type of show is raised), the demand for this type of show rises, but at a diminishing rate. It turns out that, under reasonable assumptions about cross-effects (of v on Ψ and w on Π), the same results hold as in the simpler model in the case where it was assumed the manager was maximizing the audience of elite-type shows: an increase in subsidies and donations will cause w to decline at a moderate rate as v rises.[25]

The consequences of growing government support for the performing arts, culminating in the experience of Holland's theaters in the period from 1965 to 1975, may be traced heuristically with the help of the model. We may begin by assuming that in the 1960s the managers of Dutch theaters had only a moderate preference for elite-type shows. They were perhaps maximizing their total audience at a point such as a in Figure 1. As subsidies rose they moved from a to r and then to s, still using popular shows to subsidize elite shows. Along this path, prices of popular as well as of elite shows were declining.[26] The NPO sector must have been encroaching on the market of the commercial theater. In the late 1960s, under pressure of the Tomato Movement and of other student groups, the managers of NPO theaters changed their policy: henceforth, they chose their mix as if they were maximizing the audience of elite shows. With a constant level of subsidies, they moved from a mix indicated by point s to one on the same contour indicated by point t. The drastic decline in w concommitant with this move would have been associated with an increase in Ψ, thus reducing the NPO's competitiveness with the commercial sector.[27] With an increase in subsidies, a manager still pursuing the maximization of v would have traveled along the line from t to u until he encountered a capacity limit. Along this path Ψ would have remained approximately constant. Any further increase in subsidies would have compelled the NPO to give up one unit of w for every unit increase in v, as it moved from point u to point m in Figure 1 along the capacity constraint. This, as I have already explained, would have caused another round of increase in Ψ, tantamount to a further loss in the NPO's competitive position vis-à-vis the commercial sector in the market for w. If enough NPOs behaved in this manner, as I believe Dutch theaters did in the early 1970s, the joint effect of their output decisions would be tantamount to a withdrawal of the nonprofit sector from the market for popular shows. This behavior would be sufficient to explain the extraordinary revival of the commercial theater during the first half of the 1970s, which regained much of the ground lost to the NPOs during the 1960s.

In the Dutch story government subsidies played a predominant role, private donations a negligible role. Still, if the model is to have wider application, it may be useful to dwell on the factors determining the level of donations (so far considered exogenous like subsidies). Henry Hansmann (1981), in his model of the performing arts, which inspired my own attempt at modeling the impact of outside financial support on the output of art services, assumes that donations in a one-product NPO will be a constant fraction of the surplus enjoyed by consumers of the product. This consumers' surplus is approximated by the area under the conventionally drawn demand

curve. It is easily shown that the effect of a marginal increase in
subsidies on this surplus must be positive. In my view this is an
unrealistic treatment of donations, at last in Europe where
foundations do not give matching grants contingent on government
support. In particular, the positive effect of government subsidies
on donations postulated by Hansmann is hard to reconcile with the
negative association between donations and subsidies revealed by the
European experience. In any event, as far as strictly private
donations are concerned, I would argue that patrons of the performing
arts are more likely to donate money to their favorite organizations
if they fear that, in the absence of their donations, the show will
not go on. Granted that the size of their potential donation will be
partly determined by their consumers' surplus -- a measure of how much
they would be willing to give rather than do without the service
altogether -- the fraction of that surplus they will be willing to
give may well be inversely correlated with their expectations of the
level of output of the NPO (as long as they consider that level to be
beyond their own individual influence). If so, the fraction of
consumers' surplus donated will be a number from zero to one,
diminishing with v. As is explained in greater detail in the
mathematical note, the effect of an increase in government subsidies
will be to increase donations at a diminishing rate until some
critical value of v is attained. From that point on, further
increases in subsidies will cause donations to decline and eventually
cause them to go down to zero. When donations are on a rising
trajectory, their effect is to reinforce the impact of increasing
subsidies on v. Conversely, on a falling trajectory, they will
diminish the impact of increasing S on v. (Needless to say, if
government subsidies are tied to matching funds from private sources,
donations will be more strongly correlated with subsidies than this
model would lead one to expect.)

We are now ready to explore the consequences for consumer welfare
of increasing the level of government subsidies proferred to NPOs. We
have found so far that NPO managers were able to exercise discretion
in their output mix in meeting the no-profit-no-loss constraint and
that subsidies, by relieving them of the financial necessity of
producing popular shows that they had no personal interest in staging,
could reinforce their personal inclination to put on mainly elite
shows. If "consumers' welfare", as experienced by consumers at each
point in time, is our criterion, then it is pretty obvious that a
manager concerned only with putting on elite shows will act in such a
way as to reduce welfare if he receives larger subsidies. This is so
almost by definition since shows are only "popular" if they please
consumers, and any reduction in the number of popular productions
and/or tickets sold to such shows must reduce their welfare. A more
analytical way of looking at the matter is to argue that since profits
are being made on w and losses on v, the marginal rate of substitution
of consumers, equated to the ratio of market-clearing prices Π and Ψ,
cannot be equal to the relative marginal costs of the two types of
shows. As long as marginal rates of transformation (ratios of
marginal costs) are not equal to marginal rates of substitution for
consumers, Pareto-optimality cannot be achieved.[28] Operating the
model in reverse gear, we can readily see that a cut in subsidies, by
inducing an increase in w and a reduction in v, is likely to enhance

welfare. All this of course only applied if and when managers, by imposing their own tastes, pursue a policy at odds with their customers' preferences. A manager maximizing a function of v and w with reasonable weights attached to both may well promote welfare when subsidies are increased by putting on more of both kinds of shows.

The introduction of quality variables, specifically identified in the analysis in the mathematical note with the number of productions of v and w, does not substantially affect our conclusions on the welfare implications of massive subsidies. Under the "normal conditions" defined in the note, some of the subsidies will be used by the NPO maximizing the audience size for, or the quality of, elite shows to increase quality and some to lower Π and widen the audience attending these shows. But as long as the increase in subsidies is associated with a reduction either in the size of audiences attending popular plays or in the number of productions of popular plays, consumers' welfare will be adversely affected.

To these pessimistic arguments, we may counterpose the idea that elite-type productions have a positive long-run impact on welfare. That is, as consumers are exposed to more difficult works -- more complex patterns of symbols in terms of Scitovsky's (1975, chs 1 & 2) conception of art -- they gradually get to understand and appreciate them.[29] Their relative demand for v-type productions increases. Post hoc, these changes in taste validate the manager's choices. Strictly speaking, this infant-industry argument for subsidies tending to promote elite productions requires that the increase in demand be sufficient not only to bring about a state of affairs where the (v, w) combination chosen by the manager in each period maximizes intertemporal consumer utility but where the increase in consumer's surplus eventually generated is sufficient to compensate for the temporary losses in welfare incurred before the change in taste took place. The argument, in any case, is of doubtful empirical validity. If culture consumers were so malleable, there would be no need to increase subsidies through time as Holland, Germany, and Sweden have done on such a massive scale.

The remaining arguments in favor of massive subsidies to NPOs promoting nonpopular, money-losing cultural ends turn on Bildung. These arguments do not necessarily imply that an elitist minority need impose its tastes by social compulsion on a recalcitrant majority, for example, by milking subsidies through manipulation of the political process. Consumers may not enjoy "serious" music or theater, now or after prolonged exposure. Yet, they may be willing to vote to subsidize music and theater, or to elect representatives who will promise to subsidize them, because they regard high-culture offerings as being, in one way or another, important to their community or to the nation as a whole. I leave to political scientists and sociologists the task of ascertaining how widespread such an attitude toward merit goods may be. But even if the voter should favor art as Bildung, I am not sure that the NPO is the right conduit for large-scale subsidies to achieve this cultural end. There is no guarantee that managers of NPOs, whose policies may be influenced by career and professional considerations having nothing in common with the Bildung aims accepted by voters, may, if given too much leeway, move away from optimality, whether welfare is defined in terms of consumers' sovereignty or according to some other, broader notion.

V. CONCLUSION

In conclusion, the performing-arts organizations in Western
Europe are the recipients of generous government subsidies, which have
undoubtedly given much satisfaction to at least a minority of the
population, contributed to the cultural education of another segment
of the public (partly overlapping with the first), and added to the
luster of the states and cities that spent their tax monies on these
activities. The United States has only recently begun to emulate the
European pattern in this regard, but it has not gone nearly as far in
the direction of public support for the arts as European governments
have done. The European experience occurred in a sociopolitical
environment that differs in essential respects from the one prevailing
here. European organs of government are less responsive to popular --
not to speak of populist -- pressures than ours. Class cleavages,
which are more profound than they are in this country, make Europe's
common citizens more ready to accept the cultural leadership of its
elites. Any policy that would use tax monies to subsidize high
culture to the point of virtually giving it away free for the benefit
mainly of better-off citizens (as in the case of Swedish opera) would
be considered profligate and inequitable by the wide American public.
In a culturally very heterogeneous country such as the United States,
the claims for public support are too many to be all addressed, let
alone satisfied. At the same time, a policy lavishing subsidies on a
few activities, especially of an elite sort, is likely to be resented
both by the public at large and by unsuccessful claimants. Arts
organizations risk losing the sympathy of the broad American public if
they press their demands for government support beyond the point of
compatibility with its basic values.

FOOTNOTES

I am grateful to Avner Ben-Ner, Henry Hansmann, Daniel Levy, Paul
DiMaggio, Richard R. Nelson, Susan Rose-Ackerman, and John Simon for
their very helpful comments (empirical, theoretical, or of both kinds)
on an earlier draft of this paper.

1. In the United States, also, private patronage and associations or
    cooperatives played a key role in supplying orchestral music in
    the second half of the nineteenth century (see below). But, in
    contrast with the German experience, state and municipal organs of
    government in the United States did not take over the
    responsibility for financing orchestral music in the first quarter
    of the twentieth century.

2. The arts may have benefited from the gradual dismantling of the historical *Verzuiling* system whereby each major social group, including especially the Protestant and Roman Catholic communities, had received, and was left to administer, a portion of government support. Since there had been no organized constituency concerned primarily with the arts, there had been little support for art activities. On *Verzuiling* and its decline, see Kramer (1979, 155-73).

3. Interview with Bernt Langenberg, director of the Verenigung van Nederlandse Toneelgeselshapen (Association of Netherlandish Theater Societies), June 1980.

4. Data supplied by the Verenigung van Nederlandse Toneelgeselschapen. Attendance at other performing arts, including symphonic music, where repertory was not nearly to the same extent influenced by the demands of the activists, also fell, but much less drastically.

5. In the second half of the eighteenth century, an observer complained that theatricals at Yale "had turned the College into Drury Lane" to the detriment of "the more solid parts of learning" (cited in Miller 1966, 263).

6. Except for a few short-lived ventures in the 1890s. For details, see Jack Poggi (1966, 102).

7. In the U.S. and especially in Canada there is evidence to show that government and private support for the performing arts are substitutes. See Globerman (1980, 73).

8. It is interesting in this connection to recall the examples of Würtemberg in the period 1818 to 1820 and Sweden in the late 1860s when democratically elected representatives balked at the lavish expenditures on royal establishments.

9. The Strasbourg national theater, unlike the other national theaters, is organized as a "public corporation of an industrial and commercial character."

10. An ordinance of 14 October 1945 deemed all "theatrical activity" to be "commercial in nature" but excluded national theaters from this definition (Hue 1979, 30). Several Parisian orchestras (Concerts Colonne, Lamoureux, and Pasdeloup) are also organized as associations but, for some unfathomable reason, they are not denied the opportunity of engaging in regular commercial activity. (I assume that a concert is neither more nor less commercial from a legal viewpoint than a theatrical performance for which tickets are sold.)

11. At the I.S.P.S. meeting where the findings in this paper were first presented, one participant commented that the level of public support for the performing arts in Europe and the United States would look very different if military bands and high school

theatricals and orchestras were included in the statistics of public support. In support of this view, Mr. Richard Magat brought to my attention a news release by U.S. representative Fred Richmond who points out that, in the recommended federal appropriations for 1982, $89.7 million were earmarked for military bands as against $88 million for the National Endowment for the Arts as a whole. In France, 84 million F. were spent in 1979 for all the musical activities of the Ministry of Defense (chiefly military bands), a sum equal to just over one-fifth of the Ministry of Culture's budget for music and dance subsidies of all sorts and 5.6 percent of estimated government support for music at all levels (data supplied by France's Conseil Economique et Social, cited by Xavier Dupuy in an unpubished doctoral dissertation at Université de Paris I). Since this paper concentrates on the behavior of nonprofit organizations competing with privately owned organizations in the market place, the narrower definition used here may be more appropriate than one that would include government support for the arts in the military and in schools. In any event, the more comprehensive data are not available on a comparative basis.

12. In Germany, the "public" theaters had an audience of 17.3 million persons in 1973/74, and the private theaters, including cooperatives, of 4.7 million persons. In Holland, the audience of "subsidized theaters" was 1.4 million in 1969/70, of private and other unsubsidized theaters about 180,000. In 1974/75, for reasons that will be discussed in part IV, the audience of subsidized theaters shrank to 907,000 while the audience of private and other nonsubsidized theaters rose to an estimated 750,000. (Information obtained from the Association of Dutch Theater Companies in Amsterdam). Since Dutch orchestras and ballet companies are all subsidized foundations or associations, the balance of the entire sector clearly favors "nonprofits."

13. Holland is probably exceptional in the degree to which nontraditional art forms such as the puppet theater and pantomime are publicly subsidized. But even in Holland, the line is drawn between modern dance, which is deemed worthy of support, and exhibition ballroom dancing or figure skating which are not. As far as I can make out, jazz and pop music are not regularly subsidized in any Western European country.

14. The Economist (London) published an estimate of this share, which it set at 59 percent for 1975, without supplying details on how the figure was calculated (cited in Throsby and Withers 1979, 146).

15. Expenditures on the newly constructed Centre Beaubourg in Paris are kept separately. In 1973, capital expenses for the Centre came to 126 million F. compared to 95.6 million F. spent on total current and capital support for the theater and 93.7 million F. for the opera. (France, Ministère de la Culture 1977, 23, 34.)

16. On the basis of data published by Dick Netzer (1978, 64, 88, 93, 95), I estimated 1974 federal support for the performing arts (as defined in Table 5) at roughly $39 million, state support at $30 million, and local (municipal and county) support at $25 million. Total support for the arts (performing arts plus visual arts) in that year amounted approximately to $79 million at the federal level, $60 million at the state level, and $60 million at the local level. Compare the data for 1975 in Netzer (1978, 95).

17. In the French national theaters, personnel expenses range from two-thirds to four-fifths of total expenditures. In the Paris Opera, salaries came to over three-quarters of total expenditures in 1974. Purchases of goods and services amounted to 17 percent of total expenses. (France, Ministère de la Culture 1977, 176, 227.)

18. Some theaters, such as De Twentse Schouwburg, are owned jointly by the municipality and a local foundation. In Amsterdam De Brakke Grond Theater is part of a building complex owned by the (private) AMO-Bank, which, via a management firm, rents the facility for 65,000 Ft a year to a Foundation called Theater Unie. Property relations between and among municipalities, foundations, private firms, and theater associations are too tangled to be described in detail here. (They are summarized in Netherlands, Ministerie van Cultuur 1976, 26-27.)

19. About one-third of all performances in Maisons de la Culture in 1977/78 consisted of music, theater, opera, and dance; movies represented 53 percent of the total. (France, Ministère de la Culture 1980, 10.)

20. Interview material (Ministère de la Culture et de la Communication). On the other hand, it is said that the 0.5 percent deduction on personal income is automatically taken by most French taxpayers whether they donate to charities or not, so that it has no real effect on giving.

21. The model has the same basic structure as the one developed by Henry Hansmann in his "Non-profit Enterprise in the Performing Arts" (1981). The differences between my model and his are the following: (1) popular and elite productions are explicitly segregated· (2) a capacity constraint is introduced limiting the total number of tickets sold per day; (3) private donations are treated differently; (4) the influence of the NPO's output decisions on its competitive position vis-à-vis the commercial sector is examined.

22. Costs, in particular, will vary with the number of days during which each type of show is staged.

23. The line marked d(NR)/dv = 0 is the locus of combinations of v and w that would be selected by a manager maximizing w as S and D increased.

24. That is, the own-effect of w on Ψ is always absolutely greater than the cross-effect of v on Ψ.

25. It may also be noted that the contours will shrink not only when subsidies and donations decline but when production costs increase faster than the sale of tickets, a symptom of "Baumol's disease." The erosion of demand due to competition from movies, television, and phonograph records, if it were not matched by a reduction in costs, would also have that effect.

26. The inverse demands functions for Π and Ψ in terms of v and w were assumed to be such that a simultaneous increase in both arguments must reduce price.

27. The reason Ψ must rise as the output-mix is shifted from point s to point t is this: the shape of any contour is elongated in the vertical direction because, by assumption, w is more popular than v, hence with a given level of subsidies, the audience level w at point 1 that could attracted if w were maximized is greater than the level of v at point t where v is maximized. Hence, for any mix of v and w such as the one at point s, which would be chosen if v and w were equally preferred (or at least if w were not strongly preferred), the contour must have a slope with an absolute value smaller than unity. This implies that any gain in v from point s to point t must be associated with at least as large a loss in w. But, since the impact of w on Ψ (the "own-price effect") must be greater than that of v (the "cross-effect"), the price-raising effect of the decrease in w must be greater than the price-reducing effect of the smaller increase in v.

28. This is not to deny that a subsidy given to a one-product enterprise might increase welfare by reducing the gap between price and marginal cost (a point stressed by Hansmann). What is going on here, however, is that the subsidies make it possible for the manager to alter the NPO's output-mix in a way that is increasingly inimical to consumers' interests.

29. This type of consumer behavior has been modeled by Roger McCain (1979).

BIBLIOGRAPHY

Barnum, P. T. 1871. *Struggles and triumphs*: *forty years' recollections, written by himself.* New York: American News Company.

Baumol, H., W. Baumol. 1980. On finances of the performing arts during stagflation: some recent data. *J. of Cultural Economics,* 4 (2)(December): 1-14.

Bourassies, J. 1875. *Les spectacles forains et la Comédie Française.* Paris: E. Dentu.

Burkhauser, R. V., M. Getz. 1982. What federal subsidies will buy: the case of symphony orchestras. Department of Economics and Business Administration, Vanderbilt University, Working Paper No. 81-W18. Nashville: 1-18.

d'Arschot, R. 1974. *Theater and music in Western and Northern Europe 1960-1972.* Report prepared for the Ford Foundation. New York. (Duplicated)

Deutscher Bühnenverein. 1974. *Theater-statistik 1973/74.* Koblenz: Peter Steffgen.

Deutscher Bühnenverein. 1979. *Theaterstatistik 1978/79.* Koblenz: Peter Steffgen.

de Varine, H. 1977. Le soutien privé à l'action culturelle dans le cadre local et régional. Ministère de la Culture et Communication, Service des Etudes et de Recherches. Paris. (mimeo)

DiMaggio, P. 1981. The impact of public funding on organizations in the arts. Program on Non-Profit Organizations Working Paper No. 32, Institution for Social and Policy Studies, Yale U. New Haven, Conn.

DiMaggio, P. 1982. Cultural entrepreneurship in nineteenth-century Boston: the creation of an organizational base for high culture in America. *Media, Culture and Society,* 4(1): 33-50.

Fabrizio, C. 1975. Le projet Súedois de démocratie culturelle: Essai de comparaison avec la situation française. *Notes et Etudes Documentaires,* No. 4205-4206(22 July): 11-72.

Ford Foundation. 1974. *The financing of the performing arts: a survey of 166 professional non-profit resident theaters, operas, symphony, ballet, and modern dance companies.* New York.

France, Ministère de la Culture et de la Communication. 1980. *Données statistiques d'ensemble sur les maisons de la culture.* Paris. (mimeo)

France, Ministère de la Culture et de l'Environnement. 1977. *Annuaire statistique de la culture, données de 1970 à 1974.* Vol. 2. Paris: La Documentation Française.

Globerman, S. 1980. An explanatory analysis of the effects of public funding of the performing arts. In *Economic policy for the arts*, ed. W. S. Hendon et al. Cambridge, Mass.: Abt Books.

Hansmann, H. 1981. Non-profit enterprise in the performing arts. *The Bell J. of Economics*, 12(Autumn): 341-61.

Herterich, F. 1937. *Theater und Volkswirtschaft.* Munich and Leipzig: Verlag Duncker and Humbolt.

Hue, J.-P. 1979. *L'état et les nouvelles formes du théatre depuis 1968.* Doctoral Thesis, Université de Rouen, Faculté de Droit et de Sciences Economiques. Rouen.

James, E. 1981. Cross-subsidization by non-profit organizations: theory, evidence and evaluation. PONPO Working Paper No. 30. ISPS, Yale U. New Haven, Conn.

Kramer, R. M. 1979. Governmental-voluntary agency relationships in the Netherlands. *The Netherlands J. of Sociology*, 25: 155-73.

Magnin, J. 1909. *Les théatres municipaux de la province.* Le Mans: Impr. C. Blanchet.

McCain, R. 1979. Reflections on the cultivation of taste. *J. of Cultural Economics*, 3(1): 30-52.

Miller, L. B. 1966. *Patrons and patriotism: the encouragement of fine arts in the United States 1790-1860.* Chicago and London: The U. of Chicago Press.

Netherlands, Central Bureau voor de statistiek. 1979. *Statistiek inkomsten en uitgaven van de overheid voor cultuur en recreatie 1975.* The Hague: Staatsuitgeverij.

Netherlands, Ministerie van Cultuur, Recreatie en Maatschappelijk Werk. 1976. *Toneel ter zake: Een onderzoek naar de exploitatie - uitkomsten van gesubsideerde toneel voorstellingen.* The Hague: Staatsuitgeverij.

Netherlands, States General of the. 1977. Tweede Kamer, 1976-77 session. Nota orkestenbestel. The Hague: Staatsuitgeverij.

Netzer, D. 1978. *The subsidized muse: public support for the arts in the United States.* Cambridge, London, New York, New Rochelle, Melbourne, Sidney: Cambridge U. Press.

No Author. 1964. Le théatre en République Fédérale d'Allemagne. *Notes et études documentaires*, no. 3119 (15 September).

Nye, R. B. 1960. *The cultural life of the nation 1776-1830.* New York: Harper and Row.

Peacock, A. T., C. Godfrey. 1976. Cultural accounting. In *The economics of the arts*, ed. M. Blaug. London: Mark Robertson.

Poggi, J. 1966. *Theater in America: the impact of economic forces.* Ithaca: Cornell U. Press.

Schuster, M. 1972. *Income taxes and the arts: tax expenditures as cultural policy.* Unpublished Ph.D. dissertation, Department of Urban Studies, M. I. T. Cambridge, Mass.

Scitovsky, T. 1975. *The joyless economy.* New York: Oxford U. Press.

Sweden, Ministry of Education and Cultural Affairs, Department of Cultural Affairs. 1970. *The state and culture in Sweden.* Stockholm: The Swedish Institute.

Sweden, Statistika centralbyran. 1976. *Statistik arsbök for Sverige 1976.* Stockholm.

Throsby, D. D., G. A. Withers. 1979. *The economics of the performing arts.* New York: St. Martin's Press.

Versillier, M. 1973. *La crise du théatre privé.* Paris: Presses Universitaires de France.

Wahl-Ziegler, E. 1978. *Theater und Orchestra zwischen Marktkraften und Marktkorrektur: Existenzprobleme und Uberlebenschancen eines Sektors an Wirtschaftstheoretischer Licht.* Göttingen.

19
Energy and Agricultural Development in the Third World

Robert L. West

I. INTRODUCTION

We owe to Lloyd Reynolds the observation that economic development is an activity -- and development economics is a chronicle of wisdom extracted from practical experience. The decade past, with its sequence of rude surprises, has provided a variety of new economic development experiences such as those described by Bela Balassa, Henry Bruton, and Robert Triffin in earlier chapters of this volume. In consequence, development economics has been enriched by an array of new derivative propositions. Two such propositions concern us here, each an important reformulation of development doctrine reflecting Third World experience in the 1970s.

We have a new appreciation of the relationship between energy use and economic growth. The profoundly changed conditions of energy availability which emerged in the last decade are seen, in retrospect, as introducing a bleaker period for the world economy and, specifically, reduced growth prospects for non-oil producers of the Third World (Reynolds 1980; Lewis 1980; Dohner 1981).

New insights articulated in the 1970s have also given us a reformulation of agriculture-in-development theory, a keener perception of agricultural sector performance in successful development experience, and new criteria for evaluating agricultural development strategies (Reynolds 1975; Reynolds 1977, Chapters 3, 4, 11; Mellor 1976).

We enter the 1980s in possession of an improved grasp of development strategy -- an agriculturally-based and employment-oriented strategy -- and with enhanced understanding of means to promote successful development performance, yet deeply suspicious of how future energy shocks will impact on Third World prospects. But just how, and to what extent, will widespread adoption of the preferred agricultural development strategy -- with its appropriately adapted new technologies, its packages of inputs and practices, and its labor-absorbing emphasis -- encounter the constraints and depressing influences attributed to the energy requirements of economic growth? Will successful pursuit of the new economics of agriculturally-based growth intensify the future energy management problems of all, or some, developing countries?

No consensus has emerged with respect to the answers to these questions despite a virtual flood of literature on the subject of energy for agriculture (one U. S. Department of Agriculture bibliography contains 2,613 citations on this subject for 1973-79: USDA 1979). In general, the basic, if guarded, optimism for prospects of agriculturally-based growth does not appear to have been intersected by the pessimistic expectations for energy-related dampening of growth performance.

From farm-level studies -- including studies of crops which define the major Third World agricultural systems -- there is ample indication of very high marginal energy inputs and marginal rates of substitution associated with the adoption of improved agricultural technologies. Some observers have expressed concern that high energy prices and supply insecurity may constrain adoption of new production methods. A few analysts, such as the authors of the Global 2000 report, foresee a dangerous interaction between the energy and agricultural sectors, but this view has been directly contradicted by critics. Insofar as rural activities are identified as a potentially significant source of energy management difficulties for developing countries, this has usually referred to the "other energy crisis:" pressure for expanded use of traditional energy sources -- notably, firewood and charcoal -- and the increased prospect for degradation of forest, soil, and water resources (see Fallen-Bailey and Byer 1979; UNCTAD 1980).

In general, the economic literature and the views expressed by planners have tended to be sanguine about the commercial energy requirements of agriculture and other rural activities. Economists and planners have also generally discounted the sometimes alarming views expressed by those agronomists and ecologists who foresee a possible explosion of energy demand in developing country rural areas as improved agricultural methods gain widespread adoption (Hirst 1974; Pimentel, Dritschilo, Krummel, Kutzman 1975; Pimentel 1976).

There have been several independent reasons for the general disregard in the development economics literature of a possible energy requirement crisis associated with agricultural development. First, a reliable body of information about patterns of energy use in the agricultural sectors of developing countries was wholly missing until nearly the end of the 1970s. Second, the available case studies of energy use in agricultural production are chiefly concentrated on activity in industrialized countries, do not lend themselves readily to conventional farm management analysis, and tend to show very modest use of commercial energy in the agricultural pursuits of developing countries (Leach 1976; FAO 1976, 81-111). Third, the technology assessment literature reporting on energy flows associated with different economic activities and patterns of resource allocation has been accompanied by a methodological dispute about the appropriate role of net energy analysis which, to some, appeared to challenge traditional economic techniques. The public exchanges on points of methodology and interpretation may have acted to obscure the empirical evidence as well as cast doubt on the policy interpretations (Gilliland 1975; Huettner 1976; Herendeen and Bullard 1974; Costanza 1980).

There has been in the 1970s virtually no coordination of agricultural and energy planning at the national level in developing countries. This is strikingly evident, for example, in the country surveys compiled for the U.S. Department of Energy World Energy Data System, reporting on the energy management organizations of a large number of developing countries. At both the national planning agency and the international organization levels, agriculturalists and energy analysts have acknowledged the "firewood crisis," relating to the growing scarcity of traditional fuels, and have expressed interest in a few specific interactive cases such as the energy requirements of fertilizer production and proposals for expanded production of methanol and ethanol, but have almost wholly ignored the agricultural sector in defining goals for energy demand management (see, for example, the survey by the World Bank Energy Department Staff, Fallen-Bailey and Byer 1979). Very often, the viewpoint expressed by agricultural policy planners has been that, given the absolute importance of improved performance of agricultural-lifestock production activities, it is the duty of the energy-management agencies and the energy industry to deliver whatever will be required to fulfill agricultural sector goals.

Insofar as missing basic data have contributed to these results, the prospect for reassessment has been strengthened by the substantial efforts to improve reporting on energy sources and uses in developing countries which were stimulated by the energy shocks of the 1970s. The available information at the beginning of the decade was the product of a long-standing system of data collection, coordinated by the United Nations Statistical Office, on commercial energy production and international trade (United Nations Statistical Office, Series J.). In the latter half of the 1970s significant supplementary efforts to collect and standardize data on sectoral uses of both commercial and nonconventional energy have been made by national agencies, the industry, the specialized agencies of the United Nations, and the Organization for Economic Cooperation and Development (International Energy Agency, OECD 1979). Improvements in analysis of these data, and particular attention to assessment of the energy flow in agriculture, have been contributed by scholars and assisted by private foundations (see, for example, studies cited by Leach 1976; Darmstadter, Dunkerley, and Alterman 1977; studies summarized by Fluck and Baird 1980).

In part II we will display the kind of information on sources and uses of energy which has recently become available, drawing on a data base assembled with support of the Rockefeller Foundation for ongoing studies of changes in the management of energy resources by developing countries over the decade of the 1970s. We will inspect the data for fifty developing countries in the base-line year, 1970, and discuss in some detail the conventions which apply to estimation and interpretation of national energy balances.

In part III we will examine the uses of energy in agricultural production and conduct a preliminary reconnaissance of this new body of information to see if it appears to confirm or contradict an optimistic judgment that , in general, developing countries will be able to accommodate readily the energy requirements of proposed strategies for agricultural development.

In part IV we will enquire whether the cross-country patterns of information on farm-sector energy consumption suggest the existence of systematic linkages between rural development strategies and the relative intensity of energy use in the agricultural sector.

II. SOURCES AND USES OF ENERGY IN DEVELOPING COUNTRIES

For more than thirty years the Statistical Office of the United Nations has assembled information from national reporting agencies and the energy industry on production, stocks, and international trade in commercial energy materials and products. Throughout the decade of the 1970s this information has been available on an almost comprehensive worldwide basis, for 192 nations and territories, at a level of detail distinguishing more than 100 products and grades of materials. To facilitate aggregation and comparison, heat content coefficients are employed to convert the products and materials into units of a standard coal equivalency of 7000 calories/gram. The energy data for developing countries in this study are fully reconciled with this United Nations reporting basis.

Traditional fuels which lie outside the definitional boundaries of commercial energy are widely utilized in developing countries. Much the most important is wood. Information on fuelwood (volume) and charcoal (weight) production and trade is gathered by the U.N. Food and Agricultural Organization and this has been employed to estimate the wood data in this study. To compare fuelwood with other energy sources and uses introduces a kind of indeterminancy not shared by commercial energy. The heat content of a given quantity of wood, subjected to combustion under conditions corresponding to the measurement of heat coefficients for other energy sources, varies by specie, dry or green condition, and moisture content. These specifications are not available for fuelwood actually used in any country. To compare fuelwood with other energy sources we must guess what these conditions of wood may have been, or adopt a set of assumptions permitting conversion of wood into coal equivalency units. We adopt assumptions, for common application to all the developing countries of this study, which result in a conversion ratio of one cubic meter of wood equal to .2175 metric tons of coal equivalency, or about 1.5225 billion calories per cubic meter of firewood. A heat equivalency coefficient for the species of wood used as fuel in the United States, at bone dry conditions, would be nearly double this value and some energy analysts, such as the projects staff of the World Bank Energy Department, conventionally use a coefficient for international comparisons of wood use that is two-thirds higher than that employed in this study. While we believe a heat rating much greater than used here cannot be justified for the subject of this study, it results in a substantially lower fuelwood to commercial energy ratio t an reported elsewhere (on the energy equivalency of wood, see Hughart 1979; National Academy of Sciences 1980, esp. 166). To minimize distortion resulting from the indeterminancy of the wood heat rating, we assign all fuelwood and charcoal to household consumption, although as much as one-tenth of this fuel in developing countries may be used in food processing and similar activities outside households (in some countries the proportion may approach 20 percent: Arnold 1978).

Tables 1A and 1B show the 1970 uses of commercial energy and fuelwood-charcoal in fifty large and medium-sized, market-oriented countries located in the eight most important farming regions of the Third World. These countries have been selected on the basis of their comparability with respect to energy management and agricultural development activities. The major oil-exporting and oil-processing countries are excluded, as are all nations and territories of less than one million population in the 1970s; these excluded nations confront quite different problems of energy and agricultural policy management and their distinctive patterns of sectoral energy use cannot be interpreted in the same way as other countries in the farming regions where they are located. A few nations in the eight farming regions cannot be included in this study for other reasons: Bangladesh, which was not an independent nation throughout the 1970s and where estimates for former East Pakistan introduce unacceptable observational errors; Lebanon, for which comparisons are distorted by hostilities during the years of civil war; Taiwan, for which the United Nations agencies did not report, separately from mainland China, the range of information necessary for making intercountry comparisons; and four francophonic African nations where some production data are missing. These omissions are regrettable but will not materially affect our findings; the fifty selected countries accounted for 93 percent of the 1970 apparent consumption of commercial energy of all oil-importing nations and territories located in the eight farming regions.

"Total Consumption" of Table 1 comprises domestic production of power and energy materials plus net imports, adjusted for changes in stocks and deducting non-energy uses of these materials for such purposes as petrochemical feedstocks, paints, road asphalts and the like. It is a convenient aggregate for making intercountry comparisons. In 1970 the fifty countries of this study used about 122 million metric tons coal equivalent (mtce) of fuelwood and 395 mtce of commercial energy; this volume of commercial energy can be compared with other components of worldwide energy use. In 1970 the 192 nations, territories and dependencies covered by the United Nations reporting system consumed 6,877 million mtce of commercial energy. Developed market economies consumed 4,312 million mtce, centrally planned economies 1,987 million mtce, and developing market economies 578 million mtce -- 8.4 percent of world total, shared among 140 nations and territories. Twenty of these nations were major oil exporters or oil-processing economies, and they used slightly less than one-fourth of the developing countries' total (139 million mtce). About 5 million mtce were used by 49 small countries, each with less than one-million population, and the balance of 434 million mtce by 71 large developing countries.

Among the large oil-importing Third World economies, about 30 million mtce were consumed by Bangladesh, Lebanon, Taiwan and the four omitted francophonic African countries; 9 million mtce by developing countries in farming regions other than the eight inspected here; and 395 million mtce by the fifty countries, as shown in Tables 1A and 1B. The fifty countries, although using only six percent of the world total, accounted for 90 percent of commercial energy consumed by all oil-importing developing countries in 1970. It appears that they also used a slightly greater proportion of fuelwood consumed in all developing countries. We are not likely to be seriously misled about energy use in rural areas of the oil-importing Third World by inspecting the patterns of energy use in these fifty countries.

The wide range of variation among developing countries in their relative reliance on different energy sources is also illustrated in Tables 1A and 1B, where the use of each major energy source is shown

TABLE 1A
Energy Uses by Sector, 1970
(Thousands of MTCE)

	Households: Consumer End-uses	Intermediate Inputs	Agriculture On-Farm	Services Sector	Industry-Energy Sector	Transport Sector	Total Consumption
				All Fifty Countries			
Total	167,675	349,355	5,431	7,726	239,770	96,431	517,030
Wood	122,339	-	-	-	-	-	122,339
Fossil Fuels: Direct Use	30,829	285,643	5,431	5,518	178,952	95,742	316,472
Electr.Gen.Transf.Loss	8,502	38,500	-	1,294	35,799	407	46,002
Electricity	6,004	26,216	-	914	25,019	282	32,220
				India			
Total	30,670	90,346	976	2,084	66,840	20,445	121,016
Wood	21,968	-	-	-	-	-	21,968
Fossil Fuels: Direct Use	6,946	73,043	976	1,706	50,107	20,254	79,989
Electr.Gen.Transf.Loss	1,062	10,468	-	229	10,123	115	11,530
Electricity	694	6,835	-	149	6,611	75	7,529

TABLE 1B

	Households: Consumer End-uses	Intermediate Inputs	Agriculture On-Farm	Services Sector	Industry- Energy Sector	Transport Sector	Total Consumption
23 Petroleum-Dominant Countries							
Total	61,522	198,507	3,373	3,743	137,497	53,894	260,029
Wood	29,331	-	-	-	-	-	29,331
Fossil Fuels: Direct Use	21,594	161,745	3,373	2,628	102,251	53,494	183,339
Electr.Gen.Transf.Loss	6,905	23,973	-	727	22,984	262	30,878
Electricity	3,694	12,789	-	389	12,262	139	16,483
26 Wood-Dominant Countries							
Total	75,483	60,503	1,082	1,899	35,433	22,092	135,986
Wood	71,040	-	-	-	-	-	71,040
Fossil Fuels: Direct Use	2,308	50,836	1,082	1,166	26,594	21,994	53,144
Electr.Gen.Transf.Loss	650	2,944	-	223	2,693	30	3,594
Electricity	1,483	6,725	-	510	6,146	68	8,208

Note: Heat loss distributed; excludes imputed heat loss and nonenergy uses.
Sources: See "Note on Statistical Sources."

for groups of the fifty countries. India is the only developing country for which coal is the most important single source of domestically consumed energy; it is, therefore, shown separately in Table 1A and elsewhere in this study (India contains large areas of several different farming systems and is considered to be a separate farming region in the Third World). In 23 countries petroleum is the most important energy source, constituting more than half of all energy consumed, and these countries appear as the "petroleum-dominant" group; for the balance of 26 countries, shown as the "wood-dominant" group, fuelwood is the single most important source of energy consumed by each in 1970. This distinction between petroleum- and wood-dominant countries is of great importance in defining and evaluating national energy management problems; as we will find below, it also closely corresponds to the distinction between countries in the wheat and rice farming regions as contrasted with countries in other farm-system regions of the Third World.

Throughout this study, the sector definitions of the International Energy Agency have been adopted although the conversion factors remain those of the United Nations. By IEA convention, total energy requirements of the country are attributed to internal consumption in the energy-producing sector itself or to the "first purchaser" from the energy sector of the power and energy products. The first purchasers are classified as industry, transportation, and household-commercial; household-commercial includes agricultural, private commercial, all governmental, and residential users. This somewhat awkward sectoring derives from the nature of the primary data source, the energy industry record of power and products purchased by categories of customers and intermediate suppliers, which consolidates into these sectors (see International Energy Agency 1978, esp. Chapter II; International Energy Agency 1979, pp. XVII-XXV; and discussion in Darmstadter, Dunkerley, Alterman 1977, Parts I and II.) For the 50 developing countries of this study, sectoral uses were computed by tracking about 50 specific energy products to their consumers, using public power agency and energy-industry information about product sales to classes of customers. Thus, for each country and each source of energy, the energy units of Total Consumption have been distributed to a recorded use in the energy-producing sector, to an industrial purchaser, to a transportation sector purchaser, or to a household-commercial sector user.

The household-commercial energy consumption shown in Tables 1A and 1B is disaggregated into the categories of Households, Agriculture, and Services. The on-farm agricultural use of fuels has been computed by a method (two-stage process analysis) developed by the U.N. Food and Agriculture Organization, as described in part III. Services, representing energy use by government and by private suppliers of trade and other services, has been estimated by fitting energy-coefficients for the fifty countries to data on governmental recurrent non-personnel expenditures and the value-added in trade and private services industries; the Services estimates are subject to large error terms and only indicate the probable orders of magnitude. The balance of energy purchased by the household-commercial sector is shown in Tables 1A and 1B as consumed by Households.

The columns of Tables 1A and 1B may be compared to the columns of an input-output table, recording the power and energy (physical quantities) used as inputs by the intermediate sectors composing the inter-industry matrix, and consumed by final-demand end-users. To improve this analogy to the conventional input-output format, the energy directly purchased by government (part of that shown in the Services sector), by investors (a portion of that included in the Industry and Transport sectors), and by users of personal vehicles (included in the Transport sector) should be shown together with the Households sector as constituting energy delivered to the final-demand bill of goods. By reference to this analogy, it should be evident that the classification of "consumer end-uses" and "intermediate input" uses of energy in Tables 1A and 1B is only approximate. The latter category is overstated by inclusion of some energy delivered directly to both governmental and private end-users, not employed by them to produce other goods and services. The sectors of the Table do not, of course, identify the ultimate consumers of energy in the economy; almost all of the energy delivered to the Industry sector, for example, is subsequently embodied in the products of this sector and ultimately consumed in that embodied form by a final-demand end-user of industrial products. We may note, also, that because the Households sector does not record the fuel and lubricants purchased by members of households for personal vehicles, this omission understates the private consumption of energy and inflates the Transport sector. But this has a modest effect on the data for most developing countries where only a small part of vehicular fuels and lubricants is used by households directly for personal transportation.

The energy recorded in Tables 1A and 1B includes wood and fossil fuel products directly consumed by each sector; the coal, oil, and natural gas used as boiler fuel in thermal stations is embodied in the electricity generated and is indirectly consumed by the sectors in the electricity purchased by each. Electricity delivered to each sector, whatever its mode of generation, is shown at its intrinsic heat value of 0.123 mtce per 1,000 kilowatt-hours. No heat loss is imputed to primary electricity generation, i.e., by hydro and geothermal stations, but the difference between the coal equivalency of the fuels burned in thermal plants and the intrinsic heat value of the electricity generated by those plants is recorded as "electrical generating transformation loss." Where this is distributed among the sectors in proportion to the amount of electricity consumed (as in Tables 1A and 1B), rather than attributed to the energy sector alone, this is indicated by the note "heat loss distributed." A comparison of the intrinsic heat value of electricity consumed with the corresponding electrical generating transformation loss provides a crude index of the effect on energy use of the ratio of primary to thermal-generated power. As may be seen in Table 1B, the wood-dominant countries obtain a much higher proportion of electricity from hydro sources than do the petroleum-dominant countries -- one contributor to the lower commercial energy consumption per capita and per unit of value-added in the wood-using countries.

It is in this form -- commercial energy use per capita or per value unit of real output -- that international comparisons of energy consumption are usually made. Table 2 contains a set of such measures for the fifty developing countries. The top panel reproduces the

TABLE 2
Commercial Energy Use Ratios, by Sector, 1970

	Intermediate Inputs	Agriculture On-Farm	Services	Industry	Transport	Total Consumption (a)
Energy Uses (Millions of mtce)						
All Fifty	349.4	5.4	7.7	239.8	96.4	394.7
India	90.3	1.0	2.1	66.8	20.4	99.0
Petr-Dom.	198.5	3.4	3.7	137.5	53.9	230.7
Wood-Dom.	60.5	1.1	1.9	35.4	22.1	64.9
Energy Uses per capita (Kg coal equiv.)						
All Fifty	282.9	4.4	6.3	194.2	78.1	319.6
India	167.6	1.8	3.9	124.0	37.9	183.7
Petr-Dom.	482.9	8.2	9.1	334.5	131.1	561.2
Wood-Dom.	212.6	3.8	6.7	124.5	77.6	228.2
Value Added (Billions of real 1970 US dollars) (b)						
All Fifty	608.1	163.9	226.4	184.2	35.0	608.1
India	163.1	74.4	41.4	39.1	8.3	163.1
Petr-Dom.	297.5	57.7	122.5	100.4	18.1	297.5
Wood-Dom.	147.4	31.8	62.6	44.7	8.6	147.4
Energy Use per Thousand Dollars Value-Added (Kg coal equiv.)						
All Fifty	574.5	33.1	34.1	1,301.7	2,755.2	649.1
India	553.8	13.1	50.4	1,709.5	2,463.3	607.1
Petr-Dom.	667.1	58.5	30.6	1,369.5	2,977.6	775.3
Wood-Dom.	410.5	34.0	30.3	792.7	2,568.8	440.7

Notes: (a) Energy Total Consumption includes consumer end-uses.
       (b) Local currencies converted at purchasing power parities.

commercial energy aggregates from Tables 1A and 1B and shows the sectoral use per capita in kilograms coal equivalent (kce). In the bottom half of Table 2 are shown values of sectoral real output for the groups of countries. Sectoral real output has been computed by converting sectoral value added (sector gross domestic product in factor values as reported in local currency by the national statistical agencies) to a common unit of currency, 1970 U.S. dollars, using the purchasing power parity conversion ratios for 1970 estimated by the United Nations International Comparison Project (Kravis, Heston, Summers 1978). Sectoral energy use per 1,000 U.S. dollars of 1970, in kilograms coal equivalent, is shown in the bottom panel of Table 2.

By all such measures, total commercial energy consumption of these fifty countries is far below the levels reported by industrial societies. Even when account is taken of the differences in real income and the effect of excluding traditional fuels, a great gap remains in the intensity of energy use per capita and per unit of real value added. Instructive comparisons can be made with the set of similar measures for the nine major industrial societies, in 1972, presented in a Resources for the Future study, where the comparative analysis of sectoral energy use has employed essentially similar data sources and methods of estimation. The 320 kce total commercial energy consumption per capita, shown for the fifty developing countries in Table 2, contrasts with 1972 per capita consumption of 11,567 kce in the United States, 4,638 kce in France, and 4,000 kce in Japan. Real per capita Gross Domestic Product in purchasers'·values, all in 1970, were $4,790 in the United States, $3,506 in France, and $2,836 in Japan as compared with $550 for the fifty developing countries ($330 for India, $810 for the petroleum group, and $600 for the wood-dominant group of countries). Commercial energy consumption per thousand dollars of real value added, 649 kce for the fifty developing countries as shown in Table 2, was 2,050 kce in the United States, 1,110 kce in France, and 1,169 kce in Japan (Darmstadter, Dunkerley, Alterman 1977, Appendix B, with nonenergy uses deducted and comparisons on the basis of GDP in factor values; real GDP from Kravis, Heston, Summers 1978, Table 1).

Comparisons of sectoral energy use can help to identify the sources of these differences between developing and industrial societies. The Agricultural and Services sectors in developing countries show energy use per capita about one-tenth that of the Western European industrial societies and Japan. We will explore agricultural uses in the next part of this paper. For the Services sector, the predominant origin of this great proportionate difference in energy use can be readily identified: about 80 percent of energy consumption in this sector of industrial countries is for conditioning space in buildings. Climatic differences and the low level of space-conditioning commitment in developing countries account for the great bulk of the Services sector energy-use gap.

Comparisons of household end-uses of energy in developing and industrial societies are difficult to interpret, both because of the climatic variances and the very substantial use of fuelwood and other traditional fuels in the developing countries. As among the groups of developing countries shown in Tables 1 and 2, however, it is evident that consumer end-use of commercial energy in households is a small part -- less than 10 percent -- of total national consumption in the coal and wood-dominant countries and less that 15 percent of total consumption in the petroleum-dominant countries, far below the household share reported by industrial societies.

By contrast, the levels of energy use per thousand dollars of real value added in the Industry and Transport sectors of the fifty developing countries are within the range of energy/output ratios reported by industrial societies. The 1,300 kce for the fifty developing countries shown in Table 2 for the Industry sector may be compared with 3,080 kce in the United States, 1,210 kce in France, and 2,070 kce in Japan in 1972 (Darmstadter, Dunkerley, Alterman 1977, 103-108, data adjusted to total value added basis). While Transport sector consumption of energy per capita and per unit of real output is highly varied among industrial societies -- United States use per capita is three times that of Japan -- the 2,755 kce per thousand dollars of real value added for the fifty developing countries shown in Table 2 is at the low end of the range reported for the industrial countries.

In summary, energy use per unit of real output in the modern, urban-based industrial activities of developing countries, and in transportation, are close to the levels found in industrial societies. The great contrasts are in space conditioning (both commercial and residential), in other household end-uses by consumers, and in agriculture.

III. ENERGY REQUIREMENTS OF AGRICULTURAL PRODUCTION

The data on agricultural sector energy consumption shown in Tables 1 and 2 -- measuring the energy content of commercial fuels delivered to farms for use in food, fiber and livestock production -- are representative of the kind of information that has been assembled by energy balance accountants to record the energy requirements of Third World agriculture. The magnitudes are similar to estimates reported by the U.N. Food and Agriculture Organization for continental regions of the world, as would be expected since the data shown here have been computed by a method paralleling that of the FAO (but on a country-by-country basis rather than for geographic regions.) The data are also roughly comparable to agricultural sector energy use estimates for developed market economies with large primary-commodity producing industries (FAO 1977; International Energy Agency 1979, Vol. II).

The assessment of this information has generally led to conclusions that may be inferred from inspection of Table 2. The absolute level of commercial energy consumed in the agricultural sector is very low. Its proportion to total energy consumption, or to all uses of energy as intermediate inputs, is in the one to two percent range. Energy use in agriculture is very modest when contrasted with consumption in the industrial and transport sectors. These intersectoral contrasts do not change materially when comparisons are made of groupings of countries with substantially different levels of gross national output or with quite different structures of productive activity. At the same time, there evidently is substantial variation among countries in agricultural energy use per capita and per unit of real output. This range, which appears to be about four or five to one for the country groupings shown in Table 2, is judged to reflect (at the level of aggregate energy use by the agricultural sector, and for groups of countries) the very wide variations in the energy requirements of different production methods observed in farm-level studies (compare FAO 1977, 91-105; Leach 1976; Fluck and Baird 1980).

But other inferences have been drawn that cannot be confirmed by inspecting information of the kind appearing in Table 2. From cross section data for groups of countries, showing that fuels used in agricultural activities on-farm are only one or two percent of total energy consumption in high per capita income countries as well as in low per capita income countries, it has been inferred that a future transition by developing countries to more energy intensive production methods in agriculture will impose no significant burden on their future overall requirements for energy. This conclusion is sometimes bolstered by the observation that among industrial countries in recent decades, where commercial energy input per hectare and per agricultural worker has risen very substantially, the proportion of total energy use devoted to agricutural production at the end of this period is only one or two percentage points higher than at the beginning of the period (Pimentel 1974). In sum, the future development of Third World agriculture is expected to result in higher ratios of energy use to other sectoral inputs and to sectoral real output, but the absolute amount of energy used in agriculture and its relation to other uses of energy by the developing countries are both expected to remain modest.

There are three reasons why these may be dubious inferences to draw from the data presented in the energy balances of developing countries. First, the on-farm use of fuels recorded for the agricultural sector substantially understates the total energy requirements of crop and livestock production and omits kinds of energy use that are likely to grow most rapidly as agricultural development strategies are implemented in developing countries. Second, the presentation of agricultural energy use by the conventional (e.g., continental) groups of countries masks the relevant range of national variation; the intercountry differences are much greater, and the intersectoral ratios of energy use show much greater variation, than has been apparent from averages for groups of countries containing different farming systems. Third, the consistently low proportion of national energy use devoted to agricultural production -- in countries with relatively high incomes, productivity, and energy intensity in agriculture as well as in countries with more primitive agricultural sectors -- may be a result attributable to a specific past developmental process, marked by a dominant agricultural development strategy and a constrained set of available options. The proposed new development strategy -- agriculturally based and employment oriented -- may be found to have very different energy-requirement implications. Taken together, these three reasons call into question the conventional conclusion that the requirements of agriculture will impose no great future burden on energy management among developing countries.

Table 3 contains estimates of total 1970 energy use in agricultural production for the fifty countries. It shows both the on-farm use of fuels, as reported in the energy balances, and the

TABLE 3
Energy Use in Agriculture by Farming Regions, 1970
(Thousands of MTCE)

	All Fifty Countries	India	Asian: Rice	N.African–Mid.East: Wheat	American: Wheat Livestock	American: Corn-Beans-Roots	East African: Corn	African: Millets-Sorghum	African: Roots-Tubers
On-Farm Fuels									
Farm Machinery	4,210	492	174	895	1,062	1,439	56	57	35
Irrigation	1,222	484	88	484	41	91	2	25	7
Total	5,432	976	261	1,380	1,103	1,530	58	83	42
Off-Farm Inputs									
Fertilizer	11,669	3,976	1,828	2,617	327	2,572	115	183	51
Farm Machinery	2,203	247	87	507	496	777	26	45	18
Irrigation	173	76	14	60	6	14	0	3	1
Total	14,046	4,299	1,929	3,183	830	3,363	141	231	70
Total Energy Use in Agriculture	19,479	5,276	2,190	4,563	1,933	4,893	199	313	111
[N.B. Econ. Active Population in Agriculture (Millions)]	(300.0)	(151.3)	(37.2)	(29.5)	(2.3)	(28.3)	(10.6)	(23.5)	(17.3)

TABLE 4
Agricultural Outputs and Inputs by Farming Regions, 1970, per Member of Economically Active Population in Agriculture

	All Fifty Countries	India	Asian: Rice	N.African-Mid.East: Wheat	American: Wheat Livestock	American: Corn-Beans-Roots	East African: Corn	African: Millets-Sorghum	African: Roots-Tubers
Outputs									
Cereals (Kilograms)	951	753	1,138	1,403	9,622	1,591	382	488	266
Other Field Crops (Kilograms)	943	470	725	916	6,575	3,190	897	680	1,538
Value-Added ($ PPP)	547	492	480	784	3,093	940	235	298	302
Inputs									
Cropland (Ha)	1.57	1.09	1.11	2.34	17.14	2.75	0.85	1.71	1.65
Perm. Pasture (Ha)	2.77	0.09	0.06	1.91	72.03	11.26	4.77	5.96	4.65
Irrigated Area (Ha)	0.22	0.20	0.15	0.63	1.25	0.23	0.01	0.06	0.02
Fertilizer(Kg x 10)	2.14	1.32	2.93	4.35	11.46	5.62	0.76	0.37	0.20
Tractors (per 1000)	3.05	0.73	1.06	6.66	95.23	11.04	1.18	0.54	0.45
Energy Inputs									
On-Farm (Kg c.e.)	18.11	6.46	7.03	46.72	469.79	54.12	5.45	3.53	2.40
Off-Farm (Kg c.e.)	46.82	28.42	51.86	107.80	353.44	118.98	13.31	9.83	4.03

major categories of agricultural production inputs for which energy is embodied when the input is delivered to the farm-gate. In energy balances the consumption of energy embodied in these off-farm produced inputs is recorded in the sector where the inputs are manufactured or processed -- in the Industry sector for domestically-produced farm inputs or in the embodied energy of imports if they are produced abroad. The method of preparing these estimates for each of the fifty countries closely follows a technique developed by the U.N. Food and Agriculture Organization and is based on FAO information about equipment stocks, deliveries, use rates, and fuel consumption requirements. These data show energy used in the process of agricultural and livestock production, only, and do not include energy use attributable to investment activities such as improvement or extension of land and water resources, additions to equipment stock, or inventory buildup (this contrasts with FAO reported data for geographical regions: see FAO 1977, 95-103). We also exclude all off-farm product processing, energy-use in the food chain beyond the farm-gate, and such service "margins" as off-farm trade and transportation (including transport of the farm inputs). Finally, we omit all uses of energy in the farm household not directly attributable to crop and livestock production, and a range of minor production inputs such as pesticides and similar chemicals.

This conservative accounting for the energy requirements of agricultural sector production reveals that the on-farm fuel use is only about one-fourth of the total energy consumed. By omitting the energy use represented by fertilizer and other chemical inputs, as much as 85 percent of energy consumed in some farming systems is unrecorded in the energy balance sector information. In the total energy use in agriculture, as represented in Table 3, the balance between machinery fuel and fertilizer-water control varies among the regions but the fertilizer-irrigation use is predominant in all but the wheat-livestock farming system of Latin America. In 1970 about 4 percent of all commercial energy used as intermediate inputs in the fifty developing countries was devoted to irrigation and fertilizer: the total agricultural production energy requirements were slightly more than 5.5 percent of all intermediate uses of energy.

The energy and other key agricultural inputs, together with summary output data for agricultural products, are recorded in Table 4 for the fifty countries, distributed among eight Third World regions in which they are located. Each region is characterized by a specified agro-climatic and socio-economic system of agriculture. (For description of these characteristics and country listings, see National Academy of Sciences 1977, Report of Study Team 4, Subgroup A).

The farming regions generally correspond to the wood versus petroleum-dominant categories. All but one (Burma) of the 17 countries in the wheat, wheat-livestock or rice regions are petroleum-dominant. All but one (Liberia) of the 19 countries in the millets-sorghum, roots-tubers, and corn regions are wood-dominant. In the mixed (corn-beans-roots) region of Latin America, 5 heavily-forested and generally low-productivity countries are wood-dominant, and the 8 other countries are petroleum-dominant.

Within a farming region, the system of agriculture is characterized by a particular quality and mix of natural resources, specified climatic conditions, and a distinctive product mix; but a variety of production technologies may be in simultaneous use. Comparison of energy use in agricultural production by countries located in one region should reveal differences primarily attributable to variations in agricultural technologies employed. Comparisons of energy and other input uses in different regions should reveal differences primarily attributable to variations in agroclimatic and natural resources conditions, but will also record inter-regional differences in production methods and technologies. Because a specified set of climatic and resource conditions is usually associated with a distinctive product-mix, a region is often identified by its dominant products, as illustrated by the labels assigned to the farming regions of Tables 3 and 4. Where we find closely similar product mixes, whether in groups of countries within one region or in different regions (as is the case for the East African Corn and the American Corn-Beans-Roots regions), we will consider differences in the use of energy and other inputs per unit of real output as attributable to the variation in agricultural technologies employed.

There are great differences in the relative proportions of inputs employed, and in energy used, as among the major farming regions of the Third World. With half of the economically active population in agriculture and a third of the cropland, India consumes slightly more than one-quarter of the energy used in agriculture by all fifty countries. But fully one-third of the energy consumed in agriculture by all fifty countries is used in the two farming regions of Latin America by one-tenth of the farming population on one-quarter of the cropland.

To illustrate the range of variation among regions, Table 4 shows summary indicators of agricultural outputs and inputs per member of the economically active population in agriculture. If we identify productivity with value-added per person engaged in agriculture, and energy intensity with sectoral inputs per agricultural worker, the eight farming regions reveal a wide span of differences. There are only modest differences among the three low-productivity farming systems of sub-Saharan Africa, but the energy and other inputs employed per person in agriculture are much greater in the Asian systems of intermediate productivity, in the high productivity wheat regions, and in the corn-roots farming system of Latin America. We may observe that the variation among farming systems in energy use per person and per unit of real output is substantially greater than indicated in the conventional comparison of country-groupings by geographic area. A comparable range of interregional variations in energy consumed is found when productivity differences refer to real output per hectare of cropland (or total arable land).

We can summarize these observations about sectoral energy use in a cross-section of large developing countries. We find that the output elasticity of energy use in agriculture is very high, there are great differences in output per agricultural worker (or hectare), but the ratio of energy use in agriculture to total energy production-inputs in the economy is small for all the developing countries. Direct inputs of farm fuels are found to be 1-3 percent of total-national intermediate uses of energy, and all energy use in agricultural production is 5-6 percent of production-inputs for the economy as a whole. Moreover, the ratios are about the same, on the average, for countries with low farm incomes and with high farm incomes. This same conjunction of findings -- high rates of energy use per added unit of agricultural output, great variation of average product per unit of land and labor input, and a stable ratio of energy intermediate inputs in agriculture compared with the economy as a whole -- also emerges from time-series data for developing countries over a sufficient span of time that incomes per capita rise significantly.

IV. ENERGY AND AGRICULTURAL DEVELOPMENT

In this summary of findings there is an apparent contradiction. The high input elasticities and wide variation in productivity per worker and per hectare might be expected to result in a rising proportion of energy use in agriculture as per capita incomes rise. The same inference might be drawn from the micro, farm-level evidence of very great increases in energy use associated with adoption of improved agricultural methods. But these expectations are confounded by the low, stable share of agriculture in total intermediate use of energy observed in both the cross-section and time-series data showing national patterns of energy use.

Across the experience represented by these fifty countries -- with substantial differences in industrial structure, levels of productivity and incomes -- there appears to have been a common result: intermediate use of commercial energy in agricultural activity has grown in close correspondence with energy use in other productive sectors. To what extent is this attributable to common features of the development strategies pursued in these countries? One hypothesis is that this result is directly traceable to the urban-industrial emphasis in development-promoting policies, and is the expected outcome of the transfer of resources among sectors encouraged by those policies. We will explore the arguments underlying this hypothesis. In a concluding section of part IV we will note how the appearance of resource constraints and altered development strategies may change the pattern of energy use in the future.

A. Intersectoral Resource Transfers and Energy Uses

The argument that there is a close association between development strategy and the pattern of energy uses that we have observed departs from the familiar observation that a broadly-shared set of policies has been implemented in these countries, in particular to transfer resources from traditional to improved methods of agricultural production -- and out of agriculture into (predominantly) urban-based activities. Over a span of the post-war decades, the structural changes accompanying the economic growth of these countries have been characterized by:
   -- high growth rates of population and labor force, accomodated in part by migration out of agriculture and in part by growth in the number of low-productivity, low energy-using agricultural units at the extensive margin of arable land;

-- concentrated areas of high energy-using agricultural development to satisfy demand for food and fibers in the urban growth centers, and for export;

-- agricultural development "balanced," and usually led, by rapid growth of energy-intensive, urban-based industrial and similar activities.

It is this pattern of structural change, seen as the intended outcome of an urban-industrial strategic emphasis in development, which has been subjected to severe criticism over the past decade. The critics cite the evidence of labor displacement in many areas of agriculture and the modest rates of labor absorption in the high-growth sectors of industrial and other urban activities. At the same time, the social consequences include growing disparities in the distribution of both rural and urban incomes, the latter associated with growth in the proportion of the labor force in the urban informal sector, in low-productivity services, and in the ranks of the unemployed.

More than a decade ago Lloyd Reynolds identified these consequences of growth-promoting strategies in a "slack labor" economy, where expansion of modern sector activity was accompanied by persisting open and disguised unemployment and where wages and prices were not effective in clearing factor markets (Reynolds 1969; 1969a). He sketched out the structural characteristics of such an economy consisting of multiple sectors, each characterized by distinctive production and distribution relations, and he emphasized the pervasive influence of public policies directing the allocation of resources among and within the several sectors. A great volume of subsequent work, in the genre pioneered by Reynolds, has explored the labor-allocation and income-distribution dimensions of various growth strategies in dual and multiple sector economies.

Acknowledging that multiple-sector models may be too complicated for general analytical solutions, Reynolds counseled their use in simulations to explore the consequences of their structural linkages and the differing values of key variables in the system (Reynolds 1969, 98-100). Adopting this approach, we may trace the simulated distribution of energy use and of productive factors among the sectors of a "slack labor" economy where growth and structural changes approximate the characterization we have given of an urban-industrial development strategy.

The study of factor allocation among productive activities is a familiar use of multiple-sector models (such as the "labor absorption" model specified by Henry Bruton and Charles Frank 1977). A model readily adaptable to our purposes is a sectoral energy requirements model, designed to generate projections of factor use (labor and intermediate-inputs) and of intersectoral factor transfers among four kinds of productive activity in (1) a rural-traditional sector, (2) an improved-agricultural sector, (3) an urban-traditional sector, and (4) an urban-modern sector. Different production techniques are utilized in each sector. In the urban-modern sector, production is expressed as a function of input aggregates, following the Berndt-Wood procedure for partitioning inputs entering the production of goods and services for final demand (see Berndt and Wood 1979). Marketing of agricultural production occurs only in the improved-agriculture sector and output in this sector expands to accommodate demand for food and fibers at stable urban-rural terms of trade. To emphasize intersectoral transfers in the simulation, technical change is concentrated in the urban-modern sector and production relations in the other sectors approximate fixed factor proportions of energy, land and labor. (A full specification of the model is given in West 1981.)

An abstract model of this kind is a crude instrument for interpreting the economic behavior of developing societies. Our purpose, however, is the more limited one of illustrating the argument that there may be a close association of development strategy with the pattern of energy use we have found in the fifty countries of this study. Inspection of the model-simulated sectoral distribution of output, energy use, and employment of labor may also be rewarding for a second purpose. It will illustrate some of the sources of ambiguity in evaluating national energy use data.

Table 5 presents the simulated distribution of real output, labor use, and intermediate-uses of energy over a span of three decades. The parametric values are those found in evaluating energy use patterns in Thailand during the postwar period, with labor units adjusted to average earnings of one real-output unit in the rural traditional sector at year zero. The model is driven by the growth of the labor force, utilized capital in the modern sector, and technical change in the modern sector production relations. The simulation of Table 5 is based on an assumed 2.6 percent growth rate of the economically active population, 4 percent annual growth of utilized capital, and 1 percent annual increase in the efficiency with which both capital and labor are employed in the modern sector. While this corresponds to one meaning of neutral technical change, the policy behavior we have assumed to maintain stable rural-urban terms of trade and the specified wage-determination mechanism have the effect that both factor intensity and relative factor shares are altered in the modern sector. In the Hicksian sense, the technical change is factor biased. The intensity and the factor bias of technical change, in turn, determine the sectoral distribution of output, labor, and energy use -- given the year-zero values of budget-shares, relative factor shares, income elasticity of demand, and wage rates in the rural sectors.

The performance shown in Table 5 would be judged a modest success by reference to growth of output and productivity. Real output of the economy grows at above 4.3 percent annually and output per member of the economically active population rises by two-thirds over the thirty years. Real output per worker rises in both rural and urban sectors. The familiar urban-industrial emphasis is evident in the structural changes. Urban output is 40 percent of total at the beginning and 80 percent at the end of thirty years, while rural-urban migration has a corresponding effect on the labor force: the urban labor force is 27 percent of the total in year zero and 78 percent in year 30. But only 44 percent of the labor force has found employment in the modern sector at the end of the period and the proportion of urban labor in informal or traditional occupations is the same at the end as at the beginning of the simulation. If we measure "slack labor" by the proportion of the total labor force in rural and urban traditional sectors, the absolute number is greater after thirty years than at the

TABLE 5
Simulated Sectoral Distribution of Output, Labor, Energy Use

	Year 0	Year 10	Year 20	Year 30
Real Output: Total	3,000	4,433	6,770	10,720
Modern Sector	1,000	1,949	3,760	7,194
Urban-traditional	200	390	752	1,439
Improved-Agriculture	560	835	1,244	1,867
Rural-traditional	1,240	1,259	1,014	221
Econ.Active Population: Total	2,000	2,585	3,342	4,320
Modern Sector	333	603	1,078	1,913
Urban-traditional	200	390	752	1,439
Improved-Agriculture	225	334	497	747
Rural-traditional	1,242	1,259	1,014	221
Energy Intermediate Inputs	1,727	2,597	3,905	5,875
Modern Sector	1,634	2,459	3,699	5,566
Improved-Agriculture	93	138	206	309

Notes: Simulated sectoral allocation of output, labor force, and
        energy-use by projection model, as described in text, for
        modern-sector income elasticity of demand for agricultural
        products = 0.6 and ratio of real wages in the modern and
        improved-agriculture sectors to real income in traditional
        sectors = 1.5 (see West 1981).

        Details may not add to totals due to rounding.

beginning of the period; a rapid decline occurs in the final decade of the simulation, but the "slack labor" sectors still contain nearly forty percent of the labor force in year 30. Moreover, the growth of the labor force in improved-agriculture is much below the growth of employment in the modern-sector and -- with no technical change in improved-agricultural production methods and with fixed rural-urban terms of trade -- no improvement occurs in earnings per farmer in the sector. The simulation has the characteristics for which the results of an urban-industrial development strategy have been faulted.

Some of the key structural changes associated with successful pursuit of this development strategy, as illustrated by the simulation, are indicated in Table 6. While rural output falls sharply as a proportion of total, the output of the improved-agriculture sector about keeps pace with overall growth of the economy. The bulk of the "slack labor" migrates from the traditional rural sector to the informal urban sector. After an initial modest increase, the ratio of total energy use to total real output declines sharply. But the proportion of agricultural to total intermediate uses of energy is unchanged. All of these results are traceable to a common source: the transfer of resources among the sectors, where each sector has distinctly different factor requirements. In this very simple case, the factor proportions are unchanged in all but the modern sector and the intersector transfers are the outcome of the development strategy pursued -- i.e., the concentration of capital formation and technical change in the urban modern sector, the allocation of nontraditional inputs to improved-agriculture in a manner to maintain stable terms of trade, and the wage-determination policy in the improved-agriculture sector.

That there may be more image than reality in many of the most widely-used indicators of energy relationships is illustrated by the energy/output elasticities of the simulation, for which decennial values have been computed as the ratio of proportionate rates of growth, as shown in Table 7.

The reality, in this case, is that each added unit of real output in the modern sector (and for urban output as a whole) has required the same added amount of energy as an intermediate input. The modern sector elasticity of energy-use has been constant with respect to growth of output throughout the thirty years. Similarly, the energy elasticity with respect to output in the improved-agriculture sector is constant. Detectable inputs of energy are only found for production in these two sectors. But other resources have been transferred among the sectors -- including the labor and land factors -- in association with the changes in the structure of production occurring over the thirty years. The fall in the elasticity for the overall energy/output ratio is attributable to the intersectoral shifts of resources and outputs; the same pattern of change (but not the same magnitude) would appear for any other trend-values of technical change in the modern sector, or no technical change at all. Similarly, the high and rising elasticity of energy-use for growth of rural output is entirely attributable to transfer of resources out of traditional-rural activities, with no change at all in the added energy-inputs required at the margin in any line of production in either of the rural sectors.

TABLE 6
Simulation Results: Indicators of Structural Changes
(Ratios)

	Output Ratios		Labor-Force Ratios		Energy-Use Ratios	
	Rural Sectors/ Total Output	Improved-Agricul./ Total Output	"Slack labor" Ratio	Improved-Agricul./ Modern Sector	(Index) Total Energy/ Total Output	Improved-Agricul./ Modern Sector
Year 0	0.601	0.187	0.721	0.675	100.0	0.057
Year 10	0.472	0.188	0.638	0.555	101.9	0.056
Year 20	0.333	0.184	0.529	0.461	100.3	0.056
Year 30	0.195	0.174	0.384	0.390	95.3	0.056

TABLE 7
Simulation Results: Decennial Energy-Use Elasticities
with Respect to Output

	Total Output	Urban Sectors	Rural Sectors	Improved-Agriculture
First decade	1.050	0.605	2.681	1.000
Second decade	0.963	0.614	5.415	1.000
Third decade	0.886	0.622	-5.305	1.000
All 30 Years	0.962	0.613	8.375	1.000

Note: Elasticities computed as the ratio of proportionate rates of growth.

Source for Tables 6 and 7: Simulation results shown in Table 5.

Until we have energy-use and factor-input information in a form that distinguishes production by sectors, where production relations differ among the sectors, the interpretation of differences among countries or through time with respect to labor and energy use will contain this ambiguity. It may be plausible, although it cannot be confirmed, that the historically-observed high marginal rates of energy-use with growth of agricultural output are chiefly attributable to inter-sectoral transfers of labor, with little or no effect of change in the production methods employed in either traditional or improved-agriculture sectors. The historically-observed stable ratio of agricultural to total intermediate uses of energy may, similarly, be attributable to the process of resource transfers among sectors that are associated with the development strategy and policies pursued, such as those of the simulation. If this is, or has been historically, the dominant reality, then at any moment of time, such as 1970, a cross-section of developing countries (having shared experience with a common development strategy) might consist of some countries with sectoral-patterns similar to year zero of Table 5, others similar to year 10, and so on. They would have significantly different production structures, different patterns of labor-force distribution, different levels of per worker output and income, but the same proportion of total energy used in agriculture. Even comparing groups of countries from different farming regions, where there exist significantly different input-requirements for different crop mixes, those variances in the patterns of energy use may be obscured by the dominant influence of the shared development strategy experience.

Some modest support for this argument may be found in the observation that, within both the wood-dominant and the petroleum-dominant groupings, there are countries with sectoral distributions similar to year zero, others similar to year 10, and so on. For the fifty countries taken together, the sectoral distribution of output, labor, and energy-use is very much like that shown for year 20 of Table 5.

B. Energy Requirements of Land-Saving Techniques

Whether or not this hypothesis accounts for the energy-use patterns of the past, it is an inadequate guide for the future. Quite apart from the effect of increase in the relative cost of energy inputs, a powerful influence derives from the circumstance that the era of expanding agricultural output at the extensive margin of land is drawing to a close in many developing countries. The constraint of land and water availability is a sufficient reason for the accelerated introduction of land-augmenting change in production techniques in many countries. To this may be added the effects of pursuing more labor-using and rural-oriented development strategies.

These changes occur gradually but they have been underway for a considerable period in countries with a severe land constraint. Prior to 1970, the "green revolution" in rice-growing regions, and related techniques for increasing productivity in wheat and corn areas, had been introduced on a modest scale in some of the fifty countries. These countries show consistently higher energy/output ratios in agriculture, compared to other countries in the same farming region.

Despite difficulty in distinguishing the effects of technical change in agriculture from the effects of sectoral resource-transfers, the evidence of much higher energy use-rates (particularly as embodied in chemical inputs) associated with higher yields supports the presumption that we observe, in part, the high energy-using elasticity of improved agricultural techniques introduced. From an inspection of differences in energy use in agricultural production of countries with relatively high per hectare (and per worker) productivity as compared with countries in the same farming region but with low per hectare productivity, it appears that all forms of land-augmenting technical change require substantially greater energy inputs.

The character of this evidence may be illustrated by looking within two of the farming regions of Tables 3 and 4, to compare inputs for very similar product mixes in low and high productivity countries. Table 8 shows, on a per hectare basis, the average real output and the quantities of inputs used to attain that output, comparing two high productivity Asian Rice Region countries with three low productivity Asian Rice Region countries; a similar comparison is made for thirteen high productivity and four low productivity countries in the African-Latin American Corn Regions. We interpret the comparison of high-versus low-productivity countries, in the Asian Rice case, as showing the effects of technical differences in production methods which are land and capital-saving but labor-using. The comparison, in the Corn Regions case, illustrates technical differences in production methods which are capital-using, but land and labor-saving.

There does not appear to be any substantial difference· in the labor or energy inputs per hectare in the traditional agricultural activities of the Asian Rice Region countries, and only modest differences in the traditional-sector agricultural production of the Corn Regions countries. In the Asian Rice Region, there is no substantial intercountry difference in the estimated relative distribution of resources between the traditional and improved-agriculture sectors. The differences in energy use per hectare, per worker, and per unit of real output shown in Table 8 apparently reflect, predominantly, the differences in production techniques within the improved-agricultural sectors.

In all comparisons of this kind we have inspected, raising real output requires more than proportionate increase in energy inputs. Moreover, in comparing high productivity with low productivity countries with similar product mixes, and where there is clear evidence of more land-saving methods of production in the former, the high productivity countries show a consistently higher proportion of total intermediate energy devoted to the agricultural sector. This is the only systematic explanation we have found for the observed differences, among these fifty countries, in the ratios of agricultural to total intermediate uses of energy.

Higher ratios of energy inputs to real output in agriculture, and higher ratios of energy use in agriculture relative to nonagricultural intermediate uses, are what we should expect from the introduction of land-augmenting technical change -- where production relations are otherwise unchanged and where the urban-rural terms of trade adjust to the intersectoral transfer of labor and other resources called forth by the intensity and factor bias of the technical change introduced. With respect to the intersectoral allocation of labor, this is the

470

TABLE 8
Comparison of Inputs and Output per Hectare, for Low- and High Productivity Countries, with Similar Crop-Mix

| | Asian Rice Region | | Corn Regions | |
	Low Productivity	High Productivity	Low Productivity	High Productivity
Machinery services (Kg c.e.)	6.87	5.20	9.08	28.52
Irrigation services (Kg c.e.)	2.39	3.95	0.20	1.35
Fertilizer (Kg. c.e.)	15.18	137.50	12.69	33.10
Labor (manyears)	0.90	1.35	1.16	0.36
Output (real value: in $ PPP)	255	1,025	274	342
N.B. Energy-use				
On-farm energy (Kg c.e.)	6.76	7.23	6.38	19.87
Total energy (Kg c.e.)	24.44	146.64	21.98	62.96

Sources: See "Note on Statistical Sources." Farming regions as in Tables 3 and 4.

case investigated in the dual-sector models of John W. Mellor and Uma Lele (Mellor 1974; Lele and Mellor 1981). Adapted to the distinction between traditional and improved methods of production, the Mellor-Lele model shows that technical change in agriculture with land-augmenting effect is expected to increase labor use in both the improved agricultural sector and in urban modern-sector activities. However, the employment of labor in agriculture relative to employment in the urban modern sector is expected to fall in all but the exceptional case of high elasticity of factor substitution in improved-agriculture in conjunction with an increase in (Solow-units) labor efficiency. (A matrix of the parametric values governing labor allocation is in Lele and Mellor 1981; see also West 1981.)

This is the nexus of technical change in agricultural production methods and goals of rural development strategy we wish to emphasize. Where land-augmenting methods are introduced -- perhaps driven by rural population growth and disappearance of prospects for expansion of traditional farm units into an extensive margin of arable land -- a sharp increase in the energy-intensity of production is expected. In conditions where governmental intervention does not wholly frustrate the tendencies toward equilibrium in product and labor markets, energy use may be expected to rise relative to the economically active population in agriculture. Policies directed toward expanding employment in agriculture will accentuate the rise in energy-use relative to agricultural labor, the energy-use to real-output ratio, and use of energy in the agricultural sector relative to other national intermediate-uses. These effects flow from the nature of the agricultural technology which will fulfill the dual requirements of land-saving and of increasing labor efficiency under conditions of land-water constraint; this calls for expansion of irrigation and of chemical inputs, both relatively energy-intensive techniques. (On the requirements of technical improvements, with special application to Asian farming systems, see the typology developed by Bartsch 1977, Chapters 2, 3, Appendices.)

C. Conclusions

We do not have data on the range of parameters necessary to determine the degree to which intercountry differences in the agricultural methods employed, within farming regions, may account for the differences in sectoral distribution of energy and labor -- and to isolate this source of influence on factor allocation from the effects of intersectoral resource transfers of the kind and origin described in part IV A. However, this new body of information on energy use, for agriculture and other productive sectors of large developing countries, does permit many cross-country comparisons to be made of differences in factor proportions in agricultural production. Such comparisons consistently show differences in energy and labor use with the expected sign, and large magnitudes of difference in the relative inputs of total energy in agricultural production, such as are illustrated in Table 8.

From a preliminary reconnaissance of these sectoral energy balances, the hypothesis of part IV A and the expected effects of land-augmenting technical change described in part IV B are not obviously inconsistent with the intersectoral distribution of factors found in these fifty large developing countries. It is plausible that the urban-industrial emphasis of development strategy, shared by these developing countries in the postwar period, may be an important factor in accounting for the intersectoral distribution of energy-use and of labor found in these data. It is also plausible that the appearance of land-water constraints, and the introduction of technical changes in agricultural production to accommodate those constraints, are likely to alter the patterns of sectoral distribution for both energy-use and labor in the future -- and this result may be accelerated or intensified by a shift of policy emphasis toward greater rural and employment-generating concentration.

Energy-input requirements in agriculture, direct and indirect, could increase very rapidly in relation to other uses of energy. In an era of high and rising energy costs, these possibilities of a shifting pattern of energy demand appear to warrant careful monitoring to ensure that national energy management does not choke-off the process of agricultural development. Until we attain more adequate insight into the energy-use consequences associated with technical improvements in Third World agriculture, it seems imprudent to assume that the choice of rural development strategy is independent of an energy-requirements constraint.

NOTE ON STATISTICAL SOURCES

Commercial energy sources shown in Tables 1A and 1B are from the United Nations Statistical office data tape, with up-dates and adjustments of data for 1970, corresponding to publication of World Energy Supplies 1972-1976, Statistical Papers Series J No. 21. The definitions and coefficients appearing in that publication, pp. v-xxviii, apply. Computation of electricity at fossil-fuels equivalent values followed the procedure described in the text (p. 453). Wood and charcoal data are from the Food and Agriculture Organization of the United Nations, Yearbook of Forest Products, various issues; conversion to heat equivalent units followed the procedure described in the text (p. 448).

The sectoral distribution of energy uses of Tables 1A and 1B is based on energy balance sheets, 1970-1976, assembled by a project team directed by the author. Information on sectoral distribution was obtained, as available, from national agencies of each country, international organizations, and two international oil companies which kindly provided data on categories of customer sales and estimates of total energy use. Disaggregation of the conventional household-commercial sector proceeded by (a) estimation of agricultural on-farm uses (as described below); (b) application of energy-use coefficients to constant-price series for value added in public and private services; and (c) assignment of the residual to the category of consumer end-uses.

Table 2 "value added" estimates are based on United Nations Yearbook of National Accounts Statistics presentations of gross domestic product by kind of economic activity, in producers' values, in accordance with the Former System of National Accounts, to show gross domestic product in factor values. Conversion to 1970 U.S.

dollars is by use of the purchasing power parity rates for 1970 estimated by Kravis, Heston, and Summers (1978). Population data are from International Monetary Fund, International Financial Statistics. 1978 annual edition.

Table 3 data have been computed for each country following the procedure developed by the FAO and reported in State of Food and Agriculture 1976, pp. 81-111. The regional energy coefficients as shown in Tables 3.4, 3.9, 3.10, 3.11, 3.12, and the sources cited have been used. Country data on equipment, machinery, installed irrigation facilities, and fertilizer consumption are from the FAO Yearbook of Production, supplemented by information collected for the FAO 1979 conference on "Agriculture: Toward 2000", and for the United Nations Water Conference, Mar del Plata, of 1977. Data on irrigation equipped areas have been adjusted to the regional totals of Water for Agriculture, a report prepared by the FAO for the 1977 conference.

Country data on economically active population, in agriculture and total, are from the FAO 1973 report on "Agricultural employment in developing countries," (FAO 1974) with some adjustments as subsequently reported in the FAO Production Yearbook issues.

Table 4 (except data on energy inputs and economically active population) has been compiled from country data on production as reported for 1970 by the FAO Production Yearbook tape of mid-1979. The classification of countries by farming regions follows the National Academy of Sciences, National Research Council, Report of Study Team 4, Subgroup A, as reported in Supporting Papers: World Food and Nutrition Study (National Academy of Sciences 1977). ·

BIBLIOGRAPHY

Arnold, J.E.M. 1978. *Wood energy and rural communities*. Prepared for 8th World Food Congress, Jakarta. Rome: FAO.

Bartsch, W. H. 1977. *Employment and technology choice in Asian agriculture*. New York: Praeger Publishers.

Berndt, E.R., D. O. Wood. 1979. Engineering and econometric interpretations of energy-capital complementarity. *Amer. Econ. Rev.*, 69(3): 342-54.

Brown, M. 1966. *On the theory and measurement of technological change*. Cambridge: The University Press.

Bruton, H., C. R. Frank, Jr. 1977. Mathematical Appendix. In *Income distribution and growth in less-developed countries*, ed. C. R. Frank, Jr. and R. C. Webb, 565-75. Washington, D.C.: The Brookings Institution.

Costanza, R. 1980. Embodied energy and economic valuation. *Science*, 210: 1219-24.

Darmstadter, J., J. Dunkerley, J. Alterman. 1977. *How industrial societies use energy*. Baltimore, Md.: The Johns Hopkins U. Press for Resources for the Future.

Dohner, R. 1981. Energy prices, economic activity, and inflation: a survey of issues and results. In *Energy prices, economic activity, and inflation*, ed. K. Mork. Cambridge, Mass: Ballinger Pub. Co.

Fallen-Bailey, D. G., T. A. Byer. 1979. *Energy options and policy issues in developing countries*. World Bank Staff Working Paper No. 350. Washington, D.C.: The World Bank.

Fluck, C., C. D. Baird. 1980. *Agricultural energetics*. Westport, Conn.: Avi Pub. Co.

Food and Agriculture Organization of the United Nations. 1974. Agricultural employment in developing countries. *The state of food and agriculture 1973*. Rome: FAO.

Food and Agriculture Organization of the United Nations. 1977. Energy in agriculture. *The state of food and agriculture 1976*. Rome: FAO.

Food and Agriculture Organization of the United Nations. 1977a. *Water for agriculture*. Prepared by the FAO for the United Nations Conference, Mar del Plata, March 1977. Rome: FAO.

Gilliland, M. W. 1975. Energy analysis and public policy. *Science*, 189: 1051-56.

Herendeen, R. A., C. W. Bullard. 1974. *Energy costs of goods and services*. Document 140, Center for Advanced Computations, U. of Illinois, Champaign-Urbana.

Hirst, E. 1974. Food-related energy requirements. *Science*, 184: 134-38.

Hogan, W. W., A. S. Manne. 1979. Energy-economy interactions: the fable of the elephant and the rabbit. In *Advances in the economics of energy and resources*, Vol. 1, ed. R. S. Pindyck. Cambridge, Mass.: JAI Press.

Huettner, D. A. 1976. Net energy analysis: an economic assessment. *Science*, 192: 101-04.

Hughart, D. 1979. *Prospects for traditional and non-conventional energy sources in developing countries*. World Bank Staff Working Paper No. 346. Washington, D.C.: The World Bank.

International Energy Agency, Organization for Economic Cooperation and Development. 1978. *Energy balances of OECD countries 1974/76*. Paris: OECD.

International Energy Agency, Organization for Economic Cooperation and Development. 1979. *Workshop on energy data of developing countries*. Volume I. Proceedings: summary of discussions and technical papers. Volume II. Basic energy statistics and energy balances of developing countries 1967-1977. Paris: OECD.

Kravis, I. B., A. W. Heston, R. Summers. 1978. Real GDP per capita for more than one hundred countries. *Econ. J.*, 88(June): 215-42.

Leach, G. 1976. *Energy and food production*. Guilford, Surrey: IPC Science and Technology Press Ltd.

Lefeber, L. 1973. Income distribution and agricultural development. In *Development and planning: essays in honour of Paul Rosenstein-Rodan*, ed. J. Bhagwati and R. S. Eckaus. Cambridge, Mass.: The MIT Press.

Lele, U., J. W. Mellor. 1981. Technological change, distributive bias and labor transfer in a two sector economy. *Oxford Econ. Papers*, 33: 426-41.

Lewis, W. A. 1980. The slowing down of the engine of growth. *Amer. Econ. Rev.*, 70(3): 555-64.

Mellor, J. W. 1974. Models of economic growth and land-augmenting technological change in foodgrain production. In *Agricultural policy in developing countries*, ed. N. Islam. New York: John Wiley & Sons.

476

————, 1976. *The new economics of growth*: *a strategy for India and the developing world*. Ithaca: Cornell U. Press for the Twentieth Century Fund.

National Academy of Sciences, National Research Council. 1977. *Supporting papers*: *world food and nutrition study*. Volume II. Washington, D.C.: NAS.

National Academy of Sciences. 1980. *Firewood crops*: *shrub and tree species for energy production*. Washington, D. C.:NAS.

Organization for Economic Cooperation and Development. 1977. *World energy outlook*. A Report of the Secretary-General. Paris: OECD.

Pimentel, D. 1974. Energy use in world food production. *Environmental Biology*. Cornell U., Ithaca, N.Y., Report 74-1.

Pimentel, D., W. Dritschilo, J. Krummel, J. Kutzman. 1975. Energy and land constraints in food protein production. *Science*, 190: 754-61.

Pindyck, R. S. 1979. *The structure of world energy demand*. Cambridge, Mass.: MIT Press.

Reynolds, L. G. 1969. Economic development with surplus labour: some complications. *Oxford Econ. Papers*, 21(1): 89-103.

————, 1969a. Relative earnings and manpower allocation in developing economies. *The Pakistan Dev. Rev.*, IX(Spring): 14-34.

————, 1975. Agriculture in development theory: an overview. In *Agriculture in development theory*, ed. L. G. Reynolds, 1-24. New Haven: Yale U. Press.

————, 1977. *Image and reality in economic development*. New Haven: Yale U. Press.

————, 1980. Economic development in historical perspective. *Amer. Econ. Rev.*, 70(2): 91-95.

Sonenblum, S. 1978. *The energy connections*: *between energy and the economy*. Cambridge, Mass.: Ballinger Pub. Co.

United Nations, Statistical Office. *World energy supplies*. Annual. Statistical Papers Series J. New York: United Nations.

United Nations Conference on Trade and Development. 1980. *Energy needs of developing countries*. Report Prepared by the UNCTAD Secretariat for the Committee on Transfer of Technology. New York: United Nations.

U.S. Department of Agriculture. 1979. *Energy for agriculture: a computerized information retrieval system*. Bibliographies and Literature of Agriculture no. 5, Compiled by B. A. Stout and C. A. Myers. Washington, D. C.: USDA.

West, R. L. 1981. A multisector model for energy-use and labor projections. International Energy and Resources Study Paper 1981-4. Fletcher School of Law and Diplomacy. Tufts U. Medford, Mass.

Contributors

WALTER ADAMS, Distinguished University Professor (Economics) and Past President, Michigan State University

BELA BALASSA, Professor of Political Economy at the Johns Hopkins University and Consultant to the World Bank

R. ALBERT BERRY, Division of Social Sciences, Scarborough College, University of Toronto

HENRY J. BRUTON, John J. Gibson Professor of Economics, Williams College

CARLOS F. DIAZ ALEJANDRO, Professor, Department of Economics, Yale University

JOHN C. H. FEI, Professor, Department of Economics, Yale University

RICHARD B. FREEMAN, Professor of Economics, Harvard University, and Director of Labor Studies, National Bureau of Economic Research

RAYMOND W. GOLDSMITH, Professor of Economics Emeritus, Yale University

PETER GREGORY, Professor, Department of Economics, The University of New Mexico

G. K. HELLEINER, Professor, Department of Economics, University of Toronto

JESSE W. MARKHAM, Professor, Law & Economics Center, Emory University

J. MICHAEL MONTIAS, Professor of Economics, Institution for Social and Policy Studies, Yale University

CYNTHIA TAFT MORRIS, Professor of Economics, The American University

HOWARD PACK, Professor, Department of Economics, Swarthmore College

HUGH PATRICK, Director, Economic Growth Center, Yale University

FREDERIC L. PRYOR, Professor, Department of Economics, Swarthmore College

GUSTAV RANIS, Frank Altschul Professor of International Economics at Yale University

MICHAEL P. TODARO, Professor of Economics, New York University, and Senior Associate, Center for Population Studies, Population Council

ROBERT TRIFFIN, Institut de Recherches Economiques, Universite Catholique de Louvain, Louvain La Neuve

ROBERT L. WEST, Professor of International Economics, The Fletcher School of Law and Diplomacy, Tufts University

Index

482